MW00782942

The Adams Papers

SARA MARTIN, EDITOR IN CHIEF

SERIES III

GENERAL CORRESPONDENCE
AND OTHER PAPERS
OF THE ADAMS STATESMEN

Papers of John Adams

Papers of John Adams

SARA GEORGINI, SARA MARTIN,
R. M. BARLOW, GWEN FRIES, AMANDA M. NORTON,
NEAL E. MILLIKAN, HOBSON WOODWARD
EDITORS

Volume 20 • *June 1789 – February 1791*

THE BELKNAP PRESS
OF HARVARD UNIVERSITY PRESS
CAMBRIDGE, MASSACHUSETTS
AND LONDON, ENGLAND
2020

Printed in the United States of America

Funds for editing *The Adams Papers* were originally furnished by Time, Inc., on behalf of *Life*, to the Massachusetts Historical Society, under whose supervision the editorial work is being done. Further funds were provided by a grant from the Ford Foundation to the National Archives Trust Fund Board in support of this and four other major documentary publications. In common with these and many other enterprises like them, *The Adams Papers* has continued to benefit from the guidance and cooperation of the National Historical Publications and Records Commission, chaired by the Archivist of the United States, which from 1975 to the present has provided this enterprise with major financial support. Important additional funds were supplied from 1980 to 1993 by The Andrew W. Mellon Foundation, The J. Howard Pew Freedom Trust, and The Charles E. Culpeper Foundation through the Founding Fathers Papers, Inc. Since 1993, *The Adams Papers* has received major support from the National Endowment for the Humanities, and matching support from The Packard Humanities Institute, through the Founding Fathers Papers, Inc., and from The Charles Francis Adams Charitable Trust, The Florence J. Gould Foundation, The Lyn and Norman Lear Fund, and anonymous donors. Any views, findings, conclusions, or recommendations expressed in this publication do not necessarily reflect those of the National Endowment for the Humanities.

∞ This volume meets all ANSI/NISO Z39.48-1992 standards for permanence.

Library of Congress Cataloging in Publication Data (Revised for vols. 9–20)

Adams, John, 1735–1826.
Papers of John Adams.

(The Adams papers: Series III, General correspondence and other papers of the Adams statesmen)
Vols. 1–6 edited by R. J. Taylor, G. L. Lint, and C. Walker.
Vols. 7–18 edited by G. L. Lint . . . [et al.]
Vols. 19–20 edited by S. Georgini . . . [et al.]
Includes bibliographical references and index.
1. United States—Politics and government—Colonial period, ca. 1600–1775—Sources. 2. Massachusetts—Politics and government—Colonial period, ca. 1600–1775—Sources. 3. United States—Politics and government—Revolution, 1775–1783—Sources. 4. United States—Politics and government—1783–1809—Sources. 5. Presidents—United States—Correspondence. 6. Adams, John, 1735–1826. I. Taylor, Robert Joseph, 1917–2004. II. Lint, Gregg L. III. Georgini, Sara. IV. Title. V. Series: Adams papers: Series III, General correspondence and other papers of the Adams statesmen.

E302.A26 1977 973.4′4′08 77–4707

ISBN 0-674-65441-2 (v. 1–2)
ISBN 0-674-65442-0 (v. 3–4)
ISBN 0-674-65443-9 (v. 5–6)
ISBN 0-674-65444-7 (v. 7–8)
ISBN 0-674-65445-5 (v. 9–10)
ISBN 0-674-01136-8 (v. 11)
ISBN 0-674-01281-X (v. 12)
ISBN 0-674-01812-5 (v. 13)
ISBN-13 978-0-674-02607-0 (v. 14)
ISBN-10 0-674-02607-1 (v. 14)
ISBN 978-0-674-05123-2 (v. 15)
ISBN 978-0-674-06557-4 (v. 16)
ISBN 978-0-674-72895-0 (v. 17)
ISBN 978-0-674-54507-6 (v. 18)
ISBN 978-0-674-91928-0 (v. 19)
ISBN 978-0-674-24466-5 (v. 20)

With great esteem for his years of service,
we dedicate this volume to
LEVIN H. CAMPBELL,
advisor and friend of The Adams Papers

This edition of *The Adams Papers*

is sponsored by the MASSACHUSETTS HISTORICAL SOCIETY

to which the ADAMS MANUSCRIPT TRUST

by a deed of gift dated 4 April 1956

gave ultimate custody of the personal and public papers

written, accumulated, and preserved over a span of three centuries

by the Adams family of Massachusetts

The Adams Papers

The acorn and oakleaf device on the preceding page is redrawn from a seal cut for John Quincy Adams after 1830. The motto is from Cæcilius Statius as quoted by Cicero in the First Tusculan Disputation: *Serit arbores quæ alteri seculo prosint* ("He plants trees for the benefit of later generations").

Contents

Descriptive List of Illustrations

1. "ADIEU BASTILLE," 1789 111

"The king is now perfectly sincere in his surrender at discretion to the states general and will do whatsoever they desire him," John Brown Cutting wrote to John Adams on 24 July 1789, shortly after the fall of Paris' Bastille prison (below). Deserted by his supporters in the clergy, nobility, and army, King Louis XVI of France accepted the National Assembly's goal of creating a constitutional monarchy. Correspondents like Cutting and the Bordeaux-based merchant John Bondfield kept Adams informed of the opening stages of the French Revolution. The author of the *Discourses on Davila* was intrigued to see what form the French government might take, given the chance of reinvention. Writing to Bondfield on 16 September, Adams asked: "In what will be the fermentations in France and the rest of Europe end? Will the spirit and the system of constitutional liberty prevail or will confusion preceed despotism?" (below).

This 1789 caricature by an unknown artist depicts the end of the ancien régime and the birth of a constitutional monarchy dominated by the third estate. The figures of a peasant, a cleric, and a nobleman represent the three estates. A towering peasant wears a tricolor cockade and acts as puppet master. A lion symbolizing the French monarchy crouches at his feet, docile in chains. Meanwhile, a cleric and a nobleman spar on the side as the peasant pulls their strings. In the background, workers dismantle the Bastille (Bosher, *French Rev.*, p. 147–148; William Doyle, *The Oxford History of the French Revolution*, Oxford, 1989, p. 107, 110–111; Ernest F. Henderson, *Symbol and Satire in the French Revolution*, N.Y., 1912, p. 44).

Courtesy of the Library of Congress.

2. CATALOG OF BOOKS IN JOHN ADAMS' LIBRARY, JUNE 1790 187

When he moved from Braintree to New York City in spring 1789, Vice President John Adams asked his wife, Abigail, to gather a selection of his books, mainly works by classical authors and political theorists touching on constitutionalism. As he drafted his *Discourses on Davila* that fall, Adams' mind often turned back to his bookshelf. He tasked Mary Palmer, a longtime family friend, with cleaning and arranging the volumes held at Peacefield. William Cranch, the Adamses' nephew and Palmer's cousin, aided by compiling a full inventory, of which the first page is shown here.

Written entirely in Cranch's hand, this is the earliest and most comprehensive catalog of John Adams' library found in the Adams Papers. Dated June 1790 by his grandson Charles Francis Adams, it is a bound book measuring 7 1/2 by 4 1/2 inches with a dark brown cover. Cranch used 48 of the pages and left four blank. He inscribed "Books at Braintree" on the front cover, and on the back cover he wrote "Catalogue of Books. 1790." He divided Adams' library into several discrete categories of law, religion, history, natural philosophy, poetry, classical literature, and reference works. Cranch recorded the author, title, number of volumes, and, occasionally, the date of publication. Adams' law books were plentiful at 138 volumes, exceeded only by historical topics at 245. Adams owned diverse works written in English, French, Latin, Greek, Italian, and Dutch. Cranch listed 873 titles in all, but by counting each volume separately, he claimed a sum total of 1,674 volumes. Cranch's final count should have totaled 2,248 volumes because he neglected to count numerous titles and a few were recorded twice. The bulk of these books are extant in Adams' library at MB (from Palmer, 25 Nov. 1789, below; *AFC*, 8:358; *Catalogue of JA's Library*).

Collection of the Massachusetts Historical Society.

3. "A SOUTH-WEST VIEW OF NEWPORT," BY SAMUEL KING, 1795 219

As 1789 drew to a close, Rhode Island remained the only state yet to ratify the U.S. Constitution. Politically divided between commercial and agricultural interests, the state legislature at first refused to call a convention. After several months of heated debate, lawmakers relented under the threat of the federal Collection Act, which would have required the state to pay high foreign tonnage duties after 15 January 1790. Delegates met in March and agreed to a bill of rights and suggested amendments before adjourning. They reconvened and ratified the Constitution on 29 May, finally entering the union.

Leading Federalists such as Jabez Bowen, John Brown, and Henry Marchant kept John Adams informed of the unfolding process. Repeatedly, they sought his influence to secure congressional intervention and petitioned for a renewed exemption from the costly duties. Intent on strengthening the fragile union, Adams viewed Rhode Island's outlier status thus: "There can be no medium. Enemies they must be, or fellow citizens, and that in a very short time" (to Brown, 15 Sept. 1789, below).

Newport artist Samuel King (1749–1819) drew this seascape in 1795, capturing the importance of maritime trade to Rhode Island's economy. It was engraved by Enfield, Conn., printer Luther Allen (1780–1821) and featured prominent landmarks, including Trinity Church in the center and, in the distance, the State House, where citizens deliberated ratification (from Marchant, 29 Aug. 1789, and note 4; from Bowen, 9 March 1790, both below; vol. 19:404–406; Oxford Art Online; Clarence S. Brigham, "Librarian's Report for the Year 1907," *Proceedings of the Rhode Island Historical Society*, 29:35

[1910]; Mantle Fielding, *American Engravers upon Copper and Steel*, Phila., 1917, p. 4; *Doc. Hist. Ratif. Const.*, 26:711, 984).
Courtesy of the Rhode Island Historical Society.

Benjamin Franklin's death on 17 April 1790 sank the world into mourning and inspired John Adams to organize his reflections on his former colleague and onetime rival. As he confided to Benjamin Rush on 4 April: "The History of our Revolution will be one continued Lye from one End to the other. The Essence of the whole will be *that Dr Franklins electrical Rod, Smote the Earth and out Sprung General Washington. That Franklin electrifed him with his Rod—and thence forward these two conducted all the Policy Negotiations Legislation and War.*" Perhaps recalling Franklin's ingenuity, Adams tried a creative experiment of his own, dashing off his whimsical "Dialogues of the Dead" essay on [*ca.* 22 *April*] (both below).

Adams' recollection of the Boston-born scientist and diplomat resonates with this oil painting by the British artist Benjamin West (1738–1820). Franklin is shown conducting his 1752 kite and key experiment, aided by cherubim who harness the electricity and collect the particles in a glass Leyden jar. West's white-haired Franklin resembles the same figure in his unfinished work "The Signing of the Anglo-American Preliminary Peace Treaty, 30 November 1782," though Franklin performed the experiment decades earlier, for which see vol. 14:x, 104 (Franklin, *Papers*, 4:360; I. Bernard Cohen, *Science and the Founding Fathers*, N.Y., 1995, p. 143; Helmut von Erffa and Allen Staley, *The Paintings of Benjamin West*, New Haven, 1986, p. 506).
Courtesy of the Philadelphia Museum of Art.

Inventors assailed John Adams with queries for patents in the months before and after Congress' passage of the Patent Act on 10 April 1790. The vice president found the task beyond his prescribed powers under the Constitution, writing to Gen. Benjamin Lincoln on 19 May: "One is harrassed through life with an hundred of these dreamers who will never take no! for an answer." Among the array of inventors was manufacturer Joseph Hague, of Derbyshire, England, who relocated to Philadelphia in 1774 and received £15 from the Pennsylvania legislature for building a spinning jenny. Hague split the prize with Christopher Tully, another inventor who put forth an identical design. Hague modeled his machine after an English version; he wrote to Adams on 13 May 1790 that he was entitled to hold the American patent (both below).

This engraving of Tully's machine appeared in the April 1775 issue of *The Pennsylvania Magazine* with a guide to how it worked. The operator fed cotton or wool through the wooden spindles in the lower frame, and then through the slide and across to the steel spindles of the upper frame. Bands connected the steel spindles to a cylinder and then to a rotating wheel, in order to spin the thread. Tully's machine was six feet long and three feet high, with 24 spindles (*The Pennsylvania Magazine; or, American Monthly Museum*, 1:157–158 [April 1775]; David J. Jeremy, "British Textile Technology Transmission to the United States: The Philadelphia Region Experience, 1770–1820," *Business History Review*, 47:28, 32 [Spring 1973]).

Collection of the Massachusetts Historical Society.

6. "A CHART OF THE INTERIOR PART OF NORTH AMERICA," DETAIL, 1790 373

Tensions flared between Great Britain and Spain from April to November 1790 as they clashed over the Spanish seizure of British ships in Canada's Nootka Sound, a lucrative spot for the fur trade as well as a link to the fabled Northwest Passage. The Nootka Sound conflict became the first major test of the U.S. foreign policy of neutrality. At the center of the Anglo-Spanish dispute over trade rights was former British naval officer and entrepreneur John Meares. Operating variously under a British or a Portuguese flag, he established a trading post at Nootka Sound in 1788, disregarding a 1493 papal bull that recognized Spain's discovery and awarded the land to Spain. In the spring of 1789 Spanish Navy commodore Don Esteban José Martinez seized four of Meares' ships and arrested the crews, thereby reasserting the Spanish claim. Intent on compensation, Meares appealed to the British foreign ministry, triggering a series of tense negotiations that ended with both nations gaining access to the region.

Meares also wrote and circulated an account of his career in the burgeoning China trade, *Voyages Made in the Years 1788 and 1789, from China to the North West Coast of America*, London, 1790. This map appeared in the book, with a preface documenting his search for the Northwest Passage. Meares instructed traders to sail from Hudson Bay to the Pacific Ocean. Nootka Sound is located in the lower right-hand quadrant of the map detail shown here (from John Brown Cutting, 3 June, and note 1; *DNB*; John Meares, *Voyages Made in the Years 1788 and 1789*, London, 1790, p. xli).

Collection of the Massachusetts Historical Society.

7. GEORGE WASHINGTON, BY JOHN TRUMBULL, 1790 397

New York mayor Richard Varick notified John Adams on 21 July 1790 that the city council "applied to the President of the United States to permit Col. John Trumbull take his Portrait" for display in Federal Hall. Adams and the Senate readily agreed to the plan the next day (both below). George Washington sat for his former aide de camp for this portrait, which pays tribute to his wartime leadership. *The New-York Journal & Patriotic Register*, 21 September, announced Trumbull's completion of the painting and set a value of one hundred guineas.

Measuring seven feet high, this presidential portrait graced the room where the first Congress met, which Trumbull called "the most elegant Room in America & in a very perfect light." As Washington reposes in victory, New York streets lie in ruins and British military forces evacuate the city by land and by sea (Washington, *Papers, Presidential Series*, 6:102–103).

Courtesy of Collection of the Public Design Commission of the City of New York. Photograph by Glenn Castellano.

8. "ROBERT MORRIS MOVING THE CAPITOL," CA. 1790 415

In July 1790 all New York congressmen voted against the residence bill, which relocated the federal capital to Philadelphia while a permanent seat of government was built on the Potomac. While John Adams anticipated relocating to a familiar city, many New Yorkers did not welcome the move, as it would damage their business profits and political influence. During the debates, New Yorkers identified Pennsylvania senator Robert Morris as their main adversary. He stood to benefit personally and professionally if the capital moved to Philadelphia. Morris was willing to settle for a short-term placement—likely hoping that after a few years, Congress might find it difficult to move again. Ultimately, Morris led the delegation that bargained with Alexander Hamilton, Thomas Jefferson, and James Madison to pass the Residence Act on 16 July.

During the debates, however, Morris suffered badly in the press, writing to his wife, Mary White Morris, on 2 July: "The Yorkers . . . lay all the blame of this measure on me, and abuse me most unmercifully, both in the Public Prints, private conversations, and even in the streets." This hand-colored cartoon, drawn by an unknown artist and measuring roughly eight by ten inches, was printed in New York. It depicts a giant Morris following the devil to Congress' new home. Morris carries Federal Hall on his shoulder and says: "Never fear I and my Black Friend will carry you safe to Philada." Gesturing at a prostitute, the devil replies: "Come along Bobby here's the Girls." Showing the spectrum of public attitudes toward the move, another man stands on a rooftop shouting "Huzza for Philad:" while a disapproving onlooker laments the "D——d dirty Work" (First Congress, Second Session, 4 Jan. – 12 Aug. 1790, Editorial Note; to Samuel Adams, 12 Sept., both below; *AFC*, 9:xi–xii; Elizabeth M. Nuxoll, "The Financier as Senator: Robert Morris of Pennsylvania, 1789–1795," in Kenneth R. Bowling and Donald R. Kennon, eds., *Neither Separate Nor Equal: Congress in the 1790s*, Athens, Ohio, 2000, p. 105; *Annals of Congress*, 1st Cong., 2d sess., p. 1040, 1737; Jefferson, *Papers*, 17:xxxiv–xxxv).

Courtesy of the American Antiquarian Society.

9. HANNAH ADAMS, BY CHESTER HARDING, CA. 1827 479

Amid the many requests for political and cultural patronage that John Adams received, a short note from a distant cousin stood out. "I request your acceptance of the inclosed dedication to my View of Religions," historian and scholar Hannah Adams wrote on 21 February 1791. "Your permission to adorn my book by prefixing your name will do me the greatest honour" (below). He replied on 10 March, ordering three copies. He requested, however, that she omit "all Titles literary or political . . . and that the Address may be only to John Adams Vice-President of the United States of America" (JA, *Works,* 9:574).

Hannah's father, Thomas (1725–1812), of Medfield, Mass., sold books and hosted boarders studying for entrance to Harvard College. Drawing on her access to literature and armed with Latin and Greek, Hannah became a noted historian of religion. She researched and wrote several works on Christianity, Judaism, and the history of New England. A copy of the 1801 Boston edition of her *View of Religions, in Two Parts*, is in John Adams' library at MB.

Boston artist Chester Harding (1792–1866), known for his oil portraits of prominent political leaders, painted the only known image of Hannah Adams. Toiling in her study, the muslin-capped author is shown seated within easy reach of her Bible, looking up from her deep reading to reflect. The Boston Athenæum exhibited this portrait in its first gallery show shortly after Harding completed it in 1827 (*AFC*, 9:240, 13:119; *Catalogue of JA's Library*; CFA, *Diary*, 3:411; Katherine Wolff, *Culture Club: The Curious History of the Boston Athenaeum*, Amherst, Mass., 2009, p. 63, 66, 68, 176).

Courtesy of the Boston Athenæum.

Introduction

"What is a federal Republic?" Vice President John Adams reflected on 12 June 1789, as the first United States Congress battled to draft legislation. "It is an association of a Number of independent Sovereign States.— Are the Seperate States in our national Government, Sovereign and independent? If they are, We had all better go home. for Heavens Sake, let us analyze our Ideas and correct our Language.— Unanimity is essential to a fœderal Republick.—" Adams' prudent shaping of his office and Congress' formation of the federal government dominate this volume, which chronicles a pivotal era spanning from June 1789 to February 1791. While members of both houses struggled to interpret the Constitution and implement an economic framework, Adams held fast to federalist ideals and etched clear boundaries for his executive powers.[1]

Meeting in New York City, Adams and his colleagues warred over how to collect revenue and where to locate the seat of government. They established and staffed the departments of justice, state, treasury, and war. The first vice president focused on steering progress in the Senate, where he broke a significant number of ties. Enduring the daily grind of politics, Adams lauded the "National Spirit" of his fellow citizens and pledged to continue laboring for the needs of the American people. "If I did not love them now, I would not Serve them another hour—for I very well know that Vexation and Chagrine, must be my Portion, every moment I shall continue in public Life," Adams wrote to his old friend and political confidant Dr. Benjamin Rush. When his duties permitted, Adams considered how to communicate his federalist principles to a wider audience. Despite the country's rapid growth, the aging revolutionary worried that Americans would

[1] To William Tudor, 12 June 1789, below.

be "tormented with a government of men and parties instead of being blessed with a government of laws."[2]

Keeping up a grueling pace in the Senate, the vice president still carved out time to create. From 1789 to 1791 Adams researched and wrote his *Discourses on Davila*. His final product, an influential set of 32 essays, synthesized American progress with the perils of French history. To his chagrin, the same *Discourses* echoed down through the rancorous political debates of the 1790s, arming critics who erroneously labeled the essay collection as evidence of his love of aristocracy. An incomplete draft of his 33d essay is printed here for the first time, as is his whimsical "Dialogues of the Dead," in which he staged a set of historical figures conversing in the afterlife as they awaited Benjamin Franklin's arrival.[3]

Once again, John Adams' candid letters reveal firsthand the joint labor of nation-building in an age of constitutions. The 301 documents printed in volume 20 of the *Papers of John Adams* show a statesman transitioning into the national spotlight after a decade of service abroad. Now that he shared a city and the opportunity for conversation with trusted interlocutors like John Jay and Thomas Jefferson, Adams reconfigured his networks of correspondence. For news of the unfolding French Revolution and the Anglo-Spanish rivalry in Canada's Nootka Sound, he turned to letters from C. W. F. Dumas, the Marquis de Lafayette, John Bondfield, John Brown Cutting, and Thomas Brand Hollis. But, overall, Adams locked his gaze on domestic affairs. He pursued intense dialogues about the state of American politics with Rush, Roger Sherman, John Trumbull, and William Tudor. After years of negotiating treaties and managing loans, Adams was restless to know how the state legislatures were developing; if economic prospects had improved in peacetime; how to uphold American neutrality; and when the newly created government entities would achieve the ideals that he envisioned.

Volume 20 captures John Adams' initial effort at providing national leadership in an era of radical change. Whether or not the union would hold, as regional interests impeded congressional action, remained his chief concern. Adams and his family moved from Brain-

[2] To James Lovell, 4 June 1789; to Benjamin Rush, 9 June; to James Sullivan, 14 July, all below.

[3] John Adams' *Discourses on Davila*, 28 April 1790 – 27 April 1791, Editorial Note; John Adams' *Discourses on Davila*, No. 33, [*ca. 16 March 1791*]; "Dialogues of the Dead," [*ca. 22 April 1790*], and note 1, all below.

tree to New York City before relocating to Philadelphia, the new temporary capital, for his next decade of public life. It was, as he admitted to Rhode Island ally Henry Marchant, a real challenge to sustain the revolutionary vigor needed to build a republic. From his perch in the heart of a bustling Senate, Vice President John Adams wrote: "United We Stand but divided We fall. Join or die. these were our Maxims, twenty five or thirty Years ago, and they are neither less true nor less important now than they were then."[4]

1. UNITING THE STATES

After the first federal Congress convened on 4 March 1789 in New York City's Federal Hall, members drafted a legislative agenda focused on enforcing the ratified Constitution and raising revenue. John Adams and his peers sought to repair public confidence in national governance. Operating under the relatively weak Articles of Confederation, the Continental Congress had foundered badly in efforts to stabilize the economy and enforce foreign treaties. Members had not achieved a quorum since October 1788. With President George Washington's election and all but two states consenting to the Constitution, the momentum for federal progress began at a steady clip. Adams, surveying his colleagues on 21 April 1789, hoped they were ready for hard work. He addressed the Senate: "A trust of the greatest magnitude is committed to this Legislature; and the eyes of the world are upon you Your country expects, from the results of your deliberations, in concurrence with the other branches of government, consideration abroad, and contentment at home—prosperity, order, justice, peace, and liberty."[5]

Every state save North Carolina and Rhode Island had congressmen in place by fall. Dual paths of legislative action, mirroring the Constitution's implied powers, quickly emerged. The House of Representatives brought the country's finances in line, while Adams and the Senate dealt with forming departments of justice, state, treasury, and war. At times, this split focus hampered overall progress. The House, for example, repeatedly deferred action on the Bill of Rights, the ten amendments to the Constitution that secured personal liberties, as they deliberated over ways to collect revenue. Presiding over

[4] To Henry Marchant, 1 June 1790, below.
[5] Vol. 19:xxviii, 418.

the Senate, Adams watched—and heavily contributed to—marathon debates on bicameral protocol. "We proceed Slowly: but in digesting Plans so new, so extensive and so important, it is impossible to bring Bodies of Man to a clear Comprehension of Things and a mutual Satisfaction without long deliberation and debate," Adams reported to his old friend James Bowdoin. Mindful of precedent, members of Congress experimented with forms of communication, creating a daily whirl of new committees and federal firsts. Their routine notes of transmittal, ferrying bills back and forth for edits or requesting signatures, do not appear in Series III since they are found in the volumes of the *First Federal Congress*. The frequency and intensity of members' exchanges on the floor vibrates through the letters printed here. Keen to make headway on a number of fronts, John Adams longed for Congress to take "bold and decisive Measures," yet he was sensible of the institution's youth.[6]

Eager to weigh in when arguments touched on constitutional interpretation and legal history, Adams developed a distinctive presence in the first Congress, as progress moved along in fits and starts. He cast the tie-breaking vote four times in the first session, when minor dilemmas of wording hindered the process. New England Federalists provided him with a rich pipeline of information and votes. Antifederalist critics like William Maclay delighted in jabbing at Adams' pride. The Pennsylvania senator's description of Adams, seated in his "great chair" at the Senate's head and rustling newspapers, was less than flattering. In Maclay's view, Adams was fond of giving "pretty speeches," though "Bonny Jonny Adams" did "show as much joy on an adjournment from Friday to Monday as ever a school-boy did at the sweet sound of play-time."[7]

In his Diary, John Adams kept fitful notes about the major debates but was too busy to comment fully in the bulk of his letters. When the session adjourned on 29 September, the first federal Congress had regulated trade and confirmed the U.S. Supreme Court justices. The president had filled his cabinet with influential department heads, including Thomas Jefferson, Alexander Hamilton, and Henry Knox. Several pressing issues were postponed for the next session, namely, the location of the capital, the creation of a post office, the establishment of patents, and, most critically, the discharging of the national debt.

[6] To James Lovell, 4 June 1789, and note 3; to James Bowdoin, 11 June; to Richard Peters, 5 June, all below.

[7] Maclay, *Journal*, p. 86, 275, 313, 385.

Departing New York City on 12 October, Adams spent his first hiatus in making a restorative solo trip to his native Braintree. Weary from six months of legislative work, he appeared with Washington and Samuel Adams in Boston, where the trio drew cheers. Writing to his wife, Abigail, on [*1*] November, Adams recalled: "The Remarks were very Shrewd— Behold three Men, Said one, who can make a Revolution when they please. There Said another are the three genuine Pivots of the Revolution." By late November, the vice president was back in New York City and ready for Congress' second session, which began on 4 January 1790.[8]

A great deal of congressional progress hinged on Adams' robust exercise of his vice presidential powers. He broke more ties in the second session than he did in any other of his tenure in the Senate, often reaping criticism for it. Meanwhile, members squared off on two complex issues, the federal assumption of state debts and the site of the national capital. Progress on all fronts gradually stalled. During the spring of 1790, petitions piled up and bills lagged. "The awful object before them, I mean the national debt, monopolizes the attention of Congress to such a degree that untill some system is digested no member of either house will be able to attend to any thing else," Adams wrote on 27 February. He was uneasy that members could not agree on a permanent seat of government. Senators from Pennsylvania and Maryland made a good case, as Adams thought, for situating the capital in proximity to lucrative western lands. In his Diary, Adams jotted down fragmentary notes on the debates, emphasizing Virginia senator William Grayson's main point: "We are about founding a City which will be one of the first in the World, and We are governed by local and partial Motives." To Adams' mind, the standstill threatened the government's credibility. Once Hamilton and Virginia representative James Madison struck their infamous bargain at Jefferson's dinner table in June, Congress swung back into action. The Residence Act, signed by the president on 16 July, eased southerners' concerns about federal power. The law stipulated the creation of a permanent seat of government on the Potomac River, with a temporary residence planned in Philadelphia for ten years. The Funding Act, passed on 4 August, also reinvigorated congressional momentum, appeasing northern demands for the federal assumption of heavy Revolutionary War debts. With a plan in place for establishing

[8] *AFC*, 8:420, 432.

the capital and collecting revenue, the union now stood on much firmer ground—with one exception.[9]

For, elsewhere, the protracted quandary of how to handle Rhode Island's outlier status—whether to inflict high foreign duties on the lone state still mulling ratification of the Constitution—hit an impasse. Throughout the fall of 1789 and stretching into the following spring, Newport and Providence Federalists like Henry Marchant and Jabez Bowen appealed to Adams seeking congressional intervention. Led by a powerful Country Party, the Rhode Island legislature favored the emission of paper money and harbored Antifederalist sentiments inimical to adopting the Constitution. Several snarled attempts at hosting new sessions of the ratification convention ensued. Adams forwarded their petitions to Congress but complained that Rhode Islanders' failure to consent indicated a deep rift in the union. "They are betraying the Rights and Interests of New England every day," he wrote on 18 June 1789. Aside from expressing his ire, Adams took no public step to meddle in Rhode Island's internal affairs, ensuring that the vice president's powers did not overreach into state business. Operating under constitutional principles meant that Congress was not authorized "to make a Conquest of that People, or to bring them into the Union by Coertion," Adams observed on 28 February 1790.[10]

Rhode Island merchants won a short reprieve from paying foreign tonnage duties until 15 January. They pleaded for a renewal of the exemption, to no avail. Congress, riven by arguments over the assumption of state debts and the federal seat, let the matter lie until April. Facing an increasingly dire situation—owing expensive duties and with scarce currency to pay them—Rhode Island capitulated. In March state convention delegates reconvened to debate amendments to the Constitution, but local factionalism again halted progress. Congress revisited the issue in April, drafting a punitive trade bill that treated the state as a foreign nation. Rhode Islanders responded by ratifying on 29 May. "Their members will join you, full fraught with State-politics, & a tolerable infusion of Antifederalism. The real friends to an efficient Government are so few," John Trumbull cautioned the vice president on 5 June, voicing the attitude of many Federalists and speculating on the changes that Adams' new peers might

[9] First Congress, Second Session, 4 Jan. – 12 Aug. 1790, Editorial Note; to Jabez Bowen, 27 Feb., both below; JA, *D&A*, 3:223; *AFC*, 9:xi–xii.

[10] From Jabez Bowen, 16 June 1789; to James Sullivan, 18 June; from Henry Marchant, 29 Aug.; from Bowen, 28 Dec.; to John Brown & John Brown Francis, 28 Feb. 1790, all below.

engineer. With the former thirteen colonies reunited in Congress, Adams and his colleagues continued the great work of making a government.[11]

When the second session closed on 12 August, Adams was relieved. It had been a period of "pretty tight service," as Abigail recalled. He presided over the Senate every day, from ten o'clock in the morning until four o'clock in the afternoon, for seven months. "Reading long Bill, hearing debates, and not always those the most consonant to his mind and opinions putting questions, Stating them, constant attention to them that in putting questions they may not be misled, is no easy task what ever Grumblers may think," she wrote. By session's end, John Adams was deeply troubled by the partisan rivalry emerging in the halls of Congress. "There is every Evidence of good Intentions on all sides but there are too many Symptoms of old Colonial Habits: and too few, of great national Views," he wrote. He believed that this enmity, which resounded in the press, undermined the government's work. Service in the Senate also took a personal toll on Adams, who wrote: "Every unpopular point is invariably left to me to determine so that I must be the scape goat, to bear all their sins, without a possibility of acquiring any share in the honor of any of their popular deeds."[12] Diligently, Adams wrapped up his duties. He directed the city council to retain the fine mahogany and crimson-velvet furniture of the Senate while Congress moved to its next home, Philadelphia. The vice president and his family lingered in New York City, savoring the prospect of a quiet month ahead. All that changed abruptly in late August 1790, when Washington sought John Adams' advice in resolving the first major crisis of American foreign policy.

2. "PRESERVE AN HONEST NEUTRALITY"

Even as the new United States was opening to the world, lawmakers like John Adams carefully measured the limits of that engagement. His incoming letters offer a sharp lens on both the country's early economic history and Americans' hopes of fortune. Reeling

[11] From Henry Marchant, 18 Jan. 1790; from William Ellery, [*ca.* 6] March; to Ellery, 19 May; from John Trumbull, 5 June, all below.

[12] *AFC*, 9:74; JA, *D&A*, 3:217–224; Bickford and Bowling, *Birth of the Nation*, p. 15–22, 29–35, 45–54; to Richard Peters, 5 June 1789; to William Cushing, 14 Sept.; First Congress, Second Session, 4 Jan. – 12 Aug. 1790, Editorial Note, all below.

from Revolutionary War debt, merchants found themselves enmeshed in the Anglo-American trade war that consumed their meager profits throughout the 1780s. In response, American entrepreneurs widened their reach, eyeing the riches of the developing China trade. They braved Barbary depredations, skyrocketing marine insurance rates, and the daily hazards of doing business without the protection of the British Navy. Adams had spent a decade viewing their plight from the Continent; as vice president, the problem came home. He encouraged explorers like Capt. Robert Gray, who circumnavigated the globe, and adventurers like Jeremiah Allen, who traveled to Empress Catherine II's Russia to trade. In New York, Adams and the Senate reviewed two treaties with Native American tribes but never formally consented to the agreements, claiming confusion over internal protocols. When Adams and the Senate replied to George Washington's annual address on 11 January 1790, they recommended a cautious approach to achieving expansion and diplomacy: "We are persuaded that one of the most effectual means of preserving peace, is to be prepared for war; and our attention shall be directed to the objects of common defence, and to the adoption of such plans . . . most likely to prevent our dependence on other countries for essential supplies." With the boundary lines of the nation still fluid, Congress monitored multiple frontiers, wary of entanglement in foreign rivalries.[13]

Then, to Americans' dismay, a major Anglo-Spanish dispute erupted over events in the small but strategic foothold of Nootka Sound. There, in late 1789, Spanish naval officers seized four cargo ships belonging to British entrepreneur John Meares and detained the crew, thereby reaffirming the Spanish claim to the region. What began as a fight over trading rights escalated into a clash of European powers by June 1790. Whether or not it advanced to war, the Nootka Sound conflict hinted at ideological and imperial consequences alike. If the British argument held, then it invalidated the 1493 papal bull affirming that land could be claimed by Spain's discovery. Further, it meant that sovereignty without settlement was no longer a viable practice. Eager to maintain their far-flung colonial possessions, Britain and Spain spent the summer arming fleets and amplifying rhetoric. "The warlike preparations in every port and corner of

[13] Vol. 19:xiii; to Roger Sherman, 20 July 1789, and note 2; from Jeremiah Allen, 29 July 1790, and note 1, both below; U.S. Senate, *Jour.*, 1st Cong., 2d sess., p. 104.

the Island are most vigourous and extensive," John Brown Cutting wrote from London on 3 June.[14]

By late spring, frantic reports of a possible Anglo-Spanish war filled the newspapers and letters that flooded John Adams' desk. The most substantial news came from Cutting, a longtime informant who supplied Adams with Meares' account, squibs from the British press, naval intelligence, and parliamentary gossip. Like many observers, Cutting perceived several ways that the United States could turn the encroaching war to its advantage. First, America might sign an offensive and defensive treaty with Britain, with the expectation that a new commercial deal would result, along with a proper exchange of ministers—thereby satisfying two of Adams' lingering desires from his time as minister in London. Alternatively, Americans might undertake the Spanish cause and help lock out the British from establishing a permanent base for trade in Nootka Sound, which was a gateway to the legendary Northwest Passage. This path would deprive the British of several generations' worth of profit. Cutting espied another, richer angle of opportunity. In exchange for U.S. aid, Spain might open up navigation of the Mississippi River to Americans. Or, Cutting speculated further, perhaps a triumphant and grateful Britain would secure the same right for its American allies. Either way, an Anglo-Spanish war sent foreign troops marching across the neutral United States.[15]

In European gazettes and American newspapers, conjectures flew thick and fast, mixed in with some facts. British militias were training in Detroit, Michigan. Spanish Army officers planned to invade St. Augustine, Florida. William Pitt the Younger held clandestine talks with Latin American revolutionaries, plotting to ensure British control of the region's gold and silver mines in the wake of a Spanish defeat. Tensions rose with each report. Americans, who had largely evaded the global conflicts that raged in the 1780s, eyed the Nootka Sound crisis with mounting apprehension. Many supported a policy of neutrality for the same reasons that Adams had laid out three years earlier: "The United States of America will take the coolest precautions, while they fulfil their engagements with honor, to maintain their neutrality inviolate. If a general and lasting war in Europe

[14] From John Brown Cutting, 3 June 1790, and notes 1–2, below; John Meares, *Authentic Copy of the Memorial to the Right Honourable William Wyndham Grenville . . . Containing Every Particular Respecting the Capture of the Vessels in Nootka Sound*, London, 1790, p. 8. See also Descriptive List of Illustrations, No. 6, above.

[15] See, for example, John Brown Cutting's letters of 14, 16 June, and 5 July 1790, all below.

should ensue, and America preserve her peace, she will be, at the close of it, the first country in the world, in point of affluence and prosperity if not in real power.—" To Adams' mind, dabbling in foreign quarrels endangered the union's hard-won liberty and risked its financial ruin. Americans watched, and waited.[16]

Though British and Spanish negotiators met in Madrid to resolve the conflict, signing a preliminary agreement on 24 July 1790, that critical piece of news did not cross the Atlantic until months later. The opening act of the Nootka Sound conflict rattled lawmakers like Washington and Adams, who hoped to "preserve an honest Neutrality," given the nation's inability to muster an army, raise a fleet, or afford a war. Beset by rumors and reports, Washington wrote to his cabinet on 27 August, seeking counsel. The president circulated a nearly identical and "secret" letter to Adams, Alexander Hamilton, Thomas Jefferson, Henry Knox, and John Jay. He asked each to assess the threat, recommend a course of action, and weigh the price of neutrality. Washington ended with a pointed query: Should the United States grant safe passage to British troops?

John Adams was the first to reply. From his perspective, maintaining American neutrality was key. Like Washington, he projected that the British would strike first at French Louisiana. This invasive maneuver would render the nation's western lands vulnerable and halt U.S. trade with the West Indies, while the British Navy's presence on the Atlantic coast would breed panic. Americans would be surrounded and occupied, and therefore he advised that they continue to pursue "a neutrality, as long as it may be practicable." In addition, the nation lacked the resources to contend with a foreign threat, a view echoed in the replies of Hamilton, Jay, and Knox. "We Should not engage even in defensive War, untill the Necessity of it, Should become apparent, or at least until We have it in our Power to make it manifest, in Europe as well as at home," Adams wrote. He flatly rejected allowing British troops to pass over U.S. soil, suggesting that Washington turn down any such request in "clear and decided" but "guarded and dignified" terms. Adams drew on the circumstance of the country's scattered population and law of nations theory to buttress his argument, decrying "a measure So daring offensive and hostile, as the march of Troops through our Territory to Attack a friend." Within the cabinet, Jefferson dissented, urging a show of force. Heeding Adams and the majority of his advisors, Washington stood

[16] From John Brown Cutting, 5 July 1790, and notes 1–2; from George Walton, 23 July, and note 1, both below; *Dipl. Corr.*, 1783–1789, 2:805.

firm and took no action. An ocean away, Anglo-Spanish negotiators spent the autumn crafting a set of conventions that awarded trade rights to both nations. Owing to British ingenuity at the bargaining table, Spain was edged out of Pacific lands and cut off from the fur trade. And the United States hung on to its neutrality.[17]

Shrewdly, Adams used the Nootka Sound crisis to press for the enlargement and development of a professional diplomatic corps. This arose from a combination of experiences, mainly the debates he saw in the Senate and his years of service in Europe. For, as Adams knew, nominations for consulships fell under the constitutional purview of the president. Adams received a wave of patronage requests for these prestigious posts from former business contacts, ship captains, and Continental Army officers trying to recoup the fortunes they had invested in the Revolutionary War. While he stressed the need for neutrality, Adams underlined to Washington how vital it was to staff U.S. diplomatic offices around the world. The failure of unofficial efforts by Gouverneur Morris and William Stephens Smith to negotiate an Anglo-American trade deal bore out his belief. Without ministers resident at listening posts in London, Paris, and The Hague, a fresh crisis might afflict the United States and do greater damage. "God knows where the Men are to be found who are qualified for Such Missions and would undertake them," he wrote. Briefly free of official duties during the Senate's adjournment, Adams seized on the Nootka Sound conflict to reiterate his statesmanship—and to assert his voice in Washington's cabinet.[18]

3. MAKING THE VICE PRESIDENCY

Americans had never had a vice president before John Adams. Nor did the supreme law of the land, the U.S. Constitution, supply a clear road map to the responsibilities and privileges of the office. Adams envisioned the role as similar to the rotating head of the States General in the Netherlands, with a touch of Roman senator. He was less certain, however, that he prevailed in a fair election. Whispers of a "dark and dirty Intrigue" haunted Adams' initial months in office,

[17] Black, *British Foreign Policy*, p. 233–256; from George Washington, 27 Aug. 1790, and notes 1–3; to Washington, 29 Aug., both below.

[18] Vol. 19:xxx–xxxi; to George Mason Jr., 4 July 1789; from Robert Montgomery, 20 July; from Sylvanus Bourne, 18 Aug.; from John Brown Cutting, 3 June 1790, 17 July; from Jeremiah Allen, 29 July; from John Codman Jr., 27 Aug.; to George Washington, 29 Aug.; to Codman, 10 Oct.; from WSS, 3 Dec., and note 2, all below.

and evidence of it trickled steadily into his mail. Slowly, he uncovered a scheme propagated by Alexander Hamilton and Col. Samuel Blachley Webb. Acting in concert, they convinced presidential electors in New England and in the southern states to cast their votes for other candidates, thereby ensuring that Adams came in second to George Washington. He did not care to expose the plot, but Adams still fumed about the flawed procedure a year later. "The Doctrine of *throwing away Votes* is itself a Corruption. a bare Motion in the House or Senate to institute an Inquiry would produe a trepidation in many hearts. Throwing Away a Vote is betraying a Trust, it is a Breach of Honour, it is a Perjury—it is equivalent to all this in my Mind," he wrote to John Trumbull. Reluctant to incite more discord in Congress, Adams turned to shaping the vice presidency.[19]

First, he sought to settle the question of his ambition, a popular complaint that had dogged Adams since his earliest days of public life. "I am not of Cæsar's mind. The Second place in Rome is high enough for me," Adams asserted as he settled into his post. He knew he lacked the public "confidence and affection" showered on Washington, a war hero who was the people's choice at the polls. The president nearly died twice during his first year in office, prompting an outpouring of popular concern that mingled, bitterly for Adams, with open hostility toward the idea of his assuming the top seat. Ever sensitive to criticism, Adams recoiled from the notion that he was anything other than the eighteenth-century ideal of a disinterested servant toiling solely for the public good. In letters to friends and former law students, he emphasized that a decade in luxury-loving Europe had not led him to abandon American morals. He acknowledged that he was no Washington. But Adams was eager to accentuate his venerable New England roots, scholarly prowess, and diplomatic expertise. "The Character of a Legislator, has in all Ages been held above that of an Hero," he wrote, adding: "A consummate Master of science and Literature, a long Experience in Affairs of Government, travel through all the known World were among the ancients thought little enough for a Founder of Nations Laws.—" It was no accident that Adams, who cast himself in cutting contrast to Washington as a lawmaker rather than a warrior, had exhibited precisely those skills.[20]

[19] To Benjamin Rush, 9 June 1789, and note 2; to François Adriaan Van der Kemp, 27 March 1790; to John Trumbull, 25 April, all below.

[20] To James Lovell, 1 Sept. 1789, and note 2; to William Ellery, 19 May 1790, and note 3; to Henry Marchant, 20 March, all below.

Second, Adams navigated the hazy charge of the vice presidency, seeking a balance between his Senate labors and the joys of writing. Presiding over the Senate was physically and intellectually demanding. The former diplomat was accustomed to life on the road rather than the "severe" strain of a desk job in Federal Hall. He persevered with the task, reflecting that "setting still in the same place, so many hours of every day, and attending to the Course of proceedings in every step, as it is some thing new to me is somewhat injurious to my health." Gradually, he acclimated to the routine of attending debates, editing bills, and signing the continuous stream of paperwork that brought political architecture to life. Between his rounds of duty, Adams tried to engage citizens in print. He proved to be an exceptionally prolific author during the first Congress. New editions of his works about American federalism and European history rolled out, including *Twenty-six Letters, Upon Interesting Subjects, Respecting the Revolution of America*; his three-volume *Defence of the Constitutions of Government of the United States of America*; and an essay series, *Discourses on Davila*. When his work in the Senate felt tedious, Adams reached out to a set of elite readers—C. W. F. Dumas, Thomas Brand Hollis, François Adriaan Van der Kemp, and others—who were enthusiastic to trade news and views.[21]

According to Adams, the American vice president should be a diligent bureaucrat with (preferably) no pretensions to higher office. A thick-skinned attitude toward the press, a trait that Adams rarely demonstrated, was also required. When a satirical ode by Edward Church sped through the states, lampooning Adams as "The Dangerous Vice ——" who loved monarchy, he struck back, but privately. One part of Church's ode that particularly riled the prickly Adams was allegedly inspired by Washington's refusal to acknowledge him at a levee. This portrait of division and jealousy at the highest level of government, Adams thought, was exactly the kind of poisonous sedition he expected from a spurned job-seeker with loyalist roots. He was surprised, though, to serve as Church's target. "Washington refused or neglected him: and he fawns on Washington and Spits fire at Adams. poor Devil! I pitty him," he complained to Cotton Tufts. His response was mild, but Adams recognized that the vice presidency offered no buffer from the press. Alternately celebratory and

[21] Vols. 10:196–252; 18:539, 544, 546–550; 19:130–132; to James Lovell, 4 June 1789, John Adams' *Discourses on Davila*, 28 April 1790 – 27 April 1791, Editorial Note; from François Adriaan Van der Kemp, 7 Jan. 1790; to Van der Kemp, 27 Feb., all below.

vicious, the constant ebb and flow of public opinion influenced Adams' approach to shaping national policy and, by extension, his role in it.[22]

The years from 1789 to 1791 brought more than a career change for Adams, who struggled to reconcile the personal and the political. Benjamin Franklin and James Bowdoin, two of his closest revolutionary colleagues, died. Adams revered Bowdoin and suggested to son John Quincy Adams, now a fledgling lawyer in Boston, that Bowdoin offered a fine role model: "Massachusetts has produced few Characters so respectable. Splendid fortune Seldom unites with so much Knowledge Integrity, Prudence and public Spirit." Adams was less charitable in remembering his fellow peace commissioner, eulogizing Franklin thus: "I can reconcile his Conduct in public affairs neither to the Character of an honest Man, nor to that of a Man of sense.—" Along with his mixed feelings about mourning Franklin, Adams suffered another kind of loss, made evident in this volume. The French Revolution's onset, which caused Adams "to rejoice with trembling," severed his exchanges with trusted confidants in Europe by early 1791. At home, partisan politics drove him apart from friends who expressed Antifederalist sentiments, including Mercy Otis Warren. Once Adams had hailed her as "the most accomplished Lady in America." Following her published critique of the U.S. Constitution, Adams changed tone. He drafted a sternly worded letter to Warren, explaining that Antifederalist resistance could trigger a bloody civil war. Some friends, Adams wrote, lost his trust if he could not stomach their politics: "As long as this indecission remains, it is impossible there should be the same confidence between them and me, which there was once.— The affection for them which I once had will never be forgotten, nor can it ever be destroyed, but confidence can never be the same, without the same foundation for it." He never sent the letter, but the break was mutual. Adams and Warren did not resume correspondence until 1803.[23]

From November to December 1790, Adams spent the congressional break settling into his new residence of Bush Hill. Although he let his outgoing correspondence lapse, reserving his energy for the forthcoming legislative session, Adams kept busy. Avidly, he collected re-

[22] Vol. 18:103; to Sylvanus Bourne, 30 Aug. 1789, and note 1; to Cotton Tufts, 16 Sept., both below.

[23] Vol. 9:64; to JQA, 8 Dec. 1790, Adams Papers; to John Trumbull, 25 April; "Dialogues of the Dead," [*ca. 22 April 1790*]; to Richard Price, 19 April; to Mercy Otis Warren, 14 Feb. 1791, all below.

actions to his writings, especially his *Discourses on Davila*. Soon, a characteristic zeal to return to public service resurfaced in Adams' letters. The political conversations centering on the Bill of Rights persuaded Adams that some wounds of partisan rivalry, no matter how deep, could be healed. He responded to Samuel Adams, the new lieutenant governor of Massachusetts, explaining that his cousin's Antifederalist critiques must not curtail their dialogue. John Adams proposed the "Sweet Communion" of a reunion. "I dont believe, that We who have preserved for more than thirty Years an uninterupted Friendship, and have So long thought and acted harmoniously together in the worst of times, are now so far asunder in sentiment as some People pretend," he wrote. Written between the lines, the vice president's message was nevertheless clear. Support of the Constitution was sorely needed at every level, or partisan politics would tear apart Congress before it passed vital legislation. The "active and ardent" rivalry developing between the state and federal governments also troubled John Adams. "Thirteen Strong Men embracing thirteen Pillars at once, and bowing themselves in concert, will easily pull down a frail Edifice," he warned Trumbull.[24]

For Adams and many of the lawmakers who filed into Philadelphia's Congress Hall on 6 December, the third session felt like a homecoming, to the site where the Continental Congress declared independence in 1776. Adams appreciated the change of scene. "Philadelphia is worth Seeing. It is a great City and has Science, Litterature, Wealth and Beauty, which deserve respect, if not Admiration," he wrote to John Quincy on 13 December 1790, as the federal gears again began to move. With the Funding Act and the Residence Act in place, members focused on the maintenance and enforcement of recent legislation. Congress approved another key piece of Hamilton's economic framework, establishing the First Bank of the United States on 25 February 1791. That step came after weeks of debate, with James Madison and others questioning the federal government's constitutional power to create such an entity, in light of the states' abilities to form branch banks. With Hamilton's vision taking root, speculation soared and real estate investment boomed. Two territories, Vermont and Kentucky, advanced toward statehood. Adams welcomed the United States' growth and relayed word of it across the Atlantic to a handful of well-connected friends in Europe. "This

[24] From James Sullivan, 2 July 1789, and note 2; to Samuel Adams, 18 Oct. 1790; to John Trumbull, 23 Jan. 1791, all below.

country, sir, is as happy as it deserves to be," he observed to Hollis. Digging back into his now familiar Senate routine, Adams almost sounded optimistic.[25]

During the third session members acted swiftly, demonstrating an acculturation to protocol and a fresh capacity for compromise, now that the Funding Act and the Residence Act were made law. They also rejected or tabled a substantial number of bills, mostly related to domestic issues such as federal regulation of the post office, compensation for widows and orphans of Revolutionary War soldiers, and the consular convention. Congress made a last push on 3 March to pass the Whiskey Act, which raised duties and laid an excise on distilled liquors, and several other acts extending Hamilton's financial plan. Yet American affairs felt unsettled as the term waned. Washington sent a message to Adams and the senators still in Philadelphia, calling for a special session on 4 March to address "certain matters touching the public good." He was anxious to finish filling government posts and sent a long list of nominations for excise supervisors, army officers, and more.

The vice president readied for another bruising round in the Senate. As the special session opened, he once again permitted himself a few brief moments of literary reflection. He contemplated how far the theory of tripartite federalism had carried the nation, and whether it could survive as a political practice. In his draft 33d essay of the *Discourses,* John Adams assessed the state of the American union and considered what came next in terms of legislative labor: "Before We attempt Discoveries and improvements, We should consider, whether the whole of a Subject is not already known: and whether it is not already as perfect as We can make it: and better than it would be with Such Innovations and alterations as are projected."[26]

4. JOHN ADAMS AND HIS LETTERBOOKS

During the span of 21 months covered by this volume, John Adams used Letterbooks 26 and 27, which correspond to reels 114 and 115 of the Adams Papers Microfilms. Both Letterbooks have been fully described in a previous volume.[27] Between September 1789 and Feb-

[25] *AFC*, 9:160, 186, 250; to Thomas Brand Hollis, 3 Nov. 1790, below.

[26] Bickford and Bowling, *Birth of the Nation*, p. 99, 100; Washington, *Papers, Presidential Series*, 7:485–486; John Adams' *Discourses on Davila*, No. 33, [*ca. 16 March 1791*], below.

[27] Vol. 19:xxxii–xxxiii.

ruary 1791, John's middle son, Charles, often served as his secretary. Occasionally, William Stephens Smith and Abigail Adams 2d performed the same duty. Many entries are in John Adams' hand, although a few unknown hands are also featured therein.

5. NOTES ON EDITORIAL METHOD

There have been no substantive changes made in the editorial method since 2007, when the editors made changes following a comprehensive review of the project's editorial practices. For a statement of the policy as then determined, see the *Papers of John Adams*, 14:xxix–xxxvii. Those interested in following the evolution of the editorial method from the beginning of the project should consult the *Diary and Autobiography of John Adams*, 1:lii–lxii, and the *Papers of John Adams*, 1:xxxi–xxxv; 9:xx–xxiii; 11:xx–xxi.

6. RELATED DIGITAL RESOURCES

The Massachusetts Historical Society is committed to making Adams family materials available to scholars and the public online. Four digital resources of particular interest to those who use the *Papers of John Adams* volumes are the Adams Papers Digital Edition; The Adams Family Papers: An Electronic Archive; The Diaries of John Quincy Adams: A Digital Collection; and the Online Adams Catalog. All are available through the Historical Society's website at www.masshist.org.

The Adams Papers Digital Edition, a project cosponsored by the National Endowment for the Humanities, Harvard University Press, and the Massachusetts Historical Society, offers searchable text for 47 of the Adams Papers volumes published prior to 2016 (excluding the *Portraits* volumes). There is a single consolidated index for volumes published through 2006, while the indexes for more recent volumes appear separately. This digital edition is designed as a complement to the letterpress edition by providing greater access to a wealth of Adams material.

The Adams Family Papers Electronic Archive contains images and text files of all of the correspondence between John and Abigail Adams owned by the Massachusetts Historical Society as well as John

Adams' Diaries and Autobiography. The text is fully searchable and can also be browsed by date.

The Diaries of John Quincy Adams Digital Collection provides digital images of John Quincy Adams' entire 51-volume Diary, which he composed over nearly seventy years. The images can be searched by date or browsed by diary volume. Access to the diaries is being expanded through the John Quincy Adams Digital Diary, the goal of which is to provide verified and searchable transcriptions alongside the digital images of the Diary. The project is supported by the Amelia Peabody Charitable Fund, Harvard University Press, and private donors.

The Online Adams Catalog represents a fully searchable electronic database of all known Adams documents, dating primarily from the 1760s to 1889, at the Massachusetts Historical Society and other public and private repositories. The digital conversion—based on the original Adams Papers control file begun in the 1950s and steadily updated since that time—was supported by the National Historical Publications and Records Commission and the Massachusetts Historical Society, and was initiated with Packard Humanities Institute funds in 2009. The catalog allows public online access to a database of nearly 110,000 records, with some 30,000 cross-reference links to online, printed, and microfilm editions of the items, or to websites of the holding repositories. Each record contains information on a document's author, recipient, and date and on the location of the original, if known.

Also of value to users of the *Papers of John Adams* is the John Adams Library at the Boston Public Library, which contains a catalog record of the marginalia entered by Adams in his books.

Volume 20 explores 21 months of John Adams' public life as he painstakingly created the office of the vice presidency, in theory and in practice. The 301 documents printed and 128 omitted should be used in conjunction with the documents for the period appearing in the *Adams Family Correspondence*, 8:367–451 and 9:1–196, wherein an additional 32 letters to or from John Adams appear. Abigail Adams' letters provide details on the family's myriad social and political obligations in Braintree, New York City, and Philadelphia, as well as their cultural travels. John Quincy Adams' correspondence with his father about the legal profession and with other family members offers a nuanced portrait of the trials and tribulations of life as a young lawyer in Boston. Scholars should also consult John Adams' *Diary and Autobiography*, 3:217–224, which he briefly resumed from 15 July 1789 to 25 January 1790 to record key debates in the Senate during the first federal Congress.

Sara Georgini
July 2019

Acknowledgments

Volume 20 of the *Papers of John Adams* is the product of the dedicated members of Adams Papers staff, past and present. We recognize the contributions of assistant editor Christopher F. Minty and editorial assistant Tess Renault during our production process. We are grateful for the support of interns Margot Rashba and L. J. Woolcock, as well as the many transcribers who labored to prepare transcripts for this and future Adams Papers volumes. Once again, we would like to thank Ann-Marie Imbornoni, who copyedited the volume and added immensely to its accuracy and style.

Over time, a project such as the Adams Papers builds a store of old and new friends whose assistance is vital to the editorial process. Jeremie Korta translated the French documents. James P. McClure of the Papers of Thomas Jefferson kindly consulted on special research topics. Robb K. Haberman of the Selected Papers of John Jay clarified details regarding Jay's labors in the U.S. judiciary. Jayne F. Carbone of the Boston Marine Society aided with queries about John Adams' membership and the contents of their institutional archives. We are grateful to the reference librarians of Harvard University's Houghton, Lamont, and Widener libraries as well as Boston University's Fineman and Pappas law libraries. At the Boston Public Library, Kimberly Reynolds, Curator of Manuscripts, and Sean P. Casey of the Rare Books and Manuscripts Department assisted with research related to John Adams' Library.

Adams Papers editors are especially indebted to the efficiency of Kenneth and Kevin Krugh of Technologies 'N Typography in Merrimac, Massachusetts, who skillfully managed the typesetting of the volume. Greek characters were set using Zeph Text, courtesy of the Loeb Classical Library. At Harvard University Press, we acknowledge the unflagging efforts of Andrew Kinney, General Editor; Tim Jones, Director of Design and Production; Christine Thorsteinsson,

Managing Editor; Abigail Mumford, Assistant Director of Production; Olivia Woods, Editorial Assistant; and Eric Mulder, Design Assistant.

We thank the Massachusetts Historical Society, which has served as a home for both the Adams Papers editorial project and Adams-related scholarship for over sixty years. In particular, we thank President Catherine Allgor; Peter Drummey, Stephen T. Riley Librarian; Carol Knauff, Vice President of Communications & Marketing; Brenda M. Lawson, Vice President for Collections; Maureen Nguyen, Vice President of Development; Will Tsoules, Vice President & Chief Financial Officer; Anne E. Bentley, Curator of Art & Artifacts; Elaine Heavey, Director of the Library; Nancy Heywood, Senior Archivist for Digital Initiatives; Ondine E. Le Blanc, Worthington C. Ford Editor of Publications; Kanisorn Wongsrichanalai, Director of Research; Conrad Edick Wright, Sibley Editor; Laura Wulf, Photographic and Digital Imaging Specialist; Mary E. Yacovone, Senior Cataloger; and all of the members of the Library–Reader Services department. As ever, the Society's Adams Papers Committee provides steadfast support for the project's success.

Guide to Editorial Apparatus

The first three sections (1–3) of this guide list, respectively, the arbitrary devices used for clarifying the text, the code names for prominent members of the Adams family, and the symbols that are employed throughout *The Adams Papers*, in all its series and parts, for various kinds of manuscript sources. The final three sections (4–6) list, respectively, the symbols for institutions holding original materials, the various abbreviations and conventional terms, and the short titles of books and other works that occur in volume 20 of the *Papers of John Adams*.

1. TEXTUAL DEVICES

The following devices will be used throughout *The Adams Papers* to clarify the presentation of the text.

[. . .]	One word missing or illegible.
[. . . .]	Two words missing or illegible.
[. . . .][1]	More than two words missing or illegible; subjoined footnote estimates amount of missing matter.
[ ]	Number or part of a number missing or illegible. Amount of blank space inside brackets approximates the number of missing or illegible digits.
[roman]	Conjectural reading for missing or illegible matter. A question mark is inserted before the closing bracket if the conjectural reading is seriously doubtful.
~~roman~~	Canceled matter.
[*italic*]	Editorial insertion.
{roman}	Text editorially decoded or deciphered.

2. ADAMS FAMILY CODE NAMES

First Generation

JA	John Adams (1735–1826)
AA	Abigail Adams (1744–1818), *m.* JA 1764

Second Generation

AA2	Abigail Adams (1765–1813), daughter of JA and AA, *m.* WSS 1786
WSS	William Stephens Smith (1755–1816), brother of SSA

JQA	John Quincy Adams (1767–1848), son of JA and AA
LCA	Louisa Catherine Johnson (1775–1852), *m.* JQA 1797
CA	Charles Adams (1770–1800), son of JA and AA
SSA	Sarah Smith (1769–1828), sister of WSS, *m.* CA 1795
TBA	Thomas Boylston Adams (1772–1832), son of JA and AA
AHA	Ann Harrod (1774–1845), *m.* TBA 1805

Third Generation

GWA	George Washington Adams (1801–1829), son of JQA and LCA
JA2	John Adams (1803–1834), son of JQA and LCA
MCHA	Mary Catherine Hellen (1806–1870), *m.* JA2 1828
CFA	Charles Francis Adams (1807–1886), son of JQA and LCA
ABA	Abigail Brown Brooks (1808–1889), *m.* CFA 1829
ECA	Elizabeth Coombs Adams (1808–1903), daughter of TBA and AHA

Fourth Generation

LCA2	Louisa Catherine Adams (1831–1870), daughter of CFA and ABA, *m.* Charles Kuhn 1854
JQA2	John Quincy Adams (1833–1894), son of CFA and ABA
CFA2	Charles Francis Adams (1835–1915), son of CFA and ABA
HA	Henry Adams (1838–1918), son of CFA and ABA
MHA	Marian Hooper (1842–1885), *m.* HA 1872
MA	Mary Adams (1845–1928), daughter of CFA and ABA, *m.* Henry Parker Quincy 1877
BA	Brooks Adams (1848–1927), son of CFA and ABA

Fifth Generation

CFA3	Charles Francis Adams (1866–1954), son of JQA2
HA2	Henry Adams (1875–1951), son of CFA2
JA3	John Adams (1875–1964), son of CFA2

3. DESCRIPTIVE SYMBOLS

The following symbols are employed throughout *The Adams Papers* to describe or identify the various kinds of manuscript originals.

D	Diary (Used only to designate a diary written by a member of the Adams family and always in combination with the short form of the writer's name and a serial number, as follows: D/JA/23, i.e., the twenty-third fascicle or volume of John Adams' manuscript Diary.)
Dft	draft
Dupl	duplicate
FC	file copy (A copy of a letter retained by a correspondent other than an Adams, no matter the form of the retained copy; a copy of a letter retained by an Adams other than a Letterbook or letterpress copy.)
FC-Pr	a letterpress copy retained by an Adams as the file copy
IRC	intended recipient's copy (Generally the original version but received after a duplicate, triplicate, or other copy of a letter.)

Lb	Letterbook (Used only to designate an Adams Letterbook and always in combination with the short form of the writer's name and a serial number, as follows: Lb/JQA/29, i.e., the twenty-ninth volume of John Quincy Adams' Letterbooks.)
LbC	Letterbook copy (Used only to designate an Adams Letterbook copy. Letterbook copies are normally unsigned, but any such copy is assumed to be in the hand of the person responsible for the text unless it is otherwise described.)
LbC-Tr	Letterbook copy-transcript (A transcript of an official letter or document copied into a volume of transcripts created for JA by Benjamin Franklin's secretary Jean L'Air de Lamotte, APM Reel 103.)
M	Miscellany (Used only to designate materials in the section of the Adams Papers known as the "Miscellanies" and always in combination with the short form of the writer's name and a serial number, as follows: M/CFA/31, i.e., the thirty-first volume of the Charles Francis Adams Miscellanies–a ledger volume mainly containing transcripts made by CFA in 1833 of selections from the family papers.)
MS, MSS	manuscript, manuscripts
RC	recipient's copy (A recipient's copy is assumed to be in the hand of the signer unless it is otherwise described.)
Tr	transcript (A copy, handwritten or typewritten, made substantially later than the original or later than other copies–such as duplicates, file copies, or Letterbook copies–that were made contemporaneously.)
Tripl	triplicate

4. LOCATION SYMBOLS

CtY-BR	Yale University, Beinecke Rare Book and Manuscript Library
DLC	Library of Congress
DNA	National Archives and Records Administration
DSI	Smithsonian Institution
ICN	Newberry Library
InHi	Indiana Historical Society
MeHi	Maine Historical Society
MdHi	Maryland Historical Society
MB	Boston Public Library
MBA	American Academy of Arts and Sciences
MBBS	Bostonian Society
MH-H	Houghton Library, Harvard University
MHi	Massachusetts Historical Society
MWelC	Wellesley College
MiD-B	Detroit Public Library, Burton Historical Collection
NjBaFAR	United States, Federal Records Center–New York
NjP	Princeton University
N	New York State Library
NHi	New-York Historical Society
NIC	Cornell University

NN	New York Public Library
NNC	Columbia University
PHi	Historical Society of Pennsylvania
PPPrHi	Presbyterian Historical Society
PPRF	Rosenbach Museum & Library
RHi	Rhode Island Historical Society
WHi	State Historical Society of Wisconsin

5. OTHER ABBREVIATIONS AND CONVENTIONAL TERMS

Adams Papers

Manuscripts and other materials, 1639–1889, in the Adams Manuscript Trust collection given to the Massachusetts Historical Society in 1956 and enlarged by a few additions of family papers since then. Citations in the present edition are simply by date of the original document if the original is in the main chronological series of the Papers and therefore readily found in the microfilm edition of the Adams Papers (APM, see below).

The Adams Papers

The present edition in letterpress, published by The Belknap Press of Harvard University Press. References to earlier volumes of any given unit take this form: vol. 2:146. Since there is no overall volume numbering for the edition, references from one series, or unit of a series, to another are by writer, title, volume, and page, for example, JA, *D&A*, 4:205.

Adams Papers Editorial Files

Other materials in the Adams Papers editorial office, Massachusetts Historical Society. These include photocopied documents (normally cited by the location of the originals), photographs, correspondence, and bibliographical and other aids compiled and accumulated by the editorial staff.

APM

Formerly, Adams Papers, Microfilms. The corpus of the Adams Papers, 1639–1889, as published on microfilm by the Massachusetts Historical Society, 1954–1959, in 608 reels. Cited in the present work, when necessary, by reel number. Available in research libraries throughout the United States and in a few libraries in Canada, Europe, and New Zealand.

Biografisch Portaal van Nederland

Biografisch Portaal van Nederland, a compendium of online Dutch biographical resources, including Repertorium van Ambtsdragers en Ambtenaren 1428–1861, *Biografisch Woordenboek van Nederland*, and others: www.biografischportaal.nl.

Nationaal Archief

Nationaal Archief, The Hague. For details on the Dumas Papers microfilm edition, see JA, *D&A*, 3:9–10.

A New Nation Votes
: Philip J. Lampi and others, comps., A New Nation Votes: American Election Returns, 1787–1825, American Antiquarian Society and Tufts University: elections.lib.tufts.edu.

Oxford Art Online
: Oxford Art Online, a compendium of online art resources, including Grove Art Online (formerly the Grove *Dictionary of Art*), the Bénézit *Dictionary of Artists*, and others: www.oxfordartonline.com.

6. SHORT TITLES OF WORKS FREQUENTLY CITED

Abernethy, *The South in the New Nation*
: Thomas P. Abernethy, *The South in the New Nation, 1789–1819*, [Baton Rouge, La.], 1961.

Adams, *Writings*
: *The Writings of Samuel Adams*, ed. Harry Alonzo Cushing, New York, 1904–1908; 4 vols.

AFC
: *Adams Family Correspondence*, ed. L. H. Butterfield, Marc Friedlaender, Richard Alan Ryerson, Margaret A. Hogan, Sara Martin, Hobson Woodward, and others, Cambridge, 1963– .

Amer. Philos. Soc., *Memoirs*, *Procs.*, *Trans.*
: American Philosophical Society, *Memoirs*, *Proceedings*, and *Transactions*.

Amer. State Papers
: *American State Papers: Documents, Legislative and Executive, of the Congress of the United States*, Washington, D.C., 1832–1861; 38 vols.

ANB
: John A. Garraty, Mark C. Carnes, and Paul Betz, eds., *American National Biography*, New York, 1999–2002; 24 vols. plus supplement; rev. edn., www.anb.org.

Annals of Congress
: *The Debates and Proceedings in the Congress of the United States* [1789–1824], Washington, D.C., 1834–1856; 42 vols.

Bickford and Bowling, *Birth of the Nation*
: Charlene Bangs Bickford and Kenneth R. Bowling, *Birth of the Nation: The First Federal Congress, 1789–1791*, Washington, D.C., 1989.

Biog. Dir. Cong.
: *Biographical Directory of the United States Congress, 1774–2005*, Washington, D.C., 2005; rev. edn., bioguide.congress.gov.

Black, *British Foreign Policy*
: Jeremy Black, *British Foreign Policy in an Age of Revolutions, 1783–1793*, Cambridge, Eng., 1994.

Black, *Law Dictionary*
: Henry Campbell Black, *Black's Law Dictionary: Definitions of the Terms and Phrases of American and English Jurisprudence, Ancient and Modern*, St. Paul, Minn., 1979, 5th edn.

Bosher, *French Rev.*
J. F. Bosher, *The French Revolution*, New York, 1988.

Bryan, *Hist. of the National Capital*
Wilhelmus Bogart Bryan, *A History of the National Capital from Its Foundation through the Period of the Adoption of the Organic Act*, New York, 1914–1916; 2 vols.

Cambridge Modern Hist.
The Cambridge Modern History, Cambridge, Eng., 1902–1911; repr. New York, 1969; 13 vols.

Catalogue of JA's Library
Catalogue of the John Adams Library in the Public Library of the City of Boston, Boston, 1917.

CFA, *Diary*
Diary of Charles Francis Adams, ed. Aïda DiPace Donald, David Donald, Marc Friedlaender, L. H. Butterfield, and others, Cambridge, 1964– .

Chernow, *Alexander Hamilton*
Ron Chernow, *Alexander Hamilton*, New York, 2004.

Col. Soc. Mass., *Pubns.*
Colonial Society of Massachusetts, *Publications.*

DAB
Allen Johnson, Dumas Malone, and others, eds., *Dictionary of American Biography*, New York, 1928–1936; repr. New York, 1955–1980; 10 vols. plus index and supplements.

Dexter, *Yale Graduates*
Franklin Bowditch Dexter, *Biographical Sketches of the Graduates of Yale College with Annals of the College History*, New York and New Haven, 1885–1912; 6 vols.

Dipl. Corr., 1783–1789
The Diplomatic Correspondence of the United States of America, from . . . 1783, to . . . 1789, [ed. William A. Weaver], repr., Washington, D.C., 1837 [actually 1855]; 3 vols.

Disney, *Memoirs*
John Disney, *Memoirs of Thomas Brand-Hollis, Esq.*, London, 1808.

DNB
Leslie Stephen and Sidney Lee, eds., *The Dictionary of National Biography*, New York and London, 1885–1901; repr. Oxford, 1959–1960; 21 vols. plus supplements; rev. edn., www.oxforddnb.com.

Doc. Hist. Ratif. Const.
The Documentary History of the Ratification of the Constitution, ed. Merrill Jensen, John P. Kaminski, Gaspare J. Saladino, and others, Madison, Wis., 1976– .

Doc. Hist. Supreme Court
The Documentary History of the Supreme Court of the United States, 1789–1800, ed. Maeva Marcus, James R. Perry, and others, New York, 1985–2007; 8 vols.

Elkins and McKitrick, *Age of Federalism*
Stanley Elkins and Eric McKitrick, *The Age of Federalism*, New York, 1993.

Essex Inst., *Hist. Colls.*
Essex Institute Historical Collections [title varies], 1859–1993.

Evans
: Charles Evans and others, *American Bibliography: A Chronological Dictionary of All Books, Pamphlets and Periodical Publications Printed in the United States of America* [1639–1800], Chicago and Worcester, Mass., 1903–1959; 14 vols., rev. edn., www.readex.com.

Ferguson, *Power of the Purse*
: E. James Ferguson, *The Power of the Purse: A History of American Public Finance, 1776–1790*, Chapel Hill, N.C., 1961.

First Fed. Cong.
: *Documentary History of the First Federal Congress of the United States of America, March 4, 1789 – March 3, 1791*, ed. Linda Grant De Pauw, Charlene Bangs Bickford, Helen E. Veit, William C. diGiacomantonio, and Kenneth R. Bowling, Baltimore, 1972–2017; 22 vols.

First Fed. Elections
: *The Documentary History of the First Federal Elections, 1788–1790*, ed. Merrill Jensen, Robert A. Becker, Gordon DenBoer, and others, Madison, Wis., 1976–1989; 4 vols.

Franklin, *Papers*
: *The Papers of Benjamin Franklin*, ed. Leonard W. Labaree, William B. Willcox, Claude A. Lopez, Barbara B. Oberg, Ellen R. Cohn, and others, New Haven, 1959– .

Hague, *Pitt*
: William Hague, *William Pitt the Younger: A Biography*, New York, 2005.

Hall, *Politics without Parties*
: Van Beck Hall, *Politics without Parties: Massachusetts, 1780–1791*, Pittsburgh, 1972.

Hamilton, *Papers*
: *The Papers of Alexander Hamilton*, ed. Harold C. Syrett, Jacob E. Cooke, and others, New York, 1961–1987; 27 vols.

Haraszti, *Prophets*
: Zoltán Haraszti, *John Adams and the Prophets of Progress*, Cambridge, 1952.

Heitman, *Register Continental Army*
: Francis B. Heitman, *Historical Register of Officers of the Continental Army during the War of the Revolution*, rev. edn., Washington, D.C., 1914.

Hoefer, *Nouv. biog. générale*
: Jean Chrétien Ferdinand Hoefer, ed., *Nouvelle biographie générale depuis les temps les plus reculés jusqu'à nos jours*, Paris, 1852–1866; 46 vols.

JA, *D&A*
: *Diary and Autobiography of John Adams*, ed. L. H. Butterfield and others, Cambridge, 1961; 4 vols.

JA, *Defence of the Const.*
: John Adams, *A Defence of the Constitutions of Government of the United States of America*, London, 1787–1788; repr. New York, 1971; 3 vols.

JA, *Discourses on Davila*
: [John Adams], *Discourses on Davila: A Series of Papers on Political History Written in the Year 1790, and Then Published in the Gazette of the United States*, Boston, 1805.

JA, *Earliest Diary*
The Earliest Diary of John Adams, ed. L. H. Butterfield and others, Cambridge, 1966.

JA, *Legal Papers*
Legal Papers of John Adams, ed. L. Kinvin Wroth and Hiller B. Zobel, Cambridge, 1965; 3 vols.

JA, *Papers*
Papers of John Adams, ed. Robert J. Taylor, Gregg L. Lint, Sara Georgini, and others, Cambridge, 1977– .

JA, *Works*
The Works of John Adams, Second President of the United States: with a Life of the Author, ed. Charles Francis Adams, Boston, 1850–1856; 10 vols.

Jay, *Selected Papers*
The Selected Papers of John Jay, ed. Elizabeth M. Nuxoll and others, Charlottesville, Va., 2010– .

JCC
Journals of the Continental Congress, 1774–1789, ed. Worthington Chauncey Ford, Gaillard Hunt, John C. Fitzpatrick, Roscoe R. Hill, and others, Washington, D.C., 1904–1937; 34 vols.

Jefferson, *Papers*
The Papers of Thomas Jefferson, ed. Julian P. Boyd, Charles T. Cullen, John Catanzariti, Barbara B. Oberg, James P. McClure, and others, Princeton, N.J., 1950– .

Jefferson's Memorandum Books
Jefferson's Memorandum Books: Accounts, with Legal Records and Miscellany, 1767–1826, ed. James A. Bear Jr. and Lucia C. Stanton (*The Papers of Thomas Jefferson*, Second Series), Princeton, N.J., 1997; 2 vols.

JQA, *Diary*
Diary of John Quincy Adams, ed. David Grayson Allen, Robert J. Taylor, and others, Cambridge, 1981– .

JQA, *Writings*
Writings of John Quincy Adams, ed. Worthington Chauncey Ford, New York, 1913–1917; 7 vols.

Laurens, *Papers*
The Papers of Henry Laurens, ed. Philip M. Hamer, George C. Rogers Jr., David R. Chesnutt, C. James Taylor, and others, Columbia, S.C., 1968–2003; 16 vols.

LCA, *D&A*
Diary and Autobiographical Writings of Louisa Catherine Adams, ed. Judith S. Graham and others, Cambridge, 2013; 2 vols.

Lodge, *Peerage*, [year]
Edmund Lodge, *The Peerage and Baronetage of the British Empire*, London, various years.

Maclay, *Journal*
Journal of William Maclay, United States Senator from Pennsylvania, 1789–1791, ed. Edgar S. Maclay, New York, 1890.

Madison, *Papers, Congressional Series*
The Papers of James Madison: Congressional Series, ed. William T. Hutchinson, William M. E. Rachal, and Robert Allen Rutland, Chicago, 1962–1991; 17 vols.

Madison, *Papers, Presidential Series*
The Papers of James Madison: Presidential Series, ed. Robert Allen Rutland, J. C. A. Stagg, Angela Kreider, and others, Charlottesville, Va., 1984– .

Mass., *Acts and Laws*
Acts and Laws of the Commonwealth of Massachusetts [1780–1805], Boston, 1890–1898; 13 vols.

Mazzei, *Writings*
Philip Mazzei: Selected Writings and Correspondence, ed. Margherita Marchione and others, Prato, Italy, 1983; 3 vols.

MHS, *Colls.*, *Procs.*
Massachusetts Historical Society, *Collections* and *Proceedings*.

Morison, *John Paul Jones*
Samuel Eliot Morison, *John Paul Jones: A Sailor's Biography*, Boston, 1959.

Morris, *Papers*
The Papers of Robert Morris, 1781–1784, ed. E. James Ferguson, John Catanzariti, Elizabeth M. Nuxoll, Mary A. Gallagher, and others, Pittsburgh, 1973–1999; 9 vols.

NEHGR
New England Historical and Genealogical Register.

NEQ
New England Quarterly.

New-York Directory, [year]
New-York Directory [title varies], issued annually with varying imprints.

OED
The Oxford English Dictionary, 2d edn., Oxford, 1989; 20 vols.; rev. edn., www.oed.com.

Oliver, *Portraits of JA and AA*
Andrew Oliver, *Portraits of John and Abigail Adams*, Cambridge, 1967.

Oliver, *Portraits of JQA and LCA*
Andrew Oliver, *Portraits of John Quincy Adams and His Wife*, Cambridge, 1970.

Oxford Classical Dicy.
Simon Hornblower and Antony Spawforth, eds., *The Oxford Classical Dictionary*, 3d edn., New York, 1996.

Philadelphia Directory, [year]
Philadelphia Directory [title varies], issued annually with varying imprints.

PMHB
Pennsylvania Magazine of History and Biography.

Repertorium
Ludwig Bittner and others, eds., *Repertorium der diplomatischen Vertreter aller Länder seit dem Westfälischen Frieden (1648)*, Oldenburg, 1936–1965; 3 vols.

Richards, *Shays's Rebellion*
Leonard L. Richards, *Shays's Rebellion: The American Revolution's Final Battle*, Philadelphia, 2002.

Rush, *Autobiography*
The Autobiography of Benjamin Rush: His "Travels through Life" Together with His Commonplace Book for 1789–1813, ed. George W. Corner, Princeton, N.J., 1948.

Rush, *Letters*
Letters of Benjamin Rush, ed. L. H. Butterfield, Princeton, N.J., 1951; 2 vols.

Schama, *Citizens*
Simon Schama, *Citizens: A Chronicle of the French Revolution*, New York, 1989.

Schama, *Patriots and Liberators*
Simon Schama, *Patriots and Liberators: Revolution in the Netherlands 1780–1813*, New York, 1977.

Sibley's Harvard Graduates
John Langdon Sibley, Clifford K. Shipton, Conrad Edick Wright, Edward W. Hanson, and others, *Biographical Sketches of Graduates of Harvard University, in Cambridge, Massachusetts*, Cambridge and Boston, 1873– .

Stahr, *John Jay*
Walter Stahr, *John Jay: Founding Father*, New York, 2005.

U.S. House, *Jour.*
Journal of the House of Representatives of the United States, Washington, D.C., 1789– .

U.S. Senate, *Exec. Jour.*
Journal of the Executive Proceedings of the Senate of the United States of America, Washington, D.C., 1789– .

U.S. Senate, *Jour.*
Journal of the Senate of the United States of America, Washington, D.C., 1789– .

U.S. Statutes at Large
The Public Statutes at Large of the United States of America, 1789– , Boston and Washington, D.C., 1845– .

VMHB
Virginia Magazine of History and Biography.

Warren-Adams Letters
Warren-Adams Letters: Being Chiefly a Correspondence among John Adams, Samuel Adams, and James Warren (Massachusetts Historical Society, *Collections*, vols. 72–73), Boston, 1917–1925; 2 vols.

Washington, *Diaries*
The Diaries of George Washington, ed. Donald Jackson and Dorothy Twohig, Charlottesville, Va., 1976–1979; 6 vols.

Washington, *Papers, Confederation Series*
The Papers of George Washington: Confederation Series, ed. W. W. Abbot and others, Charlottesville, Va., 1992–1997; 6 vols.

Washington, *Papers, Presidential Series*
The Papers of George Washington: Presidential Series, ed. W. W. Abbot, Dorothy Twohig, Jack D. Warren, Mark A. Mastromarino, Robert F. Haggard, Christine S. Patrick, John C. Pinheiro, David R. Hoth, and others, Charlottesville, Va., 1987– .

Washington, *Papers, Revolutionary War Series*
The Papers of George Washington: Revolutionary War Series, ed. Philander D. Chase, Frank E. Grizzard Jr., Edward G. Lengel, David R. Hoth, and others, Charlottesville, Va., 1985– .

Winter, *Amer. Finance and Dutch Investment*
Pieter J. van Winter and James C. Riley, *American Finance and Dutch Investment, 1780–1805*, New York, 1977; 2 vols.

WMQ
William and Mary Quarterly.

Young, *Democratic Republicans*
Alfred F. Young, *The Democratic Republicans of New York: The Origins, 1763–1797*, Chapel Hill, N.C., 1967.

VOLUME 20

Papers

June 1789 – February 1791

Papers of John Adams

From Samuel Barrett

Honored & dear Sir, Boston 1 June 1789

On Advice of my very excellent Friend the hon^be^ Mr Bowdoin I inclose you Copies of my Letter to Major General Knox & his Answer, with a rough Draught of a Letter to his Excellency the President of the United States; requesting you to peruse them & to give me your opinion as to the best Mode of Conducting my intended Application, & if you approve of this mode & see any Prospect of Success to let me know what Alterations are necessary to be made in the Letter that I may perfect it & forward it to you to be presented with such Information as you may think proper to give, as I am a perfect Stranger to the President; but I am persuaded that every Purpose of such a Letter will be better accomplished by your Recommendation alone.[1]

You Sir will be the earliest acquainted with the Arrangements to be made & can instantly form a Judgment what Place may be suitable for me & what Probability there is of my obtaining it— Your advice & Patronage will be of the first Importance to me, as under the Conduct thereof alone I can ever accomplish my Wishes—& for your Goodness I shall ever esteem myself under the highest Obligations—

I can with Pleasure refer to Governor Bowdoin General Lincoln, Mr Gorham Judge Wendell[2] Mr Strong, Mr Dalton, Mr Lowell, Mr Ames, General Knox & Mr Gerry Mr Cranch & to several other Gentlemen, for such Testimonials as may be requisite

I am, / Honored & dear Sir / With the highest Respect / Your very hum^l^ Ser^t^ Samuel Barrett

PS. What think you of the Clerkship of the Federal Court, itinerant or domestic?[3]

With the domestic I might perhaps retain the Office of a Justice of the Peace, & recieve the Benefits of it, without Interference—& both would yield me a competent Support.

The clerkship will probably be in the Gift of the Court; but your Recommendation would give me Favor with the Justices of that Court—

RC and enclosures (Adams Papers).

[1] Samuel Barrett (1739–1798), Harvard 1757, of Boston, had served as a judge of the Mass. Court of Common Pleas since May 1787. Barrett enclosed copies of his 11 May 1789 letter to Gen. Henry Knox, the secretary of war; a 24 May recommendation letter from Knox; and a 1 June Dft of his appeal to George Washington (all Adams Papers). JA replied on 11 June, below, prompting Barrett to revise his request. He petitioned the president a week later, soliciting the clerkship of the U.S. Supreme Court and listing JA among his references. Barrett did not earn a federal post. John Tucker was appointed clerk of the Supreme Court on 3 Feb. 1790 (*Sibley's Harvard Graduates*, 14:135, 140–141; 18:520, 522; *Worcester Magazine*, 17 May 1787; Washington, *Papers, Presidential Series*, 3:33–35; *Doc. Hist. Supreme Court*, 1:158, 160).

[2] Oliver Wendell (1733–1818), Harvard 1753, of Boston, was a Suffolk County probate judge from 1780 to 1788 and served alongside Barrett on the Mass. Court of Common Pleas (*Sibley's Harvard Graduates*, 13:367, 371–372, 373).

[3] For the evolution of the Judiciary Act of 1789 and JA's thoughts on the president's appointments, see his letter of [*10 July 1789*] to Francis Dana, and note 2, below.

To James Lovell

My dear Friend— New York June 4th 1789—

By the last post I was favoured with yours of the twenty first of May: Mr Duncan I presume has not come on—neither by his letter or your own am I made acquainted with his Views or the Object of his Wishes— I can only say to him as to all others, that his application must be made to the President and it ought to in writing[1] Your testimony in his favr will have weight— I thank you Sir for your blessing—your reason for not writing me, is not a good one—for although I have no spare moments Yet if I had any, should not judge them the proper moments to read or to answer Your Letters— I should devote hours of Buisness and of Pleasure to that service— I have no kind of animosity or antipathy to the Gentleman whose name you mention:[2] but I know of no merits or pretensions that he has, which can give him hopes of interfering with your Claims to an Employment long possessed hardly earned, and faithfully executed— I find the personal service which my Office renders indispensable somewhat severe— Setting still in the same place, so many hours of every day, and attending to the Course of proceedings in every step, as it is some thing new to me is somewhat injurious to my health:

but I hope to get the better of this inconvenience and when habit shall be formed, to find it pleasant; there is in the Senate much more of a National Spirit than you and I have been accustomed to see in Congress and much more apparent Moderation—[3] I wish the Motions of both Houses could be accelerated: but in untried Paths so many Obstructions occur, that time and Patience alone can cure them— I wish to know the spirit of the new Gov^{t} in Massachusetts: and am not without hopes it will be sufficiently National: I dont say fœderal for I think that an improper Word—

I am my dear Sir / Yr sincre Friend & servant John Adams

LbC (Adams Papers); internal address: "Mr Lovell— Boston—"; APM Reel 115.

[1] For Lovell's letter of 21 May recommending Robert Duncan for a federal post and JA's subsequent advice, see vol. 19:426–427.

[2] Lovell was engaged in a bitter public rivalry with Gen. Benjamin Lincoln, then lieutenant governor of Massachusetts, to obtain the Boston and Charlestown collectorship that ended in Lovell's defeat (vol. 19:412).

[3] Throughout the spring and summer of 1789, members of Congress struggled with their primary task of straightening out the economy. They laid down ways to ensure income, establish credit, and address the states' wartime debt while acting within the Constitution's scope. Four bills, all passed by early August, formed the core of the revenue plan: the Tariff Act, the Tonnage Act, the Collection Act, and the Coasting Act. The first pair of laws raised money by implementing a 5 percent duty on imports and established credit by upholding foreign treaties. The next two pieces of legislation enforced the revenue system by organizing regional districts, outlining federal record-keeping methods, drafting inspection standards, and constructing lighthouses. In contrast to the weak economic framework of the Articles of Confederation, the new federal legislation provided a viable infrastructure for raising revenue. There was no direct tax levied on individuals, and no excise tax set on domestic liquor. For a more expansive view of the debates, readers should turn to *First Fed. Cong.*, vols. 1, 2, 3, 10, 11.

From Benjamin Rush

Dear Sir, Philadelphia June 4$^{th:}$ 1789.

I find you, & I must *agree*, NOT to *disagree*, or we must cease to discuss political questions. I could as soon believe that the British parliament, ~~never~~ had once a right to tax America, as believe that a ~~fourth~~ major part of the citizens of New york were *federal*, or that many of the federal minority were so, from proper motives.— I know from good authority that some of the leading federalists of new york pressed the Senate at albany to relinquish the power of appointing federal senators, to the assembly, rather than risk the loss of the residence of Congress in new york.[1] But my principal Objection to the continuance in new York, is the influence which a city contaminated by having been for seven years a garrison town to a corrupted British Army, must have Upon the manners, & morals of those men who are to form the character of our Country. I already *see* the effects of this influence, and *hear* much more of it.— The citizens of Pennsylvania are truly republican; and will not readily concur in a government which has begun so soon to ape the corruptions of the British Court, conveyed to it, thro' the impure channel of the city of new york. I think Philad$^{a:}$ the most eligible Spot in the Union for the present residence of Congress— Upon this Account, I am sure it will not be preferred,— But Trenton—Annapolis—Chester town—or the Banks of the Ohio should all be prefer'd to New york.— It is the *sink* of British manners & politicks. I hope one of the last mentioned places will be fixed upon soon, otherwise such factions will I fear arise, as will convulse our government. There is more *known—said* & *felt* upon this subject that is proper to be communicated, or than will be believed while Congress is perfumed with British incense in new york.

When I speak of the *influence* of the New Eng$^{d:}$ States, I mean that influence in favor of Virtue—order, & liberty which has long been a *System* with them, but which is only felt, by fitts & starts by most of the Other States. I wish to see such an influence revived, & perpetual in our Country, & to ensure this, I wish it not to be perceived, or opposed.

When I expressed a wish for a Union in Principle & conduct of massachussets—Virginia—& Pennsy$^{a:}$—I wished only for the *predominance* of numbers & property in the legislative & executive parts of our government.[2]

I highly respect Mr Jay, but supposed, he would have been continued in his present office.—[3] After stating the Abilities—Sacrifices & services of Mr Wilson—could it be offensive to hear that he ~~was your friend, p[. . .]~~ opposed the narrow Views of those people who wished to so render your election abortive? or to dishonour you by the manner in which it was conducted?— In this he acted a manly part, and I have a right to say, that he was less influenced by personal regard, than by genuine—federal—and republican principles.— Letters from *new York* & maryland (which I saw) strongly urged him to an opposite Conduct. But he *felt*—what you have *expressed*, and could his advice have prevailed *fully*, you would have had *ten*, instead of eight Votes from Pennsylvania.—[4]

Why should we accelerate the progress of our Government towards monarchy?— Every part of the conduct of the americans tends to it. we will have but *one* deliverer—*One* great—or *one* good man in our Country. For my part, I cannot help ascribing the independance—& new government of our Country to thousands—all equally necessary & equally useful in both those great events.

This is not a time to mention nor are you in the proper place to hear, who were unfriendly to your election, in new york.

That you may never mistake any of my Opinions or principles in my future letters, I shall add to this long One,—that I am as much a republican as I was in 1775—& 6—that I consider *heriditary* monarchy & aristocracy as rebellion against nature—that I abhor titles, & every thing that belongs to the *peagantry* of government—that I love the *people*—but would sooner be banished to Iceland or Tobalski, than gain their favor by accommodating to one of their unjust popular prejudices,—that I feel a respect for my *rulers* bordering upon homage, but that I would not be jolted two hours in the Stage that plies between new york & Philad[a:] to be the prime minister of the United States,—& that I have applied for no office, & shall apply for none. Under all circumstances, I hope I shall be excused in *thinking* for myself, at all times, & upon all subjects.— To this detail of my *principles*, I have only to add one *feeling*, and that is, that I am with as much Affection & respect as I was in 1775—(notwithstanding our present contrariety of sentiment upon some subjects) your sincere friend, and / humble / Servant Benj[n:] Rush

RC (Adams Papers).

[1] Fractured by a largely Federalist senate and an Antifederalist-dominated assembly, the New York legislature struggled to choose federal members of Congress, ultimately sending representatives in April and July (vol. 19:314, 390–391).

[2] Rush was resuming his argument that given Massachusetts, Pennsylvania, and Virginia's joint support of JA for vice president, the three states would guide the choice of federal seat and the distribution of federal posts. JA was less convinced of their influence, writing: "Nor do I think that this Circumstance ought to have any Weight in Elections or appointments" (vol. 19:401, 460).

[3] With an eye on nominating heads of the new treasury, state, and justice departments, George Washington met with John Jay in early August and "had some conversation . . . respecting his views to Office." Although he was well-suited to continue as acting secretary of state, Jay informed the president that he was more interested in serving as the first chief justice of the U.S. Supreme Court, a choice strongly supported by JA (Washington, *Papers, Presidential Series*, 3:405; Stahr, *John Jay*, p. 271–272).

[4] According to Rush, James Wilson, a leading Federalist and Pennsylvania elector, intended for all ten of the state's electoral votes to go to JA in the 1789 presidential election. Wilson received at least two letters, one of 19 Jan. from former loyalist Rev. William Smith of Chester, Md., and another of 25 Jan. from Alexander Hamilton of New York, both swaying him to steer votes away from JA in order to ensure Washington's victory. The state's final vote count was 10 for Washington, 7 for JA, and 3 for various other candidates (vols. 3:56, 19:424; *First Fed. Elections*, 1:384; Israel W. Morris, "Letters of Hon. Alexander Hamilton and Rev. William Smith, D.D., to Hon. James Wilson, 1789," *PMHB*, 29:210–215 [1905]).

To Jeremy Belknap

Dear Sir New York June 5. 1789

I have this Evening received, your favour of May 30$^{th.}$ inclosed with a Sermon at the Installation of Mr Morse.[1] This elegant Discourse, I have read with the more pleasure, because that, besides the good Sense, the moral Sentiments and christian Benevolence which it breaths, I had the last Week an Opportunity of commencing an Acquaintance with Mr Morse himself, who appears to be an interesting Character and a Man of litterary Merit.

The more the Subject is considered, the sooner all Men will be convinced that human Passions are all insatiable; that instead of being extinguished, moderated or contented, they always Strengthen, by indulgence and gratification: and therefore that the only Security against them is, in Checks, whether in civil or ecclesiastical Societies.

This is no more true, with regard to the Love of Power, than it is with regard to the Love of Riches, of Fame, of honour or of pleasure. While We see and acknowledge it to be the constitution of nature; the quality to which We owe our Activity and Industry; our Virtues and our Happiness: We ought instead of quarrelling with it, to be only on our guard against its tending to abuse, to Vice and to Misery, when uncontrouled.

I thank you, Sir, for giving me, this Opportunity of assuring you, that I am with great / Esteem, your most obedient servant

John Adams.

RC (MHi:Jeremy Belknap Papers); addressed: "The Rev$^{d:}$ / Jeremiah Belknap / Boston—"; internal address: "The Reverend Mr Belknap."; endorsed: "John Adams. June 5. 1789." LbC (Adams Papers); APM Reel 115.

[1] Rev. Jedidiah Morse (1761–1826), Yale 1783, presided over the First Congregational Church of Charlestown, Mass., until 1819. Belknap sent JA a copy of his homily *A Sermon, Preached at the Installation of the Rev. Jedidiah Morse, A.M.: To the Pastoral Care of the Church and Congregation in Charlestown, on the 30th of April, 1789*, Boston, 1789, Evans, No. 21673 (vol. 19:484; *AFC*, 12:511).

To Richard Peters

Dear Sir New York ~~May 28:~~ June 5th 1789

Yesterday I had the Pleasure of receiving your Letter of the 28$^{th.}$ of May.[1] Mr Beals Intention was not to Stay in Philadelphia more than two or three days, and his absence from this Place was accordingly very short. I thank you, for your obliging Enquiries after him, and for your kind offers of Civility to others of my Friends. I hope e're long to be in a Condition to receive any Friend of yours, or Yourself if you should honour this City with a Visit. Mr Delany, I hope and presume will have no difficulty in obtaining the object of his Wishes.[2]

After an Absence of Eleven Years, it might be Presumption in me to be Sanguine in any Judgment I may form of the Temper and opinions of the People in all the States: but as far as my Information extends, I am clearly of your Mind, that bold and decisive Measures might be taken without risque.— but did you ever know a bold and decisive Assembly? especially in its youth? Although Individuals of this Character Sometimes appear, it is not always Safe to follow them, because they have not always that extent of information and that [accu]rate Judgment, which are indispensably necessary to conduct Such measures to a Successful Conclusion. and when it happens that Knowledge Experience, and Caution, are found united with Enterprize in a few, they find it impossible to impart enough of these qualities to others, to engage them to cooperate in their systems. You remember enough of this in former times; and may live to See more of it.

Your confidence in the thoughtful Temper and prudent Foresight of the President is perfectly well founded, and these qualities will be greatly assisted by proper Ministers. But the avarice of Liberty which predominates in the Breasts of our Fellow Citizens, by excluding all Ministers from both Houses ~~of the Legislature~~, in the formation of the Constitution, has rendered it extreamly difficult to conciliate the Legislature to any Plans of the Executive however Salutary. Poor Montesquieu, if he perfectly understood himself, has been wretchedly mistaken by others. His doctrine of a Seperation of the Executive from the Legislative is very just and very important, if confined to the Departments but is much otherwise, when extended to all the Individuals. Seperation is necessary, only So far as to Secure the Independence of each. but to take away from the Executive the Power of appointing to Office any Individual, is Shakling its Authority and diminishing its Independence. [on the] other Hand, depriving the People of the Power of choosing into the Legislature any Man who holds an Office under the Executive, is abridging the Liberties of the People in the most essential Point the Election of Legislators even in the lower House; and is a Diminution of the Independence both of the Legislature and its Constituents.—

There is every Evidence of good Intentions on all sides but there are too many Symptoms of old Colonial Habits: and too few, of great national Views. I am, Sir, with great / Esteem, your most obedient servant John Adams.

RC (PHi:Richard Peters Papers); addressed: "The Honble / Richard Peters Esquire / Speaker of the Assembly in / Pensylvania—"; internal address: "The Honourable Richard Peters Esq[r] / Speaker of the Assembly of Pensilvania."; endorsed: "June 5. 1789 / Hon John Adams"; notation by JA: "Free / John Adams." LbC (Adams Papers); APM Reel 115. Text lost due to fading of the ink has been supplied from the LbC.

[1] Vol. 19:481–482.

[2] Capt. Benjamin Beale Sr. (1702–1793), of Braintree, accompanied JA when he traveled to New York City in April 1789. Sharp Delany (1739–1799) was an apothecary whom Peters recommended for the Philadelphia collectorship, in a letter to JA of 14 April (Adams Papers). George Washington nominated Delany as collector on 3 Aug., and the Senate confirmed him the next day. Delany served in the post until 1798 (*AFC*, 8:341, 11:149; Michael E. Ingrisano Jr., *The First Officers of the United States Customs Service: Appointed by President George Washington in 1789*, Washington, D.C., 1987, p. 3, 5; *First Fed. Cong.*, 2:15, 20; Washington, *Papers, Presidential Series*, 2:89, 90).

From Thomas Brand Hollis

Dear Sir Chesterfeild Street June 6. 1789

your long silence gave me much uneasiness but I endeavour'd, to assign a thousand reasons which must have prevented you & some of them most natural at last however your favor restored my calm.

I should have been surprised indeed, had Cato's house stood uninjured in the general conflict for Existence life & liberty.[1] remember the glorious contest the Anxious fears the painful doubts the dreadful suspence & above all the tremendous consequences of not succeeding— yet your manly unremitting energies have overcome all these horrors staring you in the face big with calamities & woe.

But how different your fate from that of the Roman for tho success is not absolutely necessary to happiness yet in the state of doubt in which we live it seems desirable to keep alive the cause of virtue & to prevent the insolence of Vice.

What reason have you then to rejoice & to be exceeding glad & more when you recollect that some of your copatriots set out aswarm in the publick cause yet soon relinquish'd, at the approach of danger, their first love which you never forsook.

your state may be envied not regretted & upon the Balance I know which will kick the beam, as our time is short here, it is to be estimated by what we effect,—having showed your self capable &

worthy & having done what will entitle you to an exalted state in a future active life. I should not have said thus much but that your country is sensible of the same by ranking you among her first magistrates which I enjoy & approve may you do the same & fill up your measure of Virtue.

How different the state of this country! no struggles for the preeminence of virtue. Baseborn ambition Vice & dissipation predominate & is encouraged as the means of governing—was ever Royalty seen in all its dignity—was ever prostitution from the Bar from the senate & the sacred Rostrum carried to a greater height even in the times of the infamous Jemmy?[2]

the emoluments of office are the ruin of this country.

we have a new Speaker Addington a New secretary in place of sidney proofs of a change which must come & a new parliament not of long continuance.[3]

I have sent you a few tracts & papers—[4]

our college prospers & is full.

The Dissenters have been cajoled as usual.

Feuds & animosities among the family.

The Lama of Tartary has taken up his residence in England we have all the expence of Monarchy without the Splendor[5] the minister has been most fortunate in availing himself of the mistakes of his opponents who maintaind tory principles about the regency, & Pitt a Tory took up whig principles to serve his purpose & has succeeded, such is the glorious fixed principles of Politicians of my amiable Friend Mrs Adams I hear not one word, nor from her— tell her I visited her family very lately who are all well & that the character of a great lady is every day more & more visible & I might add another Epithet for she now is principal[6]

we have a sad prospect before us but I do not despair do but inform the people & they will not injure themselves.

I have sent some books to the college very various for every book has its merit & few from which knowledge may not be obtained & every thing is acceptable to a publick Library.[7]

The affair of Lazaretto's is of the utmost consequence to America—it will be in your power to promote it think of Harvard—bills of health & entrance will effect it—the plans are made out of which these are choice:—regulations & passes m[us]t exclude the Barbarians & plague—excuse the liberty & accept of the intention[8]

I hear this morning Bell will pub[lish] in the oracle [Ameri]can intelligence—may m[any] profit by it

[Washi]ngtons speech is printed—[9]

I have much to say but the ship is upon the to[. . .] how do I wish to be remember'd by the Adam's family who have saved their country.

Hawsbury will be secretary.[10]

more taxes tho we save money.

Farewell & be happy as wishes / your sincere Friend

T Brand Hollis.

RC and enclosure (Adams Papers); addressed: "To / The Honorable / John Adams Esqr / Vice President / Boston / The American Congress"; endorsed: "Mr T. B. Hollis / June 6. 1789." Some loss of text where the seal was removed.

[1] JA's most recent extant letter to Hollis was of 3 Dec. 1788. Here, he equated his public service with that of the Roman republican hero Marcus Porcius Cato Uticensis (vol. 19:356–357; *Oxford Classical Dicy.*).

[2] The "infamous Jemmy" was James Scott, 1st Duke of Monmouth, who mounted a bloody and unsuccessful challenge to James II, king of England, in 1685 (*Cambridge Modern Hist.*, 5:230, 232).

[3] Henry Addington, 1st Viscount Sidmouth (1757–1844), became speaker of the House of Commons on 8 June 1789. Thomas Townshend, 1st Viscount Sydney, served as the British home secretary until 5 June. His successor was William Wyndham Grenville, 1st Baron Grenville, who filled the post until 21 April 1791 (*DNB*).

[4] Not found.

[5] Hollis referred to the illness and recovery of King George III, likening his absence from public life to the hermetic habits of the Tibetan Buddhist priesthood. The king's health crisis prompted an outpouring of public emotion in the British press. As an example, Hollis enclosed an anonymous satirical poem, "Redeunt Saturnia Regna" (Adams Papers), mocking the monarch's return and the deeper political implications of the regency crisis following a revolution. Allegedly written "by an American," the poem opens with the lines: "See the vengeance of heavn, America cries, / George loses his reason, North loses his Eyes. / But when first they provok'd us all Europe could find / That the monarch was mad & the minister blind" (vol. 19:360; Hague, *Pitt*, p. 225–226).

[6] AA last wrote to Hollis on 5 April 1788. She wrote next on 6 Sept. 1790, telling him that AA2 had named her third son, born 7 Aug., Thomas Hollis Smith. AA also described the estate that they had rented, Richmond Hill, as a "truly enchanting" and "delicious spot" to live. Hollis may have visited John Boylston, of Bath, the cousin of JA's mother whom JA, AA, and JQA all met in England (*AFC*, 7:46; 8:xv–xvi, 252, 427; 9:99–101).

[7] To Harvard College, Hollis sent copies of John Howard's *An Account of the Principal Lazarettos in Europe* and Leopold II's *Edict of the Grand Duke of Tuscany, for the Reform of Criminal Law in his Dominions*, both London, 1789.

[8] Prior to Congress' Quarantine Act of 27 May 1796, individual states tried to manage the containment of contagious diseases. For example, in an effort to halt the spread of yellow fever in 1793, New York established a temporary hospital on Governors Island and implemented a two-week quarantine for ships arriving from Philadelphia, whereas Boston officials quarantined all incoming traffic (*U.S. Statutes at Large*, 1:474; *AFC*, 9:448; Wesley Spink, *Infectious Diseases: Prevention and Treatment in the Nineteenth and Twentieth Centuries*, Minneapolis, Minn., 1979, p. 152).

[9] Printer John Bell (1745–1831) began publishing the London *Oracle* in June 1789. In the 11 June issue, below a note that the *Oracle* intended to report on American intelligence, he printed George Washington's 30 April inaugural address (*DNB*). By midsummer, several British newspapers had reported the arrival of JA and Washington in New York City; see, for example, *London Chronicle* and London *World*, both 13 June.

[10] The London *Sunday Chronicle*, 7 June, falsely reported the imminent resignation of the Marquis of Carmarthen, British foreign minister, and named Charles Jenkinson, 1st Earl of Liverpool, as his successor.

From William Tudor

Dear Sir — Boston 6 June 1789

That I was right in my Position "that a considerable Time must elapse before the united States can arise to Greatness" I find confirmed by your last Letter.[1] That our Situation, Resources and Population may & ought to rank Us high on the Scale of Nations is indisputably true. But the heterogeneous Materials which compose our extensive federal Republic; the Jealousies, the Ignorances, & the paltry Views of paltry Politicians, will long impede our national Prgress. Why do we hear of a Faction at New York attempting to lessen the Influence of the Vice President but for the Weight he gives to the Eastern States? And why is he to have a scanty Provision for his Services, but because he contends for Dignity & Energy in the Government & its Officers? I have sometimes thought there was something in the Constitution of our Countrymen naturally opposed to Men of great Talents. Owing I suppose to their conceiving, & justly enough, that when they chuse Persons of Common Abilities to Offices they make them what they are, but Men of Genius make themselves. And what is still worse, the few great Men which God has given to a Nation, will rouse them from their Indolence & point the Way to Greatness & to Happiness. Americans have no Objection to public Prosperity, provided it is confined to a narrow Scale. And these Principles will continue to be acted upon, untill every State Constitution is annihilated, and Governors &c become what they only ought to be, Corporation Officers. We therefore hope that Congress will pass as many general Acts as possible that the national Legislative, Judicial & executive Powers may be speedily & universally felt in every part of the united States. Among other Acts, a Bankrupt Law is much wanted, & would conduce to make many Individuals feel the Force, & participate in the Advantages of the national Government more than any Thing. The numerous Debts contracted before the War, & at the Peace, with the real or artificial Scarci[ty] of Cash which is so distressingly felt throughout the whole Confederacy, calls for such a Relief. Besides the Inconveniences resulting from some States having Bankrupt Acts, some, Statutes of Insolvency, & others being without any provisional Relief. The Revenue Laws controul & command the States at Large, Bankrupt Statutes would regulate & govern the dearest, because the pecuniary Interests of every Subject of every State.—

In Consequence of one Paragraph in your last obliging Favour of 27 May, I inclose a Letter to the President, which if you approve of, I wish may be sealed & sent to him, either through the Medium of the Post Office, or as You please. I have my own Doubts on the Subject of such an Application. And therefore beg leave to trust to your Judgement for it's Propriety. The awkwardness of the Direction is humbly copied from the Stile of the House of Representatives of the United States.

I am, Dear Sir, most cordially Yours Wm Tudor

RC (Adams Papers); addressed: "His Excellency the President of / the Senate of the United States"; internal address: "President Adams"; endorsed: "Mr Tudor June 6th / Answd the 12th. 1789—" Some loss of text where the seal was removed.

[1] Tudor wrote to JA on 18 May soliciting a judicial appointment in Massachusetts. JA replied on 27 May, explaining that all applications should be directed to the president. No letter from Tudor to George Washington has been found, but see JA's 12 June response, below. Tudor did not earn a federal post, and his failure to do so bred speculation in Boston that JA's influence was "much diminished" on the national stage (vol. 19:464–465, 477–478; *AFC*, 8:412, 413).

To Benjamin Rush

Dear Sir New York June 9. 1789

No! You and I will not cease to discuss political questions: but We will agree to *disagree*, whenever We please, or rather whenever either of Us thinks he has reason for it.— I really know not what you mean by apeing the Corruptions of the British Court.[1]

I wish Congress had been called to meet at Philadelphia: but as it is now here, I can conceive of no way to get it transported thither, without tearing and rending.— I own to you, that I shall wish to remain here rather than go to any other place than Philadelphia. Congress can not be accommodated in any other than a great City.

There was a dark and dirty Intrigue, which propagated in the Southern States that New England would not vote for G. Washington, and in the Northern States that New York Virginia and South Carolina would not vote for him but that all would vote for me, in order to Spread a Panick least I should be President, and G. W. Vice President: [and this] ma[nuvire] made dupes even of two Con[necticut Electors—] I am well aware that this plott originated in N. York and am not at a Loss to guess the Men or their Motives.[2] I know very well how to make these Men repent of their rashness.— it would be easy to sett on foot an Inquiry: but it is not worth while.

That every Part of the Conduct and feelings of the Americans tends to that Species of Republick called a limited Monarchy I agree.— They were born and brought up in it.— Their Habits are fixed in it: but their Heads are most miserably bewildered about it. There is not a more ridiculous Spectacle in the Universe, than the Politicks of our Country exhibits.— bawling about Republicanism which they understand not; and acting a Farce of Monarchy. We will have as you say "but one great Man" yet even he shall not be a great Man.

I also, am as much a Republican as I was in 1775.— I do not "consider hereditary Monarchy or Aristocracy as Rebellion against Nature." on the contrary I esteem them both Institutions of admirable Wisdom and exemplary Virtue, in a certain Stage of Society in a great Nation. The only Institutions that can possibly preserve the Laws and Liberties of the People. and I am clear that America must resort to them as an Asylum against Discord Seditions and Civil War and that at no very distant Period of time. I shall not live to see it—but you may. I think it therefore impolitick to cherish Prejudices against Institutions which must be kept in View as the Hope of our Posterity.— I am by no means for attempting any Such thing at present.— Our Country is not ripe for it, in many respects and it is not yet necessary but our ship must ultimately land on that shore or be cast away.

I do not "abhor Titles, nor the Pageantry of Government"—if I did I should abhor Government itself.— for there never was, and never will be, because there never can be, any Government without Titles and Pageantry. There is not a Quaker Family in Pensilvania, governed without Titles and Pageantry. not a school, not a Colledge, not a Clubb can be governed without them.

"I love the People," with You.— too well to cheat them, lie to them or deceive them.— I wish those who have flattered them so much had loved them half as well.— If I had not loved them I never would have Served them— if I did not love them now, I would not Serve them another hour—for I very well know that Vexation and Chagrine, must be my Portion, every moment I shall continue in public Life.

My Country appears to me, I assure you in great danger of fatal Divisions, and especially because I Scarcely know of two Persons, who think, Speak and Act alike in matters of [Governmen]t. I am with real Friendship yours John Adams

RC (private owner, 1944); endorsed: "J. Adams." LbC (Adams Papers); APM Reel 115. Text lost due to fading of the ink has been supplied from the LbC.

[1] Here and below, JA quoted from Rush's letter of 4 June, above.

[2] On 25 Jan. Alexander Hamilton wrote to James Wilson outlining a plan to encourage presidential electors to cast votes meant for JA to other candidates; the goal was to guarantee that George Washington and JA would win the top two seats in that order. Throughout the first year of his vice presidency, JA pieced together the story of what he called "a corrupt Intrigue and an insidious Maneuvre," relying on various informants to fill in the details. See also John Trumbull's letter of 30 March 1790, discussing the process in Connecticut, and JA's reply of 25 April, both below. The final count was 7 for Washington, 5 for JA, and 2 for Samuel Huntington, who was also an elector (vol. 19:438; Hamilton, *Papers*, 5:247–249, 252; Chernow, *Alexander Hamilton*, p. 272; *First Fed. Elections*, 2:47).

From James Searle

Dear Sir Philadelphia 10th. June 1789.

I was duely favoured with your obliging letter of the 15th. of last Month and feel myself not a little gratified with the renewal of a correspondence with Mr. Adams, a friend for whom I feel a most exalted respect and affection.—[1]

When I took the liberty to write to you last I mentioned my happy situation in business, and my independent feelings, but I hope I have not been misunderstood by Mr. Adams in that declaration, or that I mean't that Surly haughty English independence that many make it their boast to feel; On the contrary Sir I am clearly in sentimt. with Yorick that we are all (or ought to be) Brothers in this mutable State, and depend much upon each other for Acts of Kindness and Brotherly love, Indeed it is very commode for me to think so at present, because I am going to claim the honour of being your relation in his sense of the word, and in consequence to ask a Brotherly peice of Kindness from you, which I persuade myself you will not with-hold from me.

To come to the point, I have now laying before our Council in this State An Account and a Claim which I have against the State for my Agency & Expences in endeavouring to effect a Loan for the State, and the Comptroller general of the state thro' whose office my Accts. must first pass, & who is my friend,[2] tells me that he is convinced a few lines from you to me expressive of your opinion that I took the most effectual measures on my arrival in Holland to obtain the Aforesaid loan, and that the then Situation of Affairs in Holland would not admit of my obtaining the loan, woud greatly facilitate the Settlement of my claim— Now my Dear Sir as I did myself the honour to consult you agreable to the orders I had received from the

Council before I left America, in the early Stages of that business in Holland, and as you will no doubt recollect the difficultys that attended obtaining loans at that time (the Winter of 80 & Spring & Summer 81.) I humbly request you woud take the trouble at a leisure moment of writing me a few lines on this Subject, and perhaps you may so far gratify me as to give it as your opinion that I did not dishonour the State I represented or neglect their Interests in my endeavours to procure the Loan.[3]

I hope you will pardon the liberty I am now taking wch. I coud only prevail on myself to do, as I am fully convinced of your goodness & freindly disposition to me.

I have the honour to be with every Sentiment of respect / D^r. Sir / Your most Obliged & Obed Servt.

James Searle

RC (Adams Papers).

[1] See vol. 19:449–450, 451–452.

[2] John Nicholson (1757–1800), a land speculator from Chambersburg, served as Pennsylvania's comptroller general from 1782 to 1794 (*ANB*).

[3] Searle arrived in Paris in Sept. 1780, planning to arrange a loan for Pennsylvania. Failing in his efforts with several French firms, Searle traveled to the Netherlands, where he met JA. Searle's quest was unsuccessful there as well, but he made a positive impression on JA, who observed: "Mr. Searle's Conversation is a Cordial to me. He gives a charming sanguine Representation of our Affairs, such as I am very well disposed to believe, and such as I should give myself, if interrogated, according to the best of my Knowledge" (vols. 9:453, 10:384).

From James Sullivan

Sir

Boston 10th June 1789

The Communicating our Sentiments to men in power, when done with the respect due to their characters, and without a troublesome intrusion, is at all times a mark of Veneration and esteem. upon these ideas I Venture to address a letter to the Vice President of the United states, and which he will read, when his leisure will admit a moment of heedless employment.

I am very deeply impressed with the disagreeable situation of N Carolina, Rhode Island, and Vermont. though I am very sensible that your Situation and ability have placed you far beyond the reach of my suggesting any thing new to you upon the subject, yet I wish to be indulged one word.

great expectation of happiness and prosperity are raised upon the general Government. these are still heightned by the idea of the Characters who have the administration of it. but the system, perfect as it is, or may be, or the Governors, however wise, or prudent, cannot afford to man, that perfect ease and enjoyment, which his fond hopes are reaching after, and which the Wisdom of heaven hath decreed he cannot possess.

I beleive we shall be as happy as any nation in the world, but not as happy as we expect to be: Government as Doctor Price says, being but the choice of evils.[1]

When our officers have a naked competency, and our national Debt creates Either an imaginary, or a real burthen, our people may become in some measure uneasy. the raising a revenue by Impost, is clearly the best Mode in the world; but while it was thought a virtue to prevent the British revenue raised on the Colonies, our Merchants contracted habits which Interest, or Necessity may suffer some of them to indulge, and it would be no wonder that a partial uneasiness, or possibly a limitted disaffection to a young Government, should take place for awhile. if any thing of this kind should happen, and the States above mentioned should remain unconnected with the confederated republic, they will become asylums for fugitives from Justice, and increase their number by lessening the risque of offending; and greatly serve to promote the Subversion of the Revenue and other Laws.

I could point out many Mischiefs arising from this source, and you might call them imaginary ones. but if they might really exist, it would be more useful to prescribe a remedy, but this I cannot pretend to. and yet as I dread a civil contest, and am very averse to that kind of war, which calls for halters and axes, I beg leave to mention the necessity of an Early attempt by Congress, to unite all the States; and that before any interdiction of commerce with those which are delinquent Congress should address the Legislatures of those States with Solicitude on the subject, point out to them their unfortunate Situation, and the necessity which the Republic is under of taking decided measures to bring them under the general Government, and protection. let me add, the idea of a Letter for this purpose being Signed by the President at the request of Congress. should this fail, perhaps the giving Individuals who shall take the oath of Alegiance, the priviledge of Citizens, may weaken the force, and distract the Councils of the opposition, and bring on a conviction of the necessity of a union.

however small these observations may appear to you, yet you will suffer the goodness of my intentions to apologize for them; for I assure you that I dread a delay in this important business— because I beleive, that soon after the Revenue Laws, and the restrictions on trade shall begin to opperate a present benefit will arise which may strengthen the opposition.

The People of the Eastern part of this state where I once was conversant are uneasy at having no port of delivery, or of Entry, Eastward of Portland. the shore is two hundred miles long, and they will suffer great inconvenience by being obliged to Enter at Portland, my Friends that way have urged me to write you on the subject expressing their confidence in your goodness.[2]

I am Sir with the highest / sentiments of respect your most / obedient Humble Servant

James Sullivan

RC (Adams Papers); internal address: "His Excellency John Adams."

[1] "The choice generally offered us is 'of two evils to take the least.' We chuse the restraint of civil government, because a less evil than anarchy" (Richard Price, *Observations on the Importance of the American Revolution*, London, 1784, p. 17).

[2] After the first draft of the 8 May collection bill was tabled in the House of Representatives, Pennsylvania congressman Thomas Fitzsimons introduced a second bill on 27 May. Debate centered on the establishment of ports of entry and delivery. On 2 June representatives agreed that Portland was one of the Massachusetts ports. A day later, the House added eight more ports, all in the region of present-day Maine. Rather than amend the 27 May bill, Massachusetts representative Benjamin Goodhue presented the House with a new bill on 29 June, later known as the Collection Act. Passed on 31 July, this legislation allotted twenty ports to Massachusetts, including six northeast of Portland: Bath, Wiscasset, Penobscot, Frenchman Bay, Machias, and Passamaquoddy.

As part of the establishment of a federal system of revenue, the Collection Act divided the states into districts and established ports in all states save North Carolina and Rhode Island, which were treated as foreign states owing to their pending ratification of the Constitution. Further, the act summarized the duties of collectors, naval officers, and inspectors. Collectors were responsible for examining ships' manifests, estimating and collecting duties for the U.S. Treasury, basic record-keeping, monitoring fraud, and appointing inspectors. They were entitled to fees of $1.50 to $2.50 on every ship that entered or cleared the port, of 20 to 40 cents each for every permit or certificate they issued, and at nine of the largest ports, of one half of a percent of all money collected and sent to the U.S. Treasury. By 1792, the income garnered from customs yielded over 90 percent of the federal revenue. JA received numerous patronage requests for new posts created by the Collection Act; see, for example, Stephen Hall's letter of 15 Aug. 1789, below (*First Fed. Cong.*, 1:102; 3:73, 100, 813, 814; *Annals of Congress*, 1st Cong., 1st sess., 1:433, 434, 435; *U.S. Statutes at Large*, 1:29–49; Douglas A. Irwin and Richard Sylla, *Founding Choices: American Economic Policy in the 1790s*, Chicago, 2011, p. 101).

To Samuel Barrett

Dear Sir

New York June 11th 1789—

I have received the letter you did me the honour to write me on the first of this month with its inclosures: The Letter to The President is conceived with propriety & expressed with decency. As the

Investigation of the Characters, Services, Qualifications, and all other pretensions of every Candidate for public employment, is constitutionally, in the President in the first Instance; General Knox's Advice to you was very proper, and I know of no other Course you can pursue.[1] As the Journals & debates of the House are regularly published you will have early information of all the Offices which may be created & will have opportunity to accomodate your application to the Circumstances as they rise—[2]

It would be to me at all times a pleasing Employment, if I had it in my Power, to contribute to the happiness of a deserving Man & a virtuous Family; but in this buisness is out of my sphere, I can do no more than relate the truth as far I may know it, whenever I may be interrogated concerning Facts—

I am Sir with much Esteem / Your most Obed[t] & humble Servant

John Adams—

LbC (Adams Papers); internal address: "The Honourable Sam[l] Barrett Esq[re]— / Boston—"; APM Reel 115.

[1] Frequently, JA replied to the flood of patronage requests much as he did here, reiterating the Constitution's stipulation that such nominations were a presidential power alone.

[2] Throughout the summer, American newspapers printed the full text of the judiciary bill, which included provisions for the appointment of clerks; see, for example, the *Boston Gazette*, 29 June; *Pennsylvania Packet*, 29 June. John Beckley, clerk of the House, and Samuel Allyne Otis, secretary of the Senate, contracted with private printers to publish journals that appeared at the opening of each congressional session (vol. 19:478; *First Fed. Cong.*, 1:x, 2:vii, 3:xiv).

To James Bowdoin

Dear Sir New York June 11. 1789

I have recieved the Letter you did me, the honour to write me, on the 30. of May: but have not yet had an opportunity to See M[r] Boid.[1]

Whenever that Gentleman shall appear, it will be a pleasure to me to give him all the Attention and Assistance, in my Power, which may be due to public Justice, and to your Recommendation.

We proceed Slowly: but in digesting Plans so new, so extensive and so important, it is impossible to bring Bodies of Man to a clear Comprehension of Things and a mutual Satisfaction without long deliberation and debate.

I called on Sir John Temple last Saturday and tho I was sorry to find him in so ill health, I apprehend with Exercise and Care he will get the better of his Complaint.[2]

With great Respect I have the Honour / to be, Sir, your most obedient and / most humble servant John Adams.

RC (MHi:Winthrop Family Papers); internal address: "Governor Bowdoin"; endorsed: "1789. / Letter from John Adams / Esq$^{r.}$ Vice President of / the United States. / dated New York June / 11$^{th:}$—" LbC (Adams Papers); APM Reel 115.

[1] For American sympathizer James Boyd's efforts to reclaim land near Passamaquoddy, Mass. (now Maine), see vol. 19:484–485.

[2] John Temple served as British consul general to the United States from Feb. 1785 to his death in 1798. He was married to Bowdoin's daughter, Elizabeth (vol. 17:16; *AFC*, 4:240).

To William Tudor

Dear sir New York June 12. 1789

Your Letters put me more and more out of Patience every Post.— Why, in that of the 6$^{th.}$ do you call our national Government a *federal Republick*? It is no more that, than it is Sphœrical Trigonometry. What is a federal Republic? It is an association of a Number of independent Sovereign States.— Are the Seperate States in our national Government, Sovereign and independent? If they are, We had all better go home. for Heavens Sake, let us analyze our Ideas and correct our Language.— Unanimity is essential to a fœderal Republick.— Is Unanimity necessary According to our national Constitution? Would it not ruin this Country to make it essential?— I ask again Where is the Soverignty of our Nation? Answer me, as a Lawyer and a Statesman, as a Philosopher and an Historian.

You need not be apprehensive of "any Faction attempting to lesson the Influence of the V. P.—["] He has no dread of that upon his mind.— He will have as much Weight as he ought, and he would not have more if it were offered him. He flatters himself he knows his Stops, pretty well, at fifty three or four Years of Age.— He must contend for "the dignity and Energy of Goverment" because he knows, that without dignity and Energy there can be no Government at all.

I agree most cordially with you in all the rest of your excellent Letter and will take care of that inclosed.

I am dear sir yours J.A.

RC (MHi:Tudor-Adams Correspondence); addressed: "William Tudor. Esquire / Barrister at Law / Boston—"; internal address: "William Tudor Esqr / Barrister at Law,"; endorsed: "12 June 1789"; notation by JA: "Free / John Adams." LbC (Adams Papers); APM Reel 115. Tr (Adams Papers).

To Cotton Tufts

Dear Sir New York June 12. 1789.

The last Evenings Post favoured me with yours of the 6th.[1]

Many Gentlemen are in favour of a national Excise: and Some would have the nation take upon itself all the State Debts. Mr Morris particularly: but I cannot say what will be done.

My Burthens are not very heavy: but my health is not very good.— I have been obliged to decide many questions on the Impost Bill, the Senate being equally divided.—[2] I was obliged to reduce the Duty on Molasses from four Cents, and to prevent that on Salt from being raised from 6 to 9.— My Vote on Molasses I Suppose will displease the Southern Gentlemen: but that on Salt, ought to attone for it.— so the ballance is even.

Drawbacks on Exportation Seem to be necessary to Support infant manufactures and Some branches of commerce not fully established.— But whenever the Manufacture or the Trade will bear it, it Seems to be good Policy to make the foreign consumer, pay the Duty. The Senate has rejected the Drawback on Rum; and reduced the Duty on Molasses to 2 1/2 Cents. if the Rum trade will bear it, I shall be glad. if not, it is ill Policy. My Friends the Dutch have the Art to make Foreigners pay two thirds of the Duties to the State.[3] They Suffer no Drawback when the trade will bear the Duty.

The Note inclosed in your Letter I burned as you desired as soon as I had read it: but not untill it had made too deep an Impression on my heart as well as Memory.— What Shall I do, with that tender hearted Fool?

When will Mrs A. come on? I Suffer, very much for Want of her assistance.[4]

My Love to all our Connections / yours most Sincerely

John Adams.

RC (NHi:Gilder Lehrman Coll., on deposit); addressed: "Dr Tufts"; internal address: "Dr Tufts."; endorsed: "John Adams Esq / June 12. 1789." LbC (Adams Papers); APM Reel 115.

[1] Not found.

[2] During the Senate's long-running debate over the impost bill, Richard Henry Lee recommended doubling the 6-cent duty on salt to 12 cents. William Maclay opposed the idea, arguing that the price posed a hardship for new settlers who lived far from the coast. JA broke the deadlock in the Senate by voting against raising the duty. Faced with three motions for reducing the duty on molasses, JA decided that the Senate should vote first on the proposal for reducing the duty to the highest amount, 4 cents. After the senators voted in favor, JA raised a point of order to continue

voting for the lower amounts of 3 cents and 2 cents. The Senate further reduced the duty on molasses to 2.5 cents per barrel, which the House carried without debate. George Washington signed the bill into law on 4 July. Writing to his father on 28 June, JQA reported that Boston merchants "have not . . . been so much pleased with any Act of the President of the Senate, as his turning the vote for reducing the duty to 3 cents" (vol. 19:425, 468; *First Fed. Cong.*, 9:57, 59, 68; *AFC*, 8:383).

[3] Since 1680, Dutch customs duties tended to be lower than those of competitors, allowing merchants to import goods from China, India, and Japan and sell them at a profit in foreign markets without the benefit of a drawback, or refund, of the import duty (Marjolein 't Hart, Joost Jonker, and Jan Luiten van Zanden, eds., *A Financial History of the Netherlands*, N.Y., 1997, p. 25; Jan de Vries and Ad van der Woude, *The First Modern Economy: Success, Failure, and Perseverance of the Dutch Economy, 1500–1800*, Cambridge, Eng., 1997, p. 387, 458, 459).

[4] AA left Braintree on 17 June 1789. She was accompanied by CA, Louisa Catharine Smith, and two servants, Polly Taylor and Matilda. Arriving at Daggett's Inn in Providence, R.I., on 19 June, AA and her travel party were met by a welcoming crowd of Federalists. After dining with John and Sarah Brown in a company of 22, AA toured the town and drank tea with John Francis, Abby Brown Francis, Sarah Brown Bowen, and their families. Reaching Newport, R.I., the next day via the packet *Hancock*, Capt. James N. Brown, AA stayed at the home of Henry Marchant. She arrived in New York City on 25 June (*AFC*, 8:373–375, 377–380).

From C. W. F. Dumas

Monsieur | Lahaie 13e. Juin *1789*.

L'affection dont vous m'avez honoré pendant votre séjour en Europe, & les sentimens inaltérables de mon attachement pour Votre Excellence, m'engagent à vous présenter l'expression de ma joie, à l'agréable nouvelle de l'important Poste auquel le Peuple le plus libre du monde vient de vous élire, & que votre zele pour la patrie vous a fait accepter. Puisse ce zele trouver sa récompense dans le succès la plus complet de vos travaux pour la félicité publique, dans la prospérité de votre chere famille, dans l'estime & l'amour de vos Concitoyens, dans les bénédictions de cette vie & de celle qui attend la vertu dans l'autre.

Je me suis pressé de publier votre beau Discours, coñe V. E verra par la Gazette ci-jointe de notre ami à Leide.

Je ne puis rien vous dire, Monsieur, de la vie politique de ce lieu, étant nul pour elle, coñe V.E. pourra voir par mes Lettres au Département des Affaires Etr., sur-tout depuis 7bre. dernier.—[1] Quant à la vie sociale, quoique moins agitée par les coñotions extérieures, elle n'en est pas moins disgracieuse pour tous ceux qui ne peuvent se croire heureux non seulement en dissimulant, mais en simulant: car il faut pouvoir faire l'un & l'autre. Il n'en est pas de-même, à ce que j'apprends, dans les villes: mais ici, jusqu'aux plus proches, on se méconnoît, hait, calomnie, trahit, &c. &c. impitoyablement; &

les plus vertueux en souffrent le plus. Quelques-uns succombent au chagrin, & meurent: D'autres, un peu plus vivaces, végetent tristement.— J'ai pris la Liberté de solliciter dans mes Dépeches, pour être accrédité come Chargé d'Affaires auprès de la Cour de Bruxelles, & être porteur de deux Lettres du Congrès, l'une pour la dite Cour, l'autre, à lui remettre en même temps, pour la faire passer à la Cour de Vienne, dans lesquelles on suppléeroit à l'Omission anterieure, d'avoir donné connoissance directe & formelle de l'Indépendance & de la Majesté de la Confédération Américaine.— Je pourrois aussi minuter avec la dite Cour un Traité de Comerce & d'Amitié, à conclure finalement par S.E. Mr. Jefferson avec le Ministre Impérial à Paris.—[2] Ainsi accrédité une fois pour toutes, sans avoir besoin de résider à la continue à Bruxelles, je serois plus sous la protection du Droit des Gens, & moins déprécié en ce pays. Par la même raison il seroit bon pour moi de pouvoir remettre officiellement de pareilles Lettres de notification aux Ministres Danois, Suedois, Russe, Prussien & Sarde à Lahaie, pour les faire passer à leurs Cours. Il n'y auroit même aucun Inconvénient que je remisse à Mr. Fagel une Lettre pour Leurs H.P. où connoissance leur seroit donnée directe & imédiate, de la nouvelle Constitution fédérative des Etats-unis. Cela m'y rendroit une certaine contenance & considération dans la socialité, dont on travaille sourdement à me priver tant qu'on peut. Cela désole ma famille, & me prive de *toutes* les douceurs & consolations que j'ai droit d'en attendre.— Son Exc. Mr. Jay me fait espérer, que dès que le Congrès aura terminé les affaires majeures, il voudra bien, entre les mineures donner attention à celle-ci, & faire quelque chose qui done à connoître, que quoique réprouvé du Système aujourd'hui dominant en ce pays, je ne le suis pas pour cela, & pour lui faire plaisir, de mes maîtres; & je me recomande à cet égard, come à tout autre à l'amitié & à la bonté de votre Exce. pour moi, qui suis avec le plus respectueux attachement, De Votre Excellce. / Le très-humble & très-obeissant / serviteur

Cwf Dumas

Je viens de recevoir le noble & touchant discours de S.E. Mr. le Président. Il l'envoie à Leide pour être inséré dans la Gazette.[3]

J'eus l'honneur d'écrire à V.E. au mois d'Août de l'année passée, une Lettre adressée à Boston.[4] J'espere qu'elle Lui est parvenue, & que je serai favorisé du souvenir de V.E., pour avoir des nouvelles de sa santé & de celle de Madame, à qui je présente l'homage de mes respects.

TRANSLATION

Sir The Hague, 13 June *1789*

The affection with which you honored me during your time in Europe, and my steadfast sentiments of devotion for your excellency, move me to offer my expressions of joy at the pleasant news of the important post to which the freest people in the world have elected you, and your patriotic zeal led you to accept. May this zeal find its reward in the total success of your efforts for the public good, in the prosperity of your dear family, in the esteem and love of your fellow citizens, in the blessings of this life and of the one that awaits virtue in the other.

I hastened to publish your fine speech, as your excellency will see by the enclosed *Gazette* from our friend at Leiden.

I can say nothing, sir, about the political life of this place, not knowing anything about it, as your excellency may see in my letters to the department of foreign affairs, especially since last September.[1] As for social life, though less perturbed by foreign agitation, it is no less a disgrace for all of those who cannot count themselves happy having not only to dissemble, but to pretend: for one must needs do one and the other. It is not the same, from what I gather, in the cities. But here, and even among intimates, we misapprehend each other, we hate, slander, betray each other, etc., etc., mercilessly. And the most virtuous are made to suffer the most. A few succumb to sorrow and die. Others, a little more lively, languish in sadness. I have taken the liberty in my dispatches to request that I be recognized as chargé d'affaires at the court of Brussels, and that I carry two letters from Congress, one for the said court, and the other, to hand them at the same time to be forwarded to the court in Vienna, which would amend the former omission to have given direct and formal notice of the independence and sovereignty of the American confederation. For that court, I could also compose a draft of a treaty of commerce and friendship, ultimately to be concluded by his excellency Mr. Jefferson with the imperial minister in Paris.[2] Thus recognized once and for all, and without needing to continually reside in Brussels, I would be protected under the law of nations, and not be so disparaged in this country. For the same reason, it would be good for me to be able to officially remit similar letters of notice to the Danish, Swedish, Russian, Prussian, and Sardinian ministers at The Hague so that they can forward them to their respective courts. It would be of no inconvenience to address a letter to Mr. Fagel for Their High Mightinesses, giving them direct and immediate notice of the new federal Constitution of the United States. This would lend me a certain status and consideration in social interactions, which is being secretly undermined as much as possible. This saddens my family, and deprives me of *all* of the domestic comforts and consolation that I have the right to expect. His excellency Mr. Jay gives me hope that, as soon as Congress has finished with major duties, he will be pleased to attend to this one among the minor affairs, and to do something that gives credence to the fact that, while disgraced by the system in place today in this country, I am not for all that, by my masters. And I entrust myself in this regard, as in all others, to the friendship and goodness of your excellency for myself, who am, with the most respectful devotion, your excellency's most humble and most obedient servant

Cwf Dumas

I have just received his excellency the President's noble and touching address. He sends it to Leiden to have it included in the Gazette.[3]

I had the honor of writing a letter addressed to your excellency at Boston last August.[4] I hope that it reached you, and that I will be graced by a memento from your excellency with news of your health and of Madam's, to whom I present the token of my respects.

RC (Adams Papers); internal address: "A Son Exce. Mr. Jn. Adams, Vice Présidt. du Congrès des Ets unis"; endorsed: "Mr Dumas. 13 June / 1789."

[1] Between 22 Jan. 1788 and 15 June 1789, as the Dutch political crisis made Dumas' unofficial role as the U.S. agent at The Hague increasingly more precarious, he wrote at least 32 letters to John Jay assessing the situation. Dumas' ten letters to Jay from 4 Sept. 1788 to 11 Dec. have not been found, but they were summarized in the journal of the department for foreign affairs, and drafts appear in his letterbook. Dumas reported that anti-Patriot mobs daubed Orangist colors on the door of the American legation and city officials harassed him, adding that Patriot leader Robert Jasper van der Capellen van de Marsch had fled to Paris (*Dipl. Corr., 1783–1789*, 3:605–642; Jefferson, *Papers*, 16:551; Schama, *Patriots and Liberators*, p. 144, 146).

[2] The Continental Congress commissioned William Lee on 9 May 1777 to arrange an Austro-American commercial treaty, but his 1778 mission failed. A decade later, Dumas proposed that JA and Thomas Jefferson send him to Brussels to take up the task, but, as Jefferson explained, the joint commissioners lacked the authority to do so. Dumas repeatedly presented this plan to John Jay and to George Washington but met with no success (vol. 6:125, 126, 215; Jefferson, *Papers*, 12:257–258, 359–360; *Dipl. Corr., 1783–1789*, 3:601–603, 637–639, 644–645; Washington, *Papers, Presidential Series*, 2:482–483).

[3] Editor Jean Luzac printed a two-part French translation of Washington's 30 April 1789 inaugural address in the *Gazette de Leyde*, 19, 26 June.

[4] For Dumas' letter to JA of 27 Aug. 1788, see vol. 19:338–339.

From Joseph Mandrillon

Amsterdam ce 15 Juin 1789

Monsieur Le Vice-Président,

Le tems peut sans doute avoir detruit le souvenir dont vous m'honoriez, lorsque les interêts del'Amérique vous appellerent dans differentes cours del'Europe, en quittant ces Provinces:[1] mais quand la renomée ne m'auroit pas Sans cessé rappellé votre merite, et votre personne, il m'auroit suffit de penser à l'acceuil flateur dont vous m'avez honoré ici, et aux conversations intéressantes dont vous me faisiez part, pour Savoir apprécier tout l'avantage dont je jouissois.

Reçevez je vous prie, Monsieur, mon compliment Sincere Sur la justice que vos compatriotes viennent de vous rendre en vous nommant leur *Vice-President*; il etoit naturel que le citoyen respectable qui avoit redigé leurs loix, veilla à leur exécution, et cette nommination fait votre éloge & le leur en même tems.

Je profite du départ de Monsieur Théophile Cazenove de cette ville pour vous addresser la présente.[2] Il va voyager en Amérique pour mieux la connaître, et certainement, s'il à l'honneur de vous connaitre, il ne peut que gagner infiniment pour augmenter les lumieres qu'il a dejà acquises.

Je fais des voeux, Monsieur, très Sincere pour votre bonheur & votre conservation, ainsi que pour votre chere et respectable famille, qui doit être bien heureuse de vous posseder au Sein de la gloire et de la paix

J'ai l'honneur d être avec le plus parfait respect Monsieur le Vice-Président / Votre très humble & très obéissant / Serviteur

J[h.] mandrillon

Des Académies de Philadelphie, de Haarlem &c—

TRANSLATION

Mr. Vice President Amsterdam, 15 June 1789

Time may well have abolished the memory with which you used to honor me, once American interests called you to quit these provinces and travel to other European courts.[1] However, even if your reputation had not constantly recalled to mind your merits and your person, it would have been sufficient to remember the gracious welcome that you honored me with here, and the interesting conversations you involved me in, to acknowledge all the benefits I enjoyed.

I pray you accept, sir, my sincere congratulations for the justice your compatriots have lately rendered you in naming you their *vice president*; it was natural that the respectable citizen who drafted their laws saw to their execution, and this election honors you and them at the same time.

I take advantage of the departure of Mr. Theophile Cazenove from this city to send you this letter.[2] He travels to America in order to know it better, and certainly, if he has the honor to know you, he can only add endlessly increasing enlightenment to that which he has already acquired.

I express my heartfelt wishes, sir, for your happiness and your preservation, and for your dear and respectable family, who must be quite happy to hold you in the bosom of glory and peace.

I have the honor to be, with most perfect respect, Mr. Vice President, your most humble and most obedient servant J[h.] mandrillon

Of the Academy of Philadelphia, of Haarlem &c—

RC (Adams Papers).

[1] Amsterdam bookseller Joseph Mandrillon (b. 1743), a Dutch Patriot, was guillotined in Paris on 7 Jan. 1794 (Hoefer, *Nouv. biog. générale*).

[2] Dutch land agent Théophile Cazenove (1740–1811) managed the American financial operations of four prominent Dutch banking firms and dined with JA on 30 June 1790 (*AFC*, 11:451; from Alexander Hamilton, 23 June 1790, below).

From Eliphalet Pearson

Sir, Cambridge 15 June 1789.

President Willard having resigned the office of corresponding secretary to the American Academy of Arts & Sciences, your goodness will pardon his successor, in diverting your attention, for a moment, from more important objects, while I request a favor, with which the honor of the society may be connected.[1]

At our last meeting, & upon the recommendation of Mr. Gardoqui, through General Knox, the Duke de Almodavar, & the Marquis de Santa Cruz, two Spanish noblemen, were elected fellows.[2] Not knowing the place of their Lordships' residence, & being totally unacquainted with the forms of addressing Spanish nobility, I have taken the liberty of troubling your Excellency with the certificates of their election, accompanied with official letters undirected. Permit me, therefore, to request the favor of your adding, or of your asking the Spanish minister to add, the proper superscriptions; directing each of the letters to the nobleman, named in the certificate inclosed under the same cover. The certificates, & letters thus directed, Mr. Gardoqui, I trust, will be so obliging, as to address under cover, & forward to the respective noblemen.

Be pleased, sir, to accept my thanks for Mr. Croft's letter to Mr. Pitt, which you were so good, as to send me some time since;[3] and, praying that your health, happiness, and extensive usefulness, may be long continued, indulge me the honor of subscribing myself, with sentiments of profound respect & sincerest esteem, / Sir, / Your Excellency's / much obliged & very humble servant

E. Pearson.

RC (Adams Papers).

[1] Joseph Willard acted as corresponding secretary of the American Academy of Arts and Sciences from 1780 to 1789. He was succeeded by Pearson, who held the post until 1802 (Mark G. Spencer, ed., *The Bloomsbury Encyclopedia of the American Enlightenment*, 2 vols., London, 2015, 2:1103; *Sibley's Harvard Graduates*, 18:292).

[2] The academy elected Spanish chargé d'affaires Don Diego de Gardoqui; Pedro de Luxan y Silva, the Marquis de Almodóvar, former Spanish minister to Great Britain; and José Joaquin de Bazán Silva y Sarmiento, Marqués de Santa Cruz (1734–1802), director of the Spanish Royal Academy since 1776. The 62 founding members of the academy were all Americans, but between 1785 and 1804, they selected 48 Europeans to join the ranks

(vols. 6:232, 17:19; *Elogio del Excelentísimo Señor Marques de Santa Cruz*, Madrid, 1802, p. 4; *Memoirs of the American Academy of Arts and Sciences*, 1:v, xx–xxii [1783]; 2:165–166 [1804]).

[3] Sir Herbert Croft, *An Unfinished Letter to the Right Honourable William Pitt Concerning the New Dictionary of English*, London, 1788.

From Richard Peters

Dear Sir Belmont June 15. 1789

I am honoured with yours of the 5th. instant I thank you for your kind & polite Offers of Hospitality. Experience has convinced me of your Friendship on this Head—

I find from the Reflexions occasioned by the just Observations in your Letter that I have expected too much & am therefore not entitled to the Right of complaining under Dissappointment. Tho' placed in a new Situation, we are the same People & are playing something of the old Game tho' we have changed our Pack— Allons—jouez bien votre Cartes— I am only a Stander-by & will patiently wait the Event: For, after all the grave Calculations of the gravest Politicians (among whom by the By I do not rank myself) Success in the Eyes of most Men stamps a substantial Value upon Measures— We were however very near losing our Liberty in the first Stages of the War by temporary military Expedients, under a Fear that a well organized & permanent Army might turn out dangerous to it. I wish we may not bring it again into Jeopardy by the same Fears excited by different Objects. But the Transactions of many Years past have made me somewhat of a Predestinarian in Politicks I therefore, judging of the future by what has past, I rest firmly convinced that *all will end well.*

I am happy to find by your Letter that you are likely to be settled so, as I presume, to have your Family with you. This Satisfaction of mine is on your own Account, for as a Pennsilvanian I do not desire you to be so comfortably settled where you are as not to be convinced that you could do better where all Pennsilvanians wish you— Wherever you are be assured of the sincere & respectful Esteem with which / I am your obedt Servant— Richard Peters

P.S. The Sentiments of Montesquieu on the Subject you mention have indeed been miserably construed. He was a great & sensible Man but has in many Passages of his Works rendered his Meaning obscure by a Habit of too much condensing his Ideas so as to avoid Prolixity. He is a Kind of Bible for Politicians & it fares with his as it does with the good Book—every one finds a Text to suit his own Purposes. If indeed the Text does not exactly fit, convenient Interpretations must do the Business.

RC (MHi:Adams-Hull Coll.); addressed: "His Excellency / John Adams / V President of the United States / New York"; internal address: "His Excy John Adams—"; endorsed: "Richard Peters. / June 15."; notation by CFA: "1789."

From Benjamin Rush

Dear Sir, Philada June 15th: 1789

I have been so long accustomed to regard all your opinions upon goverment with reverence, that I was disposed upon reading your last letter,[1] to suspend my belief in republican Systems of political happiness; but a little reflection led me again to adopt them, and upon this single principle, *that they have Never had a fair tryal.* Let us try what the influence of general science & religion diffused in early life, will have upon our citizens. Let us try the effect of banishing the latin & greek languages from our country. They consume the flower of human life—and by enabling us to read agreeable histories of ancient crimes, Often lead us to imitate or to tollerate them. Hitherto the factions have been fewer, & less violent in America since the year 1776 than in many monarchies in the same number of years, under less irritating, and dividing circumstances. Passions which in Europe would have vented themselves in war, here discharged themselves only in newspaper scurrility, or in inflammatory resolves, or addresses.— One thing further, my profession has taught me, Viz: that political passions produce fewer diseases in a republic than in a monarchy.— Disappointed ambition in Sweden and in Italy has produced sudden death from colics, & apoplexies,— In america, it has scarcely of *late* years produced a single hypocondriac disorder. In time, I believe the effects of the political passions upon health & life will be still less perceptable in our country. I think likewise our republican form of government, has already softned the religious passions. we have less bigottry than formerly—and while there is no court, nor monarch, no mode of worship will be preferred from interested considerations. Do you not think it will be better to raise our people to a pure & free goverment by good education, than to sink to their present vulgar habits by accommadating a goverment to them? Much has been done already to enlighten our citizens—but much more may be done.— What do you think of a federal University, & of *English* free Schools in every township in the United States?—[2]

I find we think more alike in your last letter upon a certain subject, than we did in your first.— I have a right to believe that the residence of congress in new York has always been an object of more importance in the eyes of many people, than the adoption or establishment of the federal Goverment.—

Many pious people wish the name of the supreme Being had been introduced Somewhere in the new constitution. Perhaps an acknowledgement may be made of his Goodness, or of his providence in the proposed amendments.— In all enterprizes, & parties, I believe the *praying*, are better Allies, than the *fighting* part of communities.—

I am Dear Sir with great regard / Your affectionate and / steady friend

Benj[n] Rush

RC (Adams Papers); endorsed: "D[r] Rush June 15 / ans[d] 19. 1789."

[1] Of 9 June, above.

[2] Rush's essay "To Friends of the Federal Government: A Plan for a Federal University" was published under the pseudonym "Citizen of Pennsylvania" in the Philadelphia *Federal Gazette*, 29 Oct. 1788. Rush's proposed curriculum included government, history, manufacturing, commerce, math, science, English, French, and German (Rush, *Letters*, 1:491–495).

From Jabez Bowen

Sir, Providence June 16. 1789

I Returned yesterday from attending the Gen[l] Assembly, the great matters on which the in[s.] & outs differ were bro't on. we lost the Convention by 11 Votes. The Repeal of the Tender by 9. on the whole we gain a little. but our progress is so slow that we shall never arive at our wish'd for point except something like M[r] Bensons motion in Congress, could be obtained.[1] it was usual for us to adjorn 'till August, but no such motion was made. consiquently the Assembly will not meet 'till October (except calld by Warrant.) in August the Lower house are Re:chosen. we shall do our utmost to make a Change to our wishes, but have no great prospects. The oposition which consists of the Debtors, with the midling & Lower Classes of Farmers continue firm in their oposition. and I am afraid will so Continue Their Leaders keep up a Correspondence with some of the Antifederal Members of Congress by which they are encouraged to stand out. our situation is Difficult & verry disagreable and what further steps to take we know not. wish for your advice & assistance. I think it was a great oversight in not putting the old Impost Bill in motion the first moment Congress was organized, in that case no time would have been lost, and every one would have been fully heard with patience.[2]

From the forme of the Address used by The House of Representatives of the U. States to the President, one would think that the House was composed of a Majority of Quakers, and should we have no occasion to Talk to any Bodys of Men in the old World, we might make out pretty well. but when the Respectable Republicks of America determin that no Title shall be affixed to their Head, it will be looked upon as a piece of Singularity & oddity. I hear President Manning is just arived shall call on him before I Close this as I dont mean to be troublesome by the frequency of my Letters.[3] By him I learn that no plan seems to be agreed on, that on the whole we must be endur'd with that most Excellent Virtue ~~Charity~~ Patience; and let Time bring us to that period that shall deliver us out of the hands of unjust men.

Continue to be mindful of us, and Believe me to be with the greatest Esteeme Your Excellency' Most Obedient Servant

Jabez Bowen

RC (Adams Papers); endorsed: "Governor Bowen / ~~July~~ June 16. ans^{d} 26. / 1789."

[1] The Rhode Island legislature met from 8 to 13 June. It passed an embargo on grain and approved exemptions to that act in cases of hardship, but the proposal to repeal the state's tender act lost by seven votes. An impost bill that called for a 30 percent tax on all imports was referred to the next session. More significantly, the proposal for another ratification convention failed. New York representative Egbert Benson introduced a congressional resolution on 1 June recommending that the Rhode Island legislature call for a convention. The House considered the motion on 5 June but, led by Virginia representative Alexander White, decided against it (*Records of the State of Rhode Island and Providence Plantations in New England*, ed. John Russell Bartlett, 10 vols., 1856–1865, 10:332, 334–335; *Newport Herald*, 18 June; *AFC*, 9:339; *Doc. Hist. Ratif. Const.*, 25:527, 531).

[2] In 1781 the Continental Congress approved a 5 percent tax on all imports despite the refusal of delegates from Rhode Island to support the motion. By 1786 Rhode Island was in favor of a federal impost, but New York defeated it (vol. 14:139, 140; Ferguson, *Power of the Purse*, p. 242).

[3] Rev. James Manning (1738–1791), Princeton 1762, served as Rhode Island's delegate to the Continental Congress in 1786 and was pastor of the First Baptist Church in Providence, R.I., from 1771 to 1791. An ardent Federalist, he attended the Massachusetts ratification convention, and, in Aug. 1789, he chaired the committee that drafted Providence residents' petition to Congress seeking exemption from foreign duties (*Doc. Hist. Ratif. Const.*, 7:1532; 24:42, 314–315).

To Richard Peters

Dear sir— Richmond Hill June 18th. 1789—

Success you say, in yours of the 15th. stamps a substantial value upon measures, Yet the Motto under a Picture of O. Cromwell, is not without its Justice

> Careat successibus, opto,
> Quiquis, ab Eventu, facta notanda putat.[1]

It is a saying in France, "We can never be ruined, for if our ruin had been possible, it would have been accomplished long ago, since the wisest Heads in France have been these hundred Years employed in doing all they could to effect it"— Something very like this may be said with great truth of our own Country.

Tho I think we are not out of danger of divisions, yet upon the whole I rest with you in an humble Confidence that we all will end well— I am settled on the beautiful banks of the Hudson and expect Mrs. Adams daily— Tho I shall be as happy as a Priest I shall have no Objection to as good a Residence on the Schuylkill or Delaware, if my superiors should command me to remove

Yet we have so much to do, that it would be a pitty to interrupt our deliberations with any questions about Place at present—

I am Sir, with great esteem— / Your Most Obedient

J. Adams.

LbC in WSS's hand (Adams Papers); internal address: "The Honble. Richard Peters"; APM Reel 115.

[1] "Let him come to naught, I pray, / who thinks the deed should be condemned from its result" (Ovid, *Heroides*, transl. Grant Showerman, Cambridge, 2014, Letter II, lines 85–86).

To James Searle

Dear sir— NewYork June 18th. 1789—

I have received your Letter of the 10th. and in answer to your question, I have no scruple to say, that on your arrival in Holland you appeared to me to take as effectual measures as any man could then have taken to obtain a loan to the state of Pensylvania: But that such was the situation of Affairs, that it was next to Impossible to obtain any considerable Loan for the United states Jointly or severally. I could take up your time for an hour in relating the mortifications suffered by myself in many ineffectual attempts in behalf of the United states— The invariable answer to me was "nothing can be done till the States General have acknowledged your Independence" in consequence of which, I most earnestly endeavoured to impress upon Congress in all my dispatches the Policy and necessity of sending a minister to that Republic. and it was not till a full Power was sent by Congress and acknowledged by their High Mightinesses that I was able to obtain money for the United States— Till then I could persuade nobody to undertake to open a Loan, except Mr. De Neufville[1] and all the effect of His efforts and my own—were 4000 Guilders obtain'd by him and 3000 by myself— I never heared or suspected any neglect of the interests of your Constituents or any dishonour brought upon them by your Conduct— You did me the honor to consult me very frequently, upon the Business of your mission according to your instructions: but it was not in my Power to give you better advice than I gave myself or could procure from others: and it all proved ineffectual in my own Case as well as yours—

I have the honor to be with much esteem Sir. / Your most Obedient & most Humble servant John Adams.

LbC in WSS's hand (Adams Papers); internal address: "Mr. Searle"; APM Reel 115.

[1] JA's first attempt at a Dutch loan, a 1781 contract for 1 million florins with the Amsterdam banking firm of Jean de Neufville & Fils, failed to attract investors (vols. 11:xv, 102; 12:434–435; 16:93).

To James Sullivan

Sir. NewYork June 18th. 1789—

I have received your favour of the 10th. and am obliged to you for a free Communication of Your sentiments upon some important points.

The situation of Rhode-Island, North Carolina and Vermont, must be disagreable to themselves as well as to their neighbours. Congress is not inattentive to either. What measures they may think proper to take is as yet to be determined— It is reported here that the Minority in Massachusetts are encouraging the majority in Rhode Island— A. speach from the President, a Resolution of the House or senate or both, have been thought of and proposed, but there are different sentiments concerning the Wisdom and the effects of Either— but there is no difference of opinion concerning the Conduct of Rhode-Island— They are betraying the Rights and Interests of New England every day; and their fault is less Criminal than that of Massachusetts-Men who countenance and encourage them—

You must be enough acquainted with American Politicks to perceive that the members of the middle & the south, will not be unanimously Zealous at this moment to give N. England two additional senators—

If the new Government has dominion enough over the minds and Hearts of Men to Maintain its ground in the states that have accepted it—Rhode-Island will come in, if not, the other states will go out, and the Government will expire.

Our Eastern friends seem to have reason to desire a Port of delivery Eastward of Portland, but that Bill is not yet digested— The members from that Part will endeavour to obtain what is reasonable, and I shall be glad to throw in my mite of assistance to them, in any thing in my sphere—

I am Sir. Your most Obed$^{t.}$ / & most Humble serv$^{t.}$

J. Adams.

LbC in WSS's hand (Adams Papers); internal address: "Judge Sullivan—"; APM Reel 115.

To Benjamin Lincoln

Dear Sir — New York June 19. 1789

I am honoured with yours of the 30$^{th.}$ of May, and find We are well agreed in opinion in all points.[1]

Nothing Since my return to America, has alarmed me So much, as those habits of Fraud, in the Use of Language which appear in conversation and in public writings. Words are employed like paper money, to cheat the Widow and the fatherless and every honest Man. The Word Aristocracy is one Instance. 'tho I cannot say, that there is no colour, for the Objection against the Constitution, that it has too large a Proportion of Aristocracy in it; Yet there are two Checks to the Senate evidently designed and prepared, the House of Representatives on one Side and the President on the other. Now the only feasable remedy against this danger is to compleat the Equilibrium, by making the Executive Power distinct from the Legislative, and the President as independent of the other Branches as they are of him.— But the Cry of Monarchy is kept up, in order to deter the People, from recurring to the true Remedy, and to force them into another which[2] would be worse than the disease, i e. into an entire relyance on the popular Branch, and a rejection of the other two. a remarkable Instance of this, I lately read, with much concern, in the Message from the Governor to the House.—[3] the attention and affections of the People are there tu[rned] to [their] Representatives only, and very artfully terrified with the Phantoms of Monarchy and Despotism.— Does he mean to insinuate that there is danger of a Despotism? or of Simple Monarchy? or would he have the People afraid of a limited Monarchy? in Truth Mr H. himself is a limited Monarch. The Constitution of the Massachusetts is a limited Monarchy. So is the new Constitution of the United States.— both have very great Monarchical Powers; and the real defects of both are, that they have not enough to make the first magistrate, an independent and effectual Ballance, to the other Branches. But does Mr H. mean to confound these limited Monarchical Powers, with Despotism & Simple Monarchy which have no limits? Does he wish and mean to level all Things and become the Rival of General Shase? the Idea of an equal distribution of Intelligence and Property, is as extravagant as any that ever was avowed by the maddest of the Insurgents, another Instance of the false Coin, or rather paper Money in Circulation, is the Phrase "confederated Republick" and "confederated Commonwealth."— The new Constitution might in my opinion, with as much Propriety, be denominated judicial Astrology.— My old Friend your Lt Governor, in his devout Ejaculation for the new Government, very carefully preserves the Idea of a confederated Commonwealth, and the *independent* States that compose it.—[4] Either his Ideas or mine, are totally wrong upon this Subject.— in Short Mr A. in his Prayer and Mr H. in his message, either understood not the force of the Words they have used, or they have made the most insidious Attack on the new Constitution that has yet appeared.

With two Such popular Characters at the Head of Massachusetts so near to Rhode Island: with Governor Clinton at the head of N.Y. and Governor Henry, in Virginia so near to N. Carolina: there is some reason to be jealous. a convulsion with Such Men engaged openly or Secretly in favour of it, would be a Serious Evil. I hope however that my fears are groundless.— and have too much Charity for all of them, to imagine that they mean to disturb the Peace of our Israel.

Mr Henshaw like all others must apply to the President, if he has any Views of Employment.—[5] He has never communicated to me any desire of any Thing. I believe him to be a very worthy man.

This Letter is very free, and of course confidential.

We have got down Molasses to two and an half Cents: but I was obliged to reduce it, the senators being equally divided. But when they Saw that I had reduced it to three Cents, they took the Resolution to take away the Drawback on Rum, and reduce Molasses half a Cent lower.— They have not been very Severe upon me for what they call my Partiality for thę Eaters and Distillers of Molasses.

With great Regard, I am, sir your / most obedient

John Adams.

RC (MeHi:John S. H. Fogg Autograph Coll.); addressed by WSS: "The Honourable / Benjamin Lincoln / &c. &c. &c. / Hingham / Massachusetts—"; internal address: "General Lincoln"; endorsed: "June 19 1789 / Mr. J: Adams"; notation by JA: "Free / John Adams." LbC (Adams Papers); APM Reel 115. Text lost due to fading of the ink has been supplied from the LbC.

1 Vol. 19:485–488.

2 The LbC is in WSS's hand to this point, and the remainder is in AA2's hand.

3 In his 8 June message to the Mass. General Court, Gov. John Hancock lauded members of the first federal Congress for their service, stating that "no place will be opened, to those ideas of monarchy and despotism, which have long scourged other parts of the world." The General Court responded eight days later, concurring that they shared the duty to "establish the honor of our CONFEDERATED REPUBLIC" (*Massachusetts Centinel*, 10 June; Boston *Herald of Freedom*, 23 June).

4 On 29 May newly elected lieutenant governor Samuel Adams addressed the General Court, expressing his "devout and fervent wish, that gracious Heaven may guide the public councils of the great confederated Commonwealth, and the several free and independent Republics which compose it" (Boston *Herald of Freedom*, 2 June; *New-York Packet*, 11 June).

5 For Samuel Henshaw's patronage request, see vol. 19:488.

To Benjamin Rush

Dear Sir New York June 19. 1789

Your Single Principle, in your Letter of the 15th must fail you.— You say "that Republican Systems have never had a fair Tryal."— What do you mean by a fair Tryal? and what by Republican systems.— Every Government that has more than one Man in its soverignty is a republican system. Tryals innumerable have been made. as many as there have existed Nations. There is not and never was, I believe, on Earth, a Nation, which has not been, at Some Period of its duration, under a republican Government. i. e. under a Government of more than one. all the various combinations and modifications which the subtile Brains of Men could invent have been attempted, to no other purpose but to shew that Discord Anarchy and Uncertainty of Life, Liberty and Property; can be avoided only by a perfect Equilibrium in the Constitution. You Seem determined not to allow a limited monarchy to be a republican System, which it certainly is, and the best that ever has been tryed.—

There is no Proposition, of the Truth of which I am more clearly convinced than this, that the "Influence of general Science," instead of curing any defects in an unballanced Republick, would only increase and inflame them and make them more intollerable. for this obvious and unanswerable Reason, that Parties would have in them, a greater number of able and ambitious Men, who would only understand the better, how to worry one another with greater Art and dexterity.— Religion itself, by no means cures this inveterate Evil, for Parties are always founded on some Principle, and the more conscientious Men are, the more determined they will be in pursuit of their Principle system and Party.

I Should as soon think of closing all my Window shutters, to enable me to see, as of banishing the Classicks, to improve Republican Ideas.— How can you Say that Factions have been few in America? Have they not rendered Property insecure? have they not trampled Justice under foot? have not Majorities voted Property out of the Pocketts of others into their own, with the most decided Tyranny.?

Have not our Parties behaved like all Republican Parties? is not the History of Hancock and Bowdoin, the History of the Medici, and Albizi—that of Clinton and Yates, the Same with that of the Cancellieri and the Panchiatichi.?[1] and so on through the Continent.— and We Shall find, that without a Ballance the Progress will soon be, from Libels to Riots, from Riots to Seditions and from Seditions to civil Wars.

Every Project to enlighten our Fellow Citizens has my most hearty good Wishes: because it tends to bring them into a right Way of thinking respecting the means of their Happiness, civil political social and religious.

I wish with all my heart, that the Constitution had expressed as much Homage to the Supream Ruler of the Universe as the President has done in his first Speech. The Petit Maitres who call themselves Legislators and attempt to found a Government on any other than an eternal Basis of Morals and Religion, have as much of my Pitty as can consist with Contempt.

I am my dear sir yours John Adams.

RC (private owner, 1977); addressed by WSS: "D^r. Benjamin Rush / Philadelphia"; internal address: "Dr Rush."; endorsed: "John Adams." LbC (Adams Papers); APM Reel 115.

[1] The Medici and Albizzi families were longstanding political rivals in medieval Florence, while the Cancellieri and Panchiatichi clans headed warring factions in Pistoia. JA included the history of both Italian republics in the second and third volumes of his *Defence of the Const.*, for which see vol. 19:130–132. During the 1789 New York gubernatorial election, Federalists supported Robert Yates despite his Antifederalist leanings, in an attempt to divide the Antifederalists and oust incumbent George Clinton (JA, *Defence of the Const.*, 2:103, 3:56–57; William J. Connell and Andrea Zorzi, *Florentine Tuscany: Structures and Practices of Power*, N.Y., 2000, p. 238, 319; Young, *Democratic Republicans*, p. 130–132).

To George Washington

Dear sir— Richmond Hill June 20th. 1789—

Among the Candidates for the Honour of public Employment, under the New Government there is one, whose connection in my family, and public relation to me, in the late legation to St. James's would render my total silence on his account, liable to misinterpretation, as proceeding, either from a want of esteem, confidence, or affection for him on the one hand, or to a failure of respect to The President on the other,

The Gentleman, I mean is Colonel Smith whose original, education and Services, during the late War are all better known to you, Sir, than to me, He was indeed so much a stranger to me, that, to my recollection I never heared his name, 'till he was announced as the secretary, of my Legation to Great Britain[1]

During the three Years that he resided with me in England, his Conduct was to my satisfaction—and his Character was much esteemed in England, France, spain, Portugal through all which Countries he had occasion to travel—

As his Qualifications, are as well known to you, sir, as to me, and the situations that require to be filled, and the merit of other Candidates, much better: it is not my intention to solicit any particular place for him. his inclination, as well as mine, would no doubt prefer something at home,—but if the public service require a minister to go abroad, and he should be thought a proper person, I presume he would have no objection

In England he has served three Years; is known at Court, and in the Nation, and is as much esteemed and would be as well recieved, as any other faithfull American. As all my Dispatches passed through his hands, he is well acquainted, with the rise, progress and present state, of the negotiations of the United states at that Court. I shall not however dissemble my opinion, that it would not consist with the dignity of this Nation, or Her Chief Majistrate, to send to that Country, any Character higher than a Consul, before an explicit agreement shall be made on their part, to return to your Court a Minister of equal rank—

In Portugal Mr. Smith has already executed one Commission, to the satisfaction of that Court as well as of his Constituents. With the Present Prime Minister, The Chevelier De Pinto, he has had a personal Acquaintance in London for several years, and to my knowledge is much esteemed by that wise, able, and amiable Nobleman, one of whose most earnest Wishes, it is, to form a Treaty with this Country—[2]

In Holland Mr. Smith is known to many: and I flatter myself, that, from my long residence and numerous Acquaintances in that Republic; especially among the Capitalists, Stock-Brokers, Loan-Undertakers and money Lenders who have now in their possession, obligations under my hands, for more than nine Millions of Guilders.

And from his known Connection with me, he would be, as well received, both at the Prince of Orange's Court, by their High Mightinesses, by the Corps Diplomatique, and the Nation, as any other Person—

While on one hand I shall hold myself under Obligation for whatever appointment The President may judge fit for him, I shall cheerfully acquiesse, on the other, in whatever may be the determination—

With every sentiment of Respect / and affection, I have the Honor to be / Dear sir. / Your most Obedt— / & most Humble servt—

John Adams.

LbC in WSS's hand (Adams Papers); internal address: "To / The President / of The United States—"; APM Reel 114.

[1] Despite rumors of a diplomatic assignment, WSS was nominated on 25 Sept. to serve as marshal for the district of New York, and the Senate confirmed the appointment on the same day (vol. 19:201, 202; *AFC*, 9:93, 149).

[2] For WSS's goodwill mission to Lisbon and the [25 *April 1786*] proposed Portuguese-American Treaty of Amity and Commerce, see vols. 18:256–271; 19:46, 153.

From William Tudor

Dear Sir, Boston 21 June 1789

I thank you for correcting my careless Appellation of federal Republic as applied to the National Government. We are so used to Absurdities & indefinite Terms when speaking of the great Constitution, that I am now to ask your Indulgence in future for sometimes hastily adopting Expressions which are so often improperly used by our Massachusetts Politicians. And yet notwithstanding your just Idea of the sole Sovereignty of the national Government, was a Man to tell our general Court that the Commonwealth of Massachusetts was not a sovereign & independent State they would charge him with talking Treason. They admit that Congress now is sovereign, quoad certain Purposes, and this State alone sovereign for others. This Error & nonsense they will persist in, untill the full Operation of the National Statutes, & the new Officers get into Play. And give me leave to ask if Congress is not in a Degree countinancing this Delusion? Are they not, I mean the lower House, encouraging those extreme democratic Notions which have hitherto impeded the Advancement of that full Respectability that our Country is intitled to, by refusing to admit of those Distinctions & Titles which effect so much in European Governments? The News Papers inform that even the Title of Esquire is become an Abomination in their Ears.[1] And on the same Principle so ought the Addition of Mr. to be. To act thoroughly consistent they ought to turn Quakers in Politicks, if not in Religion. This Silliness pleases Mr. Han. Mr. S. A. & Dr. J.[2] I most heartily wish all the Fools of the same Stamp throughout the Union would unite & colonize. There is Land enough upon the Banks of the Ohio for all the democratic Simpletons in the united States. There let them found a Utopia & crack Acorns with the *equal* Commoners of the Woods.

It is owing to Envy & a contemptible Pride, that our chief Magistrates are to be denied those Titles which would be expressive of their Posts, because two only can possess them. and because thirteen Excellencies would be then out titled.

I inclose You the Copy of a Petition presented to the General Court in their May session of 1788.[3] If it should not furnish an argument in favour of a national Bankrupt Act, it may furnish a very extraordinary & interesting Peice of ~~private~~ an Individual's History. The Facts alledged in the Petition were fully substantiated before a Committee of both Houses, & a Bill in favour of the Petitioner was reported, but miscarried, for various local Reasons, of no Importance now to relate.

I most sincerely thank You for your two last Letters, & for your promised Care of the one I inclosed.[4] That Letter occasioned me some Mortification. But a Wife & six Children with a sinking Profession, forbid me being the Dupe of Feelings, which, perhaps, all the Seekers & would be Devourers "of the Loaves & Fishes," are not troubled with. I hope before this Letter reaches New York You will have had the Pleasure of Meeting Mrs. Adams; that Friend of your Heart so well calculated to mitigate the Cares of your Station. Pray make my most affectionate Compliments to that Lady, & be assured of my unalterable & perfect Attachment. Wm Tudor

RC (Adams Papers); internal address: "President Adams"; endorsed: "Mr Tudor. 21. June / ansd. 28. 1789."

[1] A piece in the Boston *Independent Chronicle*, 2 April, observed that Americans' choice of titles for government officials was evidence of "a propensity . . . to monarchy" and that "Honourable and Esquire have become as common in America, as Captain is in France,—Count in Germany,—or any Lord in Italy." For the controversy over titles, including a form of address for the president, see vol. 19:445.

[2] Anonymous correspondents in several Boston newspapers identified John Hancock, Samuel Adams, and Charles Jarvis as champions of republican principles and opponents of aristocracy. Jarvis (1748–1807), Harvard 1766, of Boston, trained as a physician and served in the Mass. General Court from 1788 to 1797 (*Boston Gazette*, 9 Feb. 1789; Boston *Herald of Freedom*, 15 May; *Sibley's Harvard Graduates*, 16:378, 379, 382; *AFC*, 8:413).

[3] The enclosure has not been found, but Newburyport merchant Nathaniel Tracy submitted a similar request to Congress on 5 March 1790, recounting his service as a financier during the Revolutionary War and asking Congress to enact a bankruptcy law. Tracy indicated that he had presented the same query to the Mass. General Court, but that it had not ruled on his petition, because drafting a uniform law for bankruptcy lay within federal jurisdiction (vol. 3:327; *First Fed. Cong.*, 8:86–89).

[4] Tudor referred to JA's letters of 28 May 1789 (vol. 19:479–480) and 12 June, above. For the "inclosed letter," see Tudor's letter of 6 June, and note 1, above.

To Jabez Bowen

Sir Richmond Hill New York June 26 1789

I received your letter of June. 16: and am glad to learn that you "gain a little." If as I have learnt from Dr Manning, the leaders of your councils have an intercourse with the dissaffected in the Massachusetts, and as appears by your letter a correspondence with antifederal members of a more august body: it is probable there is a chain of communication throughout the states. If such should be the actual situation of things, would not any address of Congress, give fresh courage and spirits to the general cause of opposition? especially if it should be found, not to make any great impression on the callous minds and hardened hearts of desperate debtors?

I wonder that any class of farmers, provided they are not in debt, beyond the value of their possesions; Should continue their opposition: because their property must always lie at the mercy of those who have none, without a consistent government.

It is in vain to talk of oversights. The scene is new, and the actors are inexperienced. much light has been obtained and diffused by the discussions which have occasioned delay—and there is no remedy but patience. Why will you afflict the modesty of any gentlemen by expecting that they will give themselves titles. They expect that you their creators will do them honor. They are no quakers I warrant you and will not be offended if you assert your own majesty, by giving your own representatives in the executive authority the title of majesty. Many of these quakers, think Highness not high enough, among whom I own I am one. In my opinion the American President will soon be introduced into some farce or other in half the theatres of Europe and be held up to ridicule. It would not be extravagant the prophecy that the want of titles may cost this Country fifty thousand lives and twenty millions of money, within twenty years. I will continue to be mindful of you and will endeavour to pursuade Gentlemen to promote such a resolution as you desire, but there seems to be a general aversion to it, or rather suspicion that it would do harm rather than good.

I beg leave to return you, and the other Gent^m: of Providence and Newport my best thanks for your polite and friendly attention to Mrs Adams and her family in her late journey through your State.[1]

With esteem I have the honor to be Sir your most obedient and most humble serv^t: John Adams[2]

LbC in CA's hand (Adams Papers); internal address: "The Hon: Jabez Bowen Esqr" and by JA: "Providence"; APM Reel 115.

[1] For AA's travel to New York, see JA's letter of 12 June to Cotton Tufts, and note 4, above.

[2] Signature in JA's hand.

To Uzal Ogden

Sir Richmond hill New York June 26 1789

I have received the letter you did me the honor to write me, on the twefth of this month, with the first number of a new periodical publication.[1] I have not been able, as yet to find time to read the whole of the christian schollars and farmer's magazine, but upon looking over several parts of it, they appear to me to correspond with the title, and to be well calculated "to promote religion, disseminate useful knowledge, and afford litterary pleasure" with the best wishes for your success, I have the honor to be Sir your most obedient and most humble servant John Adams

LbC in CA's hand (Adams Papers); internal address: "The Rev^d: / Mr Ogden. Newarak / New Jersey."; APM Reel 115.

[1] Episcopal clergyman Uzal Ogden (ca. 1744–1822) served as rector of Trinity Church in Newark, N.J., from 1788 to 1805. With his letter to JA of 12 June 1789 (Adams Papers), Ogden sent the first issue of *The Christian's, Scholar's, and Farmer's Magazine*, which was published by Shepard Kollock, editor of the *New-Jersey Journal*, from April 1789 to March 1791 (*ANB*; Frank Luther Mott, *A History of American Magazines, 1741–1850*, Cambridge, 1966, p. 112).

To Eliphalet Pearson

Sir Richmond Hill, New York June 26. 1789

By my Son Charles, who arrived Yesterday, in good Health,[1] I received the Letter you did me, the honour to write me, on the fifteenth of this month with the Letters enclosed for the Duke D'Almodavar and the Marquis De Santa Cruz.— These Letters Shall be delivered as you desire, to my Friend, Don Diego De Gardoqui, by the first Opportunity and that Minister will no doubt be flattered with the Opportunity of transmitting the Honours of your Accademy to those Noblemen.

Accept my Thanks for your obliging Wishes for my Health, and believe me to be with great Esteem, Sir your most obedient / and most humble Servant John Adams

RC (MBA:American Academy, Letters, 1780–1791); addressed by CA: "M[r] Eliphalet Pearson. / Professor of Philosophical grammar, / and secretary to the academy of Arts and Sciences. / Cambridge—"; internal address: "M[r] Pearson Secretary / to the American Academy."; endorsed: "From his Excellency / John Adams L.L.D. / Rec[d.] 3 July 1789."; notation by JA: "Free / John Adams." LbC (Adams Papers); APM Reel 115.

[1] CA set to work as JA's unofficial secretary. Writing to JQA on 9 July, JA observed, "Charles has been very industrious and useful to me, Since his Arrival" (*AFC*, 8:386).

From Francis Dana

Dear Sir York June 26[th:] 1789

When you was last at Cambridge at my house, in consideration of the weight of the business of my present office, and of the feeble state of my health, I was induced to suggest to you, that if any office under the United States, which your partiality for me might lead you to think me capable of filling, and the duties of which wou'd be less burthensome than those of my present one, shou'd be open, it wou'd not be disagreable to one to be honoured with your influence and interest as a candidate for it— As nothing more particular upon the subject then passed between us, it is *possible* you might conceive I wished again to enter into the Diplomatic corps; especially if it shou'd be thought proper to send a Minister to the Court of St: Petersbourg my former residence. However gratifying that appointment might be to my ambition, yet I do assure you that nothing wou'd tempt me again to leave my Country and family. But there is an office still open for which I presume, *in confidence*, to offer myself to you only, as a candidate. I find there is a district Judge to be appointed within each of the confederated States. *That* for our State is the only office which I shou'd prefer to a seat upon our Supreme Judicial Bench. A place in the Supreme Fœderal Court wou'd be more honourable; but on account of the extent of their circuits, and of their sitting twice a year at the seat of the Federal Government, that wou'd expose me to all the difficulties arising from my present office: but for the consideration of which, I wou'd not quit it for any other in the gift of the United States, or of this State.

While on the present circuit, I find from Mr: Parsons, that he has contemplated the appointment of Mr: Lowell to the office of our District Judge, and that in consequence of it he is lead to expect Mr: Lowell wou'd appoint him the Attorney or Advocate for the United States. Both those Gentlemen wou'd fill those offices worthily. Mr: Parsons wou'd probably be the Advocate in either case.

I have supposed from the above conversation between us (however it may savour of vanity in me) that you might think of your friend for one of the Supreme Fœderal Judges. Mr: Lowell has already been in that capacity; and if the reasons I have given against accepting that office, did not exist, I shou'd not choose to stand a candidate for it against him. Perhaps there may be no impropriety in both appointments, as every State must have a district Judge, and, I think, Massachusetts, cœteris paribus, may be entitled to one Judge of the six of the Supreme Fœderal Court.

I wish now to trouble you with one declaration only viz that this is the first instance in my life of my offering myself a candidate for any office whatever, directly or indirectly: and none but the reasons abovementioned shou'd have induced me ever to have done it.

I beg you wou'd be pleased to present my sincere regards to your Lady, and to acquaint her I shall remember her request respecting Master Thomas. But to enable me the better to execute it, it might not be amiss for her to advise him to visit very frequently in our family. We shou'd be very happy to have him do it: to domesticate himself in some sort with us. I will be his friend so long as he will permit me to be so: but he must not keep himself aloof from us.[1]

I am dear Sir, / Your much obliged Friend / & obedient humble Servant FRA DANA

P.S. please to advise me of the receipt of this as soon as may be convenient

RC (Adams Papers); internal address: "Honble John Adams / Vice President of the United States"; endorsed: "Judge Dana June 26. / ans^{d} July 10. 1789."

[1] TBA was entering his final year at Harvard, and AA, writing to JQA on 30 May, asked her eldest son, "in my absence to attend to your Brother Tom, to watch over his conduct & prevent by your advice & kind admonitions, his falling a prey to vicious Company." For their involvement in the 29 Nov. 1787 student riot at Harvard, TBA and CA were required to pay for damages to the college's dining hall. AA likely made a similar request of Dana when she visited him in late May 1789 (*AFC*, 8:233, 360, 363).

To William Tudor

Dear Sir Richmond Hill June 28. 1789

I Shall not grant the Indulgence you request in yours of the 21st, most certainly: I mean that for hastily adopting Expressions, which are So often improperly used by Massachusetts Politicians. Our Fellow Citizens will never think alike nor act aright, untill they are habitually taught to Use the Same Words in the Same Sense. Nations are governed by Words, as well as by Actions; by Sounds as well as Sights.— You and I learned in our Youth from our great Masters, the Civilians, that the Summa Imperii, is indivisible. That Imperium in Imperio, is a Solecism, a Contradiction in Terms.— and We have been both taught, by History and Experience, Since, that those Instructions of our Masters were infallible oracles.

The new Constitution, however, I fear will be found to be too nearly related to such a Solecism.— It is an avowed Attempt to make the national Government Sovereign in Some Cases and the State Governments in others. it is true that as the former, embraces the whole, and the latter but Parts; as the former has the greatest Objects as War and Peace &c and a general Superintendence over all the rest, the Superiority of Rank and Dignity is allowed to it. But I nevertheless, own, that it is too clear that in a course of Time, the little fishes will eat up the Great one unless the great one Should devour all the little ones.

It is contended by Some that our new Constitution, is partly national and partly fœderal. but it Seems to me, that as far as it is fœderal, it is wholly national: as far as it is not national it is not fœderal but consists of individual, Seperate, independent and inconnected States. but in this View, it is improper to talk of the fœderal Commonwealth and the independent Republicks that compose it—because that the new Constitution, which is the only League by which they are connected together, is not a Confederation of independent Republicks, but is a monarchical Republick, or if you will a limited Monarchy. Though Names are of Importance, they cannot alter the nature of Things. The Name of President, does not alter the Nature of his office nor diminish the Regal Authorities and Powers which appear clearly in the Writing. The Prince of Orange Said to me "Monseiur, Vous allez avoir un Roi, Sous le titre de President,"[1] and his Judgment would be confirmed by every Civilian in Europe, who should read our Constitution.—

Crudities enough, to be Sure, come from a certain august Source; as you have remarked: but the People Should not mind them. The People themselves should honour their own Creation, if they mean to honour themselves. and I hope the People will assert their own Supremacy, and give the Title of *Majesty* to the President. This is the lowest that can comport with his constitutional Dignity, Authority, and Power.

I agree, entirely with you that it is Aristocratical Pride alone, that feels itself hurt, by a distinction of the President. Those who proudly think themselves his Compeers, cannot bear that he should be more than Primus inter Pares. But the common People, if they understand their own cause and Interest, will take effectual Care to mortify that Pride by making the Executive Magistrate a ballance against it which can be done only, by distinguishing him clearly and decidedly, far above all others.

I thank you for Traceys Romance, which I have Shewn and will continue to show to proper Persons, and I hope it will assist in procuring a Bankrupt Act.—[2] Your Letter to the President, I delivered immediately.[3]

Your Pupil Ames makes a very pretty figure: let me congratulate you on his fame, and that of another of your Pupils M[r] Minot, to whom I am indebted for two Copies of his History, which I am ashamed to say I have never thanked him for, as I ought in Duty to have done for the great Pleasure I received from the perusal of that elegant and judicious Composition.[4]

I am, my dear sir yours &c John Adams.

RC (MHi:Tudor-Adams Correspondence); internal address: "William Tudor Esq[r] / Barrister at Law."; endorsed: "M[r.] A. 28 June / 1789—" LbC (Adams Papers); APM Reel 115. Tr (Adams Papers).

[1] Sir, you are going to have a king, under the title of president.

[2] See Tudor's letter of 21 June, and note 3, above.

[3] See Tudor's letter of 6 June, and note 1, above.

[4] That is, Massachusetts representative Fisher Ames and historian George Richards Minot. Minot (1758–1802), Harvard 1778, of Boston, was clerk of the Mass. house of representatives from 1781 to 1792. A presentation copy of Minot's *History of the Insurrections in Massachusetts in the Year Seventeen Hundred and Eighty-Six and the Rebellion Consequent Thereon*, Worcester, Mass., 1788, is in JA's library at MB. His account, although flawed by inattention to the role of Boston politics and the difficulty of understanding and suppressing the insurgents, became the standard narrative of Shays' Rebellion (*DAB*; Richards, *Shays's Rebellion*, p. 159, 160–162; *Catalogue of JA's Library*).

To Cotton Tufts

Dear sir Richmond Hill June 28. 1789

I have received your favour of the 22.— M[rs] Adams, M[r] Charles and Miss Louisa, arrived on Wednesday the 24[th.] after a tedious Passage of five days from Newport. We are all very happy.

M[r] Samuel Tufts needs no other merit but that of being your Brother, to convince me that he has a great deal: but if he is a Candidate for any Employment he must apply directly to the first Magistrate. The Authority and Duty of the first Executive Magistrate, it is to investigate the Characters and Merits of all Competitors and the Reputation of his Reign is responsible for his faithful and impartial Use of it. I Shall be obliged to you however, for your State of M[r] Tufts's merits.[1]

M[r] Jackson, of N. Port M[r] Pickman of Salem and Mr Sargant of Glocester have applied I Suppose: for Places but this is under the Rose.[2]

I am with sincerest affection John Adams.

RC (NN:Edward S. and Mary Stillman Harkness Coll.); internal address: "D[r] Tufts."; endorsed: "John Adams Esq / June 28. 1789." LbC (Adams Papers); APM Reel 115.

[1] For Samuel Tufts' query, see Theophilus Parsons' letter of 8 July, and note 2, below.

[2] Newburyport merchant Jonathan Jackson did not receive a collectorship, but George Washington nominated him as marshal for the district of Massachusetts on 24 Sept., and he was confirmed by the Senate two days later (*AFC*, 8:313; *Sibley's Harvard Graduates*, 15:64; *First Fed. Cong.*, 2:44, 46). For the patronage requests of William Pickman and Epes Sargent Jr., see vol. 19:382, 431.

From James Boyd

Boston June 30th. 1789

Your Excellency will pardon the freedom of my addressing you, when you are acquainted with my sufferings & my present Indigence. which is such as urges me to request your Influence with Congress respecting the resolv's of this Court (relative to my sufferings) which was sent on to Congress, by Order of Government. bearing date Novr. 10th: 1786, Copy of which by the desire of the Honbe. Mr. Bowdoin. I inclos'd to the Honbe. Mr: Dalton on the 3 Int. requesting him to deliver the same to your Excelly.[1]

As your Excellency was in Europe at the time those papers were sent to Congress. I was inform'd by several Gentlemen then in Congress. that nothing respecting them cou'd be done untill your return to America as the Eastern Boundary Line was not then determin'd. Altho' that Matter is not yet fully determin'd as to the River St. Croix. I am clearly of opinion that its the Most Northern River, as that was the only one known to the Indians by the Name of St. Croix, & is the River *Mitchel* was order'd by Government to explore & take the true Course, I was present with Mitchel when the Indians (upon Oath) declaird that to be the only St. Croix—[2]

I am encouraged by my Friends who have wrote to Congress in my behalf, to hope that Congress will take Notice of my present Indigent situation & in their wisdom & goodness grant me some relief. as I am the only Refugee yet unnoticd—

with great Esteem & respect I beg leave to / subscribe my self Your Excelly / Most Obt Hbe. Servt.— James Boyd

PS. for any particulars I beg leave to refer to Mr: Dalton. who I wrote fully too—

RC (Adams Papers); internal address: "His Excellency John Adams Esq / Vice president of the United States."

[1] Seeking restoration of or compensation for his land, Boyd wrote to George Washington on 27 November. The president included Boyd's petition in his 9 Feb. 1790 message to the Senate on the eastern boundary dispute, along with a copy of the Mass. General Court's 10 Nov. 1786 resolution supporting Boyd's quest. The Senate appointed a committee to investigate the claim on 10 Feb. 1790. Six weeks later, it recommended the formation of a joint Anglo-American commission to settle the dispute, effectively reiterating John Jay's advice on the matter in his 21 April 1785 report to Congress. Boyd did not regain his lands, but on 7 April 1798 Congress passed an act for the relief of refugees from Canada and Nova Scotia. In 1812 Congress recognized that Boyd lost 50,000 acres and awarded his heirs 2,240 acres near Columbus, Ohio (vol. 19:485; *First Fed. Cong.*, 2:59, 61–62, 65–66, 373–376, 383–385; *Amer. State Papers*, 1:95, 96; *U.S. Statutes at Large*,

2:712; Edward Livingston Taylor, "Refugees to and from Canada and the Refugee Tract," *Ohio Archæological and Historical Publications*, 12:219, 239 [1887]).

2 For the dispute over the location of the Schoodic River (now St. Croix) and the significance of John Mitchell's map, see vol. 18:241–244, 296, 328–329, 399–400.

From James Sullivan

Sir Boston July 2d. 1789

When I had the honor of addressing a Letter to your Excellency, upon a subject of allowed importance to the united States, I did not indulge a hope, that you would step aside from the important concerns in which you are engaged, to acknowledge the receipt of it.[1] nor was I vain enough to imagine, that I was able to Suggest one thought, which was not fully possessed by the Learned body of Partriots in which you preside.

But having been informed that the report which you are obliging enough to mention, was generally spread round the seat of Government; and being well aware, that it could not fail to give great uneasiness, as well to the President, and Congress, as to every real friend to his Country, I threw upon paper, Such Sentiments, as might be well improved, in Some measure to contradict it. for if I beleived that the report was true, I should appear to be, Either in traiterous enmity to the united states, or very little versed in those politicks, which are founded in the feelings of the human heart, in advising to a measure that wears the appearance of coercive decision. for if what is (as I suppose) intended by the Minority here, would support that state, a coercive Experiment might be disagreeable in its consequences.

When the frame of Government for the united States, was submitted to the people, as a political proposition, it could not be conceived, that they would be intirely united in any one opinion besides that, of a federal Government being Necessary; this was not only an avowed, but I beleive a real, & general Sentiment. every one had an indubitable right to express his mind upon the subject; and he was a Coward, and unworthy of that freedom we have contended for, who would not dare to do it. I was myself, and still am, an advocate for amendments: but not for one half the *Alterations* proposed by Mr. Madison.[2] the trial by Jury, as a democratical balance in the Judiciary department, in all matters where alliens are not wholly concerned, or where the revenue is in question, (constitutionally Established), has ever been my principal wish in amendments. I may therefore be placed in what is called the minority. or if by minority is intended, those members of our State convention who voted against the Constitution, the report Your Excellency has mentioned, has very little foundation. there can be no Minority, or Majority, composed of a large number, but what must include some unprincipled men; and as it cannot be fully concluded, that all those of the Massachusetts convention, who voted for the adoption of the Constitution, were Patriots instigated by genuine Love to their Country, so the conclusion on the other Side, that all who voted against it, were Enemies to their Country, would be equally fallacious. my opinion is, and I know as much of the people of this Commonwealth, as any one man in it, that the minority (with few exceptions), both in Convention and out, are as zealously inclined to support the general Government as the majority are; they wish amendments, but they neither wish them in any other mode than the one pointed out by the Constitution, nor that the effecting them should interrupt the necessary business of the Revenue, or that of organizing the Government

There are in this Commonwealth, some men in whom the people have no confidence, who are Seeking for themselves, and who hope to succeed by Scandalizing men, whose merit, & Services, give them the preheminence with the people. they will no doubt, alarm the apprehension of good men, and create Jealousies and a want of confidence. and may thus Succeed in their enterprizes if they answer their Sinister purposes without destroying that confidence between Rulers, and Ruled, which is the bond of society, it will be fortunate. their political situation of some of them in years past, obliges them to direct their Arrows in a particular manner, and though some revolutionists are raised above their reach, yet when ever they are found vulnerable there will be no want of shafts. a grateful Country has a plaister, Sooner or later, for every wound.

perhaps some Individuals, unworthy, unprincipled, and distressed in their pecuniary circumstances, and who were in the minority in the Convention of this state, may prompt the majority in Rhode Island to wrong and destructive measures. but I do most solemnly assure you, that I beleive the report to be fabricated to serve particular purposes, and that the people in general of this Commonwealth, minority as well as majority, are as ready to Support and defend this Constitution as they would the Revolution of the states if it was in danger. the sentiments contained in the first production in the paper inclosed are those of the people in general. let me add here, that I am assured, that there are some men who have a hand in sowing these Jealousies, that would be very willing to bury the

Constitution of the united States, in the ruins of our Independence. in short these misrepresentations originate from men who have an habitual hatred to the old whigs, and are used by men who have no other politicks, than office and Emolument, and who circulate the reports to wound those who stand in their way.

I will intrude no longer upon Your Excellencys goodness; Time will discover who are the friends of the people, and of the Government the people have Established

I am with the most perfect / sentiments of Esteem your Excellen / cys most obliged & most Humble / Servant Ja Sullivan

RC (Adams Papers); internal address: "His Excellency Mr Adams."

[1] Sullivan's letter was of 10 June, to which JA replied on 18 June, both above. Sullivan wrote again on 28 June (Adams Papers), requesting JA's patronage for a judicial appointment in the newly created eastern district. JA took no action on his behalf. Sullivan resigned his post as a probate judge when, on 12 Feb. 1790, Gov. John Hancock named him attorney general of Massachusetts (Thomas C. Amory, *Life of James Sullivan*, 2 vols., Boston, 1859, 2:416).

[2] With Rhode Island and North Carolina still wavering on ratification, the Constitution's critics-turned-congressmen began to consolidate a set of amendments for discussion. James Madison, who had postponed the subject on 25 May 1789, led the charge on 8 June, brushing aside calls to delay the debate while the formation of the revenue system simultaneously occupied the House of Representatives. Anxious to identify and "provide those securities for liberty which are required by a part of the community," Madison argued that swift approval of the amendments would accelerate the process of ratification.

Since the Constitution's drafting two years earlier, JA and others had questioned why the document lacked a clear summary of individual liberties alongside the frame of government. When he sent Thomas Jefferson a copy on 10 Nov. 1787, JA asked, "What think you of a Declaration of Rights? should not Such a Thing have preceeded the Model?" JA echoed popular fears that freedom of press and conscience as well as the powers of juries lay largely unaddressed. He also contested the limited presidential veto and the need for Senate approval of nominations, but JA was willing to bend on those points in order to achieve ratification. Jefferson, who backed Madison's plan of "alterations," was more emphatic about reserving power at the state level, worrying that individual rights recently won in the American Revolution were again at stake. "This is a degeneracy in the principles of liberty to which I had given four centuries instead of four years. But I hope it will all come about. We are now vibrating between too much and too little government, and the pendulum will rest finally in the middle," Jefferson wrote to WSS on 2 Feb. 1788.

Combining and repackaging ideas from nearly 200 separate revisions that arose in the state ratification conventions, Madison proposed several amendments that mainly guaranteed personal liberties. Members put off discussion of Madison's amendments for another month as they tended to other matters. In Aug. 1789, the amendments went through several rounds of heavy revision and heated debate, mostly centered on the clauses upholding freedom of religion. Congress finally passed twelve amendments, ten of which came to be known as the Bill of Rights, on 25 September. JA signed the Bill of Rights, along with Frederick Augustus Muhlenberg, Speaker of the House, John Beckley, clerk of the House, and Samuel Allyne Otis, secretary of the Senate. Meeting the constitutional quota needed to enact it as law, ten states ratified the Bill of Rights by 15 Dec. 1791. Connecticut, Massachusetts, and Georgia did so in 1939 (vol. 19:212–213, 269–270; Madison, *Papers, Congressional Series*, 12:196, 199; Jefferson, *Papers*, 12:558; U.S. Senate, *Jour.*, 1st Cong., 1st sess., p. 96–97; Bickford and Bowling, *Birth of the Nation*, p. 51–54).

To William MacPherson

Sir Richmond hill July 4, 1784 [*1789*][1]

I have received your polite letter of the second of this month, and am obliged to you for this instance of respect and attention to me.[2] The competition for employment under the national government, is, I preceive, in Philadelphia, very numerous, and the merits of various candidates are considerable The personal knowledge of the President, and the able and faithful characters within the reach of his enquiry, from that district, cannot leave him at a loss to determine whose pretensions ought to be prevalent.

As according to my construction of the constitution the Senate have only a negative on the nominations of the President, and as I have a voice only in case of division of the Senators, the case is not likely very soon to happen, that I shall venture to put a negative on a nomination of the President supported by the suffrages of half the Senate. I should be very likely to make presumtions in favor of a constitutional nomination.

The recommendation of your friend Colo: Smith in addition to all that I have seen or heard of your character, would dispose me to wish well to your pursuits as far as they may be found consistent with Justice and public policy.

I am & & John Adams

LbC in CA's hand (Adams Papers); internal address: "William McPherson Esqr / Philadelphia"; APM Reel 115.

[1] An inadvertence.

[2] William MacPherson (1756–1813), of Philadelphia, attended Princeton College. He enlisted in the British Army before the Revolutionary War but switched his affiliation to the American cause and served on the Marquis de Lafayette's staff. Aware that Congress was on the verge of passing the 31 July Collection Act, which created the U.S. Customs Service, MacPherson joined a multitude of former soldiers and struggling merchants who petitioned JA for federal employment. MacPherson wrote to JA on 2 July, noting that he was "well aware . . . of the extreme impropriety of asking from a Gentleman in your exalted station, any thing like a promise—I mean not Sir to presume so far—I only beg leave to make known my wish" (Adams Papers).

George Washington immediately began drafting his list of nominees to stock nearly sixty ports with collectors, naval officers, and surveyors, which was printed on 8 August. Initially, MacPherson's desired post went to Samuel Meredith, who resigned in September. MacPherson was appointed and served as surveyor of the Philadelphia port until 1793 (William Henry Egle, *Some Pennsylvania Women During the War of the Revolution*, Harrisburg, Penn., 1898, p. 120, 121; Michael N. Ingrisano Jr., *The First Officers of the United States Customs Service: Appointed by President George Washington in 1789*, Washington, D.C., 1987, p. 3, 5, 14).

To George Mason Jr.

Dear Sir Richmond hill July 4 1789

With great pleasure, I received your kind letter of the twenty fifth of last month,[1] give me leave to congratulate you on your marriage, the increase of your family, and your happy settlement on your plantation.[2] I have known by repeated experience enough of the pleasure of returning from the life of a traveller in Europe, to the pleasures of domestic life, in a calm retreat in the country, to be very sensible of your situation's being enviable. I thank you Sir, for the friendly and respectful confidence in me, with which you have communicated your desires in favour of Mr Joseph Fenwick to be Consul at Bourdeaux. Your recommendation has weight with me: but you know very well that the duty of looking out for the fittest men for all employments, is by the constitution imposed on the President, who I am well persuaded will discharge it with all that fidelity which is due to his Country, and all the impartiality which becomes a father of his people. As Mr Jefferson is expected from France, perhaps no appointment will be made in that country untill his arrival.[3] Mr Fenwick is probably known to the President: if not, it will be very natural that information and Judgment will be asked of the Gent: from Virginia and Maryland, whose knowledge of the person is personal, and should therefore be taken in preference to mine, which can only be at second hand. The candidates for such appointments will in most instances be numerous, and their services, merits and qualifications various. The great Magistrate, whose right it is will I doubt not, determine among them all in a manner that will give satisfaction to the publick.

Your congratulations on my late appointments are very obliging. The Duties, of my office require a constant and laborious attention: but there is so much information, candor and dignity in the characters with whom I am associated, that application to business in concert with them is pleasure.

I am & & John Adams

LbC in CA's hand (Adams Papers); internal address: "George Mason Junr:^ Esqr / Colchester, Virginia—"; APM Reel 115.

[1] Mason's letter of 25 June (Adams Papers) recommended Maryland-born merchant Joseph Fenwick (1762–1849) to serve as the U.S. consul at Bordeaux. For the past year, Fenwick had operated, with Mason's brother John, a trading firm in the French port, which supplied wine to JA, George Washington, and Thomas Jefferson. Fenwick's main

rival for the position was John Bondfield, who had acted as the American commercial agent for Bordeaux, Bayonne, Rochefort, and La Rochelle since March 1778. When Washington nominated Fenwick on 4 June 1790, he mistakenly wrote "James Fenwick" but sent a note of correction to the Senate on 23 June. Fenwick was confirmed by the Senate on 7 June, and he served as U.S. consul to France until 1801 (vols. 6:10, 9:103; Richard C. Allen, "Nantucket Quakers and Negotiating the Politics of the Atlantic World," in Marie Jeanne Rossignol and Bertrand Van Ruymbeke, eds., *The Atlantic World of Anthony Benezet (1713–1784): From French Reformation to North American Quaker Antislavery Activism*, Leyden, 2017, p. 123; Washington, *Papers, Presidential Series*, 3:53, 54; 5:474–476; Jefferson, *Papers*, 8:158).

[2] Elizabeth Mary Anne Barnes Hooe (b. 1768), of Barnesfield, Va., married Mason on 22 April 1784. They lived on the Doegs' Neck, Va., plantation of Lexington, named in 1775 to commemorate the Revolutionary War battle, and at this time they had three children: Elizabeth, George, and William ("Notes and Queries," *VMHB*, 52:276 [Oct. 1944]; Pamela C. Copeland and Richard K. MacMaster, *The Five George Masons: Patriots and Planters of Virginia and Maryland*, 2d edn., Fairfax, Va., 2016, p. 250).

[3] On 23 Aug. 1789 Jefferson received John Jay's 19 June letter, enclosing a Senate resolution of 18 June that approved his return and named William Short as the American chargé d'affaires. Fleeing the French Revolution's upheaval, Jefferson sailed from Le Havre to Cowes, England, on 7 Oct., making a turbulent crossing via the *Clermont*, Capt. Nathaniel Colley. He arrived in Norfolk, Va., on 23 Nov., where he was greeted by citizens who thanked him for his diplomatic work, to which Jefferson replied: "That my country should be served is the first wish of my heart: I should be doubly happy indeed were I to render it a service" (Jefferson, *Papers*, 15:202–203, 496, 521, 546, 553, 556–557).

From Stephen Higginson

Sir Boston July 4: 1789—

Since I had the honour of seeing you at your own house, I have been so unwell, & so much occupied with my private Business, when able to attend to it, that I have not had an opp^y^ of writing to you, as you requested & I engaged to do. Nor can I now do more than just to inform you, that, as the British are coming fast into their old practice, of taking from hence the Rum necessary for their Factories upon the Coast of Guinea, a draw back on Our Rum exported to foreign markets is important to the Commerce of this state.[1] more than 1200 hhds have this year been called for by them; & so fond are the Africans of this spirit, that was it freed from the duty when exported thither, I have no doubt the British would soon take several thousands of hhds annually.—

as Our molasses Trade is the main branch of Business in this state, & is really the chief support of Our Cod fishery, as well as necessary to several other important branches of Our Commerce, it is a great point to have it as free as possible from unnecessary expences & embarrassments. the amount of Our export of Rum to foreign markets may now be fairly estimated at 3000 hhds a year; &

there can be no doubt of its soon amounting to twice or thrice that quantity if it was not loaded with the duty; for every market we now have for it abroad will be increasing in its use of & demand for it, unless the increase of the price prevents. two pence per gallon is no small Object in that Article, it is sufficient perhaps to secure to us permanently, or to deprive us wholly of the supply to the markets alluded to.—

it strikes me as very singular & unequal, that there should be a drawback generally upon foreign Imports when re exported; & none allowed upon a principal export of this state. If the former is admitted upon the principle of giving facility & extension to Commerce, will not the same Reason apply as strongly in the latter case. it is true the former may affect the other states more than the latter; but if to load exports to foreign markets with duties is anti commercial, if the principle be good, as a general case, it will not be objected that we shall principally be benefitted by it in this case. This would savour strong indeed of locality, & confirm the Idea here, that southern Gentlemen are jealous of, & wish to restrain us in Our Trade.—

If a drawback be refused on Rum lest the Revenue be injured, the Objection will apply as forcibly, at least, to the general provision; for surely the former case is capable of as many good Checks, as in any Case that occurs to me. the general allowance of drawbacks will give many openings, without great care is taken, to defraud the Revenue. a variety of deceptions may there be practised from the extent & complexity of the Objects; but here we have a single Article only to attend to, & this we can check in the hands of the Distillers who are few in number. I fear these hasty Observations may be too late, & perhaps not sufficiently clear & weighty to merit attention; but as I could not believe, till within a day or two, that a drawback on Our Rum could eventually be refused, I may be excused for not troubling you sooner on the subject, & it must be my Apology for now doing it thus hastily.—

Should Congress appoint the inferior Officers in the executive departments, & think it expedient to continue such in Office as have conducted well, permit me to say that I think Mr. Joseph Hiller naval Officer for Salem is one of the best in the state.[2] his integrity, accuracy & faculty of executing rigidly the duties of his Office without giving Offence, are much greater than common. I am induced to say this of him, having been lately informed, that several in that Town have applied for the Office, expecting the appointment will be made by Congress, who are by no means his equals for such a post.—

With the most respectful Regard for your Lady & family, & most sincere wishes for your health & happiness, I have the honour to be Your Excellencys most humble Servant— Stephen Higginson

RC (Adams Papers); endorsed: "The Hon. S. Higginson / 4. July. / Ans$^{d.}$ 14. 1789."

[1] For the debate over the molasses duty, see JA's 12 June letter to Cotton Tufts, and note 2, above.

[2] Joseph Hiller (1748–1814), of Boston, formerly a major in the Continental Army, was nominated by George Washington on 3 Aug. to serve as collector for the ports of Salem and Beverly, Mass., and was confirmed by the Senate the same day (Essex Inst., *Hist. Colls.*, 3:123 [June 1861]; U.S. Senate, *Exec. Jour.*, 1st Cong., 1st sess., p. 9, 12).

To Benjamin Rush

Dear Sir Richmond Hill, July 5. 1789

Without waiting for an Answer to my last, I will take a little more notice of a Sentiment in one your Letters. You Say you "abhor all Titles."[1] I will take the familiar freedom of Friendship to say I dont believe you.— Let me explain my self.— I doubt not your Varacity. but I believe you deceive yourself, and have not yet examined your own heart, and recollected the feelings of every day and hour.— What would you say or think or feel, if your own Children, instead of calling you, Sir, or Father or Papa, should accost you with, the Title of "Ben"!— Your servant comes in, and instead of Saying, "Master! my hat is much worn, will you please to give me a new one"; crys "Ben! my old hat is all in rags, and makes you the laughing stock of the Town! give me a new one."— What think you of this simple manly republican Style?

had I leisure to write Plays like Gen. Burgoine, I would undertake a Comedy, under the Title of "Government with out Title."[2] The Dramatis Personæ should be a Quaker and his Wife, ten Children and four servants. They should all live in the Same room, dine, breakfast & sup at the Same Table— they should promiscuously call each other by their Names, without Titles and live without form.— We Should See, what order, Virtue and Œconomy would ensue.— The sons would soon be married to the female servants and the Daughters to the Male. both Children & servants would soon trick and cuff the old Man & Woman.

Poh, Poh Poh! Say you all this is vulgar and beneath the Dignity of a Legislator.— Give me leave to say nothing in human Life is beneath the Dignity of a Magistrate to consider. The Principles of Government are to be seen in every Scene of human Life. There is no Person and no society, to whom Forms and Titles are indifferent.

"Look through the Deeds of Men,["] and then say whether Shenestone is not in the right, when he says in a whimsical Production called the "School-Mistress" which he wrote in imitation of Spencer.

> "Albeit ne flatt'ry did corrupt her Truth
> Ne pompous Title did debauch her ear,
> Goody, good-Woman, Gossip, n'aunt, forsooth
> or Dame, the Sole additions She did hear;
> Yet these She challeng'd; *these She held right dear*;
> Ne would esteem him Act as mought behove
> Who Should not honour'd eld with these revere:
> *For never title yet So mean could prove,*
> *But there was eke a mind, which did that title love.*"[3]

The two last Lines contain a truth so exact, so universal, and so litteral, that I declare to you, in the Course of fifty Years Experience, in various Stages of Life, among all Classes of Peope and in Several different nations I have never yet met with one Man Woman or Child, who was destitute of a Passion for a Title. Let Us consider, my Friend more reverently and therefore more truly the Constitution of human nature, and the invariable Progress of human Life and manners. Family Titles are necessary to Family Government Colonial Titles We know were indispensable, in Colonial Government; and We shall find national Titles essential to national Government. as long as Titles are respected by others, they will be esteemed by every man. but it is not to gratify Individuals that public Titles are annexed to offices. it is to make offices and Laws respected; and not so much by the virtuous Part of the Community, as by the Profligate the criminal and abandoned, who have little reverence for Reason Right or Law divine or human. These are overawed by Titles frequently, when Laws and Punishments cannot restrain them.

Think of these Things, and perhaps I may hint to you some others hereafter. Yours with Sincere Esteem John Adams.

RC (MB:John Adams MS Coll.); internal address: "The Honourable Benjamin Rush Esqr"; endorsed: "John Adams." LbC (Adams Papers); APM Reel 115.

[1] JA paraphrased Rush's letter of 4 June, above.

[2] After retiring from the British Army, Gen. John Burgoyne successfully launched a literary career and reaped popular praise for his 1786 play, *The Heiress* (*AFC*, 7:x).

[3] William Shenstone, *The School-Mistress, a Poem. In Imitation of Spenser*, London, 1742, lines 73–81.

From Theophilus Parsons

My dear Sir— Newbury Port July 8th. 1789

Conscious of the persecutions you would meet with, by applications for your influence in the appointment to offices, I had determined not to increase the number of them; but being just informed, that the President proposes to nominate as officers, for the collection of the national revenue, those persons who hold the like offices in the collection of the state revenues, unless complaint was made against them, I am compelled to trouble you on the subject. If such was openly known to be the presidents intentions, there would not be wanting well founded complaints against Messrs. Titcomb and Cross, the naval-officer, and collector of excise for this port— I must sollicit your patience, while I give a short history of the manner, in which those gentlemen came into those offices, and of their conduct afterwards—

Michael Hodge Esq., a gentleman of this town, of undoubted integrity and capacity, and of pure public principles, was, upon the first erection of the naval office, appointed to fill it; he continued in it a number of years, while the fees were receivable in paper-money, but soon after, the office being then deemed lucrative, Mr Titcomb, availing himself of his influence as a representative, procured the place for himself, to the exclusion of Mr Hodge—[1] He continued in that office two or three years until, for his misdemeanors in permitting an entry of vessels while at sea, to evade our lumber acts, he lost his election, and Mr Hodge was rechosen— Tumults arose in our governments soon after— Mr Titcomb was elected a representative and, by the influence of the malcontent party, to which he always adhered as much as he dared, he was rechosen as Naval-Officer— When the rebellion arose, he took every method, in his power, to render the government odious, and the conduct of the rebels unexceptionable, and his tools, in this town, were in a flame, when the legislature declared that a rebellion existed. Soon after that rebellion was crushed, the federal government came upon the carpet, and it was not judged expedient to attempt his removal, as it was supposed that, upon the adoption of that government, he would drop of course.

I might add, that altho', when one of our delegates in convention, the spirit of the men he was with, compelled him to the adoption of the constitution, yet, at the same time, his principles were hostile to every federal measure, & all his out-door connections were railing at the new government. Judge then my dear Sir, what must be the sentiments and feelings of people here, to see that man carefully provided for, under a government to which he is not friendly, and who has opposed every honest measure proposed in our own state government; and a man who has really, in my opinion, no moral principles to guide him in any department. Nor can the fear of loosing his property, influence him to right conduct, as that is all gone, and the house, he now lives in, has lately been taken by execution over his head.

As to Mr Cross, he obtained the Excise in the same unworthy manner— Mr Saml. Tufts, a brother of the Hon. Cotton Tufts, was the excise-officer, until Mr Cross, going representative, availed himself of the influence of that place, to procure himself chosen in his room.—[2] As to our own government, he has always been opposed to every measure, calculated to support, either it's credit, or it's energy, and has been heartily in favour of the insurgents— But to the federal government he has been openly and avowedly it's opponent—and was he an officer under it, instead of feeling grateful for the favour, he would use that very office, to create or forment an uneasiness among the people, to justify his former opposition—such is this man's temper— Besides, as he is a Collector of Our Excise, there can be no great propriety in his collecting the national revenues at the same time— It may be said, that he may resign the former office, but he will not do it, if he can hold both; and why should such a man, acquiring an office in the manner he did, still have his election to hold a lucrative and influential place under a government to which he was openly hostile—

From this view of these two men, which in my opinion is quite a just one, the good people here would feel exceedingly sore at their appointment to office—and did they conceive any information to the president, upon this subject, proper, it would be given him, signed by very respectable names— I conceive the energy of the federal government will depend much on the principles of the men, who are first appointed to Office— Our own Government has been ruined, for want of attention to this point.

Whenever men, disesteemed by the respectable part of the Community, or antifederal in their principles, are designated to Offices, the people will soon have no respect for the government— They will reason, and reason very naturally, that a government which will take it's enemies into it's bosom, and neglect it's friends, who have supported it in trying times, does not wish to have friends, or to secure to itself the public attachment— I think these sentiments are in some degree just—and if they are, I trust our beloved president will feel the influence of them— He can, with the most perfect propriety, act agreably to them— He is not obliged to court friends—and he has a weight of character, that will support him firm as Atlas— Had I the honour of his notice, I would intreat him, from my knowledge of the people in this place, and from the principles and characters of Messrs. Titcomb & Cross, to pass them by, & to nominate other characters— I would, with great humility & sincerity, tell him, that I had no personal interest depending, but that I was influenced only, by a devout attachment to a firm, energetic, federal government—

Perhaps you may ask me who are suitable men for the three offices in Newbury Port— I will give you the opinions of the respectable people here upon that subject— Mr Hodge, as the Naval Officer, they all agree in, from a sense of his merits, and from the ill-treatment he has received— Mr Tufts would make an honest, faithful, and disinterested collector of the revenues, and so would Ebenezer March Esq; and probably, no man would make a better surveyor, than Mr David Moody—[3] To speak my own ardent wishes—I hope Mr Hodge may be provided for at all events—

I have a great reliance on your good nature, when I expect your excuse for troubling you on this tedious subject— I will quit it, & take one more agreable to you— Your son is indefatigable in the office—too much so I fear; and his whole conduct gives me the greatest pleasure— May it be my fortune, to have reason to think so well of a son of mine, as I do of yours—

My particular regards wait on Mrs Adams who, I hear, is with you, and believe me to be, notwithstanding all this trouble, / Yours most affectionately Theop Parsons

RC (Adams Papers); internal address: "His Exc^y^ Mr Adams"; endorsed: "Mr Parsons / July 8. ans 1789."

[1] Gen. Jonathan Titcomb (1727–1817), Stephen Cross (1731–1809), and Capt. Michael Hodge (1743–1816) had all held various positions in town government since the 1770s. On 3 Aug. 1789, George Washington made the following nominations for Newburyport, which were confirmed by the Senate on the same day: Cross as collector of customs, Titcomb as naval officer, and Hodge as surveyor (John A. Schutz, *Legislators of the Massachusetts General Court 1691–1780: A Biographical Dictionary*, Boston, 1997; *Doc. Hist. Ratif. Const.*, 5:708; U.S. Senate, *Exec. Jour.*, 1st Cong., 1st sess., p. 9, 12).

[2] Newburyport merchant Samuel Tufts (1735–1799) was Cotton Tufts' younger brother and the former collector of duties and excise for Essex County. AA lobbied

fruitlessly on her cousin's behalf, writing to JA on 7 June: "I think Sir I have never petitioned for any office, for any Relation of mine. mr Sam[ll] Tufts of Newburry port was formerly in an office which he discharged with fidelity to the publick . . . his character as an honest industrous capable man will not be disputed, and perhaps it may not be thought amiss to bring him forward again" (*AFC*, 2:197; 8:370; 9:195).

[3] Neither Ebenezer (March) Marsh (1745–1827) nor David Moody (b. 1735), both of Newbury, earned a federal post (Schutz, *Legislators of the Massachusetts General Court 1691–1780*; Noreen C. Pramberg, *Four Generations of the Descendants of William Moody of Newbury, Massachusetts in 1635*, Newburyport, 1986, p. 46).

From James Lovell

Dear Sir Boston July 9th. 1789—

altho' this Letter is somewhat of a *public* Nature, yet I dare not address you in a consonant manner, 'till the Point is settled between *his Excellency* and *John* Adams. I apply to you, as I *feel* you in my Heart to be; satisfied that the Yeas & Nays of no public Body whatsoever concerning *Epithets* can in any measure alter *Essences*.

Dear Sir,

Sturgis Gorham of Barnstable *is* my Brother in Law, whether I wished it or not; He is less beloved by me however on that Score, than because he has been *habituated* to esteem *you*.[1] Inspired early by the *Prognostications* of James Otis jun[r] when you was on your *first* Barnstable Circuit, he has looked for an Event of *Eminence* which Time has realised; and he feels happy in considering the Merits of a young Barrister ripen'd into the Dignity of a Vice President of the United States for the Promotion of his and my Felicity in common with other Fellow Citizens. He is so situated in Barnstable as to be *locally* fit for a Collector. He has been so educated as to be fit for a *scientific* and *efficacious* officer of the Customs—is in Estate *responsible* and is deeply *interested*, personally and as a Citizen, to make a *good* Collector for the United States, in that District.

I cannot conceive how the President will nominate so great a Number of Officers as the Districts make necessary without depending much upon *Informations*; for he certainly cannot have *personal* Knowledge in such various Localities. In this Idea, I have written to M[r] Partridge who is representative of the District.—[2] I do not consider M[r.] S. A. O[3] as one whom the President will consult with Propriety—or as fit to be consulted in this Case, especially.

As on the one hand I would not seek for a Place myself unless in the full Idea of *Faithfulness*, so on the other I would not recommend any Man for any other Place but on the same Idea—

I consider this Attempt as connected with my own Reputation M$^{r.}$ Partridge's and yours so far as the President may be influenced by it, and I feel a conscientious Awe with Firmness.

I am Sir / your devoted Friend James Lovell

RC (Adams Papers); addressed: "The Vice President of the / United States. / His Excellency / John Adams Esqr"; endorsed: "Mr Lovel July 9. / ans$^{d.}$ 16. 1789."

[1] Barnstable, Mass., shopkeeper Sturgis Gorham (1742–1795), a former militia captain who was active in local politics, wrote to George Washington on 9 July soliciting a federal post; he was unsuccessful. Gorham's daughter Deborah married Lovell's son James Smith in 1786 (John A. Schutz, *Legislators of the Massachusetts General Court 1691–1780: A Biographical Dictionary*, Boston, 1997; Washington, *Papers, Presidential Series*, 3:154–155; *Sibley's Harvard Graduates*, 14:47; *NYGBR*, 45:247 [July 1914].)

[2] George Partridge (1740–1828), Harvard 1762, of Duxbury, represented Massachusetts in the House of Representatives from 1789 to 1790. He followed up on Lovell's request, writing to the president's secretary, Tobias Lear, on 27 July 1789 and to Washington on 21 Feb. 1791, to recommend Gorham and Ephraim Spooner for customs posts in Massachusetts; none earned appointments (*Biog. Dir. Cong.*; Washington, *Papers, Presidential Series*, 3:333, 7:398–399).

[3] Samuel Allyne Otis.

From William Tudor

My dear Sir Boston 9 July 1789

However you & I may have been taught by Civilians, & however History confirms the Maxim, that an Imperium in Imperio is a Solecism, this Country will continue to learn from its own limited School, & by the most expensive Experiments, those Truths which Statesmen, Legislators & enlightened Politicians have in vain pointed out to them.—

Our present Confederacy is not very unlike the Monster of Nebuchadnezzar, which was composed of Brass, Clay & Iron— It is neither completely national, federal nor sovereign, for each State has reserved some seperate & independent Powers. Was it composed of the four Eastern States only: Or did it embrace the Inhabitants from the Hudson to the Potomack; or did the Limits of Virginia & Georgia confine its Operations, the Inhabitants might soon agree in consolidated national Principles. But a Country, extensive as the present united States, so differently settled, & so widely dissimiliar in Manners & Ideas cannot easily be reduced to a homogeneous Body— Nature & Circumstances have marked the dividing Lines of the three Kingdoms that fifty Years hence will Occupy & part the present immense Territory, which, the glorious Peace of Paris, gave to the united States. Twenty years ago New England contained but one Set of People, the Middle Colonies two, & the Southern Provinces three. It may be different now. Common Dangers & Common Sufferings have had Effects in bringing Us nearer together, but it is a Monarchy alone, limited & republican if they please, that can make Us great or contented. While each State exercises the Powers of making distinct & particular Laws, independent in numerous Instances of the general Governments, although perhaps they may not amount to a direct Contravention of the Statutes of Congress, they will operate in perpetuating local & different Principles of Action, in the distant Parts of the Empire. I most heartily wish my Countrymen Freedom & an honest Independence, because Myself & Children are to participate in it, but I also wish an energetic, stable & magnanimous Government, that shall protect Us at home, and make our Country respectable abroad.

Mr. Ames & Mr. Minot are two excellent young Men, & very capable of serving their Country, in different Walks. I shew to the latter the Paragraph which so flatteringly mentions him & his History.[1] He has beg'd Me to return his Thanks for so obliging a Testimony of your Approbation of well intended Labour.

I find by the Judiciary Bill which has been printed, that my Letter to the President is superceeded by a certain Office being to be disposed of as the District Judge shall think proper. And Of that Judge whoever he may be, I shall have no Favours to sollicit.

I am with great Affection & Respect / Dear Sir / Your faithfull Friend & Servant
Wm Tudor

RC (Adams Papers); internal address: "President Adams"; endorsed by AA2: "Mr Wm. Tudor / July 9"; and by JA: "ansd. sept. 19. 1789."

[1] See JA's 28 June letter to Tudor, and note 4, above.

To Francis Dana

Dear Sir [*10 July 1789*][1]

I have received the letter you did me the honor to write on the 26th of last month and am much obliged to you for it. The Judicial bill is still under consideration of the senate, and altho' it has undergone many alterations and amendments it is imposible to say what farther changes may be made in the house of representatives.[2] The district Judges may be annihilated altogether, and the number of supreem judges as well as the number of circuits doubled. The Attorney general is now to be appointed by the President, with consent of the Senate, in course we are upon an amendment made a few days ago, if this plan continues, the Attorney Genl: will appoint persons to act for him, or the court will appoint in his appearance in the district courts. Mr Nathan Cushing, Mr Dana Mr Lowell Mr Parsons and Mr Sullivan have been mentioned here, as candidates for offices in the Judicial system. And I will say to you that another person has been mentioned for one of the judjes of the supreme court and that is chief Justice Cushing— For my own part I only wish that the best and ablest men may be brought into the public service, such as have the clearest and fairest reputations, are known to the people and have acquired weight and consequence in their estimation. Parsons I think would make an excellent attorney general, but I know not that he will be likely to be appointed. When a President has the whole continent to look through for a single officer it is imposible to guess where his choice will fix. Dana or Lowell would be the best of Judges for the district: and if Main should be a district by itself, Sewal is the fittest man. If Cushing should be a supreem judge, Dana and Sewal district Judges, could Mr H be persuaded to appoint Lowel to one of their places? Parsons I presume would be one unless he should be attorney General. If Lowell should be a supreme judge I presume Dana may district judge if he will, and vice versa. I speak only from my own conjecture however.[3] The President has representations and solicitations no doubt from many quarters, but nothing can ultimately arranged till the bill is passed.— I feel some anxiety for Nathan Cushing, whose condemnation of vessels in hard times have certainly made his name immortal, Mr Sullivan, I presume, will have representations made in his favor from several points of compass. His ambition is unbounded: but I wish his moral sentiments were as delicate and his political systems as consistent, as his ~~talents are~~ Industry is examplary and his abilities respectable. If the President should consult me, I shall give him every information in my power, with the utmost impartiality. With regard to yourself, I have no scruple to say, that any places in the judicial system would be honored by your acceptance of them in my humble opinion. Reserving always however, the chief Justices office for Mr Jay. With Mrs Adams's and my best regards to Mrs Dana I remain with & &

John Adams

LbC in CA's hand (Adams Papers); internal address: "Honble: Francis / Dana Esqr / Cambridge."; APM Reel 115.

[1] The dating of this letter is based on Dana's reply of 31 July, below.

[2] Throughout April and May, a Senate committee labored to draft the judiciary bill, thereby implementing Art. 3 of the Constitution and establishing the federal court sys-

tem. The legislation's chief architect was Oliver Ellsworth of Connecticut, a Federalist whom JA found to have "the clearest head and most dilligent hand" during his long term of public service. Ellsworth's plan placed one chief justice and five associates on the Supreme Court; in addition, a district court judge and two Supreme Court justices would serve on each circuit court. The bill created thirteen judicial districts in the eleven states that had ratified the Constitution thus far, with Massachusetts and Virginia allotted an additional district court each for, respectively, Maine and Kentucky. It established several new offices, including U.S. and state attorneys general, and federal and deputy marshals. The bill also laid out the court procedures to be used throughout the entire U.S. judiciary. Significantly, the bill upheld the Supreme Court's right of judicial review, which allowed justices to reexamine state court decisions when federal law was at issue. Defendants facing lawsuits from citizens in other states now had the option to remove their cases to a federal circuit court.

Richard Henry Lee of Virginia introduced the bill in the Senate on 12 June. It was printed twice so that members of Congress could solicit and incorporate their constituents' revisions. JQA, who recalled "a transient sight of a copy," echoed popular Federalist complaints that the Supreme Court was too small and the district judges too powerful. Others worried that the boundaries between state and federal jurisdictions were ill-defined and therefore prone to friction. Another vocal opponent, William Maclay of Pennsylvania, observed: "It certainly is a vile law system, calculated for expense and with a design to draw by degrees all law business into the Federal courts. The Constitution is meant to swallow all the State Constitutions by degrees, and thus to swallow, by degrees, all the State judiciaries."

During eighteen days of debate, senators finely parsed the bill's language, mindful of constitutional interpretation and the weight of precedent. Some, like Paine Wingate of New Hampshire, expressed concern about what it would cost to build the court system and to cover the great expense of judicial salaries. After several revisions, the judiciary bill passed on 17 July in a vote of 14 to 6. It then stalled for a month in the House of Representatives, where members were locked in fierce debate over the revenue system and proposed amendments to the Constitution. They began discussion of the judiciary bill on 24 Aug., focusing on questions of southern jurisprudence and the federal courts' ability to enforce payment of prewar debts to British creditors. The House made few substantial changes, however, and passed it on 17 Sept. without a roll call vote. George Washington signed what became the Judiciary Act of 1789 into law one week later. The president, who described the U.S. judiciary to John Jay as "that department which must be considered as the Key-Stone of our political fabric," immediately sent his list of judicial nominees to the Senate (Bickford and Bowling, *Birth of the Nation*, p. 45–49; *AFC*, 8:383; 11:205; Maclay, *Journal*, p. 117; U.S. Senate, *Jour.*, 1st Cong., 1st sess., p. 34, 42, 85; *Annals of Congress*, 1st Cong., 1st sess., p. 812, 928–929, 2239–2255; Washington, *Papers, Presidential Series*, 4:75–78, 137).

[3] Although Dana, Nathan Cushing, and Theophilus Parsons were not among Washington's 24 Sept. nominations to the U.S. judiciary, JA's overall suppositions were correct. The president nominated William Cushing as an associate justice on the Supreme Court, John Lowell and David Sewall as the district judges for Massachusetts and Maine, and John Sullivan as district judge for New Hampshire; all were confirmed by the Senate on 26 Sept. (U.S. Senate, *Exec. Jour.*, 1st Cong., 1st sess., p. 29, 30).

Nathan Cushing (1742–1812), Harvard 1763, of Scituate, formerly an admiralty judge, was appointed to the Mass. Supreme Judicial Court in early 1790, amid criticism from JA, JQA, and others that he lacked the eloquence and experience necessary for the position. He served until his resignation in 1800 (*Sibley's Harvard Graduates*, 15:376, 378; Alden Bradford, *Biographical Notices of Distinguished Men of New England: Statesmen, Patriots, Physicians, Lawyers, Clergymen, and Mechanics*, Boston, 1842, p. 121).

To Stephen Higginson

Sir

New York July 14, 1789

I received your favor of the 4th of this month, but not till the impost bill was enacted and published. In the progress of that law, through the several branches of the legislature, the arguments in favor of a drawback on rum were insisted on by several members of each house. But I think it was not shewn with sufficient evidence, nor explained with so much precision as I expected, how it would affect the exportation of that article, to Africa, the baltick, and east Indies. This is an affair of calculation; if the price without a drawback, is so high, that a freight cannot be made and a reasonable profit, and still leave the adventurer at liberty to produce it at market at a price that will bear the competition with gin, Brandy, and West India rum, the exportation will be lessened, if not annihilated. This however was not shown and proved; if it can be proved, the merchants and Manufacturers interested in the business should address a petition to the President, Senate and House of Representatives stating the fact, and praying a redress. The contest about molasses was very sharp and long continued, and the Senate on some questions pretty equally divided. I took as much pains, as I thought was justifiable and more than I expected would have been excused; but no more could be done than you see.

Give me leave to congratulate you on you marriage, and present my compliments to your lady.[1]

In great haste I am & &

John Adams

LbC in CA's hand (Adams Papers); internal address: "Honble: Stephen Higginson Esqr / Boston"; APM Reel 115.

[1] Higginson married Elizabeth Perkins (d. 1791), of Boston, on 18 June (Thomas Wentworth Higginson, *Descendants of the Reverend Francis Higginson*, n.p., 1910, p. 21).

To Thomas Mifflin

Dear Sir

New York July 14 1789

I have received the letter you did me the honor to write me on the third of this month, and I thank you for giving me an opportunity of renewing a friendly intercourse which has continued I beleive with some interruption for these seventeen years.[1]

I was early acquainted with the activity, Zeal, and Steadiness of Capt: Falconer in the cause of his country: but as the number of competitors for employment in your city, is greater than that of the offices to be bestowed, and the merits of many of them are considerable; The President will no doubt think himself obliged to seek information from all quarters and carefully weigh the merits and qualifications of every one.

In order to preserve and improve the Ballance of our constitution, it is so necessary that the nominations of the President should be revered, that I shall generally support to the utmost of my power the men of his choice, and it must be a very strong case indeed that would justify me to myself in venturing to differ from him.

I congratulate you on the prospect we have that our countrymen will by degrees recover their original national character, and thier native veneration for the wisdom and virtue of those institutions of our Ancestors, which have been so long obscured and misrepresented by passion, prejudice, ignorance, and error.

With great esteem & John Adams

LbC in CA's hand (Adams Papers); internal address: "His Excellency Thomas Mifflin / President of Pensylvania."; APM Reel 115.

[1] The Pennsylvania governor wrote to JA on 3 July to recommend Capt. Nathaniel Falconer for a customs post in Philadelphia. Falconer appealed to JA on 30 June (both Adams Papers), citing his past service in outfitting the Continental fleet and issuing loan certificates. JA replied to Falconer on 4 July (LbC, APM Reel 115), explaining that the president, "as the common father of the people, is wisely entrusted with authority to weigh all the pretensions of every competitor, is personally so well acquainted in Pensylvania, and has so many able and faithful men within his call to consult upon such matters, that my testimony in your favour, can add little weight." Falconer applied to George Washington on 8 July and was named master warden of the port in 1792 (Washington, *Papers, Presidential Series*, 3:147–148).

To James Sullivan

Sir New York July 14 1789

I have received your favor of the second of this month. The report I mentioned to you in a former letter, was spoken of to me by gentle$^{n:}$ from Rhode Island, who are good citizens. One of these assured me of the fact as of his own knowledge, that there was an intimate intercourse between some of the leading antifederalists in their State and some of the same character in Massachusetts, belonging to the neighboring counties, particularly Bristol.[1] I do not beleive however that there is any general encouragement given by those who were against the constitution, or those who voted for it with amendments; tho the Gent[n:] from Rode Island assured me that the majority in their state kept up the spirit of party, by roundly affirming that in case of a contest they should be supported by half Massachusetts.

With regard to amendments, there is no man more sensible that amendments are necessary than I am. There is not in the world I beleive a more decided friend to juries than myself, and I should chearfully concur in any measures necessary to render this admirable institution permanent and immortal. But there are other particulars, which seem to me to require amendment which have not been suggested by any of the States. The great divisions and distributions of powers on which depend that delicate equipoise, which can alone give security to liberty, property, life, or character, have not been attended to with necessary accuracy. An equilibrium of power is the only parent of equality and liberty; but the executive authority cannot in our constitution preserve an equilibrium, with the legislative; nor can the President in his legislative capacity preserve or defend himself against the two houses; nor perhaps can the representatives preserve their share against the Senate without convulsions—nor can the President and the house in concert, form a ballance to the Senate, if this house is pleased to exert the power it has and the people suffer it. I am more clearly impressed with this because I know that the equilibrium if preserved, would of itself, and by its natural and necessary operation cure every defect in the constitution: whereas all the other amendments which have been proposed, if adopted will never remedy the defect in the equilibrium and consequently will never secure the rights of the citizen.

We may study to all eternity: but I am bold to say, we never shall discover any other security for the rights of mankind but in a ballance of trusts and power. It is and ever has been amazing to me, that the people of America who boast so much of their knowledge of government, and who really understand so well the principles of liberty, should have so far forgotten the institutions of their ancestors, as to have been so neglegent of this indispensible ballance in all the State constitutions as well as in that of the united states. Untill we shall correct our ideas under this head; we never shall get right: and we shall be tormented with a government of men and parties instead of being blessed with a government of laws. In what manner the public opinion can be weaned from those errors which passion prejudice and ignorance have propagated I know not.

I am & & John Adams

LbC in CA's hand (Adams Papers); internal address: "Judge Sullivan / Boston."; APM Reel 115.

[1] The weight of new Massachusetts taxes fell increasingly on rural residents of Bristol County throughout the 1780s, stirring Antifederalist sentiment (Hall, *Politics without Parties*, p. 194, 238, 300).

From Benjamin Lincoln

Dear sir Hingham July 14th. 1789—

I had the pleasure a few days since of receiving your kind favor of the 19th. ulto—

When I first saw the new constitution I was very apprehensive that the President would not be able to maintain his ground and preserve such a stand, on the stage of our political theater, as to keep up that equilibrum essential to our enjoying all those blessings which are derived from a constitution in which the powers of the first magistrate are sufficient to ballance the other branches. If our constitution shall, on trial, be found defective in this respect, it should be mended as soon as may be. In the mean time we ought to be exceedingly attentive that we avoid every thing which may have a tendency to enervate and reduce those degrees of influence which the President may derive from the present government. I hope and trust that there will not exist in either house a wish to invade the right of the other or a desire to press upon the prerogative of the first Magistrate, their caution, in this point, will have its influence, and their conduct will give a tone to the actions of the citizens at large, who ought to know in what their real interest lies, and that the moment they are so far duped as to put an entire relyance on the popular branch, they may date their ruin; and they will know, when it is too late, that they have been jockeyed out of their reason and rights, by men who wanted either better information or better hearts.—

The conduct of our great man is no less painful to us than alarming to you. He is not, from any thing which appears, an enemy to monarchical powers— He has, I think, in frequent instances exercised those powers, and is daily pursuing a line of conduct which will enable him to carry them to a much greater length. The very message to which you refer, is in my opinion, a proof in point, however paradoxical it may seem—[1] By his frequent addresses to the people, through their representatives, and by the trumpeters of his fame they are taught to believe that he is, almost, the only guardian of their rights now remaining in the commonwealth. With these impressions and under the idea, equally erroneous, that it is the fixed design of others to enslave them the first hour they shall have the power of doing it. Mr. H—— may sport with the rights of the people and trample upon our constitution with impunity. When ever his conduct is arraigned, it is enough for him and his friend, to give out that the aristocratical junto, as those are stiled who are for a firm energetic government, want his removal that they may be in the saddle themselves the more easily to execute their nefarious purposes with success. Many of the people, not the class with which you have been much connected, seem to consider Mr. H—— as the only man in the commonwealth who can preserve the state in peace and order in freedom and happiness strange delusion! Such however are the facts and he may now go almost any lengths in acts of monarchy not limited by any other principle than his policy, that may suggest to him, (or his friends may do it) the propriety of his keeping within some bounds.—

As soon as an influential character is discovered in any town, he must however be on the right side, he is immediately nominated for a justice of the peace, this line of conduct has filled most of our towns with such officers whose influence at home, and weight in the house of representatives, many of them find means to get there, secure to their creator his darling object— I would not be misunderstood our justices are not all so there are many of them who have not bowed the knee and are men of pure mind, and independent principles— The next Gentleman who writes a book & is pointing out the danger of any order of men in the community will not I hope forget to mention the danger of so liberal, if not wanton, exercise of the power given to our governour of appointing justices

It is unfortunate for us and it may be so for the Union that such leading characters as Mr. H—— and Mr. A—— do not with more cordiality love and embrace the new constitution, they are considered by many as opposers of it and by all as men wishing for such alterations as will essentially change it.—[2] They cannot, I trust, wish its annihilation.— So far as I can judge from all I have seen and heard they want a constitution which, in my opinion, would be little more than a puppet and the play thing of the different States. Any thing which looks national or like a consolidation of the different State is thought to be one of the greatest evils which can befall us and to be avoided as such— We had better annihilate the new constitution at once than amuse and deceive the people with false ideas and groundless expectations which we shall certainly do if we suffer it to be garbled according to the wishes of all the sticklers for amendments. This will not do a national government we must have and that soon, I think we shall find it, notwithstanding the exertion of all its opposers, under our present constitution. If we can but once get our system of revenue into operation under officers, who shall not know any other rule by which to regulate their conduct than the laws of their country and shall banish from their minds every idea of temporizing, and that they are not legislators but meer executors of the law and can and will sacrifice to their duty every other consideration which may come in competition there with we shall have made great progress. We have to combat in this business long and deep rooted prejudices, and to do away the evils which have taken place in consequence of repeated popular elections— It is said that not more than one third of the duties are now collected, things must not remain so. No State can exist without more punctuality frauds in the collection of the revenue must be pregnant with the most fatal evils as they will render abortive the best devised schemes of the most able financiers. and will soon destroy that good faith without which no people can flourish and be happy.—

As soon as our revenue Laws are in full operation, we may consider the works as nearly done, for if the government is not opposed, in this tender point, and the officers of it are permitted to do their duty without interruption, as they will be here I presume, in the first instance, the novelty of the scene will be over and precedents after, will come in aid of law. Besides the moment our long exhausted treasury shall be replenished, people, friends and foes, will look up to the government with respect and will flock to our national standard as to that of a successful potintate.—

I am very happy that the duty on molasses is reduced, I wish it could be farther so, for the draw back on Rum would have given us trouble, and especially if our duties could not be collected with more punctuality than such duties have heretofore been, I hope they will, I hope so because I know it ought to be

Our general Court is in recess If it has not done things which it ought not to have done and left undone those which it ought to have done I have judged wrong

I beg you would tender my best regards to M[rs.] Adams to Col[o.] Smith & M[rs.] Smith and / believe me to be towards / you D[r.] sir all which / esteem, confidence, and / affection can make / me—

B Lincoln

NB you will, burn the above when you have read it

RC (Adams Papers); internal address: "His Excellency / The Vice President"; endorsed by CA: "Hon[ble] B Lincoln / July 14"; notation by CFA: "1789."

[1] For Gov. John Hancock's 8 June address to the Mass. General Court, see JA's letter of 19 June to Lincoln, and note 3, above.

[2] Reconciling past political differences, Hancock and Samuel Adams united in strong public support of James Madison's proposed amendments to the U.S. Constitution, for which see James Sullivan's letter of 2 July, and note 2, above. Adams favored revising constitutional language to "expressly" reserve certain powers to the states. Along with Antifederalist sympathizers, however, he yielded to the doctrine of "implied" powers advocated by Alexander Hamilton and others (John K. Alexander, *Samuel Adams: America's Revolutionary Politician*, Lanham, Md., 2002, p. 209, 211).

To John Jenks

Sir

New York July 15 1789

I received your letter of the first of this month and thank you for you kind congratulations.[1] The application in favor of Joseph Hiller to be naval officer for the port of Salem must be made by himself or friends to the President. The indispensible duties of my office render it impossible for me to give much attention to nominations and appointments in the executive departments: but if this were otherways, the opinion and judgment of the Senators and representatives from the neighbourhood, whose personal knowledge and other means of information are so much superior will and ought to have much more influence. I shall however be attentive to your recommendation, and those of others in favor of the same person, and if a fair opportunity presents, mention them, leaving the decision to that wisdom, to which the constitution has confided it

Your &

J Adams

LbC in CA's hand (Adams Papers); internal address: "M[r] John Jenks / Salem"; APM Reel 115.

[1] The Salem, Mass., merchant Jenks wrote to JA on 1 July (Adams Papers), welcoming him home from Europe and recommending Joseph Hiller, for whom see Stephen Higginson's letter of 4 July, and note 2, above.

To Benjamin Rush

Dear Sir New York July 15 1789

I have read Dr Rush, de moribus Germanorum, with pleasure.[1]

As I am a great lover of paradoxes, when defended with ingenuity, I have read also the Phillippic against Latin and Greek, with some amusement: but my reverence for those Languages and the inestimable treasures hoarded up in them is not abated. Jean Jaques Rousseau's phillippic against the arts and sciences[2] amused informed and charmed me—but I have loved and admired arts and sciences the better from that time to this— What an ingrate was he to employ arts and sciences to abuse them? and are you much better, to use the knowledge and skill you derived from Latin and Greek to slander those divine Languages

Yours Ut Supra J A

LbC in CA's hand (Adams Papers); internal address: "D^r^ B Rush—"; APM Reel 115.

[1] Tacitus, *De moribus germanorum, et de vita agricolæ*, London, 1788.

[2] Jean Jacques Rousseau, *Discours . . . des sciences & des arts*, Geneva, 1750, a copy of which is in JA's library at MB (*Catalogue of JA's Library*).

To William Thompson

Sir [*15 July 1789*][1]

I have received the letter you did me the honor to write me on the fifth of this month, and am the more earnest to give it an early answer, as from various circumstances, I have been prevented from answering that delivered by Colo; Tudor

It is so rare of late, to find a candidate for office, acknowlege the ease and independance of his circumstances, that your frankness in this particular: was the more welcome and agreable. Distress in a man's affairs, in the ordinary course of things, is so far from being a recomendation to public trust, that it ought to be an objection tho' not a decisive obstruction to him. But in the present times, when there are so many ruined men and families, whose misfortunes have been clearly occasioned not by their own fault, but by the injustice and impolicy, of their country, and whose merits and public services have been considerable; the ordinary rule seems to be inverted. Nominations an appointments to office are however wholly out of my sphere. The Vice President has a constant and laborious service assigned him by the constitution, at the head of the Legislature, which consumes all his time, strength, and spirits; and leaves him no opportunity or capacity to collect the information, or to weigh the pretensions of candidates necessary to form these arrangements, or even to give advice concerning them, except perhaps in a few instances, more particularly and personally known to him. These duties are by the constitution wisely and virtuously assigned to the first executive Magistrate, and to him therefore must your application as well as all others be made.

I am & John Adams

LbC in CA's hand (Adams Papers); internal address: "William Thompson Esq[r] / Boston."; APM Reel 115.

[1] Thompson twice appealed to JA for patronage, on 9 March and 5 July. The dating of this letter is based on Thompson's reply of 30 July, in which he described the scale of his debt and wrote that "if nothing can be obtained at present, I shall acquiesce—perhaps some Door may open before long, and I flatter myself I shall not have your Negative, unless for Substantial Reasons" (all Adams Papers). Thompson, who served as commissioner of Connecticut's public accounts from 1783 to 1787, also applied to George Washington, on 28 July 1789, but did not earn a federal post (Morris, *Papers*, 7:441; Washington, *Papers, Presidential Series*, 3:341, 343).

To James Lovell

Dear Sir New York July 16, 1789

There is no such point in dispute, as that you mention in your favour of the 9th. The only question is concerning the title of the first man. All the world sees the absurdity and feels the humiliation of giving the titled of excellency, which is only a provincial, or diplomatic title of the lowest order, to a great Prince vested with the whole executive authority of Government in a nation, who sends and receives ambassadors, who nominates and appoints Generals, Admirals and even Govenors of the western territory at least. Every body indeed feels the absurdity of giving the title of highness to an office whose dignity and authority can have no other adequate title than that of MAJESTY. But as the nation has not digested this subject, the family and the world call him "The General." so that the first civil and political magistrate in the nation is to be called by the military title of a provincial Brigadier.— Did you ever read Shenstones School mistress, in immitation of Spencer? if you have you have there seen an authority very much to the purpose, which I wish you would request Russel to put in his excellent centinel.

Albeit ne flattery did corrupt her truth
Ne pompous titles did debauch her ear

Goody, Goodwoman, n'aunt forsooth
Or Dame, the sole addition she did hear.
Yet there she challenged these she held right dear
Ne would esteem him act as mought behove
Who should not honor'd eld with there revere
For never titles yet so mean did prove
But there was eke a mind which did that title love.

The executive authority is called "the prince" and we shall never have our equal station with other nations untill our national executive, has a Princely title. If you give him only a diplomatic title he will be ranked with ambassadors—if a provincial one, he will be levelled with govenors of Colonies and Generals of armies. but never with the first Magistrates of other nations.

Mr Sturgis Gorham, I doubt not from your recommendation, would make a good collector, but his representations and sollicitations must be transmitted to the President by himself or friends.

Otis's prognostication, and Sturgis's event of eminence has amounted to just nothing at all.— a spendid pompous nothing. an office that between you and me Brother Wingate or Macclay, might execute as well as, Cecil, Chatham, Sully, Colbert or Neckar. In the scale of rational existences or intelligent natures the Farmer of Pen's hill or Stony field hill, hold in my philosophy, a rank much superior to the Vice President of Richmond Hill, though you should give him the title of Eminence, Highness or Holiness. instead of that of Excellence. He has in short not the smallest degree of power to do any good either in the executive, legislative or Judicial departments. A mere Doge of Venice, a mere "Teste de legno" or least you should not be an Italian "Head of wood" a mere mechanical tool to wind up the clock. The moment our country has wisdom to introduce a proper ballance of powers into their constitution they will cut off this head, and I myself should be ambitious of the honor of weilding the ax. Our Countrymen are Romans and Spartans only in theory. The idea of two Consuls or two Kings they cannot comprehend; nor is it proper they should. Their hearts and whole habits are against their own ignorant republican ideas. farewell my dear friend and write as often as you can to the honest Monarchical republican

John Adams

LbC in CA's hand (Adams Papers); internal address: "Hon Jame Lovell / Boston"; APM Reel 115.

To Theophilus Parsons

Dear Sir New York July 16. 1789

I have received your favor of the eigth of this month, and am much obliged to you for the frank and manly representation it contains, I wish however you had written the same things to the President. I doubt whether the President has prescribed to himself any rule so rigid as that you have heard of to appoint all men who are in possession, against whom there is no complaint of Superior merit and better qualifications are made to appear, I dare say they will have the preference, Cœteris paribus, the rule may be good to make no change, but not otherwise I have determined to lay your letter before the President, this day: because it contains information which ought not to be concealed from him. As you have began, I hope you will continue to favour us with you sentiments on public affairs.

We want all the speculations of the ingenious as well as the prayers of the faithful, and unless our Countrymen more highly favored than their prejudices, passions, follies, and errors and vices have deserved all will not extricate them from the castigating rod.

Your Testimony in favour of my John gives comfort to my inmost soul, and from my heart I wish you a double portion of the same consolation. Will you give him leave to visit us, when it suits his and your convenience.[1]

With great esteem I am & J. Adams.

LbC in CA's hand (Adams Papers); internal address: "Theophilus Parsons Esqr / Newbury Port."; APM Reel 115.

[1] From 7 Sept. to 14 Oct., JQA took a hiatus from his studies with Parsons and visited with family in New York. He met George Washington and observed sessions of Congress and the Supreme Court (*AFC*, 8:464).

From Henry Marchant

Private

Dear Sir Newport July 16$^{th.}$ 1789

I have yet to acknowledge Your Politeness and Kindness in ranking me in the List of your Friends by your Letter of Invitation to an epistolary Correspondence previous to your embarking for Europe.[1] It was truly flattering to my Pride. My leaving Congress, and being much out of the Circle of Information, whereby I might in some little Measure have repaid those Obligations which your Letters must have laid me under, prevented my making that use of the Honor Your Proposal conferred upon me, which it was my full Inclination to have done— In two Instances however I made Attempts by Gentlemen of my Acquaintance, both of whom after They were possessed of my Letters relinquished their Voyages.

I have participated in and enjoyed the Dignity Honor and Advantages in common with the rest of Our Friends and Countrymen, which Your Abillities Wisdom and Integrity have procur'd to Our dear Country.— Dear it will allways be to me, tho' a base and ungrateful Host have risen up, intermixed with Tories, Speculators and Characters which in Our dark Days had kept behind the Scene, to snatch the Honors and Advantages from, as well as to rob and plunder, every noble Adventurer in the great Cause; and who chearfully in early Day put Life and Fortune to the Hazard.— Such was the rash Rebellion in the Massachusetts:— Such has been and still is (tho' under the dignified Cloak of Law) the System of, I was about to say Government, *Power* in this State—

After having for a series of Years, nay from the Stamp Act to the Conclusion of Our glorious Revolution pursued one steady Line of Duty to my Country, sacrificeing my Time the most valuable Part of my Life; submitting to the Ravages & Destruction of the War upon my Property without repining, and indeed to the baseness of the sly and insiduous Acts of such as were ever debasing Our Cont$^{l.}$ Currency to answer their private selfish Ends— Instead of the Thousand Blessings I had anticipated for my Country, and in which I hoped to participate, at the ushering in of Peace—Instead of the Security we ever presumed we were purchasing by the arduous Struggle:—An unexpected set of Men took the Reigns of Government here, and struck such a levelling Stroke at Property, and aimed it with such a Will (if their Power could have reached as far as they looked,)[2] to have cancelled the whole national Debt— I never bought or sold a publick Security:— All I could spare I early lent either to the United States or to this State:— And this State have cancelled Their Debt, if such an Act in a future Day can be sanctioned as Law— From the Moment Their System took Place it has been out of the Creditors Power to call for his own.— Business, especially in my Profession, has been almost entirely stagnated.— Thus circumstanced I stand, strugling against a Torrent of Ignorance and Wickedness,— As one of the Minority my utmost Exertions in the Legislature, as well as out of it, have been and still are made to obtain an Adoption of the

Constitution– The Paper-Money System has been the only real Motives in the Opposition,– That out of the Way, and I am confident this State would have been one of the first for the Adoption– The Majority rather decreases; many are growing sick of Their Situation;–And I have hopes that, in the Course of the Fall or Winter Our People will open Their Eyes:– If They do, They will start with Horror from Their past Infatuation and fly to the Adoption of the Constitution, as to the Horns of the Alter:–[3] But too late to save Numbers of Widows Orphans and honest Citizens from Penury and Want, who were in Plenty and Affluence; at least in the Enjoyment of a comfortable Property–

I have often recollected several of Your prophetick Declarations– The solemn one You made on the Floor of Congress respecting the late Confederation, just as we had closed it, hath come to pass:– And what we then thought of most solemn Consideration, has proved most joyous, glorious and honorable for this Country– Your Prophetick Declaration as to myself, You will begin to believe with me will never come to pass– It will be of no Consequence to the Publick if it does not; and I hope no bad one to me. I wish ever to court the good Opinion of my Country as far as may be consistant with Honor and Probity:– I esteem, I reverence the Voice of the People, next to the Voice of God.– But They will be sometimes carried off the Ground;– Infatuation will for a Time fasten upon Them– An honest Man cannot, will not shift his Ground; but will remain steady, and pursue every Plan and make every Effort to bring Them back to a sense of Honor Virtue and Stabillity– As This State now stands, and as I stand within its Circle I know not, if any of Us will pass in *Review* before the Honorable Nominator to Offices under the now Constitution;– Or if with any Propriety we might; I feel a Delicacy and a Pain in suggesting the Thought even to one whom I know to be my Friend, and would be generous to gratify me in any reasonable Wish within His Power; and still more generous in forgiving the Impropriety of a Request, and that Partiallity we too often feel for Ourselves– I observed before that I have spent much of the Prime of Life, and that too unrewarded, but by my own conscious Feelings, in the publick Cause– After which it was tedious and urksome again to enter, and begin anew, the Circuit of Courts:– But still more disagreable I confess to find by a System of Laws little or no Business in the Profession to attend– I wish to live either by my Profession or in some Department, requiring the Knowledge of it; and in which I might in some good Measure still serve that Publick, in whose Interest I have for many Years been inlisted; and be receiving some honest Benefit to myself— I know of no Person better acquainted with my Character, Abillities, Inclinations and Sensations than my Friend to whom in *Confidence* I now write.— I have said enough; perhaps too much.— If so, He will not chide but pass it by— I know I have Friends in our mutual Friends Rich^d. H. Lee, Ol^r. Ellsworth and others in the Senate, and in the Hoñble Assembly— To His Excellency I have been personally known in sundry Interviews of a publick Nature from Congress and this State, as well as in my private Character; but I know not that I am known to Him as of the Profession.

I mention no particular Respects to Them thro' You Sir, as I do not wish at present it should be known I had written this Letter—

I hope M^rs. Adams, Son &c had a pleasant Passage thro' the Sound, and a happy meeting with M^r. Adams in Health— My Dear Sir, You perceive with what Freedom I have wrote, notwithstanding the accummulated Honors bestowed upon my Friend— I beleive Him in private Life the same, He ever was.— In publick the same,— extending His Usefulness as His Country has enlarged His Circle and increased His Opportunities— In my small Circle I too pride myself in being the same, wishing every Increase of Good to my Country, and of Honor and Glory to Him who thro' divine Providence hath done so much for it; and happy in subscribing myself His most / assured Friend / and humble Servt.

Henry Marchant

RC (Adams Papers); internal address: "The Honble John Adams Esqr. / Vice President New York."; endorsed by CA: "Mr Merchant July 16"; and by JA: "ans^d. Aug. 8. 1789."

[1] JA's first extant letter to Newport, R.I., lawyer Henry Marchant was that of 10 Sept. 1779, reflecting on their shared experiences in the Continental Congress and the state of American maritime power. Marchant (1741–1796), University of Pennsylvania 1762, delivered Newport's petition for duty exemptions to Congress in Sept. 1789. Five months later, he introduced the bill that led to the state's final ratifying convention, where he acted as a delegate and voted to adopt the Constitution in May 1790. Marchant served as a U.S. judge for the district of Rhode Island from 1790 until his death (vol. 8:136–137; *Doc. Hist. Ratif. Const.*, 24:315).

[2] Closing parenthesis has been editorially supplied.

[3] Adonijah and other fugitives won asylum in Jerusalem by holding on to the horns of the altar (1 Kings, 1:50–53).

To Roger Sherman

Dear Sir Richmond Hill July 17. 1789

I have read over with Pleasure, your Observations on the new federal Constitution, and am glad of an opportunity to communicate to you my opinion of some Parts of them.[1] it is by a free and friendly Intercourse of Sentiments that the Friends of our Country may hope for Such an Unanimity of Opinion and Such a Concert of Exertions, as may sooner or later produce the Blessings of good Government,

You Say "it is by Some objected, that the Executive is blended with the Legislature, and that those Powers ought to be entirely distinct and unconnected; but is not that a gross Error in Politicks? The united Wisdom and various Interests of a nation Should be combined in framing the Laws, by which all are to be governed and protected, though it would not be convenient to have them executed by the whole Legislature. The Supreme Executive in Great Britain is one branch of the Legislature, and has a negative on all the Laws; perhaps that is an extreme not to be imitated by a Republic, but the Negative vested in the President by the new Constitution, on the Acts of Congress, and the consequent Revision, may be very useful to prevent Laws being passed without mature deliberation; and to preserve stability in the Administration of Government. And the Concurrence of the Senate in the Appointment to office, will Strengthen the hands of the Executive, and Secure the Confidence of the People, much better than a Select Council and will be less expensive."—

Is it then "an extreme not to be imitated by a Republic, to make the Supreme Executive a Branch of the Legislature, and give it a Negative on all the Laws?" if you please We will examin this Position, and See whether it is well founded. in the first Place what is your definition of a Republic? Mine is this, *A Government, whose Sovereignty is vested in more than one Person*. Governments are divided into *Despotisms*, *Monarchies*, and *Republics*. A *Despotism* is a Government, in which the three Divisions of Power, the Legislative, Executive and Judicial are all vested in one Man. A *Monarchy* is a Government, where the Legislative and Executive Powers are vested in one Man; but the Judicial, in other Men. in all Governments the Sovereignty is vested in that Man or Body of Men, who have the Legislative Power. in Despotisms and Monarchies therefore, the Legislative

Authority being in one Man, the Sovereignty is in one Man. in Republicks, as the Sovereignty that is the Legislative Power is always vested in more than one, it may be vested in as many more as you please. in the United States, it might be vested in two Persons, or in three Millions or in any intermediate Number, and in every Such Supposeable Case, the Government would be a Republic. in conformity to these Ideas Republics have been divided into three different Species, monarchical, Aristocratical and Democratical Republics. England is a Republic: a monarchical Republic it is true: but a Republic Still: because the Sovereignty, which is the Legislative Power, is vested in more than one Man: it is equally divided indeed between the one, the few, and the many: or in other Words between the three natural Divisions of Mankind in every Society; the monarchical, the Aristocratical and the Democratical. it is essential to a monarchical Republic, that the Supream Executive Should be a Branch of the Legislature, and have a Negative on all the Laws.— I Say essential because, if Monarchy were not an essential Part of the Sovereignty the Government would not be a monarcharcical Republic. Your Position therefore is clearly and certainly an Error, because the Practice of G. Britain in making their Supreme Executive a Branch of the Legislature and giving it a Negative on all the Laws, must be imitated, by every Monarchical Republic.—

I will pause here if you please—but if you will / give me leave, I will write you, another Letter or / two upon this subject. mean time I am with / unalterable friendship yours John Adams.

RC (MHi:Foster Family Autograph Coll.); internal address: "The Honourable Roger sherman Esq."; endorsed: "Vice Presidents / Letter July 17. 1789." LbC (Adams Papers); APM Reel 115.

[1] Connecticut representative Roger Sherman, who served alongside JA on the committee to draft the Declaration of Independence, articulated Federalist revisions to the Constitution against the backdrop of his state's ratification convention. Between 15 Nov. and 20 Dec. 1787, he issued a series of essays as "Countryman," intended to assuage public fears that federal power would eclipse state governments and suppress individual liberties. Here and below, JA referred mainly to Sherman's essay "Observations on the new Federal CONSTITUTION," which appeared in the *New-Haven Gazette*, 7 Jan. 1788. Writing as "A Citizen of New Haven," Sherman described the political institutions defined by the Constitution and upheld the separation of powers. In line with JA's views, Sherman assured readers that "the Constitution appears to be well framed to secure the rights and liberties of the people and for preserving the governments of the individual states, and, if well administered, to restore and secure public and private credit, and give respectability to the states both abroad and at home" (JA, *D&A*, 2:391–392; Mark David Hall, *Roger Sherman and the Creation of the American Republic*, N.Y., 2013, p. 113–116).

To Roger Sherman

Dear sir Richmond Hill July 18. 1789

In my Letter of Yesterday, I think it was demonstrated that the English Constitution is a Republic, and that the Regal Negative upon the Laws, is essential to that Republic: because that without it, that Government would not be what it is a monarchical Republic, and consequently could not preserve the Ballance of Power between, the Executive and Legislative Powers, nor that other Ballance, which is in the Legislative between the one, the few and the many, in which two Ballances the Excellence of that form of Government, consists.

Let Us now enquire, whether the new Constitution of the United States is, or is not a monarchical Republic, like that of G. Britain.— The Monarchical, and the Aristocratical Power, in our Constitution, it is true are not hereditary: but this makes no difference in the nature of the Power, in the nature of the Ballance, or in the name of the Species of Government.— it would make no difference in the Power of a Judge, or Justice, or General, or Admiral, whether his Commission were for Life or Years. his authority, during the time it lasted would be the Same, whether it were for one Year or twenty, or for Life, or descendible to his eldest son.— The People The Nation, in whom all Power resides originally, may delegate their Power, for one Year, or for ten Years, for Years or for Life, or may delegate it in fee simple, or fee Tail, if I may so express my self or during good behaviour, or at Will, or till further orders. A nation might unanimously create a Dictator or Despot, for one Year, or more, or for Life, or for Perpetuity with hereditary descent. in Such a Case, the Dictator for one Year, would as really be a Dictator during the Time, his Power lasted, as the other would be whose Power was perpetual and descendible.— a Nation in the Same manner might create a Simple Monarch, for Years, Life or Perpetuity, and in either Case the Creature would be equally a Simple Monarch during the Continuance of his Power. so the People of England might create King, Lords and commons, for a Year, or for several Years, or for Life—and in any of these Cases, their Government would be a monarchical Republic, or if you will a limited Monarchy, during its continuance, as much as it is now, when the King and Nobles are hereditary. They might make their house of commons hereditary too. what the Consequence of this would be it is easy to foresee: but it would not in the first moment make any change in the legal Power, nor in the name of the Government.

Let Us now consider what our Constitution is: and see whether any other name can with propriety be given it: than that of a monarchical Republic, or if you will a limited Monarchy.— The Duration of our President is neither perpetual nor for Life, it is only for four Years: but his Power, during those four Years, is much greater than that of an Avoyer, a Consul a Podesta, a Doge, a Statholder, nay than a King of Poland.— nay than a King of Sparta.— I know of no first Magistrate, in any Republican Government, excepting England and Neuchattel, who possesses a constitutional Dignity, Authority and Power comparable to his.— The Power of Sending and receiving Ambassadors of raising and commanding Armies and Navies, of nominating appointing and commissioning all Offices—of managing the Treasures, the internal and external affairs of the nation—nay the whole Executive Power, co extensive with the Legislative Power is vested in him: and he has the Right and his is the Duty to take Care that the Laws be faithfully executed.— These Rights and Duties, these Prerogatives and Dignities, are so transcendant, that they must naturally and necessarily excite in the Nation all the Jealousy, Envy, Fears, Apprehensions and Opposition, that is so constantly observed in England against the Crown.

That these Powers are necessary I readily Admit. That the Laws cannot be executed without them: that the Lives, Liberties, Properties and Characters of the Citizens cannot be Secure, without their Protection is most clear. But it is equally certain I think that they ought to have been Still greater, or much less.— The Limitations upon them, in the Cases of War, Treaties, and Appointments to Office and especially the Limitation, on the Presidents Independence as a branch of the Legislature, will be the destruction of this Constitution, and involve us in Anarchy, if not amended.— I shall pass over all these particulars for the present, except the last: because that is now the Point in dispute between You and me.

Longitude and the Philosophers Stone, have not been sought with more Earnestness by Philosophers, than a *Guardian of the Laws* has been Studied by Legislators from Plato to Montesquieu. but every Project has been found to be no better, than committing the Lamb to the Custody of the Wolf, excepting that one, which is called *A ballance of Power*.— a Simple Sovereignty, in one, a few, or many has no ballance, and therefore no Laws. a divided Sovereignty without a ballance, or in other Words, where the division is unequal is always at War, and consequently has no Laws. in our Constitution the Sovereignty, i.e the Legislative Power is divided, into three Branches. The House and Senate are equal, but the third Branch, tho essential is not equal.— The President must pass Judgment upon every Law—but in Some Cases his Judgment may be overruled. These Cases will be Such as attack, his constitutional Power, it is therefore certain he has not equal Power to defend himself, or the Constitution or the Judicial Power, as the Senate and House have.

Power naturally grows.— Why? because human Passions are insatiable. but that Power alone can grow which is already too great, that which is unchecked. that which has no equal Power to controul it. The Legislative Power in our Constitution, is greater than the Executive, it will therefore encroach—because both Aristocratical and democratical Passions are insatiable.— The Legislative Power will increase, the Executive will diminish.— in the Legislature, the Monarchical Power is not equal, either to the Aristocratical, or democratical—it will therefore decrease, while the others will increase. indeed I think the Aristocratical Power is greater than either the Monarchical or Democratical. that will therefore Swallow up the other two.

in my Letter of Yesterday, I think it was proved, that a Republic might make the Supream Executive an integral Part of the Legislature. in this it is equally demonstrated as I think, that our Constitution ought to be amended, by a decisive Adoption of that Expedient.

if you dont forbid me, I shall write you again, / Yours sincerely

John Adams

RC (MHi:Foster Family Autograph Coll.); internal address: "The Hon. Roger Sherman Esqr." LbC (Adams Papers); APM Reel 115.

From Jeremy Belknap

Much respected & dear Sir Boston July 18. 1789

It was a very singular pleasure to me to receive a Line from you approving the discourse which I did myself the honor to send to you; the good opinion of such a Gentleman as Mr Adams & the very great honor wch he has done me will not easily be effaced from my remembrance.

Not till this Week have I met with the political annals of George Chalmers printed in London 1780 in one Vol 4to.[1] From what little I have as yet had Opportunity to read of the work, I conceive the author to have the spirit of indefatigable enquiry which is necessary in a historian, tho' I think not so much of that Candor which is becoming in judging the characters & actions of those who have trod the Stage before us— The reason of my mentioning him to you is to introduce an enquiry whether you know the Man—Whether he be an American refugee or an Englishman—a Lawyer I think he is—& whether there is or is likely to be a second volume of his work. When I observe his having had access to the papers in the plantation Office, I feel a regret that an Ocean seperates me from such a grand repository. how necessary to form a just judgment of the secret springs of many American transactions!

The want of public repositories for historical materials as well as the destruction of many valuable ones by fires, by war & by the lapse of time has long been a subject of regret in my mind. Many papers which are daily thrown away may in future be much wanted, but except here & there a person who has a curiosity of his own to gratify no one cares to undertake the Collection & of this class of Collectors there are scarcely any who take Care for securing what they have got together after they have quitted the Stage. The only sure way of preserving such things is by printing them in some voluminous work as the Remembrancer—but the attempt to carry on such a work would probably not meet with encouragement— the publication of Gov[r] Winthrop's journal labours & I fear will come to nought.—[2]

You have done what I wished in *publishing* the Letters to D[r] Calkoen, a Copy of which I was favoured with the Sight of by M[r] Cranch before this publication was made. It is certainly an important point in the History of our Revolution that it was the work of the people at large & not of any party or faction as our Enemies have affected to believe. There is another point which ought to be as fully ascertained & that is that our Opposition to Great Brittain did not originate in a desire of Independence, but that we preserved our loyalty & affection to the Crown of Great Brittain as long as was practicable considering the immense provocation which we received.

Pray my dear Sir is it a fact that Baron Kalb was sent over hither by the Court of France to sound the inclinations of the Americans after the Repeal of the Stamp-act & that he found us so passionately attached to the British nation as to report the impossibility of attempting a seperation?[3]

You will pardon me for thus intruding on your more important engagements—& if you think me too forward or impertinent in my enquiries, suggest to me the propriety of being less so & you shall be obeyed—for really Sir I have a regard for your Character little short of veneration.—

Believe me therefore y^r truly respectful / & much obliged friend & humble Ser[vant] Jere Belknap

RC (Adams Papers); addressed: "The Honourable / Mr Adams / Vice President of the United States / New York"; endorsed: "Rev. Jeremiah Belknap. / July 18. ans^d. 24. 1789." Some loss of text where the seal was removed.

[1] The same edition of George Chalmers' *Political Annals of the Present United Colonies, from Their Settlement to the Peace of 1763* is in JA's library at MB. Chalmers (1742–1825), a prolific Scottish antiquarian, studied law in Edinburgh and practiced in Baltimore. Appointed chief clerk of the British Privy Council's Board of Trade and Plantations in 1786, Chalmers drew on official records to publish various historical works (*Catalogue of JA's Library*; *DNB*).

[2] Then comprising two manuscript volumes, the journal of Massachusetts Bay Colony governor John Winthrop (1588–1649) circulated widely in early American antiquarian circles. Connecticut governor Jonathan Trumbull Sr. (1710–1785), Harvard 1727, toiled with secretary John Porter to transcribe the journal for publication, but he died before finishing the task. Belknap, inspired by London editor John Almon's monthly newspaper of Anglo-American politics, *The Remembrancer*, sought to preserve the new nation's past through publication. He recovered Winthrop's journal from Trumbull's Lebanon, Conn., estate and brought it home to Boston.

In 1790 Noah Webster published a Hartford, Conn., edition of Winthrop's account entitled *A Journal of the Transactions and Occurrences in the Settlement of Massachusetts and the Other New-England Colonies, from the Year 1630 to 1644: Written by John Winthrop, Esq. First Governor of Massachusetts: And Now First Published from a Correct Copy of the Original Manuscript*. A third volume of Winthrop's manuscript, discovered in 1816, was temporarily deposited with the Massachusetts Historical Society, which Belknap founded in Jan. 1791 (*The Journal of John Winthrop, 1630–1649*, ed. Richard S. Dunn, James Savage, and Laetitia Yeandle, Cambridge, 1996, p. xi, xvi, xxii; *Sibley's Harvard Graduates*, 8:267, 268, 298; *DNB*; Louis Leonard Tucker, *Clio's Consort: Jeremy Belknap and the Founding of the Massachusetts Historical Society*, Boston, 1990, p. 93, 115, 116).

[3] Maj. Gen. Johann von Robais, Baron de Kalb (1721–1780), of Hüttendorf, Germany, gathered political intelligence for the Duc de Choiseul, French minister of war and foreign affairs, during his travels through Amsterdam and London in 1767. Arriving in Philadelphia on 12 Jan. 1768, and observing Americans' fury with the British parliament over a new wave of taxes, Kalb reported that the Stamp Act "affair is very far from being adjusted." Intending to learn specifics about the colonists' military capabilities, Kalb described a rising tide of violence within the provincial assemblies of Massachusetts and Pennsylvania. He sailed to New York City two weeks later and made side trips to Boston and Halifax to gauge the political mood. Kalb informed the French ministry that Americans, while liberty-minded, would not invoke foreign aid, expecting that independence would evolve naturally in time. With his mail repeatedly intercepted and no reply from Choiseul, Kalb returned to Paris in mid-June. He sent Choiseul a memorandum listing British Army forces stationed in the colonies, which the minister dismissed as inflated. Kalb continued to report for several months on American affairs despite Choiseul's indifference (Reneé Critcher Lyons, *Foreign-Born American Patriots: Sixteen Volunteer Leaders in the Revolutionary War*, Jefferson, N.C., 2014, p. 141, 145–147; Friedrich Kapp, *The Life of John Kalb: Major-General in the Revolutionary Army*, transl. Charles Goepp, N.Y., 1884, p. 46–71).

From Samuel Mather Jr.

Sir London 19[th.] July 1789

My Friend Robert Young Esq[r.] of Warwick Court Holborn having lately published an Essay on the Powers and Mechanism of Nature, in which he has advanced some new and important Doctrines,[1] which he wishes may be investigated by the Philosophers of America, has desired me to distribute a few of them to the Persons, whom I know to be the most eminent for their Learning and love of the Sciences—and as I know of none more so than Your Excellency, I am to request You will be pleased to accept of the herewith inclosed Book from him—and I am very happy in the opportunity it gives me of congratulating Your Excellency on your appointment to the very high and important Office to which You have been chosen by your Country, and in the execution of which, I wish You may meet with all the Success and satisfaction which I am sure your Endeavours for the Public Good will merit—

If You should be so obliging as to acknowledge the receipt of my Letter, be pleased to direct for me, to the care of Sam[l.] Rogers Esq[r.] N[o.] 23 Charlotte Street Portland Place.[2]

I have the Honor to be with very great Respect and Esteem— / Sir / Your Excellency's / most obedient / and most humble Servant

Sam[l.] Mather

RC (Adams Papers); internal address: "His Excellency / John Adams Esq[r.] / &c &c &c—"

[1] Loyalist Samuel Mather Jr. (1745–1809), former chief clerk of the Boston customs office, returned to America and became a major shareholder in the Connecticut Land Company. He sent Robert Young's *An Essay on the Powers and Mechanism of Nature*, London, 1788. While living in England, AA attended Young's scientific lectures, and a copy of this work is in JA's library at MB (vol. 17:50; Chaim M. Rosenberg, *Yankee Colonies Across America: Cities upon the Hills*, Lanham, Md., 2015, p. 39; *AFC*, 8:25, 26; *Catalogue of JA's Library*).

[2] Samuel Rogers (1764–1804), Harvard 1765, was a Boston merchant who resettled in London in 1778. Holding the power of attorney for many of his fellow loyalists, he assisted with their compensation claims and operated a banking firm on Charlotte Street (*Sibley's Harvard Graduates*, 16:211, 212).

From Edmund Randolph

Dear sir Williamsburg July 19. 1789.

Your friendly answer to the letter, which I took the liberty of addressing to you in favor of Col[o.] Heath, has increased the attachment, which your civility to me in 1775, and your public conduct since, first produced My application in that gentleman's behalf being founded on a conviction of his worth, I conceived, that it might not be improper to make that worth known to all those, who might eventually decide on his pretensions.[1]

I am almost unable to inform you, where my uncle, Mr. Jenings, is, or how he is employed.[2] I have not received a letter from him for five months; and indeed he communicates so little concerning himself, that, notwithstanding his affectionate letters, he is almost a perfect stranger to me. Among the few particulars, however, which have fallen from his pen, respecting himself, his esteem and veneration for you have been the most considerable. In both I beg leave to assure you, that I cordially concur, and that I always am, / Dear sir, / your obliged and obt. serv Edm: Randolph.

RC (Adams Papers).

[1] Randolph last wrote to JA on 12 Feb. (Adams Papers), recommending retired Maj. Gen. William Heath (1737–1814), of Roxbury, for a federal post. JA replied on 25 May, instructing Randolph to apply to George Washington (LbC, APM Reel 115). Heath had been soundly defeated in the election for Massachusetts lieutenant governor two years earlier. While JA thought highly of his military service, he observed in 1776 that "Heath unfortunately has not a Reputation, equal to his Merit." Heath did not receive an appointment in the Washington administration (vol. 4:444; *AFC*, 8:99).

[2] Edmund Jenings, who frequently dined with JA in London, lived near Kensington Square and engaged in scholarly pursuits until his death on 27 July 1819 (vol. 19:144; Virginius Cornick Hall Jr., comp., *Portraits in the Collection of the Virginia Historical Society*, Charlottesville, Va., 1981, p. 128).

To Roger Sherman

Dear Sir Richmond Hill July 20. 1789

There is a Sense, and a degree, in which the Executive, in our Constitution, is blended with the Legislature: The President, has the Power of Suspending a Law; of giving the two Houses an Opportunity to pause, to think, to collect themselves, to reconsider a rash Step of a Majority; he has the Right to Urge all his Reasons against it, by Speech or Message; which becoming Public is an Appeal to the Nation— But the rational Objection, here is not that the Executive is blended with the Legislature: but that it is not *enough* blended; that it is not *incorporated* with it, and made an *essential* Part of it.— If it were an *integral* Part of it it might negative a Law, without much Noise, Speculation, or Confusion among the People. But as it now Stands, I beg you, to consider—it is almost impossible that a President Should ever have the Courage to make Use of his partial negative. what a Situation would a President be in, to maintain a

Controversy against a Majority of both Houses, before the Tribunal of the Public. To put a stop to a Law, that more than half the Senate and House, and consequently We may Suppose more than half the Nation, had set their hearts upon.? it is moreover possible, that more than two thirds of the Nation, the Senate and House, may in times of Calamity Distress, Misfortune and ill success of the Measures of Government from the momentary Passion and Enthusiasm, demand a Law which will wholly Subvert the Constitution. The Constitution of Athens was overturned in such a moment by Aristides himself.— The Constitution Should guard against a Possibility of its Subversion.— But We may take Stronger ground and assert that it is probable, that Such Cases will happen and that the Consitution will in fact be Subverted, in this Way.— Nay I go farther and Say, that from the constitution of human nature and the constant Course of human Affairs it is certain, that our Constitution will be Subverted, if not amended, and that in a very Short time, merely for Want of a decisive negative in the Executive.

There is another Sense, and another Degree, in which the Executive is blended with the legislature, which is liable to great and just Objection; which excites Alarms, Jealousies and Apprehensions in a very great degree.— I mean 1. the Negative of the Senate, upon Appointments to Office; 2. the Negative of the Senate upon Treaties, and 3. the Negative of the two Houses upon War.— I Shall confine my self at present to the first. The Negative of the Senate upon Appointments, is liable to the following Objections. 1. It takes away, or a least it lessens the Responsibility of the Executive—our Constitution obliges me to Say, that it lessens the Responsibility of the President. The blame of an hasty, injudicious, weak or wicked Appointment, is shared So much between him and the Senate, that his part of it will be too Small.— Who can censure him, without censuring the Senate, and the legislatures who appoint them? all their Friends will be interested to vindicate the President, in order to Screen them from censure. besides if an Impeachment is brought before them against an officer are they not interested to acquit him, least some part of the Odium of his Guilt Should fall upon them, who advised to his appointment.

2. It turns the Minds and Attention of the People, to the Senate, a Branch of the Legislature, in Executive matters. it interests another Branch of the Legislature in the management of the Executive,. it divides the People, between the Executive and the senate: whereas all the People ought to be united to watch the Executive, to

oppose its Encroachments, and resist its Ambition.— Senators and Representatives, and their Constituents, in short the Aristocratical and Democratical Divisions of Society ought to be united, on all Occasions to oppose the Executive, or the Monarchical Branch when it attempts to overleap its Limits. But how can this Union be effected, when the Aristocratical Branch has pledged its Reputation to the Executive by consenting to an Appointment.

3. It has a natural Tendency, to excite Ambition in the Senate,— An active, ardent Spirit, in that House, who is rich, & able; has a great Reputation and influence,; will be solicited by Candidates for Office. not to introduce the Idea of Bribery, because, tho it certainly would force itself in, in other Countries, and will, probably, here when We grow populous and rich, yet it is not yet, I hope to be dreaded.— But Ambition must come in, already.— A Senator of great Influence, will be naturally ambitious and desirous of increasing his Influence. Will he not be under a Temptation to Use his Influence with the President as well as his Brother Senators, to appoint Persons to Office in the several states who will exert themselves in Elections to get out his Ennemies or Opposers both in senate and House of Representatives, and to get in his Friends, perhaps his Instruments.? Suppose a Senator, to aim at the Treasury Office, for himself, his Brother, Father, or son—suppose him to aim at the President's Chair, or Vice Presidents, at the next Election—or at the Office of War, foreign or domestic affairs, will he not naturally be tempted to make Use of his whole Patronage his whole Influence, in Advising to appointments, both with President and senators to get such Persons nominated, as will exert themselves for Elections of President Vice President, senators and H. of Representatives to increase his Interest and promote his Views.— in this Point of View I am very apprehensive that this defect in our Constitution will have an unhappy Tendency to introduce Corruption of the grossest Kinds both of Ambition and Avarice into all our Elections. And this will be the worst of Poisons to our Constitution—it will not only destroy the present form of Government, but render it almost impossible to substitute in its Place any free Government, even a better limited Monarchy, or any other than a Despotism or a Simple Monarchy.

4. To avoid the Evil, under the last head, it will be in danger of dividing the Continent, into two or three Nations, a Case that presents no Prospect but of perpetual War.

5. This Negative on appointments, is in danger of involving the Senate in Reproach, Obloquy, Censure and Suspicion, without do-

ing any good.— Will the Senate Use their Negative or not.— if not; why Should they have it—many will censure them, for not Using it. many will ridicule them, call them Servile &c—if they do, Use it. The very first Instance of it, will expose the Senators, to the Resentment not only of the disappointed Candidate and all his Friends; but of the President and all his Friends; and these will be most of the Officers of Government, through the nation.

6. We Shall very soon have Parties formed—a Court and Country Party. and these Parties will have names given them, one Party in the House of Representatives will support the President and his Measures and Ministers—the other will oppose them. a Similar Party will be in senate— these Parties will Struggle with all their Art, perhaps with Intrigue—perhaps with Corruption at Every Election to increase their own Friends and diminish their opposers. Suppose Such Parties formed in senate, and then consider what Factious divisions We shall have there, upon every Nomination.

7. The Senate have not time. The Convention & Indian Treaties.

You are of opinion "That the concurrence of the Senate in the Appointments to Office, will Strengthen the hands of the Executive, and secure the Confidence of the People, much better than a Select Council, and will be less expensive" but in every one of these Ideas, I have the Misfortune to differ from you.[1] 1. it will weaken the hands of the Executive, by lessening the Obligation, Gratitude and Attachment of the Candidate to the President. by dividing his Attachment between the Executive and Legislative which are natural Ennemies.— Officers of Government instead of having a Single Eye and undivided Attachment to the Executive Branch, as they ought to have consistent with Law and the Constitution, will be constantly tempted to be factious with their factious Patrons in the senate. The Presidents own Officers in a thousand Instances will oppose his just and constitutional Exertions, and Screen themselves under the Wings of their Patrons and Party in the Legislature. Nor will it Secure the Confidence of the People. The People will have more confidence in the Executive, in Executive matters than in the Senate.— The People will be constantly jealous of factious Schemes in the senators to unduly influence the Executive, and of corrupt bargains between the senate and Executive, to serve each others private Views. The People will also be jealous that the Influence of the senate will be employed to conceal, connive and defend guilt in Executive offices, instead of being a guard and watch upon them and a terror to them. a Council selected by the President himself at his Pleasure, from among the senators, Representatives and Nation at large, would be purely responsible. in that Case, the Senate as a Body would not be compromised. The senate would be a Terror to Privy Councillors. its Honour would never be pledged to support any Measure or Instrument of the Executive, beyond Justice, law, and the Constitution. Nor would a privy Council be more expensive. The whole Senate must now deliberate on every Appointment and, if they ever find time for it, you will find that a great deal of time will be required and consumed in this service. Then the President might have a constant Executive Council now he has none.

I Said under the Seventh head that the Senate would not have time.— You will find that the whole Business of this Government will be infinitely delayed, by this Negative of the Senate on Treaties and Appointments.— Indian Treaties and Consular Conventions have been already waiting for months and the senate have not been able to find a moment of time to attend to them.—[2] and this Evil must constantly increase. so that the Senate must be constantly Sitting, and must be paid as long as they Sit.

but I have tired your Patience. Is there any Truth or Importance in these broken hints and crude surmises? or not? To me they appear well founded and very important. I am / with usual Affection Yours

John Adams

RC (MHi:Foster Family Autograph Coll.); internal address: "The Hon. Roger Sherman"; endorsed: "Vice President's / Letter July 20th. 1789." LbC (Adams Papers); APM Reel 115.

[1] For Sherman's opinion, see JA's letter of 17 July, and note 1, above.

[2] Senators inherited two major foreign policy items from the Continental Congress: approving the pending Fort Harmar treaties of 9 Jan. and the new Franco-American consular convention. The first treaty, negotiated by Gen. Arthur St. Clair, governor of the Northwest Territory, with the leaders of the Wyandot, Delaware, Ottawa, Chippewa, Potawatomi, and Sac nations, was intended to restore property and regulate trade, simultaneously compensating the tribes with $6,000 in goods for land taken. St. Clair's second treaty was with the Six Nations of New York and featured the same terms. The Mohawks were absent from the negotiations and therefore excluded from the agreement.

Acting under Art. 2 of the Constitution, George Washington sent the Fort Harmar treaties, along with supporting documents and a report from Gen. Henry Knox, to the Senate on 25 May for approval. Still sorting out the process of supplying advice and consent for foreign treaties, the Senate formed a committee on 12 June to examine the materials. On 22 Aug. the president also took the unusual step of appearing before the Senate to seek advice regarding negotiations with the Creek, retreating with "sullen diginity" once he realized the debate's scope. Four days later, the committee advised the Senate to consent to the first treaty, which it did on 8 Sept., but made no mention of the second agreement, with the Six Nations. Although Washington and the Senate operated as if both treaties were valid, the agreement with the Six Nations was not filed with the U.S. State Department until 1797.

The Senate made swifter progress with the consular convention, which was the last foreign agreement forged by the Continental

Congress and the first consented to by the Senate. Signed and sent by Thomas Jefferson to John Jay on 14 Nov. 1788, the convention defined the duties and privileges of French and American consuls. For the convention's evolution, which was hampered by American perceptions of French plans for espionage and clashes over Franco-American shipping, see Jefferson, *Papers*, 14:55–66, 67–180. Washington sent it to the Senate on 11 June 1789. Members again debated how to provide the advice and consent that the Constitution mandated. They followed the route of, first, reviewing a treaty that was negotiated under the prior government and, second, seeking guidance from a former department head. On 17 and 21 June senators asked Jay to examine the translation of the text, which he approved in a report of 25 July. The convention was unanimously consented to by the Senate four days later (Washington, *Papers, Presidential Series*, 2:391–392; 4:51–53; *First Fed. Cong.*, 2:152–163; Maclay, *Journal*, p. 128–131; Francis Paul Prucha, *American Indian Treaties: The History of a Political Anomaly*, Berkeley, Calif., 1994, p. 57, 73–74, 76; U.S. Senate, *Exec. Jour.*, 1st Cong., 1st sess., p. 6–9).

From Robert Montgomery

Sir Alicante 20 July 1789.

The honour I had of an Aquaintance with your Excellency Shortly after your arrival at the Court of Varsailles; and some friendly letters you was pleased to write me after my return to Alicante, together with my affection for the United States to which you have rendered so many signal services, Impel me to take the liberty of addressing you at this time with my Sincerest Congratulations on your being Ellected Vice President; accept Sir of my warmest wishes for your wellfare and happiness, and may that Success and Prosperity which has so much distinguished your Character continue to attend you thro' a long And useful Life.[1]

As by a long residence here as a Merchant I have aquired a tolorable knowledg of the Language and manners of the People, and the Intrests of this Countrey with respect to Ours and of Ours with respect to this; I may be able occationally to give such Informations on those points as your Station of second Legislator of our Countrey may require for your goverment in frameing any laws respecting our commerce with Spain, in which should you think I can be any way useful I Shall be highly honoured by recieving any of your Commands

As Madrid is at so great a distance from every part of the Coast of Spain; a person who Resides there cannot be of Such immediate service to our Vessels and the Active part of our commerce as may often be required, which will I Suppose make it Necessary to follow the Example of Other Nations, and appoint Consuls in the Principal Ports, whoes business it will be to attend to those matters in perticular, and Give such advices to Congress as may be prudent and useful in that Line, and as I have by approbation of the Honorable M^r^

Jay and Mr. Carmichael continued to do the office of Consule ever Since the Independance, I hope you will do me the honour to confirm me in it, and you may depend on my utmost Exertions to be useful and Give every Satisfaction to the United states, with honour to your recommendation, being with the greatest respect and Veneration / Dear Sir / Your Excellency's Obedient and Affectionate / Humble Servant Robt Montgomery

RC (Adams Papers); internal address: "His Excellency the Honorable John Adams."

[1] Irish-born merchant Robert Montgomery (b. 1754) solicited Thomas Jefferson for a consular appointment in Spain on 22 May 1787, stating that he had operated "the first American House of Commerce" there since 1776 and that John Jay would vouch for him. Throughout JA's and Jefferson's diplomatic tenure in Europe, Montgomery regularly reported on the Barbary corsairs' movements, plague conditions in Spain, and the plight of the American captives in Algiers. His brother John also petitioned JA on his behalf, writing on 16 Feb. 1790 and 28 June (both Adams Papers). George Washington nominated Robert Montgomery as consul at Alicante on 19 Feb. 1793. He was confirmed by the Senate the next day and served until his death in 1823 (Jefferson, *Papers*, 11:376; Franklin, *Papers*, 26:242; U.S. Senate, *Exec. Jour.*, 2d Cong., 2d sess., p. 130, 131; Philadelphia *National Gazette*, 21 Feb. 1824).

From Roger Sherman

Sir— New York July 20th. 1789

I was honored with your letters of the 17th. & 18 Inst. And am much obliged to you for the observations they contain— The Subject of Government is an important one, and necessary to be well understood, by the citizens & especially by the legislators of these States. I Shall be happy to receive further light on the Subject, and to have any errors that I may have entertained corrected.

I find that writers on government differ in their difinition of a *Republic*. Entick's Dictionary defines it, "*A commonwealth, without a King*" I find you do not agree to the negative part of his definition.[1] What I meant by it was—a government under the authority of the people—consisting of legislative, executive and judiciary powers, the legislative powers vested in an assembly consisting of one or more branches, who together with the executive are appointed by the people, and dependent on them for continuence by ~~frequent~~ periodical elections, agreably to an established Constitution, and that what especially denominates it a *Republic*, is its dependence on the *public* or *people* at large without any hereditary powers. But it is not of so much importance by what appellation the government is distinguished, as to have it well constituted to Secure the rights, and advance the happiness of the Community.— I fully agree with you Sir, that it is optional with the people of a State, to establish any form of Government they please, to vest the powers, *in one*, *a few* or *many*, and for a limited or unlimited time, and the individuals of the State will be bound to yield obedience to such government while it continues; but I am also of opinion that they may alter their frame of government when they please, any former act of theirs, however explicit to the contrary notwithstanding.

But what I principally have in view is to submit to your consideration the reasons that have inclined me to think that the qualified negative given to the Executive by our constitution is better than an absolute negative:— In Great Britain where there are the rights of the nobility as well as the rights of the common people to Support, it may be necessary that the Crown should have a compleat negative to preserve the balance;—but in a *Republic* like ours, wherein is no higher rank than that of common citizens, unless distinguished by appointment to office—what occasion can there be for such a balance? It is true that some men in every Society, have natural and acquired abilities Superiour to others, and greater wealth. yet these give them no legal claim to offices in preference to others, but will doubtless give them some degree of influence, and justly, when they are men of integrity, and may procure them appointments to places of trust in the government, yet they having only the Same common rights with the other citizens what competition of Interests can there be to require a balance? besides while the real estates are divideable among all the children, or other kindred in equal degree, and Entails are not admitted, it will operate as an agrarian law, and the influence arising from great estates in a few hands or families, will not exist to such a degree of extent or duration as to form a System, or have any great effect.

In order to trace moral effects to their causes & *vice versa*—it is necessary to attend to principles as they operate on mens minds.— Can it be expected that a chief Magistrate of a free and enlightened people on whom he depends for his election and continuance in office, would give his negative to a law passed by the other two branches of the legislature if he had power? But the qualified negative given to the Executive by our Constitution, which is only to produce a revision, will probably be exercised on proper Occasions, and the legislature have the benefit of the President's reasons in their further deliberations on the Subject, and if a sufficient number of the members of either house should be convinced by them to put a negative upon the Bill it would add weight to the Presidents opinion & render it more Satisfactory to the people.— but if two thirds of the members of each house after considering the reasons offered by the President Should adhere to their former opinion, will not that be the most Safe foundation to rest the decision upon? on the whole it appears to me that the *power* of a compleat negative if given would be a dormant and useless one and that the provision in the constitution is calculated to operate with proper weight, and will produce beneficial effects.

The negative vested in the Crown of Great Britain has never been exercised since the revolution, and the great influence of the Crown in the legilature of that Nation is derived from another Source, that of appointment to all offices of honor & profit, which has rendered the power of the Crown nearly absolute.— So that the Nation is in fact governed by the Cabinet Council, who are the creatures of the Crown, the consent of Parliament is necessary to give Sanction to their measures, and this they easily obtain by the influence aforesaid.

If they should carry their points so far as directly to affect personal Liberty or private property the people would be alarmed and oppose their progress. but this forms no part of their System, the principal object of which is *revenue*, which they have carried to an enormous height. Where ever the chief Magisgrate may appoint to offices without controul, his government, may become absolute or at least oppressive. therefore the concurrence of the Senate, is made requisite by our Constitution.

I have not time or room to add, or apologive. I am with great respect your obliged humble Servant Roger Sherman

RC (Adams Papers); internal address: "The Vice President of the United States"; endorsed by CA: "Mr Sherman / July 20"; notation by CFA: "1789."

[1] John Entick, *The New Spelling Dictionary*, London, 1772.

To Peter Cunningham

Dear Sir New York July 21. 1789

I have received your favor of the thirteenth of this month, from the hand of Mr McGuire, and am much obliged to you for the information of your welfare, and the situation of your family.[1] A country life like yours, retired on a farm is sedom acceptable to a man educated in a city and accustomed to the sea: and therefore your inclination to return into the active world is no surprise to me. Yet there is more safety, more tranquility, and perhaps better prospects for your family, in your present course. What opening there may be, for the employment of your talents in the public service, I am not at present able to conjecture. But I should be obliged to you, if you would write me, in confidence an account of your former actions and services, which will at least be a pleasure to know, if I should never have an opportunity to make use of it to your advantage.

My Family consists of a daughter and three sons. The former is married to Col: Smith and has presented me with two grand sons. My Eldest son, John, is in the study of the law at Newburyport with Mr Parsons— Chas had his degree this month and is now with me— Thomas will take his degree next year.

By this detail you will see, what you knew however very well before that I am not a young man. But I shall never be too old to wish well to your prosperity and that of your family: being with great esteem, Yours J A

LbC in CA's hand (Adams Papers); internal address: "Peter / Cunningham Esqr / Pomphret"; APM Reel 115.

[1] Peter Cunningham (1750–1827), JA's first cousin, served aboard the Continental vessel *Hazard* during the Revolutionary War (*AFC*, 2:341–342). Cunningham, who was struggling as a farmer in Pomfret, Conn., wrote to JA applying for a naval post on 13 July (Adams Papers). He did not receive a post in the Washington administration, and this is the last extant letter between Cunningham and JA.

To Alexander Hamilton

Sir Richmond Hill July 21. 1789

Mr Charles Adams, my Second son, the Bearer of this Letter, I beg leave to introduce to you.— He took his degree at our University of Cambridge this Year, and is destined to the Study of the Law.— I wish to get him into some office in New York, and should give the Preference to yours[1]

But there are two Contingencies, one possible the other probable in the Way. The first is that Congress may force me to Philadelphia or the Lord knows where: the other that you may become a Minister of State, or some other Thing better or worse than the Practice of the Bar, but, however, incompatible with it.

As it is my Intention that my Son Shall board with me, he must follow, wherever Congress shall lead me— If you should leave the Bar, Some other Arrangement must be made for him.

He may go into Town, and come out, with me every day, and attend your Office, from between ten and Eleven, to between three and four. When Your Business presses, he may attend earlier or latter as you shall direct.

If you will take him into your Office immediately, Subject to these Contingencies, I shall be obliged to you, and ask the favour of you to mention to me your Terms. The Circumstances of my Family and Fortune will not permit me to be generous: but it is my determination, in every Circumstance of Life, to be just.— With great Esteem I have the Honour to be, sir your most / obedient Servant

John Adams.

RC (DLC:Alexander Hamilton Papers); internal address: "Col Hamilton."; endorsed: "21 July 1789 / John Adams"; notation: "COPIED." LbC (Adams Papers); APM Reel 115.

[1] Following his Harvard graduation in June, CA studied law with Hamilton from July to September (*AFC*, 8:334, 401). When Hamilton stepped in to serve as treasury secretary, CA removed to a new law office, for which see JA's letter of 19 Sept. to John Laurance, and note 1, below.

From Benjamin Rush

my dear friend, Philadelphia July 21st. 1789.

From an unfortunate concurrence of circumstances, I find myself under the influence of the same difficult command in corresponding with the Vice President of the United states, which the King of Syria gave to the Captains of his chariots.—

"Fight ye not with small or great, save only with the KING of Israel."—[1]

The subjects upon which we differ are *monarchy—titles*—& the *latin & greek languages*.

I repeat again that Republicanism has never yet had a fair tryal in the world.— It is now likely to be tried in the United states. Had our goverment been more completely ballanced; that is, had the President possessed more power, I believe it would have realised all the wishes of the most sanguine friends to republican liberty. Licentiousness—factions—Seditions & rebellions have not been restrained by monarchy even in Great Britain. They have been more numerous in that country than in any of the *less* free monarchies, or *more* free republics of Europe.— The factions—Seditions—& rebellions of Republics arise wholly from the want of checks or ballances, and from a defect of equal representation. The wisdom of modern times has discovered, & in part remedied these evils.— we may hope therefore that our republican forms of Goverment will be more safe, and durable than formerly. when we reject a republic, I wish we may adopt an absolute monarchy, for Goverments (like women among whom it is said no One, between a virtuous woman & a prostitute ought ever to please) should know no medium between absolute ~~freedom~~ Republicanism & Absolute monarchy. There cannot be a greater absurdity than to connect together in one goverment, the *living* principle of liberty in the people with the *deadly* principle of tyranny in an heriditary monarch. They must in time with the best ballance in the world overset each other. They are created with implements of war in their hands. Fighting will be natural & necessary to each of them to preserve an existence. From a Variety of circumstances, the victory 99 times in an 100 will be in favor of the monarch—& hence will arise the annihilation of liberty.—

An hundred years hence absolute monarchy will probably be rendered necessary in our country by the corruption of our people. But why should we precipitate an event for which we are not yet prepared?— Shall I at five & twenty years of age, because I expect to be an old man—draw my teeth—put on artificial grey hairs & bend my back over a short cane?— no—I will enjoy the health & vigor of youth & manhood, and leave Old age to take care of itself.— I will do more. I will husband my health & vigor, & try to keep off Old Age as long as I can, by temperance, proper cloathing simple manners—and the practice of domestic Virtues.

The characters you so much admire among the ancients were formed wholly by republican forms of goverments.—

Republican forms of goverment are more calculated to promote Christianity than monarchies. The precepts of the Gospel, and the maxims of republics in many instances agree with each Other.

Please to take notice that when I speak of a Republic, I mean a Goverment consisting of *three* branches, and each derived at different times & for different periods from the PEOPLE. Where this circulation is wanting between rulers & the ruled, there will be an obstruction to genuine goverment. A king or a Senate not chosen by the people at certain periods becomes a sebimus—a Bubo or an Abscess in the body politic which must sooner or later destroy the healthiest State.—

A simple democracy, or an unballanced republic is one of the greatest of evils. I think with Dr Zubly that "a Democracy (with only one branch) is the Tevils own governement." These words he uttered at my table in the Spring of 1776, upon my giving as a toast the "commonwealth of America."[2] At the same instant that he spoke these words, he turned his glass upside downwards, and refused to drink the toast.

I have no objection to men being accosted by the titles which they derive from their Offices. Mr President—M^r^ vice president—senator—Councillor Judge—or even Constable—may all be used with propriety, but why should we prefix *noble*, *honourable*—or *elective* to them?— Such epithets are a transgression of a rule in composition which forbids us to use unnecessary adjectives, inasmuch as they always enfeeble the sense of a Sentence. I cannot think with you that titles overawe or restrain the profligate part of a Community. The very Atmosphere of London is impregnated with the sounds of "my Lord"—"my Lady," "Right honourable"—"your honor"—"Sir John & Sr. James," and yet where will you find more profligate manners than among the citizens of London?— The use of titles begets pride in rulers & baseness among the common people.— Among the Romans whom you so much admire, Cæsar was Cæsar—& Scipio was Scipio in all companies.— The conquered provinces I believe first introduced titles. Among the Quakers the highest degrees of order are preserved without titles.— But if we begin with titles in the United States, where will they end? A new Vocabulary must be formed to provide for all the officers of the federal & state goverments, for the states still retain the power of creating titles. If titles are given to Men must not the women be permitted to share in them? By what rule shall we settle precedency? Shall a law, or a title Office be necessary for this purpose?— In a word my friend, I see no end to the difficulties—disputes—and Absurdities of admitting titles into our Country. They are equally contrary to reason and religion, and in my opinion are no more necessary to give dignity or energy to a Goverment, than Swearing is to govern a Ship's crew, or Spirituous liquors to gather in the fruits of the earth.—

Upon the Subject of the latin & greek languages I shall only ask two questions.—

who are guilty of the greatest Absurdity, the Chinese who press the feet into deformity by small Shoes, or the Europeans & americans who press the brain into Obliquity by Greek & Latin?—

Do not men use Latin & Greek as the scuttlefish emit their ink on purpose to conceal themselves from an intercourse with the common people?

Indeed my friend I owe nothing to the Latin & greek Classicks, but the turgid & affected stile of my youthful compositions, & a neglect of English grammar. At 22 years of Age I read Lowth introduction to the Grammar of our language,[3] and Hume's history of England, as also some of Swift's Works. By means of these Authors, I learned to put words together, and If I possess at this time any knowledge of Stile or language, I owe it to my having nearly forgotten the Greek, and suspended for many years the delight with which I once read the Roman poets and historians.

I Often look back with regret upon the four years I spent at an Academy on the borders of maryland & Pennsylvania in learning the Latin & greek languages,—and had not my master (a pious Clergyman & an industrious farmer) taught me during those years the first principles & duties of Christianity, and at the same time given me habits of *labor*, which produced some knowledge in moral affairs, I should wish the memory of those years blotted out of my mind for ever.[4]

I expect to prevail in the United states in my Attempt to bring the dead languages into disrepute,—for my next Attack upon them shall be addressed to our American ladies.— They are not perverted by any prejudice upon this subject.— They will hear from me the language of reason and nature,—and their influence will render my opinions sooner or later universal. From the Character you Once gave me of Mrs Adams, & which I have had confirmed by all who have ever conversed with her, I anticipate Support from her in my Undertaking.

If the years spent in teaching boys the Greek & Roman mythology, were spent in teaching them Jewish Antiquities, and the Connection between the types & prophesies of the old testaments, with the events of the new, 'dont you think we should have less infidelity, and of course less immorality & bad goverment in the world?—

My friend the late Anthony Benezet—One of the greatest and best men that ever lived, used to say that "the height of all Charity was to bear with the Unreasonableness of Mankind."—[5] Men love ~~the splendor of~~ Royalty,—titles—and the Latin & Greek languages. They make wars—enslave their fellow creatures—distil—and drink Rum—*all* because they are not governed by REASON.

I have only to beg your pardon for the length of this letter, and to assure You that no difference of sentiment upon any subject can alter the respect and regard with which I am my D^{r} sir / Your sincere / friend

Benj$^{n:}$ Rush

RC (Adams Papers); endorsed: "Dr Rush. July 21. / ans^{d} 24. 1789."

[1] 1 Kings, 22:31.

[2] A native of St. Gall, Switzerland, John Joachim Zubly (1724–1781) was the founding pastor of the Independent Presbyterian Church in Savannah, Ga. Zubly, a loyalist who favored Anglo-American reconciliation and served as a delegate to the Continental Congress, was briefly banished from Georgia for sending secret political reports to the royal governor, Sir James Wright (vol. 4:353; *Biog. Dir. Cong.*).

[3] Robert Lowth, *A Short Introduction to English Grammar*, London, 1762.

[4] Rush's early teacher was his uncle, the Calvinist clergyman Samuel Finley (1715–1766), who operated a school in West Nottingham, Md., and later served as president of Princeton College (Rush, *Letters*, 1:2, 9).

[5] French-born abolitionist Anthony Benezet (1713–1784), a Huguenot refugee, converted to Quakerism while living in London. He immigrated to Philadelphia in 1731 and worked as a teacher, establishing an evening school for the city's African-American population in 1750. An advocate of pacifism and temperance, Benezet wrote influential antislavery essays in the 1760s and 1770s; several of his works are in JA's library at MB (*DNB*; *Catalogue of JA's Library*).

To Roger Sherman

Dear Sir New York. July 22. 1789

As the Citizens of these States, are all Legislators, or Creators of Legislators, it is, as you observe in your favour of the 20th., necessary that Government Should be well understood by them. it is necessary too that We Should understand it alike. That We should all agree in Principles, and the essential Parts of Systems. to this end it is necessary that We understand each others Language, and agree in the deffinitions of Terms, especially Words of Art. if We do not, our Intercourse with each other, will be a Series of political fraud. for Example. The Constitution, Art. 4. Sect. 4. Says "The United States Shall guarantee, to every State in this Union, a Republican form of Government." in order to determine, what is the meaning of the Word Republican, We must enquire what is a Republick? Look into Entick's or Perry's dictionary.[1] They define it "a Commonwealth without a King"— Look into Johnson and Sherridan. They define it "A State, in which the Power is lodged in more than one.["]— The Readers of Entick, will therefore understand that the Constitution renders it their Duty to be King killers— The Readers of Johnson, will understand that the Constitution has guaranteed to them the Rights of their Ancestors, and the Solid Blessings of English Liberty. Is this Government, my Friend? or is it Paper Money? Is it thus that We are to cheat or be cheated? Let Us take a little pains to understand one another, and then to make ourselves understood by the People.— You and I, will never be reproached, by the People that We have deceived them. The Deffinition of Entick and Perry, is as ignorant as the pedantical Schoolmasters who made it.— All Writers ancient and modern from Plato and Aristotle, all Courts present and passed—all the Universities of the World, are against them.— all these Authorities have ever agreed, that Lacedemon was a Republic, tho it had, for Seven hundred Years, hereditary Kings: that Poland is a Republic, tho it has a King: and that England is a Republick tho it has hereditary Kings.

But, Sir, are Words to be abused in this manner? if our popular Government is to be conducted by the *Abuse of Words* We are undone.— The vicious Part of the Community, will avail itself of this Instrument of Government, more than the Virtuous. Are We, employing another *Abuse of Words* in the Name President.? Are Americans So Simple, as to be amused with a Name.? The Prince of orange Said to me, in March 1788 "Sir You are going to have a King under, the Title of President."[2] This Princes Judgment, upon this Occasion, would be approved by Sidney and Harrington, Cicero and Livy, Plato and Aristotle, every one of whom, upon reading our Constitution would pronounce the President, a King—[3]

Dft (Adams Papers); docketed by JA: "Republicks."

[1] William Perry, *Royal Standard English Dictionary*, Worcester, Mass., 1788.

[2] For JA's final audience at The Hague with William V, on 7 March 1788, see vol. 19:284–285.

[3] JA never sent this Dft, likely opting to continue the conversation when he dined with Sherman on 28 Aug. 1789 (Sherman to JA, 21 Aug., MHi:Adams-Hull Coll.).

From Jabez Bowen

Sir— Providence July 22d. 1789

I was honoured with your favour of the 18th. of June[1] for which I return you my Thanks, and was happy to hear of the safe arival of Mrs Adams and family.

our Rulers continue as obstinately opposed to the Federal Government as ever, and I have no Idea that they ever intend to call a Convention; they are striving to alienate the minds of the people at large by exagerating the amount of the Salleries allowed the Members of Congress, and take hold of every Topick that in any measure answers their wicked purposes; I am still of opinion if Congress could send and Enquire of the State in a pretty plain & firm Tone the Reason why they do not take up the great Question of the Constitution in the mode Recommended by the Grand Convention and the Resolve of Congress, that it would stagger their *Mermadons*; and occasion the people to look to the Minority to get them out of the Dillemma they are now in.

In Establishing the Judiciary System; was in hopes to have seen some stroke that would have saved the publick & private Securities of the Inhabitants of this State that have been obliged to put them off in other States to save them. I see no remedy if the Bill pass as first proposed.

This will be Delivered you by the Rever'd Mr Hitchcock, who I Recommend to your particular Notice as a worthy Character in the Clerical line.[2] your noticing him will be obligeing one who with every sentiment of Esteeme Remains your Excellencys Most obedient and humb. Servant

Jabez Bowen

RC (Adams Papers); endorsed by CA: "Govenor Bowen / July 22"; notation by CFA: "1789."

[1] Bowen likely meant JA's letter of 26 June, above, for no letter of 18 June has been found.

[2] Enos Hitchcock (1745–1803), Harvard 1767, of Springfield, Mass., had served as minister of the First Congregational Church in Providence, R.I., since 1 Oct. 1783. In his Fourth of July oration of 1788, Hitchcock urged Rhode Islanders to ratify the Constitution and thereby join "an entire revolution in policy and government, the most important that ever marked the progress of human society" (*Sibley's Harvard Graduates*, 16:475, 479, 480, 482, 483).

From James Sullivan

Sir

Boston 23d July 1789

I have to acknowledge the honor of receiving your Letter dated the 14th July. as to the subject respecting an opposition to the constitution of the united states, there are no doubt men in every society whose desperate Fortunes render them alike Enemies to all Government, but the people with very few exceptions, and these by no means important consider the Government of the united states as the palladium of their Liberty and a System which at all events is to be supported. there are in it imperfections which we all wish to have cured and hope that Wisdom and Experience will point us to the remedy— That matter of Trial by Juries I must always repeat is a matter of consequence with me. but should the Executive Legislative and Judicial powers be properly balanced the security of trial by Jury would grow out of that balance naturally. if there is an objection against that balance of power in the minds of the people of this Country, it has arisen from the Exorbitant power of the Crown while we were a part of the british Empire. perhaps as we had no representative in Parliment the reasoning is wrong to conclude that an Executive power here possessing the same prerogatives as a King there did would be dangerous to us, but will not Time and reasoning bring all right?

we are a young nation; and I conceive that the several separate powers will gain strength from time to Time as the Limbs in an animal gain strength and proportion by age, and that there will see a period (God give it Soon) when the Constitution of the united States will arrive at compleat perfection and will after in Time like that of other Countries decline: but in the mean time every aid will be given by the patriots which can be applied without convulsing the whole frame. perhaps in this moment when such an intire confidence is placed by the people in the men at the head of Government many Masterly and [Efficaous] strokes may be given to insert in some measure the equlibrium wanting

we have nothing new here all is peace quietness & patient Expectation for blessings which no form of Government can bestow.

I am Sir with sincere / friendship to you & your Lady / To whom pray present my Comp$^{ts.}$ / Your most obedient Humble / Servant

Ja Sullivan

This Days paper is inclosed[1] tomorrows I have ordered to be thrown into the mail

RC (Adams Papers); internal address: "His Excellency Mr Adams"; endorsed by CA: "Judge Sullivan / July 23^{d}" and by JA: "ans$^{d.}$ sept. 21. 1789."

[1] The enclosure has not been found.

To Jeremy Belknap

Dear Sir New York July 24. 1789

I have, this morning received your Letter of the 18$^{th.}$, George Chalmers, I have Seen in London. He is a Scot, who adventured to Maryland and practised Law,. When Hostilities commenced, he fled to the British Army in N. York. He has much of the Scornful, fastidious Temper of his nation; has been a very bitter Tory: but is a laborious writer. There is no Second Volume of his Annals, and as he has had the Art of obtaining Some Employment under the present Ministry, I Suppose it probable, that he will neither find Profit nor Pleasure to tempt him, to labour longer at Annals.

Mr Fenno asked my Leave to publish the Letters to Kalkoen, and I consented.— There was never any other Reason for printing them, more than a dozen Volumes of others, but this, that the originals of them, were on loose Papers, instead of proper Letter Books; and consequently in continual danger of being lost.—[1] Mr Jay has Surprized me, Since I came here, by Shewing me, Six folio Volumes of my dispatches to Congress, recorded in a beautiful hand. He has taken the Same prudent Care of the Dispatches of all the other American Ministers abroad—so that this branch of our History is well Secured.— Private Letters however, are often wanted as Commentaries on publick ones.— and many I fear will be lost, which would be necessary to shew the Secret Springs.[2]

There are Several Circumstances, which I wish were preserved Somewhere, of much Importance, to this End, which are in danger of being lost—respecting the *opposition to Bernard and Hutchinson* and British Ministers and Measures in the Massachusetts—to the *formation of the Union of the Colonies* in 1774—to the *organization of our Army in 1775*—To the *Negotiations in France, and Holland*—and to many other Events.

some of these ought not to be public, but they ought not to be lost.— My Experience, has very much diminished my Faith in the Veracity of History.— it has convinced me, that many of the most important facts are concealed.— some of the most important Characters, but imperfectly known—many false facts imposed on Historians and the World—and many empty Characters displayed in great Pomp.— All this I am Sure will happen in our American History.

The Idea, that a Party or Faction should demolish thirteen, established Governments, and erect as many new ones, in opposition to the Sense of the People, and in opposition to large Armies and powerful Fleets, is ridiculous.—

The Anecdote of Baron De Kalb, that you enquire after, never came to my Knowledge.— De Kalb was in America, before the War, and not long after the Peace of 1763, but it was accidental; owing to shipwreck as I have heard—very probably he might make Such a Report that the Americans were indissolubly attached to England to the French Ministry: but I dont believe he ever was sent by them.

After the Loss of Canada, the vast Addition to the naval Power and commercial Advantages of England, allarmed the French very much and there is no doubt, that the thought of assisting the British Colonies to throw off the yoke, occurred to them—as the Loss of America now rankling in the hearts and tingling in the Veigns of the English nation, is every day suggesting to them, Projects of Assisting the Spaniards of South America to Seperate from Spain. Monsieur Le Roi, a french Accademician, who had been acquainted with Dr

Franklin in England, upon introducing him at Paris to some Members of the Accademy of Sciences, Said *Voila Monsieur Frankland, qui est de ce Pays la en Amerique, qui nous debarrassera, un jour de ces Angloises.*[3] This Le Roi told me in Presence of Franklin who Said he remembered it very well.— This sentiment I doubt not had its Influence in procuring Franklin to be elected a Member of that Accademy.— But it was a vague tho general Presentiment—and no explicit Advances were ever made to him or any one else by the French Court, till 1775.—

I Shall have more occasion for Apology than you have, if I proceed. The oftener you write me, and the more you enquire of me the more you will oblige, sir your / most obedient John Adams

RC (MHi:Jeremy Belknap Papers); internal address: "The Rev^d. Mr Belknap."; endorsed: "John Adams July 24. 1789." LbC (Adams Papers); APM Reel 115.

[1] JA's *Twenty-six Letters, Upon Interesting Subjects, Respecting the Revolution of America* was printed in London in 1786. John Fenno printed JA's sixth letter to the Amsterdam lawyer Hendrik Calkoen in his *Gazette of the United States*, 22 April 1789. By June Fenno had issued the first of two American editions, and he also reprinted the letters in his newspaper between 14 Oct. and 26 Dec. (vol. 10:199).

[2] For John Jay's archiving of diplomatic correspondence, see vol. 19:125, 126, 162.

[3] French physicist Jean Baptiste Leroy (1720–1800), a member of the Académie royale des sciences since 1751, conducted electricity experiments with Benjamin Franklin at Passy. The U.S. minister to France, who steered Leroy's 15 Jan. 1773 election to the American Philosophical Society, found Leroy to be a key supporter of the patriot cause. As JA recalled Leroy's quip: "Here is Mr. Franklin, who is from that country of America, which will one day rid us of those English" (*AFC*, 3:183; Franklin, *Papers*, 8:359, 19:278; Hoefer, *Nouv. biog. générale*).

To Benjamin Rush

My dear Friend New York July 24. 1789

I have persecuted you, too much with my Letters.— I beg you would give yourself no trouble to answer them, but when you are quite at Leisure, from more important Business or more agreable Amusement.

I deny; that there is or ever was in Europe a more free Republic than England, or that any Liberty on Earth ever equalled English Liberty, notwithstanding the defects in their Constitution.

The Idea of admitting absolute Monarchy into this Country, either in this or the next Century Strikes me with horror. a little Wisdom at present, may preserve a free Government in America, I hope for ever—certainly for many Centuries.

I agree with you, that hereditary Monarchy and hereditary Aristocracy, ought not yet to be attempted in America—and that three ballanced Branches, ought to be at Stated Periods elected by the People. This must and will and ought to continue, till Intrigue and Corruption Faction and Sedition Shall appear in those Elections to Such a degree as to render hereditary Institutions a Remedy against a greater Evil.

I learned in my Youth, from one of my Preceptors. Vattel. B.2. c.3 ss.41. that "a Nation may grant to its Conductor, what degree of Authority and what rights it thinks proper: it is equally free, in regard to the Name, the Titles, and honours, with which it would decorate him. But *it is agreable to its Wisdom, and of Importance to its Reputation, not to deviate, in this respect, too much from the Customs' commonly received among civilized Nations.* Let Us Still observe, that it ought to be directed there by Prudence, to proportion titles and honours to the Power of its Superiour and to the Authority with which it would invest him. Titles and Honours, it is true, determine nothing; they are vain names and vain Ceremonies when they are ill placed: but who does not know the Influence they have, on the Thoughts of Men? *This is then a more Serious Affair than it appears at the first glance.* The Nation ought not to degrade its conductor, by too low a Title. it ought to be Still more careful not to Swell his heart with a vain name, by unbounded honours; So as to make him conceive the Thoughts of arrogating to himself a Power answerable to them, or to acquire a proportionable Power by unjust Conquests. on the other hand, an important Title may engage the Conductor, to Support with greater firmness the Dignity of a Nation. Conjunctures determine the Prudence which observes in every Thing a just Proportion."[1] All the Reading Observation and Reflection of thirty or 35 Years, have confirmed these Truths in my mind.

Among the Romans Scipio was Imperator, and Cæsar was Pontifex Maximus.— They were Tribunus Sacer, Pater conscriptus, and Patronus excellentissimus, on all Occasions, and the Prolocutor of the Senate, was Prince of the Senate. There is not a grosser Error, in the World, than the common saying that the Romans had no Titles.

We come now to your Question, which has great Weight and solidity. "If We begin with Titles where will they end?" it is true, as you Say, "the States Still retain the Power of creating Titles." or at least they may claim it.— You ask another very important and difficult Question "By what Rule Shall We Settle Precedency.?["]

I will neither undertake to answer, Where We shall end, nor to determine the Rule— But this I will venture to say, that We never shall have, either Government or Tranquility or Liberty, untill Some

Rule of Preceedency is adopted, and some Titles settled. The question is not whether Titles shall be admitted into our Country. They are already in it, and you will annihilate the Nation before you will eradicate them.— The question is whether Provincial, Titles or Diplomatic Titles, can preserve or Acquire Consideration at home or abroad to a national Government.— I totally deny that there is any Thing in Reason or Religion against Titles proportional to Ranks and Trusts. and I affirm, that they are indispensably necessary to give Dignity and Energy to Government— and on this ground alone I am an Advocate for them. in my private Character, I despise them as much at least as any Quaker, or Philosopher on Earth.

You may depend on being the Contempt, the Scorn and the Derision of all Europe, while you call your national Condutor, General or President— You may depend on another Thing—the State Governments will ever be upper most, in America in the Minds of our own People, till you give a Superiour Title to your first national Magistrate.

The most modest Title you can give him, in any reasonable Proportion, to the Wealth, Power and Population of this Country and to the constitutional Authority and Dignity of his office is "His Majesty, the President." This is my opinion, and I Scorn to be hypocrite enough to disguise it.— Miracles will not be wrought for Us. We dont deserve them.— if We will have Government, We must Use human and natural means. Titles and Ranks are as essential to Government, as Reason and Justice.— in short government is nothing else but Titles Ceremonies and Ranks. They alone enable Reason to produce Justice.

I am with Usual Esteem and regard / dear sir your

John Adams

RC (MB:John Adams MS Coll.); internal address: "D[r] Rush."; endorsed: "Jn[o.] Adams." LbC (Adams Papers); APM Reel 115.

[1] Emmerich de Vattel, *The Law of Nations; or, the Principles of Natural Law*, London, 1759–1760, Book II, ch. iii, sec. 41, a copy of which, with significant annotations, is in JA's library at MB (*Catalogue of JA's Library*).

From John Brown Cutting

My Dear Sir Bordeaux 24th July 1789

By a vessel that departs from hence in half an hour bound for the Potowmack I send you some authentic papers which contain details of the late revolution in the government of France.[1] M[r] Jefferson's last letter to me is dated on the 16th. He confirms most of the facts contained in the printed letter of M. Nairac and in the "Extrait d'une lettre de Paris"—and concludes by remarking that tho' the people of Paris are still in such a heat in consequence of the late bloodshed that they distrust the royal word and continue arming—yet that he (Mr Jefferson) believes that the king is now perfectly sincere in his surrender at discretion to the states general and will do whatsoever they desire him.[2] All the troops that were lately assembled in the vicinity of Versailles and Paris are actually on their march to the frontier towns of the kingdom

The Queen, it is whisperd, has retired into a Convent of which she is foundress—for the present—near Versailles. Madam De Polinac has escaped to England. Count D'Artois has fled to his brother in law the King of Sardinia. The Condee's, Conte's Marschal de Broglio and those ministers and instruments of the court cabal who had the temerity to assemble forty thousand troops to overawe, or dissolve the states general and crush every hope of a thorough national reform have been most egregiously out-general'd and miserably defeated.[3] A number of those capital culprits will be impeach'd. The soldiers the subaltern officers, the inferior clergy the lower middling and opulent classes in the cities and many patent nobles and great land holders in the country are so united in sentiment upon this great occasion and the spirit of the nation is so hot for the measure that nothing can prevent it but a miraculous mitigation of the public temper. M. Neckar on the contrary and Count Montmorrin, the two honest ministers whose dismission from office of late exile was the signal of conflict between the Court and Country—will doubtless be re-instated[4]

On the 17th of July the King entered Paris guarded by the burgers only and the late President of the Commons, M. Bailly, now Mayor of Paris delivered to him the keys of that capital with a speech which I am told was to the following effect. "These keys that Henry the fourth restored to the City which he had conquer'd; in the name of the City are now restored to his descendent whom we have conquer'd."[5]

The Marquis La Fayette being nominated by the armed Burgers of Paris commander in chief of their forces the states general approved the appointment and the king countersigning his commission has confirmed it. At this moment it is unquestionably the first command in the nation. The most moderate accounts state the number of armed people in Paris at two hundred thousand.

The french troops for refusing to butcher their fellow citizens when that blind old bigot De Brolio,[6] instigated by a corrupt junto of courtesans and courtiers, not only commanded but endeavoured to seduce them to do it by an offer of the whole pillage of Paris—it is said have not only in general acquir'd credit but a part of them in particular have obtain'd renown and the universal applause of the country for their gallant deeds in behalf of their bleeding brethren the burgers, in whose ranks they fought till the mercenary germans were repuls'd and then led on the same city band to attack the arsenal and storm the bastile. In the display of this honourable generous and manly spirit which guided, emulated and guarded those neighbours whom they were commanded to slaughter the corps of french guards was greatly distinguish'd—especially in that daring assault of the bastile the success of which dismayed their enemies and still astonishes the nation. This same bastile is now level'd in the dust and razed to its lowest foundations. Most of the french guards I understand and many soldiers also of other royal regiments are now incorporated with the armd burgers of Paris who with reason love & cherish them and from whose associations they are never again to seperate. Perhaps this single circumstance may partly account for the immense number of parisians in arms—now under command of the Marquis. The same soul and spirit pervades the provinces—nor does it appear that in any quarter of the kingdom there exists the shadow of an opposition to the measures of the states general nor one murmur of sympathy in favour of the court or king.

In a word the monarch & his ministers mistook the temper of the times and grossly miscalculated both in despising the intrepidity of citizens and disbelieving the patriotism of soldiers. I rejoice that their error is as irretrievable as it is conspicuous. I rejoice that the people are triumphant—that the rights of man are asserted—that freedom prospers—that tyranny withers—and that despotism is dying—in France.

Will Mrs Adams and yourself have the goodness thus abruptly to accept my best compliments and believe me always to be / with unalterable affection / and respect / Your Most Obed Servt.

John Brown Cutting

RC and enclosure (Adams Papers); internal address: "John Adams Vice President of the United States."; endorsed: "Mr Cutting. 24. July / 1789."

[1] Cutting enclosed a copy of his 21 July letter to Thomas Jefferson, describing the opening stages of the French Revolution and the formation of the National Guard, the civil militia led by the Marquis de Lafayette to curb the "ferment" of street violence in

1. "ADIEU BASTILLE," 1789
See page xi

and around Paris. Cutting wrote: "I have seen and heard both in Paris and Bordeaux enough to convince me that the flame of liberty which is now kindled in France will consume every relic of feudal and papal tyranny that yet lingers within her confines together with the clumsy buttresses of unlimited prerogative: and that the genius of free government may spring like a phoenix from their ashes and permanently inhabit a new european edifice." Cutting sent this letter, one of the first comprehensive reports that JA received of the French Revolution, via the *Washington*, Capt. Bond, which reached New York City in late September (Jefferson, *Papers*, 15:293–296; *New-York Packet*, 8 Oct.). For the onset of the French Revolution, see Descriptive List of Illustrations, No. 1, above.

[2] Jefferson and others read an account of the chaos in Paris written and distributed by Paul Nérac, a deputy from Bordeaux. Cutting believed that Nérac's article, not found, briefly soothed the protesters, writing that its "moderating efficacy was immediately manifest. The patriots of Paris it appear'd had overcome diciplin'd mercenaries and cut the throats of a few obnoxious chieftains. But even had the event of that conflict prov'd otherwise nothing cou'd daunt or diminish the spirit of all ranks of people here in support of the national assembly, nor suppress open demonstrations of its fervency" (Jefferson, *Papers*, 15:293, 296).

[3] As mob violence mounted in the weeks following the Bastille's fall, King Louis XVI and Queen Marie Antoinette wove in and out of public view. Prominent members of the court, including Charles Philippe, Comte d'Artois, scattered abroad. On 15 July the king ordered Victor François, Marshal de Broglie (1718–1804), to move troops out of Paris (William Doyle, *The Oxford History of the French Revolution*, Oxford, 1989, p. 108, 110, 112, 122, 451).

[4] Royal advisors who urged Louis XVI to assent to the liberal restructuring of government powers under the June formation of the National Assembly now faced the king's purge. After being dismissed on 11 July, finance minister Jacques Necker was invited to return to his post five days later by order of the National Assembly. Armand Marc, Comte de Montmorin de Saint Herem, the foreign minister, was also dismissed but regained his post (Bosher, *French Rev.*, p. xvii, l, 128; John S. C. Abbott, *The French Revolution of 1789: As Viewed in the Light of Republican Institutions*, 2 vols., N.Y., 1887, 2:522).

[5] Jean Sylvain Bailly (1736–1793), who served as mayor of Paris from 1789 to 1791, presided over the 20 June Tennis Court Oath, which marked the National Assembly's formal creation and its public commitment to drafting a national constitution. After meeting with Bailly, Louis XVI proceeded to the Paris town hall, where he donned a tricolor cockade (Hoefer, *Nouv. biog. générale*; Bosher, *French Rev.*, p. xvii, 131, 133).

[6] JA socialized with Broglie in Paris in 1778–1779. Broglie was a cousin of the Chevalier de La Luzerne (JA, *D&A*, 2:295, 396; Hoefer, *Nouv. biog. générale*).

From James Lovell

My dear honoured Friend — Boston July 26th. 1789—

I had often considered your Situation, before the Receipt of your Letter of the 16th, and I had hoped you would "Possess yourself in *Patience*." If you already draw a Picture Teste di legno and talk of sharpening an Ax for Decapitation, what am I to look for in the Run of a Twelvemonth?

I do not like your diminutive italien Idea. You who are said to be more than half british ought to have called yourself a spare Rudder or Mainmast; and that would have given me a fine oppertunity to comment upon the *Parsimony* of those who will not pay for a *good* one when the Length and Risk of an Enterprise demand such a precautionary Duplicate. Once more however I recur to the Tëte-de-bois—tis a delphic one you must own; and you are to expect the *dilectable* Chance of being applied to in all Cases of *Difficulty*; I do not mean when the *Judgement* of the Senate is in *Reality* at Moieties, For, that will not be the Event one Time in Fifty, while 49 Times relative Contingencies of *Popularity* will balance the Votes and your oracular Decision will have the Praise or Blame. "You have decided in Favour of the *Power* of the Prime *because* you look up to that Goal." If I did not know you well I would not write thus to you. A *weak* Man only would be discouraged by such Suggestions of the Base. All whom you esteem here are pleased with your Vote. But better than that, I know you have your own Approbation upon your own Principles which lead regularly to *impavidum* ferient ruinæ.[1]

I feel at this Period redoubled mortifications that you was not at Home when I dined with your Lady and conversed with Doct[r.] Tufts upon the *Point of Time* when the continental Government was to affect our Laws of Revenue. He conceded to my Idea that we could not be deranged 'till the compleat Organization of Congress, when I expected a Proclamation from the President directing the Continuence of the offices & officers of the Confederation *till further orders*, and providing against any Derangements in the individual States, where the new Constitution might be naturally supposed to interfere—*till the legislative measures of Congress should be in Operation.*—

I have 8 or 9 Causes of Libels to be tried this Week some of them as high as twelve hundred pounds; and I am told most of the Bar are engaged together for mutual Assistance to defend upon the principle that *no Impost Law has been in Force here* since —— I know not when.

"Congress" are to have such and such Powers—"and to make all Laws which shall be necessary and proper for carrying into Execution the foregoing Powers and all other Powers vested by this Constitution in the Government of the United States"[2]

If these Seizures of mine are acquitted all the Duties I have collected in *the Period*, be it what it may, are to be refunded.— It was upon that Paragraph of the VIIIth Section, that I fixed for the Termination of my State Collection of Impost. what say the Merchants of N york or Philad[a.] respecting State Duties? Is it only here that Doubts exist? I can give only one of two Reasons why a Proclamation did not appear. The Idea at Head Quarters must have been either that Nobody could *suppose* we had a Right here to Impost or that nobody could *doubt* but that we had it— yet, in Fact, there is a *great Division of Sentiment* upon the Point.

I have directed the Attorney General to go forward by Demurrer or Appeal. And I had advised the supreme Judges to converse upon the Subject as they were riding the Eastern Circuit or smoaking their Evening Pipes together.

Have we *now* the Right of *Tender*? In my opinion the *Constitution* decides that without the necessity of any *Law* of Congress. Can a Pyrate be *now* tried? *our* Law is sufficient till congress *promulge* one. This last Principle avails in the Impost. Excuse my Impertinence in showing my Opinion, while I meant to intreat yours.

I salute You and your Lady and Family cordially. Pardon the Slovenlyness, I have detained the Postmaster already too long from his Office

Your devoted Friend James Lovell

RC (Adams Papers); endorsed: "M[r] Lovell. 26. July. Ans[d] / 1. sept[r.] 1789."

[1] "If the firmament were to split and crash down upon him, he would remain unafraid when hit by the wreckage" (Horace, *Odes and Epistles*, transl. Niall Rudd, Cambridge, 2004, Book III, Ode 3, lines 7–8).

[2] Here, in the left margin, Lovell wrote: "Sec VIII last paragraph." He referred to Art. 1, sect. 8, of the Constitution, known as the "elastic clause," which granted incidental powers to Congress, thereby strengthening the new federal government in a way that the Articles of Confederation had not done.

From Roger Sherman

Sir— New York July [27] 1789[1]

I received your letter of the 20th Inst. I had in mine of the Same date communicated to you my Ideas on that part of the constitution, limiting the Presidents power of negativing the acts of the legislature.— And just hinted some thoughts on the propriety, of the provision made for the appointment to offices, which I esteem to be a power nearly as important as legislation.

If that was vested in the President alone, he might were it not for his periodical election by the people—render himself despotic.— It was a Saying of one of the Kings of England. That while the King could appoint the Bishops and judges he might have what Religion and Law he pleased.

It appears to me the Senate is the most important branch in the government, for aiding & Supporting the Executive, Securing the rights of the individual States, the government of the united States, and the liberties of the people, The Executive Magistrate is to execute the laws, the Senate being a branch of the legislature will naturally incline to have them duly executed, and therefore will advise to Such appointments as will best attain that end.— from the knowledge of the people in the Several States, they can give the best information who are qualified for offices, and though they will as you justly observe in Some degree lessen his responsibility, yet their advice may enable him to make Such judicious appointments as to render responsibility less necessary—

The Senators being elegible by the legislatures of the Several States, and dependent on them for reelection will be vigilant in supporting their rights against infringement by the legislature or executive of the united States.— And the government of the union being federal, and Instituted by the several States for the advancement of their Interests, they may be considered as So many pillars to Support it. and by the exercise of the State governments, peace and good order may be preserved in places most remote from the Seat of the Federal government, as well as at the centre. And the Municipal and federal rights of the people at large will be regarded by the Senate, they being elected by the immediate representatives of the people, & their rights will be best Secured by a due execution of the laws.— what temptation can the Senate be under to partiality in the trial, of officers whom they had a voice in the appointment of, can they be disposed to favour a person who has violated his trust & their confidence? The other evils that you mention that may result from this power appear to me, but barely possible. The Senators will doubtless be in general Some of the most respectable citizens in the States for wisdom & probity, superiour to mean and unworthy conduct—and instead of undue influence to procure appointments for themselves or their friends, they will consider that a fair and upright conduct will have the best tendency to preserve the confidence of the people & of the States. They will be disposed to be diffident in recommending their friends & kindred, lest they Should be Suspected of partiality, and the other Members will feel the same kind of reluctance lest they Should be thought unduly to favour a person because related to a member of their body.— So that their friends and relations would not Stand so good a chance for appointment to offices according to their merit as others.

The Senate is a convenient *body* to advise the President from the Smalness of its numbers. And I think the laws would be better framed & more duly administred if the Executive and judiciary officers were in general members of the legislature, in case there Should be no interference as to the time of attending to their Several duties— this I have learned by experience in the government in which I live, & by observation of others differently constituted.

I See no principles in our constitution that have any tendency to Aristocracy, which if I understand the term, is, a government by Nobles independent of the people, which cant take place in either respect without a total Subversion of the Constitution. and as both branches of Congress are elegible from the Citizens at large & wealth is not a requisite qualification, both will commonly be composed of members of Similar Circumstances in Life. And I See no reason why the Several brancheses of the government Should not maintain the most perfect harmony, their powers being all directed to one end the advancement of the public good.

If the President alone was vested with the power of appointing all officers, and was left to Select a council for himself he would be liable to be deceived by flatterers and pretenders to Patriotism, who would have no motive but their own emolument, they would wish to extend the powers of the Executive to encrease their own importance, and however upright he might be in his intentions, there would be great danger of his being misled, even to the Subversion of the constitution, or at least to introduce such evils as to interrup the harmony of the government & deprive him of the confidence of the people. but I have Said enough upon these Speculative points, which nothing but experience can reduce to a certainty.

I have the honor to be / with great Esteem & Respect / Your obedient / humble Servant

RC (Adams Papers); internal address: "His Excellency John Adams Esquire"; endorsed: "Mr Sherman / July"; notation by CFA: "1789."

[1] Blank in MS. The dating of this letter is based on Sherman's retained copy (MHi:Foster Family Autograph Coll.).

From William Tudor

Dear Sir Boston 27 July 1789.

Our Citizens here disapprobate the Compensations, as they are called, which have passed the lower House of Congress. They generally think that the Salary of the Vice President should have been Ten thousand Dollars, A Guinea Per Diem for the Representatives, & six Dollars for a Senator. As it now stands, the first Sum is a Disgrace to the Government; & is here considered as arising from Party Views & illiberal Policy.[1]

The Constitution intended a Distinction in the Rank & Dignity of the Senate as being the Upper House of Congress, & that Difference, ought to be extended to Pay as well as to Place.

Our Profession are waiting with some Impatience for the Judicial Appointments. Mr. Dana & Mr. Lowell are supposed to be the Candidates for the Supreme Bench. Neither I believe (indeed the latter I know)[2] would not, accept the District. A certain Probate Judge is supposed to have taken great Pains to obtain this Post.[3] To no Person but to Yourself, unless my Letter to the President should be quoted against the assertion, have I ever hinted a Wish to be noticed in the Places that must soon be disposed of. But you will now give me leave to say that I should be pleased with an appointment to some Office (the Advocateship is now out of the Question) which my Education might enable me to discharge the Duties of. I am now advancing to forty, & as the Profession is at present circumstanced, the Spirits & Feelings are too often affronted, for a Gentleman not to wish a Removal from the Drudgery of earning, & the Mortification of asking for fees, which are now become paltry. More than this, on such a Subject, I ought not to say even to you, Sir. And less, at this Juncture, I might perhaps hereafter regret, to have communicated.

I am, Dr Sir, / yours Wm Tudor

RC (Adams Papers); internal address: "Vice President Adams."

[1] After lengthy debate, on 24 Sept. Congress passed the Compensation Act, which set the president's annual salary at $25,000 and the vice president's at $5,000. On 28 Aug. the House approved a bill to pay all members of Congress $6 a day (vol. 19:416; Bickford and Bowling, *Birth of the Nation*, p. 21; U.S. Senate, *Jour.*, 1st Cong., 1st sess., p. 65–66).

[2] Closing parenthesis has been editorially supplied.

[3] Nathan Cushing.

To Benjamin Rush

Dear Sir Richmond Hill July 28. 1789

"The Characters, I So much admire among the ancients," were not "formed wholly by Republican forms of Government"—[1] I admire, Phillip and Alexander, as much as I do Themistocles and Pericles, nay as much as Demosthenes— I admire Pisistratus, almost as much as solon: and think that the Arts, Elegance, Literature and Science of Athens, was his Work and that of his sons, more than of any or all the popular Commanders or oraters.

The two Republicks of Antiquity, that I most admire are Sparta and Rome, and these were both monarchical Republicks.— Athens indeed was ballanced, with great Care and some Art, till Aristides overturned the Constitution to make himself popular, and acquire the Title of just, so that I think the Man who voted to ostracise him because he was called just by the Mob, was a Man of Sense, Spirit and Virtue.—

You doubt whether Titles overawe the profligate.— You ask where do I find more profligate manners, than among the Citizens of London?— I am almost disposed to answer You, by Saying, in Boston, in New York, in Philadelphia.— I assure You, my friend I wish my dear Countrymen had less Vanity and more Pride. The Advantages We have, over Europe, are chiefly geographical— I see very little moral or political Preference.— as far as I can judge there is as much Vice, Folly, and more Infidelity Idleness Luxury and Dissipation, in any of our great Towns, in Proportion to Numbers, as in London.— But the Question Should be what would be, the degree of Profligacy in London, if there were no Titles? and I Seriously believe it would be much greater than it is.— Nay I dont believe it would be possible to Support any Government at all, among Such Multitudes without Distinctions of Rank and the Titles that mark them.— According to what I have Seen in England, as well as France Holland Spain and Germany, there is nothing Strikes and overawes the most abandoned of the Populace so much as Titles.

Whether Titles beget Pride in Rulers, or not is not an Argument.— Would you reject every Thing that begets Pride? if you do you must reject Virtue, which begets the most exquisite, exalted and unconquerable Pride.— You must reject Laws, Government, offices of all Kind, and even Religion. Spiritual Pride, has grown out of Religion. Would you reject religion.—

Men who will be made proud by a Title, will be made so by an office without a Title.—

But Why Should Titles beget Baseness among the common People?— Respect, Reverence, Submission and Obedience to the Laws and lawful Magistrates You would wish to see both in the virtuous and vicious of the common People. if Obedience cannot be obtained from the vicious without begetting Baseness, by which I suppose you mean fear, why should you object to that.— But Titles have no Tendency to beget Baseness in poor Men who are virtuous, more than offices without Titles.— But I must insist that Laws are made and Magistrates appointed on Purpose, to create Fear, & Terror in the Minds of the vicious, and if Titles will Save you the Expence of Gallows, Stocks Whipping Posts, or the Pain of employing them, why not Use them? if Titles will do instead of Armies and Navies, or any Part of them, why reject them? Dont the Gallows beget Baseness in the common People?— Would you have no Gallows? dont a prison beget Baseness? Would you have no Prison?— dont all Sorts of Punishments beget Baseness? would you abolish all Punishments?

You Say the conquered Provinces first introduced Titles into the Roman Empire.— But in this I believe you are mistaken.— had the Kings of Rome, no Titles?— Vir amplissimus—Vir Clarissimus. Vir amplissimus Consul.— Vir Summus. These were familiar among them, in the Simplest times.

Historians indeed never use Titles.— but Titles were Used in Life, and had their Influence.—

1 The Romans conferred Titles very early, e.g. Manlius, Capitolinus, and very late as Scipio Africanus.— These Titles, were very common and had great Influence, for they carried with them the Ideas of Tryumphs and Glory, beyond any Titles in our Times.

2 They managed their Agnomen, Cognomen and Nomen in a manner, to influence the People, as much as our Titles.— Cicero tells us, what was their Custom "Nomen cum dicimus, cognomen quoque et agnomen, intelligatur, oportet."[2]

1 The Prænomen was, our Christian Name. 2. The Nomen was the Name of a Race, or Gens.— as all descended from Julus the son of Eneas the son of Venus, were called Julii, and were accounted divine. 3. The Cognomen distinguished different Families of the Same Race. for Gens signified the whole and Familia a Part.— Those of the Same Gens were called Gentiles, (whence our Word Genteel and Gentleman)— Those of the Same Family Agnati. 4 The Agnomen, like Scipio Africanus and Scipio Asiaticus, has been mentioned before.— Julius Signified the Gens and Cæsar the Familia.

As these Families and Races, happened to be of consular Prætorian, or Tribunitian Dignity, or even only of patrician Dignity, their names carried more Influence, than the Titles of Princes, Dukes, Marquises, Earls Barons do at this day in Europe, for We must always recollect, that these Families and Offices were all consecrated: and consequently Struck the Roman Mind which was certainly more Superstitious, if not more religious than ours, with an holy Awe.— in order to form some Idea of the religious Veneration, approaching to Adoration, which the Roman Policy inspired into the Minds of their Citizens towards their Magistracies and the Races and Families which exercised them We must recollect their, Leges Sacratæ. and what was a Lex Sacrata? Sacratæ leges Sunt, (inquit Festus) quibus Sancitum est, qui quid adversus eas fecerit, Sacer alicui deorum Sit, cum familia, pecuniaque.—[3] There were several of these Sacred Laws, by which all their Magistrates were protected. The Lex Sacrata, passed upon the holy Mountain, for the Security of the Tribunes, is in Dionysius as follows "Tribunum nemo in ordinem redigito, neque invitum quidquam facere cogito, nec verberato, nec alium verberare jubeto. Si quis contra fecerit, Sacer esto, et bona ejus Cereri Sacra Sunto: et qui eum occiderit, purus a cæde esto.— hanc legem omnes juraverunt Seque et Posteros in Sempiternum observaturos.["]—[4] only consider the Effect of taking an Oath by all the People to observe this Law.

Now sir, I contend, that as Consuls, Præters, Tribunes &c were consecrated Officers, the Title of Sacrosanctus belonged to them all, and was little short of that of Sacred Majesty.— I Say farther that Patres Conscripti, was an higher Title than My Lords, or most Honourable, and that the Names of Sacred Gentes, et Familiæ, had greater Influence among the Romans than modern European Titles.

Never Let me again hear the Romans quoted, as neglecting or despizing Titles.— if I do, I will persecute You with more latin. Yours affectionately John Adams

RC (MB:John Adams MS Coll.); addressed: "Dr: Benjamin Rush / Philadelphia"; internal address: "Dr Rush."; endorsed: "Mr Adams."; docketed: "Mr Adams to / Dr." LbC (Adams Papers); APM Reel 115.

1 JA was quoting from Rush's letter of 21 July, above.

2 When I say name, it should be understood that both the cognomen and the agnomen are included (Cicero, *De Inventione*, Book II, lines 24–25).

3 "Sacred laws are laws that have the sanction that he who breaks them becomes accursed to one of the gods, together with his family and property" (Festus, *The Beginnings of Rome: Italy and Rome from the Bronze Age to the Punic Wars, c. 1000 to 264* B.C., transl. T. J. Cornell, Oxford, 1995, p. 449).

4 "Let no one compel a tribune of the people, as if he were an ordinary person, to do anything against his will; let no one whip him or order another to whip him. If anybody shall do any one of these things that are forbidden, let him be accursed and let his goods be consecrated to Ceres; and if anybody shall kill one who has done any of these things, let him be guiltless of murder" (Dionysius of Halicarnassus, *The Roman Antiquities*, transl. Earnest Cary, 20 vols., Cambridge, 1943, 6:89).

From Francis Dana

Dear Sir Cambridge July 31st: 1789

I did not receive your very obliging favour of the 10th: inst: till yesterday, when I returned from the eastern Circuit. I have heard that the Judicial bill has been passed in the Senate without any alterations respecting the general plan of the judicial system. But you seem to think great changes may be made in it in the house of Representatives—that the district Judges may be annihilated altogether, and the number of Supreme Judges as well as the number of Circuits doubled. It appears to me indispensably necessary to have district Judges who shall have jurisdiction of all Admiralty matters, and whatever may in any way concern the Revenue. This I mean as to the begining of things; and that all causes at Common Law, whether between the Citizens of different states, or foreigners and Citizens, shou'd originate in the Supreme Common Law Courts of the respective States, wherever the Justices thereof are appointed during good behaviour, and have fixed permanent salaries annexed to their offices; but that where this is not the case, that all such Causes may be originated in the federal district Court, or if you please *shall* be so originated, with the right of appeal to the Circuit Court, upon either plan, when judgment shall be given against the foreigner or the Citizen of another State, but no appeal from the judgment of the Supreme Common Law Courts when the judgment shall be in their favour: it appearing reasonable to me that every Citizen ought to sit down quiet under the judgments of their own Supreme Courts. A provision of this nature wou'd probably have the happy effect of bringing on a speedy establishment of the Sup: Com: Law Courts upon their only proper ground, in every State where they are now differently constituted. It has been my opinion from the first, that an augmentation of the Judges of the Supreme Federal Court wou'd be found necessary, say to nine; but I do by no means think so as to the number of Circuits. The Circuit Courts are to be holden twice a year in each State which will be sufficient, at least for some years to come. I understand an idea is gaining ground in the House of Representatives, of annihilating the district Judges, and throwing all the Admiralty & Revenue Causes originally into the State Sup: Judicial Courts. This wou'd, in my opinion, be exceedingly impolitic, as it wou'd not only be difficult to withdraw such Causes from their Jurisdiction when it shou'd be found inconvenient to continue them under it, but wou'd also infallibly have a strong tendency to render those Courts, if they shou'd discharge their duty in Revenue Causes, very unpopular, serve to lessen that opinion of their impartiality, which ought ever to be kept up among the people at large, to weaken their authority, and of course the respect for the Laws, and for Government itself; These appear to me but a part of the fatal consequences which wou'd ensue from such a temporizing system. Tho' œconomy is held up as the ostensible ground of such a system, yet it seems to be in realty nothing less than an unpardonable thirst for popularity— I have seen a letter from a Representative, in which he says, that when Salaries are under consideration (alluding to the judicial System) nothing less than 2, or 3000 Dollrs: comports with the ideas of some Gentlemen; because they say no Man of Respectability in the Law wou'd accept any office under such a salary. What may be the case of certain Law characters I do not know: but I shou'd think 1500 wou'd not be rejected by any one in this State who shou'd be appointed district judge, and a considerably lesser sum might do in the smaller States—[1]

I agree with you touching the characters you have named as Candidates for the Judicial Departments, except the Gentleman whose condemnations, you say, have immortalized his name. He is a friend of mine, a good federal character: but, *between us*, not fit for such an appointment. He is not a Lawyer.[2]

Whether in the case you mention, the Governour cou'd be persuaded to appoint Mr: L. I am much at a loss. I *fear* he wou'd rather nominate Sullivan or Hitchbourn, if he thought his Council wou'd advise to their appointment.—

I was sincere when I told you that I did not wish for an appointment upon the Sup: Federal Bench. Our Chief Justice or Lowell wou'd be worthy Members of that Court. yet I doubt whether the former wou'd accept of a Seat there, on account of their distant employment at certain times. His abilities are equal to that station. Jay wou'd give universal satisfaction, but I have thought he wou'd rather prefer his present office. The Gentn: you mention for the District of Main is not only the fittest Man, but the *only fit one* within that District: But our present Sup: Jud: Court must not be entirely changed: for to tell you a truth, I know not where their places can be equally well filled. I shou'd dread the appointment of some persons, under the present Administration, as the greatest curse that could fall on this Commonwealth. You know whom I allude to.

I feel myself infinitely obliged to you for the favourable sentiments you have been pleased to express of me. It is my highest ambition to merit in some degree the good opinion of all good men.

We beg your & your Lady's acceptance of our most sincere regards, and we shall be ever happy in keeping up that friendly connection which has been formed between us.

I am, dear Sir, with much respect & esteem / Your obliged friend & humble Servant FRA DANA

RC (Adams Papers); internal address: "The honble the Vice President / of the United States"; endorsed by CA: "Judge Dana / July 31."

[1] The Judiciary Act of 1789 set the Supreme Court's annual salaries at $4,000 for the chief justice and $3,500 for each associate justice. Yearly compensation for district judges varied from state to state, ranging from $800 to $1,800 (Judicial Salaries, www.fjc.gov/history/judges/judicial-salaries-supreme-court-justices; *Doc. Hist. Supreme Court*, 1:666, 719, 722, 723).

[2] Nathan Cushing.

To Joseph Hardy

Sir — Richmond hill Aug[t] 6 1789

In 1779 at Bilbao I was solicited for releif by a number of American seamen who had been captured by the English and turned adrift in Portugal. These wandered to Spain with much difficulty and in great distress. I had no means of supplying them: but M[r] Gardoqui very generously offered to assist them upon my advice.[1] The article in his account, ought to be allowed him with interest and thanks. I only regret, that the multiplicity of other cares, prevented me from doing justice to my own feelings as well as to the honor of this Country by remitting the money to Bilbao from Holland, when I had money of the public in my hands— I am & John Adams

LbC in CA's hand (Adams Papers); internal address: "M[r] Hardy"; APM Reel 115.

[1] Two days after reaching Bilbao, Spain, in mid-Jan. 1780, JA dined with merchant Joseph de Gardoqui and solicited aid for fifteen American prisoners who had escaped from Portugal. Gardoqui agreed to furnish them with "Cloaths to the Amount of six dollars a Man." JA explained that while he lacked any formal authority to make the request, he "believed Congress would do all in their Power to repay him." Hardy (d. 1813), who acted as the first clerk in the comptroller's office of the Treasury Department from 1789 to 1791, facilitated Gardoqui's claim (JA, *D&A*, 2:431, 432; 4:236; Franklin, *Papers*, 38:19; Washington, *Papers, Presidential Series*, 2:439).

From John Brown Cutting

My Dear Sir, — Bordeaux 6 Aug 1789

Before this reaches You I hope You will have authentic accounts of the late revolution in France.

At such a distance from Paris it is difficult to asscertain the truth of such important transactions as have continually taken place since the 14th of July, at court and in the capital. By Cap[t] Bond of the Washington I inclosed you a parcel of pamphlets and newspapers which afforded You I hope some satisfaction.

I now add a few more. This City was beautifully illuminated last night in honor of M[r] Neckar's reinstatement in office.

No new administration is yet formed— The establishment of a national constitution it is thought will precede that measure; meanwhile those ministers who did not manifest their guilt by fear or flight continue to perform the functions of their respective offices.[1]

I sit off for Paris tomorrow, whence you shall again hear from me if Mr Jefferson be not sailed.

I take advantage of a ship that sails in a day or two for Philadelphia[2] to transmit this scrawl to You and am, with much respect and attachment / Your Mo. Obed^t:^ Ser^t:^ John Brown Cutting

RC (Adams Papers); internal address: "John Adams Vice President of the United States."

[1] Despite the popular momentum for political change in the wake of the 20 June Tennis Court Oath, the National Assembly's committee to draft a constitution struggled from 6 July 1789 to 3 Sept. 1791, riven by internal politicking and complex debates over defining the rights of the citizen in conjunction with the powers of the king. France's new constitution was finally adopted on 3 Sept., and Louis XVI consented to it eleven days later (Bosher, *French Rev.*, p. 133–146).

[2] Cutting likely sent this letter via the *Pallas*, Capt. Collins, which reached Philadelphia in early Oct. 1789 (Philadelphia *Independent Gazetteer*, 14 Oct.).

From John Lowell

Dear Sir Roxbury Augt. 7th. 1789—

Although I have had frequent Occassions to sollicit in Favour of my Friends, (or such other Charecters) as I have thought might be usefully employed in public Business, my early Habits, which in all Cases influence our Sentiments, have been such that I have never conversed or written on any such Subject when immediately affecting myself, 'thõ I have been of Opinion that Custom, & the Expectation of the World, having created different Ideas even in Persons of the greatest real Delicacy of Mind, that this Habit might lead me into an unnecessary Reserve, & be only false Delicacy, but I have been obliged to combat it with great Efforts;—I have always entertained such an Idea of your Friendship, & had such a Confidence in the Rectitude of your Sentiments, that I can say with much Sincerity that there is no Person to whom I should with more Freedom commit myself in such a Case than to you.— the general Voice, not only of my Circle of Friends & Acquaintance, but of others has so frequently & freely informed me, that in the Arrangement of Appointments under the new Constitution, it was probable I should be thought of to sustain the important & hoñble Office of an Associate Judge, that I supposed it would not be necessary for me to interfere in the Business, or on that Occassion break thrõ the Habit I have explained to you, and that if I should be thought capable of doing Service to my Country in that Line, I should not have Occassion to trouble my Friends on that Subject; but as I have received Letters from two of our Friends at New York, which have drawn me out farther than I before thought necessary, I could not omit opening myself to you, for I should feel guilty of not using that Confidence which I really possess;—[1] The Appointment is so important in its Nature to our Country that I dare not assume a Confidence in my own Qualifications for it, I am too much concerned to judge impartially, and I have a Sense of Reputation & I flatter myself of Rectitude too great to wish if it was in my Power that my own Judgment should decide that Point; all I intend is to mention those Circumstances, to you, which in Case your own Opinion coincides with the Partiality of my Friends might have their Weight when compared with those that may attend other Candidates.— I am so far advanced in my professional Line, that I find my young Bretheren & Children pressing fast on my Heels, & many of them possessing so much real Merit, & having a Warmth & Vigour of Imagination, to be found only in youth, & so necessary with other Qualities to the shining Part of our Profession, that I see very plainly my Situation among them will soon be less agreable than it has been— I have sustained a Commission under Congress, which has been repeatedly executed in Philadelphia & New York, within the Knowledge & observation of most of the leading Charecters in the Union, & I have acquired a personal Acquaintance with many of them; If the Confederation (too rotten I confess to have been thoroughly repaired) had been amended by additional Powers given to Congress, respecting Trade Revenue &c this Commission would without doubt have drawn to it Cognizance of these Matters; the new Court will take up specifically the Powers of that Commission, entended it is true, & rendered more important; the gentlemen who were with me in it have been taken out of Office, by very hoñble Appointments; one of them having two years since been a member & President of Congress, which vacated his com̃n: the other is now a Senator. I am the only one whom the new Appointments will discharge & supercede, this will undoubtedly produce a Question in the Minds of those who have been acquainted with these Facts, respecting the Cause of my being omitted; I can avoid seeing the gentlemen at a Distance, but so universal has been the prevailing Opinion in this state & New hampshire, that I should be reappointed, that I must meet the Question

& Condolance of most with whom, I shall converse; If however the Defect of Qualifications is the real Cause, however painful it may be, it is so just, that it ought to be acquiessed in without a Murmur.— A Gentleman of our State, of whose merit no Man entertains a greater Idea, I have heard has been proposed to fill this office,[2] that he will fill it honourably there can be no Question; whether he wishes or would incline to exchange his present Office for it I know not, but I conceive he will not feel himself neglected, or hurt if it should not be proposed to him; he now holds in the State a very respectable Com$^{n.}$, perhaps as respectable as any in it, & he receives the Satisfaction of Knowing that he possesses the Esteem of all whose Esteem he would wish for, the Enemies of our local Peace alone would rejoice at his Removal; the Friends of it would be satisfied that he was still doing good how far & how long he would be able to go thro the Fatigues of an Associate Judge, which if the proposed Arrangement takes place will call him far from Home, at the most inclement Seasons of the Year I cannot tell; But my dear Sir who will take his Place in Massachusetts? If the Question is answered by saying, the Senior Judge undoubtedly for on any other Principle I take it the whole Bench will be broken up; who will supply the Vacancy? can any body answer for the whims & Caprices of —— The present Court of Mass$^{a.}$ harmonize, & are fœderal, all disposed to support the Government of the Union, will they continue to do so in the Contingency supposed? & is it of small Consequence to the general Good that in such a State as this, at such a Time, this Point should be put at Risque— but I know I reason under the Influence of Personality, I have opened myself with unbounded Freedom to you my Friend, & wish your Judgment alone to decide.— If this Occassion is pretermitted I am left alone, to the Gratifications of those Enemies, who, thõ not numerous, have taken much Pains to mortify me, because they conceive I have not bowed down to their Idol; our Friends Lincoln & Lovell, I trust will be placed out of their Reach— I have great Reason to suppose that among the good Men who may promote the Appointment of so respectable a Charecter as our Ch. J: some will be found of another Class who wish to give Pain & Dishonor to me, I have been told that some of this Description have been already suggesting the Measure.— I am ashamed of being so long on this Subject you will however by it have the fullest Evidence of my entire Confidence.— I have only intended to suggest some Things, which perhaps might not have occurred to you without; I have an Interest in the happy Establishment of this

Government, far superiour, after all, to any personal Event in this Business, which my Family & Country claim & which I would not have receive a Detriment to avoid my own Humiliation—

I am with real Esteem / your most obed^{t} Serv$^{t.}$ J Lowell

August 9$^{th.}$

I have just heard that Gen$^{l.}$ L is appointed Collector of Boston it will gratify all good Men with us—

RC (Adams Papers).

[1] Lowell last wrote to JA on 30 Jan. (Adams Papers). The two "Friends at New York" who spurred along Lowell's quest for a federal judgeship were likely Massachusetts congressmen Fisher Ames and Elbridge Gerry, who wrote to him on 28 July and 1 Aug., respectively, regarding George Washington's approach to the nomination process (John P. Kaminski, *George Washington: A Man of Action*, Madison, Wis., 2017, p. 62–63).

[2] William Cushing.

From John Bondfield

Sir Bordeaux 8 Aug 1789

A ship Sailing in the morning as it interests you to know the state of the Nation.[1] I have the pleasure to advice you that the appearances promises perfect accomplishment of the Revolution,

All the Chiefs in opossion are fled. the National assembly proceed, and are advanct in the Ground Work of the Constition, the most Liberal that to this has been held out to any Social Body, not Excepting America,

Inclosed I have the honor to transmit you two Papers refering to your Ideas the fermentations and the State in which all parties were Situated.[2]

A perfect Calm at present reigns in the Capital and the Provinces, all the Nation form One National Army, all are regimented, on an Instant in Case of need ready for the field fortunately no Enemies appear, The Regular Troops instruct the New Levies in Military dicipline

many Referances in the Grand Assembly to the American Institutions. Mr Jefferson is not without application for Council he has openings and I beleeive has some influence in the present plans—

With due Respect I have the honor to be / sir / Your most obedient / Servant John Bondfield

RC (Adams Papers); internal address: "The Hon^{be} John Adams Vice President of Congress."

[1] Bondfield probably sent this letter via the *Pallas*, for which see John Brown Cutting's letter of 6 Aug., and note 2, above.

[2] The enclosure has not been found.

From James Bowdoin

Sir Boston August 10. 1789

As it is the duty of every good citizen to counteract, as far as he can, any measures that may operate injuriously to the Public, I am constrained to inform you of a plan, which if successful, will have that operation in the important department of the Administration of Justice in this Commonwealth.

We have a perfect Confidence, and are therefore happy, in the Gentlemen, who now constitute our Supreme judicial Court: but it is the wish of some intriguing Individuals to get themselves Seated upon that Bench: and for this purpose, it is their design, that the chief Justice, Mr. Cushing; who is a most worthy character, should be appointed to the federal Bench. In that case they expect, and have reason to expect, his place will be supplied by a man totally disagreeable to all the other Justices; and whose appointment will probably, or rather certainly, occasion the resignation of most or all of them: in which case they have little room to doubt of their own appointment.

To secure effectually the completion of this *laudable* manœuvre, they have been for some time past exerting themselves in every possible way: and it is probable, that before this time you have been made sensible of their exertions. In short, Sir, to be perfectly explicit, if Mr. Chief Justice Cushing be appointed to the federal Bench, the consequences abovementioned will assuredly take place.

I have a high regard for Judge Cushing; and think the public Good necessarily connected with his continuance in the Office of chief Justice: which he holds with great dignity to himself, and advantage to the Commonwealth.

As you wish the peace and happiness of the Commonwealth, you will permit me, with the Friends of good government, to hope, you will use your influence with his Excellency the President of the United States, for preventing the Evil, that will arise from the removal of Mr. Cushing from the Office of Chief Justice: especially as there is a Gentleman here, every way qualified, who 'tis said, has been recommended to the President, for the federal Bench.— I mean the honble. John Lowell esqr., who was one of the Admiralty Judges under the late federal Constitution; and with whose person and character you are perfectly well acquainted.

With the most disinterested esteem, I have the honour to be, sir, Yr. Excy's most obt. hble servt.

James Bowdoin

RC (Adams Papers); internal address: "His Excellency / Mr. Vice-Presidt. Adams."; endorsed: "Govr Bowdoin / Aug. 10. 1789."

From Stephen Higginson

Sir

Boston Augt. 10: 1789

I never yet have had occasion to solicit an appointment either for myself or my friends, nor do I love to interest myself in matters of the kind; but, when there is an appearance of danger from any proposed appointment, it seems to me to be the duty of every good Citizen, to give such information as appears to be material. upon this ground only I shall now take the liberty of stating to you, some of the Evils which are here thought inevitable, should Mr. Cushing, Our present chief Justice, be removed to the federal Bench; a measure, which several Letters by the last post inform us, would probably be taken. you know, & every One acknowleges, his Abilities & many good qualities; which render him a proper person for the Office referred to, & which make him of the highest importance to this commonwealth in his present Station. Our present Bench are very respectable, they harmonize to an unusual degree, they love & respect each other, & they are all federal. by means of these qualities Sentiments & union, they act with dignity & decission; & they form the greatest Barier we have, by much, against popular frenzy, & the influence of popular Demagogues. Should that Bench be broken up, or much changed, it would probably give rise to more mischief, & would certainly give more pain to the good Citizens, to the friends of government than any thing that can happen. It is an Event which his Brethren, the Bar, & the best of Our Citizens would depricate exceedingly—for the certain consequence would be, the appointment of a man, with whom some, if not all the others would refuse to sit—at least such is the Opinion of all that I am acquainted with.— It is indeed an Event, which the popular party here would much rejoice at, & which they have been labouring to bring about. they certainly wish much to derange that Bench, & to place on it some men of very opposite Characters; & they sometime since intimated that it would happen ere͂ long. But as no One concieved it in any degree probable, & every One supposed that Mr. Lowell would be the man; no measures have been taken to guard against it, & perhaps no information of this kind before given to you.—

I hope you may not consider this communication as improper or ill timed, I assure you that it's made upon public principles only. though your particular friends, & the best men in this State are much alarmed at the Idea of such a change; yet it may happen, from various causes, that none of them may write to you upon this Subject.— Mr. Cushing is in the highest estimation with every good man here, & but for the particular circumstances of the Case, they would wish him to be removed, if he desired it; which is doubted however by many. But as Mr. Lowell is considered as equally qualified for the place with Mr. C:, & from the Offices he before held has been viewed as the only fair Candidate—&, as such great injury is considered as inevitable to the State from the removal of Mr. Cushing, those who are the common friends of both the Gentlemen, & the best friends to Government, & to those who administer it, would be much pleased at the appointment of the former, but would lament exceedingly that of the latter—

I have given you Sir freely & honestly what I suppose to be the general Sentiments of the most respectable men among us. you will pardon the freedom I have taken, & give credit & weight to the communication so far only as you think it merits.— I have wished to trouble you with some of my own Ideas as to Revenue & commerce; but my time has been taken up by Journeying &c to recover my health, & my nerves are so weak that I write with much difficulty & labour—& this must apologise for the present hasty Scrawl not being copied.— please to present my own & Mrs Hs. respects to your lady &c. With much respect I have the honour to be your Excellencys very huml Servant— Stephen Higginson

RC (Adams Papers); internal address: "His Excellency John Adams Esqr"; endorsed: "Mr Higginson Aug. 10. / 1789 / ansd. Septr. 21."

From Stephen Hall

Portland 15 Aug. 1789.

My very Dear & much honoured Friend;

Permit me overwhelmed with grief & chagrined at disappointment to beg your kind attention for a minute. I am grieved, because my pretensions to the Office I sollicited were certainly far better grounded than his, who holds the Appointment: I am chagrined, because my expectations were with reason high.[1]

I think it not vanity to say I have some degree of personal merit; and some publick Seals of Government, with papers (even complimentary) accompanying, which I have on file, witness some small Services I have rendered the publick.

In the year 1779 I served them, at my own Expence, as Commander of the Troops at Falmouth, and met with the approbation, & received even the Compliments of the Government of the Massachusetts. In the year 1780 I again voluntarily served them as Secretary to General Wadsworth, Commander in the eastern Department.[2] Altho' there was no establishment originally made for a Secretary in that Department; yet the State saw fit to offer me handsom Compensation; but I chose to enjoy their gratitude, rather than accept their pay farther than to reimburse my expences. I continued my endeavours to serve the publick without remission to the end of the war; and then confined my self to my domestick affairs, pleased with the reflection that I had contributed my mite to the service of my Country.— With such pretensions, incouraged by the friendship of some of the most eminent Gentlemen in Congress, I flattered my self that Government would favor me with some degree of attention. But when I experienced your Goodness and Condescention in favoring me with a line, I tho't my self certain of success; especially as Mr. Wingate had informed me that the President himself had not forgotten me since he knew me at Cambridge: And I think success must have attended me, had it not been for Mr. Thatchers very great zeal in serving his particu[lar] friends; for whom I find provision is made at every Port in this eastern part of the Government, where he had them.— If Mr. Thacher has endeavoured to serve them merely because they were his friends, and not because of their deserts, & of their capacity to serve the publick, I think he has done wrong: If he has made use of a certain Recommendation in favor of Mr. Fosdick (of which Mr. Wingate can particularly inform You, and also how it was obtained) I think he has imposed upon the President, and personally injured me.

Had others, who have pretensions similar to mine, been appointed; I should only have been disappointed; but should not have been grieved: But to see the appointment conferred upon a person, to whom his most zealous friends cannot with truth ascribe any peculiar personal merit, and he himself would not pretend to any services he had ever rendred the publick, is truly aggravating.

To say he sustained the Office before, is not true: He was only a Naval Officer; and that Office he had not long sustained; and the manner in which he obtained it from those much more deserving reflects no great honor upon him.— But so it is.— It is done— He has obtained his appointment— He has practiced, & has prospered.— I am not envious; but I am grived. The cause of my grief I think would have been prevented, had things been known as they really are: But perhaps it cannot now be removed. I think however it will shortly be found that a Naval Officer will necessary at this Port; as I think there is, and I am told so by Gentlemen in trade, much more business to be done in this District, than in either of the Districts of Portsmouth, or of Newbury-Port: or there may be some other agreeable Appointments to be made that I know not of. I should suspect the Collection-Bill suggests an intervening Officer between the Collectors & the Treasury; as I find the Collectors are to settle their Accounts once in three months, or oftener.

I still wish for an agreeable Employment under Government; and shall most gratefully acknowledge your kindness in befriending me, if any should present.— Relying upon your Goodness to excuse the freedom I have taken, & the trouble I have given You, permit me to subscribe my self with every sentiment of Respect & Gratitude, / Your Excellency's / most obedient and obliged, / humble Servant;

Stephen Hall

RC (Adams Papers); internal address: "His Excellency John Adams. Esqr."; endorsed: "Mr Stephen Hall / Aug. 15. 1789." Some loss of text due to wear at the edge.

[1] Stephen Hall (1743–1794), Harvard 1765, of Westford, Mass., was the chaplain at Boston's Castle William and Harvard College's liaison to the Mass. General Court. After the Revolutionary War, Hall became a prominent supporter of Maine's separation from Massachusetts. Anticipating that excise posts would develop as "the grand federal wheel begins to move," Hall first sought JA's patronage in a letter of 23 Feb., recalling their shared journey from Fishkill, N.Y., to Baltimore in 1777 (Adams Papers). JA replied to Hall's requests on 26 June 1789, promising that "if the President should make any inquiries of me concerning the pretensions of the candidates, I shall faithfully relate to him all I know of your education and character" (LbC, APM Reel 115).

Despite earning the recommendations of Gen. Benjamin Lincoln and New Hampshire senator Paine Wingate, Hall did not receive a post, nor did he approve of the men who did. On 3 Aug. George Washington nominated Nathaniel F. Fosdick as collector for the ports of Portland and Falmouth, and he was confirmed by the Senate the same day. Fosdick (1760–1819), Harvard 1779, of Marblehead, Mass., sent a letter of support to the president from the citizens of Portland, where he had acted as collector since 1787. Hall was especially incensed by the actions of congressman George Thacher (1754–1824), Harvard 1776, who represented the combined district of York, Cumberland, and Lincoln, Maine. Hall lobbied JA and Washington for various excise posts over the next four years, without success (*Sibley's Harvard Graduates*, 16:165, 167, 169; U.S. Senate, *Exec. Jour.*, 1st Cong., 1st sess., p. 10, 13; Washington, *Papers, Presidential Series*, 1:235; 2:298, 329;

Biog. Dir. Cong.; Hall to JA, 19 Feb. 1791, 2 March 1793, both Adams Papers).

[2] Gen. Peleg Wadsworth (1748–1829), Harvard 1769, of Duxbury, Mass., arrived in Boston in March 1780, charged with commanding "all such men as shall be raised for the defence of the Eastern parts." Hall aided Wadsworth as a tutor to his son, John, and as a secretary (*Sibley's Harvard Graduates*, 16:165, 167, 169; 17:291, 296).

From Roger Sherman

Augt. 16th [1789]

Mr. Sherman returns his respectful compliments to the Vice-President, and would have done himself the honor of Waiting on him to Dine on Thursday next but he was previously engaged.[1]

RC (MHi:Adams-Hull Coll.); docketed by JA: "Card."

[1] By early August, JA and AA had oriented themselves to the social responsibilities that came with the vice presidency. Owing to the city's summer heat and a scarcity of cooks, AA waited until mid-August to set up weekly dinners for the social elite, which complemented Martha Washington's Friday evening levees. On Thursdays the Adamses regularly hosted 24 guests, with congressmen, like Sherman, and their wives crowding into Richmond Hill's single dining room. Between legislative sessions, making and receiving visits also consumed the Adamses' time. AA recalled returning over sixty calls "in 3 or 4 afternoons" and hosting unplanned visitors who arrived at breakfast to meet with JA (*AFC*, 8:397, 399, 406). Multiple dinner invitations dating from JA's vice presidency, including loose notes accepting and declining, are in MHi:Adams-Hull Collection.

To Henry Marchant

Dear Sir

New York August 18 1789

I have received your kind and obliging letter of the 16 of July, and am sorry that the extream heat of the weather, and a constant attendance on the duties of an office which is somewhat laborious and fatiguing, have prevented my giving it an earlier answer. The approbation you are pleased to express of my public conduct, is a great satisfaction to me. It is true that I have run through a course of dangers, hardships and fatigues by sea and land, and a series of perplexed negotiations among various nations, and at different Courts, which have never fallen to the lot of any other American, and scarcely to any other man. But although I may flatter myself that under the favor of heaven, I have had as much success as could have been rationally expected; Yet I find myself obliged with you to lament; that our Countrymen have not availed themselves of the advantages, which Providence has placed in their power. After a generous contest for liberty of twenty years continuan[ce] Americans forgot wherein liberty consisted— After a bloody war in defence of property, they forgot that property was sacred—after an arduous struggle for the freedom of commerce they voluntarily shackled it with arbitrary trammels, after fighting for justice as the end of government, they seemed determined to banish that virtue from the earth. Rhode Island has carried all these errors to their extreams: but there is not any State in the union, which is wholly free from the same mistakes. I should denominate this conduct guilty as well as erroneous, if I were not sensible that it has been owing to the loss of that ballance in our governments which can alone preserve wisdom or virtue in society— The whole continent seems at present sensible that much has been wrong, and desirous of reformation But there are obstacles in their way, among which the unatural conduct of Rhode Island is not the least— You will add greatly to your merits towards your Country by your exertions to bring your fellow Citizens into a right way of thinking in this Respect— It is very true, that several of those loose conjectures of an imagination wandering into futurity, which you are pleased to dignify with the magnificent appellation of prophetic declorations have been brought to pass in a singular manner, for some of which I had much less reason to offer, than for that which has not been accomplished, relative to youself. This however is still not impossible, nor perhaps improbable.

The solemn declaration which you call prophetic, and say has come to pass, made on the floor of Congress, respecting the late confederation, just as we had closed it, I do not distinctly recollect— I should be much obliged to you if you would write me, as particular an account of it as you can recollect. Hæc olim meminisse juvabit.—[1]

I must now thank you for your polite and friendly attention to my family when at New Port. They speak with much gratitude of the civilities they received both there and at Providence—and we live in hopes of seeing you in senate before another year is compleated.

I am Sir Your friend J Adams

LbC in CA's hand (Adams Papers); internal address: "The Hon[ble] Henry Merchant"; APM Reel 115. Some loss of text due to an ink blot.

[1] "It will some day be a joy to recall" (Virgil, *Aeneid*, transl. H. Rushton Fairclough, Cambridge, 1916, Book I, line 203).

From Sylvanus Bourne

Respected Sir— Boston Augt 18th 1789—

It gives me sensible pain to be under the necessity of troubling you further with my personal Concerns amid the weight of your public Cares: but entertaining the fond hope that you are not totally disinterested in my welfare, I am prompted to observe to you, that upon my arrival here I found Mr Keith had been pushing all possible force for the Marshalship of this District a place which I mentioned to your Excellency the day before I left New york, I had requested of the President: the above circumstance of Keiths warm application may render some more pointed exertions on my part necessary and that I should thro some able friend acquaint the President that relying on the force of your recommendation & others upon another Account. I had neglected to accompany my request for the marshall with any specific vouchers—but which if necessary I have the happiness to suppose I can obtain from the most respectable of my fellow Citizens who are cordial in their wishes for my success— under this impression I have taken the liberty to enclose a line to the President which humbly hope you will do me the fav^{r} to hand him if not militating with the delicacy of your official situation or personal Dignity. I should be extremely hurt to ask any thing improper—& your refusal of it, if so will be my just return: but if not I cannot but entertain sanguine wishes of success from the medium of conveyance—[1]

Genl Lincoln & Govr Bowdoin not knowing of my wishes for the marshalship have given Keith letters, but say they should have been happy in giving me the preference, & yet hope from which they have mentioned in my behalf in another Case, joined to my other recommendations that I may eventually succeed in my wishes—

I am sorry to use so many egotisms in my letter which the Case alone can justify—

Any assistance my much Esteemed Sir—which you may afford me in procuring a reputable situation in my Countrys service will be received with affection & remembered with gratitude by him who is with all that Respect & Esteem which your Abilities command & your virtues inspire / Your obliged & Devoted / servant

Silva^{s} Bourn—

PS—

If you should think that your relating the circumstances of the

Case to the President would render a delivery of the letter unecessary; you will withold it. I submit to your judgment a matter in which my feelings are much interested & the hopes of my friends—

My best respects to Mrs. Adams & Family—

RC (Adams Papers); internal address: "His Excellency John Adams Esqr— / Vice President / of the / United States"; endorsed: "Mr Bourne Aug. 18. / ansd 30. 1789."

[1] Merchant Sylvanus (Silvanus) Bourne lobbied JA, George Washington, and Thomas Jefferson over several months for various positions, including marshal for the district of Boston and U.S. consul at Lisbon. In June 1790 Bourne was named "Consul of the United States of America, for the Island of Hispaniola, and for such other islands."

Gen. Israel Keith (1751–1819), Harvard 1771, of Easton, Mass., became a justice of the peace for Suffolk County following his service in the Continental Army. He appealed to Washington for a position on 18 July 1789, subsequently sending letters of recommendation from James Bowdoin and William Heath. Keith did not earn a federal post and moved to Pittsford, Vt., to establish an ironworks in 1791 (vol. 19:375–377; Washington, *Papers, Presidential Series*, 2:364–366, 3:234).

From William Cushing

Dear Sir, Scituate August the 22d. 1789—

I hope you will excuse my indolence as to writing; but I ought before now to have expressed my thanks for your favor of the Second volume Hollandois, which has afforded me a great fund of entertainment & instruction:[1] you accomplished a great work and of a variety of thoughts arising upon the occasion, this is one—that the minister of a mighty monarch appears to make but a small Figure before a minister of a scarcely existing state. I wish your present office & Situation may be agreeable; though an inflexible adherence to the rule of right & the public good may produce opposition if not trouble; & I fear your compensation will not be equal to the circumstances.—

You were reduced lately to a [nice] Situation to be obliged to turn a point of Prerogative, but rightly turned, I think.—

I was absent Seven weeks on the Pownalborough Circuit; on our return (Mrs. Cushing with me) we Stopped two nights at Judge Sargeant's; where we had the pleasure of Seeing Mr. & Mrs. Shaw & your youngest son, who were well. And there I had the pleasure of seeing a letter of yours (en confidence) wherein you state some difficulties or defects respecting Supremacies &c.[2] As to the Legislative & Judicial, it seems to me, they will work their way; as to the Executive—there's the rub. Assuming the State debts would be a capital Stroke, if practicable.

I would propose a question upon the Constitution of the U. S., on the third Section of the third Article, & Second Section of the fourth Article, *Respecting treason*, whether there be any kind of treason which may be tried by a particular state, consistent with the Constitution, & if any what kind. For the Constitution declares what shall be treason against the United States—determines a mode of evidence, gives Congress power to declare the punishment; & the Second Section of the third Article extends the Judicial power to all cases arising under the Constitution;—and yet the Second Section of the fourth article seems to suppose a State may have Jurisdiction in a case of treason.

Another question is, whether the power of our Supreme J. Court of this state, of trying piracies & felonies committed upon the high Seas, by force of the ordinance of Congress of 5th. April 1781, is not now at an end. It seems, a Small vessel of about 30 tons, which touched in at Cape Elizabeth, while we were at Portland, was piratically run away with from the Coast of Africa, according to the account given us, on examination by the three hands on board. We ordered them committed, till duely discharged.[3]

I must take the Liberty to remind you of our friend N. C.[4] the late maritime Judge, who behaved, for ought I know, with propriety in his office, who has been a Staunch invariable friend to the cause of liberty & his Country, & at the Same time a Supporter of good government & good men—exerted himself much & got nothing—of any consequence. The office of District Judge would Seem naturally to fall to him, & I must desire your attention, if you think proper, to that matter. Indeed I have heard something which makes me suppose, you have thought of him already.— I have never had the honor to See or be known to his greatness & goodness, the President (I can give titles though Congress can't) And if I had,—a word of yours would outweigh many of mine.—

Mrs. Cushing joins in best respects to you & Mrs. Adams. I am, Sir, your affectionate humble Servant— Wm Cushing—

RC (Adams Papers); internal address: "His Excellency / John Adams Esq— / Vice president of the / United States— / City of / New york"; endorsed: "C J. Cushing / Aug. 22. 1789. / Ansd. sept. 14."

[1] JA likely sent his "Letters from a Distinguished American," for which see vol. 9:531–534, 536–588.

[2] Vol. 19:472–474.

[3] Although the details of this case are unknown, Cushing's reference to the problems of the wartime judiciary is clear. Acting under Art. 9 of the Articles of Confederation, the Continental Congress on 5 April 1781 established a string of admiralty courts to handle

"the trial of piracies and felonies committed on the high seas," but it was unclear what force they held under the new federal government (*JCC*, 19:354–356).

[4] For the controversy over Nathan Cushing's judicial appointment, see JA's letter to Francis Dana of [*10 July 1789*], and note 3, above.

From John Brown

Dr. Sr. Providence Augt. 24th. 1789

The Federalest of this State *are very much Alarmed* that the Tunnage Act should be as is generly Supposed to be put in force Immediately on all Vessells of this State, tho the produce of the State may go Free of Impost, the Federalests are allso further Agreaved by a Law of this State which makes them First pay a Contenentell Impost hear in Spetia, which will not Exempt them from the payment, of the Fourreighn Duty when Exported to Aney State of the Union,[1] had Congress Thought proper to have put the produce of the State on a Simmular Footing with the property of the Merchants who are nearly all Federal their Feelings would not have been So much wounded but will the property of the Anties go untouched it Seems by the preceedings of the House of Representitives in Congress the Federals of this State or the allredy too much Oppressed are to Undergo the Severity of their Friends. the Navigation of the State belongs 9/10th. to the Federal partey who in Lue of paying aney Extreonary Tunnage or Impost are Justly Intituled to Every Indulgence of Congress, Such as paying no more Tunnage nor Impost than is pd. by the Other States, at Least the Federalest of this State thinks them Selves Intituled to this Lennity, till the Anties of the State has had Some Notice pd. them from Congress by Some proibition or Resstrictutions Against their property as well as Against ~~their Opponents~~ that of the Federalest,

I ad no more thinking it Impossable that the Act Can pass the Sennet as it has the Representitives, & I Can not Account for their Conduct in no other way than as a Descire to bring the Federalest before them by way of Potition, when perhaps they may Conclude, the Case of the State at Large Must be tacon up

I am with all Due Respect / Your Obt Humble Servt.

John Brown

RC (Adams Papers); internal address: "The Honobl. John Adams Esqr."

[1] For Rhode Islanders' petitions to Congress seeking exemption from foreign duties, see Henry Marchant's letter of 29 Aug., and note 4, below.

From Edward Bancroft

(Francis Street Bedford Square)
London August 29th. 1789.

Sir

As Dr. Jeffries is about to return to America, I have desired him to take charge of a Letter from, & of two Volumes lately Published by, Major Jardine of the British Artillery, an acquaintance of mine to whom I lent your three Volumes on the Science of Government, with which he has been greatly pleased.[1]

Dr. Jeffries has at last determined to fix his residence in the United States a determination which gives me great pleasure, as I am persuaded it will not only prove advantageous to himself but to those of our Countrymen who may hereafter need his professional Assistance. To you who know his merits my testimony in their favour would be superfluous: But perhaps it may not be altogether useless for you to be informed of the Opinions of more competent Judges, such as Dr. Warren[2] and others who are at the head of the medical Profession in this Country, and who after a multitude of opportunities of properly estimating his talents & acquirments in the healing arts, uniformly speak of them in Terms of the highest Commendation. and I am confident, those in America who may either call for his aid or recommend it to others, will never have occasion to regret their doing so.

To Dr. Jeffries I must refer you for such information as you may desire respecting men & things here— I cannot however conclude without offering you my cordial Congratulations upon that Choice of the United States by which you have been lately placed in the most important & distinguished Situations, which I have no doubt of your continueing to fill to your own honor & their greatest benefit.

I beg my most respectful Compliments to your Lady & to Mrs. & Col. Smith, and that you will beleive me to be with the greatest Sincerity & respect / Sir / Your most faithful / & most Devoted Humble Servant

Edwd. Bancroft.

RC (Adams Papers); internal address: "His Excellency John Adams Esq."; endorsed: "Dr. Ed. Bancroft / Aug. 29. 1789."

[1] Loyalist John Jeffries, who was the Adamses' physician in London, returned to Boston in November with his second wife, Hannah Hunt Jeffries, and reopened his practice five months later. Bancroft sent a copy of Alexander Jardine's *Letters from Barbary, France, Spain, Portugal, &c.*, London, 1788, which is in JA's library at MB. Jardine (d. 1799), a former British Army officer and diplomatic agent, shared cultural observations

from his 1771 mission to Morocco and subsequent travels in Europe (*Sibley's Harvard Graduates*, 15:425–426; *Catalogue of JA's Library*; *DNB*).

[2] Dr. John Warren (1753–1815), Harvard 1771, of Cambridge, was a surgeon and a founder of the Massachusetts Medical Society (vol. 3:357; *Sibley's Harvard Graduates*, 17:655–669).

From Henry Marchant

private

Dear Sir, Newport Aug$^{t.}$ 29$^{th.}$ 1789

Yours of the 18$^{th.}$ just came to hand— M$^{r.}$ Jackson was in town some time past— I was attending a Court in the Country and lost the Pleasure of seeing Him— He left word with a Friend of mine that He wished to see me as he had a verbal Message from You to me—[1]

I learn the Heat has been excessive at the Southward and fatal to many— Your confined Situation requires an Attention to your Health, which you ought not to neglect—

I cannot conceive it possible for Congress to adjourn so soon as I find reported by a Committee— The Business enumerated by that same Committee as necessary to be done previous to the Adjournment, I should think would occupy the Time of Congress for Months, unless happily, & which I hope is the Case, You dispatch Business with greater Facillity than the former Congress were ever able to do—[2]

There are many Matters I wish to converse upon with some Person of Information, Judgement & long Experience in Our publick Affairs— It is a long Time since I enjoyed that Satisfaction—

You wish me to give You a particular Account of the *prophetick Declaration* made on the Floor of Congress just as the former Confœderation was concluded—

When my Friend has all His Feelings wound up, upon an important Subject, and Vent must be given:— He has a Manner of Expression so peculiar to Himself, and so striking to the Heavens, that the Impression as from a stroke of Lightening is left behind, while the Flash and Sounds—The mode of Expression is lost or forgotten— His Words I will not engage to recollect with exactness—

The Articles of Confœderation on being completed, the Members by Rotation were called to place their Signatures to them.— this being concluded;—a Pause and perfect Calm succeeded— He sat and appeared full of thought.— He rose.— "M$^{r.}$ President,"— His Cane sliped thro' His thumb and fore-Finger with a quick Tap upon the Floor.— His Eyes rolled upwards,—His Brows were raised to their full Arch.—

"This Business Sir, that has taken up so much of Our Time *seems* to be finished:— But Sir, I now upon this Floor venture to predict, that before Ten Years, this Confœderacy like a Rope of Sand, will be found inadequate to the Purpose; And its Dissolution will take Place

Heaven grant, that Wisdom and Experience may then avert what We have most to fear"—

I never knew a greater Solemnity upon the Mind, of the Members— It was near the usual Time of Adjournment— Congress was adjournd—[3]

I am obliged to You Sir, for the Hopes You express of seeing me in the Senate, before another Year Expires— that this State will adopt the Constitution in the Course of this Fall or Winter, I greatly flatter myself

The Minds of many are changed in Favour of it; the last week we had a new Choice of Members for the lower House, and there are considerable Alterations for the better— In Our last Tryal of that Question we came within seven— the upper House being elected for the Year, we have most to fear from them— But Sir, however it may be in the Minds of my Friends abroad and at Home; I confess, I am almost weary of so publick a Character,—And could my Friends consistantly with their own Sentiments of me—suffer and promote me to some more fixed Station, more immediately adapted to my Profession it would abundantly more agree with my Wishes—

I take the Liberty to enclose You a Copy of a Petition to Congress from this Town, upon the Subject of foreign Tonnage &c exacted upon Our Coasting & other Vessells, by the officers of the Customs at New-York—

The Town of Providence have also petitioned, but I have not seen their Petition, and I hear they have appointed two Gentlemen to attend Congress to inform their Petition;—[4] But it was presumed here, there would be no hearing of them upon the Floor of Congress, therefore this Town have not sent any Person with theirs; but instructed me as Moderator of that Meeting to forward it to Congress as I should think proper— Supposing that as it is upon the Subject of Revennue it must be taken up in the first Instance in the House of Representatives, I have enclosed the Original to the Speaker— I should be sorry if I have been mistaken in the Mode—

It would not have been a Matter of *Surprize* if the Nonacceeding States had been left intirely upon the footing of Foreigners— But the Lenient Spirit of Congress appears conspicuous in their Acts— While therefore we were happy to find, that all our Produce &c was to be admitted free of Duty,—and that the foreign Goods we might import into the United States would be recd. upon the same footing with the acceeding States, and as far as we saw, no Clause in any of the Acts of Congress, exacted a foreign Tonnage upon Our Vessells;—We were surprised to learn that a foreign Tonnage was exacted by the Officers on Our Vessells.— Either We or the Officers are mistaken— Upon the Supposition they are warranted so to do, it is indeed mortifying to find the only Distinction between the Subjects of the States in the Union and Us, put upon those of this State,—the Merchantile Interest, the most Zealous Advocates for the Adoption of the new Constitution— For while the Produce of the Farmer is imported into any of the United States Duty free, The Merchant in whose Vessell they are carried pays a foreign Tonnage—

Indeed this will not be the Case,—for He must lay up his Vessell and the common Coasters, which are of very publick Utillity also, if this Duty is exacted.— And the Produce of this State must be carried in Bottoms of the States in the Union—

It certainly could not be the Wish of Congress that such a Distinction should take Place; or that the Ardour & patriotick Spirit of all the Advocates for the Constitution should thus be depressed, & by such a Distinction mortified and left to be pointed at by those who have been altogether opposed to it.—

I confess I have undergone much upon this Occasion, And I survive merely upon the Expectations that, Congress will agreably to the Sense and Construction we put upon those Acts, so explain them, as that this Exaction may be stoped— This indeed Sir is a Matter of much Consequence to the trading and fœderal Interest of this States; I wish it may be thoroughly investigated, and that as early as possible, for a total Stagnation has taken Place— We also wish that before Congress adjourn Provision may be made,—that if in the Recess of Congress the present nonacceeding States should adopt the Constitution, they should be immediately admitted to all the Advantages of it—

This Letter has got to such a tedious Length that asking Pardon for the Trouble I give, with my sincere Respects to Mrs. Adams & Your Family I must hasten to subscribe myself / with all possible Esteem / Your most devoted / Friend & Servant Henry Marchant

RC and enclosure (Adams Papers); internal address: "The Honble John Adams Esqr. / Vice President of the / United States &c—"

[1] This was probably Newburyport merchant Jonathan Jackson, then serving in the state senate (*AFC*, 8:313; *Biog. Dir. Cong.*).

[2] The opening session of the first federal Congress adjourned on 29 September.

[3] For JA's denial of this account, see his 17 Sept. reply to Marchant, below.

[4] As citizens continued to agitate for a ratification convention amid internal political strife, Rhode Island's "rogue" status grew costly. Under the Collection Act, Rhode Islanders faced steep tonnage duties because of their foreign status. Federalist merchants like Marchant perceived an opportunity to resume their push for ratification of the Constitution. He enclosed a copy of Newport, R.I., residents' 28 Aug. petition to Congress seeking exemption from the payment of foreign duties and underlining their desire to join the union. Marchant and Isaac Senter carried it to Congress in early September. The Federalist corps in Providence, R.I., generated a similar petition on 27 Aug., which was delivered by James Manning and Benjamin Bourne at the same time (vol. 19:405–406; *Doc. Hist. Ratif. Const.*, 25:577–582; Washington, *Papers, Presidential Series*, 3:596–597; from Jabez Bowen, 31 Aug., below).

To Sylvanus Bourne

Dear Sir New York August 30th 1789

I have received your letter of the 18th of this month and have communicated that to the President, which was inclosed in it. The particular office you sollicit by that letter, will be sought by numbers: and among them probably will be men advanced in life, incumbered with large families, in necessitous circumstances, perhaps occasioned by public services, by depreciated public promises & &— The President will as he ought, weigh all these particulars and give the preference upon the whole as justice humanity and wisdom shall dictate.

There is another gentleman who has applied for it whose pretensions perhaps will have great weight and will be supported by recommendations of the first sort. I must caution you my dear sir against having any dependance on my influence, or that of any other person— No man I beleive has influence with the President. he seeks information from all quarters and judges more independantly than any man I ever knew. It is of so much importance to the public that he should preserve this superiority, that I hope I shall never see the time that any man will have influence with him beyond the powers of reason and argument.

Who is it, pray that has been honoring—Vice —— in poetry.[1]

J A.

LbC in CA's hand (Adams Papers); internal address: "Mr S Bourn"; APM Reel 115.

[1] JA probably saw an advertisement in the 22 Aug. *Massachusetts Centinel* for a "genuine satire," an anonymous poem by Edward Church entitled "The Dangerous Vice ——," Boston, 1789, Evans, No. 21736. Church (1740–1816), Harvard 1759, was a Boston mer-

chant whose repeated rejections for a diplomatic post triggered his attack in print. His popular poem mocked JA as a royalist who was compromised by pride and a love of European luxury, calling him "a Stickler for a crown, / Tainted with foreign vices, and his own, / Already plotting dark, insidious schemes, / Already dubb'd a King, in royal dreams." AA, who circulated Church's name as the author, was disappointed that JA's views on presidency and monarchy went unexamined. "I could wish that the Author might be fully known to the publick with regard to the subject of a proper title for the Pressident mr A never has or will disguise his opinion, because he thinks that the stability of the Government will in a great measure rest upon it," she wrote (vol. 18:103; *AFC*, 8:404). For JA's reaction to Church's piece, see his letter to Cotton Tufts of 16 Sept., below.

From Jabez Bowen

Sir, Providence August 31. 1789

By the operation of the Commercial Regulations of the United States, those that have been friends, and for adopting the New Constitution in this State, are like to be exceedingly oppressed as well as Mortify'd. your Laws say that the productions & Manufactures of the Country shall be imported Duty Free by this the Farmers (who compose the Anti federal party) are highly favour'd, the Collecter of New York says that the Coasting and other Vessells that belong to the Citizens of R^{d} Island must pay the Tonnage as Foreigners this puts an end to the Coasting Trade among us, and will bring great Distress on the Inhabitants of the Seaport Towns who almost to a Man have been for establishing the Federal Government. this operates in so untoward a manner, and is so mortifying to us that we shall loose all our influence among the people and they will turn their Eyes to the other kind of people to help them.

Indee I think it must be a verry unnatural and forced Construction of the Law to make us Foreigners. we certainly were a part of the U— S— and are liable to a proportion of the Debts. we Live on or within the Lands given up to the Union and were invited to joyn in mending the old Constitution. but a majority of the State tho't it did not need it. you that tho't it did, have procurd and framed a New one. you have not so much as given us any Notice of your proceedings nor invited us to come in and Try the New Government, but on the Contrary have framed a Code of Laws that shut us out of the Union, and have not waited a propper time for us to Conquer old prejudics and Recover our Senses.— from the late Election of Representatives we have every Reason to think that a Convention will be Order'd when the Genl Assembly meets in October. that, in all Novemb^{r} it may be know wheather we adopt it or not, on the whole we Intreat you in the most earnest manner to attend to the

Petitions of the Town of Newport Providence &c for Releving us at present so far as not to insist on the Foreign Tonnage and giving us liberty to carry other Merchandize on Paying the Dutis &c. This is a matter of the greatest importance to the well being of this State in general, and will operate as sevearly and much in the same way that the infamous Port Bill did against the Town of Boston.

Do[r] Isaac Senter and Benjamin Bourne Esq[r.] are appointed to come on and present the Petition your favourable Notice of them will be verry pleasing to one who is with the Highest Esteem Your Excellency Most Humb Servant Jabez Bowen

was out of Town when M[r] Bourne went forward.

RC (Adams Papers); endorsed: "Jabez Bowen / ans[d.] 18. sept. 1789."

To James Lovell

Dear Sir New York September 1 1789

I have not yet answered your letter of the 26 of July. You guess well—I find that I shall have all the unpopular questions to determine: and shall soon be pronounced Hostes Republicani generis—[1] What they will do with me I know not, but must trust to providence. You insinuate that I am accused "of deciding in favor of the power of the prime: because I look up to that goal" That I look up to that goal sometimes is very probable because it is not far above me, only one step, and it is directly before my eyes: so that I must be blind not to see it— I am forced to look up to it and bound by duty to do so, because there is only the breath of one mortal between me and it— There was lately cause enough to look up to it, as I did with horror, when that breath was in some danger of expiring.[2] But deciding for the supreme, was not certainly the way to render that goal more desirable or less terrible: nor was it the way to obtain votes for continuing in it, or an advancement to it. The way to have ensured votes would have been to have given up that power.— There is not however to be serious, the smallest prospect that I shall ever reach that goal our beloved Chief is very little older than his second—has recovered his health and is a much stronger man than I am— a new Vice President must be chosen before a new President— This reflection gives me no pain: but on the contrary great pleasure: for I know very well that I am not possesed of the confidence and affection of my fellow Citizens, to the degree that he is. I am not of Cæsar's mind. The

Second place in Rome is high enough for me. Although I have a spirit that will not give up its right, or relinquish its place whatever the world or even my friends, or even you who knew me so well may think of me, I am not an ambitious man. Submission to insult and disgrace is one thing: but aspiring to higher situations is another. I am quite contented in my present condition and should not be discontented to leave it. Having said too much of myself let me say something of you. The place of Collector would undoubtedly have been yours if the President could have found any other situation for your friend Lincoln—it was from no lukewarmness to you I am certain. But the public cause demanded that Lincoln should be supported, and this could not be done any other way— If after some time any other permanent place should be found for him, you, I presume, will come in collector. He sailed yesterday in good health for Georgia and may heaven prosper him with all happiness honour and success— It is a very honorable embassy: and will produce great and happy effects to these states— I am John Adams

LbC in CA's hand (Adams Papers); internal address: "Honble James Lovell"; APM Reel 115.

[1] Enemy of the people of the republic.

[2] Suffering from "a very large and painful tumor" on his left thigh and a "slow fever," George Washington was unable to fulfill many of his presidential duties between June and September. Doctors diagnosed the condition as an "anthrax" infection, and the streets around his Franklin Square mansion were roped off so that carriages would not disturb the president's rest. On 17 June the tumor was removed. A painful and public recovery followed. Like JA, James Madison understood the political repercussions of Washington's ill health: "His death at the present moment would have brought on another crisis in our affairs." The president's long recovery stretched into September, and by the 8th he returned to his duties. "Upon the whole, I have more reason to be thankful that it is no worse than to repine at the confinement," he wrote (Washington, *Papers, Presidential Series*, 3:76–77, 4:1; Madison, *Papers, Congressional Series*, 12:258).

From William Maclay

Sepr. 1st 1789

Mr Maclay's Compliments wait on the Vice President of the united States, begs leave to inform him, That he is in so ill a State of Health, That he cannot have the honor of dining, with him on Friday next—[1]

RC (MHi:Adams-Hull Coll.); addressed: "Honble Vice President of the / United States—"; docketed by JA: "Card / 1789."

[1] Suffering from ill health, William Maclay of Pennsylvania requested a leave of absence from the Senate from 20 July to 17 Aug. and again from 2 to 20 Sept. (*First Fed. Cong.*, 14:763).

From Sylvanus Bourne

My respected Sir— Boston Sept 8th 1789—

I was honoured by the due Receipt of your obliging favr. of Augt 30th for which you have my Cordial thanks— I am fully sensible of the justness of your Observations, relative to the Presidents nominations, and doubt not, they will be all made free from any partial biass whatever, and on the principles of humanity, Wisdom, & justice to his Country, whose best interests, have been his uniform Study & pursuit; no personal dissappointment will ever excite in my mind a distrustful idea of the good wishes of my friends towards me—convinced of the uncertain nature of these kind of applications—

I have yet some hopes of a registership in the Judiciary to which Object Mr Jay may have it in his power to assist me essentially— Should I be eventually defeated in my wishes for a domestic Office, I would wish the favr of your opinion upon the subject of my original intent of going as Consul to Cadiz— you once observed to me while at Mr Jay's that if Harrison did not go you thought it clear for me— Harrison has repeatedly told his friends here, that he did not wish to go unless a salary was affixed to the office; but I will consent to go without, depending on forming some mercantile connection & the chance of a future moderate grant from Govt: should the President be inlined to favr my views I suppose it to be fully within his power to originate this appointment if unaccompanied by a pecuniary Stipend & should he think it of public advantage & that I am capable of rendering public service herein—he can send down his nomination before the Senate rise this Session— in a leisure moment will you please to inform me on this Subject.—[1]

Prompted I hope by justifiable motives I have chosen this crisis to obtain some employ in my Countrys Service but if foiled in every attempt—I shall not yet despair—by fortitude, industry, & persevarance in private pursuits to be able to support that character & Reputation in the world without which Life will be to me scarce an Object of desire— I sometimes am led to think it a curse to possess any Ambition & to look with envy on the stupid, senseless part of Mankind, who are willing to tread on the same "dull pace from day to day"

Dr Sir I suppose the poem you allude to—to be the infamous production of a disappointed expectant by the name of *Edward Church*,[2] who tainted by his Brother's treacherous blood, would hope to poison the public mind— but a Character like your's Sir built on the broad basis of tried Integrity, superior Ability and an ardent love of your Country manifeted by a series of painful services, is not to be shaken by the envenomed shafts of Envy—or the rancourous ebulitions of a corroded mind—but shall remain unsullied in the grateful sentiments of the virtuous part of your Countrymen, till time shall be no more, and after that curtain shall drop, which will open to your view, the more peaceful scenes of a future existence—

Please to tender my best Respects to Mrs Adams & the rest of your good Family believing me to be with unfeigned Essteem & Respect / Your Obliged & devoted / Servt Silva: Bourn

RC (Adams Papers); internal address: "His Excellency John Adams Esqr—"; endorsed: "Mr Bourne / Sept 8. 1789."

[1] Alexandria, Va., merchant Richard Hanson Harrison acted as the unofficial U.S. consul at Cádiz, Spain, until 1786. George Washington nominated Harrison to the post on 4 June 1790, and he was confirmed by the Senate three days later. Seeking a stable salary, Harrison declined the post on 6 Jan. 1791. Thomas Jefferson recommended John Codman Jr.'s brother, the Portland, Maine, merchant Richard Codman, in February, but the post remained vacant until 1793 (vol. 18:148; *AFC*, 1:135, 9:105; U.S. Senate, *Exec. Jour.*, 1st Cong., 2d sess., p. 47, 49; Washington, *Papers, Presidential Series*, 1:229–231).

[2] For Edward Church's satirical poem, see JA's 30 Aug. 1789 letter to Bourne, and note 1, above. His brother was Dr. Benjamin Church, who became a British spy (vol. 3:index; JA, *D&A*, 3:384).

To William Cushing

Dear Sir New York septr 14, 89

I have not yet acknowledged my obligation to you for your favor of Augt 22. if my hasty scrawls written in gloomy times and desperate circumstances, have furnished you an amusement for a vacant hour I am glad of it.

My present office is as agreable to me as any public office ever can be: and my situation as pleasing as any on this earth, excepting Braintree. My compensation will be straightened to such a degree, that to live among foreign ministers, travelling Americans, Govenors, Chancellors, Judges, Senators and Repre in a style which my unmerciful Countrymen exact of all their public men, will require the consumption of the whole of it with the whole income of my private fortune added to it: and after all I shall be but poorly accommodated. But I have often been obliged to apply to myself what one of my predecessors in the Corps diplomatique in Holland, wrote to his master. The President Jeannin, Ambassador from Henry 4th of France, wrote him from Holland "Sire I have been so long used to labour a great deal, and profit little, that the habit is familiar, and I am contented."[1] Jeannin however profited more and labored less, and never ran the gauntlet among halters, axes, libels, Daggers, cannon balls, and pistol bullets as I have done, nor performed one half of the immense journeys and voyages that have fallen to my lot.

Every unpopular point is invariably left to me to determine so that I must be the scape goat, to bear all their sins, without a possibility of acquiring any share in the honor of any of their popular deeds— If legislative, my friend, and judicial work their way, and the executive has not weight to ballance the former, what will be the consequence? an unballanced Legislative is a tyranny, whether in one few or many. A more important question, than yours concerning treason, never was proposed upon any part of the constitution: and upon the right decision: of it will, in my opinion, depend the existence of government. Two sovereignties against which treason can be committed can never exist in one nation or in one system of laws.— We should soon see officers of the national government indicted convicted and executed for treason against the seperate states, for acts done by virtue of their offices and in discharge of their duty. The clause you refer to in ss: 2 Art 4 is this "A person charged in any state with treason, felony or other crime who shall flee from justice, and be found in another state, shall, on demand of the executive authority of the state from which he fled, be delivered up, to be removed to the State having jurisdiction of the crime" But this in the case of treason can mean only that the traitor may be tried, by the national judicial in the State where the crime was committed according to those words in ss: 2 Art 3 "The trial of all crimes, except in cases of impeachment shall be by Jury: and such trial shall be held in the state where the said crimes shall have been committed.[") I am not enough acquainted with the subject of Pyracy to form any opinion.

The character, biography and merits of our friend N—C. has been long since laid before the President, in as handsome terms as I was master of, and if he is passed by it will be from public motives only, I presume. I hope he will bear it with magnanimity: but I know not the Presidents intentions. M^rs^ A joins with me in kind comp^ts:^ to Mrs Cushing & yourself— Your letters sir are not like hundred I receive— They contain profound and useful enquiries, a continuance of them will be a favor to J Adams

LbC in CA's hand (Adams Papers); internal address: "C Justice Cushing"; APM Reel 115.

[1] JA read and admired the tactics of French diplomat Pierre Jeannin (1540–1622), who negotiated the Twelve Years' Truce of 1609 between the northern Netherlands and

Spain (JA, *D&A*, 2:398; Hoefer, *Nouv. biog. générale*). JA's mention of Jeannin suggests that he had begun composing his reflections on the civil wars that afflicted Henry IV's reign, for which see John Adams' *Discourses on Davila*, 28 April 1790 – 27 April 1791, Editorial Note, below.

To John Lowell

Dear Sir New York Sept[r.] 14. 1789

I received your Letter of the 7th in due Season and have delayed my Answer, in hopes it might be more determinate. I have received also Letters from Governor Bowdoin and M[r] Higginson on the Same Subject.[1] The Contents of these Letters appeared to me of Such Importance, that I thought it my Duty to lay them before the President, as [in]formation that he ought to be possessed of;—Since which I have had more than one personal Conference with him on the Subject;—What his decision will be I am not able to say. Applications and Recommendations and Representations are made to him from all Parties. M[r] H. & M[r] A. are not Silent,[2] any more than others who are more zealous for the new Gov[t.]— The President Examines and weighs with great Attention and Care, and determines according to Principles which he has laid down for himself, which in general are good & wholesome.

For my Part, I am So clearly convinced, of the Necessity of an *Unity* in the Executive Authority of Government, and of the Propriety of having all Appointments vested in one Breast, that I wish my Friends would excuse me from interfereing on any Occasion. The Daily Labour, of my Attendance in Senate, is fatiguing, the delicacy of finding proper times to converse with the President, on Appointments, renders it difficult, and after all, my information can be but partial, when his, is compleat.— Especially as I am to be made the Scape Goat, on whom all the sins of Unpopularity are to be laid.— My Exertions for Lincoln, have torn open an hornets Nest at Boston, and my Vote for the Presidents Power of Removal, according to the Constitution, has raised from Hell an host of political and poetical Devils.—

I have waited on the President expressely in behalf of our Friend Jackson: He listenened Attentively to all my Representations: but I found that other Characters were in contemplation, meritorious Officers in the late Army and amiable Men, it must be confessed.

In all Events, my Friend, Suffer not these Things to affect your Spirits or your Happiness.— You may have cause to rejoice, that you have met a disappointment, if even that should happen.— Things are not enough settled, to make any Place desireable.

at least this is still the Opinion of, dear sir / Your old Friend and faithful humble / sert John Adams

RC (Pequot Library Association:Monroe, Wakeman, Holman Coll., on deposit at CtY-BR); addressed: "Hon[ble] [. . . .]"; notation by JA: "Free / John Adams." LbC (Adams Papers); APM Reel 115. Text lost where the seal was removed has been supplied from the LbC.

[1] James Bowdoin's and Stephen Higginson's letters were of 10 Aug., both above.
[2] John Hancock and Samuel Adams.

From Nicolaas & Jacob van Staphorst and Nicolaas Hubbard

sir Amsterdam 14 September 1789

On the 26th: last Month only, we received your respected favor of 2 Decbr to our Predecessors, accompanying the Second and Third Volumes of Your Defence of the American Constitutions, to compleat the Setts presented us; For which Mark of your Friendship and Remembrance, Please accept our hearty Thanks.—[1]

Your departure from Europe, has been followed by Events of infinite importance indeed; Here the Flame caught by your glorious Revolution, has been smothered for a time, But in France it appears to have made such Progress, as will We hope ensure to that populous & happily situated Country, a Constitution of Freedom, the Basis of which is already laid by a declaration of the sacred and inalienable Rights of Mankind. Should this grand Work be carried to Maturity, of which there is a good prospect, its Consequences will spread all around, and this Country certainly not feel them the last.—

The Dread of this great Revolution already alarms the Foes to the natural Liberties of Mankind, and may probably cause an Embrasure in Europe, that by involving the different powers of this Quarter of the Globe, would prove highly advantageous to your Commerce and Credit in Europe, The present State of the latter of which confirms in the fullest manner, what We have often assured to you in person, that its Revival depended solely upon the Establishment and Operation of an efficient and respectable Government in the United-States: As the Parent of the American Credit in this Country, You Sir, cannot but be more than ordinarily interested in its progress and Situation, Wherefore We are certain to gratify you, in communicating more early perhaps than You would know thro' your Official Channel, the purport of the Letter the Commissioners of the American Loans here address per this Conveyance to your Treasury-Board, To the inclosed Copy of which We have only to subjoin, that Your Four per Cent Bonds are now One to Two per Cent above par, and the Five per Cents from 96 to 99 per Cent, So that they now appear most respectably among the other Loans negotiated here, with the appearance of going still higher, and thus will be rendered easy the raising here on favorable Terms, what further Sums the United-States may stand in need of.—

We beg you to accept our most sincere Congratulations upon this Situation of the American Credit here, as well as upon the successful Operations of Your new Federal Government, and your Appointment to the very distinguished Post You occupy in it; Which We wish you a long Enjoyment of, not doubting but You will discharge it with equal Assiduity and Abilities as You have manifested in all your former Employs, Which have secured you the most flattering Recompence, the Esteem and Gratitude of your Fellow Citizens.—

Mrs: Van Staphorst joins in presenting our most respectful Compliments to Mrs: Adams; And requesting that when in our power to render you any useful or agreeable Offices here, You will not spare us, as it will at all times afford us real Satisfaction to convince you how truly and respectfully We are / sir / Your most obd hble Servt.

N & J. Van Staphorst & Hubbard

RC and enclosures (Adams Papers); internal address: "John Adams Esqr.—"; endorsed: "Vanstaphorsts and / Hubbard. 14. Septr / 1789."

[1] JA last wrote to the Dutch banking firm of Nicolaas & Jacob van Staphorst on 2 Dec. 1788, expressing thanks for gifts sent to his family and commenting on political news (FC, Adams Papers). For Nicolaas Hubbard, who joined the firm from 1789 to 1801 and later interacted with JQA and TBA, see *AFC*, 11:index.

With this letter, the firm enclosed a Dupl and two copies of its 11 Sept. 1789 report to the Board of Treasury, outlining the state of American credit in Europe as well as Thomas Jefferson's failed attempt to transfer the debt to France, for which see Wilhem & Jan Willinks' 1 Feb. 1790 letter, and note 1, below.

To John Brown

Sir New York Septr: 15. 89

I received in due time your favor of August 24, the subject of which has since been under the deliberation of both houses. The act, which has been the result of their attention to the petitions of New

Port Providence and other towns, will appear to you, probably before this letter.[1] Whether it will in all respects be conformable to your wishes, I am not able to say: but it seemed to be the greatest lenght that some of the best informed members, thought it safe to go. We are all very sanguine in our hopes, that you will send us members of both houses, before the 15 of Jan$^{y:}$, indeed on the first monday in December. All unkind questions will then be done away. But if unhappily Rhode Island should not call a convention; or calling one not adopt the constitution, something much more serious than has ever yet been done or talked of, will most probably be undertaken. We have very often been irritated with rumors of correspondences between the Antis in your state and those in Massachusetts, New York, Virginia, N Carolina &. and even with insinuations of intrigues with British emmisaries These are very serious reports. such intercourses are extreamly criminal in the citizens of the Union, and hostile at least in those who are not— If the citizens of Rhode Island place themselves in the light of correspondents with criminal citizens of the Union, or in that of ennemies to the United States, their good sense will suggest to them, that the consequences will be very speedy and very bitter. I rely upon it therefore, that unless your state is devoted and abandoned to the judicial dispensations of heaven, that your people will open their eyes before it is too late. This is the very serious advice of one who has ever been and still is the hearty friend, but who must cease to be so when they become the enemies of the united states. There can be no medium. Enemies they must be, or fellow citizens, and that in a very short time. I am sir & & J Adams

LbC in CA's hand (Adams Papers); internal address: "John Brown Esqr Providence. R.I"; APM Reel 115.

[1] For Rhode Island's petitions to extend the exemption on foreign duties, see Henry Marchant's letter of 29 Aug., and note 4, above.

To John Bondfield

Sir New York Septr 16, 89

I have received the letter you did me the honor to write me on the 15 of May. and take this opportunity to return you my thanks for your polite congratulations. It is now five months within a few days since I entered on the execution of my office: and although I had many apprehensions from the novelty of it, and from my own long habits formed to different scenes of life, in the course of a ten years residence abroad in Paris, London and the Hague; yet I have not found much injury to my health or depresion of spirits. The greatest pleasure I enjoy is in the reflection that I am now employed in doing everything in my power to form a system of policy and Finance that may enable us to pay those debts both at home and abroad which I had so great a hand in contractting. You will always oblige me sir by transmitting me any information concerning the public affairs of France in whose happiness and prosperity I am not a little interested.

In what will be the fermentations in France and the rest of Europe end? Will the spirit and the system of constitutional liberty prevail or will confusion preceed despotism?

If you can send me a cask of claret such as you sent me at the Hotel De Valois, Rue de Richelieu, and another of Vin De Grave to be delivered to me at my house at New York, at your *Risque* and can contrive to receive your pay at the time and place of delivery, I should be much obliged to you.[1]

I am sir Yours & & J Adams

LbC in CA's hand (Adams Papers); internal address: "John Bondfield Esqr / Beurdeux"; APM Reel 115.

[1] For JA's 1780 wine order from Bondfield, see vol. 9:128.

To the Comte de Sarsfield

My dear Count New York Septr 16 1789

Your friendly letter of the 23 of April, has laid me under obligations to you which it shall be my endeavour to discharge.[1]

It will ever be a pleasure to me to hear of your health and happiness: and perhaps you may have a curiosity to hear of mine.— I have been here about five months, and without missing a single day, (excepting one when my own salary was under consideration, and delicacy induced me to absent myself) have constantly attended the Senate. Such constancy in attending to the deliberations of such an assembly, on such a variety of buisiness, and the continual exercise of speaking, are laborious service, and will endanger my health. Hitherto, however, by good air at home, and regular daily exercise at vacant hours, I have preserved a good share of health and spirits.— We are very anxious about the state of Europe, and that of France in particular. Will the states general claim authority to controul the crown, or will they be contented to advise it? Mixed in one assembly with the commons, will not the nobles be lost? Out numbered and out voted on all occasions? If in earnest a constitution is to be established you must separate the Nobles by themselves and the Commons must be placed in another assembly; and the Clergy divided between the two. In short your legislature must have three branches, and your Executive and Legislative must be ballanced against each other, or you will have confusions: Let my acquaintance the Marquis of Condorcet say what he will. But my friend, you may take the word of one who speaks from experience, dear bought experience! when a man suffers himself to be drawn in by the current which leads to a revolution, he knows not where he is going. He will soon find himself in a torrent which he can neither resist nor guide. Winds, tides and waterspouts which no wisdom could foresee will occur. Ignorace, if not knavery will intervene, and by means of passions, imagination, superstition or enthusiasm carry away the confidence of the people from truth virtue and the public good— Humiliations and mortifications innumerable if not total ruin will be his lot.— If however humanity on the whole is a gainer, a Philosopher will find some consolation. You will oblige me always by your letters as well as by presenting my most affectionate respect to M Le Duc and M[e] La Duchess de lu Vauguion and by accepting the compliments of my family as well as the repeated assurances of the sincere friendship of J Adams

LbC in CA's hand (Adams Papers); internal address: "Le Comte Sarsefield"; APM Reel 115.

[1] Vol. 19:427–428.

To Cotton Tufts

My dear Friend New Yo[rk Se]pt. 16. 1789

I have rec[d] all your Letters, and the Post Office is very faithful.[1] The Heat has been excessive and my daily Toil Somewhat exhausting besides a very extensive Correspondence, without a Clerk. Pray let M[r] Cranch if he will be so good look over the Account, as he did formerly.

Have you read Ned Church's fragment.? What Passion, or what Principle, could put it into that fellows head? I never injured, or offended him. I never saw him— He did not call on me. He never asked any Thing of me.— Washington refused or neglected him: and he fawns on Washington and Spits fire at Adams. poor Devil! I pitty him.— it is however good Verse and will do me honour.— so i'l enjoy it.—

The Fellow Su[pp]osed it impossible but the first must always be jealous of the Second; and on this principle expected to recommend himself at Court by abusing a Rival: but in this he mistook the Characters both of the first and Second, between whom there is the most perfect Harmony and good Understanding.

I must soon write again / Yours John Adams

RC (NHi:John Adams Coll.); addressed by CA: "Hon[ble:] Cotton Tufts / Boston"; internal address: "The Honourable Cotton Tufts Esq"; endorsed: "Rec[d.] Sep[tr.] 23[d.]—"; notation by JA: "Free / John Adams." LbC (Adams Papers); APM Reel 115. Text lost where the seal was removed has been supplied from the LbC.

[1] The most recent extant letter to the Adamses was Tufts' of 20 July to AA, outlining the sale of JA's farming tools and livestock as well as the leasing of the Adamses' land in Braintree (*AFC*, 8:392–393).

To Henry Marchant

Dear sir New York Sept[r.] 17. 1789

Your kind Letter of Aug. 29, gave me much pleasure.

There is more Confinement, in my present Situation than in any, that I have been in these thirty Years: and another Evil is come upon me, under which I suffered formerly, but from which I have been wholly relieved during my Absence from America.— Publick Speaking ever gave me a Pain in my Breast, which was not only troublesome for the time, but dangerous for the future. My present Office not only obliges me to a constant and close Attention of Mind, but to continual Reading and Speaking, which has again affected, La Poitrine, as it used to do, and raises many doubts how long I shall be able to go on.

Your Account of the *Prophecy* is humorous enough: but you must be mistaken in the Point of time. I left Congress on the 11[th.] of Nov. 1777 (that Year which the Tories Said had three Gallows's in it meaning the three sevens 777) just as Congress had gone through the Confederation, but before it was Signed. My Name is not to that Confederation. So that the Prediction must have been uttered either at York Town, a day or two before I left it, or before, at Philadelphia. I recollect Some Expressions of that Sort, on the Floor of Congress in Philadelphia, immediately after the Determination that the Votes Should be by States, and not by Numbers a Point which Wilson and I laboured with great Zeal. After that determination and some others,

I own, I gave up that Confederation in despair of its Efficacy or long Utility.

Congress have passed a Law, as you Solicited but a Clause has been introduced relative to Rum &c which perhaps your People may not relish so well.[1] It is now the Universal Expectation that your State will come in before Winter.— but if the Public should be disappointed, some thing very unpleasant will undoubtedly be the Consequence.— It would not be difficult for Congress to make the Unsocial Rhode Islanders, See, and feel, that the Union is of Some importance to their Interest and Happiness.— Winning however by Mildness and Condescension is much more agreable.

My oldest Son, arrived here Yesterday, very full of Gratitude for the Kindness and Attention of your Family to him at Newport.

Deacon Sayward of York, who was a timid Tory, Said to me at Dinner with the Judges on the Eastern Circuit in June 1774 "Mr Adams, you are chosen to go to Philadelphia as a Member of Congress. it is a weighty Trust, and I beg leave to recommend to you as a rule of your Conduct, the Doctrine of our former Minister Mr Moody. at the Declaration of the War of 1745, he preached a Sermon from those Words, *And they know not what to*[2] *do.— His Doctrine from the Words was, that in times of private or publick Calamity Distress or Danger it was the Duty of a Person or a People to be very careful that they do not do, they know not what.*"[3]

This Doctrine of Mr Moody I would very humbly and earnestly recommend to the Faith And Practice of every Member of the Rhode Island Legislature and Convention. and if you please you may give them this Advice of Deacon Sayward to a Member of Congress, without mentioning my Name in the Newspapers. I am / sir affectionately yours

John Adams

RC (MHi:Adams Papers, All Generations); addressed by CA: "Honble Henry Marchant / New Port R.I."; internal address: "The Hon. Henry Marchant / Newport."; endorsed: "Recd. Oct. / 7. 1789"; and: "Letter from / His Exccellency / John Adams / Esqr. Vice President / of the United States / of America dated / New York Sepr. 17 / Answered Decr 19 / 1789."; notation by JA: "Free / John Adams." LbC (Adams Papers); APM Reel 115.

[1] For the congressional battle over the molasses duty, which affected the Rhode Island rum trade, and JA's role in settling it, see his letter of 12 June to Cotton Tufts, and note 2, above.

[2] In the LbC, CA replaced "to" with "they."

[3] While riding the eastern circuit in the summer of 1774, JA noted the influence of York, Mass. (now Maine), merchant Jonathan Sayward (1713–1797), a loyalist who was active in town politics and served as a deacon in the First Congregational Church. Dining with Sayward in June, JA found him to be an "artfull, selfish, hypocritical Man." Sayward quoted a 1745 sermon given by Rev. Samuel Moody (1676–1747), Harvard 1697, in the

York church, mustering support for the Louisbourg expedition, which JA called an "oracular Jingle of Words, which seemed, however to contain some good Sense" (*AFC*, 1:110, 111, 116, 120–121; JA, *D&A*, 3:307).

To James Sullivan

Sir New York Septr 17, 89

In your letter of the 18th of August, you ask why we may not have as much paper in circulation in proportion to our circulating silver and gold, as Great Britain has in proportion to hers?[1] Give me leave to answer you without hesitation. We may as soon as we shall have any credit.— We have none. No man of common sense will trust us. As soon as an unlimited democracy tyrannized over the rich, no man of property was safe. If ever an unlimited Aristocracy shall tyrannize over the poor, and the moderately rich at once, the greater portion of society will not dare to trust the less. But if a government well ordered mixed and counterpoised should take place, and in consequence of it the commandment *Thou shalt not steal*, be observed, then and not till then you may circulate what paper you may find necessary— But I doubt very much whether our circumstances will require any paper at all. The cash paid in imposts, will immediately be paid to creditors and by them circulated in society

I am sir & John Adams

LbC in CA's hand (Adams Papers); internal address: "Judge Sullivan."; APM Reel 115.

[1] Sullivan, who had successfully defended participants in Shays' Rebellion, was anxious to address the ongoing scarcity of paper currency (Richards, *Shays's Rebellion*, p. 41). He wrote to JA on 18 Aug., comparing America's financial plight with that of Britain and suggesting the creation of a national bank for economic relief: "I do not like private Banks because it enriches private men & does no good to the public, but I beleive a public bank may Emit paper equal to the money we possess. the people when pressed for Money will be prone to blame the Government for their distresses" (Adams Papers).

To Jabez Bowen

Sir New York Septr 18. 89

I am honored with your letter of 31 of August. Your complaint against our laws was well founded but we have passed a law which I hope will give satisfaction. This was done in full confidence, that you will adopt the constitution and send us senators and Representatives before next session. If we should be disappointed I presume that serious measures will be suggested, to let your Anti's know that their interests are connected with ours, and that a desperate conspiracy of unjust men are not able to do so much mischief as they fattered themselves they had the power to do. D[r] Sender and M[r] Bourne did not give me an opportunity of shewing them the civilities which your recommendation entitled them to, and my own inclination prompted. The turbulent State of Europe ought to be a motive with us to get into order as soon as possible, and Rhode Island especially ought to feel the impropriety of her conduct in embarrassing themselves and their neighbors as they have done. out of the union there is no hope for your people but misery to themseves and mischief to others.

I have been happy in the company of my old friend M[r.] Marchant of NPort whose success in his negotiation I hope will recommend him to the favorable attention of his Country. I have known him these five and thirty years the same honest candid and sensible man

With esteem & & & John Adams

LbC in CA's hand (Adams Papers); internal address: "Hon Jabez Bowen / Providence"; APM Reel 115.

To William Tudor

Dear Sir New York Sept. 18. 1789

Yours of July 9 & 27 are unanswered.

I cannot reconcile myself to the Idea of a Division of this Continent, even fifty Years hence. great Sacrifices ought to be made to Union, and an habit of Obedience to a well ordered, and judiciously limited Government, formed at this early Period. a Dissolution of the Union involves Consequences of so terrible a kind, that I think We ought to consent to an Unity of Executive Authority at least, if not even to a Consolidation of all Power in one national Government rather than Seperate. We must first, however make a fair Tryal of the present system.

The Compensation to the Vice President, is, to be Sure, a Curiosity.— But the fault is entirely in the Massachusetts. There is not a State in the Union so weak in its Policy as that. There is not and never was these 15 Years any Union or Harmony among her Delegates

They never had a head—those whose Vanity pretended to be foremost had no heads on their shoulders. The Consequence has been, that altho the first Men have been produced by that state tho their military Power has been equal to almost all the rest: tho their commercial Advantages are superiour to any other; Yet they have the Reputation of nothing: their Commerce has been half ruined, and their Liberties nearly overwhelmed.— I Seriously think that their whole State Policy has been weaker than any in the Union.

The Opposition to the V. P. salary originated in Massachusetts.— Massachusetts moved to cutt off 500£ of my Salary in Europe immediately after I had made them a Peace. If that State is not made a signal Example of Vengeance against Injustice and Ingratitude, it will not be because it has not deserved to be.—

Other States reward their Benefactors. King, only for manœuvring Congress out of their design to go to Philadelphia has been nobly rewarded.— But a Man may drudge forever for Massachusetts and die a beggar,; nay what is worse die in disgrace. God forgive them.

how the President will decide, on the judiciary Appointments I know not.— There is no system nor Harmony among the Men from Massachusetts—One recommends one, and another another. Dont you be chagrin'd, mortified humiliated nor vexed Let it go as it will.

I am, sir yours John Adams

RC (MHi:Tudor-Adams Correspondence); addressed by CA: "William Tudor Esqr: / Boston—"; internal address: "Judge Tudor"; endorsed: "Mr. Adams 18 Sept / 1789"; notation by JA: "Free / John Adams." LbC (Adams Papers); APM Reel 115.

To John Laurance

Sir New York Septr: 19 89

My second son the bearer of this letter as soon as he was out of College was entered as a student at Law in the office of Colo: Hamilton upon certain conditions, one that if I should remove from New York, he should be at liberty to remove with me, and another was that if Hamilton should be made a minister of State his pupil should look out another patron. The latter condition being now realized, I send my son to you sir in order to know upon what conditions you will take him into your office.[1]

If it should not be inconvenient to you to receive him I should be obliged to you for your answer. I must still make a condition that I may be at liberty to take him with me wherever I may go. He will board with me, and attend your office as he did Col Hamiltons, from ten in the morning till three in the afternoon. John Adams.

LbC in CA's hand (Adams Papers); internal address: "Honble John Lawrance Esqr."; APM Reel 115.

[1] Once Alexander Hamilton assumed his new duties as first secretary of the U.S. Treasury, CA transferred his clerkship to the law firm of John Laurance (1750–1810), a former judge advocate general who had served as a New York delegate in the Continental Congress. CA opened his own practice on 20 Aug. 1792 in Hanover Square (*Biog. Dir. Cong.*; *AFC*, 9:300).

From Jeremy Belknap

Dear Sir Boston Sepr 19 1789

Your last favor of the 24th July should not have been so long without a reply had I not supposed that your attention must be so employed by the great national business as to leave You no leisure for a Correspondence with me— Indeed had the Occasion been pressing I might have taken advantage of your very obliging offer, to propose Questions to you; but as another time would do as well for me I thought it decent to wait till the adjournment of Congress might render it more agreeable to you—

The kind reception which my first Vol of the History of NHamp̃ has met with & the earnest solicitation of my numerous friends have prevailed with me to attempt another Volume,[1] which I should have begun sooner had my situation & Circumstances permitted— I am now engaged in it—& when I come to speak of the *late times* that we have passed through I shall very probably have some Questions to ask you.— One occurs to me now— The seizure of the Fort & Stores in NH in Decr 1774 was in consequence of a Prohibition of exporting Ammunition from Great Brittain—& I have a Copy of a private Letter from a Gent^n: in Office on the other side of the Question wch says "Positive proof was had from Holland that military stores to the amount of £400,000 sterlg were actually ordered & purchased from North America & were shipped to various Ports among the Islands & on the Continent. This caused an alarm, Col Lee of Marblehead it is said actually received a proportion & dispersed them.[2] He has reimbursed himself by the £800 voted to pay their minute Men, which was raised on Credit. This is truly the secret history of all the business."

If this is fact I think you must have known it & I should be glad you would (if it be proper) give me some acc^o of the Transaction or if this should lead to any other Information I would wish to have it. You observe that "many false facts are imposed on Historians & the world"— I am fully sensible there is great danger here—& therefore will endeavor to guard against it—& how can I do this better than by enquiring as far as possible into both sides of a controversy—& of those persons who were in the secrets of both parties?

Another of your observations strikes me very forcibly "some of the most important Characters are but imperfectly known, & many empty Characters displayed in great Pomp—all this I am sure will happen in *our* history"— The reason that I take such particular notice of this—is that I have been for some years preparing for a biographical History of America I.e a Collection of the Lives of the eminent Characters which have appeared on our Stage—ab initio—a specimen of what this work will be I have given in the Lives of Govr Winthrop, Sir Ferd Gorges—Capt John Smith & Friend Wm Penn which have been published in the Columbian Magazine—[3] I am daily making Collections for the prosecution of this Work but the completion of the NH histy must be made before I can go about this in earnest— When I do I shall probably give you some further Trouble with my Questions— Bernard & Hutchinson must make a part of the Group— With respect to the latter I wish to know how he passed his last days in England— I think they must have been extreemly dark & dismal.

I can give you one piece of Information which I doubt not will be agreeable. The Clergy in this Town have agreed to preach on the subject of "paying tribute & custom to whom tribute & custom are due" as a Gospel duty—& particularly necessary at this Time when our new Government is just put in motion—& is administred in such a manner as to be "a terror to evil doers & a praise to them that do well"—[4] Some of us have already spoken on the subject & (excepting that it was not a very agreeable Entertainment to the Ladies, as being rather out of their sphere) I have the pleasure to find that our discourses are approved by the judicious— I am just setting out on a Journey as far as Portsm^o & shall as opportunity presents recommend this subject to my Brethren in the maritime towns—

Adieu my dear Sir May Heaven preserve you for a long time an Ornament & blessing to your Country—& when assaulted by the invenomed darts of Malice

Hic Murus aheneus esto
Nil conscire sibi—[5]

I am with great respect Sir / y^r much obliged & most / hble serv^t

Jere Belknap

RC (Adams Papers); endorsed: "Dr Belknap. sept 19. / ans^d. 26. 1789."

[1] A copy of Belknap's three-volume *History of New-Hampshire*, Phila., 1784–1792, is in JA's library at MB (*Catalogue of JA's Library*).

[2] Col. Jeremiah Lee (1721–1775) was a prominent merchant in Marblehead, Mass. (vol. 4:476).

[3] Belknap was compiling his two-volume *American Biography*, Boston, 1794–1798, several copies of which are in JA's library at MB. He seized on the invitation of Philadelphia editor William Spotswood to print sketches of early colonial figures, including John Winthrop, Sir Ferdinando Gorges, Capt. John Smith, and William Penn, in the *Columbian Magazine* throughout 1788 and 1789 under the pseudonym "The American Plutarch." His notes for two additional volumes, which the historian did not complete before his death on 20 June 1798, are in MHi:Jeremy Belknap Papers (Louis Leonard Tucker, *Clio's Consort: Jeremy Belknap and the Founding of the Massachusetts Historical Society*, Boston, 1990, p. 40–44; *Catalogue of JA's Library*).

[4] Belknap inverted the third and seventh verses of Romans, 13.

[5] "Be this our wall of bronze, to have no guilt at heart" (Horace, *Epistles*, transl. H. Rushton Fairclough, Cambridge, 1926, Book I, epistle I, lines 60–61).

To Stephen Higginson

Sir — New York Septr 21, 89

Your favor of August 10th was duly received and immediately communicated with several other letters on the same subject to the President. His determination which will be made on the best principles and from the purest motives, as well as the most universal information, for he receives letters and makes enquiries from all quarters, we shall soon know. Altho' it is most probable to me that Mr Lowell will be the judge, yet if it should be otherwise, I apprehend your fears of an appointment to the place of C Justice of the State are not founded— Mr Hancock is not of a character strong enough to venture on such a nomination, and his Council would not consent to the appointment, if he did. It would have an happy effect if all the judges of the national supreme Court, would be taken from the chief Justices of the several states. The superiority of the national government would in this way be decidedly acknowledged. All the judges of the states would look up to the national bench as their ultimate object.— As there is great danger of collisions between the national and state judiciaries, if the state judges are men possesed of larger portions of the people's confidence than the national judges, the latter will become unpopular. This however is a subject which cannot be very accurately asscertained. It is easy to determine who a C Justice is, but not so easy to say who has most of the public confidence. The morals of the nation and perfection of the constitution; The national character, public credit, private confidence, public liberty, private property: every thing that is sacred, prescious or dear, depends so much upon these judges, that the President will choose I presume with caution. In Massachusetts happily there are several among whom he cannot make a wrong choice. The majority of the Senators and representatives from that state have recommended Lowell.

Your "Ideas of revenue and commerce" I should be glad to receive, as well as any other information relative to the affairs of this nation, whose wellfare is near my heart, Tho' it is not probable it will ever be in my power to do it much service. My own opinions of what is necessary to be done, to secure the liberty, and promote the prosperity of this Country if not singular, have too small a number of supporters to be of much use: May heaven grant that tradgedies and calamities may not in time convince Americans, when it is too late, that they have missed the tide in the affairs of men. Democratical powers equally with Aristocratical powers pushed to extremeties, necessarily produce a feudal system; this Country has already been very near the brink: within a short space of seeing hostile armies commanded by factious leaders, encamped on every great mountain and defended by a Barons castle. And if more pains and care than any disposition for has yet appeared are not taken to limit and adjust our national government, to raise it decidedly above the state government, and to prevent collisions of sovereignties, we may yet be not so far removed from a scene of feudal anarchy as we imagine. Thus you see I begin to be a *croaker*. Tho' the character is not natural to me.

J Adams

LbC in CA's hand (Adams Papers); internal address: "S Higginson Esqr / Boston"; APM Reel 115.

To James Sullivan

Sir — New York Sept 21, 89

Your letter of the 23 of July remains unanswered. There is in the United States and the regions to the southward of it a body of people, possesed of too much of the public confidence who are desperately in debt, and therefore determined all or any government, which shall have power to compel them to pay. Untill the property possesed by some of these men shall change hands, no government will be consistent in this Country. Trial by jury by the judicial bill and by the amendments to the constitution, already passed I imagine is secured to the utmost of your wishes.

The exorbitance of the power of the crown as it was exercised in this Country before the revolution was not generally complained of—it was the authority claimed by Parliament, and the attempt to increase the power of the crown and to diminish and annihilate, the power of our legislatures which gave the alarm. The legal perogatives of the crown were asserted and contended for by M[r] Otis M[r] Thatcher and M[r] S Adams in speeches and writings constantly, as essential to the protection of the rights of the people, and the liberties of the subject.

Whatever there is of danger in England at present from the power of the crown, arises not from its having an overballance, but it arises from the Aristocracy's having an overballance. The truth of fact is, that the people on one side and the crown on the other are each of them singly weaker than the Aristocracy; and as power increases like a snow ball, by rolling, if the influence of that Aristocracy; should increase much farther so strong an union will be formed between the people and the crown in opposition to it, that the King will be absolute If a few leading characters among the great landholder's were united as they were by the late Coalition administration, the Constitution would be overturned. King and people both would be prisoners to an oligarchic Junto. King and people would then unite to pull it down, as they did.—

You hope that our limbs will gain strength by time.— Indeed they will. But what limbs? Will the weak ones gain, and the strong ones loose? This would be contrary to nature and experience. The strong arm by constant exercise grows stronger, and draws the juices and nutrition from the weaker. If at our first setting out the executive power is not a counterpoise to the legislative; and if in the legislature, there be not a mediating power, sufficient at all times to decide the disputes between the poor and the rich; we shall not have law, nor consequently liberty nor property. The older we grow the more those ideas of equilibrium to which we were born and bred will wear out of the minds of the people, and Barons wars of a thousand years may be the miserable fate of America as it has been of Europe— A little longer delay might have exibited the feudal scene in America—Hancock Encamped upon Beacon hill, and Lincoln on Pens hill the one entitled Duke of Tremontain and the other duke of the blue hills—Washington encamped on mount Vernon and Henry on some other hillock—Clinton on one side of Hudsons river and Yates or a Livingston on the other. Pushing to extremities either Democratical or Aristocratical powers without attending to a ballance, produces a feudal system as naturally and, necessarily, as the collision of flint and steel produces fire.

I may expose myself to abuse and misrepresentations by such sentiments as these: but I have uniformly entertained them, and hence will discover who is in the right.— I have run the gauntlet too long among libels, halters, axes daggers, cannonballs and pistol bullet, in the service of this people, to be at this age afraid of their injustice. Those who wish for anarchy and civil war will not easily gain me over to their party.

I am sir & & & J Adams.

LbC in CA's hand (Adams Papers); internal address: "Judge Sullivan"; APM Reel 115.

To George Walton

Dear Sir New York Septr 25, 89

The duplicate via Charlestown of your letter of the thirtieth of August, never reached my hand till a day or two before the nomination took place to the office of Judge of the district of Georgia. As I had the pleasure and advantage of a particular acquaintance with yourself, and the misfortune to know nothing at all, but by a very distant and general reputation of the gentleman nominated, I should have been ill qualified to make an impartial decision between the candidates.[1] I feel upon all occasions I own, a particular pleasure in the appointment to office of Gentleman who are now well affected to the national Constitution who had some experience in life before the revolution and took an active part in the course and conduct of it.

Union peace and liberty to North America, are the objects to which I have devoted my life: and I beleive them to be as dear to you as to me. I reckon among my friends all who are in the communion of such sentiments: tho' they may differ in their opinion of the means of obtaining those ends. I will not say that an energetic government is the only means: but I will hazard an opinion that a well ordered, a well ballanced, a judiciously limited government, is indespensably necessary to the preservation of all or either of those blessings. If the poor are to domineer over the rich, or the rich over the poor, we shall never enjoy the happiness of good government: and without an intermediate power sufficiently elevated and independant, to controul each of the contending parties in its excesses, one or the other will for ever tyrannize. Gentlemen who had some experience before the revolution and recollect the general fabric of the government under which they were born and educated and who are not too much carried away by temporary popular politicks, are generally of this opinion. But whether prejudice will not prevail over reason passion over judgment and declamation over sober enquiry is yet to be determined J Adams

LbC in CA's hand (Adams Papers); internal address: "His Excellency G Walton / Augusta"; APM Reel 115.

[1] Born in Cumberland County, Va., George Walton (1750–1804) represented Georgia in the Continental Congress and later served as a chief justice and governor of the state. He wrote to JA on 30 Aug. (Adams Papers) seeking patronage (*Biog. Dir. Cong.*).

To Jeremy Belknap

Dear Sir New York Sept$^{r.}$ 26. 1789

Yesterday I received your favour of the 19$^{th.}$ and learn with Pleasure your design to pursue your valuable History of New Hampshire.

The Anecdote of "Positive Proof from Holland that military Stores, to the amount of 400,000$^{£}$ st. were ordered and purchased from N. America," is wholly unknown to me. that Col Lee of Marblehead ever "rec^{d} or dispersed" any stores I never heard nor that he was "reimbursed by the 800$^{£}$ voted to pay minute Men".— I am ignorant of the whole, nor do I believe any Part of it.— Sir Joseph York at the Hague was supposed and I beleive truely to have Spies in every Tavern in Amsterdam, who fabricated more lies than they discovered or communicated Truths; and this I doubt not was one of the former: if indeed the British Ministry had any Such Information.[1] Your Governor or Lt. Governor can tell you, with certainty whether there is any foundation for the Rumour. I believe there was absolutely none.— We should all have been comforted with even the faintest hope of Such Relief at that Time, and if there had existed even a Report of the Kind that any of Us believed, I should not have failed to have heard of it.

You have very good Reasons, from Hutchinsons Vanity his Love of Flattery, and his particular Pride in the Love and Admiration of New Englandmen, to suppose, that in a foreign Country Scantily supported, with numerous family Connections dependent on him, and still more numerous objects ruined by his Wiles, despised by one half the nation, neglected by the other, and not even much admired at Court, his latter days must have been "dark and dismal."— But I am unable to give you particular Information concerning him. Nobody where I was in England was fond of talking of him.— I heard a Report that he laid violent hands on himself, but it was from so poor an Authority, that it is scarcely worth while to enquire into the Truth of it.— if there had been any foundation for it, the Story would have made more noise.— I have heard too of Mortifications he received at Court, from Slights of the King at his too earnest Zeal to bring forward his Brother Foster upon all Occasions.[2] whether these particulars are not beneath the Dignity of Biography to mention, You are the best Judge, next to Dr Kippis that I know.[3]

The Subject chosen by the Clergy, does honour to their Patriotism as well as Piety. The Morals and Religion, as well as the Property and Liberty of the People of this Country, have Suffered extreamly, from a Loss of the Sense of the Duty of submission to Government. if the Press should not pull down as fast as the Pulpit can build up, the Design of the Clergy in all Events laudable, will have very happy Effects.

Happy are you sir, to contemplate in learned Ease and Leisure, the Course of Events, and at the same time that you contribute largely to the Entertainment & Instruction of your Country and Posterity, raise a Monument more durable than marble to yourself.— Unhappy am I, to be destined to Spend two thirds of my Life in defending this People, against an Host of Ennemies, I might have said against an Host of Nations, and the remaining third, in feebleness and Infirmity, against their own Ignorance Folly and —— I will not say more.

I have not been asssulted by Malice.— Ned Church has been actuated by the purest motives of Patriotism for any thing that I know.— I never injured nor offended him. I know nothing of him. There has not been a Word exchanged between him and me, this dozen years that I know.— if it was not Patriotism it was mere Caprice, or the lust of fame. Let him have it, tho he who burnt the Temple could not obtain it.—

With great Esteem, I have the honour / to be, sir your most obedient &c

John Adams

RC (MHi:Jeremy Belknap Papers); internal address: "The Reverend Jeremiah Belknap. / Boston"; endorsed: "John Adams Sept 26. 1789." LbC (Adams Papers); APM Reel 115.

[1] Sir Joseph Yorke (1724–1792) served as British minister to the Netherlands from Dec. 1751 to Dec. 1780. In his dispatches to Congress, JA reported that Yorke masterminded the "Swarms of Agents" who circulated anti-American propaganda in the Dutch press (vols. 6:61, 10:177).

[2] Fleeing Massachusetts for London in June 1774, Thomas Hutchinson initially enjoyed a warm reception at George III's court and established himself as a sponsor of loyalist refugees. But public attitudes gradually

changed, and false rumors about the former Massachusetts royal governor's poverty and unpopularity dogged Hutchinson until he died of apoplexy on 3 June 1780. Boston-born judge Foster Hutchinson (1724–1799), Harvard 1743, benefited from his older brother's political power, receiving an appointment to the Mass. Superior Court of Judicature in Aug. 1769. He moved to Halifax in 1776 and his estate was confiscated. After a protracted settlement with the British government, likely facilitated with his brother's aid, the judge received £510 and a pension.

JA, who was "melted" by accounts of Thomas Hutchinson's revolutionary ordeal, heard that he had committed suicide from the British home secretary, Thomas Townshend, 1st Viscount Sydney. Although JA did not believe the gossip, he later recalled seeing how his former political opponent suffered at the Court of St. James: "I know he was ridiculed by the courtiers. They laughed at his manners at the levee, at his perpetual quotation of his brother Foster, searching his pockets for letters to read to the king, and the king turning away from him with his head up" (*Sibley's Harvard Graduates*, 8:206–213; 11:237–238, 241, 243; JA, *Works*, 10:262).

[3] Presbyterian minister Andrew Kippis (1725–1795), of Nottingham, England, published a second edition of the *Biographia Britannica*, 5 vols., London, 1778–1793. Kippis frequently dined with the Adamses in London. Writing to Belknap in 1795, JA recalled: "I have been often a delighted Hearer of Dr Kippis in the Pulpit" (*AFC*, 7:155–156, 10:424; JA, *D&A*, 3:188, 193; *DNB*).

To Richard & Charles Puller

Gentlemen New York Septr 27 1789

When I had my audience of leave of his Britannic Majesty, orders were given to the master of the ceremonies Sir Clement Cotterell Dormer, to pay me the sum of money that was customarily given by his Majesty to ministers Plenipotentiaries from powers in amity with his court, upon like occasions. But as my departure was earlier than Sir Clement could receive the money from the treasury he desired me to name my banker that he might know where to pay the money, as soon as he should receive it. I accordinly named the house of Messrs C and R Puller in broadstreet buildings; presuming that the money was in your hands I drew a bill for three hundred pounds about a year ago upon your house, and sent with the first sett a letter of advice informing you of all these particulars and pointing out another for you to apply to for the money in case Sir Clement should not have paid you. But it now appears that the first of the sett and the letter of advice were lost at sea in the ship which carried them.[1] The second of the sett arrived but without the letter of advice, which amidst a multiplicity of cares I had neglected: and consequently came back protested and occasioned me a loss of about thirty or thirty five guineas for interest and damages. I am now determined not to loose my present, for if I should give it up, it would do no honor to his Majesty nor service to the nation, but would only be swallowed up, by some peculating clerk— I therefore request the favor of you to apply to Sir Clement Cotterel Dormer for the money, who will readily pay it. As soon as you have received it, you will please to write me; or if any difficulty is made about it let me know that, and I can easily find a way to make a noise about it to the discomfiture of those who may be in fault— When the money is in your hands please to order for me as good a gold snuff box with the kings picture as can be made for an hundred pounds, as good a gold watch as can be made for fifty and send me these insured, and the rest in Cash insured or bills of exchange. The rest will be employed in another manner here for the honor of his Majesty

J Adams

Upon second thought you may send the remainder after pay for the box, and watch, in two silver servers and four silver candlesticks with the kings arms upon them J Adams

LbC in CA's hand (Adams Papers); internal address: "Messrs C and R Puller / Broadstreet buildings"; APM Reel 114.

[1] The letter lost at sea was likely JA's of 28 Aug. 1788 to the London banking firm regarding his diplomatic honorarium (LbC, APM Reel 113). JA recorded a payment of £255, part of the "customary present" upon taking leave of the Court of St. James, in his accounts for 1788. He transferred the funds from the Pullers to the Dutch firm of Wilhem & Jan Willink and Nicolaas & Jacob van Staphorst (vol. 19:494). See the Pullers' reply of 6 Jan. 1790, below.

From Pierre Deschamps

Monsieur Cadiz Le 29. Septre: 1789

Il m'a été informé que je dois m'adressér a Vr̃e Excellençe; Je le fais avéc confiançe. C'est au Sujet de deux balles de Lainages qui furent chargées a Londres pour mon compte sous la marque PSD No 1 & 2. Sur le nre La Concorde, qui Fut pris par un de vos Corsaires dans sa traversée venant içy: ce nre était neutre, ainsi que moi etant Français; attestation que Je remis du consul de ma nation; Çelle de la facture qui monte £ Sterlins 820:4s:8d:; et le connaissement en ma faveur a monsieur Franklin a Paris pour les reclamér; Je reçeus la reponçe Suivante.

"a challiot prés Paris le 9: Deçembre 1777:

Mr. Monsr Franklin m'a remis comme Deputé du congrés pour L'Espagne, la lettre quil a reçeu de Vous relativement aux marchandises appartenantes avous prises par un de nos Corsaires.

J'ay l'honneur de vous avertir la dessus, que la copie de tous les papiers sur cette affaire a été expedié au congrés, et que vous pouvés comptér Sur leur Justiçe.

Je vous envoye au meme temps une lettre adressée a tous nos Capitaines et Commandants, que Je vous prie de Vouloir bien montrér a tous Ceux qui Viendront dans vos ports.

Vous Aurés la bonté d'etre persuade Mr. qu'il n'y a rien plus contraire aux Intentions du congrés que de faire tort, ou de le Souffrir d'etre Fait au sujet des nations neutres.

J'ay l'honneur d'etre avéc la consideration la plus Distinguée Monsr. vr̃e tres Humble & trés obt Sr: Arthur Lee"

Faites moi la Graçe Vr̃e Exce de me dire comment le Congrés a reglé Çet objet afin que je puisse me conformér a çe que Je la prie de me faire l'honneur de me prescrire.

J'ay Celui D'etre avéc Respect / Monsieur. / de Votre Excellençe / Le tres Humble et trés / Obeissant Serviteur. Pre: Deschamps[1]

TRANSLATION

Sir Cadiz, 29 September 1789

I have been informed that I must address myself to your excellency; I do so with confidence. It is about the two bales of woolens which were loaded in London on my behalf under the label PSD No 1 & 2 on the vessel *La Concorde*, which was seized by one of your privateers upon its crossing hither. This vessel was neutral, as I was French; an attestation of which I remitted, from my Nation's consul, along with the bill which amounts to £820.4s.8d and the bill of lading in my name, to Mr. Franklin in Paris to reclaim the sum. I received the following reply:

"From Chaillot near Paris, December 9, 1777:

Mr. Franklin remitted to me, as the agent of Congress to Spain, the letter that he received from you regarding the merchandise belonging to you and taken by one of our privateers.

I have the honor to inform you in regards to this, that a copy of all of the papers on this affair has been delivered to Congress, and that you may count on their justice.

Meanwhile, I am sending you a letter addressed to all of our captains and commanders that I beg you to show to all who enter your ports.

Please have the goodness to know, sir, that there is nothing more contrary to the intentions of Congress than to do harm, or to suffer it done to the subjects of neutral nations.

I have the honor to be, with most distinguished consideration, sir, your most humble and most obedient servant, Arthur Lee."

Do me the honor your excellency of telling me how Congress handled this affair so that I may act in accordance to what I beg you to do the honor to prescribe.

I have the honor respectfully to be, sir, your excellency's most humble and most obedient servant. Pre: Deschamps[1]

RC (Adams Papers); internal address: "Monsieur Adams, Vice, President du Congrès."

[1] For the claims of Deschamps and other neutral ship captains who demanded compensation for the seizures made by American privateers, see Franklin, *Papers*, 25:69–71. Congress took no action, and JA did not reply to Deschamps' letter.

From William Tudor

Dear Sir Boston 30 Sept. 1789

Your Letter of 18th. I received last Evening & it was particularly acceptable as I had experienced much Uneasiness from the Time which had intervened since your last Favour. Notwithstanding your kind Hint at the Close of it, I was chagrined, greatly so, by reading the Paper of this Morning.[1] Not, because I was not named as a Judge, for I think the Judges from this State are well selected & I know their Pretensions in various Respects better founded than any I could lay claim to—But the Appointment of the Attorney for the District of Massachusetts, has disappointed me. The Man who has obtained that Place has built up a very handsome Estate in Consequence of his Agency for Most of the Refugees who had Debts due to them in this Country, & which most lucrative Employment he got by the Sollicitations of his Father while he continued in England as a Refugee. I never heard of any Attachment or Services shewn by his Family to this Country, but something very different the public Acts of this Commonwealth attest to.—

But my Humiliation is forgot in the Assurance of the Continuance of your Friendship, & I have now only to regret the occasioning You Trouble in my behalf; & that I ever wrote a Line on the Subject to the President. Blessed is the Man who never expecteth for he shall never be disappointed. This Beatitude in future I will make my own, & thus I bid adieu to the Subject forever.

It is singular that Massachusetts should continue "Nothing" from a Want of System & Union in her Delegates. And what is still more disgraceful that Her paltry Policy, & debasing Œconomy should withhold a Compensation for the noblest Services of her ablest Citizens. Had the Vice President been born on the other Side the Potomac, how greatly would his Foreign services & American Merits have been estimated! As he belongs to New England, it is to be left to Posterity to do Justice to his Character, his Talents & his unparralleld Negotiations. And with such a glorious future Prospect, a Man ought to be content to be a Beggar—say the ungrateful, the Envious & the Miserly.

I am most truly yours Wm Tudor

RC (Adams Papers); addressed: "His Excellency / The Vice President of the United States / New York"; internal address: "President Adams"; endorsed: "Mr Tudor 30 Sept. / 1789."

[1] Tudor was reading the 30 Sept. *Massachusetts Centinel*'s list of nominees for the federal judiciary.

From James Sullivan

Sir Boston 2d October 1789

I have to aknowledge the honor of receiving yours of the 17th & 21st. instant

In my Letter of the 18th of agust, I suggested to your consideration, the idea of encreasing the circulating medium of the united states, by some kind of paper Credit. I hinted that I beleived, the duties, and Impost, Established, would call for more cash than is in circulation within the union, and that there was no Instance in any Country where one half of their medium passes through the public Treasury annually. in your obliging answer, you reply, that the money, as soon as received into the Treasury, will be again paid to the creditors of Government, and so be passed immediately into circulation. And that the states are destitute of that Credit which is necessary to the support of a paper Currency. these positions may be both True, but I am by no means convinced of the certainty of the one last mentioned, provideded the Government is administred with firmness moderation and prudence.

I have been in the Country upon business where money would have appeared if there had been any, and do assure you, that since my first introduction into the world, I never new so much complaint, or saw so much foundation for complaining. Our Common people have more money than the Peasants of other Countries, but you know Sir, that their Lenders in the revolution engaged that they should have more. their habits of expenditures cannot be suddenly changed without great convulsions, and perhaps civil wars. it is no easy task to learn to bear poverty with patience. but I only mean this as an apology for having troubled you on the subject. and urge the matter no further: Time decides upon all things.

I have read with great pleasure yours of the 21st., wherein you mention with great strength of expression, your determination to urge with integrity, those political principles which tend to give Government a proper balance, and consequently to secure to the people, those rights, for which all good Governments are instituted. I beleive the people are too sensible of your Services to treat you ill, and that your fellow Citizens are too much enlightned to persecute a Real friend. if you are ever injured it will be by those, who from a real regard to the principles of Despotism abhor every one who took an Active part in the late revolution, or by them who have no idea of Government, but as it affords them wealth and Emolument. these will Court you while you are in power to serve them, but the moment your old friends, and the People at large shall be induced to neglect you, these men will fatten on the triumph.

I might complain of being used not so well as I think I had a right to Expect; I engaged early in defence of my Countrys freedom, God knows it was on the purest, and most disinterested Principles. I spent the prime of my life in Legislative, and Judicial Capacities with no Emolument but paper money. I have, while there, been threatned with Halters, Gaols, &c. by men who are now in the warm Embraces of Government.[1] when the People by an unhappy combination of circumstances were exceedingly oppressed, and a number of them run mad, I took those healing Measures on our small scale, which Necker is taking in the great world: and Established without shedding blood by the civil arm, peace, and Tranquility. for I believe, that in all civil commotions, the less blood there is shed by the civil Authority, the more lasting the Succeeding peace will be. when the Constitution of the united states was submitted to the Consideration of the people, notwithstanding the Enthusiastic fervour which then reigned, I was honest enough to express my wishes for such amendments as I considered Essentially necessary to guard those rights which my Countrymen have bled to preserve, and for no other amendmends than what congress have agreed to. but *for this*, I find myself neglected by the national Government. as I do not want an office for the Emolument of it, so I can make myself very happy with the Esteem and Love of the People in private life.

Your ideas of an equipoise of powers in civil Government are always entertaining, and Instructive to me: and I am generally cautious of expressing Opinions to one, on whom the Learned world looks with so much respect as they do on you, but out of respect to you, I will venture to offer a few observations.

All writers upon civil Government agree, that there naturally exists three powers, which in a free Government can never be united in one man, or in one body of men: that such a Constitution as these writers speak of ever existed, compleat in all its parts I have yet to learn. the Europeans pretend that their orders of nobility are aristocratic bodys forming one balance, of the three powers, but it appears to me, that the Nobility in every Kingdom in Europe are an Artificial, and not a Natural branch of Government, and that the People at Large, while they suffer much by, derive no other benefit from them, than what arises from the wars between them and the soveregn power: without any regard in Either for the rights of the people.

When the united states declared themselves Independent, they became seperate sovereignties: and according to Montesque, and other writers, the people were both Sovereign, and subjects. their Magitratrates were their ministers to Execute the Laws, while the body of the People were the supreme Legislatures.

Upon the adoption of the General Government, a part of this Sovereignty was Yeilded, but the several states yet possess a great Share of that Sovereignty, over the subjects, and property they held before

In the departments of the General Government I cannot find any provision *expressly made* for the three great powers so much talked of. The President under certain advisory checks, holds the Executive Power; the senate, and House, under the Check of the Presidents negative hold the Legislative Authority, the senate is said to be a substitute for an aristocratic body, but while the two Houses of the Legislature, in the several states choose the senators, they are still but the representatives of the People, though introduced by a sort of double refinement in election.

An aristocracy, as I conceive of it, Must be independent both of sovereign and People, hence it follows that a Democracy cannot admit the appearance of an Aristocratic body. when I say an Aristocracy is independent of the Sovereign and the People, I mean that they are so, as to their future Existance and duration.

The Supreme Judicial holds that office during Good behaviour, which is a Tenure quite incompatible with the Ideas of an Aristocracy, but this Tenure however pompous it may Sound, when coolly examined will be found to be no more than a Tenency at will. and what is worse it depends upon the Legislative branch for existance. though the Judges are appointed by the supreme Executive, during good behaviour, and their Salaries irrevocably fixed by the Legislature, yet they may be impeached by the House, and tryed and removed by the Senate. therefore should there ever be a Time, when the President, House and Senate, shall agree upon a Law for changing the Constitution, and the Judges shall refuse to carry it into Execution, they may be removed by one branch of the Legislative power, and their Seats filled with men who will Act in consort with the other powers of state. then where is the Conterpoise which is so much talked of? it may be answered that the Judges will have integrity and firmness Enough to do right. that no doubt is the case with the Present Bench, nor is their Danger of a Violation of the Constitution in the Present age. but these observations if they have any weight, may be used to prove all Constitutional checks, and balances to be unnecessary.

The Method taken by all the Governments that I know any thing about to support themselves, and counterpoise their systems, is to rob the People of their wealth, their Liberty, and their understanding, and to press them down with standing Armies, and all this under pretence of defending them from a foreign power, which could not make them more unhappy, even by a Conquest. but this can never be the case in America; because the People have got a habit of understanding their own Interest, and cannot loose the use of arms.

But I am by no means aware, that the insufficiency of the Judicial, to counterpoise the other powers of Government in the plan adopted by the People of the united States, can ever become dangerous. the constitution has made as I conceive full provision in this case. the Existance of the states with uncontroulable, and Sovereign powers in some things, is preserved and guarentied by the General Government. and are necessary to the Election of Presid^t. Vice President, and Senators, the Legislature of each hath certain honors, rights, and priviledges which they will Jealously defend, and their very Existance as Soveregn states depends upon the preservation of the balance of the New general Government. to these I look as the most powerful checks, and contemplate them as possessing all the powers Necessary both to Counterpoise the Union, and to defend the people against the Encroachments which may in future ages be attempted upon their Liberty.

This species of balance may no doubt be attended with all the evils which You mention as flowing from the Encampment of great men, in the various parts of the Continent, but there can be no way to prevent it, unless by the mode of European Governments, that is to rob the people of the power of acting at all. for Nature has irrevocably established it, that where man has the power of doing good, he has the power of doing evil, You must therefore rob the people of the power of free agency, or they may do wrong.

In a Government where the People have any share of freedom, and possess any quantity of property, the beam of balance will be alway vibrating, and will Turn more, or less according to the agitation of the Surrounding Atmosphere, or other accidents. this flows forever from the imperfection of man, and must for the sake of the rights of human Nature, be born in the political, as we bear storms, and Tempests, in the Natural world

The dependence I have for Peace and good order, is in the wise administration of all our Governments, and in the intelligence and goodness of my Countrymen. they possess property, and hope for more, and have given full Evidence of their wishing for a Government to protect them in the enjoyment of it. they have indeed unhappily fallen into such mistakes and irregularities, as will Essentially injure them, but I beleive their habits are quite averse to the frequent repetition of them.

should the americans ever become ignorant, poor, and undisciplined, a strong state may be erected on the ruins of freedom, but I beleive they never will. should such a Government succeed, it will wan voluptuous, Arrogant, arbitrary, and cruel, and finally like the Roman, & other Empires will die of wounds received from its own hands.

should there ever be an unhappy Controversy between the General Government, and the particular states, a division of the whole into two or more states will be the probable Consequence, when the northern states will contend still for freedom. but how Long they will hold a free Constitution, the Century in which the Controversy shall take place may determine.

At present we can be in no danger while the General Government is administred with Impartiality; moderation, and Prudence. an attempt to alter the Constitution or to infringe the Rights of the particular states, would undoubtedly kindle a fire to be quenched only with blood.

I do not give you the trouble of reading this, supposing you would be instructed by it. or that any thing I can write will be entaining to you: but I wish you to beleeive that I am fully convinced, that the happiness of a people, depends much upon the principles of the Government under which they Live, and that I am firmly of opinion, that the *United Independence* of America must be preserved by moderation, Prudence, & Virtue, as certainly as it was acquired by Wisdom, Valour and firmness.

I have the honor to be / with sentiments of the highest / respect your most obedient / and most Humble Serv[t] Ja Sullivan

RC (Adams Papers); internal address: "His Excellency John Adams Esq[r]."

[1] Sullivan, a longtime supporter of John Hancock, fiercely opposed the rise of James Bowdoin, claiming that he headed a "party in this commonwealth composed of the seekers of emoluments" and "old anti-revolutionists." JA did not reply to this letter, and Sullivan did not resume their correspondence until 23 April 1795. In the interim, JA remained wary of his motives, sternly warning JQA that Sullivan was "a Savage, whose trea[chery] I would advise you to avoid like a Pestilence. . . . A more false and faithless Character is Scarcely to be found" (*AFC*, 9:113; *Sibley's Harvard Graduates*, 15:311).

To Thomas Brand Hollis

Dear Sir, Boston, October 28, 1789.

It was not till the last evening that I had the pleasure of your favor, with the pamphlets. They were sent to New-York, but had not arrived when I left it. Mrs. A. has sent the letter back to me.[1] Accept of my thanks for the kindness.

This town has been wholly employed in civilities to the president for some days, and greater demonstrations of confidence and affection are not, cannot be given, in your quarter of the globe to their adored crowned heads.[2]

I wrote to you, my dear friend, a year ago, by a vessel which was lost at sea, and have been much mortified that I have not been able to write to you oftener.[3] But we are men of business here, whether we will or no; and so many things that give us only troble crowd in upon us, that we have little time left for those which would afford us pleasure.

My country has assigned me a station, which requires constant attention and painful labor: but I shall go through it with cheerfulness, provided my health can be preserved in it. There is a satisfaction in living with our beloved chief, and so many of our venerable patriots, that no other country, and no other office in this country, could afford me.

What is your opinion of the struggle in France? Will it terminate happily? Will they be able to form a constitution? You know that in my political creed, the word liberty is not the thing; nor is resentment, revenge, and rage, a constitution, nor the means of obtaining one. Revolutions perhaps can never be effected without them: but men should always be careful to distinguish an unfortunate concomitant of the means from the means themselves: and especially not to mistake the means for the end.

My most cordial regards to all our friends, and believe me to be ever yours,

John Adams.

MS not found. Printed from Disney, *Memoirs*, p. 35–36; internal address: "Thomas Brand-Hollis, esq."

[1] Hollis' letter was of 6 June, above, which AA forwarded on 20 October. JA visited Braintree from 12 Oct. to late November, returning to New York by 1 Dec. (*AFC*, 8:427, 464; Washington, *Diaries*, 5:503).

[2] George Washington's intent was to tour New England and thereby "acquire knowledge of the face of the Country the growth and Agriculture there of and the temper and disposition of the Inhabitants towards the new government." He left New York on 15 Oct. and reached Boston nine days later. A large procession—comprising Massachusetts officials, merchants, and clergy—greeted the president. Newpapers described in detail the banners, cheering, and singing that accompanied the city's welcome reception for Washington. JA declined an invitation to travel with the president, but he joined Washington's party in Boston, where they dined in a large company and visited Harvard College. JA reported that the "charming" Virginian enjoyed a "cordial and Splendid reception," and that he believed the tour would "do much public good." Pausing at Newburyport, Washington heard JQA's 4 Nov. address, which hailed the president as "the friend, the benefactor, the father of his Country."

Washington's first public tour took in nearly sixty towns and stretched to Maine. Notably, he omitted Rhode Island, which had yet to join the union. In his diary, Washington recorded his impressions of people, agriculture, and manufacturing. Looking over the houses and farms that dotted Massachusetts, Mount Vernon's owner observed that there was "a great equality in the People of this State—Few or no oppulent Men and no poor." Suffering from a cold and an inflammation in his left eye, Washington moved quickly through New Hampshire and Maine, drawing his first excursion to New England to a close by early November. He turned south at Portsmouth, N.H., and headed for New York, reaching the city on 13 November. For a map of his tour, see Washington, *Papers, Presidential Series*, 4:200–201 (Washington, *Diaries*, 5:453, 460–497; *AFC*, 8:421, 425, 432, 445–446, 447; Boston *Herald of Freedom*, 27 Oct.; Newburyport *Essex Journal*, 4 Nov.; Washington, *Papers, Presidential Series*, 4:163).

[3] Not found.

To Marston Watson

Sir

Braintree November 7. 1789

The Letter you did me the honour to write me, on the thirtieth of September, has been to New York; and from thence transmitted to this Place; but it never reached my hand, till the night before last.[1] The Sentiments of Esteem for my private Character, expressed by Gentlemen who are probably Strangers to me, are very obliging: and the approbation of my public Conduct abroad, lays me under Still greater Obligations.

The Fisheries, are So essential to the Commerce and naval Power of this Nation, that it is astonishing that any one Citizen Should ever have been found, indifferent about them. But it is certain that, at a Time, when there were Reasons to expect that more than one foreign nation would endeavour to deprive Us of them, there were many Americans indifferent, and not a few even disposed to give them away.— A Knowledge of this was the first and Strongest motive with me to embark for Europe a first and a Second time.— after all however, the final Preservation of the Fisheries was owing to Causes so Providential that I can never look back upon them without Reverence and Emotion. Your Approbation, sir and that of your Friends of the Part I acted in that Negotiation, give me great Pleasure.

The Present of four Boxes of Fish, has been received in my Absence by my Family; and is in every point of View very acceptable to me. As an Amateur I shall regale myself and my Friends: as a Well wisher to the Trade I shall endeavour to make the Dish fashionable at New York: I pray You and your Companions to accept of my Sincere Thanks, for the favour, and my best Wishes for their Pleasure Profit and Prosperity, in the Prosecution of the Fisheries. May You and they live to see a Commerce and a naval Power growing out of your Occupations, which shall render this, the first and most respectable of maritime Nations. I am, sir, with my best Comple / ments to your Friends and much Esteem for / yourself your most obedient and most / humble servant John Adams

RC (WHi:Signers of the Declaration of Independence Autograph Coll.); internal address: "Marston Watson Esqr / Marblehead"; notation: "Copy of a letter of John Adams / to Marston Watson Marble Head / Fisheries." FC (Adams Papers).

[1] For Watson's letter of 30 Sept. (Adams Papers) and gift of "very fine" fish from the residents of Marblehead, Mass., see vol. 19:400.

From George Walton

sir, Augusta, 7 November, 1789.

You have my thanks for the letter which you did me the favor to write to me on the 25th. of september last; and while I express some small disappointment on the subject of it, I beg leave to give you the assurance of a chearful acquiescence. I know that disappointment has often been the cause of opposition and faction: but I trust that I have made a better estimate of men, and of the blessings of society and good Government, than to suffer myself to be governed by its influence. As a proof of this I take the liberty of repeating my application, in the same line, and to the same persons, for employment under the general Government.— Report says, at this place, that M^r.

Rutledge has declined accepting the appointment as one of the associate Judges; and the policy of diffusing the appointments will, no doubt, continue to operate. In this view I stand upon the same ground as Mr. Rutledge did; and with respect to pretensions, if they do not evidence themselves, they ought not to be attended to. In any event your approbation will console me.

The sentiments you express upon the general principles of Government, and of the present condition of America, are perfectly satisfactory to my mind; and, as to Office, I have felt, perhaps, too confident on that foundation: but I can truely assure you, that, since the 1st. day of July 1776, my conduct, in every station in life, has corresponded with the result of that great question which you so ably and faithfully developed on that day—a scene which has ever been present to my mind. It was then that I felt the strongest attachments; and they have never departed from me.

Should any principle, dangerous to the present views of future welfare, be generated in this quarter, or any thing otherwise eventful present itself, I will take an early occasion of communicating with you; and should you feel it justifiable to withdraw your attention from the engagements of your situation, and somtimes write to me, I shall be particularly obliged: for in truth, sir, / I am, with the greatest respect and / esteem, / Your most obedient servant,

Geo Walton.

Colonel Gunn,[1] who is now with me and very well, desires his respectful compliments.

I have just heard that Mr. Drayton, of South-Carolina, is recommended. I am not acquainted with him: but the fact is, that, altho a native, he was a british subject, and a british judge, during the whole Revolution. What idea will be formed of Justice, if such men are preferred?—[2]

RC (Adams Papers); internal address: "His Excellency, / John Adams."; endorsed: "George Walton / 7. Nov. 1789."

[1] Savannah lawyer James Gunn (1753–1801) served as a Georgia senator from 1789 until his death in 1801 (*AFC*, 11:96).

[2] On 24 Sept. 1789 George Washington nominated John Rutledge Sr. as an associate justice for the U.S. Supreme Court, and Thomas Pinckney as a district judge for South Carolina. The Senate confirmed both nominations two days later. Writing separately to Washington on 27 Oct., Rutledge accepted the appointment while Pinckney declined. By 18 Nov. Washington had tapped Charleston, S.C., lawyer and planter William Drayton, a former chief justice of the province of East Florida, to serve instead of Pinckney. Drayton was nominated on 9 Feb. 1790 and confirmed the next day (Washington, *Papers, Presidential Series*, 4:114–115, 305–306; *First Fed. Cong.*, 2:43–45, 48, 58–59, 61, 62; *AFC*, 8:124).

From C. W. F. Dumas

Monsieur Lahaie 15e. Nov. 1789

Après avoir présenté à Votre Excellence, dans une précédente, l'expression de mes sentimens sur son élevation au Poste éminent qu'Elle occupe, permettez, Monsieur, qu'en les confirmant j'y ajoute aujourd'hui de nouvelles félicitations sur les dignes Coopérateurs au bien public, qu'Elle vient d'acquérir par la nomination aux Postes éminents de Secretaire d'Etat, Chef de Justice, & Trésorier genl., de personnages d'un mérite aussi grand, & universellement applaudi, que le sont Leurs Exces. MM. Th. Jefferson, Jn. Jay, & Al. Hamilton.— Mon coeur, comprimé par tout ce que je vois se passer autour de moi en Europe, se dilate à l'idée d'une Administration, telle que le sera celle de la Confédération Américaine entre des mains si sages & si habiles. Vous ferez honte, Messieurs, &, s. p. à Dieu, la leçon la plus salutaire, à cette Europe; j'ose le prédire.— Dans ce moment j'apprends que le Département de la Guerre est pareillement rempli par S.E. Mr. le Genl. Knox;[1] & je differe de finir la présente, pour le mander à Mr. Luzac, afin qu'il l'ajoute au reste que je lui ai déjà comuniqué.— Dieu le bénisse aussi avec touts les autres, le Législatif, l'exécutif, le judiciaire, le maritime, tout le peuple Américain, Madame votre Epouse, famille, & votre Excellence, de qui je suis avec le plus respectueux attachement, le très-humble, & très-obéissant servit. Cwf Dumas

TRANSLATION

Sir The Hague, 15 November 1789

After having presented to your excellency, in a previous letter, the expression of my sentiments on your rise to the prestigious office that you hold, allow me, sir, to confirm them and add today new congratulations on the dignified collaborators for the public good whom you have recently acquired by the election to the prominent offices of secretary of state, chief justice, and secretary of the treasury, of individuals of equally great merit, and as universally applauded, as their excellencies Messrs. Thomas Jefferson, John Jay, and Alexander Hamilton. My heart, wrung by all that I see happening around me in Europe, expands at the idea of an administration like the American Confederation in such wise and skillful hands. You will bring shame, the most salutary lesson, sirs, and if it please God, upon Europe; I dare predict it. This moment, I have learned that the Department of War is likewise filled by his excellency General Knox;[1] and I leave

off finishing the present letter in order to send it to Mr. Luzac so that he may add it to the others that I have already delivered to him. God bless him too, with all the others, the legislative, the executive, the judiciary, the maritime, all the American people, madam your wife, family, and your excellency, of whom I am with the most respectful attachment, the most humble and obedient servant.
Cwf Dumas

RC (Adams Papers); internal address: "A S. E. Mr. Jn. Adams."

[1] News of the appointments of Alexander Hamilton, John Jay, Gen. Henry Knox, and Thomas Jefferson reached Dumas by mid-November. While the *Gazette de Leyde* remained quiet on the news, the British press reported favorably on the new department heads, singling out Knox as "extremely well qualified," and observing that "the New Government seems to be much liked, and an opposition is scarcely heard of" (*Dipl. Corr., 1783–1789*, 3:650–651, 653–654; London *English Chronicle*, 21 Nov.).

From John Bondfield

Sir
Bordeaux 20 Nov 1789

I am this day honor'd with your favor of the 16 September

I am happy to find that the affairs of America are in a state to fix a permanent line of Reimburssment, becoming thereby truely independant.

Notwithstanding the weight of Opossion against the leading Members of the National Assembly, the steddy perseverance of the few and the effectual support of the Marquis de La fayette in whose hands are the reigns of the National Troops. that the Motions made by the Patriote Committees are decretted by a Powerful majority

The Revolution is Compleat unless you regard leaving in the Person of the King a Susperiur Power and an hereditary Succession, [. . .] abuses both have limits that render the nation a Curb to infractions

the distinction of orders are Vanish'd, the Incorporated Bodies are Supprest, all provincial distinctions of charters Privalidges and Customs are destroy'd the formadable Body of the Parliaments and all Religious Orders Supprest. The Estates of the Clergy Sequester'd for the benefit of the Nation applicable to the discharge of the National Debt, the Courts of Justice suspended to the Establishment of a New Code—

The Old Mansion is thus entirely demolish'd and the materials are colected to A heap to be destroyd by time The Plan of the New fabrique is before the House of Assembly They have begun by the Ground Work, by a New division of the Kingdom into 80 equal parts of 36 by 36 Leagues. called Departement, the 80 departments into 9 equal divivissions of 6 by 6 Leagues call'd Com̃unes or Districts. The Communes into 9 equal Divissions of 2 by 2 Leagues called Cantons or Primaires The Names of the Old Provinces have no longer existence

The present deliberations are imploy'd in organizing the Municipality's. The Represtations are to take Rise from the Cantons or Primaires in the proportion of Population of 1 to 600 to form the provincial assemblys

from these outlines you see a methodique order establish'd by the Moteurs of the Revolution and all personalties being set asside and a general chain of Popular measures pursued. the People at large approve the measusurs and smother the murmurs of the discontented[1]

The Austrian Netherlands [. . .] in Arms have Publish'd their manifest against the Souveregnety of the Emperor, but their ~~principals~~ motifs not springing from Liberal Principles but from Religious fermentations fomented by discontented Religious Orders who were supprest by order of Gouverment it is posible their resistence may prove a Civil Slaughter without reaping any Solid advantages.[2]

I shall ship by the french Pacquet that will leave this in ten or fifteen Days the wine you have pleased to Commission[3]

If on application that will be made to you for Supplies of Wheat and flour from the Ministry of france should be complied with permit me to Solicite your Influence in my favor as your Agent for the Receipt of the Cargoes that may be addrest to this port[4]

with respectful Attatchment I have the Honor to be / Sir, / Your most Obedient / Humble Servant John Bondfield

RC (Adams Papers); internal address: "The Honble John Adams Esq Vice President of Congress"; endorsed: "Bondfield / 20. Nov. 1789." Some loss of text due to an ink blot.

[1] After the National Assembly's abolition of the three estates and renunciation of special privileges for provinces on 4 Aug., the French Revolution's political progress gained pace. The assembly dissolved all monasteries and convents on 28 Oct. and then confiscated church property amounting to an estimated 2.5 billion livres. As Bondfield pointed out, Louis XVI held some power, but on 14 Dec., that, too, changed when the assembly established new municipal governments and courts. By 15 Feb. 1790, France was divided into 83 departments of roughly equal size (Bosher, *French Rev.*, p. 140, 145, 148–149).

[2] Beginning in 1781, Joseph II, emperor of Austria, conducted a two-year program of political reforms that stripped away the power of the Roman Catholic Church in the Austrian Netherlands. In a rapid series of edicts, he suppressed monastic orders and reallocated their funds. He cut off formal contact with officials in Rome and rejected the authority of papal bulls. The emperor pushed through these changes without the consent of the States General, provoking his critics in the Democrat and Statist parties to join

forces with the Catholic clergy in revolt. In Dec. 1789, the States General proclaimed Joseph II's deposition and the establishment of a short-lived Republic of the United States of Belgium. After Joseph II's death on 20 Feb. 1790, his brother and successor, Leopold II, recaptured the Austrian Netherlands (*Cambridge Modern Hist.*, 6:648–655).

[3] JA received his wine order of 16 Sept. 1789, above, via the French packet *Suffrein*, Capt. Le Grand, which arrived in New York on 15 May 1790 after a 53-day voyage from Bordeaux (New York *Daily Advertiser*, 17 May).

[4] Hailstorms, drought, and a severe winter ravaged the French wheat crop in late 1788, inciting bread riots. As the shortage continued and bread prices skyrocketed, Thomas Jefferson noted that bakers set quotas, weekly subscriptions were collected to feed the poor, and dinner party guests were asked to bring their own bread. He relayed France's need to at least one Virginia planter, Alexander Donald, who shipped 10,000 barrels of flour in Jan. 1789.

Although the grain shortage was often blamed on embattled finance minister Jacques Necker, other members of the French government drew Jefferson into the food crisis. On 6 July Honoré Gabriel Riqueti, Comte de Mirabeau, falsely informed the National Assembly that Jefferson had promised Necker that the United States would send "a large supply" of wheat and flour to ease the famine. Seeking confirmation, the Marquis de Lafayette contacted Jefferson, who denied the claim. Mirabeau retracted it two days later, but the damage was done. Several of Jefferson's exchanges with the ministry appeared in the French press, and in an unflattering light. On 6 Nov. Mirabeau put forth a new motion in the assembly, requesting that the United States pay its Franco-American loans in grain. Although he was unsuccessful, additional American shipments of wheat and flour reached Bordeaux in Jan. 1790 (Jefferson, *Papers*, 15:243–256; Schama, *Citizens*, p. 305, 324; Washington, *Papers, Presidential Series*, 4:282–284; Hamilton, *Papers*, 6:230).

From Mary Palmer

Sir

Braintree Novr 25th 1789

I beg leave to inform you that Princes Chronology is now in the office, unless the same fairy who bro't it has carried it away again—[1] Since you left us I have repeatedly search'd for it to no purpose & had given it over, but chancing to go in yesterday this Book Struck me as one I had not seen & was quite sure was not on the shelf the day before, taking it up I found it to be the very one you seem'd so anxious to recover— If this intelligence will give pleasure enough to attone for my boldness in writing to the Vice President I shall be happy.

I have not yet executed any part of the commission with which you were pleased to honour me but am determin'd health permitting to do my best in cleaning & setting the Books in order This I cant do but in a warm spell of weather as our finances are too low to afford a fire in that room— My intention was to take a Catalogue & transmit to you, but Cos: W Cranch says he is commisioned to do this part, which is much better on many accounts for I shou'd have been sadly put to it to write Greek & Hebrew, as well as puzzled in spelling the other languages—[2]

Mamma & sister join with me in wishing D[r] Adams an agreable journey & happy Meeting with his family—also in repectful compliments to his Lady & love to Mrs & Miss Smith

I am Sir your hum[le] Servant Polly Palmer

RC (Adams Papers); endorsed: "Polly Palmer / 25. Nov. 1789."

[1] Thomas Prince, *Chronological History of New-England*, Boston, 1736.

[2] Mary Palmer (Polly, 1746–1791) was the niece of AA's sister Mary Smith Cranch, and a resident at Peacefield. JA admired Palmer's skill as a writer, telling AA that "her Narration is executed, with a Precision and Perspicuity, which would have become the Pen of an accomplished Historian." William Cranch (1769–1855), AA's nephew, worked with Palmer to compile JA's book list, which the vice president used to select volumes for his New York home (*AFC*, 1:18; 2:27, 67; 8:385; *Catalogue of JA's Library*). For more on JA's book catalog, see Descriptive List of Illustrations, No. 2, above.

From Hendrik Fagel

Monsieúr. a la Haÿe ce 30 novembre 1789

La lettre, dont voús m'avés honoré le 26 de Maÿ m'est bien parvenúe dans son temps, avec le second, et troisieme tome de Votre Oúvrage, qué je desirois beaucoúp d'avoir, a caúse de son contenú interessant.[1] La maniere, dont voús avés developpé vos principes sur̃ la meilleúre forme de gouvernement ne peut etre qu'approuveé generalement, et il seroit a soúhaiter, qu'il pút etre súivi par toút, mais les circonstances ne permettent pas toújoúrs de le mettre en exécution. J'ai appris avec ún veritable plaisir, Monsiéur, qué le nouveaú gouvernement voús a choisi, comme Vice-President, dont j'ai l'honneúr de voús feliciter. Soús votre sage direction, et celle de Votre Illústre Chef, on ne peút, qué bien augurer poúr la Republiqué des Etats Unis, à laquelle je souhaite toúte sorte de bonheúr et de prosperité, avec la conservation de la paix, quí voús convient, aússi bien qu'a noús. Dieú veuille noús l'accorder longtemps.

Notre ami commún, Dr Maclaine a eté tres sensible a Votre souvenir.[2] Il voús donnera lui meme de ses nouvelles. Il ne me reste, qué de voús assúrer de la haute estime, et de l'attachement respectúeux, avec lequél j'ai l'honneúr d'etre, / Monsieúr / Votre tres humble et / tres obeissant serviteúr H. Fagel.

TRANSLATION

Sir The Hague, 30 November 1789

The letter that you honored me with of the 26th of May reached me in due time, along with the second and third volumes of your work, which I greatly desired to have because of its interesting contents.[1] The way in

Catalogue of Books in
this Library.

June 1790.

Law.

Abridgment of State Trials, by Salmon. vol. 1. fol:
Accomplish'd Attorney . . . 1. 8vo
Archerley's Brittannic Constitution . 1. fol
Burlemaque Nat. Law 1st Vol.
Burrows Reports . . 3. 4to
Blackstones Commentaries . . . 4. quto
——— Appendix . . . 1. 8vo
——— Law tracts . . . 1. .
Barnardiston's Reports . . . 2. fol.
Book of Rates . . 1728 . . . 1. . .
Bridgman's Conveyances . 1725 — — — 1 . .
Booth, of Real Actions . . . 1. .
Barrington's observations on the Statutes. 1. qto.
Burns Justice abridged by Greenleaf . . 1. . .
Burn's Justice . . . 4. 8vo
Burns Ecclesiastical law. . . . 4. . .
Barnes's Notes . . . 2
Bacon's Element of the Common law . . 1. 4to
Bacons Abridgment . . . 5. fol.
Beccaria on Crimes and Punishments . 1. 8vo
Comberbach's Reports . . . 1. fol.
Comyn's Digest . . . 5. fol
Cokes Reports. 1680. 11 parts. . . 1. . .
Coke's Entries . . . 1. . .
Cokes Reports 12th & 13th parts . . 2. . .

46

2. CATALOG OF BOOKS IN JOHN ADAMS' LIBRARY, JUNE 1790

See page xi

which you have developed your principles on the best form of government can only be broadly approved of, and it is to be hoped that it may be followed everywhere, yet circumstances do not always allow it to be implemented. I was genuinely delighted when I learned, sir, that the new government chose you as vice president, for which I have the honor of congratulating you. Through your wise guidance and that of your illustrious leader, one can only anticipate good things for the republic of the United States, for which I wish every kind of happiness and prosperity, with preservation of peace, which is as agreeable to you as it is to us. May God grant us it for a long time yet.

Our mutual friend, Dr. Maclaine was very touched by the memory of you.[2] He will give you his news. It remains only for me to guarantee you the high esteem and respectful attachment with which I have the honor to be, sir, your most humble and obedient servant. H. Fagel.

RC (Adams Papers).

[1] Vol. 19:474–475.

[2] Rev. Archibald MacLaine, Presbyterian pastor of the English Church at The Hague, had last corresponded with JA in 1783 (vol. 15:45–46).

From Wilhem & Jan Willink

Sir.— Amsterdam 8, Decem[r:] 1789.—

Shortly after we had the pleasure of paying you our respects under date of the 30 April, we were honor'd with your Letter of 2 Decem[r:] A.P.;[1] for it's contents we pray you to be assured of our Sincere thanks, & to do us the Justice to believe that we shall with pleasure embrace every opportunity that may present for cultivating our private Correspondence, that you express such a desire of continuing.—

We have as yet only been enabled to send the first Volume of your defence of the American Government to the several Gentlemen as desired, instead of receiving the compleat sett from M[r:] Dilly, we have only recẽd the first & third Volumes; on which we addressed him, requesting to be furnished with the Second Volume that we might comply with your directions without delay, in reply he informed us that fifty Copies of that volume were Shipp'd us per the Margaretha in Sept[r:] 87. & that as he cou'd not find the Capt[ns:] receipt for the parcell, he presumed it had been transmitted us, We immediately made enquirey of the Ships Broker who informed us that she arrived here the 5 Oct: 87. but that he cou'd get no intelligence of any such parcell having been on board, which we wrote M[r:] Dilly desiring he wou'd send us fifty other Copies, as it was not natural to suppose that you shou'd suffer thro' any neglect or omission of his, for had he given us proper Information in due time of the Shipping, we shou'd have taken the necessary care to have made application for them on the Vessels arrival, he now informs us in reply to this, that he can say nothing further respecting the Books, but that he will write you concerning them, in which case you will now be enabled to give him a reply.

The present Political Situation of Europe renders it rather difficult to ground any opinion on the future events that may arrive, we hope nothing will tend to involve our Republick into a War, the blessings of Peace are invaluable at all times, but especially when we see them at the greatest distance, at least they are rendered the more so then, because the impossibility of enjoying them is greater.—

We are highly gratified to observe that the chief offices under your new Government, are filled by such Characters as give universal Satisfaction, & shall be truly happy to learn the continuation of such Steps, as will procure a great degree of respectability to your Executive, as well as Legislative authority.—

Our Ladies consider themselves particularly obliged by your kind remembrance of them, & have requested to join us in best respects to you & Mrs: Adams.—

With assurances of our Sincere respect & Esteem, we have the honor to Subscribe ourselves / Sir.— / Your most obedt: & hble Servants.

Wilhem & Jan Willink

Mr: Dilly never wrote us the least word at the time of his Shipping the Copies of the Second Volume, thus it was not in our power to have made enquirey respecting them 'till we recēd information of the Transaction—

RC (Adams Papers); internal address: "To / The Hoñble J. Adams"; endorsed: "W. and J. Willink / 8. Decr. 1789." Dupl (Adams Papers).

[1] For these exchanges, which concerned the Willinks' distribution of JA's *Defence of the Const.* as well as the maintenance of his Dutch investments, see vol. 19:355–356, 434–435.

From William Smith

Sr. Boston. 14th Decr. 1789.—

By direction of the Boston Marine Society, I have the honor to forward you by the Honble. Mr. Otis a Certificate of your admission as a Member of that Society the 6th of November 1768.—[1]

I am with Respect / Yr H Sert. Wm. Smith.

RC (Adams Papers); internal address: "His Ex$^{y.}$ John Adams Esq$^{r.}$"

[1] Boston merchant William Smith's enclosure has not been found. Established in June 1742 and incorporated on 2 Feb. 1754, the Boston Marine Society was mainly made up of ship captains who provided aid to indigent colleagues, shared reports on coastal trade, and sought to improve knowledge of navigation. According to the organization's minute books, JA did not attend any meetings but remained a member until his death (vol. 19:468; Nathaniel Spooner, comp., *Gleanings from the Records of the Boston Marine Society*, Boston, 1879, p. 3, 7, 8, 11–12, 34, 104, 105, 190–191).

From James Lovell

Sir — Boston Decr 19$^{th.}$ 1789.

Though I know your extreme Delicacy as to any Interference in the *executive* Affairs of the U.S$^{s.}$ yet to you I *must* apply; for, Heaven & Secretary Jackson know I may be chagrined in an Attempt to *address* the President.

I am in Dread least an Action should take Place which will renew the Vigour of the Opponents & damp the Spirit of the Friends of Government: And, it will be out of Time to await the Motions of a *deliberate* Legislature

The enclosed Copy of a Letter will explain my Dread.[1] If it appears well-founded and of sufficient Importance to call for a speedy Remedy, a very mild but efficacious one may be suggested. The President may see the *circular Instruction* of Octr 31$^{st.}$ and advise that it be *immediately* followed by another stating the Point "to appear, upon Review, to be of such a Kind as to need, perhaps, Legislative Attention"; and therefore proposing to the Collectors to stay all Proceedings therein "till they hear *again* from the Treasury.["]

I am totally rong in my Conceptions of the Business, or else it may be expected that one single Suit commenced in each of the States would produce a Multitude of News paper Suggestions of a very unpleasant Sort both respecting the General Government and its new Law Courts.

Am I consummately *impudent* in this Application? Whatever may be your Judgement of it, you may be assured I will attribute so much of that Charge to myself as to keep my Doings herein a *profound Secret*.—

I am endeavouring to break the Neck of some Enemies to the french Consulate here. You must know I admire that Institution, because by the Kings Ordonnances it's Chancery has all the Spirit & Essence of our *Jury of Equals*.

The *Herald* inclosed proclaims my first Onset, as the Printer of it did not feel my sly Knock at *his* Licentiousness so sensibly as to refuse me the Use of his Types.[2]

Here, I am aground: For, as your Lady has *all* my Regards, what have I left for You? The Jus Mariti[3] must relieve me. Demand your Quantum from the Bone of your Bone or as RTP Esquire would quaintly gallicize it—from *that* Bonne of *You* Bon.

James Lovell

RC and enclosure (Adams Papers); internal address: "His Excellency / John Adams"; endorsed: "Mr Lovel 19. Decr. / 1789."

[1] Lovell enclosed a copy of his 17 Dec. letter to Benjamin Lincoln, expressing reluctance to comply with the collector's 16 Dec. request for a record of Boston imports from 1 to 10 August. Once the Tariff Act took effect on 1 Aug., importers were required to pay certain customs, but they were allowed a grace period until local collecting houses were established; in Boston, they were formally created on 10 August. Lovell argued that an interim collection was unfair to importers who had sold their goods and that it targeted ports with better records. Responding to critics, Alexander Hamilton sent a circular letter on 31 Oct. to the nation's port collectors stipulating that while customs must be collected to fund the debt, moderation was key. The backlash continued, and on 30 Dec. Hamilton again issued a circular letter. There, the treasury secretary admitted that the new policy was problematic, and he recommended that Congress revise the plan in its second session (Hamilton, *Papers*, 5:478–479; 6:39, 290).

[2] Despite his lack of an appointment, Lovell continued to monitor the politics of the port. When Philippe André Joseph de Létombe, the French consul at Boston, was suspected of forcing a French intendant to sign for supplies that may not have been delivered, Lovell intervened in the press. He trained his criticism on Létombe's accuser, Louis Baury de Bellerive. Originally from St. Domingue, Bellerive (1754–1807) was a French officer who fought in the Continental Army and aided in the suppression of Shays' Rebellion. Claiming that the charge was "false in the groundwork," Lovell issued a four-letter defense of Létombe, which began appearing in Edmund Freeman's *Herald of Freedom* the day before Lovell wrote this letter to JA. Bellerive fired back via the same newspaper, replying that Lovell had "too much of my contempt to merit further notice" (vol. 14:159; Boston *Herald of Freedom*, 18, 22, 25 Dec. 1789, 5 Jan. 1790; *Reports of Committees of the House of Representatives Made during the First Session of the Thirty-second Congress*, Washington, D.C., 1852, 147:1; *AFC*, 9:173). On the mounting significance of fraud in New England ports, see Stephen Higginson's letter of 21 Dec. 1789, and note 1, below.

[3] The legal right of a husband to acquire his wife's estate by virtue of marriage (Black, *Law Dictionary*).

From Henry Marchant

Newport State of Rhode Island &c Decr. 19th. 1789—

Dear Sir,

Yours of the 17th. of Sepr. I have been honored with.— I truly esteem myself so by every Mark of Your Attention— Your unexpected Visit to Boston prevented an Answer sooner— My Concern as a Friend to my Country is awakened at the Account You give of some disagreable Symptoms attending Your Breast upon close attention, and in publick speaking. How we can spare You from the first I scarce can tell.— But you must somewhat abate in the Severity of it— As to the latter, Reading &c, I would advise that You let one of the Clerks do all the publick Reading, even every Motion made— I know many Explanations and Observations, Opinions &c &c must be expected from the Chair; but you have a peculiar Faculty of speaking multum in parvo—

I was very glad to find upon my Return that my Family had found out your Son:— He had taken up Lodgings and could not be tempted to release them. His very agreable Manners and Improvements rendered Him too entertaining to cause any Regret, but that of His too suddenly leaving the Town— We hope Mr. Adams and His, will never pass Us without Notice—[1]

You must be right, and I stand corrected as to the Time of the Prediction &c I heretofore alluded to— It must have been,—I well remember it was at Philadelphia— The Matter, and the Effect of it, as it struck my Mind, and to all Appearance every Member present I never can forget.— I have mentioned it a hundred Times, tho' not the Author, save to a very few—

You may remember when I had the Honor of seeing you at New-York last Sept.— I informed You, Our Assembly had been called specially, after I left Newport.— That it boded no good;—and I was confident the Govr. had been induced to it, by His Friends who were alarmed at what might take Place in the New House at Octr. sessions,— And therefore were determined by some Means or other, if possible to raise some Difficulty in Their Way:— It turned out so:— The special Assembly, (at which I arrived in Time to be mortified with Their Conduct)—directed Town-Meetings to be called to give their new Members Instructions— Those New members had been appointed in Consequence of the Alteration which had greatly taken Place in the Minds of the People as to the Paper Mony System: But the People still not so much relenting in Their Opposition to the New Constitution did indeed instruct Their Members agt. a Convention— Upon Consultation out of the House, we found most of the new members would have risked giving a Vote for a Convention, if the Disposition of the People had been any way flattering, of Success in a Convention— This not being the Case, it was thought prudent, the members should conduct agreably to Their Instructions, thereby to continue Their Credit with Their Constituents, till They might be induced to more favourable Sentiments of the New Constitution— With this Opinion the old Fœderal Members politically coincided Our Assembly again sits the second Monday of January— The Ground is considerably changed since the Instructions given last October. The Amendments have been sent forth by Congress, And North Carolina by a very large Majority have acceeded to the Union, And for which I sincerely give You Joy.

What effect those Circumstances may have we cannot possitively conclude. We have been often deceived in Our Hopes, and I do not wish to be sanguine— As to interested Motives, I know of none of much Importance, that we can advance to Our Country Members that have not been already urged, that will operate till the next Fall upon Them—While Our merchantile Interest on the fifteenth of January will be in a most deplorable State— It has been an unhappy Circumstance hitherto, that nothing could be done by which the merchantile and Country Interest should be affected at the same Time,—And unless the merchantile Interest is indulged till next Fall, They must suffer and severely too, at least nine Months before the Country Interest can be much affected— This however upon the Supposition that there should not be a voluntary giving up of former Sentiments, or the Measures of Congress should not prove sufficient Inducements to lead Our People to a Spirit of Condescention—

I was at New Haven the begining of Novr. where I placed my Son under President Stiles, in the second Year.—[2] I arrived there two Hours after His Excellency The President, had left the Town on His Return to New-York—[3]

I hope You have refreshed Your Body and Spirits by Your Journey; and that you found Mrs. Adams & Family well— Be pleased to present my Respects & Compliments—

I am most truly / Your old and / sincere Friend

Hy: Marchant

RC (Adams Papers); internal address: "His Excellency John Adams Esqr."; endorsed: "Marchant. 19. Decr / 1790 / answered March 20."

[1] Passing through Newport, R.I., on 10 Sept. and again on 6 Oct., JQA briefly recorded meeting Marchant and his wife, Rebecca Cooke, on 11 Sept. (*AFC*, 8:417, 445; D/JQA/14, APM Reel 17).

[2] William Marchant (1774–1857), of Newport, Yale 1792, later served as chief justice of the Court of Common Pleas in Rhode Island (Dexter, *Yale Graduates*, 5:30).

[3] As part of his New England tour, George Washington visited New Haven from 17 to 19 Oct. and met Gov. Samuel Huntington, Lt. Gov. Oliver Wolcott Sr., and Mayor Roger Sherman. The president heard two addresses, one by state lawmakers and another by Congregationalist clergy, and replied with thanks for the "tender interest which you have taken in my personal happiness, and the obliging manner in which you express yourselves on the restoration of my health." After a trip to Yale College, Washington learned about the area's linen manufacturers and glassworks (Washington, *Diaries*, 5:463–466, 467; *Connecticut Journal*, 21 Oct.).

From John Paul Jones

Dear Sir, Amsterdam Dec$^{r.}$ 20. 1789.

The within documents, from my Friend the Count de Segur Minister Plenipotentiary of France at S$^{t.}$ Petersburg, will shew you in some degree my Reasons for leaving Russia, and the danger to which I have been exposed by the mean subterfuges and dark Intrigues of Asiatic Jealousy and Malice.—[1] Your former Friendship for me, which I remember with particular pleasure and have always been ambitious to merit, will I am certain be exerted in the Use you will make of the three Peices I now send you, for my justification in the Eyes of my Friends in America, whose good opinion is dearer to me than any thing else.— I wrote to the Empress from Warsaw in the beginning of October, and sent her Majesty a Copy of my Journal; which will shew her how much she has been deceived by the Account she had of our Maritime Operations last Campagne. I can prove to the World at large that I have been treated Unjustly, but I shall remain silent at least till I know the fate of my Journal.

It has long been my intention to offer you my Bust, as a mark of the respect and attachement I naturally feel for your Virtues and Talents. If you do me the honor to accept it, I will order it to be immediately forwarded to you from Paris.[2]

I intend to remain in Europe till after the opening of the next Campagne, and perhaps longer, before I return to America. From the troubles in Brabant, the preparations now making in Prussia and in this Country &$^{c.}$ I conclude that Peace is yet a distant object, and that the Baltic will witness warmer work than it has yet done.[3] On the death of Admiral Greig,[4] I was last Year call'd from the Black Sea, by the Empress, to command a Squadron in the Baltic &$^{c.}$ This set the invention of all my Enemys and Rivals at work, and the event has proved that the Empress cannot always do as she pleases: I do not therefore expect to be call'd again into Action.

Present I pray you my respectful compliments to M$^{rs.}$ Adams, & beleive me to be, with sincere Attachement, / Dear Sir, / Your most obedient / and most humble Servant PAUL JONES

My address is *under cover* "A Messieurs N. & J. Van-Staphorst & Hubbard à Amsterdam."

NB. M$^{r.}$ Jefferson will inform you about my Mission to Denmarc. I received there great politeness & *fine Words*. That business may soon be concluded, when America shall have created a respectable Marine.[5]

RC and enclosures (Adams Papers); internal address: "[His Ex]cellency John Adams Esquire Vice President of the United-States &c. N. York." Some loss of text due to a cut manuscript.

[1] With this, his last extant letter to JA, Jones enclosed copies of three French-language documents, all summarizing his naval activities in the Russo-Turkish War and defending him from rape allegations brought forward by Katerina Goltzwart (Koltzwarthen) of Germany. The enclosures, held in the Adams Papers, were a 21 July letter of support from Louis Philippe, Comte de Ségur, to Armand Marc, Comte de Montmorin de Saint Herem; a 21 July article in the *Gazette de France* bolstering Jones' professional reputation and announcing his impending return from St. Petersburg; and a 26 Aug. letter of recommendation sent from the Comte de Ségur to Jean François, Chevalier de Bourgoing, and Antoine Joseph Philippe Régis, Comte d'Esternon, the French ministers to Hamburg and Prussia, respectively. The scandal, as well as Jones' friction with leading Russian naval admirals, led to his permanent ouster from Catherine II's court. In an attempt to repair his public character, Jones drafted his "Narrative of the Campaign of the Liman," which was not published until 1830. No reply by JA to this letter has been found. Suffering from jaundice and nephritis, Jones died in Paris on 18 July 1792 (vol. 19:332; *Repertorium*, 3:119, 131; Morison, *John Paul Jones*, p. 382–390, 401).

[2] Jean Antoine Houdon sculpted a bust of Jones in 1780, but the naval commander evidently did not send it (Morison, *John Paul Jones*, p. 201; Jefferson, *Papers*, 19:588–591).

[3] Jones' intuition about the state of foreign relations in Europe was largely correct. Both Prussia and the Netherlands encouraged the emergence of an independent Belgian republic, with the intent of weakening Austria. At the same time, the Russo-Swedish War stretched on in the Baltic, ending on 14 Aug. 1790 with the Treaty of Varala. The Russo-Turkish War drew to a close with the Treaty of Jassy, which was signed on 9 Jan. 1792 (vol. 19:42; Black, *British Foreign Policy*, p. 199, 205–206, 214; *Cambridge Modern Hist.*, 6:782).

[4] A native of Inverkeithing, Scotland, Sir Samuel Greig (b. 1735) was an admiral in the Russian Navy who played a pivotal role in its victory over the Ottoman fleet at the 1770 Battle of Chesma Bay. He died of fever in late Oct. 1788 (*DNB*; William Stewart, *Admirals of the World: A Biographical Dictionary, 1500 to the Present*, Jefferson, N.C., 2009, p. 150).

[5] For Jones' role in the dispute with Denmark over prizes taken by the Continental frigate *Alliance* during the Revolutionary War, see vol. 15:333–334.

From Stephen Higginson

Sir Boston Decr. 21: 1789

I intended myself the honour of a little conversation with you, before you went to Congress, as to the trade of this State. We are suffering very much for want of a proper inspection of Our exports. that We now have, under the State Laws, is, as to most Articles, worse than none—it serves to conceal & encourage frauds of every kind in preparing Our exports for market.[1] We surely can supplant Ireland in every open market, with Our Beef pork & Butter; & we can vie with the British in the various kinds of pickled fish, at any foreign port, where We are admitted. in every instance, where the

Shipper has been personally attentive to have these Articles well put up, We have had the preference, both on account of the quality & price; but, very few of Our exporters are good Judges of those Goods themselves, & fewer still can find time for such attention.— I know of no way of getting Our exports into good repute abroad, but by a strict inspection of them; & to effect this, there must be a System with a responsible man of good character & information at the head of it, in each State. let him be answerable to the Shipper who sustains any loss by having bad goods delivered him, that have passed inspection, or been branded by an inspector— let him have the power to appoint & remove persons under him, & oblige him to give large Security when he enters into office

He will then take care, that none but faithful men & such as can give him ample Security shall act under him.

Every One then will feel a responsibility; & their interest will induce them all to do their duty. the fees which are now paid to no purpose by the Trade, are nearly sufficient for the purpose. Our exports are such as call for more than common care in fitting them for market; but the attempts made by the State to regulate them have done more hurt than good. the Towns appoint such, & as many as they please, without any regard to character or qualifications; & We can hire, for the fees, the brands of many officers, or obtain their certificates for Goods which they have never seen.— Our Beef, pork, Butter, pot & pearl ashes, pickled fish of various kinds, flax Seed & Lumber, constitute a large proportion of Our exports in value, as well as in bulk; & all these articles require inspection.— This must be made a responsible & a respectable department, or nothing can be effected. Governments can not find proper men in every Seaport in this State for inspectors but a good principal residing here can; nor can the trade bear the expence & loss of time, which must attend Our having only one place of inspection. every facility sh$^{d.}$ be given, & every expence saved to the exporter; but the regulation of exports should be such as will give safety & confidence to the Shipper, as to the quality, & tend to bring them into good repute abroad.—

I can not but consider your Revenue System as very defective, without such a responsible man at the head of a large district. every petty Collector in our out posts now feels quite independent, having no One within 300 miles that can call his conduct in question; & I am sure that ten times the amount of the Salary proper for such an Officer will this year be lost, for want of his influence care & inspection. But this defect I think will soon be remedied.— it will be seen by so many, & the loss to the public will be so evident to all who attend to the Subject, that I am persuaded Comptrollers or Inspectors of districts will be appointed.— I should think that one man of ability & activity—well acquainted with Our Commerce in all its branches might be sufficient for the NE States.—

We suffer very much in this State from the unequal trade We now have with the British. They take from us in Our Vessels, even in their home ports, only such articles as they can not do without; & in their Colonies They will not admit us with any thing, on any terms. Our Oil is loaded by them with an enormous duty when in their own bottoms, & prohibited in Ours; & yet theirs is the best market We can find for the most valuable kind. We are totally deprived of the intercourse We had with their Islands, newfoundland, Canada & nova Scotia; They are not permitted to draw from Us, even in their bottoms, the Supplies They want, except in times of uncommon scarcity, or some particular Articles, which They can no where else get without great trouble & expence. But they have nearly the same advantages in Our ports, They used to enjoy. other foreigners do but little interfere with them in carrying Our exports to market; &, they as yet can vie with us, & must have a large share in that branch, the tonnage &c notwithstanding. This inequality ought not to continue, but the difficulty is how to remove it. Should We at once adopt a resentful, restrictive System, the effect may be to increase the Evil. We may lose their markets for Ashes flax Seed & white Oil &c, which would injure the trade of this State very much, without gaining any thing to balance it; for We could not much profit by their being excluded Our carrying trade, as We now pursue that branch as far as We have the means, or think it for our interest. The Government of the union has now so much the appearance of respectability & efficiency, the British may be brought, perhaps, by wise & prudent measures to view it as meriting attention, & to have some respect for its movements & decissions. I should hope more from open & calm negotiation than retaliation.— If We exclude them as Carriers, We must tempt others by high freights to carry Our produce. the nothern States alone can not for a number years carry off all the produce of America, unless the Business be made much more productive, to call our main efforts & attention that way; & this can not be done without causing a great alarm & much uneasiness in the southern States.— the NE States, & particularly this feel chiefly the weight of the British restrictions—the others never had much intercourse with nova Scotia NLand or Canada; & their exports to Britain are not affected like Ours.— as the carrying Business is a great Object with the British, We may gain somewhat by negotiation, as an equivalent for their enjoying it; & in this the southern States may feel & go along with us. But if We attempt in the first instance to restrain the British, Our southern friends may get alarmed, & leave us without support; & should We succeed in drawing them into Our Views, We may both be disappointed in the effect produced upon the British.—

I feel the necessity of having a more equal & reputable trade with the British; but I am not yet satisfied that We can either compel or conciliate them to more reciprocal terms—the latter however at present is, in my mind, more eligible & promising.—

I have taken the liberty of suggesting to you in a hasty manner these loose Ideas for your consideration. if they prove of no use, nor throw any new light upon the Subject, you will excuse the manner when assured that the intention is good.—

With much respect I have the honour to be / Sir your most huml Servt—

Stephen Higginson

RC (Adams Papers); internal address: "His Excelly. John Adams Esqre—"; endorsed: "Higginson 21. decr / 1789."

[1] Echoing Higginson's concerns, four anonymous letters focusing on fraud in the export trade appeared in several Massachusetts newspapers between 13 May 1789 and 17 Jan. 1790. The series printed in the Boston *Independent Chronicle*, 24, 31 Dec. 1789, 7 Jan. 1790, argued that it was "better . . . to annihilate the Excise than continue it under its present regulations and system." Although the commonwealth relied on excise revenue to fund general expenses, a surge in deception on the docks meant that the state did not receive revenue from sales of tea, rum, and other "valuable articles," which were sold locally but misreported as exports. Bonds to foreign ports were canceled and blank certificates were issued, laying down a paper trail that neatly masked the fraud. Troubled by the potential decline of key exports like butter and beef, the letters warned that these criminal practices had crept in from the coast and now flourished in many towns despite the collectors' oversight: "Hear this, ye, Rulers, and blush, that your laws are so easily evaded." On 4 March the Mass. General Court passed an act to raise public revenue by means of a well-regulated excise, but it did not address the regulation of exports (vol. 19:225; *Massachusetts Centinel*, 13 May 1789; Boston *Independent Chronicle*, 24, 31 Dec., 7 Jan. 1790; Mass., *Acts and Laws*, 1788–1789, p. 462–476).

From Jabez Bowen

Sir

Providence Decmr 28. 1789

I Congratulate you on the accession of No. Carolina to the general Government. our *Antis* are Thunderstruck at the News more especially as the Majority was so large.[1] I have waited several Days to find out what they intend to do wheather to agree to Call a Convention, or stand out longer; in hopes that something would Turn up to perplex the New-Government. They are not well agreed among themselves. But the Heads of the party lately proposed (at one of their Night meetings) that the Duties on all Goods Imported should be put verry low (say one pr Cent.) and that our Ports should be opened to all the World (or in other words that R^d Island should be the *St Estatia*[2] of the North).[3]

The Consequences of such a proceedure can be better seen into by you Sir than by me—and I have no Idea that Congress will suffer such a set of people to remain *impure* in the verry middle of their Teritorys.

Our Genl: Assembly meets on the second Monday of January—when we shall muster all our Forces to procure a Vote for a State Convention. if we fail 'tis proposed by the most Respectable Inhabitants of the Towns of Newport Providence Bristol &c to seperate from the State Government provided Congress will protect us, and we wish to know thro some safe medium wheather This Idea meets the approbation of Congress, or wheather some different mode will be adopted to Oblige us to submit, when 49 parts out of 50, is for the adoption, and one half of the 50th part are of the same mind

I hope and Intreat that Congress will not think of Restricting our Trade as that will but Distress the Federal Towns and will be well pleasing to our *Antis.* in a word we shall be happy to fall in with any measures that will be adopted by Congress for the Compleating the Union. if Congress would Answer the Letter Received from this State[4] before your Adjornment and State in short the necessity that there was of Their Committing the Consideration of the Federal Governm^t to the People in the way prescribed by the Grand Convention and by the old Congress and perhaps hint that it was necessary that something should be done before the first of April it might, bring some of them to consider of the necessity of Acting soon on the Business—

I fully intended to have seen you when at Boston but was prevented by *Indisposition*, please to present Mrs Bowens & my Comp^s to Mrs Adams— I Remain with the highest Esteeme Your Excellency Most Obed^t. & Verry Hum^le Servant Jabez Bowen

P.S. in a Letter to the president I lately asked the Question about our seperation. it may not be amis to let him know that I have wrote to you on the same subject &c—[5]

RC (Adams Papers); internal address: "Excellency John Adams—"; endorsed: "Jabez Bowen / Decr. 28. 1789."

[1] As in Rhode Island, North Carolina's delay in ratifying the Constitution was engineered by a powerful Antifederalist party in the state legislature that favored the emission of paper money. North Carolina citizens objected to dominant federal power, a standing army, congressional control of elections and commerce, and the lack of a bill of rights safeguarding individual liberties. Largely shaped by class divisions, public attitudes toward the Constitution in North Carolina were aggravated by a 1788 election season rife with fraud and street violence. Meeting in convention that summer, North Carolinians proposed 26 amendments and resolved to hold off on considering it any further for ratification until they were approved.

Economic interdependence, Federalist press campaigns, the need to subsidize military defense, the prospect of paying foreign tonnage duties, and the birth of a federal government with a formal Bill of Rights—all of these factors combined to erode Antifederalist sentiment statewide by the early autumn of 1789. North Carolina delegates reconvened on 16 Nov. to debate the Constitution, which they adopted five days later in a vote of 194 to 77, becoming the penultimate state to join the union (Albert Ray Newsome, "North Carolina's Ratification of the Federal Constitution," *The North Carolina Historical Review*, 17:290, 291, 293–299 [Oct. 1940]).

[2] Blocking attempts at ratifying the Constitution and hosting secret night meetings, Rhode Island's Antifederalist contingent made claims like this in the press for several months. On 25 Feb. 1790, for example, the *Newport Herald* printed a letter that exhorted citizens: "Let the Constitution be immediately rejected, we have dallied with it too long for our interest,—the Revenue Act of the State be repealed,—and our ports thrown open to all the world, commerce will then revive, and agriculture and manufactures flourish. . . . We shall exceed St. Eustatius in its most flourishing state" (*Doc. Hist. Ratif. Const.*, 26:734).

[3] Closing parenthesis editorially supplied.

[4] Acting at the General Assembly's behest, Gov. John Collins wrote a memorial to George Washington and Congress on 19 Sept. 1789, reiterating Rhode Islanders' "Attachment and Friendship to their Sister States, and of their Disposition to cultivate mutual Harmony and friendly Intercourse." Collins sought exemptions on the costly foreign tonnage duties that his constituents now faced. He explained that Rhode Islanders, while "strongly attached" to the principles of democracy, perceived in the Constitution "an Approach . . . towards that Form of Government from which we have lately dissolved our Connection, at so much Hazard and Expence of Life and Treasure." The president forwarded Collins' letter on 26 Sept. to Congress, where it was tabled. In the following weeks, Collins' memorial was widely published in the American press (*Doc. Hist. Ratif. Const.*, 25:599–600, 605–607).

[5] Bowen made a similar report on the state of Rhode Island politics in his 15 Dec. letter to Washington, indicating that news of North Carolina's ratification of the Constitution would "have some weight with the opposition" (Washington, *Papers, Presidential Series*, 4:410–412).

From Charles Carroll

Dear Sir Annapolis 29th. Decr. 1789.

Our Legislature did not rise till late in the night on the 26th instant. I have been obliged to attend the whole Session; constant attendance & application have injured my health; it is now so precarious, & delicate, that I am fearful of undertaking a journey to New York at this inclement Season of the year. If my attendance, for want of a Sufficient number of members to compose a Senate, can not be dispensed with, I shall be under the necessity of resigning my Seat. The executive of this State is authorised to appoint my successor, during the recess of the Assembly, in case of my resignation. I wish to execute, to the best of my power, the trust, with which I have been honored by my country, but I am confident, my fellow citizens would not require me to hazard my life, or health in the execution of it.

I hope to be able to set out for New York in the beginning, or at furthest, by the middle of March. If I can not have leave of absence so long, be pleased, Sir, to impart to me the determination of the Senate on this point, that my successor may be appointed without loss of time, who may immediately, or very soon after his appointment repair to New York, to take his seat in the Senate I beg you to present my respectful compliments to the members of the body over whom you preside.[1] I remain with great regard and esteem / Dear Sir / yr. most obdt. hum. Servt. Ch. Carroll of Carrollton

RC (NHi:Gilder Lehrman Coll., on deposit); addressed: "His Excellency / John Adams Esqr. / Vice President / of the United States. / New York."

[1] Charles Carroll of Carrollton (1737–1832), who had been JA's colleague in the Continental Congress, took his seat in the Senate on 15 March 1790. He represented Maryland in the Senate until 1792, while continuing to serve in the state senate until 1800 (vol. 4:28; *First Fed. Cong.*, 1:258; *Biog. Dir. Cong.*).

First Congress, Second Session

4 January 1790 – 12 August 1790

Editorial Note

Congress reconvened for its second session on 4 January. Deadlocked over two entwined issues—the federal assumption of state debts and the site of the American capital—John Adams and his Senate colleagues passed waves of legislation defining naturalization, patents, and copyrights, and establishing national entities like the U.S. Coast Guard. Members of the House labored to craft an economic system that would create and collect revenue while observing the constitutional limits of federal and state power. An antislavery petition, submitted by Benjamin Franklin and others in early February, wrenched the debates anew, intensifying regional factionalism. Like many New England Federalists, Abigail Adams hoped for the adoption of the state debts, anxious that "there will be sufficient courage in the Legislature to take so desicive a step . . . it is one of the main pillars upon which the duration of the Government rests."

During this session John Adams' tie-breaking power crested in the Senate. Between 21 May and 28 July he invoked it a dozen times to modify various bills' phrasing and to keep dialogue flowing. It was a busy spring and summer for the vice president, who balanced Senate duties with a new set of social obligations and the publication of his *Discourses on Davila*. Meanwhile, the congressional membership expanded to welcome representatives from the final two states to ratify the Constitution, North Carolina and Rhode Island. Though he was deeply committed to public service, Adams' early enthusiasm for his post notably flagged amid the partisan rivalry of Congress. "Whether in public or private Life, I live and die a zealous active friend to my Country. There are many Things which want Attention. Many Things wrong, which cannot be set right but by Correspondence or Consultation among Men of Knowledge— Our Morals, Our Commerce, our Governments all want Reformation," he wrote to John Trumbull on 2 April (NIC:Moses Coit Tyler Coll.).

George Washington delivered his annual message to both houses of Congress on 8 January. Lawmakers crowded the Senate chamber in Federal Hall to hear the president's report on his first nine months in office. Washington hailed North Carolina's ratification of the Constitution and celebrated the "rising credit and respectability of our Country—the general and increasing good will towards the Government of the Union." He urged a number of key improvements, namely, the establishment of naturalization protocols, a uniform currency, and a postal service. In a speech that was widely reprinted in the American press, Washington championed the advancement of arts, sciences, and literature. He also advised greater attention to military preparedness and a stronger defense of the southern and western frontiers. Singling out the members of the House, who were mulling how to manage the federal debt, the president stressed that "support of the public Credit" was "a matter of high importance to the national honor and prosperity."

When John Adams and the Senate drafted their 11 January reply to Washington, they laid out a long agenda of domestic policy goals. Foremost were issues of domestic order, in the form of raising "indispensable" military troops; addressing relations with Native American tribes on the western frontier; improving communication through the creation of a post office and mail routes; and launching a uniform system of weights and measures. But the dilemma of how to generate and sustain revenue underpinned the session's debates. Determined to succeed where the Continental Congress had stumbled, John Adams and his congressional colleagues tried to hammer out an economic plan that appeased all rising factions.

Both of the main unresolved issues found their way to Thomas Jefferson's dinner table in late June. At a private supper hosted by the secretary of state, James Madison and Alexander Hamilton brokered a bargain, accepting the federal assumption of state debts in exchange for siting the national capital on the Potomac River. The Residence Act of 16 July articulated southern power in shaping congressional progress and, within a few months, uprooted John Adams and his family for Philadelphia. The exact location of the capital on the banks of the Potomac River was undefined. Philadelphia, meanwhile, would serve as the federal seat for the next decade.

On the legislative front, an equally significant measure of the second session was the reduction by $3.5 million of the assumption figures listed in the Funding Act of 4 August, which benefited larger states like Massachusetts and Virginia. When the members wrapped up business on 12 August,

John Adams was pleased with Congress' new momentum. But he was weary of the partisan struggle festering in the legislature, the president's cabinet, and the press. "If you meddle with political subjects, let me Advise you to never loose sight of Decorum. Assume a Dignity above all Personal Reflections: and avoid as much as possible a Party Spirit. The true Interest and honour of your Country should be your only Object," John Adams wrote to John Quincy on [*ante* 8] September (*AFC*, 9:3, 106; Bickford and Bowling, *Birth of the Nation*, p. 55–73; Washington, *Papers, Presidential Series*, 4:543–549; Elkins and McKitrick, *Age of Federalism*, p. 155–156, 159–160; Madison, *Papers, Congressional Series*, 13:245).

From Richard & Charles Puller

Sir London 6 January 1790

We are duly favoured with Your Letter of the 27th September last which We take the opportunity of the first Packet to answer & to acquaint You what We thought You must have known before this Time, that Soon after Your departure Sir Clement Cotterell paid us agreable to Your directions the Sum of three Hundred Pounds being the usual present deducting fifteen pCt. as the Customary allowance to Him for the Business passing through His Hands & We accordingly in the Account We settled with Messs. W & J Willink & N & J van Staphorst of Amsterdam of the Monies paid You passed the Sum of Two Hundred & fifty five Pounds to their Credit on the 4th April 1788 which Accounts We supposed You would have been acquainted with & We therefore having no Money belonging to You in Our Hands were surprised when Your draft for £300 was presented to Us with out any Letter of Advice & We wrote to our Friends Messs. Willink to have their directions about it but they answered that they did not know at all on what Account said draft was drawn & could give no orders about it.[1] This Explanation We imagine will clear up the Business to Your Satisfaction & We must therefore wait further directions from You relative to the Snuff Box & other Things & We beg leave to assure You We shall be always happy in any opportunity of being Serviceable to You here.

We have the Honor to remain Always / Sir / Your most obedient humble Servants C & R Puller

RC (Adams Papers); internal address: "John Adams Esqr."

[1] For JA's diplomatic honorarium from the British court, see his letter to the firm of 27 Sept. 1789, and note 1, above.

From John Jeffries

Sir Boston, 7, Jan^y: 1790—

I lately received a pacquet from Dr Bancroft, containing the inclosed for you.—[1]

By the date &c of the Doctor's to me, it appears, that it was designed for me at Rathbone place, London; but not being seasonably to meet me there, has been forwarded by a friend, the latter end of October last.—

The Doctor likewise mentions two Volumes said to accompany it;—but these, the friend who forwarded the Packet, informs me were not sent with it; nor have I, upon enquiry, been able to get any information about them, further than that they were not sent.—

Were it not for this circumstance; and that it is possible, the Letter may contain some other matters than respecting myself, I would not, (after so many personal intrusions, honoured with as many indulgencies from you) have added this to the many, and important obligations I owe you & yours.

As I intend improving the earliest good opportunity for England, it renders it improbable I shall again have the honour of paying personally my respects to you or Lady,—will you permit me in improving this, to renew my most grateful acknowledgments for the professional confidence, and the honourable friendship you afforded me in London; and to assure you, that I did at that time, and ever shall lament, that my abilities and every other pretension on my part, were so very little worthy of it.—

My dear Mrs J. who is now in the straw, (having blessed me with a Son) laments even more than myself, that she can not have the pleasure of paying her respects to Mrs Adams—we unitedly tender her our best and most respectful wishes.—[2]

If she should visit this part of the Continent before we leave it, it will afford us singular satisfaction, to have the pleasure of seeing her.—

If Sir, supported as you are, by such able and more important friends, on both sides the Atlantick, there should be anything in which I can in any way be useful to you, or any friend of yours, I shall be made happy in proving the obligation I owe you, and tho I may not presume more, will engage for fidelity and attention.—

With my most cordial congratulations for the honourable situation which you so deservedly hold; and best wishes that you may succeed to the next, whenever Providence may make it eligible, I request to subscribe, as I feel, your obliged, affectionate friend, and very respectful humble Servant J: Jeffries

RC (MHi:Adams-Hull Coll.); endorsed: "Dr Jeffries."

[1] Jeffries enclosed Edward Bancroft's letter of 29 Aug. 1789, above.

[2] Hannah Hunt Jeffries (1764–1835) gave birth to George Jaffrey Jeffries (1789–1856) on 21 December. She wrote to AA on 9 Jan. 1790 (MHi:Adams-Hull Coll.), thanking her for being a "kind Patroness" to the family (*Boston Courier*, 29 Sept. 1835; *NEHGR*, 15:16, 17 [Jan. 1861]).

From François Adriaan Van der Kemp

Sir! Kingston. 7 Jan. 1790.

Long before I read your Excell: *defence of the Constitutions* &c I saw their Criticism bÿ the Reviewers, which enlarged my desire of perusing itself, flattering mÿ with the idea, that I should acquire a fair opportunity of Sending Some Strictures upon it to Mr. Adams; because the first announcing a fear of a to ardent Love for Democracÿ, and the following declaration, that those fears were lessened, raised the idea, that, perhaps, it was to favourable for Aristocratic. I perused Sir! your Excellent work and was Sorrÿ, in finishing this business, that I could find no faults nor essential remarks enough, to excuse the Liberty of writing, to the vice-president, if the Same man had not give me an encouragement bÿ honouring my in Holland with his familiar acquaintance, and persevering in the Same benevolent manners to this new countrÿman.

There no american dares censure with greater freedom than I all what I think worthÿ of it, though he maÿ do it perhaps, nameless, in a more illiberal manner than I, not a Singl american I believe is entitled to give the Same praise to a literarÿ composition of this kind, than your friend, without encurring the danger of being Suspected of flatterÿ— there I enjoÿ the Satisfaction of living happÿ and unenvied, there no Politic fear or hope can dasele mÿ eÿe and the purtÿ of mÿ intentions can be doubted of by Mr. Adams.

I admire your elegant, curious performance, abounding with Such a large Stock of ancient and modern learning, and Profound, true and judicious Political remarks, that, upon the whole, I dare it compare to the most useful writings of our best modern authors, and Sincerely wished, that it was perused by everÿ Sensible American, and devoured by everÿ Lover of Religious and civil Libertÿ—

Everÿ page increased mÿ desire of finishing a volume—and the last encouraged me to recapitulate the whole, and I dare not saÿ, if I must more admire your convincing reasonings, or your persuasive argumentations, or your happÿ comparisons and easÿ language, or the Subtiletÿ and art, with which the recommendation of the present adopted constitution is interwoven in everÿ letter—in everÿ argumentation—it is alwaÿs *carthaginem delendam esse censeo.*[1] And this art Sir! So striking everÿ where is to be more admired, there these letters, had been produced upon *the Spur of* a Particular occasion, which made it necessarÿ to write, and publish with precipitation—["]that Scarce a moment could be Spared to correct the Stile adjust the method, pare of excrescences, or even obliterate repetitions["] (III. 500)—[2] if your patience is not yet tired in reading Such a contininuation of harsh barbarism, and I am vain enough to believe that Mr. Adams is not without curiosity of knowing my opinion about it maÿ I then guess at *that Spur of a Particular occasion,* or communicate mÿ thoughts upon it? I dare Saÿ I maÿ—and in my opinion was Mr. Adams the Soul of the Philadelphian convention—or if that is to much, and the honourable members could not bear, to be animated in this waÿ, but trusted enough upon their own abilities to erect this new edifice—than Mr. adams framed, if it not arranged, all the essentials materials of this Report, inspired the one and other with these Sentiments, and amused first the Europeans with this elaborate performance, in order to have this form universallÿ approved in Europe, before it was adopted by the different States—in the persuasion, that Such an approbation could not be then favourable to the adoption—

At present I must venture Some Remarks, of no great consequence, who in part, perhaps, wil be approved bÿ their illustrious writer.

T.i. pref. xiv. *Even the venerable magistrates of Amersfoort*—&c this example, if it must be adduced, wanted Some elucidation, in a note, for everÿ English or american reader; perhaps Some Dutchman know the Particular event of this Small city, to which in this place is alluded—

—— xvi. *de Paw*—wil not be known to manÿ americans—for their use, the addition in a note of, author of the *Recher: Philos: Sur les* Americains would have been Sufficient.[3]

—— xvii. *called* without expectation, and compelled without previous *inclination*—was perhaps the case of a large number of the common people, in the citys and in the countrÿ—but I think not, that Mr. Adams wil affirm the Same of the leading man, and principal characters of America, although there maÿ be one or other perhaps between them, who could Saÿ with truth *I was called without expectation, and compelled without previous inclination.*

your Eulogium of a trial by Jurÿ—of the danger of a Standing armÿ, and recommandation of the militia, continually (P. 95. 168)[4] with manÿ curious and beautiful passages, as that of the three aristocratical virtues. p. 129, wil be in the eÿes of Some jealous american an atonement—for your often repeated inculcation—of perpetual rulers—(P. 71) hereditarÿ magistrates &c vol. III. p. 282 (283. 296. 297. 307.) I believed it is your Sentiment—I wished to See it explained—at large and defended. will a hereditarÿ Senat not diminish, in time, the prorogatives of the president, and the privileges of the people?[5]

281. upon what authority is it, that you Say, that Harmodius—&c *from* MERE PRIVATE *revenge*? can it be Sufficiently proved?[6]

346. Is your Explication of the Law of the 12 tables—with regard to the *dissecare* preferable to that more human, bÿ which the *dissecare*, alone is understood of the goods—*dividee in partes*, So as it is explained in Europe bÿ Eminent Publicists?[7]

It would be a desirable undertaking if a Adams would perform the arduous task which he offered to Mr. Smith (p. 369) or would rather complÿ with our wishes in furnishing america with a historÿ of the Revolution, there no man wil Surmount So easÿ all—the (389) enumerated difficulties, as the author of the *defence of the Constitutions &*.[8]

Vol. ii P. 181 *Ruccellai—Luigi alemanni*—it Seems Sir! you took no notice, that there were in that conspiration two principal men of the Same name—Luigi alemanni—the one fled to Venice with Danobi Buon del monte, the other was beheaded at that time with Jacupo de Diacceto. The First was the author of a noble Poem *La coltivasione* &—[9]

201—the expedient of Niccolo Cauponi makes me remember a Similar expedient, used bÿ the magistracy of Middelburg in Zeeland, about the middle of this centurÿ—[10]

there was a violent commotion of the mob—originated bÿ a licence, to certain countrÿ people to bring their merchandises to market—this commotion was fomented more and more by one Smÿtegeld a calvinist preacher, a most popular man, who Swaied the multitude, and domineered them, as he pleased bÿ his fanatical and irresistable eloquence. the commotion was raised to Such a pitch—that the magistrates feared for their property and lives. one of them advised to Send a deputation to Dr. Smytegeld, and implore his intercession—[11] according to this Resolve two members went to Smytegeld for his good Endeavours— He refused—he was a minister of the gospel—of a kingdom not of this world—he could not meddle with Politiks.— upon his refuse, the magistrates urged him faster— than the preacher—you never go to the church Sirs! and come to me alone, because you are in danger—no—I wil—I Shal not hear your petitions—or the whole bodÿ of the magistrates must given a promise that they go to church wednesday next—and than I shall appease the citisens. the Magistracÿ appeared en corps. Smytegeld—after Psalm-Singing knocked with his hand—in a tremendous manner the pulpit, and asked who is there— he answered, the Magistracÿ of Middelburg— I hear not— he knocked a Second time "who is there" the States of Zeeland I hear not. he knocked for the 3^d^ time, who is there— answered J. C. what Saÿd mÿ Lord? give to Cæsar, what is Cæsars—to god wat is god!

In his Sermon he gives the most insolent delineation of the different members of the Magistracy, in their Politice capacities—public & privat character, omitting nothing, that could Scandalise them— he finished his Sermon—without a word to the people—but after the Psalm-Singing—before the benediction—he Stood Some minutes immoveable—looked to heaven with compassion—and then upon his auditorÿ, unfolded his hands—and Spoke with a eloquence—peculiar common to him—"People of Middleburg—this was the moment—in which I would bless you—I your beloved Smytegeld—I would bless you with the darlings blessings of my heavenly Father—but I cannot— I have heard of Some riots and commotions—and thus I cannot— damnation, damnation is yours if you persevere— I—know—you have heard I know—you have unworthÿ—vile Sinners for you Magistrates—this is true—but—nevertheless—they are your Magistrates—and as Such—obedience is due to them, though they are wrong— the almighty Shal judge them— Let it Suffice— yours is obedience— I cannot bless you fearing that one or other of this congregation had a part in these commotion—perhaps a few—perhaps no one. what Should I be glad—people—citisens—let us see—the almighty's eyes are upon is—he—who is a good citisen, who wil be obedient raise this moment—raise his right hand—his fingers—and renew with me the oath of obedience[″]—and in the Same moment, the whole congregation joined the preacher—he blessed them—and everÿ man was quiet—

P. 311. was there not a harsher Epithet Sir! for a merchant than merchants, with unblushing heads. I allow, it is adjusted to the matter—but it cannot please a merchant—who is a exception upon this rule.

Vol. III. P. 10. is filled by all the members for one Week &c. not exact—the rotation is properlÿ speaking *bÿ* the different Provinces—everÿ Province enjoys the præsiduim a week—not bÿ members.

So just Sir! as your censure was T. i. p 123 upon the Sundaÿ Law and warden act—So unpleasing and hurting wil be to everÿ Pharisaical or fanatical ear the use, which you made of Some words—which however no person wil convince of your orthodoxÿ in these articles—I mean the Passages T. ii p. 422 Trinity in unity. III. p. 157. confusion of Languages— ib. 187. with regard to the devil. 363. Fall and milennium. 332. in Trinity[12]

the omissions of these few words would have deprived me, with the few—of a Smile—but your work of not one beauty, nor your reasonings of their Strength—it can work no good—but hurt the writer by à unthinking bigotted rabble, and Mr. Adams admonished his friend, to "be prudent in regard of Theological matters in America—at your arrival[”]—[13]

For america's prosperity I wished that our illustrous President had been in the Same Sentiments upon the Cincinnati, which you expressed with So much truth and So emphatically p. 207–9.[14]

your placing the vindiciæ contra Tyrannos p. 211. between 1640 and 1660 seems to me, if I am not mistaken, an anachronism— This book was of a more early date. I posses an edition of this work, printed Francof, 1608—and this Surely was not the first. Spaguis, who give it to Fr. Hottoman, *Bibl. p.* 522 and Thuanus in his Francogallia Lib. 57 fol. 49 shows it Sufficiently—and the first autor makes mention of an edition Edinbergi 1579—another edition—in Latin and French is of 1580 or 1581, as i wel remember— Theod: Beza had the care of edition, printed in the Netherlands—and this perhaps was the reason, that it was adjudged to him.[15]

Who was that *Shase*, which you mentioned p. 219? Was that the head of the late insurrection in Massachusetts?

I was much pleased by your Strictures upon Cincinnatus (226) and the due tribut paid to the memorÿ of Spurius Melius and Manus Manlius—who tragical fate I pitied, as Soon, as learnt to read Roman historÿ (240–2–4) 244–257.[16] what you Sai of the Roman Nobles p. 287 is literaly true of the Dutch in the abjuration of Philip the II— the people then changed of masters and loosed, bÿ the state Resolution of 1581, all that Political influence, which they enjoyed under the government of charles the V and Philip the ii.[17] The unanimity, required in the 7 united Provinces, is not general, as your Excellency's opinion Seems to be, it is alone required in few capital points as *peace, war truce, taxes* and in the different Provinces—in everÿ point of incumbrance (291. col. 1355) othewyse few foreigners will be able to make the true and judicious reflections upon the Hollanders, as you penned it. 355— 291. 379. 462. if all the Patriots had been convinced of those truths—perhaps they would not have been Subdued, nor been the tools of few aristocratical man.—

what is the reason Sir, there you alledged p. 905—two authorities in which the principles, which you defended, had been acknowledged, that you gives your readers but one—the report of the convention of 17 Sept 1787. and omitted the ordinance of Congress of 13 July.

Thus I have finished mÿ remarks— if you Excell̄. had read them with patience, and can pardon the trouble, which I had given—than mÿ following lines wil want no excuse by the vice-president— there theÿ wil enable him, to Show—that under the present constitution Personal merit—and liberal arts are duelÿ encouraged, and that the personal property of everÿ citisen is protected, compatible with the Safety and intrest of the whole— I wil mention the last, and reserve a particular letter for the first—

You remember Sir! that Mr. de Nÿs and I, were constrain, to *depose* in the power of the States of the Province of Utrecht, before our enlargement, the Sum of fortÿ five thousand or 7500 £ N. york currencÿ in order, as it was Said, to recover out of this Sum, the damages caused by our direction to the Province of Utrecht and city of Wÿck-by Duurstede. we ardentlÿ wished to recover if not the whole, at least a part of it, and, neverthles al remonstrances in our favour, this affair is in the Same State, by my late information, as at my departure from that countrÿ—[18]

The onlÿ waÿ of Succes for us, Seems to me, if the congres or the President wil judge it convenable to interpose, and I doubt of one Single recommendatorÿ letter to the American agent at the Hage, one note of him to the States general wil do the matter, believing firmly that the Stadholder wil profit of this opportunity of humiliating Some aristocratical Leaders in that Province, who joined him in the revolution, and whose adsistance he wanted for a time to Subdue the people. It wil not be objected bÿ your Excellencÿ that this affair happened, before I was an American Citisen, or, that Congress cannot middle with the domestical affairs of the Dutch Republic, of decide the right or wrong of the then contending parties, because, if one of this had taken place I would not trouble your Excell: with a Single line upon this matter.

That I was at that time no citisen of America matters not— this would prove to much, if this was admitted as a valuable plaÿ— Suppose, I had been a merchant—I had valuable engagements—Some made in behalf of this countrÿ, whose paÿments wer not acquited—I emigrated to America—after Some time the paÿment was refused—Should I not have a right to appeal to the Congres for their intercession? The Sum of 45000 gl. was not a due paÿment, was not required as a *fine*, but a lone to be [ramptised] as a Securitÿ for those, damages, which *maÿ* be found to be occasioned by our direction—So that Supposing those damages, true or false, amounting to 30 to 40000 Gl. there Should neverthles be 5000 gl our undoubted property, whose recovering Seems to me as justifiable, as anÿ mercantile debt—and this evinces, that an conditional intercession in mÿ particular favour, to recover Such a Sum, as maÿ the residuum, can never be Stiled a meddling in the Domestical affairs of the republic, or a decision between the contending parties. Such an intercession is practised often bÿ the Dutch Republic—lately enough in the case of chomel en Jordain, Merchants of Amsterdam against the house of Zanowiech, whose cause was espoused, clandestinely, by the Noble Senat of the Venetians—[19] Such a conditional intercession must be applauded by the Dutch Ministerÿ, conscious enough, that they behaved not in that manner against the Americans—when they, in the time theÿ refused Mr. Adams a public audience as minister,[20] enrolled and mustered at Nymegen the Hessian and anspachian troops— Shut the gates to make desertion impossible, and maket use of the garrison to watch this vile troupeau. If mÿ petition is lawful—and practicable—if it can be effected—with decencÿ as wel as without inconveniencÿ then I dare implore this act of protection as a right, and then, I am Sure, I wil be in need of no other argument, to obtain the powerful intercession of your Excellencÿ upon this matter.

Let me join another matter—in regard—to the encouragement of personal merit—and liberal arts—

Mr. S.S.G. Mappa, late Commander of the armed citisens in the province of Holland, one of the eminent characters Among the patriots, in regard of Political knowledge, undaunted bravery, and distinguished, personal merit, is arrived in New-york, with his familÿ—with a view, to Settle in this State. Upon advice of distinguished characters in Europe, and friends to America—with advice of Embassador Jefferson, he brought with him a complete Letter-founderÿ not alone for the western, but for the oriental languages—at the value, at least of 20000 gl. Hol. or about 3500 £ New-york's currencÿ—[21]

To this moment, there is, as far as i know, not a Single Letter-founderÿ, in America, and the Printers must purchase them in England or Scotland— What a valuable acquisition then for America—if Congres think it worth anÿ encouragement, and what is more easÿ than this—a tax upon the importation of forein Letter-types wil do everÿ thing—[22] Such a tax can hurt no bodÿ, as Europeans and be of an infinite profit to american literature, if that gentleman can Supply enough—of the beauty and quality—at the Same rate—and this, I doubt not, or is possible, bÿ a tax upon importation— this wil be, an improvement, how Small it may be, for the public revenue, encrease the literarÿ performances, and Supplÿ us with Greek & oriental books, printed in America, now purchased at a high price in Holland and England—

Excuse Sir! this troublesome letter— it is the last time, that I Shal be importunate in this manner. Honour us with your favourable remembrance, and be persuaded that no American is with higher Sentiments of respect and esteem than I.

Sir / Your Excellency's / most obedient and obliged Servant

Fr. adr. Vanderkemp.

RC (Adams Papers).

[1] Van der Kemp referred to Marcus Porcius Cato Censorius' closing remark in the Roman senate: In my opinion, Carthage must be destroyed (*Oxford Classical Dicy.*).

[2] Here and below, Van der Kemp accurately cited from all three volumes of JA's *Defence of the Const.*; see also JA's response of 27 Feb., below.

[3] Cornelius de Pauw, *Recherches philosophiques sur les Américains; ou, Mémoires intéressants pour servir à l'histoire de l'espèce humain*. The 1770 and 1777 Berlin editions of this work are in JA's library at MB (*Catalogue of JA's Library*).

[4] Closing parenthesis has been editorially supplied.

[5] Van der Kemp wrote the previous three words in the left-hand margin and marked them for insertion here.

[6] Athenian aristocrat Harmodius (d. 514 B.C.) was executed following his failed assassination of Hippias the tyrant (r. 527–510 B.C.). After the Spartans expelled Hippias, Harmodius was proclaimed a hero (*Oxford Classical Dicy.*).

[7] Compiled in 451–450 B.C., the Twelve Tables served as the earliest code of Roman law. In his *Defence of the Const.*, JA wrote that the bankruptcy law listed in the Twelve Tables permitted creditors to execute and "dissect" debtors, distributing their body parts as payment (*Oxford Classical Dicy.*; JA, *Defence of the Const.*, 1:346).

[8] JA framed the first volume of his *Defence* as a series of letters to WSS. He concluded with two tasks for readers: to compare the ancient and modern forms of federalism that might shape Congress' powers and to gather the documents needed to write a comprehensive history of the American Revolution (JA, *Defence of the Const.*, 1:364, 384–392).

[9] Cosimino Rucellai (1495–1520) was the patron of a prominent intellectual circle in Florence that included aristocrats Luigi di Tommaso Alamanni, Zanobi Buondelmonti,

and Jacopo da Diacceto. Rucellai also supported the poet Luigi di Piero Alamanni (1495–1556), who published *La Coltivazione*, Paris, 1546 (Anthony M. Cummings, *The Maecenas and the Madrigalist: Patrons, Patronage, and the Origins of the Italian Madrigal*, Phila., 2004, p. 23, 24–25, 184, 185, 209; John P. McCormick, *Machiavellian Democracy*, Cambridge, 2011, p. 40, 41).

[10] Florentine politician Niccolò di Piero di Gino Capponi (1472–1529) commanded the city's militia (Keith Christiansen and Stefan Weppelmann, eds., *The Renaissance Portrait: From Donatello to Bellini*, New Haven, 2011, p. 145; Nicholas Baker, *The Fruit of Liberty: Political Culture in the Florentine Renaissance, 1480–1550*, Cambridge, 2013, p. 102; Paget Jackson Toynbee, *A Dictionary of Proper Names and Notable Matters in the Works of Dante*, Oxford, 1898, p. 273).

[11] Dutch Reformed preacher Bernardus Smytegelt (1665–1739), of Middelburg, Zeeland, gained fame for his fiery sermons against the African slave trade (*Handbook of Dutch Church History*, ed. Herman J. Selderhuis, Bristol, Conn., 2015, p. 356).

[12] JA observed that if Congress passed Sabbaterian legislation restricting commerce on Sundays, then citizens would remain "as free as they desire to be" (JA, *Defence of the Const.*, 1:123–124).

[13] JA advised Van der Kemp to be prudent about gleaning both "religious Principles" and political affiliations within New York State's Dutch community (vol. 19:252).

[14] In his *Defence*, JA reiterated his view that the Society of the Cincinnati's growth exemplified a national thirst for aristocracy, and he recommended its voluntary dissolution. For JA's longstanding criticism of the association, see vols. 15:468–469, 16:xxiv.

[15] This work was Stephanus Junius Brutus' *Vindiciae Contra Tyrannos*, Edinburgh, 1579. The Huguenot author was likely either Philippe du Plessis Mornay (1549–1623) or Hubert Languet (1518–1581). Latin editions were printed in Frankfurt in 1608 and, as Van der Kemp noted, by Theodore Beza in Amsterdam in 1660. A French translation appeared in 1581. Another Huguenot, François Hotman (1524–1590), published his *Francogallia* in 1573 (Daniel Lee, *Popular Sovereignty in Early Modern Constitutional Thought*, Oxford, 2016, p. 123; Stephanus Junius Brutus, *Vindiciae Contra Tyrannos*, ed. George Garnett, Cambridge, Eng., 1994, p. lxxxv, lxxxvi).

[16] Spurius Maelius (d. 439 B.C.) alleviated a famine by supplying corn, while Marcus Manlius Capitolinus (d. 384 B.C.) repulsed an attack by the Gauls in 390 B.C. Both Roman noblemen faced charges of tyrannical ambition and were executed (*Oxford Classical Dicy.*).

[17] Representatives from the Dutch provinces of Brabant, Flanders, Utrecht, Gelderland, Holland, and Zeeland gathered at The Hague on 26 July 1581. In an Act of Abjuration that marked a turning point in the Dutch Revolt, they deposed Philip II, king of Spain, and declared independence (*Cambridge Modern Hist.*, 3:254).

[18] For the imprisonment of Van der Kemp and Sir Adriaan de Nijs, see vol. 19:244. Van der Kemp continued his efforts at restitution, for which see his letter of 17 March 1790, and note 1, below.

[19] Styling himself as "Count Zanovich," the Albanian swindler Stiépan Annibale (1751–1786) duped Simone Cavalli, the Venetian representative at Naples, into writing letters of recommendation. Armed with Cavalli's introductions and several forged ones, Annibale defrauded the Amsterdam banking firm of Chomel & Jordan in 1772, amassing bills of exchange and diamonds. The firm appealed to the Dutch government for compensation, and officials replied by threatening Venice with an embargo. In return, the Venetian government confiscated Annibale's property and offered to pay 10,000 ducats to settle the claim. In 1786 Annibale was arrested in Amsterdam and committed suicide in prison (Mary Lindemann, *The Merchant Republics*, Cambridge, Eng., 2014, p. 209–210; W. Carew Hazlitt, *The Venetian Republic: Its Rise, Its Growth, and Its Fall, 421–1797*, 2 vols., London, 1900, 2:318–319).

[20] For JA's 19 April 1781 memorial to the States General and the path to Dutch recognition of American independence, see vols. 11:272–282; 12:xv.

[21] Dutch Army colonel Adam Gerard Mappa (1754–1828), a Patriot refugee originally from Delft, arrived in New York City on 1 Dec. 1789, bearing letters of introduction from Van der Kemp and Thomas Paine. Mappa, who had met with JA in Amsterdam to inquire about emigration, had spent Christmas dinner with the Adamses at Richmond Hill. By 1794 he left the printing business and became an agent for the Holland Land Company. Van der Kemp wrote to JA on 9 Jan. 1790

(Adams Papers), recommending Mappa's "bravery & knowledge" (*DAB*; Mappa to JA, 16 Feb. 1825, Adams Papers).

[22] Contrary to Van der Kemp's view, type foundries existed elsewhere in the United States, including Benjamin Franklin's press in Philadelphia. While the Tariff Act of 1789 did not single out fonts, they were subject to a 7.5 percent duty as metal manufactures (Isaiah Thomas, *The History of Printing in America*, 2 vols., N.Y., 1874, 1:27–30; Douglas A. Irwin, *Clashing over Commerce: A History of U.S. Trade Policy*, Chicago, 2017, p. 77).

From Pierce Butler

sir. New York January the 9th. 1790—

I feel very sensibly the impropriety of Your Address to me in senate yesterday—[1] As it was a very indellicate departure from the line of Your Official duty, I did expect that You woud, while in the Chair, have made at least the same Apology You did out of it—namely, that You meant me no offence.— The strong desire I have of promoting and preserving harmony in that branch of the Legislature induces me to take no further notice of it at this time; but if ever anything similar to it takes place again, I shall in justification of my own feelings, and of the situation in which I stand on that floor, be under a necessity of personally resenting it—

I am / sir / Yr Humble servant P Butler.

RC (Adams Papers); internal address: "His Excy the Vice President of / the United states."

[1] The Irish-born Butler (1744–1822), a merchant of Charleston, S.C., and New York City, represented South Carolina in the Senate from 1789 to 1796 and again from 1802 to 1804. Although no mention of Butler's confrontation with JA appeared in the official record, William Maclay's *Journal* offers a hint of detail. Following George Washington's 8 Jan. 1790 address to Congress, Butler complained that "the speech was committed rather too hastily" and then "made some remarks" on the Senate floor. JA called Butler to order. As Maclay wrote: "He resented the call, and some altercation ensued." Butler's chief objection was that JA and Washington had embraced British parliamentary ritual with its "mimickry of royalty, state and parade." AA later cautioned JA that Butler was "unsteady and wavering" in his conduct (*AFC*, 10:264; *Biog. Dir. Cong.*; Maclay, *Journal*, p. 174; *The Letters of Pierce Butler, 1790–1794: Nation Building and Enterprise in the New American Republic*, ed. Terry W. Lipscomb, Columbia, S.C., 2007, p. 1).

To John Trumbull

My dear Sir New York January 13. 1790

I am at length determined to omit no longer to write to you.— You read yourself to death. this let me tell you, is a Sin and a crime. Whether it is not of a deeper die, than, intemperate Indulgences of the Bottle or the Girl, is a Case of Casuistry. You know best whether You are guilty of it, or not. if you are I enjoin upon You, Pennance, either of a Walk of five miles a day, all at one time before dinner, or a Seat in some house of Representatives, at your option.

Given under my hand at New York this 13. of Jan. 1790

John Adams.

RC (MiD-B:William Woodbridge Papers); addressed: "John Trumbull Esqr / Counciller at Law / Hartford"; endorsed: "Honl. John Adams / Feby 13. 1790"; notation by JA: "Free / John Adams."

From Sylvanus Bourne

Respected & Dr Sir— Boston Jany. 17th 1790—

I am pleased to find that the President in his late Speech to both Houses of the American Parliament has specifically called their attention to foreign Affairs and to those necessary provisions, preliminary to his nominations in that Department[1]

The rising consequence of this Country in the scale of Nations will doubtless be a subject of much political & commercial speculation in the European World—while I conceive that our own interest & more especially the product of our Revenue is intimately connected with the extension of our Commerce & having our intercourse with other Powers secured by explicit treaty or Contract & no longer subject to the uncertain tenure of legislative decrees—to effect these & other valuable purposes—deputations in the Diplomatic & Commercial lines will probably soon take place—a Secretaryship in the former—or a Consulate in the latter are Objects which I trust a not unworthy Ambition still prompts me to indulge the hope of obtaining & in prosecution of which I expect to be shortly at New york

I have just finished the second reading of those Volls. of your defence of the American Constitutions which you politely gave me at Mr Jay's and I'll assure you Dr Sir I am delighted with the generous sentiments they contain in favr. of the happiness of mankind—while my mind has been illumined & informed in the best means by which that Happiness is to obtained & secured under a free & equal administration—every avenue to the human Heart is there fully explored, the true direction of the political magnet discovered, and the great Arcana in the science of Government which has puzzled Philosophers & Statesmen of old are there completely developed—and the mode of reducing its principles to practice so as best to subserve the interest of human Nature is rendered clear and intelligible—

Pardon my interruption of your time thus far—while with the Compliments of the Season you will please to tender my best Respects to your good Lady—M^r^ & Mrs Smith &c believing me / With Unequivocal Esteem / & Respect / Your Obed^t^ & Obliged / Servant—

Silv^a.^ Bourn

RC (Adams Papers); addressed: "His Excellency / John Adams Esqr. / Vice President of the United / States. / New york"; internal address: "His Excellency John Adams Esqr."; endorsed: "Silvanus Bourne / March 17. 1790"; notation: "pr post."

[1] For the president's first annual address to Congress on 8 Jan., see First Congress, Second Session, 4 Jan. 1790 – 12 Aug. 1790, Editorial Note, above. Senators Ralph Izard, Rufus King, and William Paterson drafted a reply on 11 January. Led by JA, they presented it three days later at George Washington's residence on Cherry Street, pledging to uphold the president's plans. Representatives George Clymer, John Laurance, and William Loughton Smith prepared a reply from the House on 12 Jan., promising that the question of public credit would be "among the first to deserve our attention." As AA reported: "The *House* condescended to go in a body to the President with their answer to his speech, tho' many of them warmly opposed it, yet as the Senate, with their president at their Head, had done it, they did not know how very well to get over it" (Washington, *Papers, Presidential Series*, 4:546–549; *AFC*, 9:5, 6–7).

From Pierre Charles L'Enfant

Sir. new york January the 17. 1790—

In may '89. while I was Engage in supperintending some work at the Congress House Mr Ottis requested I should Direct the Execution of Several matter wanting in the Secretary office & committee Room's to the Senate—such as *writing desk's tables* & *presses for papers* which I accordingly ordered to be done and the cost thereof to be charged in a bill to the Senate of the United states for whose private use the Saide Aarticles were Intended.[1]

your Excellency will be pleased to observe that the provision that had been made By the City for to defray the Expenditure of the building did not comprehended any thing Beyond such movables as were of most immediate necessity for to Furnish & decorate the tow Grand Room's ([viz] that of the Senat & that of the house of Representatives) and that it had been understood that any articles as Should besides be wanted for the Internal accommodation Should be provided for by the Congress themselves.

this being well known the clark of the House of representatives applied to me for severals articles similar to the above mentioned which I ordered into his office and the cost thereof was paid By that house on the account being delivered to them at the end of thier last session. the application made to me by M^r^ ottis was of a much later date to that which I had received from the clark of the House of representatives and the circumstance of the account being paid by that house well known of him. upon what ground dose M^{r} ottis persist in is objection to *W. Carter* Bringing in his bill to him for those objects which he himself has directed the Execution of. I cannot conceive—and my desir to see justice done to a deserving work men Induces me to sollicite here your Excellency goodness in his behalf[2]

the motive will I hope plead in Excuse for the liberty I am taking in availing of the opportunity for subscribing my self / With great respect / your Excellency / most humble & most / obeident servent.

P. C. L'Enfant—

RC (Adams Papers); internal address: "His Excellency / the president of the senat of the united states."

[1] The New York City Council hired L'Enfant to remodel and expand Federal Hall, where the Continental Congress had met since 1785. Reconstruction of the edifice cost $65,000, financed by local taxes and a lottery. The three-story building boasted marble floors, offices, committee rooms, and public galleries. Members of the House convened on the first floor, while JA and the Senate met on the second floor (Bickford and Bowling, *Birth of the Nation*, p. 9–10).

[2] L'Enfant's query to Samuel Allyne Otis, the Senate secretary, has not been found. The architect referred to money owed to Winsen Carter, a cartman living on Lumber Street (*New-York Directory*, 1790, Evans, No. 22724).

From Henry Marchant

East Greenwich State of Rhode Island &c Jan$^{y:}$ 18$^{th.}$ 1790

Respected Sir,

We may at Length congratulate each other on well founded Expectations of a speedy Adoption of the Constitution by this State. Agreably to the Information in my last, Our Gen$^{l.}$ Assembly sat at Providence the last Week.[1] The Opposers were to a Man upon the Ground except one sick. The Town of Warwick having four Members, had heretofore a heavy Majority against Us, and had instructed against a Convention— But on the Day on which the Assembly was to set, rallied Their Town to the largest Town meeting ever known, having upward of two hundred Votes in, but were beat by a Majority of Eleven in Favour of Instructions for a Convention— We brought on the Question in the lower House of Assembly for a Convention last Fryday, the very Day on which the Indulgence granted by Congress expired— After a Debate of four Hours, the Question was taken, and carried by five Majority— The upper House immediately took up the Subject— This was the old House, and Our Hopes were faint— On Saturday They nonconcured with Our Vote by one Majority,—and sent Us a Bill for calling Town meetings again to take Their Sense and Instructions— The lower House immediately nonconcured, and sent up another Bill in nearly the same Form as Our first, lengthening the Time one Week for Election of Delegates:— In the mean Time every Exertion was making with the Members— However at ten o'Clock in the Evening They nonconcured with Our second Bill and adjourned to the next morning. Yesterday, being the Sabbath, without sending down the nonconcurence— In the Morning They sent it down to Us, with another Bill, for calling upon the Towns for Instructions— We nonconcured with this, and once more (You will smile) sent Them the Substance of Our former Bills, varying again the Time for appointing Delegates and the setting of the Convention— One of the Members of the upper House now absenting Himself, The Question being called, Their was a Tie, and the Governor turned the Vote, for a Convention—

We were happy to find that many of Our Opposers appeared very happy the disagreable Business was over—many promised They would give no further Opposition:—not the least Timper was shewn—

The Govr. is requested to forward the Proceedings to the President of the United States, with a Request that the Indulgence before granted may be continued, for such Time as Congress shall think proper— The Election of Delegates for a Convention is fixed to the second Monday of February; and the Meeting of the Convention to the first Monday of March— As I have not a reasonable Doubt, but the Constitution will be adopted, and I have never held up any Thing to Congress, but what the Event has justified—I must sincerely wish Congress will gratify Our Wishes—And as some Vessells have sailed since the fifteenth of March for some of the United States and others will sail before such further Indulgence may be granted, I must further wish, that in granting this, They will add, that such Tunnage and Duties as may be paid by Our Vessells, other than are paid by Subjects of the United States may be returned— All this is granting no further than was granted to North Carolina upon Their having appointed a Convention, and under the Expectation of an Adoption of the Constitution— I am confident this Indulgence will give Us at least ten Votes in Our Convention; and have a Tendency to reconcile hundreds of Our People—

I must be supposed to have a tollerable Idea of the Dispositions of Our Citizens.— Few have had greater Opportunities of obtaining

3. "A SOUTH-WEST VIEW OF NEWPORT," BY SAMUEL KING, 1795
See page xii

such Knowledge— I have not hesitated to give a decided Opinion that Congress would meet Us, with every cordial Mark of Approbation; and almost pledged myself for Success in Our Application— Be so kind Sir, as to present my Respects to the President, and to the Gentlemen of my Acquaintance—And If I have Your own favourable Sentiments of this Request, inform Them, that a steady and arduous Friend in this Business begs Their Attention to, and hearty Concurrence in, this Soliscitation

With every Sentiment of Regard I am, / Your most devoted / Friend & Servant Hy. Marchant

NB—

private

There is some Reason to presume that Mr. H—l and Mr. B—d of this State have made some Interest for the Plan of D—t J—e The latter under the Friendship of Judge L—d of T—n now in Congress— If Incouragement to either, should be early given It may become a delicate Matter afterwards to do what might be most wished—[2]

RC (Adams Papers); addressed: "His Excellency / John Adams Esqr. / Vice President of the / United States &c / New York"; internal address: "His Excellency John Adams Esqr. / Vice President &c"; endorsed: "Mr Marchant / Jan. 18. 1790 / ansd March 20."

[1] Eyeing the 15 Jan. deadline for exemption from foreign tonnage duties, the R.I. General Assembly met in Providence on 11 January. Six days later it called for a new session of the ratification convention on 1 March and asked Gov. John Collins to appeal to Congress for a renewal of the exemption (*Doc. Hist. Ratif. Const.*, 25:665–667). Congress' next step was to draft the Rhode Island trade bill, for which see JA's letter of 19 May to William Ellery, and note 2, below. For Rhode Island's economic interdependence on the union, see Descriptive List of Illustrations, No. 3, above.

[2] While Rhode Islanders deliberated over ratification, the creation of federal departments beckoned to early applicants like David Howell and William Bradford. Both Howell (1747–1824), Princeton 1766, and Bradford (1729–1808) were lawyers and Federalists who sought the aid of Massachusetts representative George Leonard (1729–1819), Harvard 1748, of Taunton, in soliciting a district judgeship. They were unsuccessful, and Marchant prevailed in gaining the post (*Doc. Hist. Ratif. Const.*, 24:312, 314, 315; *Biog. Dir. Cong.*).

From Thomas McKean

Sir, Philadelphia January 20th. 1790.

This will be handed to you by Mr; Francis Bailey, printer of the Freemans Journal in this city. I esteem him as an intelligent, ingenious & honest man. He has lately invented a simple method of making ornaments, devices and even types for securities, certificates and other public papers, which cannot possibly be counterfeited.[1]

As soon as his invention shall be made known, it can be used by any printer, and no patent could secure him much benefit from it: He therefore hopes for employment from Congress in the line of his business so long as he may deserve it, as the only reward for his discovery. With this view he goes to New-York, and requests me to do him the honor of introducing him to you, and solliciting your patronage. Your countenance and recommendation will oblidge an industrious & worthy character.

Be pleased to make my compliments acceptable to M^rs; Adams, Colo: & M^rs; Smith, and permit me to subscribe myself, what with great sincerity I am, / Sir, Your most obedient humble servant

Tho M:Kean

RC (Adams Papers); internal address: "His Excellency John Adams Esquire.—"

[1] Francis Bailey (ca. 1735–1815), former printer for the Continental Congress and the state of Pennsylvania, had published the Philadelphia *Freeman's Journal* since 1781. Bailey developed a form of printing type that he claimed could not be counterfeited "by the most ingenious Artists in sculpture, or by any other means." Bailey petitioned both houses of Congress for the exclusive use of his invention, garnering prominent supporters like Pennsylvania senator Robert Morris and George Duffield, pastor of Philadelphia's Third Presbyterian Church. On 20 Jan. 1790 Duffield wrote to JA (Adams Papers), recommending Bailey as "a man of great integrity; & I think, I may safely say, universally esteemed by his Acquaintance for his honesty & uprightness."

From 2 to 26 Feb., a House of Representatives committee considered Bailey's petition and passed a bill in support of it. It was sent to the Senate on 2 March, where it foundered, likely because of Alexander Hamilton's negative report on the efficacy of Bailey's invention. On 4 March the Senate opted to postpone discussion of Bailey's request until a "bill to promote the progress of useful arts shall be taken into consideration," for which see Richard Cranch's 22 Jan. letter, and note 1, below (Washington, *Papers, Presidential Series*, 5:89–90; *AFC*, 1:216; Hamilton, *Papers*, 6:277–278; *Annals of Congress*, 1st Cong., 1st sess., p. 988).

From Richard Cranch

My dear Brother | Boston Jany. 22^d 1790.

This will be delivered to you by my esteemed Friend M^r. Nathan Reed, who was a very worthy Tutor to your eldest Son, and to mine, when at the University. He is a Gentleman whose acquaintance with the Principles of Natural Philosophy and the Mathematicks is very extensive, and he is more particularly well versed in the application of those Principles to the purposes of constructing usefull Machines.[1] And he appears to me to have such a natural Turn and original Genious that way, as, if encouraged, may prove of very great advantage to the Publick. He has exhibited to the Academy a number of Drafts of Machines of his invention or improvement, which, having been [ca]refully examined by their standing Committee, have been highly approved; and Mr. Reed is now desirous of submitting them to the Examination of Congress by such a Committee as they may please to honour him with for that purpose; hoping that if any of them should be approved, he may be so happy as to obtain a Patent, or such other encouragement as may enable him to carry them into execution for the publick Benefit. Our good Friends Doctr. Holyoke,[2] Doctr. Tufts and several other learned Members of the Academy have expressed their approbation of several of Mr. Reed's Inventions and Improvements, in a Paper by them subscribed, and given to him, which I wish you would read as containing my Sentiments also.

I heartily recommend Mr. Reed to your Notice and Friendship, and am, with Sentiments of highest Esteem and Affection, your obliged Brother Richard Cranch

[Ple]ase to give my best Regards to Sister Adams and your whole Family. We are all well at Braintree Weymo. &c.

RC (Adams Papers). Some loss of text due to the removal of the seal and a torn manuscript.

[1] Nathan Read (1759–1849), Harvard 1781, of Warren, Mass., petitioned Congress on 8 Feb. for "an exclusive privilege for constructing" his mechanical inventions, which included improvements on the steam engine. Members of the House referred Read's request to a committee which on 16 Feb. presented a bill "to promote the progress of the useful arts." The bill passed both houses of Congress, after minor amendments, by 5 April. George Washington signed the Patent Act five days later, ushering in a new system for American inventors to retain ownership of their innovations. The act established a patent board, first manned by Thomas Jefferson, Gen. Henry Knox, and Edmund Randolph, that reviewed all citizens' proposals for "any useful Art, Manufacture, Engine, Machine or Device, or any improvement therein not before known or used." Applicants paid between $4 and $5 to process submissions, which included a drawing or model of the invention. Under the act, the State Department held the power to issue patents extending to fourteen years.

Read broadened the scope of his application in subsequent petitions of 16 and 23 April; all proved unsuccessful, as a number of inventors competed to dominate the new steam-engine industry. He pressed on with additional inquiries, and in April 1791 the board "agreed to grant patents to all the claimants of steam-patents . . . without taking it upon themselves to ascertain whether those claimants were really the inventors, as they severally alleged in their petitions." Read's patent was issued on 26 Aug. (*Biog. Dir. Cong.*; *First Fed. Cong.*, 1:271–272, 277–278, 282; 3:288–289; David Read, *Nathan Read: His Invention . . . of the True Mode of Applying Steam-Power to Navigation and Railways*, N.Y., 1870, p. 111, 113, 115–116).

[2] Edward Augustus Holyoke was the former president of the Massachusetts Medical Society (vol. 17:605).

From William Cranch

Sir, Boston Jan. 24. 1790 Sunday.

I wrote you some time ago, & desired Mr Lovell, who told me he should see Mr Ames before he left Dedham, to forward it by him. Your Son Tom writes me that you have not recieved it. I shall enquire of Lovell what he did with it. It contained several letters, one to Mrs Smith, one for Louisa, one or more for my Aunt, one for Tom & one for Charles.[1]

Our Legislature is now sitting. A question has arisen, "whether persons holding offices under the national Government similar to those prohibited by our State Constitution, have a right to hold their seats in our Legislature." A joint Committee was chosen, who reported that they had no right. The Report was not accepted by the Senate. The numbers were 13 to 11. The house accepted the Report by a majority of 137 to 24.— However, the Senate still think that they have a sole right to judge of the quatifications of their own members, & are determined to pay no regard to the judgment of the House. The Consequence is that Mr Gore has quitted his seat in the house, while Mr Jackson remains still in the Senate.[2]

Mr Gardner, the Member from Pownalboro', entirely regardless of Popularity, as he himself says, & excited only by patriotic principles & passions, has been urging an enquiry into the State of the law & its Professors in this Commonwealth. On the first day of the Session, he inform'd the house that he intended the honour of making a motion on the next Tuesday. On tuesday, after a long Exordium upon Prejudice, which I suppose you have seen verbatim in the Centinel, he very pompously made his motion. The consideration of it was postponed till thursday, when in a verbose, florid speech he stated many of the pernicious practises of the lawyers & Justices of the Peace; he dwelt long upon the illegality of the Bar-Call or Bar meeting, which he affirmed to be a monster whose father was Tom Hutchinson—that it was no less than an illegal Conspiracy against the laws and that if the Attorney Gen[l.] had done his duty, they would have been indicted long before this time. Here he betrayed his cloven-foot—for while he affirmed, as an instance of their arbitrary proceedings, that they would not permit his Son to be recommended to the Court, untill he had studied 3 years regularly, he discover'd the passion which kindled his Zeal. He said that the Bills of

Cost were unjust—that the law against Champerty had cut its own throat, by inflicting a punishment upon both the parties. After stating these & some other malpractises, he was desired to read to the house what amendments he had to propose. Upon which he produced a *Bill* consisting of 21. Chapters, each Chapter containing 8 or 10 sections, a detail of which he read to the house. The most remarkable heads were these, as well as I can remember. A clause against perjury—against Champarty & maintenance—a fee bill—against lawyers exercising the judicial powers of Justices of the Peace,—destroying the distinctions between contracts under Seal & those which are not—destroying special pleadings—permiting all kinds of demands between the same parties to be contained in one writ—preventing Estates tail from being created for the future, & providing a cheap & expeditious method of barring those already created—that Deeds shall be construed more liberally & according to the *Intention* of the parties—rendering the forms of Declarations more simple—In fact making every man a Compleat Lawyer. The bill is committed to a Committee of one member from each County,—[3]

The Govr. has appointed Mr Paine, to the office of Judge of the Supreme Court. An Attorny Genl is not yet nominated. It is said the vacancy is to be filled by Judge Sullivan. The other judge it is supposed will be either Mr Sprague or Judge Nathan Cushing. If Mr Sprague should be chosen the Office of Sheriff of the County of Worcester will be vacant & Mr Greenleaf is not disqualified for holding it again. But the popular opinion must be first sounded upon that point—[4]

I rec^d. a letter from your Son at Newbury Port, dated Jan. 18.[5] he was then well— I have the Honor to be Sir your grateful & affect^e. Nephew Wm. Cranch.

RC (Adams Papers); endorsed: "W. Cranch. Jan. 24. 1790 / ans^d March 14."

[1] These letters, carried by Fisher Ames, have not been found.

[2] The controversy centered on the Mass. General Court's interpretation of Art. 9 of the Massachusetts Constitution of 1780, which stipulated that a member who accepted a state post could not simultaneously retain his seat in the state legislature. When Christopher Gore was named the first U.S. attorney for the district of Massachusetts, he faced pressure from local lawmakers to resign from the Mass. house of representatives. In his printed letter of 29 Jan., Gore argued that the article applied only to certain posts. His colleagues in the house of representatives disagreed, and ultimately Gore yielded his seat. Massachusetts senators thought differently on the question. In a 20 Jan. vote of 13 to 11, they permitted Jonathan Jackson to retain his seat while serving as a federal marshal (*ANB*; *Massachusetts Centinel*, 23, 30 Jan.).

[3] Lawyer John Gardiner (1731–1793), who represented Pownalborough, addressed the Mass. General Court regarding legal reforms on 19 Jan., and his speech was printed in the

Massachusetts Centinel the next day. Gardiner's draft of an extensive new law code featured a chapter on champerty, the practice by which a third party carried on a lawsuit, at his own cost and risk, with the expectation of collecting a share of any profits made in the result. Looking to trim frivolous lawsuits, Gardiner accused several colleagues in the state legislature of engaging in champerty, which he deemed "wild, unconstitutional, and highly injurious to the great body of this people" (*AFC*, 9:10–11; *Massachusetts Centinel*, 20, 27, 30 Jan.; Black, *Law Dictionary*).

[4] Gov. John Hancock appointed Robert Treat Paine and Nathan Cushing to serve as associate justices on the Mass. Supreme Judicial Court in early 1790. John Sprague remained sheriff of Worcester County until 1792 (vol. 4:204; *AFC*, 7:176, 9:32; Boston *Independent Chronicle*, 28 June 1792).

[5] Not found.

From George Walton

Sir, Savannah, 28 January, 1790.

Being on a circuit of our Superior Courts, & finding a Vessel ready to sail for New-York, I embrace the occasion of congratulating your zeal on the effectual opperation of the federal Government. Its quick progress to its present stage is a phenomonen in the history of mankind. But in such new and perplexed concerns a perfect combination of the various parts cannot be expected; and it is a problem which experience only will solve, whether some parts of the proceedings of the first Session of the National Congress will not be found to have exceptions. To me it appears that the Judiciary system is too ponderous, expensive and unwieldy; and its iron teeth too frightful for the condition of the Southern States.[1] It is too unqualified. The right of the writ of Capias ad Satisfaciendum in the first and last instance, under our circumstances, and without any bankrupt provision, will, I fear, produce much uneasiness. Should the british debts be entirely and at once sued for from Virginia inclusive South, the consequences would be ruinous. That these debts remained so heavy is ascribable to the depredations of the War; and I ever thought ought to have been made an object of national consideration. With respect to this State I dont think we are affected, as those debts were confiscated prior to the Treaty of Peace; and all acts of confiscation already passed were recognized and confirmed by the Treaty. In another capacity I was called upon to give an opinion on this ground last year; and the state of facts made on that occasion I will do myself the pleasure to enclose to you, & shall be particularly obliged by any observations you shall see fit to make there upon.[2]

The principle of the general Representation in the national Government being according to numbers, this State has lately adopted a measure to encrease hers, by disposing of a part of her vacant territory to three private Companies.[3] This measure will, no doubt, be ascribed to other motives by some: but, although I was not a member of the legislature, I am well assured & believe that the true ground of the act was what I have mentioned. While human nature continues the same, Governments will always act from a sense of its own Interest and aggrandisement.

I did myself the pleasure to write to you some little time since from Augusta; and the sentiments then expressed will always continue to govern me.[4] I am full of zeal for the prosperity of the United-States; and I am the servant of this state.

Colonel Gunn requests that this letter should be the Vehicle of his respects to you; & that I would add that he is extremely anxious to be with you: but that he was under the necessity of attending the court now sitting. In Schermehan he will certainly sail.[5]

With great & sincere respect & Esteem, I have the honor to be, Sir, / Your mo. Ob. Servt.   Geo Walton.

RC (Adams Papers); addressed: "His Excellency, / John Adams; / New-York—"; endorsed: "George Walton / 20 Jan. 1790." Filmed at 20 January.

[1] Although the Judiciary Act of 1789 recognized state jurisdiction over common law, it mandated that the U.S. Supreme Court could rule that a state law was unconstitutional—a form of judicial power that met with resistance in the southern states. Specifically, Walton referred to the second article of the Process Act of 1789, which permitted defendants to be jailed until their debts were paid in gold or silver. This provision disadvantaged debtors in the southern states, where specie was scarce and prewar debts to British creditors lingered (Abernethy, *The South in the New Nation*, p. 38; *Doc. Hist. Supreme Court*, 4:108–109, 114–115, 179).

[2] Enclosure not found.

[3] The Georgia legislature passed the Yazoo Act on 16 Dec. 1789, selling over 25 million acres, which make up modern-day Alabama and Mississippi, to three groups of private speculators. The South Carolina Yazoo Company purchased 10 million acres for $66,964; the Virginia Yazoo Company bought more than 11 million acres for $93,741; and the Tennessee Yazoo Company acquired 4 million acres for $46,875. Georgia lawmakers gave the companies two years to pay, further requiring them to secure the territory and remove Native American claims to the land. But the massive sale fell through after the legislature stipulated on 11 June 1790 that the state treasury would accept payment only in gold, silver, or paper money issued after 14 Aug. 1786 (George R. Lamplugh, *Politics on the Periphery: Factions and Parties in Georgia, 1783–1806*, Newark, N.J., 1986, p. 67–68, 71).

[4] Of 7 Nov. 1789, above.

[5] The sloop *Jenny*, Capt. Cornelius Schermerhorn (1756–1826), sailed from Savannah, Ga., on 1 April 1790 and reached New York on 11 April. Sen. James Gunn took his seat in Congress two days later (*Georgia Gazette*, 1 April; New York *Evening Post*, 25 March 1826; *New-York Journal*, 15 April 1790; *First Fed. Cong.*, 1:284).

From Richard Price

My Dear Friend　　　　Hackney Feb$^{y.}$ 1$^{st:}$ 1790

This comes to you with a Discourse which has been much talked of here; and which, I hope, you will accept as a Small testimony of my gratitude and respect.[1] It is an effusion of zeal in the cause of human liberty and virtue; and, 'tho a Subject of censure with many in this country, I can be confident that you will approve the Spirit of it, and the general Sentiments it contains.

I thought myself greatly favoured by the letter which I received from you at the beginning of last Summer; and it is impossible I Should ever forget the kind attention with which you have always honoured me.—[2]

You must probably feel the Same Satisfaction and triumph in the late Revolution in France that I have felt. It appears to me that most of the events in the annals of the world are but childish tales compared with it. But the united States of America have the glory of having led the way to it. The new constitution of France deviates in Some respects from those Ideas of the best constitution of governm^{t} which you have with So much ability explained and defended. But this deviation, as France is Situated, Seems to have been unavoidable; for had not the Aristocratical and Clerical orders been obliged to throw themselves into one chamber with the Commons, no reformation could have taken place, and the regeneration of the Kingdom would have been impossible: And, in future legislatures, were these two orders to make distinct and independent States, all that has been done would probably be soon undone. Hereafter, perhaps, when the new constitution as now formed, has acquired Strength by time, the national Assembly may find it practicable as well as expedient to establish, by means of a third estate, Such a check as now takes place in the *American* governm^{ts}, and is indispensible in the British governm$^{t.}$—

Remember me very kindly to Mrs Adams. May you be long continued happy in one another and in your connexions. I feel myself in the decline of life. An indolence is increasing upon me, and a disposition to be encumber'd and burden'd by every little business that comes in my way. I rejoyce in your usefulness and eminence, and the just respect which has been Shewn you by the united States. The new federal governm$^{t:}$ has, I hope, now acquired Such a firm establishm^{t} as will make it the means of extricating the united States from difficulties and rendering them permanently prosperous and happy.

Hoping never to be forgotten by you, I am, with Sentiments of warm affection and respect, / ever yours Richd Price

May I request the favour of you to convey to Mr Smith the pamphlet I have directed to him, and to deliver to him and to Mrs Smith my kind respects?[3]

RC (Adams Papers); addressed: "John Adams Esq:"; endorsed: "Dr Price. Feb. 1. / ans^d Ap. 19. 1790."

[1] Price sent his *Discourse on the Love of Our Country*, London, 1789. Drawn from a 4 Nov. 1789 speech that he gave in London, Price's work connected the onset of the French Revolution to the same political ideologies that spurred the American Revolution (Arthur Sheps, "The American Revolution and the Transformation of English Republicanism," *Historical Reflections*, 2:7 [Summer 1975]).

[2] For JA's 20 May letter to Price, see vol. 19:469–470.

[3] The pamphlet has not been found, but it may have been a second copy of the discourse sent to JA, for which see note 1. Price's most recent letter to WSS was of 28 July, commenting on political conditions in France. He thanked WSS for conveying American news, thereby countering the "nonsense" he heard about the "Dictatorship" of George Washington (*The Correspondence of Richard Price*, ed. W. Bernard Peach and D. O. Thomas, 3 vols., Durham, N.C., 1983–1994, 3:237–239).

From Wilhem & Jan Willink

Sir Amsterdam 1 febr 1790

We beg leave to refer to our last respects of 8 dec̃:, since wh^ch. time we continue without your agreable favors, we are now paying the intrest due on the 4 PC. Obt: and request Your Sending us the Coupons of yours & to dispose of Said amount; it is highly agreable to us to see the American Credit on a respectable footing, in consequence the 5 PC: Obt: are advanced at 99 1/2 PC: and the 4 PC: Sell at a premium of 2 PC: on acc^t. of the Lotery, the management we kept in it, we flatter ourselves will assure us the satisfaction of the United States & your personal knowledge in how much the influence of our Credit has contributed to it will assure us your benevolence. We think it our duty to inform you as our Friend ab^t: the letter we write with M^sr. V Staphorst to the Treasurer Hamilton Esqr. of the applications made to the Court of france to transfer to Speculaters the debt of Congress pay^e.[1] Part in money Part in france Stocks to great advantage of the undertakers, who made application to borrow on said American debt here, on terms very advantageous to money Lenders, wh^ch. they Could easily pay out of the profit that

Should result to them from this operation, whch. measure the Houses considered highly detrimental to the Credit of the United States, as the obligt. of their Loans should necessary decline, whenever people could obtain much higher intrest of Obt: funded on a debt of the Same United States & those Speculators Possessed of such a considerable debt became in Some measure Masters of the Credit here whch. they had no reason to maintain & obliged to Satisfy their engagemts. Should be in the necessity to get money on Said debt at any condition & by those advantages make it absolutely impossible for the United States to borrow here at a reasonable Condition at the Simple intrest of 5 PCt. after all our endeavours to put a Stop to it in Paris, & by the knowledge Of the desire of Congress to Pay if not of the Principal the arrears of intrest at least to france, the houses considered the best measure to make it almost impossible to the Speculators to agree, to make the obtaining of money if not impossible, highly difficult to them, in order to maintain the Credit of the United States & keep the faculty to borrow for them, the houses took on themselves to open a Loan under approbation of the United States for 3 Mills of *f* at 5 PC. in full Confidence, that our motives Should be Considered in the true light & be highly approved, the more as we get it on the terms of the first Loan, and Sacrifis a great Profit offered to us by the speculators either to be partners or commissioners whch. we thought our duty to decline.

some Members however may blame the Liberty we have taken, but we flatter ourselves of the equitable Judgment of the States, that our motives will be done Justice and considered as it is truely, a determination for the intrest of the United states, there we regretted infinitely your & Mr. Jefferson's absence to be able to Consult the Ministers in a Matter of Such delicacy.

In case of any remarks on our conduct We hope you'll be so kind to be a favourable interpreetor of the Sincerity of our Sentiments there nothing than a Sense of our duty & attachmt. to the intrest of the United States could bring us to the dermination & make us decline a considerable profit to maintain their Credit & the faculty, to borrow on advantageous terms in full reliance on your friendship we hope to hear from you, well assured that we'll always retain a proper Sense of Your benevolence

We request our Sincere Compliments to your Lady & remain with great esteem / sir Your most Obedient servants

Wilhem & Jan Willink

RC (Adams Papers); internal address: "The Hon[l:] John Adams Esqr / Newyork"; endorsed: "Willinks. 1. Feb. 1790." Dupl (Adams Papers).

[1] Following JA's and Thomas Jefferson's departures from Europe, the supervision of American foreign loans reverted to U.S. treasury secretary Alexander Hamilton. On 28 Jan. William Short, the U.S. chargé d'affaires in Paris, forwarded a 25 Jan. letter from the Dutch loan consortium to Hamilton apprising him that on 1 Feb. it would open a fifth loan, of 3 million florins, to be reimbursed between 1801 and 1805. The agreement was mainly identical to the previous four contracts, and it halted Jefferson's plans to transfer American debt to revolutionary France. Despite lacking a U.S. minister to authorize it, the Dutch bankers publicly advertised the loan, and Hamilton approved it on 7 May 1790, pending the finalization of plans for the federal assumption of state debt (vol. 19:289; Hamilton, *Papers*, 6:210–218, 409).

To Benjamin Rush

Dear sir New York Feb. 2. 1790

I cannot give up my dear Latin and Greek although Fortune has never permitted me to enjoy so much of them as I wished.— I dont love you the less however for your Indifference or even Opposition to them. Pray do you carry your Theory so far as to wish to exclude French Italian, Spanish and Tudesque?— I begun to fear that your multiplied phisical and other Engagements had made You forget me— But am much obliged to you for introducing M[r] Andrew Brown, to whom I wish success.—[1] I congratulate You, on the Prospect of a new Constitution for Pensilvania.—[2] Poor France I fear will bleed, for too exactly copying your old one.

When I See Such miserable Crudities approved by Such Men as Rochefaucault & Condorcet I am disposed to think very humbly of human Understanding. Experience is lost on poor Mankind! O how I pitty them without being able to help them.

Write me when you can

Yours &c John Adams

RC (NN:Harkness Coll.); internal address: "D[r] Rush."

[1] Rush wrote to JA on 26 Jan. to recommend printer Andrew Brown, publisher of the *Philadelphia Gazette*, who had been "very instrumental . . . in circulating federal sentiments thro' our state" (Adams Papers). Brown (ca. 1744–1797), originally from Ireland, opened a "young ladies' academy" in Lancaster, Penn., that was "more liberal than had before been contemplated in this country" (New York *Diary*, 16 Feb. 1797).

[2] For the Pennsylvania Constitution of 1790, see Rush's reply of 12 Feb., and note 2, below.

From Charles Dilly

Dr Sir, Londo; 3d Feby 1790.

I shd. not have troubled you with a Letter—but upon the peculiar instance of having received a Letter from Messrs; Wilhem of Amsterdam, a few Months ago; in which he states in consequence of the receipt of a Letter from you—he has made Enquiry about your Volumes of the Defence of the American states &c—but cannot find any of the *Second* Volume—[1] I immediatly returned for answer—Fifty Copies of that Volume were Shippd the 8th; Sepr; 1787—on board the *Maraggratha, Capt; Doorn*[2]—and on the 27 March following 50 Volume 3d— It is strange if the Parcels containing the 1st. & 3d Volumes had been opened—That the omission of the second Volume Shd not have been found out for the space of two Years. I directed upon the receipt of a second Letter last Novr; Mr; Ingram, my Shopman and—who has the conduct of all orders—and Parcels going into the Country—or Shipped for Exportation—To state the Day—and date of Sending the Parcels. Supposing Mr. Wilhem may have written to you on the Subject—I thought it expedient in me to explain that no imputation of neglect shd. be placed to my charge of omitting to forward an Equal Number of the 2d Volume as I did of the First & Third. As a greater Number of the second Volumes were sent to Amera; than the Third—I have not a Copy of the second to make up a set—and—on this acct. I have requested a friend to Enquire of Mr; Mc. Kean whether his Booksr;[3] has any of that Volume left, above the Number of the Third—and shd. it be so, to return—Ten or a dozen Copies of that Volume only—as I have First—and Thirds.

The Copies of Dr: Gordons Hist: of the American Revolution After the Subscribers were supplied—amounted to about Two hundred and they are now all sold—which is a fortunate circumstance to the Worthy Doctor—who is now fixed with a small congregation at St. Neotes about Fifty miles North of Londo;— He is a Worthy honest Man—contented with a trifle—and lives happy and chearful with his Little Flock.[4] I hope your Lady and Family Enjoy the blessing of health—and with my sincere wish for the continuation of all other temporal comforts—I rest Dr sir, Your faithful & Humbl Servt;

Chs; Dilly

RC (Adams Papers).

[1] See the Willinks' letter of 8 Dec. 1789, and note 1, above.

[2] The *Margaretha*, Capt. Klaas Doorn, departed Gravesend on 25 Sept. 1787 and arrived in Amsterdam on 5 Oct. (London *Public Advertiser*, 27 Sept.; London *Gazetteer and New*

Daily Advertiser, 24 Dec.; from Wilhem & Jan Willink, 8 Dec. 1789, above).

3 JA sent copies of his *Defence of the Const.*, via Thomas McKean, to be sold at the South Second Street bookstore of Thomas Dobson (1751–1823), an Edinburgh native and a leader of Philadelphia's literary scene (JA, *Works*, 10:269; *Jefferson's Memorandum Books*, 2:887; John Rennie Short, *Representing the Republic: Mapping the United States, 1600–1900*, London, 2001, p. 103).

4 Rev. William Gordon was preaching at St. Neots in Huntingdonshire, England (vol. 18:241).

From John Trumbull

Dear Sir — Hartford February 6th. 1790—

Your letter found me on my return from the session of our Superior Court at Haddam—since which, I have attended a three weeks session of our County Court here.[1] So that I have had little leisure to prepare for my defence in a capital Trial.

To your charge of *reading myself to death*, I now propose to plead double by leave of the Court. My first Plea is that I am yet alive. Lord Hale advises Courts to be cautious of condemning any Person for Murther, unless it be clearly proved, that the man, supposed to be murdered is actually dead—[2] I have looked over my Books & cannot find a single precedent of any man, indicted & hanged for Self murder.

In the next place, I shall plead not guilty *infra sex annos*— It is hard if there is no act of limitation in the case. From the year 1777 to the year 80, I resided in my native town in a part of the country, where I could have no more Society than a Hermit, & had no other amusement but my Books. I injured my health gradually by continual reading & writing—for I determined to be the most learned Man in America; But hurt my constitution still more by attending all the Courts in two adjacent Counties, thro' the storms & snows of the severe winter of 80—[3] In the spring of that year I found my nerves relaxed to the utmost degree of debility. I had a shock of an uncommon kind, which I scarcely survived. It came on with a coldness, & loss of pulsation, tho' not of feeling in all my limbs, which gradually extended itself nearly to the trunk of my body, attended with violent headach & palpitation of the heart— It left me subject to faintness, vertigo, loss of appetite, frequent turns of sick-headach, & every symptom of nervous decay. Before the close of that year my physicians pronounced me in the last stage of a consumption— I discarded them, & undertook to prescribe for myself. I removed to Hartford in 81, by way of experiment, as Yorick went to France, to run away from death. Since that time I have been gradually regaining health, & tho' sufficiently an Invalid, am able to transact more business in my profession, than any Lawyer in the County. Nor do I attend more to my studies, than is necessary to preserve the reputation I have gained in my profession, & do justice to the Causes in which I am engaged. Besides the want of health, I have had many disadvantages to combat in attempting to rise to eminence as a Lawyer. No man can be a judge of his own manner of speaking—but my friends have early been careful to inform me, that except a tolerable fluency, with some degree of animation, I possessed no one talent of a public speaker; that my voice was harsh & disagreable, my gestures stiff, my pronunciation naturally thick & inarticulate, & my style void of that sonorous pomp, which captivates the ears of a vulgar audience— That no genius can excell in more ways than one, that I must be content with my literary reputation, & give up all hope of excellence at the Bar. I was not willing to be so content—but what could be done— I had only two resources left—*Learning* & *Fidelity* to my Clients—I have tried them & they have availed me. Nor have I any rival in my business in my own County. In the last Superior Court, I argued every cause tried before them, during a fortnight's session, except one— At our County Court just now closed, I lost only three causes—I argued more than twenty— It is alledged that I have too great influence with the Courts, especially the County Court— But the secret is, that I judge my causes before I try them, & will try none that I think desperate. So much for boasting— I observe the alternative penance you propose me— I own myself too indolent for the five miles walk a day, & had rather submit to the seat in a house of Representatives— But I have little inclination for either— Many of my friends have urged me to attempt promotion in the political line— I have as yet purposely avoided it, & avoided it with great ease—as I have not one popular talent in my whole composition, & would not give up my right of speaking & writing my sentiments on men & measures, and of personally attacking all, whom I have viewed, as enemies to the Public, for any office or honour, I could expect in the States. And I firmly beleive that I have been of more service, in that way, to my country, than I could have been, if courting popularity, I had been able to act in any official character. I have by these means made myself many enemies—but I hug myself in the independence of my situation, & laugh at the storm, that rattles on my roof. I hope however, that the Stability of the new Government, will supersede the necessity of political Satirists.— If the public find they want me in any other way, they will call for me, but I shall never solicit their votes, which I consider as conferring burthens & not favors.

Thus much & perhaps too much, I have written on myself by way of vindication. I shall now take up a more important subject, and in return for the advice received, (for I do not choose to be in any Man's debt) address some hints to the Vice-President, relative to his own political situation, & the strictures made upon his conduct by his Enemies. I shall ask no excuse for my assurance, & am certain my motive needs no Apology.

Be it remembered then, that the Vice-President is a native of New England, & that the inhabitants of the Southern States are not yet entirely cured of their local jealousies—that without any considerable advantages from the pride of family, or the favours of fortune, he has raised himself to that eminent station, solely by his personal merit, & the importance of his public services—& that this circumstance has provoked the pride & raised the envy of many of the Southern Aristocrats, who suppose themselves born to greatness, & cannot bear to be eclipsed by merit only— That this Party are endeavouring to represent his character in an unfavorable light, & if possible prevent his ever rising to the first office in the States, whenever a vacancy shall happen.[4] The obloquy they have endeavoured to raise against him, as having deserted his republican principles, & become fond of the splendor, & titles of monarchical Courts, is well known, & needs no remark, because it has nearly subsided in the New England States, where his character is known & justly appreciated—it may perhaps still be a subject of unjust censure in the southern States— But must there at length subside, as their people, who are an age behind us in political knowlege, become convinced of the necessity of energy in the executive Department. But they attempt an attack on another ground, & endeavour to render him unpopular in the Senate, the principal theatre on which his political talents can now be exerted. They assert that the Constitution gives the President of the Senate no right to mingle in their debates—that he can on no occasion with propriety offer his sentiments at large, except when he is requested to give information respecting the affairs of foreign courts, which have fallen under his personal observation, or when in case of an equivote, he states his reasons on giving his casting voice. They add that as a public Speaker, the talents in which he excells all others, are force of argument & strength of language, approaching to sarcasm, and expressive of some degree of contempt for the opinions & reasonings of his adversaries—that in consequence, whenever he mingles in debate, he offends those whose sentiments he opposes—while the party he supports are not always pleased, as his idea of the necessity of affording his assistance is a tacit reflection on them, as incompetent advocates of a good cause—that he who mingles in debate subjects himself to frequent retorts from his opposers, places himself on the same ground with his inferiors in rank, appears too much like the leader of a Party, & renders it more difficult for him to support the dignity of the chair, & preserve order & regularity in the debate—while he gives his enemies frequent opportunity by reporting casual expressions, which have fallen in the warmth of argument, to misrepresent his opinions & designs, with little danger of detection—as the doors of the Senate are always shut.

Of the truth or justice of these remarks I am no judge—but I have heard them so frequently made, & sometimes by men who I am sure are not unfriendly, and in every other respect have the highest esteem for your abilities & character, that I thought it my duty to communicate them—especially as on so delicate a subject it was doubtful whether You would hear of them in any other way— I should have chosen to hint them in a personal interview, but my business has disappointed me of a visit to New York, which I had intended in the course of this winter.

I congratulate You on the favorable Prospect of the firm establishment of our Government— The proceedings of the last Session are generally approved— The clamours attempted to be raised on the subject of Salaries have died away—and our most sensible men would rather see an augmentation in one or two instances than a considerable diminution in any.

Vesting in the President the power of removing all officers in the executive department is a most important amendment of the Constitution in the only part in which I ever thought an amendment essential, or a defect absolutely necessary to be supplied. The other proposed amendments are very harmless at least— The Article, which establishes the right of Trial by jury in all cases at common law, I should object against, as holding out a false light, because in many cases, it must be absurd, if not impossible to carry it into execution—but the very objection shows that it is not dangerous.

The establishment of Fœderal Courts entirely separate from those of the States was another measure of equal importance, the effect will not be immediately seen, but will be eventually of the highest consequence. In a word, though there are sundry members of Congress, whose opinions on Government have never advanced beyond the crude ideas of pure Democracy which we imbibed at the beginning of the Revolution, the Majority appear sufficiently enlightened to carry every necessary measure, for establishing an energetic Government, armed with power for our Protection & Defence

Excuse the length of this Letter, which has far exceeded my intention— Please to present my most respectful Compliments to M^rs. Adams—and believe me to be with the highest respect & most sincere Attachment—Dear Sir / Your obliged & most Obed^t. / Humble Servant John Trumbull

RC (Adams Papers); endorsed: "Mr Trumbull / Feb 6. Ans^d March 9 / 1790."

[1] Trumbull received JA's letter of 13 Jan., above, after attending the session of the Conn. Superior Court in Haddam, which opened on 12 Jan. (Jesse Root, *Reports of Cases Adjudged in the Superior Court and Supreme Court of Errors from July, A.D. 1789, to June, A.D. 1793*, 2 vols., N.Y., 1899, 1:481).

[2] A copy of the 1736 London edition of Sir Matthew Hale's *Historia Placitorum Coronæ*, 2 vols., is in JA's library at MB (*Catalogue of JA's Library*).

[3] After teaching school in Wethersfield, Conn., and studying law with JA in the 1770s, Trumbull returned to his native Watertown, Conn., to pursue a dual career as a poet and judge (*ANB*).

[4] Regional interests were embedded in the longstanding debate over the federal seat. Calling JA "the presumptive successor to the presiding magistrate," James Madison warned that the New Englander's tie-breaking vote in the Senate "will render his administration an ominous period for the Potomac" (Madison, *Papers, Congressional Series*, 12:426).

From Benjamin Franklin

Sir, Philadelphia Feby 9th: 1790

At the Request of the Pennsylvania Society for the Abolition of Slavery, I have the Honour of presenting to your Excellency the enclosed Petition, which I beg leave to recommend to your favourable Notice.[1] Some further Particulars respecting it, requested by the Society, will appear in their Letter to me, of which I enclose a Copy, and have the Honor to be, / Sir, / Your Excellency's / most obedient / & most humble Servant B Franklin

Presid^t of the Society.

ENCLOSURE

Philadelphia Feb^ry. 3^d. 1790

To the Senate & House of Representatives of the United States,

The Memorial of the Pennsylvania Society for promoting the Abolition of Slavery, the relief of free Negroes unlawfully held in bondage, & the Improvement of the Condition of the African Race—

Respectfully Sheweth,

That from a regard for the happiness of Mankind an Association was formed several years since in this State by a number of her Citizens of various religious denominations for promoting the *Abolition of Slavery* & for the relief of those unlawfully held in bondage. A just & accurate Conception of the true Principles of liberty, as it spread through the land, produced accessions to their numbers, many friends to their Cause, & a legislative Co-operation with their views, which, by the blessing of Divine Providence, have been successfully directed to the *relieving from bondage a large number* of *their fellow Creatures of the African Race*— They have also the Satisfaction to observe, that in consequence of that Spirit of Philanthropy & genuine liberty which is generally diffusing its beneficial Influence, similar Institutions are gradually forming at home & abroad.

That mankind are all formed by the same Almighty being, alike objects of his Care & equally designed for the Enjoyment of Happiness the Christian Religion teaches us to believe, & the Political Creed of America fully coincides with the Position. Your Memorialists, particularly engaged in attending to the Distresses arising from Slavery, believe it their indispensible Duty to present this Subject to your notice— They have observed with great Satisfaction, that many important & Salutary Powers are vested in you for "promoting the Welfare & *securing the blessings of liberty to the People of the United States*." And as they conceive, that these blessings ought rightfully to be administered, *without distinction of Colour*, to all descriptions of People, so they indulge themselves in the pleasing expectation, that nothing, which can be done for the relief of the unhappy objects of their care, will be either omitted or delayed—

From a persuasion that equal liberty was originally the Portion, & is still the Birthright of all Men, & influenced by the strong ties of Humanity & the Principles of their Institution, your Memorialists conceive themselves *bound to use all justifiable endeavours to loosen the bands of Slavery* and promote a general Enjoyment of the blessings of Freedom. Under these Impressions they earnestly intreat your serious attention to the Subject of Slavery, that you will be pleased to countenance the *Restoration of liberty* to those unhappy Men, who alone, in this land of Freedom, are degraded into perpetual Bondage, and who, amidst the general Joy of surrounding Freemen, are groaning in Servile Subjection, that you will devise means for removing this *Inconsistency from the Character of the American People*, that you will promote Mercy and Justice towards this distressed Race, & that you will Step to the very verge of the Powers vested in you for discouraging every Species of Traffick in the Persons of our fellow Men.

B Franklin
Presid^{t} of the Society

RC and enclosures (DNA:RG 46, Records of the U.S. Senate); internal address: "His Excell^{y} John Adams Esq$^{r.}$ / Vice President of the United States"; endorsed: "2^{d} Sess: 1$^{st:}$ Con: / Letter / from B. Franklin to / the Vice President en- / closing a Petition from / the Society for the Abolition / of Slavery. / February 9th / 1790."; and on the enclosure: "2^{d} Sess: 1$^{st:}$ Con: / Memorial / of the Pennsylvania Socie / ty for the Abolition of / *Slavery*. / February 3rd / 1790."

[1] With his final extant letter to JA, Franklin sent this memorial from the Pennsylvania Society for Promoting the Abolition of Slavery. Formed in 1774, the society reorganized in 1787 under Franklin's leadership, with Quaker merchant James Pemberton (1723–1809), of Philadelphia, acting as a vice president. Pemberton secured Franklin's signature on two copies of the petition and then requested that he forward them to both houses of Congress. On 15 Feb. 1790, JA laid the petition before the Senate, where discussion ensued but no further action was taken. The petition found greater traction in the House, where it aggravated regional tensions over the national assumption of state debts and the site of the federal seat. From 11 to 12 Feb., representatives considered three antislavery petitions sent by Quakers, including this one, and referred them all to committee. The committee presented a report on 8 March that called for humane treatment of enslaved persons "while on their passages to the United States," observing that the Constitution curbed congressional regulation of the states' participation in the African slave trade. Members debated the report throughout March, with Elias Boudinot of New Jersey supporting the cause of abolition and William Loughton Smith of South Carolina leading the opposition. In a vote of 29 to 25, representatives agreed to include a copy of the report in the official record, but they took no further legislative action (Philadelphia *Freeman's Journal*, 23 May 1787; Philadelphia *American Daily Advertiser*, 14 Feb. 1809; *First Fed. Cong.*, 1:242; 3:294, 295–296, 316, 321, 332, 334, 335, 337, 341; 9:202; *Annals of Congress*, 1st Cong., 2d sess., p. 1465–1466, 1503–1514, 1516–1525).

From Benjamin Rush

Dear Sir. Philadelphia Feb: 12th 1790.

Ever since the last week in Octo^{r} I have been engaged in composing & delivering a new Course of lectures on the theory & practice of medicine in the College of this city.[1] This arduous business has employed me so closely that it has seperated me from my friends,—detatched me from all Other pursuits—and—what I regret most of all, has deprived me for a while of the pleasure of your Correspondence.— Altho' we hold different principles upon some Subjects, yet I cannot help loving and respecting you. You were my first preceptor in the Science of Goverment. From you I learned to discover the danger of the Constitution of Pennsylvania, and If I have had any merit, or guilt in keeping the public mind Awake to its folly, or danger for 13 years, you alone should have the Credit of the former & be made responsable for the latter. But my dear Sir I learned further from you, to despise public opinion when set in competition with the dictates of judgement or Conscience. So much did I imbibe of this Spirit from you, that during the whole of my political life, I was always disposed to suspect my integrity, if from any Accident I became popular with our Citizens for a few weeks or days. The reformation of our State goverment has completed my last political wish. Hitherto I have never known a defeat, or final disappointment in any One of them. I ascribe my Successes wholly to my *perseverance*. I claim this Virtue ~~publicly~~ boldly, since all my enemies admit of my possessing it, at the time they deny me every other Virtue or quality of a politician.—

The experience I have had in public pursuits, has led me to make many discoveries in the human heart that are not very favourable to it.— I shall leave some of them upon record by way of beacons to deter my children from engaging in public life.— One of them will be that "a politician can never suffer from his *enemies*."— The folly—the envy—and the ingratitude of his *friends* are the principal Sources of his sufferings.

Such is my apathy *now* to public Affairs that I often pass whole weeks without reading our newspapers.— I have never Once been within the doors of our convention, nor have I broken bread with a single member of the body who compose it.[2] Heaven has been profuse in its gifts of family blessings to me. My dear M[rs] Rush is every thing to me that a friend—a companion & a wife should be to any man. Our children are affectionate—& dutiful,—& promising as to their capacities for acquiring knowledge.— Nineteen out of twenty of my evenings are spent in their Society.

I see many ~~of my friends who began their political Service with [. . .]~~ men high in power or affluent in office, who in the year 1776 considered me as One of the firebrands of independance. I feel the effects in a debilitated Constitution of the midnight Studies which I devoted for 16 years to my Country— I see nothing before me during the remainder of my life, but labor and Selfdenial in my profession—and yet I am happy. I envy no man—and blame no man. O! Virtue—Virtue—who would not follow thee blindfold!— I want nothing but a heart sufficiently grateful to heaven for the happiness of my family & my Country

I do not reject the modern languages as a part of Academical education. I have found much more benefit from the French, than I ever found from the latin or Greek, in my profession. I have found some advantages from a knowledge of the Italian, & have been entertained by reading Spanish Books. My partiality to these languages, is one of the reasons of my having quarelled with the dead languages of Greece & Rome.—

with great regard I continue D[r] / Sir yours very affectionately / & sincerely Benj[n:] Rush

RC (Adams Papers); addressed: "The Hon[ble:] / John Adams Esq[r:] / Vice president of the / United States / New-York."; internal address: "The Hon[ble:] John Adams Esq[r.]"; endorsed: "D[r] Rush Feb. 12. Ans[d.] 17[th.] / 1790."

[1] Since 3 Nov. 1788, Rush had lectured on chemistry and "the practice of physic" at the University of Pennsylvania (Rush, *Letters*, 1:532).

[2] Throughout the 1770s and 1780s, two political factions arose in Pennsylvania, the Constitutionalists, who produced the 1776 state constitution, and the Republicans, who advocated for a system closer to JA's frame of government in the Massachusetts Constitution of 1780. Seeking to amend the document, delegates met in Philadelphia from 25 Nov. 1789 to 2 Sept. 1790. Republican James Wilson and Constitutionalist William Findley dominated the convention. They formed the coalition that resulted in the Pennsylvania Constitution of 1790, which established a bicameral legislature and gubernatorial veto power while ending property qualifications for voters and state officials (Joseph S. Foster, "The Politics of Ideology: The Pennsylvania Constitutional Convention of 1789–90," *Pennsylvania History: A Journal of Mid-Atlantic Studies*, 59:122, 123, 125, 126, 129, 134, 137, 138 [April 1992]).

From Jabez Bowen

Sir Providence Feb[r] 15. 1790

I doubt not but You have been inform'd that our Gen[l] Assembly have order'd a Convention to be called to meet a South-Kingston the first Monday of March. the Delegates were Chosen the 8[th.] of this Month and from the Returns we Count Thirty Two Federals and Thirty Eight Antis—so that the Battle will go hard against us if some methods cannot be hit upon to affoard us some help. as I hinted in a former Letter[1] so I repeat it in this, if Congress would take up the Letter that was sent from our General Assembly and give them a firm and Spirited Reply it would be of great service. they might let them know that Congress Consider the Teritory of R[d] Island as a part of the United States that if a part of the present Inhabitants did not Choose to Live under the Federal Government they would be permitted to sell Their Estates &c. but that the people of R[d] Island must of necessity be united with the Rest of the American States. the same wicked disposition continues among the Leaders as heretofore and Congress can do nothing that is good or praise worthy but every of their Acts and found fault with.

we shall do every thing in our power *per* fas *aut nefas* to accomplish our ends—as we really look on the people as Dluded and facinated at present, and seem determined to oppose with Forc of Arms every effort that can be made for the Establishing the Federal Government, if a firm Arm could be laid on us to let them feel and see that Congress was Determined that something should be done and that soon it would have a good Effect.

The present plan of the oposition is to adjorn the Convention to September by which time they say Congress will do so many unjust things that several of the great States will be ready to Revol, and that R^{d} Island remaning a Free & Independent State will put her self at their head. &c with many other Extravegant plans.

on the whole if something could be sent on from Congress to look as if it was spontaneously done. addressed to the Convention I really believe it would have a great weight in producing a favourable determination of the Question.

with Esteeme I Remain Your Excelly / most Obedient Humb Servant

Jabez Bowen

RC (Adams Papers); internal address: "Vice President U$^{d.}$ States"; endorsed: "Jabez Bowen / 15. Feb. ans$^{d.}$ 27 / 1790."

[1] See Bowen's letter of 28 Dec. 1789, above.

To Benjamin Rush

Dear Sir Richmond Hill [17] Feb. 1790[1]

I had heard, before I rec^{d} your Letter of the 12th, of your new Engagements in the Colledge added to your extensive Practice and other virtuous Pursuits: and therefore was at no loss to account for your long Silence.

I have no Pretensions to the Merit of your manly and successful opposition to the Constitution of Pensilvania: but I am very willing to be responsible for. any Consequences of its Rejection.[2]

I have never despised public opinion deliberately. if I have ever expressed myself lightly of it, it was in haste and without caution. on the contrary It is always to be respected and treated with decency, even when in Error: but never to be made the Rule of Action against Conscience,—it is seldom, and only in small Matters to be followed, implicitly. it is a Wave of the Sea in a Storm in the Gulph Stream, except when it is the Result of methodical Councils or secret Influence. It Should be guided and aided, as well as informed by those who are in Possession of all the Secrets of the state. in no nation that ever yet existed, were all the Facts known to the whole

Body or even a Majority of the People, which were essential to the formation of a right Judgment of public affairs. The History of this Country for the last thirty Years, affords as many proofs of this Truth as that of any other Nation. how many times, both at home and abroad have our affairs been in situations, that none but Madmen would have thought proper to be published in detail to the People.

You are not the only one, who has Seen and felt The Jealousy Envy and Ingratitude of Friends.

> "I love my friend as well as You
> But why should he obstruct my view"[3]

contains a Truth, which has laid the foundation for every Despotism and every Absolute Monarchy on Earth. it is this Sentiment, which ruins every Democracy and every Aristocracy, and every possible Mixture of both, and renders a mediating Power, an invincible Equilibrium between them indispensible. never yet was a Band of Heroes or Patriots able to bear the sight of any one of them constantly at their head, if they saw any opening to avoid it. Emulation almost the only Principle of Activity, (except Hunger and Lust) is the Cause of all the Wars Seditions and Parties in the World. What is most astonishing is, that We Should be so ignorant of it, or inattentive to it. and that We should not See, that an independent Executive Power, able at all times to overrule these Rivalries, is absolutely necessary.

The charming Picture you give me of your Domestic Felicity, delights my inmost soul: but revives in me a lively regret for the ten years of my Life, that I lost:—when I left my Children to grow up without a Father.

There are two Parties my friend, who have united in some degree, to obscure the fame of the old Whiggs. The Tories are one, and the Young Fry is the other. By the latter I mean a sett of young Gentlemen who have come out of Colledge Since the Revolution, and are Candidates for fame.— There is a Sett of Men in this Country, who have hazarded too much, laboured too much, suffered too much, and Succeeded too well, ever to be forgiven. Some of these unfortunately are not men of large Views and comprehensive Information, and have adopted destructive systems of Policy. Were it not for this last Consideration, you would hear their Cause pleaded in Accents that would make Impressions on every honest human heart.

You, my dear sir, enjoy the Esteem of the honest and enlightened and are perhaps more usefully and happily employed than others in places of more Eclat.— There is no Man however that I should see with more Pleasure in public Life, especially in Congress.

With a Knowledge of the modern Languages it is so easy to acquire the ancient, and the ancient are so great a step towards the Acquisition of the Modern, that I cannot help, putting in a Word more in favour of Greek and Latin.

I am, my dear Sir your Friend John Adams

I forbid You, on pain of what shall fall thereon from giving me a Title in your Letters. I Scorn, disdain, despize, (take which Word You will) all Titles.

RC (private owner, 2019); internal address: "Dr Benjamin Rush"; endorsed: "J. Adams." LbC (Adams Papers); APM Reel 115.

[1] The dating of this letter is based on the placement of the LbC in the Letterbook.

[2] JA, who issued his 1776 *Thoughts on Government* as a counter to Pennsylvania's early model of government, was pleased with the wave of new state constitutions that spread to Georgia and South Carolina (Jefferson, *Papers*, 20:306).

[3] Jonathan Swift, "Verses on the Death of Dr. Swift," lines 17–18.

From Charles Storer

dear sir, Troy. 23d. February. 1790.

From the friendship you have always expressed for me I am led to acquaint you with some circumstances in which I am interested & to request your advice & assistance— Pardon me this liberty, which I should not have taken, had not my situation required it, & but from a reliance on the same good nature to which I am already so much indebted.—

The speculation I am upon here does answer my expectations & wishes, and I am induced to look elsewhere an establishment— Without a capital it is extremely difficult to carry on business to advantage; and this, through the misfortunes of my father, I am denied the benefit of— I must therefore seek that employment, which requires the least capital, & which is more within the compass of my own abilities— From these circumstances I have turned my thoughts to a public life again, & if favored with your assistance may hope to succeed.—[1] Mr: Jefferson is appointed to the office of Secretary of State—[2] The office of his first Secretary is an appointment in his gift, & one to which I am vain enough to think myself not unequal— Being a stranger to Mr: Jefferson, I have to request your friendship to speak in my behalf— You have intrusted me with confidential matters, & I trust have never found me unfaithfull— Whatever in your good nature you may please to advance in my favor shall serve as a stimulus to merit Mr: Jefferson's esteem & confidence, and particularly to approve myself deserving your recommendation.— Since there will doubtless be many to seek this place, I would request you to write Mr: Jefferson on the subject when convenient—in order that, should he accept my services, I may be made acquainted with the result timely enough to make the necessary arrangements requisite on my leaving this place.—[3]

To be employed in a place of trust is extremely flattering to me—and to be admitted to the confidence of & habits of intimacy with Mr: Jefferson would greatly add thereto— I have therefore to request information of you on what footing his Secretary stands, and what allowance Congress has made for him—

I am fearfull you may term my application improper, as recommendation is a delicate matter—but, sir, this is between friends—this is not seeking honor & emolument—and, if it does not meet your approbation, may be checked, in deference to your opinion, which I shall at all times respect.—

Having explained myself thus openly, be pleased to communicate to me your candid thoughts in return.

[. . . .] greatly oblige me—and in the mean time [. . . .]ther that this matter remain a secret betwe[en] [. . .]

With respects to the family, I have the honor to be, dr. sir, / Your much obliged friend / & humle. servt: Chas: Storer.

RC (Adams Papers); addressed: "The Vice President / of the United States"; internal address: "John Adams Esqr:"; endorsed: "C. Storer. 23. Feb. / 1790 / ansd 20 March." Some loss of text where the seal was removed.

[1] For Ebenezer Storer's financial situation, see vol. 19:397–399.

[2] On 25 Sept. 1789 George Washington nominated Thomas Jefferson to serve as the first secretary of state, and he was confirmed by the Senate the following day. "It is not for an individual to chuse his post. You are to marshal us as may best be for the public good," Jefferson wrote to Washington on 15 December. By 22 March 1790, Jefferson had relocated to New York City and assumed his new responsibilities. He planned to retain Roger Alden and Henry Remsen Jr. as chief clerks. Alden (d. 1836), a Connecticut native, resigned on 25 July, finding the annual salary to be inadequate (Elkins and McKitrick, *Age of Federalism*, p. 52; Jefferson, *Papers*, 16:34–35, 184; 17:349–350; Washington, *Papers, Presidential Series*, 3:296).

[3] Although Charles Storer did not receive this appointment, he served as secretary to the federal commissioners who opened treaty negotiations in 1793 with the Northwest Indians in the Ohio River Valley (Washington, *Papers, Presidential Series*, 14:218–219).

From Benjamin Rush

Dear sir, Philadelphia Feb: 24. 1790.

Your remarks upon the Conduct of the tories, and the "young fry" who are now crouding into the Councils of our Country, perfectly accord with my own Observations. The present convention & assembly of Pennsylvania, and the present Corporation of Philad[a]: are all filled *chiefly* with men who were either unknown in 1776, or known only for timidity or disaffection. Your old friends have mingled with the continental money of that memorable year, and are as much forgotten as if they had paid the last debt of Nature. This part of the issue of the American Controversy has not disappointed me—for I both expected & predicted it, from a conviction that the laws of property were as exactly ascertained as the laws of matter, and that power & wealth could never long be seperated. There is one thing in which the tories have the Advantage of the Whigs. They are more Attached to each other. They have come forth in a solid column in our state, and from the violence of many of the Whigs who have been in power during the war, they have been joined by many of the most respectable republican whig Characters among us.—Had the whigs of Pennsylvania united in a good Constitution, & organised it with respectable Officers, they would have transmitted all the power of the state to their latest posterity. But this event was prevented at first by Cannon—matlack & D[r] Young, & afterwards by Reed—Bryan—and Parson Ewing.[1] The three latter reprobated the Constitution when it was first made,—but they soon discovered that it might be converted to desirable private purposes. It gratified the Ambition of Reed—the idleness of Bryan—& the Avarice and Malice of D[r] Ewing—for it was this man chiefly that directed the rage of the state against the freedom of the Quakers, by severe test laws, and against the property of the Episcopalians by robbing them of the Charter & funds of their College.[2] The combination of this triumvirate to seize the power—& treasury of the State, was the result of system. In the month of Octob[r] 1778 M[r] Reed waited upon me just as I had recovered from a bilious fever, and in a long Conversation invited me to Share with them in their premiditated Usurpation. I objected to the proposal, & told him "that he would ruin himself by taking a part in the establishment or Support of so bad a Constitution," The perfect knowledge I had of those gentlemen's characters, enabled me to detect, & expose their Schemes in every period of their Administration.— They knew this well, and hence my destruction was a favorite Object with each of them. From my taking the part of the persecuted Quakers, and Episcopalians I was represented as the enemy of the Presbyterians in our state, and so far did this calumny succeed, that it Obliged me to retreat from their Society to the Church of my Ancestors, and in which I was born, viz the Church of England. Such was the industry of Dr Ewing in circulating the above Calumny, that he reduced my business by it *among the presbyterians* in the Course of two years from near an 100, to only ten families. For these Sacrifices to my principles, I did not recieve the Support I should have done, from the friends of Order, and justice. Some of them avoided me at the time I was most persecuted, as if I had been bitten by a mad dog. Others of them joined the hue & cry against me in order to recommend themselves to the tyrants of the day—nor is this all— One of the republican party who had long seen with pain the zeal & Success of my Services, I have reason to believe employed his talents for Wit & ridicule against me in the public papers.[3] These are valuable facts for my Children. They will serve to teach them that it is much less dangerous to awaken the keenest resentment of enemies, than the envy of friends. In reviewing the history of the events which I have related, (which are now passing rapidly from the memories of most people) I feel no difficulty in exercising the Christian Virtue of forgiveness towards my enemies. They [were] open & sincere in their enmity against me. They moreover did me honor by considering me as the principal in all the measures that were taken to oppose & defeat them. But my friends were unkind—ungrateful & even treacherous, and while most of them acted a subordinate part in Schemes planned by myself, they considered me only as an instrument in their hands to effect the purposes of their Ambition or revenge.— I wish I would love them as I ought.— In reviewing their conduct and my own in the disputes in our state, I am led to conclude this narrative with the famous Spanish prayer "God deliver me from myself, & my friends."—

The real whigs find as little credit in our histories of the revolution as they meet with from the "tories & young fry." Whose heart is not affected at seeing that venerable patriot Saml: Adams traduced in so many instances by Dr Gordon?[4] What incense is perpetually offered to *One* of the military characters that acted only an executive part in the revolution,—and that too after the foundation of it was laid in principles & opinions disseminated by Otis—Quincy—Yourself—Saml Adams—Dickinson—and a few Others?— Had I leisure, I would endeavour to rescue those characters from Oblivion, and give them the first place in the temple of liberty. What trash may we not suppose has been handed down to us from Antiquity, when we detect such errors, and prejudices in the history of events of which we have been eye witnesses, & in which we have been actors?— I am sometimes disposed to question the talents of Cæsar—the Virtues of Antoninus—and the Crimes of Commodus. I suspect the well concerted plans of battles recorded by Livy to have been picked up in the barbers Shops of Rome, or from deserters from the Roman Armies.— Of the events recorded by Dr Gordon how few of them embrace the whole of their connections?— How little do we learn from them of the principles of Action in man? Of the effects of single—& compound—private & public—democratic & monarchical passions upon the human heart?— of the *Motives* of Actions in our great Men?— of the difference between Abilities & Success in enterprizes? & of the *real* characters of the patriots of the different Stages of the revolution?— To prevent my Children being deceived by the histories of the day, I have nearly filled a large Quarto volume began in 1778 with Anecdotes & characters of the principal Agents in the revolution.— Besides this Collection, I have filled two small pocket Octavos with facts connected with characters & events in 1776, & 1777—during which years I was in Congress, or in the Army.— In One of them I find the following Anecdotes. "Upon my return from the Army to Baltimore in the winter of 1777, I sat next to Jno: Adams in Congress, and upon my whispering to him, and asking him if he thought we should succeed in our Struggle with G: Britain he answered me—'yes—If we fear God, & repent of our sins.'["]— This Anecdote will I hope teach my boys that it is not necessary to disbelieve Christianity, or to renounce morality in Order to arrive at the highest political usefulness or fame.— Again—in Baltimore—I asked Jno Adams—"if he thought we were qualified for republican forms of Government["]— He said "no—and never Should be 'till we were *ambitious to be poor*"

Hereafter if agreeable—I shall send you some more extracts from these books. One of them contains your character at large—among the Gentlemen who signed the declaration of independance.[5] my Own is the shortest—and perfectly true. It consists of only these words "He aimed well."—

I thank you for your polite wishes to see me restored to public life. There was a time when I would have accepted of an Appointment abroad. My knowledge of several European languages, and of many eminent literary characters, would have added frequent opportunities to my disposition to serve my Country. I have meditated with great pleasure upon the pains I shd: have taken in such a Situation to employ my leisure hours in collecting discoveries in Agriculture—manufactures—and in all the useful Arts and Sciences, and in transmitting them to my American fellow Citizens. But the time is past—for my accepting of that or of any Other Appointment in the Government of the United states.— I already see a system of influence bordering upon Corruption established in our Country, which seems to proclaim to innocence & patriotism to keep their distance.— I have erected & decorated my little bower. Its shade is already refreshing, and its odors truly delightful.— I cannot convey to you a more lively idea of this domestic retreat than by describing the manner in which the former part of the present evening has passed in my family. At the same table where I now set, I have had the pleasure of seeing my dear Mrs Rush deeply engaged in reading Millot's Account of the manners—& laws of the ancient Egyptians—my Eldest Son—plodding over Rollin's history of Cyrus—and my second boy just beginning Goldsmith's history of England.—[6] In the course of the evening, frequent applications were made to me to explain hard words by my boys. One them who has just finished Ovid at School, asked me—"if there was such a river as the Nile, or such a Country as Egypt." my Answer to this Question led me to express my hearty disapprobation of that mode of education which makes the first knowledge of boys to consist in *fables*, and thereby leads them to reject truth, or to esteem it no more than the gross errors and fictions of the Ancient poets.—

I must not forget to mention that my eldest daughter (between 11—and 12 years of age) composed a part of this family picture. She was employed in sewing, but partook in all the Conversation of the evening.— This girl is all that the most indulgent parents could wish an only Child to be.— A compassionate heart is the principal feature in her Character. Her little Allowance of spending money is chiefly given away to the ~~lazy~~ poor. To both her parents She is dutiful and affectionate in the highest degree. In the Absence of her mama, she makes tea for me, and soothe me with a hundred little Anecdotes picked up in her Schools or in company.—

To this acct: of my family, I have only to add that my Venerable mother (now in her 75th: year) occupies a room in my house. She is often indisposed in body,—but all the powers of her mind are in their full Vigor. Such is my Veneration for this excellent parent, that

I never look forward to that hour, which must perhaps soon part us, without feeling an anguish which I cannot describe.

I have now only to beg your pardon for the length of this letter, and to request you to destroy all that part of it which relates to the private history of my dear Sir Yours / very Affectionately

Benj$^{n:}$ Rush

RC (Adams Papers). Some loss of text due to a torn manuscript.

[1] James Cannon, Timothy Matlack, Dr. Thomas Young, Joseph Reed, George Bryan, and John Ewing. Cannon, Matlack, and Young steered the creation of the Pennsylvania Constitution of 1776. James Wilson and William Findley dominated the state convention that produced the heavily revised Pennsylvania Constitution of 1790 (vol. 19:380, 388, 413; *AFC*, 10:261; Joseph S. Foster, "The Politics of Ideology: The Pennsylvania Constitutional Convention of 1789–90," *Pennsylvania History: A Journal of Mid-Atlantic Studies*, 59:129, 134 [April 1992]).

[2] Both JA and Rush condemned former Pennsylvania governor Joseph Reed's treatment of alleged loyalists, which included the public execution of two Quaker artisans in 1778. On 27 Nov. 1779 the state legislature passed an act annulling the University of Pennsylvania's charter, seizing its assets, and requiring officers and faculty like Rush to swear a loyalty oath. Lawmakers confiscated the estates of loyalists affiliated with the school, thereby establishing a lucrative endowment. Rush renounced the decision as a vindictive form of legislative overreach, briefly stepping down from his post as professor of chemistry. At the urging of Thomas Mifflin and other trustees, on 6 March 1789 the Pennsylvania legislature moved to repeal most of the act by restoring the charter and reinstating faculty (vol. 19:388; Wilbur H. Siebert, *The Loyalists of Pennsylvania*, Columbus, Ohio, 1920, p. 59–62; Rush, *Letters*, 1:289).

[3] Rush's political views, especially his public protest of capital punishment, attracted sharp criticism in the press. Writing as Philochoras, the Presbyterian minister Robert Annan (1742–1819), who presided over Philadelphia's Old Scots Church, lambasted Rush throughout the fall of 1788. Another squib claimed that the doctor "traduced the scriptures, to support a scheme which is directly repugnant to them" (Rush, *Letters*, 1:490, 491; *American Herald and the Worcester Recorder*, 23 Oct.).

[4] In his *History of the Rise, Progress, and Establishment of the Independence of the United States of America*, London, 1788, Rev. William Gordon suggested that Samuel Adams was involved in a political plot to relieve George Washington of his Continental Army command. Adams strenuously refuted the claim (Rush, *Letters*, 1:182–185; Adams, *Writings*, 4:336–337).

[5] The character sketch that Rush promised did not reach JA for several years. In composing his autobiography, Rush integrated short biographies of the members of the Continental Congress. He profiled JA as a "profound and enlightened patriot" who courted controversy during his presidency as he grew "more irritable in his temper, and less cautious in speaking of men and things." On 13 July 1816 (Adams Papers) Richard Rush sent to JA an edited copy of the sketch, in which text describing JA's alleged "prejudices in favor of the British constitution" had been excised (Rush, *Autobiography*, p. 21, 140–144).

[6] Here and below, Rush's family portrait included: Julia Stockton Rush (1759–1848), who was reading Claude François Xavier Millot's *Eléments d'histoire générale ancienne et moderne*, 9 vols., Paris, 1772–1783; John Rush (1777–1837), who was "plodding" through Charles Rollin's *Ancient History of the Egyptians, Carthaginians, Assyrians, Babylonians, Medes and Persians, Macedonians, and Grecians*, London, 1768; Richard Rush (1780–1859), who was beginning Oliver Goldsmith's *History of England: From the Earliest Times to the Death of George II*, London, 1764. Anne Emily Rush (1779–1850) and Susanna Hall Harvey Rush Morris (ca. 1715–1795), the doctor's "Venerable mother," completed the picture (vol. 19:314; *AFC*, 2:60; CFA, *Diary*, 2:5; Rush, *Letters*, 1:98, 250).

To Jabez Bowen

Sir Feb[y] 27 1790

Your letter of the 15th never reached me till yesterday I condole with you in the unfavorable aspect of your elections: but still hope that your people will cool upon reflection and that a majority of the convention may be induced to accept the constitution. It is in vain to enquire what Congress may or can do; at present they can do nothing. The awful object before them, I mean the national debt, monopolizes the attention of Congress to such a degree that untill some system is digested no member of either house will be able to attend to any thing else. When the affair of Rhode Island shall be taken up, there will be twenty different plans proposed, time must be spent in examination discussion and deliberation.

He must be less than a thinking being who can be at a loss to foresee what Congress will ultimately do with Rhode Island, if she obstinately refuses to come in— But it would not be prudent in me to predict it The opposition of Rhode Island to the impost seems to have been the instrument which providence thought fit to use for the great purpose of establishing the present constitution: I sincerely hope their infatuation may not oblige the United states to take severe measures at their expence to convince the people that their interests are in the power of their neighbours and to gain strength to the New government by punishing its rash opposers. I must finally say to you in confidence that I beleive Congress will never beg or pray or exhort your Antis to come in. They will leave them at perfect liberty—and whenever they take any steps it will not be till injuries shall be multiplied and their just resentment approved by all the world

John Adams

LbC in CA's hand (Adams Papers); internal address: "Honble Jabez Bowen / Providence"; APM Reel 115.

To François Adriaan Van der Kemp

Sir New York Feb. 27. 1790

Your agreable Letter of the 9. Jan. has lain too long unanswered.— Mr Mappa, I should be happy to present to the President and to Serve in any other Way in my Power.[1]

Your Criticisms upon "the defence" deserve more Consideration than I have time to give them.

I can Say for myself, and I believe for most others, who have ever been called "leading Men," in the late Revolution, that We were compelled against our Inclinations, to cutt off the Bands that United Us with England, and that We should have been very happy to have had our Grievances redressed, and our Dependance continued—and this Disposition continued with me, untill Hostilities commenced.— then indeed I thought all future Connections impracticable.

I will candidly confess, that an hereditary Senate, without an hereditary Executive, would diminish the Prerogatives of the President and the Liberties of the People. But I contend that hereditary descent in both, when controuled by an independent Representation of the People, is better than corrupted, turbulent and bloody Elections. and the knowledge You have of the human heart will concur with your knowledge of the History of nations to convince you that Elections of Presidents, & Senators, cannot be long conducted in a populous, oppulent and commercial Nation, without Corruption, sedition and Civil War.

A Discourse upon Fæderative Republicks and an History of the American Revolution, are both Undertakings too extensive for my Forces, unless I should retire from all Employments public and private, and devote the Remainder of my Life to writing.

Your Story of Smytegeld is very droll.

The Vindiciæ contra Tyrannos was written by Languet earlier as you Say than the time of the long Parliament but it was then reprinted in England and translated.

Shase was the Wat Tyler of the Massachusetts.—

I omitted the ordinance of the 13. July 1787 because I had not room for it in the Volume.[2]

how far it will be proper for[3] the President to interpose, in your favour in your affair in Holland, I pretend not to say. My Advice is that you write to the President, Stating the whole of the Facts and requesting his assistance by his Minister, as far as may be proper. it will probably produce an Instruction to assist you at least in a private Way.

I was Surprized to find that you had given Such particular Attention to my Volumes, and am much flattered with your favourable opinion and ingenious Compliments. The Necessity of Reaction to counterpoise Action, is pursued further than it ever was before in any Age or Language that I know of. The opinion is as ancient as Zeno as We learn from Diogenes Laertius.— I think this may be asserted without Hesitation that every Example in History proves that Peace,

& Liberty, can be united only by the Equilibrium of three Branches, because there is not one Example to be found of Peaceful Liberty without it.— and it is not to be wondered at because human Passions are all insatiable— They will move and increase in motion untill they are resisted. This quality in Men explains all the Phænomena in Government.

I am flattered in Letters from Europe, with Compliments that the Science of Government has not been so much improved Since the Writings of Montesquieu &c But notwithstanding this, the Books will not be much read.[4] So far from flattering they offend the Passions and counteract the Views of all Parties—of Courts Kings and Ministers—of senates Aristocrates and all the Pride of noble Blood—and of Democrates and all the Licentious Rabbles, who wish to fish in troubled Waters.— a Wish for Unlimited Power is the natural Passion of each of these orders, and no Doctrine pleases but that which flatters the ruling Passion. Whether human Reason will ever get the better of all these Prejudices and be able to govern Such Passions I know not. I will never cease to preach my favourite Doctrine, untill I die

yours with much Esteem John Adams

RC (PHi:Francis Adrian Van der Kemp Coll.); internal address: "Mr Fra Ad. Van der Kemp." LbC (Adams Papers); APM Reel 115.

[1] See Van der Kemp's letter of 7 Jan., and note 21, above.

[2] JA alluded to the Northwest Ordinance of 1787 at the end of his *Defence of the Const.*, arguing that the "magnitude of territory, the population, the wealth and commerce, and especially the rapid growth of the United States" warranted the establishment of a constitutional government (vol. 19:146; JA, *Defence of the Const.*, 3:505).

[3] In the LbC, CA wrote instead, "in the power of."

[4] For the composition and reception of JA's *Defence of the Const.*, see vols. 18:544, 546–550; 19:130–132.

To John Brown & John Brown Francis

Gentlemen New York Feb. 28. 1790

Your Letter of the 16th. I recd only by the Post of last Wednesday.—[1] I am really much affected at the obstinate Infatuation of So great a Part of the People of Rhode Island. It is inconceivable how men of common Sense can reconcile Such a Conduct to their Understandings men of common Honesty, to their Consciences; or men of human Feelings, to their Hearts.

Do the Antis of Rhode Island expect that the Congress of twelve States will Send them a Petition, to pray them humbly, to take a

Share in the great Council of the Nation? or do they wait for the President to Send them an Ambassador in great Pomp and State to negotiate their Accession to the Union?

The Inhabitants of Rhode Island are Freemen and I presume will be treated like Freemen. Congress will not think themselves authorised, by the Principles they profess, to make a Conquest of that People, or to bring them into the Union by Coertion. If the Convention should reject the Constitution or adjourn without Adopting it, Congress will probably find it necessary to treat them as they are, as Foreigners, and extend all the Laws to them as such. This will be disagreable because it will involve our Friends in Inconvenience as well as others. But You know that in all national Calamities, the Same Fortune attends the good and the Evil the Just and unjust. Providence itself does not distinguish, and Nations cannot. If the Lime, the Barley and all other Articles whether of foreign or domestic Growth or Manufacture, should be Subjected to a Duty, it would soon shew your People that their Interests are in the Power of their Neighbours.

The benign Influence of the new Constitution upon the Commerce, Manufactures and Agriculture of the Country, has been already Seen and felt, in as great a degree as the most Sanguine Admirer of it, could have reasonably expected. If the People of your State will not be convinced either by Reasoning or Experience, what can be done? but to let them have their Way, and treat them like Aliens as they choose to be considered?

I cannot however doubt, but that when the Convention meets and begin to think converse and debate upon the Subject a majority of reasonable Men will be found.

I am Gentlemen, with great / Regard your most humble servant

John Adams

RC (RHi:John Brown Papers); internal address: "Messieurs Brown and Francis / Providence." LbC (Adams Papers); APM Reel 115.

[1] In a letter of 16 Feb. (Adams Papers), the Providence mercantile firm informed JA that Antifederalists continued to thwart Rhode Island's ratification of the Constitution and sought JA's intervention, hopeful that Congress would respond directly and forcefully to Gov. John Collins' 19 Sept. 1789 memorial, for which see Jabez Bowen's letter of 28 Dec., and note 4, above.

To William Ellery

Dear Sir New York Feby 28 1790

Many months ago I received a kind letter from you, which by some odd accident or strange fatality has never been answered,[1] I really know not how this happened: but I hope you will excuse it and beleive me to be as I am, at all times ready to promote your views, expressed in it as far as I may have opportunity and ability. We are very greatly dissapointed in the election of Delegates to your Convention. We are told that a majority are unfriendly to the union of the nation. I still flatter myself however, that when the members assemble they will see objects in a new light and feel affections for their sister states which they have not yet been sensible of. It is now become of more importance than ever, for your State to act right, as it will not be possible much longer to extend that lenity and indulgence, which has been hitherto granted. Since the accession of North Carolina, I have learned with certainty that a correspondence has been maintained between your Anti's and theirs, and I wish to know whether the hopes of your opposition are still supported by secret communications from Virginia or Boston. Insinuations of that kind are thrown out here.— What can any Gentlemen mean? Can they coolly or warmly wish to raise a storm? The national debt engages all attention at present: but when that is over if Rhode Island should be still refractory, something must be done.

I should be glad to hear from you Sir, and will be a better correspondent for the future. being with great and sincere esteem and regard / Your^{s} John Adams

LbC in CA's hand (Adams Papers); internal address: "Honble William Ellery / New Port"; APM Reel 115.

[1] Ellery last wrote to JA on 30 March 1789 (Adams Papers), soliciting a judgeship and requesting that his son, also named William, assume his position in the Rhode Island loan office. On 14 June 1790 George Washington nominated the elder Ellery as collector of the port of Newport, R.I., and he was confirmed the same day. He held the post until he died on 15 Feb. 1820 (U.S. Senate, *Exec. Jour.*, 1st Cong., 2d sess., p. 51; *Biog. Dir. Cong.*).

From Stephen Higginson

Sir Boston march 1: 1790—

Since I had last the honour of writing to you, the vacancies in our supreme Court have been filled up;[1] & the event has proved, that you knew better the character of our Chief than many of Us did, who expected different persons from those who have been appointed. there was however, We are told, a severe struggle between his inclinations & his fears. certain it is, that one person of the profession counted upon a Seat on that Bench; & it was a long time before he was reluctantly given up.—

The report of the Secretary of the treasury has much engaged the attention of our Assembly, & of the people abroad.[2] it is very generally admired; & men of information, I find, grow more attached to it upon reflection. the rate of interest proposed, the assumption of the State Debts & adjustment of Accounts between the States & the Union, & the distinction made between foreign & domestic Creditors are very generally pleasing. there are some however both within & without doors, who would wish to embarass the System. They use every exertion to create an opposition to it; but they have hitherto failed of making any impression, & will not be able, I trust, to urge the legislature to any disagreable points. the acquisition of m^r^ Dane, by a vacancy in the Senate, has given Them new hopes; & their Efforts will be renewed in the way of Amendments, if not by a remonstrance against assuming the State Debts. They mean, it is said, to create an opposition in the national Senate, upon whom they expect to make an impression, They being chosen by the state legislatures. This mode of opposition, it is said, was recommended by m^r.^ Lee; & to make it the more efficacious will be systematically pursued in all the States.[3] to favour their Views, m^r^ Dane has reported an Amendment, by which the Senators are to be chosen all at the same time in future, for the term of four years, & subject to a recall by an order from their Constituents. whether this will pass the two houses, appears very uncertain; but the principle of action, & the object in View is very apparent.— what may be the effect upon any of your members, should it pass, you will have an opp^y^ of observing; but every new evidence of the disposition from which such propositions originate, will certainly serve to strengthen the hands of the Union. by such conduct people are taught to look up to the federal Government, for safety & protection; & the importance of the state legislatures will be thereby lessened in the Eyes of the people.

My own Views & intentions, as to future life, have lately undergone a great change. I have the last year been so arranging my Business, as to be able to leave it whenever I pleased. with a property nearly equal to a support, I meant upon a future opening to have entered again into political life. But some recent losses, to the amount of 15000 dollars, to me very unexpected, have so diminished my Capital, that I must now abandon that Object. my time must in future be devoted to Business of a private & safe kind; or I must take some station in the executive branch of Government where I can derive, at least in part, my support from the public. two principal reasons have decided to a pursuit of the latter. I wish for a situation less confined & more active, on account of my health, which is too slender already; & I am desirous of rescuing the property which remains to me, from the vicissitudes of my present Situation. with these impressions, I have decided to offer myself a Candidate for some new Office, which I presume must soon be instituted in the Revenue. if it be decently respectable, & tolerably productive, I should gladly embrace it; for I am quite tired of the changes incident to my present situation, which no care or forecast of my own can guard me ag^t.— That of Inspector, should m^r. Hamiltons System obtain, would meet my Views.— persuaded that nothing but proper qualifications, will determine your Voice in my favour, I shall urge no other consideration to engage you to aid me in the pursuit. But fancying myself, perhaps too fondly, qualified for such a station under Government; I mean only to ask, that so far as my private Views may comport with the public interest in your mind, I may enjoy your Support. you have some knowlege of me yourself; & I wish to have my principles & qualities fully known to you. I have no right to presume upon your personal friendship; this may be due only, perhaps, to a more intimate acquaintance, than I have the honour to claim. no man has been more decided in his opinions & conduct in favour of the new Government, when no Views of this kind existed in my mind; nor will any man labour officially more to promote its dignity & happiness, than I shall, under such an appointment.—[4]

I have been considering the Secretarys proposal of new duties, & his mode of collecting Them. the amount of the duties, & the novelty & energy of the collection seemed rather alarming at first; but they are both necessary to the object in view. to lessen the rate, will render the means incompetent to the End; & to abate of the vigour, proposed in his mode of collection, may entirely defeat the whole System. accustomed to Laws, weak in their principles & loose in their construction, & to modes of collection feeble & irregular, habits of Evasion have been here too generally contracted. it is idle to depend on the personal honour or patriotism of those who are to pay. firmness & force may be absolutely necessary to secure a due collection; They are the more so, because of the habits alluded to. the great difficulty is to have the System efficient without distressing Our trade, by drawing the Duty from the Importer before he can have received it from the retailer or consumer, or by establishing such Checks as will retard & obstruct Business. The former will increase an Evil now too generally felt, the want of capital; &, as the Bill now stands may create uneasiness. the latter can be obviated only by an attentive discharge of the inspectors duty, in giving every facility compatible with a regular collection, & consistent with the principles of the Bill. Should it be executed with attention & address, no injurious obstructions need take place; nor should I apprehend, in that case, any great clamour or uneasiness. very much will depend upon the executive Officers, especially in the outset.—

An excise Act is now before Our Assembly. the old One is to be repealed; & a new mode of collection is proposed, with some features taken from M$^{r.}$ Hamiltons plan, but not more efficient than the old One.[5] Though Excises have become very unpopular here, from the inequality & iniquity which resulted from the operation of the old Act, there was a majority in both houses for taking up a new one.— Some urged it to provide in part for the interest on the Debts, others were zealous for it to pay off the Court, & defray other current expences. this produced a warm debate on the question of appropriation, which ended by applying it to the Debt with an ill grace. So much temper was excited, that There is yet some doubt whether it will obtain. but if it should, being appropriated to pay the interest on the Debt, it will fall of course when the Debts shall be assumed by Congress; & will prove to be no more a bar to a general excise.—

I inclose you a paper containing a Speech of m$^{r.}$ Austins in the Senate, which may serve to shew you the Spirit & the Views of a party, who are aided & supported by some of Our great folks.—[6]

With much real respect I have the honour to be Sir your very hum^{l} Servant— Stephen Higginson

PS: I have since obtained a copy of m$^{r.}$ Danes report which I inclose you. it will give some Idea of the feelings & Views of those people who are opposed to Government—

RC (Adams Papers).

[1] Higginson last wrote to JA on 21 Dec. 1789, above.

[2] Alexander Hamilton's first report on the public credit, sent to the House of Representatives on 14 Jan. 1790, introduced a new economic framework. Inspired by the fiscal models of Jacques Necker and William Pitt, Hamilton called for the establishment of a national bank and the federal assumption of state debts, with reduced annual interest payments. He drew lessons from the failure of past efforts to replenish and stabilize the economy, which relied on selling western lands, negotiating foreign loans, and creating a federal impost. Hamilton reminded Congress that lingering obligations from the

Revolutionary War represented "the price of liberty."

Intense debate over the treasury secretary's sweeping proposal continued throughout the spring, as James Madison and Hamilton battled against each other in the political arena while their factions grew louder in the press. By 8 Feb., representatives agreed to debate Hamilton's complex report in the form of eight summary resolutions. Particularly contentious were the secretary's options for debt relief, and his strategy to trade government securities at par, which triggered a flurry of speculation and led Madison to repudiate Hamilton's plan. After addressing the House on 11 Feb., Madison presented an amendment on 20 Feb. that discriminated between original and current debt-holders, in an effort to curb speculation of formerly depreciated government bonds and to prevent stock fluctuations. Hoping that it would prove to be "the desisive day with respect to the question," AA made her first visit to the House on 22 Feb. and watched with the crowd as Madison's plan was rejected in a vote of 36 to 13 (First Congress, Second Session, 4 Jan. 1790 – 12 Aug. 1790, Editorial Note, above; Hamilton, *Papers*, 6:51–168; *AFC*, 9:14, 17, 18; Chernow, *Alexander Hamilton*, p. 297–305; Madison, *Papers, Congressional Series*, 13:xix).

[3] Beverly, Mass., lawyer Nathan Dane (1752–1835), Harvard 1778, served in the state senate from 1793 to 1799. Dane articulated Antifederalist complaints that concurred with those of Virginia's Richard Henry Lee, who objected to the lack of a bill of rights to protect personal liberties and observed that without amendments, the Constitution placed "the happiness of the people at the mercy of Rulers who may possess the great unguarded powers given." Dane's enclosed report has not been found (*Doc. Hist. Ratif. Const.*, 4:434; 8:32–33; *ANB*).

[4] Higginson wrote to George Washington on 17 March 1790 soliciting a customs position and enclosing a 13 March letter of recommendation from James Bowdoin that touted "his general knowledge, close application to business, and strict probity." Higginson did not earn a post (Washington, *Papers, Presidential Series*, 5:239–241).

[5] From February through May, Massachusetts state representatives debated the repeal of the excise act, which would have ended the commonwealth's only means of paying creditors. Instead, lawmakers sought to put pressure on the federal government by setting higher duties on imports, and they unveiled a rigorous new collection system. By 4 June, Massachusetts legislators resolved that state excise and import taxes would expire when the U.S. government assumed all state debts (Hall, *Politics without Parties*, p. 324–325).

[6] The enclosure has not been found.

From William Ellery

Dr. Sir, Newport [*ca.* 6] March 1790—[1]

Engaged as you are in public business, and this State not having shown a disposition to join the Union I did not wonder, although I could not but regret, that my letter should remain so long unanswered.—

I wish that our affairs now afforded a prospect of a speedy accession.—

Before you receive this letter you will have heard of the proceedings of our Convention.—[2] They met, framed a bill of rights, collected a long string of amendments to the Constitution, ordered them to be laid before the people at the annual meeting for proxing for Genl. Officers and chusing representatives, and adjourned to the fourth monday in May.— Unless something is done by Congress which will make the Antis feel they will in my opinion adjourn again and again.—

The Feds will continue to exert themselves;—but the Antis appear to be steeled against the most powerful addresses to their reason, their passions and their interest.— It is the opinion of many that they are supported and hardend in their opposition from the quarters you mentioned;—but it cannot yet be reduced to a certainty.— The report of the Comm̃ee of your State, appointed to consider what further Amendments are necessary to be added to the Constitution of the United States, will give an handle to our Antis to put off our accession.— If it is the wish of your State that this State should speedily become a member of the federal government it appears to me that their conduct is altogether impolitic.—

Some of our Antis have had the courage to say, that if the State stood out but six months longer, there would be such insurrections in the other States as would overturn the New Government;—and that their opposition would be the salvation not only of our own but of the thirteen States.—

Others talk as if they really thought Congress would still extend their lenity and indulgence to the trade of this State.— When the Federal members of the Convention, in order to obtain an adjournment to the last monday in March, represented in strong, pathetic terms, the distresses in which the Sea-port towns would be involved at the expiration of the Act reviving the suspension of the navigation Act, an Anti replied that they were in no danger,—that upon an Application of the merchants further indulgence would be granted;—for Congress would do any thing to favour their friends.—

The operation of the navigation act will have no influence upon the Antis until the fall, and then they will probably rather pay an advanced freight, and receive less profit upon what they may have to export to the other States, than accede to the Union.—

Something must be done.—

An address to the Gen[l.] Assembly at their Session on the first wednesday in May next, setting forth the advantages which will result to the United States and this State from her accession, and the necessity which Congress will be under to use rigorous measures if she should still persist in her opposition might answer the purpose.—

A requisition of our quota of the public debt with a declaration that, unless it was collected at the time assigned, an equivalent would be distrained would have a good effect.—[3]

If Congress have a right to consider us as a part of the United States, and to extend their Gen[l.] Government to us, and would make a declaration that they have such authority, and would exercise it if the State did not adopt the Constitution, I have no doubt but that it would be adopted at the next Session of the Convention.—

Wisdom as Father Sherman used to say, in difficult cases, is profitable to direct, and the great Council of the United States are possessed of a large share of it.—[4]

Uncertain as it is when this State will adopt the New Government; yet it must sooner or later become a member of the Union, and federal Officers be appointed for it.—

I am greatly obliged to you for the assurances you have given me of your readiness to promote my views.—

When I first wrote to you my view was, through your influence and that of other friends, to obtain the Office of a district Judge, I have since thought that the Office of Collector of the Impost for this district would be more beneficial and suit me better.— I was sometime Naval Officer of this State, while we were under the British Government, and was a Commissioner of the Admiralty under Congress;— so that the business of the customs would not be altogether new to me if I should be so happy as to be appointed a Collector of this district.— The present custom-house Offrs. of this district are a worthless sett of Antis.— Who are the candidates for the federal collectorship I do not know;—but if early and long public services,—and losses in the cause of liberty and my country can give any pretensions to an office I shall not be behind the foremost candidate, and if an addition to these, I should be favoured with your recommendation to the President & Senators I should not doubt of success—

With great esteem and regard / I am Yr. friend & servt.

William Ellery

RC (Adams Papers); internal address: "John Adams Esqr. / Vice-President &c"; endorsed: "Mr Ellery March 1790."

[1] Ellery was replying to JA's letter of 28 Feb., above. The dating of this letter is based on the adjournment of the first session of Rhode Island's ratification convention on 6 March.

[2] Gov. John Collins (1717–1795), a Newport, R.I., merchant who served from 1786 to 1790, won his office by supporting the emission of paper money. Collins broke from Country Party interests in January by casting the tie-breaking vote in favor of a ratification convention, which triggered his political downfall (*Doc. Hist. Ratif. Const.*, 24:312–313).

Seventy delegates met in Little Rest (now Kingston) for the first session of Rhode Island's ratification convention, which met from 1 to 6 March. A ten-man committee drafted a bill of rights to send out for the towns' consideration along with a list of proposed amendments. Henry Marchant urged his fellow delegates to approve the bill of rights, which they did on 6 March in a tight vote. But the draft amendments, including a censure of the Constitution's lack of a ban on the African slave trade, languished in debate. Rhode Island Federalists who sought to wind up the ratification process were again blocked by Antifederalists, who gained an adjournment until 24 May in order to incorporate their constituents' perspectives. The bill of rights and the draft amendments were widely reprinted; see, for example, Providence, R.I., *United States Chronicle*, 11 March; *Providence Gazette*, 13 March; *Maryland Journal*, 2 April; and Charleston, S.C., *City Gazette*, 22 April (*Doc. Hist. Ratif. Const.*, 26: 898, 899, 981).

[3] Rhode Island last paid $2,593,353.30 for the requisition in 1787, in nearly worthless paper currency (Frank Greene Bates, *Rhode Island and the Formation of the Union*, N.Y., 1898, p. 111).

[4] At 69 years old, Connecticut senator Roger Sherman was the oldest member of Congress when he arrived in March 1789 (Mark David Hall, *Roger Sherman and the Creation of the American Republic*, N.Y., 2013, p. 122). Ellery's related allusion was to Ecclesiastes, 10:10.

From Henry Marchant

Sir, Newport March 7th. 1790—

It is mortifying to be beat in a good Cause, without Sense or Argument, but merely by Self-Will and vile Principles— Our Convention sat all the last Week— Our News-Papers I suppose will give You the particulars— It was with Difficulty I could get a Motion for the main Question upon the Journalls— And Adjournment was determined upon by the Anties before they met Us, in their private Conventions:— And they held nocturnal Conventions the whole Week, for the Purpose of carrying their own Measures, and for settling their Arangements for the genl. Election— the Dep: Gov: Owens, President of the Convention, did not hesitate to say out of Doors, that an Adjournment of the Convention was necessary to insure their Election— He is proposed for Govr.—Collins having been their weak tool long enough—[1] O——s is a Man of more Subtilty—a profound Hypocrite—at the Gen: Assembly after the Vote for calling a Convention; He took me by the Hand, and altho' He had voted against it, He declared I could not more rejoice than He did— He had voted as He had done He said, because the People round Him were averse to the Measure as yet, but were coming over fast; And He had no Doubt the Constitution would be adopted as soon as the Convention met.— Yet He now came with the greatest Zeal for an Adjournment— He still holds up the Idea that it will soon be adopted—

the great Objection which had been made by one of their Leaders—Jona. Haszard a Delegate in the former Congress[2]—was the mode of proportioning the Tax by Numbers;—instead of the former Method— The Word Tax,—partial Tax &c sounded in the Ears of the People, had been alarming; but when an Amendment for that Purpose was brought forward—His own Party failed Him; and We had a Majority of six for the Mode fixed by the Constitution— they were now left without any formidable Objections— We took Notice that there had been a Number of things suggested out of Doors, which we were surprised, none would now father, or even mention— In short they were beat out of all their strong Holds— We agreed to their Bill of Rights, copied nearly from New-York, and their Amendments taken mostly from New-York, with their Darling Paper Money Amendment copied from our dear Sister North Carolina—[3]

What was now left, but that we should Adopt the Constitution?— It must be sent to the People, for the *Consideration* of the Towns!— And I expect next to hear the Amendments must be sent to Congress, to see if they will agree to adopt them, previous to Our adopting the Constitution— And this will be the sine qua non, of many—

Their Majority when we met was twelve agt. the Constitution— Could We have brought on the Question, I presume we should have been beat by four— wheather We shall succeed in getting that four is uncertain— they had Instructions from their Town to vote for the Constitution, but a few Days before the Convention met; and were directed not to vote for any adjournment, without the greatest Necessity; and then not beyond the first of April.— But they paid no Attention to their Instructions— How they may yet be opperated upon is uncertain— I have done giving, for I have almost lost my, Hopes of Success— Misery will fall upon the Merchantile Interest; and upon poor Newport most heavily:— Wood & Flower will rise to an extravagant Price— the Farmer will not begin to feel till next Fall, unless Congress provide otherwise— Pray Sir, what must become of Us? what more can we do, if the Constitution is not adopted at the Adjournment of the Convention the 24th. of May And what will be the Measures of Congress in that Case?— If we adopt the Constitution the Anties hope to be able to send forward their own Creatures;— And expect the Recommendation of their Senators &c will be sufficient to procure Appointments to their own peculiar Friends

I fear Congress may adjourn, before they may be able to pass the proper Bills for collecting the Revenue &c &c should We adopt the Constitution the last of May:— For it must be sometime in June, before Our Assembly will meet to choose Senators &c— Will there be a Necessity that Our Senators &c should be appointed and be in Congress, previous to Congress's passing the necessary Bills and making all the proper Arangements?— I wish to be advised hereon— I had the Honor to write You Sir the 19th. of Decr. and 18th. of Jany. last— I could wish barely to know they were recd.— We want the best Advice.— what we may *fear*, what *We* may *hope* should we faill at last—

My Family join me in Respects to Mrs: Adams and the Family— With sincere Esteem I am / most respectfully / Your very humble Servt.

Henry Marchant

RC (Adams Papers); internal address: "His Excellency / John Adams Esqr. / Vice President &c / New York—"; endorsed: "Marchant March 7 / 1790. And March / 20."

[1] Deputy governor Daniel Owen (ca. 1731–1812) was a Glocester, R.I., blacksmith and an Antifederalist. He presided over both sessions of Rhode Island's ratification convention (*Doc. Hist. Ratif. Const.*, 24:315).

[2] Newport lawyer and Antifederalist Jonathan J. Hazard (1731–1812), a leading figure in Rhode Island's Country Party, represented South Kingstown at both sessions of the ratification convention. On the morning of the third day, Hazard and Marchant clashed over the question of taxation. Both men acknowledged that the new nation was "over loaded with Debt . . . like a Cloud cast upon us." They disagreed over whether the apportionment of taxes should be calculated according to population or wealth, an issue that had long polarized Rhode Island's rural and commercial towns (same, 24:314; 26:917, 918).

[3] Like other states, Rhode Island supported a bill of rights that safeguarded personal liberties. Rhode Islanders also sided with North Carolina lawmakers in attempting to protect the ability to produce their own currency via an amendment, stipulating that Congress should not interfere with the states' emission of paper money, nor should it engage in selling the states' public securities (*Doc. Hist. Ratif. Const.*, 26:997–1002; Walter Clark, comp., *The State Records of North Carolina*, 30 vols., Goldsboro, N.C., 1886–1914, 22:51–52).

To John Trumbull

Dear Sir

New York March 9. 1790

Coll Humphreys; at the Levee, this morning, delivered me Your kind Letter of Feb. 6, for the favour of which you cannot imagine how much I am obliged to you.— not less delighted with Your frank communications respecting your own affairs, than Satisfyed with your friendly cautions to me, I shall make a kind of Commentary, or at least some marginal Notes upon both. I rejoice in your health, and your Success at the Bar as well as in your Learning and Fidelity to your Clients. You are building on a Rock that will never fail you. But I must repeat my request that you attend to Air and Exercise, and that you do not avoid a share in public Life— the last however is less the Dictate of Affection to you, than of Regard to the Public and myself, for I can give you no Encouragement from Experience to hope for any Thing but Care and Labour.— I will Say no more concerning Yourself at present: but come to the Observations that relate to me.— You talk of my Ennemies: but I assure You I have *none*. I am the Ennemy of no Man living; and I know of none who is an Ennemy to me.— I have injured no Man alive—I have not intentionally offended any Man: and I know not that I have actually offended any. This I think gives me a right to Say that I have not an

Ennemy.— But "The V.P. is a Native of New England." To this Charge, I plead guilty the fault is irrepareable, and I am reconciled to the Punishment which New England has already joined the southern States, in inflicting, for it, and to such as I know they will hereafter join in inflicting. God Save me from myself and my Friends is a Proverbial Prayer, and no Spaniard had ever more reason to offer it up than I have.— "The V.P. has no considerable Advantages from the Pride of Family." This I deny. My Father was an honest Man, a Lover of his Country and an independent Spirit. and the Example of that Father, inspired me with the greatest Pride of my Life, and has contributed to support me, among roaring Billows yawning Gulphs and burning Fevers. I must dilate, a little upon this important Subject. My Father Grand Father, Great Grandfather and Great Great Grandfather, were all Inhabitants of Braintree and all independent Country Gentlemen—I mean Officers in the Militia and Deacons in the Church. I am the first who has degenerated from the Virtues of the House so far, as not to have been an officer in the Militia nor a Deacon. The Line I have described makes about 160 Years, in which no Bankruptcy was ever committed no Widow or orphan was ever defrauded no Redemptioner intervened and no Debt was ever contracted in England. Let others Say as much.— My Father was a Farmer and a Tradesman,[1] all the rest were farmers I know and Tradesmen I believe—and the greatest fault, I ever found with any of them was that they did not educate me to their Farms and Trades.— My Mother was a Boylston one of the richest Families in the Massachusetts for above an hundred Years, and certainly not obscure, Since Harvard Colledge is indebted to it for very generous Donations and all Christendom for Inoculation for the Small Pox.[2]

But although I am proud of my Family, I should be very much mortified, if I thought that I enjoyed any share of public or private Esteem, Admiration or Consideration, for the Virtues of my Ancestors. By my own Actions I wish to be tried.— But The V.P. has had no Considerable Favours of Fortune. This I deny, and boldly affirm that he has been the most fortunate Man in America without Exception. in the public service, he has escaped death in more shapes than any Man, not excepting any officer of the army. He has escaped Death, in stormy Seas, leaky ships, threatning Diseases Cannon Balls and private Daggers, with a long train of &cas. But if by Fortune is meant private Property, his paternal Estate and his own Acquisitions before he turned Fool and Politician would out weigh the Ballance of many of those, who ride with Six horses owned in England or Elswhere— But is it not provoking, that the V.P. should be abused for the Obscurity of his Birth and the smallness of his Fortune; and at the same time abused for telling People that they have Prejudies in favour of Birth and Fortune?

When I Said I had no Ennemy, I did not mean to deny that I was envied—but Envy is not Enmity.— But Envy need not labour to prevent me from being President. there is no danger. The President is happily likely to live longer than the V.P.—and if it Should be otherwise ordered, the V.P. has no desire to be P.— He would retire to his Farm with more pleasure than ever he accepted any public office. Whether this is believed or not is a matter of Indifference at present. The World may possibly be convinced of it, by unequivocal Proofs, sooner than they imagine.— The Accusation of "fondness for the Splendor of monarchical Courts" has no Effect on me. I started fairly with my Countrymen. I published to the World with my name, my honest sentiments of Government, with the Reasons on which they were founded, at great length in three solid perhaps ponderous Volumes. these opinions are not changed, and if my Countrymen disapprove them, they are perfectly at Liberty to reject them and their Author together. I will neither falsify nor dissemble my Opinions on that Subject, if it were to obtain all the Gold of Ophyr, added to Presidencies or Royalties.

The other charge is less founded.— I have never given my sentiments at large upon any question, but once. Then I asked leave, and it was granted, seemingly with Pleasure. it was upon the great Question of the Presidents Power of Removal. at other times I have only occasionally asked a question or made a Single observation, and that but Seldom.— if these are faults they are easily corrected, for I have no Desire ever to open my mouth again, upon any question.— I am So far, from a desire of talking that I have never in any one Instance given my Reasons, for my Judgment in any of those many Cases in which the senate has been equally divided, and in which I suppose no Man would call in question my right of discussing the question at large.

No my Friend— The Observations you have heard are only Revivals of old grumblings when I was a Member of Congress from 1774 to 1778—or they may be observations on private Conversation— When I have company of friends at my own Table, and I feel very easy and happy, I sometimes hear such Strange sentiments, as arrouse me to some earnestness and perhaps warmth of Expression, and without meaning or thinking of offence to any Mortal, I may have hurt the Feelings of some of the Company. Your Friend M[rs] Adams sometimes objects to me on this head.—

You are the first who has ever hinted to me, that any Exception has ever been taken in senate—excepting about ten months ago M[r] Gerry mentioned to me that he had heard something of this kind hinted in Conversation.

To be candid with you, the situation I am in, is too inactive and insignificant for my disposition, and I care not how soon I quit it.— While in it, however I wish to do my Duty, and avoid giving just offence and you cannot oblige me more than by communicating to me, with the same Confidence and Openness, whatever you hear objected to my Conduct.

I mentioned to You three Volumes, and wish to know whether I have ever sent You a sett of them? if not, and I could find a Conveyance I would beg your Acceptance of one, for I wish to know your sentiments of it.[3] I am, my dear sir / with great Esteem and sincere Affection / your Friend John Adams

P.S.

Encore. All their Arts or rather Absurdities, cannot make me unpopular. I am, and they know it, more popular in their own States than they are. I was so fourteen Years ago, and by means of their own Constituents forced Numbers of them to vote with me, much against their Inclinations. The Lyes that have been circulated in the Southern States do me good. one was that I never came to Senate but with six horses, and often with an Escort of twelve horsemen.— There is, much too large a Proportion of both Houses who from Ignorance, Timidity or positive Antifæderalism, vote for Measures which you and I know would Subvert the Constitution. These are Sure to find me in their Way. What am I to do? Act a low Cunning? a dirty Craft? a vile Hypocricy? a base dissimulation? You know me too well to believe it possible.— Your Informers my Friend are young Men, who knew not Joseph or Tories who are associated with them.— John Adams has done Services for North America, of which no Man is ignorant, and which cannot be forgotton. They appear to be least of all known and felt in New England. The southern Gentlemen I must confess have shewn a better disposition to do me Justice than New Englandmen have. The two Men who envy me most, as you must know if you reflect, have Elections in New England much in their Power, and these have used their Influence in both Houses of Congress, to cramp me, more than the southern Gentlemen have.

This is confidential, you see wholly, I mean the whole Letter.

RC (private owner, 1959); internal address: "John Trumbull Esqr." LbC (Adams Papers); APM Reel 115.

[1] In the LbC, JA added, "I know; so were my grand father Great Grand father and great great Grand father."

[2] Boston physician Zabdiel Boylston (1679–1766), a great-uncle of JA, introduced smallpox inoculation in America in 1721 (vol. 8:366).

[3] For Trumbull's views on JA's *Defence of the Const.*, see his 14 March 1790 reply, below.

From Jabez Bowen

Sir Providence March 9th. 1790

Your favour of the 27th. ulto. came safe to hand yesterday.

I attended the Convention last week and after choosing a President &c we heard the Constitution Read by paragraps with the objections which were verry few and of no great importance, and were fully answered a Committe was then appointed to draw a Bill of Rights with such Amendments as they tho't necessary. which they Reported and after the necessary discussion they were Received.

A Motion was then made to Adjorn. which was carrid by a Majority of *Nine*. The Bill of Rights with the Amendments were Order'd to be Printed and sent out to the people to be consider'd of by them at the Annual Town Meetings. to be held on the Third Monday of April and the Convention Adjorned to the Twenty fourth Day of May—[1]

We are not much disappointed in the event but much Mortify'd; more especially as we cañot see any end to our sufferings, if good arose to the Ud States from our opposition to the five per Cent Impost— I fancy your Excellency will be obliged to Rack your Invention to point out the advantages that can possibly arise to the United or to this particular State from our late determination.

We had five old Tories in the Convention who would keep a Day of Thanksgiving on hearing that the Federal Government was dissolved, and some of the principle officers carrid away prisoners to Babilon alsius[2] G.B. we had many of Desperate Circumstances and the principle heads of the Papermoney faction, all added their strength together made the Collom to firm [. . .] broken, and these same people never will come [. . .] so long as they can possibly keep a

Majority [. . .] the Convention we are almost discouraged from making furthur Exertions. our best Citizens are looking out to dispose of their property, and to Remove out of the Government. the Restrictions on Trade will fall intirely on our *Friends* at which the oposers of the Fed$^{l.}$ Government will be will pleased. so that on the whole we begin to turn our Eyes back on the Country that we left and must all turn Tories, for any thing I can see.

be so kind Sir as to let the President know how our Convention has ended and that the Friends of the Federal Goverment are in disponding Circumstances, at present.

We would willingly Receve the necessary Officers for Collecting the Impost; if Congress would Order them to be appointed.

I Remain with much Esteeme Your / most Obedient & verry Humb Servant Jabez Bowen

PS. as the Freemen at large are to take up the Amendments on the 17$^{th.}$ of April I cannot help reminding you that it will be a good oppertunity for a Remonstrance or Adress from Congress to the People stateing the Reasons for their Adopting & the probable Consequences of their Rejection

RC (Adams Papers); addressed: "His Excellency / John Adams / Vice President United States / New York"; internal address: "John Adams Vice president U^{d} States."; endorsed: "Jabez Bowen / March 9. 1790 / ans$^{d.}$ March 20 1790"; notation: "Free." Some loss of text where the seal was removed.

[1] For Rhode Island's ongoing ratification convention, see William Ellery's letter of [*ca.* 6] March, and note 2, above.

[2] Bowen referred to 2 Kings, 24:15.

From Jeremy Belknap

Dear Sir Boston March 10 1790.

By your indulgence in permitting me to ask you any questions, I am emboldened to send you one of my circular letters; by which you may see that I intend to leave no practicable source of information unexplored. If it should be in your power to suggest any thing relative to either of the topics mentioned, I should be happy in receiving the communication.

There is another point about which I wish for satisfaction, & I know no person more capable of giving it than yourself. The annalist Chalmers had free access to the Plantation Office in London; where he found many things much to his purpose.[1] There are also doubtless many which might serve mine; but I cannot go to Europe. Can you tell me, Sir, whether that Office is under such regulations as that an American might have access to it—& if it is, do you know of any person who might be employed—& do you think a search there could be made without any considerable expense?

I am D^r sir with much Respect / Y^r obliged & obed^t Servt

Jeremy Belknap

RC (Adams Papers); internal address: "Hoñ Dr Adams—"

[1] For George Chalmers' scholarship, see Belknap's letter of 18 July 1789, and note 1, above.

To John Trumbull

Dear Sir New York March 12 1790

Your Letter of Feb. 6. has made So deep an Impression that it may not be amiss to make a few more Observations on it as it respects both of Us.

Your Friends have been very indiscreat and certainly have not done You Justice.— Fluency and Animation are Talents of a public Speaker which alone will go a great Way. I have known Several rise to Fame and extensive Practice, at the Bar, and afterwards to Influence in the Legislature and Power in the State, with very little else to recommend them.— if to these, are Added Learning and Fidelity, they will never fail to raise and Support a great Character sooner or later.— I have never had the Pleasure to hear you in public, but your Voice in Conversation is neither harsh nor disagreable, nor is your Pronunciation thick or inarticulate. Your Gestures are no more Stiff than Elsworths and every other Connecticut Man and if you were to live one Year in Boston or New York would be as easy as those of any of their Inhabitants. Your Style is very proper for the Bar. it is easy, clear and elegant: void of Fustian and Bombast to be Sure: but these qualities would offend more than they would impose upon. You need not therefore be anxious on these heads. Your Wit Satire and other Talents have made many dread you, I doubt not, and endeavour to lessen you in the popular Esteem: but you have plainly and fairly got the better of them all: and therefore I would not advise you to take Vengeance on them on one hand, nor trouble yourself about their Mortification at your Success on the other.

Let me come now to the more awkward and unpleasant Task of Saying something more of myself.— it is more than twenty Years that the American Newspapers have been throwing out hints of the Lowness of my Birth and the Obscurity of my Family. These generous and Philosophical Intimations have been carefully copied, with large Additions and Decorations in the English Newspapers, and from these translated into all the Languages and Gazettes of Europe, and now they are repeated again with as much Ardour as ever.— if I had been the Son of an Irish, Scotch or German Redemptioner, or of a Convict transported for Felony, there could not have been more Noise about it, or a more serious and weighty affair made of it.— I am the last Man in the World who will ever claim a benefit from the ~~popular~~ Democratical and Aristocratical Prejudice in favour of Blood.— But pushed as I am upon this point I will add, and Posterity will confirm it, I am the last Man in the United States, who should have any Occasion for it. But if I had neither done nor suffered nor hazarded any Thing for this Country, I am one of the last Men in the United States, who ought to be ashamed of his Family or to Suffer the Smallest Reproach, Disgrace or Reflection on Account of it. a Saxon Family by the Name of Adami, came over to England at the Time of the Saxon Conquest, and after settling in the Country translated their Latin Name into the English Plural Adams. They have multiplied exceedingly in England, and are now Scattered in great Numbers in Lincolnshire, Essex, Devonshire, the Isle of Wight, and most other Counties in England as well as in London and Westminster. many of them are opulent, some of them Magistrates Judges &c about the Year 1628 one of the Family who was wealthy but a Nonconformist, became a Member of the Plymouth Company and an Assistant in the first Charter to the Massachusetts Colony, and as You may see in Prince's Chronology, one of the most active, zealous and influencial Men in procuring the Resolution to transport the Patent to New England. About two years after my Ancestor came over with Eight sons and a considerable Property, Settled in Braintree and became an original Proprietor and a large Proprietor in that Town, and every foot of the Land he owned with great additions is now possessed by his Posterity in that Place. having been a Country Gentleman in England, and consequently a Maltster, as all the Landed Gentlemen are, he sett up a Malt House, which I have seen: as his Grandson sett up another in Boston which now belongs to the Lt. Govr.— A more industrious a more virtuous and irreproachable Race of People is not to be found in the World. I really never knew a vicious Man of the Breed.— I have therefore good Reason to despise all the dirty Lies that are told in the Newspapers. Let this Descent be compared with the Descent of any of the Grandees of any Part of America and I shall have no Reason to blush.—[1] I have Reason to blush however for the low Cunning, the mean Craft of those who talk and Scribble upon this subject. I have cause to blush, and I do blush at the Meanness and Inconsistency of the American public for tolerating this Insolence and much more for encouraging it. But I will tell you a Fact, and the longer You live, the more you will be sensible of it, the American Families who have been conspicuous in Government have more Pride Vanity and Insolence on Account of their Birth, than the Nobility of England or France have. and it is more difficult for a new Man to conquer Envy in this Country than it is in any Country of Europe: notwithstanding all our basted Equality and Philosophical Democracies.

The Charge of deserting my Republican Principles is false. My Principles and system of Government are the Same now as they ever were. And if I have ever acquiesced in Measures more democratical, it was in compliance with dire necessity, and a despair of resisting the fury of a popular Torrent excited by Men as ignorant and blind in this matter as the lowest of the People. before any Government was sett up, in Jan. 1776 I wrote & printed at Philadelphia a Pamphlet, recommending a Ballance of three Independent Branches. This Pamphlet Suggested to the Convention at New York their Idea of a Constitution. Mr Duane who was one of its framers told me as soon as it was done that it was done in Conformity nearly to my Idea in my Letter to Wythe.[2] in 1779, I drew the Plan of Government for the Massachusetts, which without me they could not have carried. Though they injured themselves by departing from my Ideas with regard to a Negative in the Governor, and by giving the Election of Officers of Militia to the Men. The Constitution of the United States is borrowed much too servilely from that of Massachusetts and now Pensilvania and Georgia have adopted the same, with some Improvements.[3] I have therefore been consistant in these Principles and to that Consistency and Constancy America is now Indebted for all the Peace order and good Government she has.— Without it she would have been at this hour in all Probabity in a civil War. and if my Advice had been more exactly followed, the shame of America would have been avoided, I mean her Breaches of Faith, her Violations of Property, her Anarchy and her Dishonesty.

I can conceive of no other Reason than this, Why I am singled out to be the Subject of their eternal Clamours about my Birth. if they could find a Spot in my moral Character or political Conduct they would not harp so much upon this string.— But the Principles of

Government which I have always embraced and professed, as they well know are such as they now Want and as the People now feel the necessity of. They have no Chance against me in this Way. Sam. Adams, R. H. Lee. P. Henry and many others are so erroneous in their Principles of Government as to be now growing Unpopular, and the Tories and Yonksters think they shall soon get them out of their Way. But John Adams remains an Eye sore to be a little more particular. There is a sett of Smart Young Fellows who took their degrees at Colledge, Since the Revolution in 1774 who are now joined by the old Tories in opposition to the old Whigs. many of these latter by their Obstinate Attachment to the Ignorance and Error of the Author of Common sense, are giving all possible Advantages against themselves. But Your Friend is not in this Predicament. and nothing remains but lies about his Birth and Conduct, to get him out of the Way.— Why else am I singled out? Three Presidents of Congress, have been sons of French Refugees Farmers and Tradesmen—surely not a more honourable Descent than that of an whole blooded English Family among the first settlers of the Country, constantly holding respectable landed Estates and enjoying the unvariable Esteem of their fellow Citizens.[4] The American Ministers abroad the Chief Justice, the Ministers of State, the Governors of States the President himself have not one Iota of Advantage of me in Point of Blood. Hancock and Washington had Splendid Fortunes. I had not. I have therefore surely bribed no Votes, nor dazzled any Man by my Wealth.— I am however and have been all my Days as independent a Man as either of them and more so too. because I have never been so much in debt, and have always lived more within my Income.

As to "Fondness for the Splendor of Titles" I will tell you an Anecdote.— The Second Day, that I presided in Senate, last April, the two Houses enjoyned me to receive the President and Address him in Public.— Upon this I arose and asked the Advice of the Senate, by what Title I should address him? The Constitution had given him no Title. it either intended that he should have none: and in that Case Honour or Excellency would be as much a Violation of it as Highness or Majesty. if We now addressed him by the Title of Excellency, We should fasten that Epithet upon him and by it depress him, not only below Ambassador from abroad and his own Ambassadors, but below the Governors of Seperate States &c— upon this arose a Gentleman in great Zeal, said he was glad to hear the Proposition;[5] that this was the precise moment to determine it: agreed in the Necessity of giving a Title that would be respectable Abroad;

and moved that a Committee should be appointed to consider and report what Title should be given to the President and *Vice President*.— Here was the blunder. I had Said nothing about Vice President.— But can one do when We are compelled to cooperate with Men, who are no Politicians? This blunder was Seized, in order to throw the blame of Titles on me.— But my shoulders are broad enough to bear it.

You Suppose me to be envyed in the southern States more than in the Northern. here You or I are mistaken. The real Envy against me is in the Northern States, and in two Men H. and A.[6] and they are their Friends who raise most of the idle Conversation about me. Their are many Gentlemen in the southern states who would prevent any northern Man from ever rising high in the public Esteem if they could: but they have no Objection against me more than any other. Emulation and Rivalry, arises between south and North as well as between Individuals. these Competitions have ever been a sourse of discord, Sedition and civil War, and unless some effectual Ballance for them is provided, I dread the Consequences. We may live to see from this Cause every great popular Leader, followed by his Clann, building a Castle on a Hill, and acting the Part of a feudal Chieftain. The Age of Chivalry and Knight Errantry may come upon Us in America. The melancholly prospect of this has induced me to wish for an Executive Authority independent and able to counterpoise the Legislative, and compose all feuds.

The Idea of the Leader of a Party, is easily conceived and propagated, from the Part I have been obliged to Act, in the question of the Presidents Power of Removal from office. I was unfortunately obliged to decide all those questions the Senate having been equally divided. There was all the last session about half the Senate disposed to vote for Measures that would as I thought weaken the Executive Authority, to a degree that would destroy its capacity of ballancing the Legislature, and consequently, in my Idea, overturn the best Part of the Constitution. This Principle I must pursue, tho it may give occasion to a Party to represent me as a Leader of the opposite Party. as to order in debate, I think there has never been any difficulty in preserving it.— I have attended the Supream Court of Justice in Gallicia in Spain, the Parliament of Paris, the assembly and Courts of Justice in Holland, and both Houses of the British Parliament as well as Congresses, senates Councils and Houses in america, and I never Saw more order in any one, than has been constantly observed in senate Since I sat in it.

Who your Informers were I know not— You say they are not unfriendly to me. but it is most certain they have been deceived, or they have misrepresented. for the facts they reported to you are not true. New England men, my friend, are more of Statesmen than they are of Politicians. The Old Whigs have lost much of their Influence. I am now obliged to act openly, in conformity to my invariabe professed Principles, which they well know, against them. Mr Hancock Mr Sam. Adams, Mr R. H. Lee—P. Henry—Govr. Clinton and General Warren with twenty others, with whom I acted in pulling down the British Government, are now not very cordially supporting the new[7] Government. They mistake their own Interest as I think as well as that of their Country. This however must necessarily produce a Coldness towards me. while those against whom I acted for many Years to their mortification, altho We now Act together, you may Suppose have not forgotten their ancient feelings. in this situation, public Life is not very agreable to me. I pray for long Life to the President with as much Sincerity as any Man in America. I have more pressing Motives to wish it, than any Man. I sincerely think him the best Man for his Place in the World and I very much doubt, whether if it should be the Will of Heaven that he should die, any other Man could be found who could Support the Government. if there is any one, I would give Way to him, with Pleasure, and retire to my farm. I never will act in my present Station under any other Man than Washington. But who can We find—Mr Jay, Mr Jefferson Mr Maddison. I know very well that I could carry an Election against either of them in Spight of all Intrigues and Maneuvres. Yet I would not do it, if I thought either could govern this People. But I know they could not, so as to give Satisfaction while I should be in the Country. I should find myself become all at once the Idol of a Party. my Character and services would be trumpetted to the Skies—and I should find myself forced in spight of myself to be placed at the head of a Party.— I will never be in this situation. if Circumstances should force it Upon me—I will at all Events quit the Country—if I spend the rest of my Days in a Garrett in Amsterdam. thank Heaven however the President is in a vigourous Health and likely to live till the Government has a fair Tryal whether it can be supported or no.— I could now quit my Place and retire without much Noise or Inconvenience, and if there is the least Uneasiness to the danger of the Government I am very willing to quit it. The System of Policy, in my Salary and in some other Things seems to have been to compell me or provoke me to retire.

I have written to You in Confidence with great freedom, because I have the highest Esteem for your Abilities and the Utmost Affection for the qualities of your heart John Adams

RC (PPRF); internal address: "John Trumbull Esqr." LbC (Adams Papers); APM Reel 115.

[1] For a comprehensive account of the English Adamses' immigration to America, and their establishment of a brewing business later owned by Samuel Adams, see JA, *D&A*, 3:254.

[2] First published in Philadelphia as a pamphlet in April 1776, JA's *Thoughts on Government* grew out of his advice to William Hooper and John Penn, who were drafting the constitution of North Carolina. JA's blueprint of a balanced, tripartite government also circulated to George Wythe of Virginia, Jonathan Dickinson Sergeant of New Jersey, and James Duane of New York (vol. 4:65–93).

[3] After ratifying the Constitution on 2 Jan. 1788, Georgia lawmakers embarked on a lengthy effort to bring local government in line with the host of federal powers. To reassess the 1777 state constitution they held three conventions to develop a set of revisions. Comprising four articles, the new Georgia constitution established a bicameral legislature that selected the governor, judges, and attorneys. It remained in effect until 1798 (Melvin B. Hill Jr. and G. LaVerne Williamson Hill, *The Georgia State Constitution*, 2d edn., N.Y., 2018, p. 7–9).

[4] The three presidents of the Continental Congress who claimed Huguenot roots were Henry Laurens, John Jay, and Elias Boudinot (*ANB*).

[5] For Richard Henry Lee's 23 April 1789 motion and the ensuing debate over executive titles that consumed the Senate for several weeks, see vol. 19:445.

[6] John Hancock and Samuel Adams.

[7] In the LbC, the next word is "Constitution."

To William Cranch

Dear Sir New York March 14. 1790

Your favours of Decr 15. Jan. 24. and Feb. 17 are before me, and I thank for your Attention, and hope for a continuance of it, though I am not a punctual Correspondent to You.[1]

To the original of the Bar Meetings I was a Witness, as I was also to their excellent Effects in the Progress of them. They introduced a Candor and Liberal[ity] in the Practice at the Bar that were never before known in the Massachusetts. Mr Gardners Master Mr Pratt was so sensible of their Utility that when We took leave of him at Dedham his last Words to Us were "*Bretheren, forsake not the assembling of yourselves together.*"[2]

My Advice to you, and all the young Gentlemen coming Up, as well as to those, now on the stage is never to Suffer Such Meetings to go into disuse, let who will clamour about them: for as I know the Body of the Law will never consent to any illegal or dishonourable Combinations, so on the other hand their deliberations together, on what is for the honour and dignity of the Bar and for the Public Good as far as their Practice is connected with it cannot but produce benign Effects.

What? is it unlawful for the Gentlemen of the Profession to Spend an Evening together once a Week? to converse upon Law, and upon their Practice: to hear complaints of unkind unfair and ungentlemanlike Practice: to compose differences: to agree that they will not introduce ignorant, illitterate, or illbred or unprincipled Students or Candidates? that they will not practice any kind of Chicanery, or take unmanly Advantages of one another, to the Injury of Clients for accidental or inadvertent Slips in pleading or otherwise? on what unhappy times are We fallen, if that Profession without which the Laws can never be maintained nor Liberty exist, is to be treated in this tyrannical manner?

But I must Stop.— ask my son if he has received two Letters from me.[3] I am / with much Esteem and affection yours

John Adams

RC (MHi:Cranch Family Papers); addressed by CA: "Mr: William Cranch. / at Judge Dawes's / Boston."; internal address: "Mr William Cranch."; endorsed: "V. President March 14 1790"; notation by JA: "Free / John Adams." LbC (Adams Papers); APM Reel 115. Text lost where the seal was removed has been supplied from the LbC.

[1] Cranch's letters of 15 Dec. 1789 and 17 Feb. 1790 have not been found, but that of 24 Jan. is above.

[2] At the age of fourteen, John Gardiner entered the office of Benjamin Prat (1711–1763), Harvard 1737, a leading Boston lawyer whom JA admired for his "strong, elastic Spring, or what we call Smartness, and Strength in his Mind." The allusion is to Hebrews, 10:25 (*Sibley's Harvard Graduates*, 10:226, 229, 238; 13:593, 602; JA, *D&A*, 1:83).

[3] For JA's 9 and 19 Feb. letters to JQA about his son's career prospects, see *AFC*, 9:14, 16.

To Stephen Higginson

Sir New York March 14 1790.

I am much obliged by your favor of the first instant with the report of the Committee: and glad to find that the bench has been filled with Characters to your satisfaction. The report of the Committee gives me concern, as it evidence of an unquiet restless spirit as it tends to encourage Rhode Island in their obstinacy: but most of all as I fear there is too much probability that it originated in the advice you mention, and is aided by some of the great folks you allude to— It is supposed to have been sett on foot in the Massachusetts to assist in raising the same spirit in Virginia, where there is at present a very general satisfaction with the national Government: though it is apprehended that this measure may revive some old uneasiness. I really fear that some of my old friends both in Virginia and Massachusetts hold not in horror as much as I do, a division of this Continent into two or three nations and have not an equal dread of Civil war. The appearance of reviving courage in this Country is very pleasing to a man as much mortified as I have been with reproaches against the Religion, morals, honor and spirit of this Country, it is rapture to see a returning disposition to respect treaties to pay debts, and to do justice by holding property sacred and obeying the Commandment "Thou shalt not steal." The worthy Clergymen throughout the United States when they pray for the Vice President petition that he may be endowed with the Spirit of his station in this petition I most devoutly join. And the most difficult part of the spirit of his station is to abstain from meddling improperly with the executive power. For this reason you must not depend upon any activity on my part to promote your views. This I can say however, that I beleive your qualifications for the office you mentioned to be of the best kind and equal to those of any man; that I shall make no opposition to you personally; and that whenever it may fall in my way, consistent with the aforesaid spirit of my station, to assist your wishes, it will give me pleasure to do it. I received sometime ago a letter from you, for which I was much obliged to you tho' I fear I have never answered it.—[1] The inspection of Merchandizes to be exported is one of the most important things this Country has to do. Next to the faith of treaties and the payment of debt, punctuality in the quality of merchandizes to be exported is the thing most wanted I will not say to support, but to restore the moral character of our Country. Pensylvania has derived such advantages from her inspection laws, that I wonder the Massachusetts should want any motive to follow her example.[2] Some of the States derive such advantages from their own inspection laws and from the want of them in New England that opposition to a general law may arise from that interest. The national debt I have long thought, must be the instrument for establishing a national government; and have the pleasure now to see that the President, his ministers and a majority in the house are of the same opinion. I have also the satisfaction to see that the ennemies and opposers of the Government are all of the same mind. The latter are accordingly exerting themselves against the assumption of the State debts, as the pivot upon which the general government will turn. The opposition however seems to be feeble, as not supported by the voice of the people This is a favorable symptom. Indeed the government appears to have had as happy an effect upon the prosperity and peace of the Country as its friends had reason to expect. it might not be too strong an expression to say that the most sanguine prophecies of its blessings and utility have been fulfilled. There are defects still in the Constitution, which if they are not supplied by degrees as it gains strength will produce evils of a serious kind. John Adams

LbC in CA's hand (Adams Papers); internal address: "Honble Stephen Higginson"; APM Reel 115.

[1] JA referred to Higginson's letter of 21 Dec. 1789, above.

[2] Prior to the implementation of the Constitution, Pennsylvania merchants operated under detailed inspection laws for lucrative exports like timber, meat, flour, bread, spirits, and tobacco (Albert Anthony Giesecke, *American Commercial Legislation before 1789*, N.Y., 1910, p. 75–78).

From John Trumbull

Dear Sir Hartford March 14th. 1790—

I have the honour of yours of the 9th. instant, & am happy to find that you are not displeased at the frankness of my communications. There are very few Persons to whom I would have written with equal freedom— Half the world are of the temper of the Italian Cardinal, described in the Spectator, who kicked his Spy down stairs for telling him what the world said against him—but with such I desire to have no connection.[1] Whatever may be the odds of Rank, merit or abilities, in a friendly correspondence, there must be an unreservedness, which assumes the appearance of equality— And were I to open a Correspondence with the Angel Gabriel, notwithstanding my deference to a superior nature, I must write with the same freedom as to a Mortal—or not write at all—

I fully believe that more has been said on the subjects I mentioned, at a distance, than at NewYork. Slander has her whispering-gallery, formed to increase the sound in its progress—and the distant echo of a lie is always louder than the first report.

Your distinction between Enmity & Envy is undoubtedly just— Yet the Envious are enemies of the worst kind—the most active persevering & malignant—

The People of NewEngland have often been charged with this fault. Perhaps the charge is not strictly true. We are true Republicans, & have the strongest feelings of personal Independence & universal equality. We are led by education to be jealous of Power, & to distrust those Men, who are raised to a dignity and elevation above the general rank. We are not however generally chargeable with ingratitude in our elections, towards public services, or known merit. But the moment we have raised the Man of our choice to a rank, necessary indeed in government, but disagreeable to our eyes, we wish to make him sensible of his dependence on our suffrages, to teach him to consider himself as the servant of the people, & to ascribe his elevation, not to his own merit, but to our gratuitous favour. This must be acknowleged as our general character. We hate to see great men, & endeavour to *belittle* them as much as possible. The V.P. must therefore expect to find his merits, & services depreciated among us, but may always be sure of our suffrages. We dislike an Office of such high rank, but if there must be such an one, we are satisfied with the Person, who holds it. Indeed so strong are our ideas of republican equality, that were the other world peopled only by a certain Party of New Englanders with their present feelings, they would be disgusted at the splendor of Omnipotence, & would wish to limit Almighty Power, & establish a democracy in heaven. Our most sensible & influential characters are however fully convinced of the necessity of an energetic Government, of due subordination, & of the proper checks & balances in the Administration— But most of these are Men of ambition, & can scarcely endure a superior. Indeed Ambition is universal among us— We have Presidents, not out of their leading strings & Vice Presidents by dozens in embrio.

The Gentlemen from the Southward may have more apparent politeness than those from New England, & would certainly be more liberal in the allowance of adequate salaries— But the People of the Southern States will never be fond of uniting their suffrages in favor of any Native of NewEngland—

I was entertained with the account of your honest, independent & respectable ancestry. Yours is a genealogy of which a wise man may be justly proud, but not such as a Coxcomb would boast. My ancestors in the paternal line were of the same class, except my Father, who was a Clergyman. It is a descent of which I was never ashamed. My mother on the contrary is a great genealogist, & has no small share of pride of birth— She is descended from the Stoddards of Massachusetts—but what pleased her best was, that she could trace her ancestry in the female line to a natural daughter of Charles the 2$^{d.}$ by one of his mistresses, I think it was the Dutchess of Portsmouth. Thus by the fashionable Assistance of a little honorable unchastity in the maternal line, I presume I have at this instant some drops of

Royal Blood flowing in my veins. From hearing this account often repeated in my infancy, I drew up, when I was about eight years old, & presented to my Mamma, her genealogy in burlesque; for the impudence of which I deserved and received a good box on the ear.[2]

While I am on this Subject I wish to enquire whether the Rev[d.] J. Adams, Author of a small volume of Poems, I have formerly seen, containing an Elegy on the Death of a M[rs.] Turell, some imitations of parts of the Revelations &c was not of your family— He was certainly a Man of poetical genius, & of a taste more correct than the New England Writers of his age.[3]

I shall hardly allow You to ascribe to the favour of fortune your frequent escapes from death and danger in the public service. It was the hand of heaven, that conducted the American Revolution, & provided & preserved the proper Instruments for our success. Providence raised a Washington & Greene &c to command our armies, & a Franklyn, Jay &c to conduct our foreign negociations. It preserved your life to accomplish the important treaty with Holland, to give M[r.] Jay the necessary assistance in settling the terms of Peace with Great Britain, & to be VicePresident of the United States. On this subject I own myself an enthusiast. In the late illness of the President, when we had an account, that his Physicians despaired of his recovery, I offered to ensure his life for a sixpence, because I was convinced, that America could not do without him as yet.

Your present situation, tho' as You observe it is in some degree inactive, is by no means insignificant or uninfluential. In the equal division of Parties in the Senate, You have had sundry questions of great importance to decide. Could the grand point of the President's Power of removal have been carried without your assistance & influence? Yet that very debate has left a great share of rancour in the minds of those, whose visionary plans, political ignorance, & frivolous arguments, You on that occasion detected & exposed—

Solitude & retirement, at which you hint, certainly form no scene for the exercise of activity, or the acquirement of significance.— All things, I firmly believe, will be & continue right. The Batteries of Slander will waste themselves in noise & smoke, or destroy themselves by being overcharged.

The first Volume of your *Defence* &c, I purchased, lent & have lost it. I have seen but one set of the Continuation here, which I borrowed & hastily perused. I can therefore at present only give my sentiments in general. Your Principles in Government appeared to me just, & your arguments for them unanswerable— I am so little versed in the History of many of the modern Republics, which You have detailed, that I could only thank You for the information You afforded on those subjects— But on the Constitutions of Greece & Rome, I felt my vanity complimented at every line, by finding your opinions coincident with those I had for many years entertained about them. Indeed it is a long time since I have read with any patience the herd of writers, who scribble eulogiums on the antient Republics, or form similar Utopias for modern States.

I know not that I should object to any of your opinions— Yet on one subject, on which indeed I am not certain of yours, I will venture a single remark. I am exceedingly doubtful, whether any imitation of the Pageantry of foreign Courts would, in the present age & according to the feelings of my Countrymen, contribute to strengthen the fæderal Government— Our national Character is very different from that of the Populace of Europe. What in that country "dazzles the croud & sets them all agape,"[4] excites in our Yeomen nothing but envy, contempt & ridicule. Let our Government be possessed of real strength— It will not need the aid of ostentation. We are sufficiently enlightened to detect the imposition of pageantry—& I fear our Government would gain as little benefit by it, as one of my dearest Friends, Col. H——s, has acquired from the French Silks & Laces, in which he returned from Europe—[5] He is happily weaning himself from that his almost only foible—and I cannot with to see our Government dressed in his cast suits.

What may be politic on this subject in the next generation, I will not undertake to say.

I shall conclude with an observation in answer to a Query in your last letter.

Art & dissimulation are the very Antipodes to your character, & You know me too well to imagine I should recommend them. The utmost exertion of your influence and abilities, on all subjects on which the happiness of America & the force of her Government depends, in such ways as are best calculated to continue & extend that influence, & crown those abilities with deserved success, is expected by your friends & the Public. We look to You for important additions, to those services, You have already rendered to your Country, which as You justly observe can never be forgotten, & for which, I trust You will find that America will not be eventually ungrateful.

Please to offer my best Respects to Mrs. Adams, & believe that with the highest attachment & regard / I have the honor to be, / Dear Sir / Your most obedient / & obliged humble servt. John Trumbull

RC (Adams Papers); endorsed: "Mr Trumbul. 14. March. / ansd 2. April. 1790."

[1] In *The Spectator*, No. 439 (24 July 1712), Joseph Addison related the tale of a spy who tells his employer that many see him as "a mercenary rascal" and coward. Irate, the cardinal "rises in great wrath, calls him an impudent scoundrel, and kicks him out of the room."

[2] Trumbull's parents were Rev. John (1714–1787), Yale 1735, and Sarah Whitman Trumbull (1718–1805), of Watertown, Conn. (Dexter, *Yale Graduates*, 1:544, 545).

[3] Rev. John Adams (1705–1740), Harvard 1721, of Boston, was a Congregationalist minister who demonstrated a prodigious bent for learning languages and writing poetry, but he was not related to JA's family. Trumbull read the 1745 edition of the clergyman's *Poems on Several Occasions, Original and Translated*, which contained his elegy "To the Rev. Mr. Turrell, on the Death of His Vertuous Consort, Daughter to the Rev. Dr. Colman. Mar. 26. 1735," p. 94–102, Evans, No. 5527 (*Sibley's Harvard Graduates*, 6:424, 425, 426).

[4] Milton, *Paradise Lost*, Book V, line 357.

[5] Diplomat and author David Humphreys returned to America in May 1786 (vol. 18:154).

From François Adriaan Van der Kemp

Sir! Kingston. 17. March 1790

After your Excellency's advice, for which I am much obliged, I wrote, by this Sloop to his Excellencÿ the President, State the affair, and requested his interference, so far, as He maÿ think proper, and I flatter mÿself, that it wil be promoted bÿ you in the Same manner.[1] But this occasion Sir! is to favourable, not to make use of it in enlarging—for a moment upon a particular article of your favour— Perhaps, Some time or other, you Excellencÿ maÿ find leisure, to gratifÿ mÿ curiosity, and honour me with a farther communication of his thoughts upon a matter, if al not interestful to us, Surelÿ not indifferent, and certainly of the highest moment to our Posterity—perhaps to our children. Ought I remember—that a hereditarÿ Senat is this Subject.

Permit me before to reflect Sir! that what you please, to call compliments received from Europe, is reallÿ no more than homage paid to truth—of So more value, because I am persuaded, that most of them, who paid that tribute, were made Proselytes to a doctrine, of which they had, before, none of verÿ confuse Ideas— this, I candidly allow, was mÿ case, who, meaning to be an adept in the Doctrine of Republican government, was Soon convinced, that I was not initiated in this So Simple mÿsterÿ—now it is revealed—and bÿ this cynosure, I made Such progress in a Short time, that I dare guess—to be not a great difference between our thoughts upon the Stability of, and the degree of civil Libertÿ inhering in last French Revolution—

I Should have desired Sir! there you had given So open and candid, morning warnings to the americans in regard, what theÿ have to do, and to fear, if they chuse to preserve their Political independencÿ and civil libertÿ, though some of these warnings maÿ, at first view, be verÿ disagreable to Short-Sighted—intrested—or ambitious Americans. There you, more than once and I Sincerilÿ believe, upon solid reasonings upon experience, intimate your fear—that the elections of Presidents and Senators will not be continued—for a long time, without corruption—Sedition &c there you Showed with a finger a remedÿ—against it—in your opinion—necessarÿ though otherwise not desirable— I should have desired, that Mr. Adams had discussed this matter a little farther, and explained—how this chance wil—or can be introduced—without Sedition—and civil war—and in wat manner that hereditarÿ Senate wil be continued after his first creation. Whether the Same reasonings wil not be as conclusi~~fes~~ against the elections of the house of representatives, as wel against the Senator and president?— being there perhaps So much reason for fear of briberÿ and corruption—when but one representative can be chosen for 30 or 90000 citisens

But Sir! it Seems not alone, the introduction wil meet the difficulties—feared be elections consequences of the most Serious nature will be unavoidable by the continuation. Shall the ofspring of certain families—the Possessors of a cetain tract of Land be chosen for the first hereditary Senators? or Shall the Legislative Bodies—or Executive Power of the different States make choice of a certain number? In case of a vacant Seed—who Shal have the Power of creating a New Senator or Peer? the President? the Senat? the house of Representatives? or both Houses—of all the three? Perhaps it would be of utility to the United States, if Kentuckÿ and Vermont, acknowledged as independant States, in alliance with us, could be persuaded to trÿ what Succes from a hereditarÿ president and Senators with a house of representatives might accrue to the State, in removing briberÿ—corruption and Sedition, in promoting civil Libertÿ—

Should it not be more desirable Sir! Supposing that the elections of a President and Senators—for one or more ÿears, was preferable, in case Such elections could be effected without fear for briberÿ—Sedition—to dismember the commonwealth—in two or more ~~Royal~~ independant Governments—as Soon as the population, opulence and commerce was increased to that degree, that everÿ part—could be compared to the whole at present? Would it not be easier to preserve peace between two, three or more States upon the Continent—than between 14 or fifteen States—of Such different intrests—united together by a feeble fee—in the possession of Such a population, opulence and commerce, as wil be the case in half a centurÿ—but more than enough, if your Excellency is not discontent with it; and excuse the trouble I had occasioned—being persuaded, that Your Excellency maÿ receive more elaborate and useful Political productions, and offerings of Services—though I dare adfirm, that not one of them, wil be with higher and Sincerer esteem and respect, than I.

Sir! / Your Excellency's most obedient / and obliged Servant

Fr Adr. vanderkemp.

RC (Adams Papers); endorsed: "Fr. Ad. Van der Kemp / Kingston. 17. March / ans$^{d.}$ 27. 1790."

[1] Van der Kemp also wrote to George Washington on 17 March, seeking restitution amounting to "45000 Guldens—or 7500£ New-yorks Currency" for the fine paid to end his 1787 imprisonment in the Netherlands. Washington referred the query to Thomas Jefferson, who responded on 31 March 1790, informing Van der Kemp that, as there was no minister resident at The Hague following JA's departure, the American government lacked a diplomatic channel to address the grievance (to Van der Kemp, 27 Feb., above; Washington, *Papers, Presidential Series*, 5:244, 245).

To Jabez Bowen

Dear Sir New York March 20 1790

If your state would as you hint in your letter of the 9th all turn tories and go back to Britain openly; I should not be obliged to rack my invention to point out the advantages which would result to the United States. For as this would oblige us to chastise the treachery, insolence and ingratitude of your people, it would be an exemplary vengeance to all others whose hearts are no better than theirs: and consequently would sufficiently strengthen the national government. A remonstrance or Address from Congress would employ them better than the Quaker petition: but there are other things which await their decission, of much more import than either. As I know it to be impossible that Congress should interpose by an address; so I hope they will no more interpose by their lenity: but treat Rhode Island in all points as a foreign state. If your people are desirous of trying their strength and their wit with us, I am for joining the issue. I shall feel for you and some others. But I say "Come out from among them"[1]

John Adams

LbC in CA's hand (Adams Papers); internal address: "Hon Jabez Bowen. Providence"; APM Reel 115.

[1] 2 Corinthians, 6:17.

To Joseph Mandrillon

M[r] Mandrillon. New York March 20 1790

The letter you did me the honor to write me, the 15th of June last did not arrive till yesterday. The memory of the time I passed in Holland, and of the esteem I conceived for several meritorious characters, and among others for M[r] Mandrillon will I hope never be effaced. The elegant compliments you are pleased to make me, on my election to the dignity of Vice President of the United States of America, deserve my respectful acknowledgments. M[r] Theophilus Cazenove will I hope find this Country prosperous in its commerce agriculture and manufactures, as well as happy in its enjoyment of civil and religious liberty. I wonder indeed that more of the patriots of the United provinces, especially those who are in banishment, have not ventured over the Atlantic. Innocence, peace and liberty may be here found in abundance; they have it in their power to bring wealth along with them and wealth may be increased in this Country faster than in any other, at least by fair means. Can you give me any account of our old friend Cerisier?[1] J Adams

LbC in CA's hand (Adams Papers); internal address: "Mr Joseph / Mandrillon"; APM Reel 115.

[1] In 1789 Antoine Marie Cerisier, editor of the *Gazette de Leyde*, launched the *Gazette universelle*, a political newspaper in Paris, with the aid of Joseph François Michaud and Pascal Boyer (Adrien Favre, *Histoire de Châtillon-sur-Chalaronne*, Ceyzériat, France, 1972, p. 91; Hoefer, *Nouv. biog. générale*).

To Henry Marchant

Dear Sir New York March 20. 1790

Your favours of 19. Dec[r.] 18. Jan. and 7. March are all before me.— I am much obliged to you for the accurate and useful Information, in all of them. It is a mortifying Thing to be obliged to take so much Pains with a Man to prevent him from Setting Fire to his own House, when he knows that he must burn the whole Town with it.

I can give you no other Advice my Friend than to persevere, with the Same Zeal Candour Honour, Probity and public Virtue, which you have hitherto discovered and leave the Event to Time. Congress I hope will now take a firm Part and make Rhode Island Cheese Butter Lime and every Thing else *foreign*. To be trifled with again would be too much.

Can it not be discovered, who are the Men among You who carry on the Correspondence with the Antis in New York, Virginia, Massachusetts, North Carolina &c and who are their Correspondents.— Your Champions are all but poor Puppetts danced on the Wires of certain hot Spirits in other States whose Ambition is greater than their Talents or Virtues, and whose Vanity is greater Still. Nothing in all this surprizes me so much as the Blockheadly Ignorance and Stupidity of your common People, which Suffers them to be made the Dupes of Artists so unskillfull. This fact among many others Serves to shew that in Proportion as you approach in a Constitution of Government to a compleat Democracy, by the same degrees your People must become savages. The Vulgar Envy and malignity will not be content with plundering the helpless and defenceless, but they will not bear the least superiority in Knowledge nor in Virtue. They will never be content till all are equally Knaves Fools and Brutes. Equality! perfect Equality!

Your Exertions and Your Influence, my good Friend have hitherto done a great deal to procure mercy to your fellow Citizens. That Esteem and Respect in which you are held, and a few others will Still induce many to wish that the day of Grace may be prolonged.— I cannot say it will not: but I must say I believe it will not; and that I think it ought not.

There are three Sorts of Men, who are like three discordant materials in a Chimical Composition; The old Whiggs; the old Tories; and the Youngsters. The old Whiggs are hated by the old Tories and envied by the Youngsters. Hatred and Envy have therefore allied themselves together. and the old Whigs have many of them given great Advantages against themselves to this confederacy by an Obstinate Attachment to very ignorant notions and pernicious Principles of government: which will end in their ruin. But not perhaps till they have excited a civil War and involved their Country in Calamities, more dreadful than those We have escaped. Rhode Island is pursuing a Conduct more directly tending to this End than any other State.— The Character of a Legislator, has in all Ages been held above that of an Hero. Lycurgus and Solon are ranked higher than Alexander or Cæsar. The most profound and Sublime Genius, the most extensive Information and the vastest Views [have] been always considered as indispensable. a consummate Master of science and Literature, a long Experience in Affairs of Government, travel through all the known World were among the ancients thought little enough for a Founder of ~~Nations~~ Laws.— But in America Dr Young,

Common sense Pain, Samuel Adams and R. H. Lee have been our Founders of Empires.— I esteem them all.— But God knows there is no Legislator among them.— and if this poor People will not learn to discover some better Plan of Government than those Gentlemen even with the assistance of Dr Price, Mr Turgot & Dr Franklin are capable of, they will attone with their blood in a civil War for their Negligence, Rashness and Willful Ignorance John Adams

RC (MH-H:Autograph File, A); internal address: "Henry Merchant Esqr"; endorsed: "V. P. John Adams— / 1790." LbC (Adams Papers); APM Reel 115. Text lost where the seal was removed has been supplied from the LbC.

To Charles Storer

My dear Charles. New York March 20th 1790.

There is nothing improper in your application of the 23^d of Feby nor should I find fault with your seeking honor or emolument. Every man has a right to seek both. Mr Remsen has been many years in the office of foreign affairs and has qualifications and merits which preclude all competition: Mr Alden is another in a similar predicament, so that there is not a possibility of your success in your first thought.— I have shown your letter to Mr Jay who is your friend and would join me in any attempt to procure you any thing attainable. A Consul abroad without a capital and without a salary would not perhaps answer. A secretaryship to a minister abroad is but poor promotion, and perhaps this could not be obtained. The executive authority is so wholly out of my sphære, and it is so delicate a thing for me to meddle in, that I avoid it as much as possible— Yet I would recommend you to the President, in friendly terms for any thing you may think of, for which you are capable, provided it were not in competition with others whose pretensions were better founded. Nor do I think meanly of your qualifications or pretensions. You will find humiliations enough in a state of dependence in any subordinate executive department: But you must judge for yourself. Your family, education, manners are all agreable and would recommend you Clerkships in the public offices are a bare subsistence, and are so humble stations, and have so little chance for rising that I suppose you could not reconcile yourself to one of them. Let me know however your further thought.

I am with great esteem and regard yours J Adams.

LbC in CA's hand (Adams Papers); internal address: "Chas Storer Esqr / Troy"; APM Reel 115.

From James Lovell

Honored & dear Sir Boston— March 20. 1790

You will have a Visit from your old Friend Gen$^{l.}$ Warren who supposed I could certify some *Intentions* of the former Congress greatly to his Advantage— Your Namesake has done it; but I found it impossible for me upon a strict Review of the Case. As you were absent part of the Time I think it my Duty to save you the Toil of searching those Journals wherein this Business is scattered. The Sketch inclosed will show you how Congress was obliged to turn & twist under the Difficulties of a depreciating Currency, and to use sometimes Expressions of *meer Gloss*;—as upon Aug$^{st:}$ 4 & Octr 31 1788, in this present Concern.[1]

I am aware that the Gen$^{l.}$ would think this Letter to be doubly *not* helping him; but I declare it proceeds from an honest Affection for your Honor, *without* the least Wish to hinder any *fair* Advances of his Interest. But really I am not free of Doubt whether Mr Gerry's Regard for the Gen$^{l.}$ and perhaps his *individual* Intention may not add a Testimony similar to your Namesake's. This increased my Desire that you should *see for yourself*, in Case you are addressed upon the Subject. Otherwise, and, if you please, at all Events, let Lovell be *out of Sight*.

If Doctor Craigie should speak to you relative to a Peice of *Justice* due to me for which I shall furnish him with Vouchers, you will certainly aid him because it is Justice: But I hope the Secretary of the Treasury will find himself possessed of a discretionary Power similar to what resided in the old Board of Commissioners for the Renewal of *destroyed* Securities. This Goverment and all Individuals here *renewed* all Obligations which depended on Them. But the Board of Treasury of Congress have held me in Jeopardy for a Course of Years without condescending to even an Answer of any Sort since my Letter to them of January 1786—in which were inclosed all the Vouchers which the Nature of the Case would Admit and which had given the fullest Conviction here where the Robbery of my Iron Chest was committed, and the Criminals condemned and *executed*; except the State's Evidence,—whose Testimony was uniform with the Confession, at times, of the two other Wretches, that "every Scrap of Paper was burnt, from Fears of Discovery, *except* copperplate Loan-Interest Certificates,["] which the Wretches thought to be Bank Bills—good Plunder, not capable of being challenged by me or any one.

Time adds Strength to my Claim because No Resurrection of a Scrap has taken Place since Nov[r.] 1784.

I am Sir / With highest Esteem / Your most humble Servant

James Lovell

RC and enclosure (Adams Papers); endorsed: "M[r] Lovel March 20. 1790 / Ans[d] Ap. 5."

[1] James Warren visited New York City from March to May, during which time he unsuccessfully sought compensation for his prior service on the Navy Board for the Eastern Department. To aid Warren's cause, Lovell enclosed his summary of various Continental Congress journal entries and duties dated from 1776 to 1788 (*Mercy Otis Warren: Selected Letters*, ed. Jeffrey H. Richards and Sharon M. Harris, Athens, Ga., 2009, p. 223).

From James Bowdoin

Dear sir — Boston March 24. 1790

The Gentleman, by whom this will be delivered to you, is Nathaniel Appleton esq[r] the Commissioner of the Loan Office for the State of Massachusetts.[1] At the first institution of the Office in the Year 1776 he was appointed to it, and has been continued in it by the Several Boards of Treasury to the present time. Besides the approbation of those, to whom he was immediately accountable, his Conduct in the Office has met with universal acceptance; and places him in the first line of notice, should Administration think proper to continue the Office; or in its Stead establish any Similar one. His capacity for business, his application to it, and the rectitude of his character, with which you must be fully acquainted, will be considered by those, who now so worthily direct the helm, as the best recommendation.

With great respect, I have the honour to be, Sir—Yr most ob[t.] hble serv[t.]

James Bowdoin[2]

RC (Adams Papers); internal address: "His Exc[y.] The Vice President."

[1] Boston merchant Nathaniel Appleton (b. 1731) served as Massachusetts commissioner of the Continental loan office until his death in 1798 (*AFC*, 7:425).

[2] This is Bowdoin's last extant letter to JA, who learned of his old friend's illness and paralytic stroke in a letter from JQA of 9 Aug. 1790. Bowdoin died of dysentery on 6 Nov. (*AFC*, 9:105).

From Stephen Higginson

Sir— Boston Mar: 24: 1790—

Your obliging letter of the 14 instant I have received, & thank you for the friendly intentions you therein express. I did not mean to request any activity on your part, in the case alluded to; nor was I aware, that any expression I used would convey an Idea of that kind—the intention you intimate, is all I wish for, or should have tho't would have been proper for me to ask.—

It is cheering to me, to find you so well pleased with the disposition & measures of Government. it confirms me in my belief, that the Secretarys Report will be adopted in its leading essential principles; & that Our national Affairs will, by it, assume a new, & more promising appearance. you are certainly right in your Idea, that the opposition thereto has not the support of the people. Their Voice, in this State, is very obviously in favour of the proposed System—so much so, that those who have laboured to create an opposition to it, are led to desist from any farther attempts, lest they should injure their own interest.— no great effect has been visible here from the report of Mr Dane & others, on the Subject of Amendments. it was not taken up in the Senate; but is now at rest in their files, to the no small mortification of the framers.— the rate of interest proposed in the report—the exploding all intention of discriminating between the different classes of the Creditors—& the assumption of the State Debts, & the adjustment of their Accounts with the Union, do all meet the public approbation. not a man, that I hear of, ventures openly to condemn either of these principles. the public mind seems to be unusually tranquil, & pleased with the appearance, & the intentions of the general Government. nothing will turn up, I hope, to disturb this placidity. Our State elections will take place without any contest, & will probably fall upon the same persons, in general, as the last year. if a change can be made in the Senate, without much of the electioneering Spirit being raised, it is to be desired. there were last year, in that branch, too many of the family of the *Honosti*; & the insurgent spirit was often too visible in a majority of Them.—[1] The fears of the Assembly were very much allayed, by an address from the now Atty general, in which he says he shall qualify himself to be the legal defender of the Sovereignty & independence of this State. with such a defence, they must have been very unreasonably afraid, not to go home with quiet minds.[2] it is a singular circumstance, that he & his brother are openly & avowedly pitted against each other, upon that point. James may please himself upon his being the official, constitutional Guardian of the weak, against the ambition & pride of the Mighty; & Jno. is not less vain of being viewed, as the great protector of the natural right of the great fishes to eat up the little Ones, whenever they can catch them.—

I am surprised to find so little apprehension, as to the new duties proposed upon Spirits &c, among the Importers. the high rates, with the novelty & the energy of the mode of collection, might naturally have excited a general alarm. But there seems to be a general disposition, to acquiesce in whatever may be necessary to the support of Government; & a belief, that no measures will be taken, bearing hard on the trade, without necessity. This surely is a favorable appearance. there are two points, which may possibly occasion a clamour, if care is not taken. Should the duties be drawn from the Importers, before They shall have received Them from the consumer, or retailer, by the sale of the Goods, uneasiness may arise. the monied capital of Our Traders is so small, that a compulsory advance of the duty to the Government, would embarrass their business, & create a very unfavorable impression. I have suggested to the Secretary this danger.—[3] the other is, obstruction to business, for want of a constant attention of the executive Officers. the checks proposed by the Secretary appear to be necessary to a due collection of the duties. they will at times inevitably retard business, in the supply to Country Traders; but detention, which can not be avoided without hazarding the Object, must be submitted to. an extension of the delay from the inattention of the Officers, may be very injurious, & will be considered as a hardship; But this will depend very much on the appointments, & a strict requisition that they attend their duty. after some attention to the Subject, I am of opinion, that the System proposed may be here executed without any difficulty, every accomadation being given to the trade, which the case will admit of.—

Important as the inspection of Our exports is to the trade, there is no chance of obtaining one under the laws of the State. that Business must undergo a thorough reform, & be put into the hands of a new & very different set of men, to answer any good purpose. while the appointments are made by the Towns, the legislature, or the Executive, there will be no responsibility, nor proper characters in office. there never was greater venality & corruption, than has appeared in this branch. the trade have not only been subjected to the expence of the fees; but they have sustained heavy losses by the most shameless prostitution of the Officers, & no man is sure of having, even the kind of Merchandize he wants, from the official evidence which attends the Article. Our inspections are not only an expence without a benefit, but They are a snare to the ignorant, & the stranger, & have proved a curse to the commerce of the State.—

The Commerce & the fisheries of this State do yet labour, & can not flourish as they ought, till We get entirely rid of the habits of dissipation & expence contracted during the War. their influence upon those two branches are yet severely felt, by those, who are engaged in them; but time & necessity will bring Us to use that industry & oeconomy, which is necessary to our thriving in any branch of Business. Those who built Vessels soon after the peace, whether for the fishery, or foreign Trade, have suffered more by the reduction in their value, than their earnings will pay; And in the old Towns, the unusual profits from the fishery; the four first years after the Peace, were consumed in expences, which They were formerly Strangers to. But those, who live upon Cape Cod, & along the south Shore, who retained their old habits of industry & frugality, applied their gains to increase their business. These have very much extended their fishery, & will continue to thrive; while the others are declining, & will not recover, but by a change of manners, & a reduction of their expences.—

The great increase of the British & french fisheries, has tended much to check the growth of Ours. the aggregate quantity of their fisheries & Ours, the two last years, has been more than a full supply for all the markets; & the prices have naturally been lower, than either They, or We can well afford to sell at. But their loss has been very great compared with Ours. They have sunk a large part of their capital, while We, with proper oeconomy, should have sunk only a part of Our usual profits. even the last year, the cod fishery on the South Shore was a living business; but in the old Towns, They took less fish, expanded much more, & had little or nothing left to support their families. There is a strong probability, that this business will, from the causes mentioned, be in a good degree transferred from the north to the south Shore. This may be, in a national View of no great importance; but the Towns of M: Head Glocester &c may be much distressed, before they recover those habits, which alone can make them to be flourishing & happy.— We have so many advantages in this business over the Europeans who pursue it; that I have no fears of our eventually losing it. the fisheries of france & britain are so depressed, by their late losses, that They will not this year be pursued to the same extent. This may give new courage, & more profit to Us in future; & the sufferings now complained of, may tend in their effects, to give us a more decided advantage in the business, than We before enjoyed.—

The complaints, as to the want of encouragement to extend Our navigation, arise principally from the same ill habits. was this business pursued with the same industry & frugality by Us, which the Europeans practice, no new advantages need be given, by Government, to enable us to be the Carriers of Our produce to market. the carrying business ought not, upon principles of policy, to be more than equal to a decent Support to those, who pursue it. all beyond this, must tend to check cultivation, or to load Our exports too much for the foreign markets.— I am very doubtful, whether any new advantages given to those branches, by bounties &c, would tend eventually to increase them; because, till Our expences of living & carrying on business, shall be reduced to the lowest practicable point, We can not derive the greatest possible advantage from them; & that reduction will not take place, but from necessity.

These Sentiments are not popular among mercantile Men; but they are, in my mind, well founded, & will in the end be promotive of the true interest of the Country.— I have ventured to give you these hasty Ideas, for your consideration, supposing that questions relative to those Subjects may be soon brought before you.—

With the highest respect & esteem I have the honour to subscribe myself your very hum[l] Servant Stephen Higginson

PS: you will excuse my not copying this letter, from a want of time

RC (Adams Papers).

[1] For Benjamin Austin Jr., who issued a series of polemics against the legal profession under the pseudonym Honestus, see vol. 18:398–399.

[2] James Sullivan's address has not been found, but it was likely his response to public concerns that his new position as Massachusetts attorney general might conflict with his ongoing duties as a private lawyer (William Thomas Davis, *History of the Judiciary of Massachusetts*, Boston, 1900, p. 101).

[3] Two months earlier, Alexander Hamilton had proposed a combination of higher duties on domestic and imported spirits as a way to raise revenue and curb smuggling. In order to draft his economic plan, Hamilton solicited advice from Higginson. The Newburyport merchant's vision of a well-regulated federal excise helped Hamilton to frame his 14 Jan. report (Hamilton, *Papers*, 5:466–508; 6:56, 102, 103).

To François Adriaan Van der Kemp

Sir New York March 27. 1790

Your favour of March 17. is rec[d.]— The French Revolution will, I hope produce Effects in favour of Liberty Equity and Humanity, as extensive as this whole Globe and as lasting as all time.— But I will candidly own that the Form of Government they have adopted, can, in my humble opinion, be nothing more than a transient Experiment. an obstinate Adhærence to it, must involve France in great and lasting Calamities.— With all your Compliments and Elogiums of my "Defence," would you believe that neither the whole nor any Part of it, has been translated into French.? at this interesting Period: at Such a Critical Moment; would you not have expected that every Light and Aid to the national Deliberations would have been eagerly embraced? But No. The Popular Leaders have Views that one assembly may favour but three Branches would Obstruct. Such is the Lot of Humanity. A Demagogue may hope to overawe a Majority in a Single elective Assembly: but may despair at overawing a Majority of independent hereditary senators, especially if they can be reinforced in Case of Necessity by an independent Executive.

our Experience in America corresponds with that of all Ages and nations.— if you Substitute Langdon and Sullivan, Hancock and Bowdoin, Clinton and Yeates; instead of Cherchi and Donati; Neri and Bianchi Buondelmenti and Uberti Ricci and Albizi Medici and Albizi, Tolomei and Salembeni, Gieremei and Lambertacci: Cancellieri and Panchiatichi Pallavicini and Dovara— the History of New Hampshire Massachusetts & New York will be the History of Florence siena Bolagna and Pistoia. The last year, a Writer in Boston under the signature of Laco, attacked the Governor Mr Hancock in a Course of Newspapers. other Writers in other Gazettes defended him. This Paper War, wrought up the Passions of the contending Parties to an high Pitch. The Mob most friendly to the Governor made an Effigy of Laco and burnt it on the Common. They threatened too to tar and feather the Printer.[1] a Trifle you see, any Accident might have blown up these Coals to a Flame and produced broken Heads. if a Life had been lost, the Sedition would not have been easily appeased. A fermentation, Somewhat like this happened here last Spring and indeed happens in all the States at every Election of Governor. The Tendency of this to civil War is rapid.— in the National Election the last year, there was a very Subtle but a very daring Intrigue, in the Election of the Vice President. Letters were written to the southern States, representing that the Northern states would not Vote for Washington, and to the Northern States representing that Virginia, south Carolina &c would not vote for Washington; so that it was represented that Adams was likely to have an Unanimous Vote and Washington not. the Effect was that Adams had not even a Majority, for fear of his having Unanimity. The Tendency of these Things to Confusion is obvious. The Elections of Senators to Congress last year, was still more a Party Business in most of the States as their Records shew.— You desire me to shew a Remedy for these Evils and how a Change can be introduced.— I confess, Sir I can think of no Remedy, but another *Convention*.— When Bribery, Corruption, Intrigue, Manœuvre, Violence, Force, Shall render Elections too troublesome and too dangerous, another Convention must be called, who may prolong the Period of senators from six Years to twelve or twenty or thirty or forty or for Life, or if necessary propose the Establishment of hereditary Senators. how can this be done. you will ask. I answer by giving the States, a Number of Senators, in Proportion to their Importance and by letting each State choose its Senators. You will ask again how can this be done? I answer by calling a Convention to elect them. or Authorize the President to appoint them. e.g.— Let the People of New York choose a Convention and that Convention elect their Number of Senators, or Authorize the President to appoint them to hold their Places for Life descendible to their Eldest Male Heirs. in some such Way as this I conceive it may be done without Bloodshed. and if the Election of President Should become terrible, I can conceive of no other method to preserve Liberty: but to have a national Convention called for the express purpose of electing an hereditary President. These appear to me to be the only Hopes of our Posterity. While Washington lives Elections may answer. They may answer while a Dozen or two of other Characters are living.

Representatives are elected not only for short Periods but for small Districts and therefore do not interest and enflame the Passions of an whole Nation, like the Election of a national first Magistrate, or national senators. There is not therefore any danger to be apprehended from that quarter

I am sir yours John Adams

RC (PHi:Francis Adrian Van der Kemp Coll.); internal address: "Mr Fr. Adr. Vanderkemp / Kingston. New York." LbC (Adams Papers); APM Reel 115.

[1] Writing under the pseudonym Laco, Stephen Higginson issued several essays in the *Massachusetts Centinel* criticizing John Hancock, which were collected and published as *The Writings of Laco, as Published in the Massachusetts Centinel, in the Months of February and March, 1789*, Boston, 1789 (*AFC*, 8:337). For JA's previous alignment of medieval oligarchies and modern politicians, see his letter to Benjamin Rush of 19 June 1789, and note 1, above.

From Thomas Brand Hollis

Dear Sir London March 29. 1790.

I ought to have acknowledged the receipt of your favour[1] before this but indeed it is not easy to get letters conveyd to you. if by private hands they often miscarry & the publick conveyance I do not much like.— The National assembly have regulated the post only one sou for a sheet of paper by this means intellects are not taxed & the produce not applied to support pride & Luxury but a free communication of sentiments is encouraged & the citizens & their representatives correspond at no expence not fearing to have too much light.[2] may America enjoy the same advantages & preserve every means of communication of knowledge free & open & the Tyrants plea necessity never prevail with them to tax or licence any instrument or means of knowledge; paper pens wax ink or Types & it is the more incumbent on them when they recollect what they owe, to publick schools & Universal reading, emancipation from Tyranny.

your favor came by Captain Bernard who conveyed three Boxes of Books to Boston tho I have never heard from President Willard of the receipt.[3] therefore imagine his letter has miscarried which should be sorry for as it delays other matters intended for Boston. The Martyr of humanity we have lost in the plains of Chersome Howard! I sent his Books of Lazzarettos. & the D of Tuscanys code of criminal Law to induce some state in America to execute one or more of those plans which having been considerd half the trouble & expence of an ignorant builder is avoided.[4] & this to be done before any publick calamity of that kind affects them to which from the shameful permitted depredations of the Africans Pyrates & from your extended coast you are most liable to.

what a Supernatural event has taken place in Europe? your manly exertions, resistance to Despotism & glorious insurrection have occasioned & brought into execution this glorious emancipation of the world, for I cannot limit or contract its bounds, as it is now spreading through all quarters of the globe— we hear & have hopes of mexico but all intelligence is prevented as much as possible from Spain regarding that quarter— we expect confirmation from the west or Jamaica. Truth is abroad & cannot now be long concealed.

could imagination have conceived such a regeneration The hand of providence seems to direct the whole but a few months since & the French nation had no Idea that the welfare & happiness of 30 millions of people were of more consequence & importance in the scale of beings than the Pride & Luxury of one man & that man a Tyrant but thanks to heaven this truth is now universally acknowledged & maintained by every Frenchman & from equal representation results equal Laws, civil & religious liberty & where each directs the Sword he wears an equal participation of the blessings of life evincing the unbounded goodness of the author of nature leading the generations of men to scenes of perpetual improvement & of endless being. The assembly have laid open the India company &c but all their glorious acts must be known to you—but the subject runs away with me & I am lost in expectation of the immense good which will follow.[5]

we have been engaged in endeavouring to repeal the test laws but the church has taken the Alarm & the minister rejoicing has joined the clergy & we have been defeated however the subject never was so well discussed or understood[6] & will come with more force sometime hence—but the church does not know its own interest— every day the Aristocratical spirit shows its self & instead of profiting by the French government we are to be more strict & not relinquish or alter any the smallest matter least innovation should ensue from which we & you owe every thing.

I have inclosed some tracts of the times which will inform you of what is going forward here. Foxs speech was excellent—but the question became a matter of party & treated accordingly.[7]

my best respects to Mrs Adams whom I remember with affection & should be gratified with a line from her— I have inscribed one Pamphlet for her as I know her principles.[8] Farewell & remember him who esteems you sincerely & is yours. T Brand Hollis.

I must think the French always had the end in view resentment & rage has had but a small part in their revolution for upon the most candid account [not] 400 persons have lost their lives & some of them notorious aggressors & others by accident the revence was against the enormous oppression of the feudal tenures—& how small a loss to the general good acquired & which will last having knowledge & truth for its basis.

The English will be the last to reform! the French refugees are acting the same part, but more diligent that the Americans did during the contest.

RC (Adams Papers); endorsed: "Mr T. B Hollis. 29 March / ans^d.^ 11 June 1790."

[1] Of 28 Oct. 1789, above.

[2] To amplify the spread of revolutionary ideas, the French National Assembly regulated the postal system in 1790 by lowering the cost of receiving mail and by decreeing that all correspondence was confidential (Martyn Lyons, *Reading Culture and Writing Practices in Nineteenth-Century France*, Toronto, 2008, p. 172–173).

[3] For the books that Hollis sent to Joseph Willard for the Harvard College library, see Hollis' letter of 6 June 1789, and note 7, above. JA and Hollis often sent letters via Capt. Tristram Barnard of the *Mary* (*AFC*, 9:323).

[4] British prison reformer John Howard died on 20 Jan. 1790 in Kherson, Ukraine (vol. 18:95; *DNB*).

[5] Just a few days after Hollis wrote this letter, the National Assembly abolished the French East India Company's long monopoly in favor of free trade (Morris, *Papers*, 9:339).

[6] Here, Hollis wrote "understood or discussed," then numbered the words to identify his intended order.

[7] Between March 1787 and March 1790, the British Parliament debated three motions to repeal the Test and Corporation Acts, in an effort to broaden civil liberties to dissenters. Whig statesman Charles James Fox led the third attempt, which was defeated owing to opposition from William Pitt and Edmund Burke. Hollis likely enclosed a copy of the two speeches that Fox gave on 2 March to the House of Commons, which were widely praised despite the motion's loss (G. M. Ditchfield, "The Parliamentary Struggle over the Repeal of the Test and Corporation Acts, 1787–1790," *English Historical Review*, 89:551, 561, 567–569 [July 1974]).

[8] The pamphlet has not been identified, but AA replied to Hollis on 6 Sept., describing Richmond Hill and sharing family news. She summed up the political scene, observing: "That peace is in our borders, and plenty in our dwellings; and we earnestly pray that the kindling flames of war, which appear to be bursting out in Europe, may by no means be extended to this rising nation" (*AFC*, 9:99–101).

From John Trumbull

Dear Sir Hartford March 30th. 1790.

You may easily conceive how much I was pleased, & flattered by your very friendly & confidential letter of the 6th instant.[1]

At the beginning of the war, he who could advance principles the most agreable to popular pride, & the most destructive to all energetic government, was the best Whig & the greatest Patriot. Many of these, who rose into high rank at that time, were not superior as Politicians to the Levellers & King Jesus-men in the times of Cromwell.[2] As we have improved in the science of Government, they have lost their popularity. You have named several of them in your letter, not one of whom has escaped the lash of our political Satirists, & lost his influence with the intelligent part of the community by adherence to his original principles of Democracy.

I agree that the strongest *Envy* against You lies in the Breasts of the two Men You mentioned, who could not bear your elevation above them— Each of them probably flattered his own vanity with an expectation of the Rank of V. P.—Hancock particularly, after his grand manoeuvre of limping forth,

> "With all his imperfections on his heels,"[3]

to propose nonsensical amendments to the Convention of Massachusetts, supposed himself almost sure of the appointment—not knowing that the whole affair was planned & conducted as a political measure by men of more discernment than himself. These two Gentlemen have undoubtedly exerted all their influence to render You unpopular, & to some of their dependants, I am told You are indebted for an attack in metre, intended for a Satire, published some time since at the Southward— But their influence is so diminished, that they have been wholly unsuccessful in the New England States, beyond the circle of their immediate connections—

The real opposition is more to your principles, than your Person— & this prevails most in the Southern States. The People in the Southern States are half an age behind us in the knowlege of Policy & the true principles of Government— Aristocratical in their habits & feelings, they are absurdly advocates for a pure Democracy— They must certainly in time become more enlightened, and I hope, especially that the *Antient* Dominion may improve as She grows *older*.

The clamour about your Birth, as it has no foundation, has never made any impression in New England—but You are a Witness how frequently it has been echoed in the Southern Papers.

I believe You may thank New England for the penurious grant of your Salary— But I have no reason to believe that any personal insult was intended— High Salaries are always a subject of popular clamour in New England— The Votes of our Senators & Delegates on that question were calculated on motives of Self interest, to preserve their own popularity— And after all, the uneasiness on account of the *high Salaries* & wages granted at the last session was very general among us, & the clamour exceedingly loud, till it was quashed at once by the President's Tour thro' New England, & absorbed in the bombastic enthusiasm of our public addresses.

I doubt with You, whether any Man but Washington could at present support the Constitution— But were he dead, I am sure none who has been thought of as your Rival, could support it while You were living & neglected. Jefferson is little known at the Northward, & it would be impossible to persuade our Great Men in New England that he is greater or wiser than themselves. We have an high opinion of Maddison's abilities, tho' it has lately been lessened by his advocating an impossible scheme of discrimation among the public Creditors—[4] To suppose he did not perceive this impossibility would detract from our esteem of his talents— If he did perceive it, we can only ascribe his conduct to the desire of increasing his popularity in his own State, or to motives of envy against the Secretary— But we have never thought of him for V. P.—

Mr. Jay is the only Man, who possesses in any considerable degree the general confidence of the Northern States, or is talked of among us as qualified for that Office— But no Party could be formed against You in his favour among us.

There is no uneasiness to the danger or even to the unpopularity of the Government from your continuance in Office, but there would arise the greatest confusion from your resignation, which for that reason, I am sure You cannot seriously think of.

April 17th. 1790—

Thus far I had written when I had the honour to receive Yours of the 2d instant—and having been obliged to attend a fortnight's session of our Court, & severely handled at the same time by a second turn of the Influenza, which is now universal in Hartford, I have had no leisure for an earlier answer.[5]

My Mother was Grandaughter to the Revd. Solomon Stoddard of Northhampton, Brother to the Col. Stoddard You mention. That family seem not to have preserved their former importance; nor to equal in present respectability my Paternal connections, who first rose to public consequence within about forty Years.

I believe there was some inaccuracy in the expressions I used relative to the affair of the Treaty of Peace. You ask me if I know the History of that negociation— I can only inform You how it has been stated by Report—That the negociations were ready to be opened before your arrival at Paris from the Hague—That the French Court were opposed to every measure, which could tend to the strength, or aggrandizement of the States, & wished to hold us dependent on themselves—That Franklyn was disposed to give way to their demands—& that Mr. Jay was under the greatest embarassment—That on your arrival the scene changed—That You ventured on a separate negociation with the English Ambassador, & procured Terms, which the French Court were obliged to ratify much against their wills—That the whole merit of this negociation must be ascribed to Yourself & Mr. Jay—That notwithstanding your success some Members in Congress clamoured, that You had gone beyond, or contrary to, your Instructions, taken too bold a step, risqued the displeasure of the French Court &c.—

I fancy by your hints the general outlines of this story are not far out of the way— I hope You will complete the history of your foreign negotiations, which must throw the greatest light on the Account of the American Revolution.

The King of Prussia, by your extract, seems perfectly acquainted with the character of French Politics—& perhaps of the Politics of all Courts, who have any—

The Ballance, as adjusted by Congress, between the Legislative & Executive Powers cannot be given up without eventual ruin to the Government. Without the power of Removal, the President is in fact a Cypher— Washington perhaps during his Day might support himself by his personal influence— But a future President must preserve his importance, only by courting the Legislature, & caballing in the Senate or house of Representatives.

As to the advantages to be derived from some appearance of Splendor in the American Court, it is undoubtedly true, that a Medium must be observed— A parsimonious economy, & democratic plainness is as much to be avoided, as the affectation of pageantry & magnificence. Perhaps we have begun rather below the true medium; but should the Government be supported for a few years, & increase in credit & resources, a sufficient degree of pomp & splendor would naturally be introduced. I conceive there is little danger on this point, & would only observe that it is often better policy to reduce things silently & gradually to their proper situation, especially when they tend towards it by their natural bias, than to give any alarm to the prejudices of mankind by telling them openly what measures may be eventually necessary. To give an instance by way of explanation— Had your real Sentiments, principles & designs relative to the contest with Great Britain in the year 1774, been known throughout America, they would at that period have occasioned an universal alarm. When I returned to Connecticut in that year, it might have been naturally expected, that I should endeavour to show my own consequence by retailing the doctrines & opinions, I had learned in your political school. But I perceived at once that the world were not ripe for the subject, & I durst not lisp a syllable about *War* or *Independence*, though I knew You had not the least expectation of a favorable issue of the Contest on any other terms. When questioned a thousand times on the subject, I was obliged to return evasive answers, & make my acquaintance believe that the Patriots in Boston had entire faith & credit in the efficacy of Petitions & Non-importation agreements.

That Mankind are easily imposed on by show & appearance is undoubtedly true, & it may be necessary to government to take advantage of that weakness—but it may not be politic to tell the People that they ought to be imposed upon, & that we assume that appearance for the purpose of Imposition. A Conjurer or Juggler must not explain how he performs his tricks—& to his art, the science of politics is often too nearly allied.

The Remarks of Rousseau undoubtedly have force—but would not an Advocate for Democracy observe that by his own stating, his language of signs, & his splendor of robes &c have been employed in all ages as the supports of despotism, & that he is peculiarly unfortunate in his modern examples of the Pope & the Doge of Venice—[6]

I can witness from my own knowlege of the history of your life, that You have not done yourself more than Justice in the account of your exertions, services & sufferings in the public cause— Nor do I believe those services so much forgotten or disregarded as You seem to suppose— That no strong enthusiasm has prevailed in your favor is easily accounted for— An able Negotiator may do infinitely more service to his country, than a General, who fights one successful battle—but he will not be equally the object of the enthusiasm of momentary praise— To raise the enthusiasm of the People, our services must not only be useful, but brilliant—nay 'tis sufficient if they are brilliant, whether importantly useful or not. As a Writer, You never flattered the passions, or adopted the false opinions of the multitude, but have exerted your pen to oppose both. Such a writer as Payne, scribbling to the passions & feelings of the moment, will for that moment be much more applauded, but must content himself with a temporary & decaying reputation— His *Common Sense* cannot now be read without contempt & disgust.

He who serves the public honestly & faithfully must often serve them against their wills— He must often oppose them, because they will often be wrong—and he must expect the attacks of Envy & at times a general combination to depreciate his merit— From this Washington has not been exempt— A Party both in Congress & the Army at one period almost succeeded in an attempt to deprive him of his Commission, on the pretence of his deficiency in military skill. In the choice of V.P. You had certainly no rival— All that could be done by your enemies was to deprive you of a number of votes. Many of your Friends were duped on that occasion— I will inform You how it was managed in Connecticut. On the day before the Election, Col. Webb[7] came on express to Hartford, sent as he said by Col. Hamilton &c, who he assured us had made an exact calculation on the subject, & found that New Jersey were to throw away three Votes,

I think, and Connecticut two, & all would be well— I exclaimed against the measure, and insisted that it was all a deception, but what could my single opinion avail against an express, armed with intelligence & calculations— So our Electors threw away two votes, where they were sure they would do no harm.

By the way is our Secretary H. a great Politician, or only a theoretical genius— He has great abilities besure— But I doubt his knowlege of mankind— I have never spoken my sentiments on his report—but I really fear some parts of his plan are too complicated—& perhaps at this period impolitic as well as impracticable—

I am exceedingly anxious for the present situation of the Public— Many things are indeed wrong—and I believe we must suffer many more evils, before our eyes will be opened to apply the proper remedy— Yet if matters should not be precipitated, all will at last come right. This is no time to desert the public— Your exertions were never more wanted. I shall be happy in knowing your opinions on the subjects You mention. I never had any other Master in Politics but Yourself, & am too old to begin in a new school.

I have the honor to be with the greatest Respect / Your most Obed[t.] Serv[t.]

John Trumbull

RC (Adams Papers); internal address: "The Vice President."; endorsed: "M[r] Trumbul. Ans[d.] Ap. 25. / 1790."

[1] An inadvertence. Here and below, Trumbull was replying to JA's letter of 12 March, above.

[2] As prominent participants in the English Civil War, the Levellers constituted a political movement that advocated popular sovereignty, greater suffrage, and religious toleration. At first they backed Oliver Cromwell's rise, but they broke with him over questions of parliamentary power. The "King Jesus-Men" were the Fifth Monarchists, a millenarian sect that flourished in the 1650s and based its doctrine on overthrowing all regimes in preparation for the return of Jesus Christ (*Cambridge Modern Hist.*, 4:345; Bernard S. Capp, *The Fifth Monarchy Men: A Study in Seventeenth-Century English Millenarianism*, London, 1972, p. 207–208).

[3] Trumbull slightly misquoted Shakespeare, *Hamlet*, Act 1, scene v, lines 78–79.

[4] For James Madison's opposition to Alexander Hamilton's economic plan, see Stephen Higginson's letter of 1 March 1790, and note 2, above.

[5] Influenza struck the northeastern states between the fall of 1789 and the spring of 1790 (*AFC*, 9:55).

[6] Trumbull referred to Jean Jacques Rousseau, *Émile; ou, De l'éducation*, Book IV, Amsterdam, 1762.

[7] New York City merchant Samuel Blachley Webb (1753–1807), of Wethersfield, Conn., served as an aide-de-camp to George Washington during the Revolutionary War (Washington, *Papers, Presidential Series*, 3:276).

To Thomas Crafts Jr.

Dear Sir April 4th, 90

Your favor of the 31st of January I received in its season. I have at two or three several times had conversation with General Knox upon the subject of Mr Martin Brimmer Sohier; and have the General's promise to give particular attention to Mr Sohier's merit and pretensions. As the Secretary at War appeared to be well acquainted with the candidate, and to have the best disposition to serve him I doubt not you will be satisfied with his decission.[1] How is commerce and business in general at this time in Boston? Is it more or less brisk than it was a year ago? Is any benign influence felt from the new government or not? Are the Shipwrights employed? What is the price of bills?[2] Here exchange is altered twenty per Cent as some say and fifteen as others state it, in favour of the Country in twelve months.

J Adams

LbC in CA's hand (Adams Papers); internal address: "Thomas Crafts Esqr Boston."; APM Reel 115.

[1] On 31 Jan. longtime family friend Col. Thomas Crafts Jr. wrote to JA (Adams Papers), soliciting a military post for Martin Brimmer Sohier (1760–1792), who had served in the Continental Army. George Washington nominated Sohier as an ensign on 3 March 1791 (Richard M. Lytle, *The Soldiers of America's First Army, 1791*, Lanham, Md., 2004, p. 236, 237).

[2] Crafts replied to JA's queries on 17 May 1790, below. According to the 1790 port returns from Boston, a total of 1,655 ships entered, yielding $21,027 in tonnage duties between 1 Oct. 1790 and 30 Sept. 1791, in addition to a net sum of $320,430 collected on goods and merchandise. The *Columbia Rediviva*'s successful circumnavigation of the globe, completed in 1790, reinforced Boston's status in maritime trade, for which see vol. 19:xiii. Between 1 Oct. and 30 Sept. 1791, Massachusetts ports had collected $420,707 in duties, comprising one-seventh of the nation's entire collection revenue (Hamilton Andrews Hill, *The Trade and Commerce of Boston, 1630 to 1890*, Boston, 1895, p. 87–88, 90).

To Benjamin Rush

Dear sir New York April 4. 1790

The Tories as you observe in your friendly Letter of 24 Feb. are more attached to each other; they are also, We must candidly confess, more of real Politicians.— They make to themselves more merit with the People, for the smallest services, than the Whigs are able to do for the greatest. The Arts, the Trumpetts the Puffs, are their old Instruments and they know how to employ them. The History of our Revolution will be one continued Lye from one End to the other.

The Essence of the whole will be *that Dr Franklins electrical Rod, Smote the Earth and out Sprung General Washington. That Franklin electrifed him with his Rod—and thence forward these two conducted all the Policy Negotiations Legislation and War.*[1] These underscored Lines contain the whole Fable Plot and Catastrophy. if this Letter should be preserved, and read an hundred Years hence the Reader will Say "the Envy of this J. A. could not bear to think of the Truth"! ["]He ventured to Scribble to Rush, as envious as himself, Blasphemy that he dared not Speak, when he lived. But Barkers at the sun and Moon are always Silly Curs." But this my Friend, to be serious, is the Fate of all Ages and Nations. And there is no Resource in human nature for a Cure. Brederode did more in the Duch Revolution than William 1st. Prince of orange.[2] Yet Brederode is forgotten and William the Saviour, Deliverer and Founder.— limited Monarchy is founded in Nature. No Nation can adore more than one Man at a time. it is an happy Circumstance that the Object of our Devotion is so well deserving of it. that he has Virtue so exquisite and Wisdom so consummate. There is no Citizen of America will Say, that there is in the World so fit a Man for the head of the Nation. from my Soul I think there is not. and the Question should not be who has done or suffered most, or who has been the most essential and Indispensible Cause of the Revolution, but who is best qualified to govern Us? Nations are not to Sacrifice their Future Happiness to Ideas of Historical Justice. They must consult their Own Weaknesses, Prejudices, Passions, Senses and Imaginations as well as their Reason. "La Raison n'a jamais fait grande chose." as the K. of Prussia says in his Histoire de mon tems.[3]

The more Extracts you Send me from your Journals, the more will you oblige me— I beg especially a Copy of my Character. I know very well it must be a partial Panegyrick.— I will send You my Criticisms upon it. You know I have no affectation of Modesty.— My Comfort is that such vain folks as Cicero, Neckar Sir William Temple & I are never dangerous.[4]

If I Said in 1777 that ["]We Should never be qualified for Republican Governments till We were ambitious to be poor" I meant to express an Impossibility.— I meant then and now Say that No Nation under Heaven ever was, now is, or ever will be qualified for a *Republican Government*, unless you mean by these Words, *equal Laws* resulting from a Ballance of three Powers the Monarchical Aristocratical & Democratical. I meant more and I now repeat more explicitly, that Americans are peculiarly unfit for any Republic but the Aristo-Democratical-Monarchy; because they are more *Avaricious* than any other Nation that ever existed the Carthaginians and Dutch not excepted. The Alieni Appetens Sui profusus[5] reigns in this nation as a Body more than any other I have ever Seen.

When I went to Europe in 1778 I was full of patriotic Projects like yours of collecting Improvements in Arts Agriculture, Manufacture Commerce Litterature & science. But I Soon found my Error.— I found that my offices demanded every moment of my time and the Assistance of two or three Clerks—and that all this was not enough. I was obliged to make it a Rule never to go out of my ROAD for any Curiosity of any kind. J. J. Rousseau understood it very well when he Said that Ambassadors *"doivent tout leur tems á cet Objet Unique, ils sont trop honnêtes gens pour voler leur Argent.*["] *Emile Tom. 4. p. 361.*[6] if he meant this as a Sarcasm, he was in the Wrong. I never knew one who attempted or affected Philosophy, that was good for any Thing in the Diplomatique Line—and I know that every Hour that I might have employed that Way would have been a Robbery upon the Duties of my Public Character.

Your Family pictures are charming; and the tender Piety you express for your Mother, is felt by me in all its force, as I have a Mother living in her Eighty Second Year, to whom I owe more than I can ever pay. This Mother and a Father who died 30 Years ago, two of the best People I ever knew formed the Character, which You have drawn. alass! that it is no better! I Said before that Vanity is not dangerous. a Man who has bad designs is seldom or never vain. it is such modest Rascals as Cæsar, who play tricks with Mankind. read his Commentaries—what consummate caution to conceal his Vanity! contemptu famæ, fama augebatur.[7] This Tyrants and Villains always know.

Adieu Mon Ami, John Adams

Pray can you recollect a Feast at Point no Point in the Fall of 1775 and the Company that returned with You and me in a Boat and our Conversation. I want a List of the Names of that Party who returned in the same Boat with Us to Philadelphia.

RC (ICN:Herbert R. Strauss Coll.); internal address: "Dr Rush." LbC (Adams Papers); APM Reel 115.

[1] For JA's reflections on Benjamin Franklin's legacy, see his "Dialogues of the Dead" of [*ca.* 22 *April*], below. See also Descriptive List of Illustrations, No. 4, above.

[2] Dutch statesman and military leader Hendrik van Brederode (1531–1568) petitioned for greater toleration of Protestants and raised troops to aid William I, Prince of Orange, in preparation for the Eighty Years' War of 1568–1648, the revolt of the Netherlands against

4. "BENJAMIN FRANKLIN DRAWING ELECTRICITY FROM THE SKY," BY BENJAMIN WEST, CA. 1816

See page xiii

Spanish rule (Biografisch Portaal van Nederland).

[3] Often attributed to Frederick II, this was one of Rush's favorite maxims, although it did not appear in the king of Prussia's *Oeuvres Posthumes*, Berlin, 1788: Reason has never done much (Rush, *Letters*, 1:547).

[4] JA esteemed the diplomatic work of Sir William Temple (1628–1699), the English statesman who concluded the Triple Alliance of 1668 among Great Britain, the Netherlands, and Sweden (vols. 4:336; 12:245).

[5] Greedy for another's possessions; extravagant with one's own.

[6] JA quoted from Jean Jacques Rousseau's *Émile; ou, De l'éducation*, Amsterdam, 1762, a copy of which is in JA's library at MB. Rousseau observed that ambassadors "spend all their time on this sole purpose, as they are too honest not to earn their pay" (*Catalogue of JA's Library*).

[7] To act contemptuously of fame is to increase it.

To James Lovell

Dear Sir — New York April 5th: 90

I am much obliged by your favor of March 20th and very apprehensive that this is not the only letter of yours unanswered. To leave your letters unanswered is in me very bad œconomy. The General is arrived here; but has as yet said nothing to me of his business.[1] Doctor Craigie shall have all the aid in my power to give him, in his pursuit of justice in your affair: but I do not at present see how I can assist him: perhaps he may point out a path.

This day the question of the assumption of the State debts is to be put in the house; the majority will not be large.—

Pray how has the new government opperated upon commerce in Boston? Has it answered the expectations of the wise? Does it gain strength? or weakness? How is trade and shipbuilding & &

John Adams

LbC in CA's hand (Adams Papers); internal address: "Hon James Lovel Esqr / Boston"; APM Reel 115.

[1] For James Warren's compensation request, see Lovell's letter of 20 March, and note 1, above.

From John Quincy Adams

Dear Sir. — Newbury-Port. April 5th: 1790.

I have more than once mentioned to you, the state of retirement from political conversation in which I live, and the restraints which I am endeavouring to lay upon a disposition inclining perhaps with too much ardor, to feel interested in public occurrences. But it sometimes happens that I am accidentally witness to conversations upon these subjects; from which I collect some trifling information, that I imagine might at least not be unentertaining to you. In general I have supposed that your other correspondents in this quarter would anticipate me and that I should only employ your time in reading a relation of occurrences, which would not even have with you the merit of novelty. But from some late Letters I have been led (though perhaps erroneously) to imagine your correspondents here have not been so punctual in their communications, as they have been formerly, and I have supposed I might mention some circumstances which though generally known here might not be public; at New-York.—[1] It appears to me that the hostile character of our general and particular governments each against the other is increasing with accelerated rapidity; The Spirit which at the time when the constitution was adopted, it was contended would always subsist, of balancing one of these governments by the other has I think almost totally disappeared already; and the seeds of two contending factions appear to be plentifully sown. The names of federalist and antifederalist, are no longer expressive of the Sentiments which they were so lately supposed to contain; and I expect soon to hear a couple of new names, which will designate the respective friends of the National and particular Systems. The People are very evidently dividing into these two parties. What the event will be, I hardly allow myself to conjecture,

> "but my soul akes,
> To know when two authorities are up,
> Neither supreme, how soon confusion
> May enter twixt the gap of both, and take
> The one by the other."[2]

In point of measures, the Government of the United States has undoubtedly greatly the *advantage*. But while they are strengthening their hands by assuming the debts, and by making provision for the support of the public credit, the partizans of our State government are continually upon the rack of exertion, to contrive every paltry expedient to maintain their importance, and to check the operations of the Government, which they behold with terror. As they can only clamour upon subjects of importance; their active efforts are used, in appointing a premature fast, or in opposing the cession of a light-house.— In the last Session of our general Court the light-houses in this Commonwealth were not ceded to Congress. And the keeper of that at the entrance of Boston Harbour has been forbidden upon his peril to receive any directions or pay from the federal officers.[3] But the imbecillity of our Government renders all these exertions the more ridiculous: for while they endeavour to prevent the assumption of their debt, they cannot even provide for the payment of the interest upon it. And they have never yet paid for two light-houses at the entrance of this harbour, although they are so solicitous to retain them.

The History of the additional amendments to the Constitution proposed by a joint-committee of our two houses, affords further evidence of the petty arts which are used by the enemies to the national union to turn the tide of popular opinion against the national Government.[4] Mr: Austin who as I have been informed had the principal agency in that affair, never expected, that any amendments would be seriously proposed to Congress by our Legislature; and there is an internal evidence in the report of the Committee, that it was intended for a declamation to the people rather than for amendments to the Constitution. They are not even pretended to be amendments but after the long common-place rhapsody, upon the dangerous tendency of the government, when we come to the *articles*, we find them pretended to be nothing but *principles* for amendments.— The Committee consisted of seven members; of whom only four were present when this report was agreed upon. Mr: Dane who drew it up was one of the absent, and it is said, afterwards declared that he should have objected to the two last articles, (perhaps the most important of the whole number) though he drafted them himself. The two other absent members utterly disclaimed the report; and the chairman, who did not vote, was equally opposed to it. Three members only agreed upon the point; and when they produced the paper in the Senate; they obtained a vote to have a certain number of copies printed. It was then dismissed without being suffered to undergo the test of an examination, and Mr: Austin I am told, made no scruple to acknowledge that he had answered his purpose.

Yet, even when opportunities are presented, where the importance of our own Government might be really increased; some other little selfish interested principle steps in, and produces measures calculated to bring it into contempt. The appointment of N. Cushing upon the bench of our Supreme Court, has certainly not tended to increase the confidence of the people in that important branch of the government: the appointment was very unpopular; and what perhaps in a political view rendered the measure the more injudicious, is that it is not his integrity but his abilities that are called in question. But personal animosity against the characters who would have added dignity to that Station, the apprehension of giving offence to the late chief Justice, who it is said recommended his cousin too strongly, and the pleasure of removing a troublesome councillor, concurring together were too powerful even for *antifederal* principles, and produced we are told a nomination, which could be accounted for upon no other motives.— The only liberal and generous measure by which they have pursued their System has been the raising the Salaries of our Judges and I fear they would not have succeeded even in that, had not the personal interest of certain influential men, of very different principles been engaged, and assisted to promote it.— It is melancholy to observe how much even in this free Country the course of public events depends upon the private interests and Passions of individuals.

But the popularity of the general Government is, and for some time to come must continue to be disadvantageously affected, by those very exertions to support the public credit, which must eventually strengthen it so effectually. It must suffer however chiefly in the Sea-ports and among the merchants who find their interests affected by the operation of the revenue Laws. In this town and Still more in Salem there have lately been considerable clamours raised by men who have been the firmest friends to the constitution; and there is now I presume before Congress a petition from the merchants in this town, praying relief from an evil, which has excited great complaints, but which will probably be remedied without difficulty.[5]

Those people among us who are perpetually upon the search, for causes of complaint against the government, are cavilling at the dilatory manner with which the Congress proceed in their business.— The decision upon the subject of discrimination, has met with general approbation in the circles of company where I have heard it mentioned; and from the complexion of our news-papers, I have concluded that the public opinion of which so much was said in the debates, is here much in favour of the measure. I do not think indeed that the public opinion can always be collected from news-papers; but they are never silent upon unpopular topics of so great importance— Mr: Madison's reputation has suffered from his conduct in that affair; and Judge Dana is the only man I have known whose character gives weight to his opinions, that has adopted those of Mr: Madison.

The report of the Secretary of the Treasury, has in general met with great approbation. I have heard it almost universally spoken of with great applause. Yet I am almost ashamed to acknowledge, that I know not how justly it is admired, as I have never read it. This neglect has rather been owing to ~~my~~ accident than to inclination, for little as I attend to the public prints I should certainly have noticed a publication of so important a nature had I been in the way of seeing the Gazette of the United States which contains it.— I am equally ignorant of the System for the establishment of the militia; which is as much disliked as the treasurer's report is esteemed; the most favourable judgment that I have heard passed upon it was, that however excellent it might be, it would never be submitted to by the people.—[6]

I know not, but that I shall incur your censure, for departing even in this instance from the line which I have prescribed to myself, and losing the lawyer in the politician; and still more for the freedom with which I have express'd myself upon public men and measures: if I should on this occasion meet with your disapprobation, I shall without difficulty observe a more prudent silence upon these subjects in future. The opinions which I have heard express'd are no evidence of the general opinion even throughout the Commonwealth; but in some instances they have been the opinions of men whose influence is great and extensive.— But if the information contained in this Letter should compensate in your mind for its tediousness, I shall from time to time continue to give you a similar supply.

In the mean time I remain, your affectionate Son.

J. Q. Adams.

RC (Adams Papers); endorsed: "J. Q. Adams. Ap. 5 / 1790."

[1] In his most recent letters to JQA, JA provided advice on entering the legal profession and encouraged JQA to supply him with "Information on political Subjects . . . as it is given with that Freedom and Independence of Spirit, which I wish you always to preserve" (*AFC*, 9:14, 16, 36–37).

[2] Shakespeare, *Coriolanus*, Act III, scene i, lines 108–112.

[3] For the oversight of local lighthouses, see William Smith's letter of 12 June, and note 4, below.

[4] For the progress of the Bill of Rights, see James Sullivan's letter of 2 July 1789, and note 2, above. Prior to the ending of the Mass. General Court's session on 9 March 1790, a committee reported on the proposed amendments to the Constitution and recommended several major changes, such as refining senators' qualifications and powers; consulting the state legislatures when establishing a national military force; and reconsidering the imposition of a direct tax. Members adjourned without taking any action on the report (Denys P. Myers, *Massachusetts and the First Ten Amendments to the Constitution*, Washington, D.C., 1936, p. 13, 28, 29).

[5] Salem and Newburyport, Mass., merchants asked Congress for revised revenue legislation. Their petitions, which were referred to Alexander Hamilton on 9 Feb. and 9 April, respectively, spurred congressional momentum for the Funding Act of 4 Aug. (Hamilton, *Papers*, 13:175).

[6] Hamilton's first report on the public credit was partially printed in *The Gazette of the United States* from 16 to 27 January. Meanwhile, Gen. Henry Knox presented his plan for the reform of the national militia to the president on 18 January. George Washington forwarded it to Congress three days later. Knox divided and nationalized the existing

militia into three corps (advanced, main, and reserved) and suggested mandatory training for men eighteen to sixty years of age. While the federal government would organize and train the militia, the states would retain the power to appoint officers and award exemptions. Despite Knox's effort to frame military needs within constitutional limits, the proposal stirred public fears of a standing army and Congress balked at its high cost. Knox's plan of militia reform was tabled until 1792 (Washington, *Papers, Presidential Series*, 5:10–15, 24–25; Saul Cornell, *A Well-Regulated Militia: The Founding Fathers and the Origins of Gun Control in America*, Oxford, 2006, p. 66–67).

From Benjamin Rush

Dear Sir, Philadelphia April 13. 1790

Your last letter is a treasure.—[1] Every Sentence in it is full of instruction. I have often contemplated that passion in mankind to concentrate all their homage and Admiration in *One Man*, in all the revolutions which advance knowledge or happiness.— Cicero Observed it, and deplored it in the fame and power of Pompey. I have thought at last that I had discovered in this weakness in human nature, the high destiny of the Soul even in its ruins.— Does it not prove that it was created originally to concentre all its love and Adoration in One Supreme Being, and that all its Obligations are due to that Being only? Is it not the counter passion of the love of fame, which is only a misplaced desire after *immortal* life & happiness?— Are not all our follies & vices the counterfits of virtues? Are not the love of pleasure—of power—of wealth—of Activity—& of rest,—nothing but passions & propensities which have corresponding Objects held out to them by revelation, but which are at present under a false direction?— a belief that this is the case has Often afforded me great pleasure, for as I observe folly & vice to be universal, and as I believe the ~~Author~~ Creator of human Souls has in infinite wisdom made no *means* without an *end*,—and made nothing in vain, so I have derived, from contemplating the weak & corrupt passions—& desires that have been mentioned, a satisfactory Argument in favor of the tendency, and Ultimate termination of all human beings in complete and eternal happiness in every respect suited to their present tempers, but under a *new*, and *different* direction.—

Had the king of Prussia never said nor wrote another Sentence than the One you have quoted from him upon *human reason*, he would have deserved the high rank he holds among philosophers and kings.— Mr Bayle has expressed the same idea, but with much less force. "We are governed, says this great man by our prejudices, and not by our reason."—[2] What did Reason do, in the council or the field in the late American War? Were not most of ~~your~~ the wise measures of Congress the effects of passion—accident or necessity, & were not all the successful movements or engagements of our Army little else than lucky blunders? Most of the valuable discoveries in philosophy have been the effects of accident. This is eminently the case in medicine. We owe more to Quacks, who never *reason*, for useful & powerful Articles in the materia medica,[3] than to the learning of MDs:— I love to establish the truth of these prepositions, inasmuch as they lead to the beleif of a general & particular providence, *and* at the same time Show the weakness & folly of human nature. Man is indeed fallen! He discovers it every day in domestic in social, & in political life. Science—Civilization & goverment have in vain been employed to cure the defects of his nature. Christianity is alone equal to this business. Did its mild & gentle Spirit prevail in our country it would do more towards rendering our liberty perpetual, than the purest republic that my imagination, or the Strongest monarchy that yours, could devise. Let us not despair. The peaceable manner in which our Constitutions has been changed in the United States & in Pennsylvania make it probable than man is becoming a more rational creature in America than in Other parts of the World.—

I made no Note of the company or Conversation to which you allude in your letter, but as nearly as I can recollect, the company in the boat consisted of yourself—Owen Biddle—David Rittenhouse—Michl Helligas—Chas Humphries—and myself.[4] The most interesting Subject discussed was a proposal to write a letter to Lord North discovering to him (as a friend to Goverment) that there was a design among the rebels to burn some of the Arsenals in Great Britain, & to urge his Lordship to take measures to prevent it. This deception was to be practised only to shew the risk of engaging in a War with America, & that Great Britain at 3,000 Miles from her was not invulnerable. The proposition was made in a joke, but Mr Helligas was so much pleased with it, that he thought it merited Serious Attention.—

Now Attend to some more of your Speeches in the first years of the revolution.

Upon my asking Mr J: Adams what he thought of sending Mr. Dickinson to Europe as a Minister—he said—"Mr D: is the most unfit Man in the World to be sent Abroad.— He is such a friend to Monarchy, that he would prostrate himself at the feet of every throne he saw. I would prefer Dr Wetherspoon to him."—Octobr: 1776

When Genl Sullivan brought Lord Howe's proposition to Congress for a Conference, in Sepr 1776, Mr Adams said privately to me "that he wished the first ball that had been fired on the 27th of Augst: had gone thro' his head."[5] On the floor of Congress, he called the General "a decoy duck." The issue of the Conference shewed Mr A: to be right in his principles & predictions.— Upon perceiving a disposition in Congress to appoint a Committee to confer with Lord Howe, he said to me at his lodgings "that mankind were made for slavery, & that they must answer the end of their Creation sooner or later."—

I intended to have concluded this letter by transcribing your character from my Notebook—but upon reading it over, I find so many things said in favor of your principles & Conduct in the years 1775 & 1776, that I should ~~incur your disapprobation by sending~~ be suspected of flattery should I send you a copy of it. I shall give you a Specimen of the manner in which I have Observed in drawing characters by sending you that of your Colleague Robt: Treat Paine's—whose name follows yours in the note Book.—

"Robt Treat Paine— He was educated a Clergyman, and Afterwards became a lawyer. He was facetious in his manner both in public and in private. He had a certain Obliquity of Understanding which prevented his seeing things in the same light that they struck Other people. He opposed every thing, and hence he got the Name of the *Objection maker* in Congress. He was thought by his Colleagues to be cool to independance. He was a useful member of Congress, especially upon Committees where he was punctual & faithful."

In my notebook I have recorded a Conversation that passed between Mr Jefferson & myself on the 17t of March of which *you* were the principal Subject. We both deplored your Attachment to monarchy, & both agreed that you had changed your principles since the year 1776. The proofs of this change we derived from your letter to Mr Hooper which was Afterwards published in this city—upon a form of Government for north Carolina.—[6]

What say you to a visit to Philada. next Spring?— You have many friends in this city—as well as in the State. Do bring Mrs Adams along with you. After You have been feasted by our fashionable people, I will claim a family evening from you, & while Mrs Adams is engaged with Mrs Rush in enumerating the years in which they were both neglected by their husbands during the War, I will read extracts from my note book to you, & afterwards receive more materials for it from your conversation.

Take care what you say, or write to me. I wish I could whisper the same caution to some Other Gentlemen high in power & Office in New York.— Some of them will find themselves, (if they survive me) turned *inside outwards.*— I have never deceived my Country in a single instance,—nor shall I decive posterity. In my present retirement I daily hear of Acts & Speeches in New york which mark worse than British degrees of Corruption. My only consolation is, our people will not follow their rulers. They are as yet unprepared for sophisticated Goverment. There will be a change I beleive in the representation of several of the States next year. ~~It is nearly certain in Pennsylvania. This is *private* for~~ This is matter of opinion only for I am now only a Spectator of public measures, & shall probably be so indifferent as to a change in our State (if it should be proposed) as not to give a Vote at our next election.—

Adieu—yours sincerely Benjn Rush

PS: On the 20th of July 1776 I met Mr Adams in 4th Street near the Indian Queen, and received from him Congratulations on being appointed a Member of Congress. I spoke in high terms of one of my Colleagues, & said I beleived him to be an honest man. "That said Mr Adams is saying a great deal of a public Character, for political integrity is the rarest Virtue in the whole World." In a subsequent conversation at his lodgings he said "that *public* & *private* integrity did not always go to together, and illustrated the position in the character of Mr Shewell of Boston who in private life, was strictly *just*—but in public life, wholly unprincipled."—[7]

I have had Occasion a thousand times in political life to see these remarks confirmed.

This letter has been written by Adjourments.— If the Subjects of it are discordant, you must ascribe it to that circumstance.—

RC (Adams Papers); endorsed: "Dr Rush. 13. April / ans^{d} 18. 1790."

[1] Of 4 April, above.

[2] Rush referenced a popular sentiment of the French writer and skeptic Pierre Bayle.

[3] That is, pharmacology (*OED*).

[4] On 28 Sept. 1775, along with fellow members of the Continental Congress, JA and Rush made a brief excursion along the Delaware River as far as Point-no-Point (JA, *D&A*, 2:187–188; Rush, *Letters*, 1:548).

[5] Following a British victory at the Battle of Long Island on 27 Aug. 1776, Adm. Lord Richard Howe proposed a peace conference on Staten Island, N.Y. He met with JA, Benjamin Franklin, and Edward Rutledge on 11 Sept., for which see vol. 5:20–21; JA, *D&A*, 3:419–422.

[6] For JA's *Thoughts on Government*, see his letter of 12 March 1790 to John Trumbull, and note 2, above.

[7] Rush likely referred to JA's friend Jonathan Sewall (vol. 18:398).

From William Brown and John Hopkins

[*ante* 14 *April* 1790][1]

To the Honourable John Adams Vice President of the United States of America

The Petition of Wm: Brown & Jam̃. Hopkins with advice of the Honourable John Jay most humbly sheweth that they being now in Confinement in the new Goal of this City suffering under the greatest cruelty that can be inflicted on any human Person & from the Noble Character that Yr. Honour bears induces them to apply for redress hoping that if consistent Your Honour will free them from the Punishment inflicted on them. may the God of Mercy in whose hands are the hearts of Men dispose Your Honour to befriend them in granting them also their Release they having sailed out of this State. The Petition would also present to Your Honour that there is people who is well acquainted with the Captain & know him to be of an infamous Character. may the Great Sovereign whose unbounded Pity is towards the distressed make Your Honour the happy instrument in granting them Release & may every Blessing be shewed on Your Noble Character from the inhabitants of this City who advised us to apply for Redress. & as in Duty bound we shall ever pray &c.—

Willm. Brown
John Hopkins

RC (Adams Papers).

[1] William Brown and John (or James) Hopkins were accused of mutiny and attempted murder aboard the *Morning Star*, Capt. Henry Kermit, which sailed from Amsterdam to New York earlier in the spring. They were arrested upon their arrival on 20 March, tried before the New York State circuit court, and found guilty. On 14 April Brown and Hopkins were sentenced to stand one hour in the pillory, serve six months in jail, and receive 39 lashes. The dating of this letter is based on newspaper accounts of their trial. There is no indication that JA intervened in the case (*Doc. Hist. Supreme Court*, 2:22; Minutes, 13–14 April 1790, Circuit Court for the District of New York, RG 21, NjBaFAR; *New-York Daily Gazette*, 22 March; *New-York Packet*, 15 April).

From John Hurd

Sir Boston Aprl. 17th. 1790

I have the honor of your Excellency's Favor of the 5th. Currt. & acknowledge myself extremely oblig'd by the kind & friendly manner in which you have receivd & reply'd to my Letter—[1] I was apprehensive that it might not be so directly in the Line of your Office to nominate, or recommend any persons to Appointments under Congress—

yet fully perswaded in my Mind that a Word from you occasionally might have great Avail, & being unknown to the supreme Executive, I had not Resolution eno' to make my Application to the President himself

It is highly satisfactory to me, that if you have Opportunity of mentioning my Name, your Report will be much in my favor—that the Number of Candidates for Offices is very great, & many have much Merit I make no doubt from wch: Circumstance some Embarrassmts. may arise—

Doctr: Welsh was kind eno' to shew me Yr. Excellencys Letter to him, from a hint therein respecting my Friends Governr. Langdon & Judge Livermore I shall take the Liberty of writing soon to one or other of them on the subject

my old Friend Putnam indeed is no more![2] I had the pleasure to hear from him a few Months before his Death and dare say, he much regretted as well as myself that he ever quitted the Country, where, had he tarry'd he might have appeared among the principal Actors on the Stage— But he was too much influenc'd by that Veteran in Toryism Old Brigadr. Ruggles & the Chandler Family—that Party, most of 'em I beleive, especialy the Residents in Nova scotia must be sensible they made a bad Bargain in their politicks—

Nova Scotia has sufferd much by the Restraints their Governmts. have laid on the Trade from New England yet very loth to own it—they smuggle considerable on the Borders of the State, and We feel the want of a Market for great part of our fresh provisions & live Stock—

Business in Boston the Winter past has been dull by a general Complaint, a smaller proportion of Navigation than usual, if we may judge by what has been done at the Insurance Offices—& unfortunately more frequent Losses taken place—few Vessells on the Stocks building either in To. or out ports—the three federal Ships set up by subscription the year before last, stood long on hand before disposd off our Ship Building Business seems to want a Stimulus from some Quarter to give the Tradesmen of this Town their usual Hilarity— Two fresh Arrivals from London Capts. Scott & Bernard with several other Vessells within the Week past seem to give a little Spring to Business in Town just now—but Lotterys & speculations in the public Funds have been the cheif Objects of late—many of our Speculators will be much disconcerted by the last News from Congress—that the Assumption of the State Debts has receivd a Negative—the price of our Massa: State Consolidd: Notes fell immediately one Shilling in the pound, & tis supposd will fall lower—so have we often been baffled when our Expectations were rais'd to the highest

Your Excellency will please to excuse my lengthy Reply & be assurd that I am with the most cordial Respect & Esteem / your very obed[t.] hum[l] Serv[t]

John Hurd

RC (Adams Papers); internal address: "His Excellency / John Adams Esq[r.]"; endorsed: "M[r] Hurd. Ap. 17 / 1790."

[1] Boston insurance broker John Hurd (b. 1727), Harvard 1747, wrote to JA on 17 March seeking his patronage for a federal post. In an [*April 1790*] letter to mutual acquaintance Dr. Thomas Welsh, JA advised Hurd to gain the support of New Hampshire senator John Langdon and representative Samuel Livermore. Hurd did not earn a federal appointment (both Adams Papers; *AFC*, 9:34).

[2] Worcester, Mass., lawyer and loyalist James Putnam (b. 1726), Harvard 1746, was a mentor to JA in his youth. Putnam relocated to St. John, New Brunswick, Canada, where he died on 23 Oct. 1789 (JA, *Earliest Diary*, 1:92; *Sibley's Harvard Graduates*, 12:64).

To Benjamin Rush

Dear sir

New York April 18. 1790

Your letter of April 13, soars above the visible diurnal Sphære.— I own to you that avarice Ambition the Love of Fame &c are all mysterious Passions. They are the greatest Absurdities, Delusions and Follies that can be imagined, if in this Life only We had hope.

In the Boat on our Return from Point no Point, the principal Topick of Conversation was *Independence*.— an intercepted Letter early in 1775 had informed the World that I was for Independence. and my Sentiments on this head were no Secret in Congress from May 1775—[1] But I was left too much alone— The Company in the Boat appeared to me, then and ever Since, to have invited me to be of their Party, that they might all assure me in that Confidential manner, that they were of my mind and would Ultimately Support me. There was not one of the Company I believe, who in the Course of the Passage did not repeatedly Assure me, that in his opinion We must be independent.— That Evenings Conversation was a great Encouragement[2] to me, ever after.

How many Follies and indiscreet Speeches do your minutes in your Note Book bring to my Recollection, which I had forgotten forever! Alass I fear I am not yet much more prudent.—

Your Character of M[r] Paine is very well and very just.

To The Accusation against me which you have recorded in Your Note Book of 17th of March last, I plead not guilty.— I deny both Charges. I deny an "Attachment to Monarchy" and I deny that I have "changed my Principles Since 1776."— No Letter of mine to M[r] Hooper was ever printed that I know of. indeed I have but a very confused Recollection of having ever written him any Letter. if any Letter has been printed in my Name I desire to see it.— You know that a Letter of mine to M[r] Wythe was printed by Dunlap, in Jany 1776 under the Title of Thoughts on Government in a Letter from a Gentleman to his Friend. in that Pamphlet, I recommended a Legislature in three independent Branches and to Such a Legislature I am Still attached. But I own at that time I understood very little of the subject, and if I had changed my opinions should have no Scruple to avow it. I own that awful Experience has concurred with Reading and Reflection to convince me that Americans are more rapidly disposed to *Corruption* in Elections, than I thought they were fourteen Years ago.

My Friend D[r] Rush will excuse me if I caution him against a fraudulent Use of the Words *Monarchy* and *Republick*. I am a mortal and irreconcileable Ennemy to Monarchy.— I am no Friend to *hereditary limited* Monarchy in America. This I know can never be admitted, without an hereditary Senate to controul it. and an hereditary Nobility or senate in America I know to be unattainable and impracticable. I Should Scarcely be for it, if it were attainable. Dont therefore my Friend misunderstand me and misrepresent me to Posterity.— I am for a Ballance between the Legislative and Executive Powers and I am for enabling the Executive to be at all times capable of maintaining the Ballance between the Senate and House, or in other Words between the Aristocratical and Democratical Interests— Yet I am for having all three Branches elected at Stated Periods. and these Elections I hope will continue, untill the People Shall be convinced, that Fortune Providence or Chance call it which you will, is better than Election. if the time should come when Corruption shall be added to Intrigue and Manœuvre in Elections and produce civil War, then in my opinion Chance will be better than Choice for all but the House of Representatives.

accept my Thanks for your polite and obliging Invitation to Philadelphia. nothing would give me greater Pleasure, than such a Visit but I must deny my self that satisfaction. I know I have friends in Pensilvania, and Such as I esteem, very highly as the Friends of Virtue Liberty and Good Government.

What you may mean by "more than British degrees of Corruption" at New York and by Sophisticated Government, I know not.— The Continent is a kind of Whispering Gallery and Acts and Speeches are reverberated round from N. York in all Directions. The Report is very loud at a distance, when the Whisper, is very gentle in the Center. But if you See Such Corruptions, in your Countrymen, on what do you found your hopes?

I lament the deplorable Condition of my Country, which Seems to be under such a Fatality that the People can agree upon nothing. When they seem to agree, they are so unsteady, that it is but for a Moment.— that Changes may be made for the better is probable— I know of no Change that would occasion much Danger but that of President. I wish very heartily that a Change of Vice President could be made tomorrow. I have been too ill used in the Office to be fond of it, if I had not been introduced into it, in a manner that made it a disgrace. I will never Serve in it again upon Such Terms.— though I have acted in public with immense Multitudes, I have had few friends and these certainly not interested ones—these I shall ever love in public or private.

Adieu my dear sir J. Adams

RC (NHi:Gilder Lehrman Coll., on deposit); internal address: "Dr Rush." LbC (Adams Papers); APM Reel 115.

[1] For JA's intercepted letters of 1775, which were widely printed in American and British newspapers, see vol. 3:90, 92–93.

[2] In the LbC, CA wrote "comfort."

To Richard Price

My dear Friend. New York April 19 1790.

Accept of my best Thanks for your favour of Feb. 1st. and the excellent Discourse that came with it. I love the Zeal and the Spirit which dictated this Discourse, and admire the general Sentiments of it. From the year 1760 to this hour, the whole Scope of my Life has been to Support Such Principles and propagate Such Sentiments. No Sacrifices of myself or my family. No dangers, no labours, have been too much for me in this great cause. The Revolution in France could not, therefore be indifferent to me. But I have learned, by awfull Experience, to rejoice with trembling. I know that Encyclopædists and Œconomists, Diderot and D'Alembert, Voltaire and Rousseau, have contributed to this great Event, more than Locke, Sidney or Hoadley,[1] and perhaps more than the American Revolution. And I own to you, I know not what to make of a Republick of Thirty Million Atheists.

The Constitution is but an Eperiment; and must and will be altered. I know it to be impossible that France Should be long governed by it. If the Sovereignty is to reside in one Assembly: The King, the Princes of the blood, and principal Quality, will govern it, at their pleasure, as long as they can agree. When they differ they will go to War, and act over again, all the Tragedies of Valois, Bourbons, Lorrains Guises and Colignis, two hundred Years ago.[2]

The Greeks sang the praises of Harmodius and Aristogiton for restoring equal Laws.—[3] Too many Frenchmen, after the example of too many Americans, pant for Equality of Persons and Property. The impracticability of this, God almighty has decreed, and the Advocates for Liberty who attempt it, will Surely Suffer for it.

I thank you, Sir, for your kind Compliment.— As it has been the great Aim of my life to be Usefull; if I had any reason to think I was So, as you Seem to Suppose, it would make me happy. For "Eminence" I care nothing.— For, though I pretend not to be exempt from Ambition, or any other human passion, I have been convinced from my Infancy, and have been confirmed, every year and day of my life, that the Mechanic and Peasant, are happier than any Nobleman or Magistrate or King; and that the higher a man rises, if he has any Sense of duty, the more anxious he must be.

Our new Government, is a new Attempt to divide a Sovereignty. A fresh Essay at Imperium in Imperio. It cannot, therefore, be expected to be very Stable, or very firm. It will prevent Us, for a time, from drawing our Swords Upon each other: and when it will do that, no longer We must call a Convention to reform it.

The difficulty of bringing millions to agree in any measures, to act by any rule; can never be conceived by him, who has not tried it. It is incredible, how Small is the number, in any Nation of those who comprehend any System of Constitution, or Administration: and those few it is wholly impossible to Unite.

I am a Sincere Inquirer after Truth.— But I find very few, who discover the Same Truths. The King of Prussia has found one, which has also fallen in my Way "That it is the peculiar quality of the human Understanding, that Example Should correct no man. The Blunders of the Fathers are lost to their Children, and every Generation must commit its own.["][4]

I have never Sacrificed my Judgment to Kings, Ministers, nor People; and I never will. When either Shall See as I do, I Shall rejoice in their Protection Aid and honour: but I See no prospect that either will ever think as I do; and therefore I Shall never be a favourite with either. I do not desire to be.

But I Sincerely wish, and devoutly pray, that a hundred Years of civil Wars, may not be the Portion of all Europe, for the want of a little Attention to the true Elements of the Science of Government.

With Sentiments; moral Sentiments, which are, and must be eternal, I am your friend John Adams

RC (MHi:Waterston Coll.); internal address: "Doctor Price, Hackney."; docketed by JA: "Letter to Dr Price" and "John Adams / letter to / Dr Price." LbC (Adams Papers); APM Reel 115.

[1] Whig Benjamin Hoadly (1676–1761), bishop of Winchester, criticized the political idea of hereditary rule in his work *The Original and Institution of Civil Government Discuss'd*, London, 1710 (vol. 2:287; *DNB*).

[2] JA referred to the major noble families involved in the French Wars of Religion that raged between Roman Catholics and Huguenots from 1562 to 1598. For his reflections on the conflict's legacy, see *John Adams' Discourses on Davila*, 28 April 1790 – 27 April 1791, Editorial Note, below.

[3] Athenian youths Harmodius and Aristogiton tried and failed to assassinate the tyrant Hippias in 514 B.C. Executed for treason, they were publicly restored as martyrs of democracy (*Oxford Classical Dicy.*).

[4] JA loosely translated several concluding lines from Frederick II, *History of the Seven Years' War*, which was printed in the third book of his *Oeuvres Posthumes*, Berlin, 1788. All fifteen volumes are in JA's library at MB and contain significant annotations (*The Correspondence of Richard Price*, ed. W. Bernard Peach and D. O. Thomas, 3 vols., Durham, N.C., 1983–1994, 3:283; *Catalogue of JA's Library*).

From Thomas Jefferson

Sir New York 20th. April 1790

Encroachments being made on the Eastern limits of the United States by Settlers under the British Government, pretending that it is the Western and not the Eastern River of the Bay of Passamaquoddy which was designated by the name of St. Croix in the Treaty of Peace with that nation, I have to beg the favour of you to communicate any facts which your memory or papers may enable you to recollect, and which may indicate the true River the Commissioners on both sides had in their view to establish as the boundary between the two Nations.[1] It will be of some consequence to be informed by what map they traced the boundary.

I have the honor to be with the greatest respect / Sir / Your most obt. and most hble. Servt. Th: Jefferson[2]

RC in Henry Remsen Jr.'s hand (Adams Papers); internal address: "John Adams Esqr."; endorsed: "Mr Jefferson. Ap. 20. / 1790."

[1] For the longstanding issue of the American boundary with Canada and the demarcation of the Schoodic River (now St. Croix), see vol. 18:241–244, 296, 328–329, 399–400.

[2] Signature in Jefferson's hand.

To John Quincy Adams

My dear son New York April 21st. 1790

I am not willing you should want Information from the Seat of Govt: but I can do little more than send you a Newspaper.

This Day twelve months I first took the Seat in which I now sett, and I have not been absent one Moment, when the senate has been sitting, excepting one Day when my own Salary was under Consideration. This Confinement will injure my health, if I cannot soon take a Journey.

Mr Jefferson has arrived and the offices are all full— The President went yesterday to Long Island for a few days.[1]

The assumption of the State Debts labours, but it is the opinion of many that it will be agreed to at length.

The Circuit Court will sit in Boston soon. The national Courts are proceeding, in all the States. in this City the Circuit Court tryed some Persons for a Species of Pyracy, and passed sentence, but not of death.

The Elections, of senators and Reps. for next Year will soon show the sentiments of the People. J.A.

RC (Adams Papers); internal address: "J. Q. Adams." Tr (Adams Papers).

[1] Thomas Jefferson's arrival in New York a month earlier signaled that George Washington had filled his cabinet, and the president departed on 20 April for a five-day agricultural tour of Long Island. Jefferson settled into a small house at 57 Maiden Lane near Federal Hall (Washington, *Diaries*, 6:63–67; Jefferson, *Papers*, 16:277, 279).

Dialogues of the Dead

[*ca.* 22 *April 1790*][1]

Dialogues of the dead.

Charlemain Frederick, Rousseau Otis.

Rousseau. have you Seen Franklin, Since he passed the River? or has the Boat been too full of Passengers to bring him over?

Otis. I know not.— I have very little Curiosity to know.— I ~~care nothing~~ have no solicitude for Steel Rods nor Iron Points— I am very glad his Points were not over my head: They might have detained me in the Regions of Mire, for twenty or thirty Years longer. The fluctuating flashes and flourishes of chimical and electrical Experiments have no Charms for me. ~~They are as~~ transitory as Sparks meteors, as fireflies Catterpillars and Sea shells. ~~all this is~~ the frivolity and Foppery of sciene.— ~~It is~~ Morality! eternal Morality, ~~it is~~ permanent Intelligence, ~~it is~~ the Policy and Divinity of the Universe! ~~that has my Devotion~~ The Intellectual and Moral World. These have ever [commanded] my Attention and Devotion.

Rousseau. ~~They were mine too~~ And mine— But these are very apt to have the Same Effect upon all Men as they had upon Us.— They ~~produce a little Extravagance,~~ often produce a Melancholly then an Extravagance and at last a Delirium

Frederick But had not Franklin a Genius for Morals?

Otis. He told some very pretty moral Tales from the head—and Some very immoral ones from the heart. ~~but his heart~~— I never liked him: so if you please We will change the subject. Populus Vult Decipi, decipiatur was his Maxim[2]

Frederick. With all my heart—I never thought any Thing of him, as a Politician.— Congress forced me to make a Treaty with him against my Inclination.— indeed his Philosophy never made any Impression on me.— it was chiefly hypothetical and conjectural— I did not think it worth my Notice in my History of my own time. My Attention was drawn to others.

Otis. indeed my Pride was not a little flattered at the Notice, taken by so great a Prince of a ~~Character whom~~ Nation which I had so great a hand in forming.

Fredrick.— Compliments are not the Ton here—if they were I should be at no loss to return yours with Interest.— You have put all our crowned heads to the blush. We have done nothing in Comparison with you. Our successors upon Earth must all go to school to your Pupils, who went to school to you.— as to myself, I feel Small and humble in your Presence— at infinite hazard, Pains and Anxiety I scattered Blood Horror and Desolation round about me: and indeed ~~was~~ thought myself obliged to do so in self Defence. I was the greatest Warrior and statesman in Europe: but if Effects are to be the Measure of Grandeur you should be admitted the Greatest statesman that ever lived. Your Town of Boston has done more than Imperial or Republican Rome: and your Harvard Colledge, than the school of Cujacius and all the Doctors of the Sarbonne. Even my Brother Charlemain must acknowledge his Inferiority to You.

Charlemain. Very true.— I cannot recollect my own Grandeur my Vast Views, my unbounded designs, and my wonderful success, without blushing. The detestible Maxim, Mr Otis which you imputed to one of your Contemporaries, Populus Vult decipi, decipiatur, was my Maxim and I owed to it most of my Greatness.— Leo gave me the Title of Cæsar and Augustus, and Magnus: and instituted that Superstitious Farce of Consecration, which cheated all Europe for ~~Nine~~ many hundred Years. I, in my turn, tranferred to the Pope, the Authority which the Roman senate and People had anciently exercised of electing and confirming the Emperors. This infamous Bargain, as contemptible as the Artifices of two ~~Horse~~ Jockeys, establishd the temporal and spiritual Monarchies of Europe for ~~near 1000~~ many hundreds of Years— But Providence reserved for You the honour of beginning a system of Policy, which has already almost and will infallibly e'er long totally overturn the whole Conspiracy of Charlemain and Leo.

Otis. Your Majesties do me too much Honour. I lived and Acted it is true in a most important Moment. I was fashioned by Providence as a very proper Wedge to split a very hard Knot.— But I was only one of many. ~~Rousseau was~~ our Friend Rousseau had no small share in this Revolution.

Rousseau. I did nothing more than propagate the Principles of Lock. and Voltaire himself, whom I never loved nor esteemed very much did as much as I did.

Frederick. The bewetching Charms of Voltaies Wit, and the enchanting Graces of your Eloquence, made his and your Writings universally read; and as you both filled every Volume and almost every Page with some Recommendation of Liberty and Toleration; your Writings contributed very much to propagate such sentiments among all Mankind. But Reason Wit, Eloquence can do no great Things. Otis began a vast system of Policy which has sett the Reason and the Passions of all Men at Work to promote your Principles.

Rousseau. My Principles were those of Lock.— But I Swallowed Lock with too little Rumination.— Otis's Pupils the Americans have convinced Me, that Lock and I, though our Principles of Liberty were good, were totally mistaken in our Ideas of Government, and the Frame necessary to produce and preserve equal Laws.

Otis. This always surprized me. I was enraptured with the sagacity of Lock and the Eloquence of Rousseau— Yet you seemed to me, never to have considered the human heart or the History of the World. how could an Observation so obvious, escape You.— The Passions of the human heart are insatiable. an Interest unballanced; a Passion uncontrouled, in society, must produce disorder and Tyranny.

You have nothing to do therefore to preserve equal Laws but to provide a Check for evey Passion, a Reaction to every Action a Controul to every Interest, which counteracts the Laws.

Rousseau.— it is now very plain to me—but like my Master Lock I did not see it, when on Earth.

Otis. Your Error, As well as your Masters, ~~have been~~ may be corrected: but there are others more dangerous still, ~~which have not~~ which may be more difficult to eradicate.— and here I cannot acquit your Majesty of Prussia.— I fear that some other Errors may do more harm than the Intrigue of Charlemain, which he just now So candidly confessed and so ingenuously repented. I mean the Renunciation of a future state, and the Tendency to deny or doubt the moral Government of the World, and the Existence of an all perfect Intelligence. This august Company must allow me, to do more honour to Palestine and Jerusalem, than You have done to Boston and Cambridge. These Places in my Opinion would have no merit at all, if they had not respected those.— Thou shalt love the supream with all thy heart and thy Neighbour as thyself, is a Maxim of eternal Phylosophy. it is the sublime Principle of Right order and Happiness in the Universe. Affection and Confidence in the Æternal, Resignation to his Will and Affection and Beneficence to his Works as far as We are intelligent active and free, must be Truth Duty and Felicity.— How then could such Characters as these in this Company give any Countenance to Encyclopædists, Atheists and Theists, in destroying or weakening the Faith of Mankind, in this divine Phylosophy?

Charlemain. A confused and uninlightened sense of these important Truths really was one of my Temptations to my unworthy Maneuvre with Leo. So much I must Say in Palliation of my enormous Error.

Frederick, Rousseau. We both stand convicted.

Frederick— I deserved ~~to be damned~~ the extream of Punishment at least ~~to suffer long in Purgatory~~ a very lasting Purgation: But am filled with Gratitude equal to my Remorse. Gratitude that Goodness could forgive when Justice might have punished.

Rousseau. I was less guilty than you—Yet I have infinite cause of Gratitude also.

Frederick and Rousseau.— If it were permitted We would chearfully return to Earth and undergo the Pains and Anxieties of Life once more, if We might have an Opportunity of expiating our Faults by Warning Mankind against our Errors.

Quincy Nov. 24. 1813.

This little thing, was written at Richmond Hill, or Church Hill, where I lived in New York in 1789, in an Evening after the News arrived of Dr Franklins Death, and after I had retired to my Family, after presiding in the Senate of U. S. The moment when it was written is the most curious Circumstance attending it. John Adams

MS (Adams Papers); docketed by JA: "Dialogue."; notation by CFA: "Written in 1789. / See the memorandum of J A. at the end."

[1] News of Benjamin Franklin's death from pleurisy on 17 April reached JA and Congress five days later. Imitating a literary genre popularized by the Syrian satirist Lucian of Samosata (b. ca. 120 A.D.) and, more recently, by the French writer Bernard Le Bovier de Fontenelle (1657–1757), JA imagined a conversation among four historical figures who awaited Franklin's arrival in the afterlife: Charlemagne, Frederick II, Jean Jacques Rousseau, and James Otis. Another writer to experiment with this particular literary format was George Lyttelton, Baron Lyttelton, who published an example in 1760 that JA enjoyed (Jefferson, *Papers*, 19:78; *Oxford Classical Dicy.*; *Catalogue of JA's Library*; Hoefer, *Nouv. biog. générale*; *AFC*, 10:293).

JA filed away this composition, which is published here for the first time. Over two decades later, while searching "among a heap of forgotten rubbish for another paper, it Struck my Eye," JA wrote. He sent a copy to Mercy Otis Warren in Sept. 1813, remembering the piece as simply "the Effusion of a musing Moment." She replied on 12 Sept., revealing that she had been "deeply affected" by JA's essay: "The sketch in my hand in connection with some of the greatest actors who have exhibited their parts on this narrow stage of human action, is a proof of your correct knowledge of history and your capacity for comparing the ages of Charlemagne, Frederick the Great, Rousseau, and Otis, though in times so remote from each other, and drawing the results of their sentiments and transactions and the operation thereof on the moral conduct of mankind in our own age and in that of Posterity" (JA to Warren, 1 Sept., NHi: Gilder Lehrman Coll., on deposit; *Warren-Adams Letters*, 73:386–387).

[2] The people want to be deceived, so let them be deceived.

From William Smith

Sir. Boston. 24th. April. 1790.

It is sometime since I had the pleasure of addressing you[1] but as I know it will not be displeasing to know the sentiments of your countrymen, on the determination of Congress not to assume the State Debts, I wou'd mention them.— the State Creditors think they are equally entitl'd to the benefits of the Genl. Government with the Continental Creditors. their property or services were advanc'd for the benefit of their Country at the earliest period, perhaps had they not exerted themselves the Country wou'd have been subdued. they presum'd, when they so readily gave their consent to the adoption of the New Government & agreed to relinquish the funds from which they were paid *their* Interest, that the Genl. Gov^t., after receiving the resources wou'd have generously provided for their Interest equally with other Creditors. much has been said on the subject of discrimination but in this State, (in the opinion of the Treasurer) two thirds of the Debt is in the possession of the original Creditors or become the property of their Heirs. most of them were persons in trade & it is now openly said why shou'd *We*, pay duties to a government, from which *we* are, *not* to receive any benefit. must we increase the Revenue for the benefit of those, who *never* riskt their property till they cou'd purchase into the Funds at an eight of their value— these sentiments are generally express[d.] If Congress do not assume the State Debts & fund the whole Debt there is great danger that the publick revenue will sink very considerably.— the Publick Papers may puff off the increasing trade of America. but you may rely on it in this State it is on the decline. Our Fishery is discourag'd & is lessen'd One hundred sail this Spring. much was expected from the Carrying Trade. a number of fine Ships were built the last year for that business, & had they met with success numbers wou'd have been added this season. but wherever we go, we find the Harbours crouded with British Shipping which have the preference.— whilst our own Ships sail the Coast from Boston to Georgia beging a Freight.

The British have lately prohibited the importation of any goods even in British Ships which are not the produce of America— Why cannot Congress say, that no Goods, Ware or Merchandize shall be imported in British Ships but what are the Growth or Manufacture of Great Britain surely we have a right to retaliate when it is so much for our Interest. the intention of the British Act is to discourage our East India Trade. as large quantitys of Cotton have been imported from India & reship'd to Great Britain in British Ships— The scarcity of Specie is very great. all the circulating Cash we can procure goes for Duties & is immediately sent of for New-York. & from the slow movements of Congress it is uncertain whether it is to be paid back in *some Years*. the Drafts on our Bank to exchange Notes for Specie to send to New-York. has been so great lately that the Bank has stopt discounting.—! cou'd not a National Bank be establish'd & their Bills have a Currency thro' the States!— this wou'd facilitate the collection of the Revenue & essentially serve the trade of the whole Continent.— We are in hopes that Congress will reconsider the subject of assumption & fund the *whole*.— by this measure they will unite State & Continental Creditors in the support of one firm energetick Government, & make it their Interest to unite in the regular collection of the Revenue—& put an end to all *partial State* Excise Laws— if this is not done, there will be a very powerful body of State Creditors constantly opposing the proceedings of the Fœderal Government & preventing the collection of the Impost.—

Mrs. S. joins me in our best regards to Mrs. Adams & yourself.

Yr Most. H Sert Wm. Smith.

RC (Adams Papers).

[1] Of 14 Dec. 1789, above.

To John Trumbull

Dear sir New York April 25. 1790

Your favour of March 30. and Ap. 17. came to hand last night. By the "attack in Metre" you mean I suppose, that written by Ned. Church, a Cockfighting Cousin and Companion of Charles Jarvis a devoted Instrument of Mr H.— Jarvis's Mother was a Church.— This Fellow, this Ned Church, I know nothing of— I scarcely ever spoke to him in my Life.— His Traitorous Brother, I knew very well: and the Vendue Man his Father.[1]

I despair of ever seeing the "ancient Dominion" wiser. Their stupid and mulish systems have many a time brought America to the Brink of Ruin— and Rich. H. Lee, as little as you and I think of him as a statesman, is as great, as any one I ever knew from that State, excepting only Washington. Yet I am on perfectly good personal Terms with all of them.—

Mr Maddison is a studious Scholar, but his Reputation as a Man of Abilities is a Creature of French Puffs.— some of the worst ~~Actions~~ Measures some of the most stupid Motions stand on Record to his Infamy— I mean that for Compelling American Ministers at the Peace to communicate every Thing to the French Ministers and do nothing without their Consent.— You hint at Suspicions of Motives of Envy against the Secretary. I would rather hope it is Defference to Constituents. This is Defalcation enough from a Character but not so much as the other. The Jealousies and Envies of Emulation are however, The Devil.— There are Jealousies and Envies arising from Rivalries for the Places of Presidents for the Places of Governors of states, for Seats in senates, for offices of state and Judicature. and these Passions are increasing to such Extravagance as to endanger extreamly the Union of the States: and Yet nobody sees them.— There is a low Hypocricy crept in among us, a solemn dissimulation, which will not allow any Man to own that himself or any other American has the Feelings of Human Nature.— an Indifference about Rank is counterfeited and falsely pretended, while the Passion for it is eating up the Hearts of all Men, as the Spartans Fox tore out his Bowells, because he would not own that the Fox was there.[2]

as to the affair of the Peace. in Dec$^{r.}$ 1777 Congress sent me to Europe, a joint Minister Plenipotentiary, with Franklin and Lee, to the King of France. I resided there a Year, when Congress annulled the Commission, and left Franklin alone at that Court.— after a series of Adventures, which would compare with Don Quixot, Gulliver or Crusoe, I obtained the Priviledge of again Crossing the Ocean, running the Gauntlet among British Men of War and came home, in August 1779.— Congress soon determind to send me again to Europe. in Nov. 1779 I embarked with two of their Commissions in my Pocket—one as Sole Minister Plenipotentiary to negotiate a Peace—the other as Sole Minister Plenipotentiary to negotiate a Treaty of Commerce with Great Britain. I resided two Years in Europe in these Capacities. But Franklins Envy And Jealousy could not bear this. Vergennes wanted more Complaisant Ministers. Marbois could obtain no better Terms with Congress than by Uniting the Jealousies of south and middle against North, and by Uniting the Friends of four others, Franklin Lawrence, Jefferson and Jay, to obtain a new Commission for Peace, and annul my Commission to make a Treaty of Commerce; a most wicked Project of Vergennes, and basely complied with by Congress, which has hurt this Country more than Mr Maddison ever in his Life did it good. Congress sent me a Letter of Credence as Minister Plenipotentiary to Holland, and a Power to negotiate a Loan of Money. as I could not get this Business compleated, till Mr Grenville and after him Mr Oswald were at Paris, I could not go there at first.— But Copies both of Mr Grenvilles and Mr Oswalds Commissions were sent me to the Hague, and I expressed to my Colleagues by Letter My Opinion of them and my Determination not to treat, untill another Commission was given, which should expessly Authorise Mr Oswald to treat with *the Ministers of the United States of America*.[3] This opinion coincided with Mr Jays: but not with those of Franklin and Vergennes.— I arrived at Paris as soon as Mr Oswalds Commission, and before the Conferences were opened.

Franklin is gone. Peace to his Shade.— Personal Resentments and Hatreds are not to be found in my nature in public affairs. I feel no ill will to his Memory—but I owe more to Truth than to his Fame; and I owe the Truth to my Country and Posterity. The last Letter of Abuse to Congress in which he mentioned me he Said I "was always an honest Man"—[4] I wish my Conscience would allow me to say as much of him.— But from the first to the last of my Acquaintance with him, I can reconcile his Conduct in public affairs neither to the Character of an honest Man, nor to that of a Man of sense.— I have hinted at these Things to introduce an Observation which will account for much of the harsh Feelings which are expressed against me.— I have Acted a Part so decided against England, that all English Emissaries dislike me. I have acted so determined a Part against Vergennes's undoubted designs to deprive this Country of their Fisheries and Western Lands, if not to cheat Us with a Truce, that the French Emissaries are not zealously my friends. And I have been obliged to watch Franklin with so vigilant an Eye and to oppose him with so much Firmness that all his numerous Friends have been tainted with Unkindness to me.— This is the true Secret of the Scurrilous Abuse that I have suffered.— But this ought to be a Motive with all true Americans to support me and discountenance such Abuses.— If this is not done, I will perish if this Country ever finds another Man, who will act a Part as independent and disinterested. if Acknowledged Fidelity to his Country at every Risque and Expence, against her open Ennemies, her selfish Allies, her treacherous Friends and unfaithful servants, is not to Support a Man in the Minds of his Countrymen, you will soon find complaisant Men alone in public.—

For myself I can truly Say I have never deceived the People, nor any Individual.— in 1774 I was sincere in my hopes that Petitions and Non Importation Agreements would procure a Redress of Grievances, which was all I desired. War, I dreaded and Independence I did not wish. It is true, I feared, & believed that We should not avoid War or Independence—and I did not conceal this opinion from any one, who asked it.

Rousseaus Examples of the Doge and the Pope, are very apposite and very conclusive. They prove incontestibly the Efficacy of Pageantry. They prove with equal force, that this Efficacy may be applied to Evil purposes. But what is there that may not? Religion and Government have both been as ill Used as Pageantry.— Signs do not necessarily imply abuse. They have been applied to good Uses as well as bad.— if Government cannot be had, nor Laws obeyed without, some Parade, as I fully believe, We must have some Parade or no Laws.

Is there a Clergyman in Connecticut who does not wear a band.? Have they left off the distinction of a red Gate and board Fence before their Houses? Could the People of New England go through the Revolution without Liberty Trees and Liberty Poles?— Was there not as much Pomp in escorting Delegates to Congress in 1774 and 1775, as in the King of Frances Tour to Cherbourg?—[5] What was all the Parade of the Presidents late Tour through New England? We practice these Things as much as other Countries. Our Feelings prompt them as forcibly. and We can do as little without them.— Was not Mr Hancock escorted from York Town to Boston in 1777 by twelve light horse—a King of England, or a Roman Consul had no more.—[6] We practice a strange Hypocricy upon ourselves.— We ought not to shock the People: but We need not deceive them and ourselves too. Let Us be moderate and reasonable, but not false.

There is a Decency in every Thing, and the common Sense of Mankind requires an attention to it.— There is not in Europe, so much attention to it, in their common Country Churches, as there is in our New England Parishes to their Meeting Houses. Is there a Being so low, as not to be offended at the Thought of worshiping God in a Barn or a mean House? Why is Plate, and handsome Vessells, at the Communion Table so much thought of? a common black Bottle, and a Wooden Dish would do as well in Essence. Yet every Mortal Sees and feels the horrid Impropriety of such a Thought.

Whenever Mankind mean to respect any Thing they always treat it decently. Why do they build Monuments and erect Grave stones? why do they plain and paint a Coffin? Why do they cover it with a Pall? Why do they march in Procession at a Funeral? Why do they give Gloves?[7]

after such grave Examples it may seem ludicrous to descend to lesser Things—But I mean nothing ludicrous or light.— Why do the Children call Father and Mother instead of John and Tom? Why do they call one another Johnny, Jemmy and suzy—instead of John James and sue? in short in the meanest family on Earth You will find these little distinctions, Marks, signs, and Decencies, which are the Result of Nature, Feeling Reason; which are Policy and Government in their Places, as much as Crowns and Tiaras, Ceremonies, Titles &c in theirs.—

Whenever the People of America shall intend Sincerely to have any Government, they will treat it decently. But as Yet one half of them have no such Intention. They have sense enough to know that Signs and Ceremonies of a decent Kind would soon establish a Government. But as they abhor the End they oppose the means.

I thank You kindly for Your Anecdote about throwing away Votes.— Both H. and W.[8] were for me; and I really Suspect that they had some real Fears, that I might have the greatest Number of Votes.— Yet in all suppositions it was a corrupt Intrigue and an insidious Maneuvre.

Our Secretary has however I think good Abilities and certainly great Industry. He has high minded Ambition and great Penetration.— He may have too much disposition to intrigue.— if this is not indulged I know not where a better Minister for his Department could be found. But nothing is more dangerous, nothing will be more certainly destructive in our Situation than the Spirit of Intrigue.— With our delightful Symphony of Elections, of Presidents, Governors senators &c &c &c when Intrigue comes in, and is not resisted, We shall have discords of the harshest kind. I fancy I could make a curious Rattling in the World by moving an Inquiry into the Maneuvre in my Election. But if it is not repeated it had better be forgotten. If it should be repeated, it must be inquired into. The Doctrine of *throwing away Votes* is itself a Corruption. a bare Motion in the House or Senate to institute an Inquiry would produe a trepidation in many hearts. Throwing Away a Vote is betraying a Trust, it is a Breach of Honour, it is a Perjury—it is equivalent to all this in my Mind. Electors are not Despots. They have no discretionary or dispensing Power.— Let Intriguers and Dupes both consider this before another Election.— They may depend upon it, they will find in me a Man who has Patience but will not be a Sport nor a Dupe.— If a Repetition takes Place I will drag out to public Infamy both Dupors and Dupees, let who will be among the Number. With / much Esteem I am dear sir your obliged / Friend John Adams.

RC (PPRF); internal address: "John Trumbull. Esqr"; endorsed: "Hon$^{ble.}$ John Adams / Ap$^{l.}$ 25$^{th:}$ 1790—" LbC (Adams Papers); APM Reel 115.

[1] For Edward Church's satirical ode, see JA's letter to Sylvanus Bourne of 30 Aug. 1789, and note 1, above. Church's father was Benjamin Sr. (1704–1781), Harvard 1727, an auctioneer. Edward's cousin was Dr. Charles Jarvis, a longtime critic of JA. Jarvis' mother was Sarah Church (*AFC*, 8:413; *Sibley's Harvard Graduates*, 8:125, 128; 14:389; 16:376).

[2] Plutarch's *Lycurgus* told the story of a Spartan boy who concealed a stolen fox under his cloak, choosing to be disemboweled by the animal rather than reveal his theft.

[3] For JA's letters to the American peace commissioners, see vol. 13:243–244, 246–250.

[4] In his 22 July 1783 letter to Robert R. Livingston, Benjamin Franklin summed up his view of JA: "He means well for his Country, is always an honest Man, often a Wise one, but sometimes and in somethings absolutely out of his Senses" (*AFC*, 5:252).

[5] For Louis XVI's tour of the naval works at Cherbourg, see vol. 18:344.

[6] Traveling from York, Penn., to Boston following sessions of the Continental Congress, John Hancock wrote to George Washington on 25 Oct. 1777, accepting the protection of a military escort. Washington replied on 2 Nov., sending "12 Dragoons" and explaining that "the severe duty, the Horse have been obliged to perform for a long time past, has rendered many of them unfit for service, to which I must add, that we are under a necessity of keeping several—considerable patroles of them constantly along the Enemy's lines" (Washing-

ton, *Papers, Revolutionary War Series*, 11:614, 12:96).

[7] Puritans followed elaborate burial practices that included gifting gloves and jewelry to the mourners who attended funeral processions (Dorothy A. Mays, *Women in Early America: Struggle, Survival, and Freedom in a New World*, Santa Barbara, Calif., 2004, p. 102–103).

[8] In the LbC, CA wrote "H—n" and "W—b" to indicate Alexander Hamilton and Samuel Blachley Webb.

From Oliver Whipple

Portsmouth Newhamp[e.] April 26th. 1790

Most respected S[r:]

The Length of Time, Since I had the Honour of a personal Interview, and the Vicisitudes of our public Affairs, perhaps have almost obliterated my Name from your Rememberance; but you will pardon my epïstolary Introduction, when I tell you I am ambitious of your Notice, and claim a kind of Right to your favorable Attention: I reflect with emense Pleasure, that my first Efforts to tread the Paths of Science and Study, were in your hon[d.] Father's House, where I had during the Space of four Months, your friendly Attention and kind Advice; and I hope I shall not be deem'd guilty of Flattery, when I say, that from that early Period, I discover'd myself & more from the Presages of others, that your Learning, Abilities, Virtues and Industry in the Round of Science, would one Day raise you to some high Degree of Eminence, (as we see at this Day) to which I sinerely congratulate you, and in which our Country exults with the most Heartfelt Satisfaction. Since my Entering on Buisness, Portsmouth, has been the Place of my Residence, where I once had the Honour of Seeing you at my House, I have lived here eighteen Years, & always demeaned myself as a good Citizen of America and by my Industry and good Fortune, have acquired a handsome & independant Estate, but the Buisness of our Profession now grows tiresome, and I wish to leave that Drudgery, to the Junior Practiscioners, for Some more agreeable Imployment.—[1]

As the Congress are now maturing & perfecting a Plan of Finance & national Revenue, the Excise will soon be an Object of thier Attention, and when setted, of Course, Appointments will take Place, thro' the several States, should this be the Case, I most earnestly entreat your Friendship, that my Name may be handed to the President, as a Candidate for the Collection of Excise in this State; To ask Favors of this kind is perhaps novel, but my Situation in this State is very singular, I have not, nor has M[rs] Whipple a Relative in the State, our Relations are at Boston Providence & Newport, and I thank God they are those kind of People, who are feoderal, and are now, to my Knowledge, Strugling against the basest Faction that ever disgraced Society, to establish good order & Government. Our Delegates are Natives of this State, they have each thier peculiar Friends & Connections, to whom they will be attentive; Mr: Langdon my Friend & Neighbour, I beleive will not be wanting to push my Interest [. . .] the President; Mr Livermore, is a good Man, but [. . .] undoubtedly, give Prefferenc to his own Circle of Friends, as to the other Delegates of our State my small Acquaintance with them will not permit me to ask Favors; I wish if it may not be too troublesome, that you will converse with Mr: Langdon on the Subject. Mr. Dalton, Mr King, Mr. Thatcher, Mr: Goodhue, Mr Patridge, and Mr. Leonard as well as other honorable Members, are personally known to me, who if my Name is mentioned, will not be unfriendly; You may depend Sr. I shall not dishonour your Recommendation; I have the Honour to be a Majestrate in this State, hold a Colonel's Commission in the Alarm Core in this District, and lately was nominated by the Council of this State for one of the Judges of the Superiour Bench, tho' Mr Alcott, who stood before me in Nomination was appointed,[2] I do not mention these Matters with any other View, but to Show you I am not unnoticed in my own State; being a Native of America, acquainted with its Laws Constitutions, Commerce & Interest, I feel a most ardent Desire to serve her at Home or abroad, new Scenes are opening and new political Connections are dayly forming, in some Capacity methinks, I could do my self Honour, nor Stain the Character of my Country; some Persons of distinguished Character in our Country will soon be appointed, as Commissioners &c to foreign Courts, in Capacity of Secretary to such a Charge, I would gladly serve; but whatever may be my Fortune I must implore your Pardon for the Freedom I have taken, with a Person of your high Rank: I shall never cease to venerate your Character & for every Intimation in my Favor pour forth the Full[ness] of my Heart animated with every possible Sentiment of Respect, and Gratitude / I am Sr. with / the greatest Esteem, your / most obedt & very humble. / Servt:

Oliver Whipple

RC (Adams Papers); addressed: "To / The most Honble. John Adams / Vice President of the united / States— / New York"; internal address: "The most honble. J Adams."; endorsed: "Mr Oliver Whipple / 26. April 1790 / ansd. 18. May." Some loss of text where the seal was removed.

[1] Portsmouth, N.H., lawyer Oliver Whipple (1743–1813), Harvard 1766, knew JA from their early days in the legal profession. He married Abigail Gardiner in 1774. Whipple sought and failed to obtain several federal posts, despite the support of Gov. John Sullivan and others (*Sibley's Harvard Graduates*, 16:430–431; JA, *Legal Papers*, 2:363, 389). See JA's reply of 18 May 1790, below.

[2] Bolton, Conn., native Simeon Olcott (1735–1815), Yale 1761, was appointed a justice of the N.H. Superior Court on 25 Jan. (Dexter, *Yale Graduates*, 2:711, 712).

John Adams' *Discourses on Davila*

28 April 1790 – 27 April 1791

Editorial Note

Following the favorable reception of his 1787–1788 work, *A Defence of the Constitutions of Government of the United States of America*, Vice President John Adams ventured deeper into the lessons of Europe's republican past. Encouraged by Thomas Jefferson and others to pursue the subject of hereditary aristocracy as "a proper sequel," Adams mulled the skills needed for such a task, namely, greater foreign-language fluency and access to more research materials (vol. 19:5). Over the course of two years, he produced his *Discourses on Davila: A Series of Papers on Political History*. Ardent Federalist John Fenno serialized Adams' *Discourses* in the *Gazette of the United States* between 28 April 1790 and 27 April 1791. The first 22 essays appeared in the *Gazette*'s New York City edition, and the next ten were published in Philadelphia, after Fenno moved his business to the federal seat. The essays were printed anonymously but Adams' authorship was an open secret; he confirmed it to son Charles in mid-February 1792. Originally intended as an English translation of French history, John Adams' 32 essays morphed into an extensive and influential commentary on social class, religion, and revolution.

Adams embarked on the project in the fall of 1789, inspired by his reading of *Histoire des guerres civiles de France*, 3 vols., Amsterdam, 1757, which was a popular French translation of Italian author Enrico Caterino Davila's *Historia delle guerre civili di Francia*, Venice, 1630. Davila (1576–1631), a former soldier and diplomat who was a native of Padua, offered a rich chronicle of the French Wars of Religion that stretched from 1560 to 1598. According to Adams, Davila's account of the sixteenth-century struggles between the monarchy and the nobility, along with the internecine conflicts of the aristocracy, supplied a resonant history lesson for eighteenth-century events in America and France. The June 1790 catalog of Adams' library lists an English translation of Davila's text as well, but he relied on the French translation, which bears significant annotations in his hand.

In terms of structure, Adams' *Discourses* may be read in two parts. He spent the initial eighteen essays translating the first five books of Davila's history, weaving in a few brief comments. The next fourteen essays featured Adams' reflections on British economist Adam Smith's ideas of social rank and ambition as discussed in his *Theory of Moral Sentiments*. When he reached No. 31, Adams announced that he was concluding his analysis of France's "melancholy history." The final printed installment of Adams' series showcased French jurist Étienne de La Boétie (1530–1563), whose essay *Discours sur la servitude volontaire ou Contr'un* attacked both the tyranny of absolute monarchy and the modes of popular surrender to it. Though his *Discourses* fell silent in the *Gazette of the United States*, Adams found he had more to say. An incomplete draft of a 33d essay intended for his *Discourses* is in the Adams Papers. It has never previously been published and is printed below. There, Adams criticized the unicameral legislature and weak executive branch espoused by the Marquis de Condorcet in his 1788 treatise, *Quattre lettres d'un bourgeois de New Haven sur l'unité de la législation*.

To his pride and provocation, Adams found an American audience that was still eager to hear and to war over his political philosophy. Throughout the 1790s, Adams' *Discourses* repeatedly rekindled the dissent already aflame between factions of staunch Federalists and emergent Democratic-Republicans. The historical essays became a partisan lightning rod, as Congress battled through regional interests and as the French Revolution's violence rippled onto American shores. Adams' new and increasingly vocal rival Jefferson, for example, seized the opportunity to praise Thomas Paine's *Rights of Man* while denouncing Adams' "political heresies" at play in the *Discourses*. This view, coupled with sharp criticism from several "Jacobinical journals," led Adams to cease writing the *Discourses* (Jefferson, *Papers*, 20:293; *AFC*, 9:263). Characteristically, he did not wholly give up on the topic. From 30 April to 9 July 1791, Adams published a serialized translation of La Boétie's scholarship in the *Gazette*.

As with his *Defence* and other writings, John Adams had a personal perspective on how to interpret the *Discourses'* significance and scope (vols. 18:539, 544, 546–550; 19:130–132). Addressing his son Thomas Boylston on 19 September 1795, the vice president wrote: "I wish The Discourses on Davila were collected and printed as a fourth Volume, for they are in reality a Key to the whole. That Emulation in the human heart which is universal, and is not a Love of Equality but a desire of Superiority, is there develloped as the eternal & universal Cause of Parties and Factions, which renders the double Ballance indispensible in every free Republican Government" (Adams Papers).

The *Discourses* enjoyed yet other public reincarnations after John Adams was elected president in 1797. John Russell began reprinting the *Discourses* in the *Boston Gazette* from 2 September 1799 to 30 June 1800, emphasizing Adams' foresight regarding the French Revolution's descent into terror. In the 15 May issue, Russell solicited subscriptions for a book-length collection of the *Discourses*, thereby ensuring "a more durable publicity" for Adams' work. Five years later, Russell and James Cutler printed a Boston edition titled *Discourses on Davila. A Series of Papers, on Political History. Written in the Year 1790, and then Published in the Gazette of the United States. By an American Citizen.* They omitted Adams' No. 32 and set the price at one dollar. Russell and Cutler added a postscript echoing Adams' call for a balanced constitutional government. They advertised the book as "the offspring" of the author of the *Defence*, and "as correlative parts, or an *additional volume* to the above work." Savoring his copy of the 1805 edition, a retired John Adams wrote the following in the margin: "Napoleon! Mutato nomine, de te fabula narrabatur! This book is a prophecy of your empire before your name was heard" (JA, *D&A*, 3:225; *AFC*, 9:262–264, 335; Hoefer, *Nouv. biog. générale*; *Catalogue of JA's Library*; Descriptive List of Illustrations, No. 2, above; C. Bradley Thompson, *John Adams and the Spirit of Liberty*, Lawrence, Kans., 1998, p. 270–274; *Boston Gazette*, 22 April 1805, 6 June).

Drafts of 17 of the 32 published essays, as well as the manuscript of No. 33, are filmed at Adams Papers Microfilms, Reel 374. For editorial arrangements of the *Discourses* that draw on John Adams' related marginalia, see JA, *Works*, 6:221–403, and Haraszti, *Prophets*, p. 39, 165–179, 334–335. A modern reprint of the 1805 *Discourses* was issued by Da Capo Press in 1973.

John Adams' *Discourses on Davila*, No. 33

[*ca. 16 March 1791*][1]

Discourses on Davila. N. 33.

It seems by the Discourse of Boetius, that there was a strong Inclination, in some to destroy Monarchy and Aristocracy in France, as long ago as the rign of Charles the ninth and some of his Predecessors. had this been done, they ~~must either have had no Government at all~~, would probably have adopted, a Government in one Center like the present national Assembly. In some former discourse an Idea was hinted at, of throwing together a few Thoughts upon the Question whether a Sovereignty in a single Assembly, could have answered the Ends of Government in the sixteenth Century or whether it will do better now in the Eighteenth, for such a nation as France. This question may be answered by a few Remarks upon a Work, which has not been much read in America, as yet but as it is a part of American Literature and will be preserved in the Cabinets of the Curious, it will not misbecome Us to look into it.

In 1788 were published in Paris four Volumes under the Title of Researches historical and political, concerning the United States of ~~America~~ North America, in which ~~is~~ are treated their Relations and Contentions with Great Britain and of their Governments before and after the Revolution, by a Citizen of Virginia; with four Letters from a Burgher of New Heaven concerning the Unity of Legislation. As these Letters from a Citizen of New Heaven to a Citizen of Virginia, are become a Part both of French and American Literature, they will descend to Posterity, as one monument of the Principles and Opinions of this important Period. Posterity therefore will be, as the present Generation both in france and America are interested in a candid investigation of the Truths or Errors they contain: and especially as the Author of them is announced to be one of the greatest Men of this Century. When the Work first appeared in public It was conjectured that the Word "Heaven" was an Error of the Press and that New Haven was meant, and Mr Trumbull the satiric Poet of humble Virtue but independent Spirit and, immortal Fame, ~~who~~ was ~~Supposed~~ imagined, by some who knowing he belonged to connecticut knew not that he was a Citizen of Hartford, to have attempted in prose to ridicule ~~of~~ a Government in one Assembly. But upon considering the concluding part of the dedication, and after reading the four Letters themselves it was conjectured that the New Jerusalem was meant, and the Plan of Government imagined for the Millennium only.[2] It now appears however that this Work has been followed by several others published with the Names of the Duke de la Rochefaucault and the Marquis of Condercet, referred to as serious Argument in the national Assembly, and that that assembly has itself adopted the Idea ~~of Mr Turgot~~ it must therefore now be given Up, that this Work was designed to delineate a Government for Men, before the coming of the New Heavens and the New Earth.

These Letters in 1788 were probably written in Answer to the Defence of the American Constitutions the three Volumes of which were all printed and some of them dispersed in France before the End of 1787. This would be probable enough, from the known Friendship of the Writer for Mr Turgot, which induced him formerly to write his Life and his Panegyrick: but it is certain, from many passages in the Letters themselves, in which the Defence, tho not named is so clearly alluded to that it cannot be mistaken. The Writer is a Man of science, but no Experience; of Letters of some kinds, but unacquainted with History as well as the Writings on Government; little ~~acquainted with~~ skilled in the human heart, not at all conversant with the World. This is all demonstrated by his Letters: and what is more whimsical Still, it appears manifest enough that he has undertaken to answer a ~~Book~~ Work without reading it.

A Desire of Reformation in Government, as well as in morals, and Religion, is a proof of an amiable disposition, and benevolent Wisdom. a Passion, for improvements in Arts and discoveries in science, is always laudable and where it is accompanied with Talents, merits and Seldom fails to obtain the Admiration of mankind. But it should be remembered that many a Man feigns a passion which he never felt: others pretend to Talents they never possessed.

There is an Italian proverb of sterling Sense, Se Sta bene non se move. If you Stand well, dont move. A maxim of Wisdom generally just and universally so with this Addition, *Unless you have good reason to believe you can Stand better*. Before We attempt Reformation We Should be Sure of two Points. 1. That there are Errors, and Abuses, or at least imperfections, which can be corrected. 2. What those Errors, abuses or imperfections are. Before We attempt Discoveries and improvements, We should consider, whether the whole of a Subject is not already known: and whether it is not already as perfect as We can make it: and better than it would be with Such Innovations and alterations as are projected.

As all Things are best illustrated by Examples, it may not be amiss to alledge one or two.

Suppose an Architect should arise and sett up Pretentions to matchless Genius, intuitive Knowledge, and exalted Invention beyond all others who had ever lived in any part of the World. He tells us gravely "Mankind have as yet discovered nothing in the Art of Building. Corinthian Pillars and all the other orders are aukward and clumsy Incumbranes. Dividing an house into various Appartements and Offices, according to the old Architecture, is all Ignorance and Empiricism. I, will teach you a new method; A method of ~~perfect~~ Unity and Simplicity. Pull down to the foundation, all your houses, cutt to pieces all your Pillars and orders, and I will build you new ~~houses~~ habitations, but at your expence however, all in one Center. Houses in which the Garrett and the Cellar, the Kitchen and the Parlour Dining Room, Dressing Room and Lodging Rooms shall all be but one Apartment. This will be Simple: all the Complications and Quackeries of the Old Architecture will be avoided by this device."

Proud as the World is there is more superiority in it, given than assumed, and a bold Pretender generally gains Attention and Obtains disciples. It is probable that our Architect would make impressions on some, for We have good Authority to say that there is no Opinion so absurd but some Philosopher has been found to mantain it. But would Mankind in General, especially the more judicious and thinking part and those who have already comfortable Dwellings, consent to destroy so much Property, waste so much labour, and turn themselves out into the open air, for the sake of Improvements So precarious and problematical.?

Another Example, equally apposite may be taken from Musick. Suppose a Person should appear and tell Us with an Air of solemnity, "that Gluck and Picini, Haydn and Handel were all quacks. Their Complications of Tenor Treble and Base were all ridiculous. But I have discovered a new Science of Musick and invented a new method of practice. a Theory and Practice of mere simplicity. reduce all your Fiddles to one String and your Organs to one Pipe. It is now discovered and made certain that Monotony Is the Perfection of the musical Art. And this is the new Musick and at present all the Tone." Would all the World, the Performers and Composers as well as Lovers And Hearers at once agree to this.? Would not some be found to say that all the great Masters of Antiquity, as well as of modern times and the present Age, before You, have thought differently. All the Examples are against you. But suppose He should reply. "Dont tell me of Examples. Examples have nothing to do in this matter. Improvement and Discovery must and shall be made. The old Musick was execrable. A better We must and will have. Away with all your Symphonies and Harmonies, your Compositions your Concords and Discords; your flatts and sharps: One simple, unique thorough bass shall bellow in your Ears forever: And then you will have no discords." "Musicians by Profession are interested to make their Science intricate and their practice complex." Must Mankind at once resign their Pleasures and Amusements to Such a decisive Pretender, without consulting their own Ears and Taste?

Another Example may be drawn from Grammar. Why should We have so complicated a system, for the ordinary conversation, and daily Intercourse of Life? Why should our Alphabets consist of so many as four and twenty Letters? cannot We do without Eight Parts of Speech? must our Pronouns have so many Cases, our nouns so many declensions, and our Verbs so many Conjugations, Voices, Moods Tenses, Numbers and Persons? Cannot a little Unity and Simplicity be introduced into this Art. The old Grammar consumes a great deal of time.— And while I am writing the federal Gazette is put into my hand with full proof that the Spirit of Unity and Symplicity is becoming epidemical. A new and universal Language is announced, invented by Professor Wolf of Petersbourg, *destitute of Words* that immediately expresses Ideas and fills the Imagination with Images and Perceptions.[3] it does not take up the fifth of the Space of any known Language. it has no Irregularities no declensions, and only one extremely simple Conjugation. Proper Names of Persons and Places may be accurately expressed by it, without the help of

Words or Letters and it may be commonly read from left to right, or from right to left at pleasure. it is not unpleasant to the Ear. And may be easily taught in any Country where there are Jews, Turks or Christians, or where the Bible or Koran is read.

What Shall We say to this discovery? or Invention? It is a Wonder, and therefore will attract Attention. But will Professor Wolf insist that We should burn all our Grammars, and cease to teach our Children any Language, till We shall be informed what his secret is? We need not contradict his Pretensions. Let him publish his Art and We shall judge. Till then We shall Use what We have and already know.—But his is a very different situation from that of our modern Legislators. Their pretended Nostrum; their Sublime Invention is nothing new. it is as old as nations and has been tried in almost every ~~nation~~ Country. There is Scarcely any nation which has not in some period of its duration, made an Essay of a Government in a single Assembly: sometimes larger and sometimes smaller in point of numbers: and they have been found to operate alike: as uniformly as the ~~Union of fire~~ Conjunction of fire and Gunpowder, has produced explosions. We need not hesitate then to pronounce the Pretension to be an Imposition. The Discovery to be nothing but a renovation of an old and very gross Error. The Invention to be nothing new, any more than Savage Life.

Naval Architecture may furnish Us with another Example. Why should a ship have three Masts? Such a multitude of Ropes and rigging and such a Variety of Sails? Unity and Simplicity, would be more conspicuous in one Mast, and in one sail.

MS (Adams Papers); notation by CFA: "never published."

[1] The dating of this MS is based on JA's mention of the Philadelphia *Federal Gazette*, 16 March 1791, for which see note 3, below.

[2] As a supplement to later editions of his four-volume *Recherches historiques et politiques*, Paris, 1788, Philip Mazzei inserted the Marquis de Condorcet's *Quattre lettres d'un bourgeois de New Haven sur l'unité de la législation*, which advocated a unicameral form of government and outlined a complex electoral process. In his preface, Mazzei lauded Condorcet but stood firmly alongside JA in upholding bicameralism as the more democratic system (Mazzei, *Writings*, 1:560).

[3] JA likely referred to the classical philologist Friedrich August Wolf (1759–1824), of Hainrode, Prussia, who taught philosophy at the University of Halle rather than in St. Petersburg, Russia, and whose academic interests reached the American press. Wolf advocated a holistic approach to humanities scholarship that focused on recovering "the science of antiquity" (Joseph Thomas, *Universal Pronouncing Dictionary of Biography and Mythology*, 3d edn., 2 vols., Phila., 1908; James Turner, *Philology: The Forgotten Origins of the Modern Humanities*, Princeton, N.J., 2014, p. 118–119; Philadelphia *Federal Gazette*, 16 March 1791).

From Amicus

Dr Sir, Massachusetts April 29th. 1790.[1]

I have ever considered the Assumption of the State Debts by Congress, as a measure necessarily flowing from the Adoption of the Constitution of the United States: That on it, the Stability, the Respect, if not the Existence of the Government, would essentially depend.— Little did I suppose, that the Gentlemen composing the house of Representatives of Congress, would determine this Subject, upon the narrow, selfish Principles, as it respects State, & State; and put out of Sight its great Importance as it relates to the United States. When I considered the many Sources of Disunion, the Difference of Climate, Habits & Manners, between the States composing the Union, I looked upon the Debts of the several States as a happy Circumstance, wch. Congress would gladly seize upon, as a cementing Principle, to give Energy, & Stability to a Government, otherwise weak from a Thousand Causes:— Little did I think, that some characters, which I have heretofore respected, and revered, would have exposed their little Souls, before the great Theatre of the World, on a Subject, that must lead mankind to suppose them under a criminal Defection, to the very Government, they exercise.—

The more I reflect upon the Plan of the Secretary of the Treasury, the more I am satisfied with it: and instead of his being thrown out of Office, like the Ministers of England, when their Plans are not supported by a Majority in Parliament the People of the United States will feel themselves interested in it, and will support the Man, for the sake of his Measures.—

The Public Creditors of the United States, are too respectable a Class of Citizens in all the States, not to have a very strong & powerful Influence, especially when there is a Disposition in the people at large, seeing that the honourable Discharge of their Debts, is perfectly within their Power, to second their Views. For the great Body of the People of every Country, when not corrupted, possess the Principles of Honour, & Honesty, in the highest Degree, and there is nothing but absolute Inability will induce them to depart from these Principles. It is for this reason, that the faith of public Engagements has been always, more sacredly preserved in free, than arbitrary Governments.

But perhaps the Gentlemen of the house of Representatives may cunningly cover their Opposition to the Assumption of the State

Debts, under the Idea, of the Contract's not being originally made by Congress, but this Subterfuge is too shallow: The Debt was contracted in a Common Cause, for common Purposes; Congress possess the whole, & only Means, whereby it can be discharged, and therefore a partial Discharge will never give Satisfaction. And what will become of the Government of the United States, without the Confidence of the People! a non-Entity very Shortly. For will the People rest satisfied with one Class of the public Creditors being paid, while another Class, equally meritorious, shall have no Provision made for their Demands? If there is a distinction of Debts, there will of course be of Creditors: If the State Creditors are referred to the State Governmts. for the discharge of their Debts, the Powers of Congress must be retrenched at least so far, as to put it in the Power of the several States to fullfill their Engagements; nor will the State Creditors rest satisfied with any thing short of it.

From this Source then, will there imeadiately rise up an Opposition to the Government, the State Creditors who might have been made instrumental to its Support, already begin to clamour agst. it, and will very shortly be in open Opposition to it. Whatever appearance, these Observations may put on, it may be depended on, I am in no wise, interested in any public Securities whatever. I can judge therefore, of the probable Effect of Congress's not assuming the State Debts, with some Degree of Impartiality. And it is with much concern, I foresee, that the Well wishers to the Government of the United States have every thing to apprehend, if the late measures of Congress are persisted in.

It appears to me there is now an excellent Opportunity for the President to express his Sentiments upon the Secretary's Report. The members of Congress having taken Sides upon this Business, will hardly relinquish their Opinions to one another, unless by the judicious Interference of the Supreme Magistrate; whose conciliating Advice and Influence might prove salutary upon this occasion. It may be said that the Presidt. may be charged with Impropriety in interfering; perhaps so; but it will be only by those Members of Congress, who at present are blinded by their Passions & Prejudices, and who find their Vanity gratified in the supposed Success of their narrow, selfish Designs. I am the more anxious for the President's Opinion at this time, as a new choice of Representatives is just at hand; ~~the President's~~ His Opinion therefore would be something like an appeal to the good Sense of the People, ~~wch. will be either rejected or confirmed~~ whereby to regulate their next choice of Persons to represent them. In England, if a Dispute takes place between the Parliament, & the King's Ministers, the King either gives up his Ministers, or dissolves the Parliament, if the latter, it operates as an appeal to the People, whether they will vindicate the Measures of his ministry, by choosing fit Persons to ~~overthrow or to~~ enforce them. ~~or not~~: By such an Appeal the elastic Principle of the Government is tried, as the reaction of ~~the President's Opinion~~ the Principle, in case there is a coincidence of Opinion, between the People & the Persons administering the Government, will give ~~confidence~~ permanency & Stability to it. Every Government ought to reflect the general Opinion, for when the Measures of it, counteract it, the great end of Government, is perverted, and the public are constrained to accept the narrow, selfish Views of a few Individuals, instead of their own enlightened, & extended Sentiments. The frequent Election of Representatives is hereby rendered necessary to pull down those, who through mistake or Design, act contrary to the general Opinion, and to elevate such, who are better qualified to discern, & to enforce it.—

The great public have had before it, the funding System of the Secretary to the Treasury. The Public Creditors did not at first seem satisfied with the Reduction of Interest, from six to four perCent: but it is left optional, whether to subscribe to the Propositions of the Secretary, or not. The public felt, that from unavoidable Circumstances, the Credit of the Securities had sunk to a very low price:— to raise them at once above par, wch. would have been the Effect of funding the Debt at six per Cent Interest would have been an injustice to those, who have parted with their Securities; to have reduced them to their Value, as sold in the public Market, or to have made a Discrimination between the Original Holders, & present Possessors, would be an injustice to the Present Possessors by not indemnifying them for the Risk they had run, & would be prostrating public Credit. For if the Securities are not to be wholly owned by the present Possessors, will the public Market give credit to the Notes of Congress in future? it is plain it would not. For the Notes being made transferable, the public Market will give the Principal, as long as, or whenever the annual Interest is punctually discharged. What then would become of this Principle, if a Discrimination between original Holders & present Possessors was to take place? It wd. be forever lost, and utterly out of the Power of Congress to retrieve it. But the advantages of the Secretary's Propositions, do not stop here, the Reduction of Interest promises us the Benefit of the Circulation of our own Debt. For if there was a great Temptation to Foreigners to become the

Purchasers of it, $w^{ch.}$ $w^{d.}$ have been the Case if it had been funded at six per Cent, the People of the States would in a few years have possessed but few of their own Securities, and the Monies raised by the Duties for the payment of the annual Interest, would be transported out of the Country, to its great Loss & Injury.—

A Perfect System of Finance taken in the present State of the Debts of the united States, is not to be expected. A compromise of Opinion upon this subject, something like the one produced by the Secretary, will probably give general Satisfaction. The Faith & credit of the united States may be preserved, whilst there is some Regard paid to the public Opinion, in consequence of the very great Depreciation of the Securities, in medio tutissimis ibis.

Every thing it appears to me stands suspended upon this important Question: If Congress assume the State Debts, Peace, Tranquility & a firm Government, will be the Result. if not, a weak, and an inefficient one, or perhaps no Government at all, may be the Consequence. The Choice lies before Congress;—Honour, or Disgrace; I hope, they'll accept the first, that we may not be again exposed to the Inconveniences of a State of Anarchy & Confusion but if they prefer the last, may the Stigma of Defection rest upon those men, who seem disposed to sacrifice the Government, to their narrow, selfish & contracted Views.

With Sentiments of the highest Esteem, I have the honour to be, Sir, / Your most $obed^{t.}$ & / very hble Servant. Amicus.

RC (Adams Papers); internal address: "To his Excellency / John Adams Esq."

[1] Although Alexander Hamilton and other writers used the pseudonym, this "Amicus" has not been identified. For the Funding Act that resolved many of the concerns raised here, see First Congress, Second Session, 4 January 1790 – 12 August 1790, Editorial Note, above.

From Eliphalet Fitch

Dear Sir Kingston $Jam^{a.}$ May $10^{th.}$ 1790

Since writing you, on the $7^{h.}$ Instant, by this Conveyance I have delivered to $Capt^{n.}$ Peters, of the Marianne, a Barrell of Sugar and a Barrell containing One dozen of old Rum and Two dozen of old Madeira Wine.— The Sugar and Rum were made on my Estate and the Wine is from my Cellar— Let me therefore present them to you.— I have requested my Mother to Send you a Packet with Some Papers relative to the Slave-Trade; and if you approve of Sending Copies to the President I would avail myself of your kind Attention therein; as you will See by the inclosed Copy of my Letter.—[1] With Sincere Esteem— / I am, Dear Sir / Yr. Mo. Obedt. Servt Elipht Fitch

PS

I do not know what Title to give to Men in America; and beg your Candour in that respect.—

RC and enclosure (Adams Papers); internal address: "The Honble. John Adams / &c. &c. &c."; notation: "Please to turn over."

[1] Boston native Eliphalet Fitch (1740–1810), second cousin to JA, was a sugar merchant. Fitch wrote to JA on 7 May (Adams Papers), announcing his plans to retire from his post as receiver general of Jamaica. Fitch sent his gift to JA via the *Marianne*, Capt. Peters, which arrived in Boston on 22 June. No letter to JA from Jerusha Boylston Fitch (1711–ca. 1799) has been found.

JA forwarded Fitch's enclosure, which contained a 10 May letter to George Washington and several pamphlets on the African slave trade. The publications were *Debates in the British House of Commons, Wednesday, May 13th 1789*, Phila., 1789, which included a key speech by abolitionist and Yorkshire M.P. William Wilberforce and *A Speech Delivered at a Free Conference between the Honourable the Council and Assembly of Jamaica Held the 19th of November, 1789 on the Subject of Mr. Wilberforce's Propositions*, Kingston, Jamaica, 1790, which was the opposition's response, made by Jamaican merchant and slave owner Bryan Edwards (Boston *Columbian Centinel*, 23 June; New York *Evening Post*, 4 Sept. 1810; *AFC*, 5:173; Ezra S. Stearns, comp., "The Descendants of Dea. Zachary Fitch of Reading," *NEHGR*, 55:400 [Oct. 1901]; Washington, *Papers, Presidential Series*, 5:391–392; François Furstenberg, "Atlantic Slavery, Atlantic Freedom: George Washington, Slavery, and Transatlantic Abolitionist Networks," *WMQ*, 3d ser., 68:266, 270 [April 2011]; *DNB*).

From Joseph Hague

Sir Williamsburg May 13th: 1790

I hope you will pardon me for my presunption to you, but the Subject being so Interesting to the Public, I take the liberty to Write you. I had the Honour to dine with you in Grosvenors square about Four Years ago, and then some conversation passed about the Manufactorys of America.[1] I acquainted you that I imported some Machiens for Carding and Spinning of Wool and Cotton, and had left them in my absence in the posssion of a person in Philadelphia and some British Faitors contrived to get them out of his possesion and sent them back to England. the Public being alarmed caused an enquiry to be made, and finding it to be an object to be noticed, and my Brother haveing been Instructed in England, how to make the different Machines for Manufactoring, the Cityzens of Philadelphia engaged him to make them a Carding Ingine and a Spinning Machine, for which he received a very Insiderable Premium, from that State, and my Brother contrary to my directions entered into an agreement with one Butlar of Philadelphia, who has made several Machines and

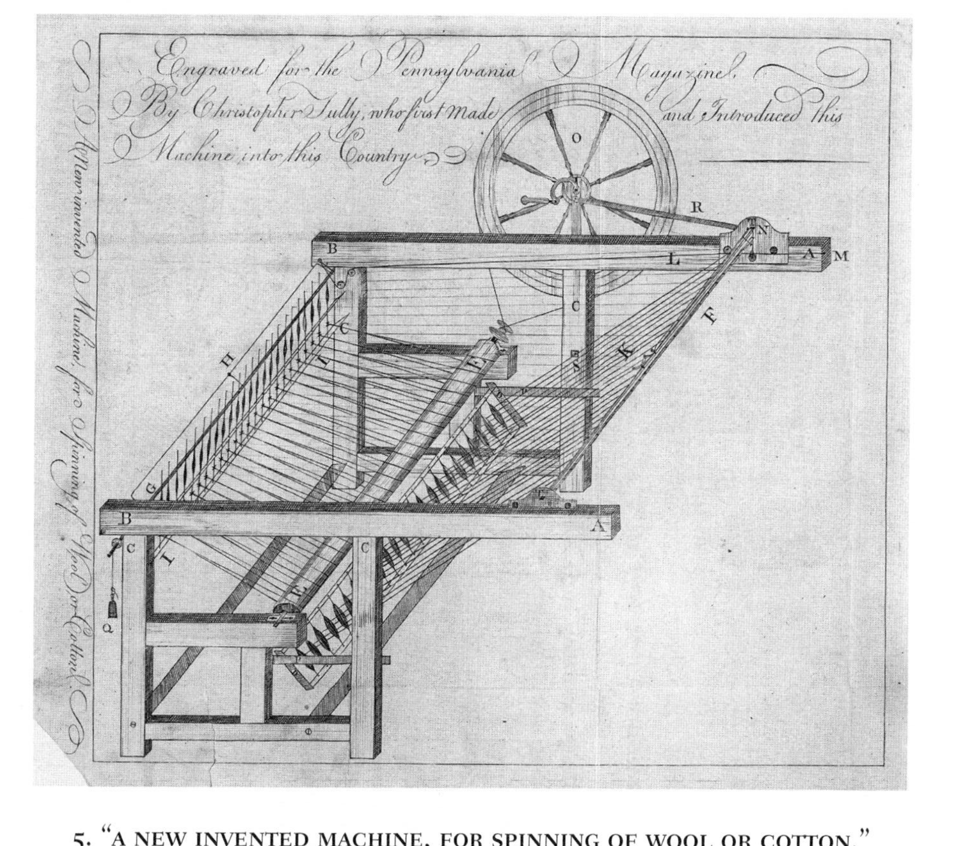

5. "A NEW INVENTED MACHINE, FOR SPINNING OF WOOL OR COTTON,"
BY CHRISTOPHER TULLY, 1775

See page xiii

not complied with is agreement I am late from England and have it in my Power to make the Machines on a more compleat plan besides several other Machines that has never been Introdust, in this country provided I can have the benifit of the Same. I understand from a late paper that patents will be granted to any of the first Introdusers of Machienery, and as me and my Brother are the Only persons that are intitled to lay the Claim, for the same Machines of Manufactoring of Wool & Cotton We can perfect the following Machines One that will Break 100 ld Wool twice over Per day which can be worked either by Water or Horse. Another that will card 30 ld Wool Per day. Another that will Spin from 9 to 12 ld wool Per day as fine as can be prodused which we dye any coular fit for the loom and then wove by Spring Shuttles.— Also the following Machine for Manufactoring of Cotton, One that will card 40 ld Per day by hand a horse or Water. Another With 40 Spindles that will draw from the roll 40 ld Per day by the Assistance of 3 Small Boys or girls and a grown person. Another with 84 Spindles that will Spin from 6 to 8 ld of Cotton Per day of a Sufficient Quality for Calicoes Jeans, Or Corduroys, and which we can also riduce so fine as to make good muslin.— I have also to inform you that I made a Spinning Mashine for Wool & Cotton as early as the year 1775 for which the records will Shew that I received a premium of £15 from the State of Pensylvania but was destroyed by the British Troops. I carried on a considirable Manufactory in the time of War and Suplied Mess Mays and Caldwell with a great Quantity of goods I have rote to One Mr John Brown who is a Member of Congress for the district of Kenticke, and crave your Aid and assistance to know how to get my Patent if I am Intitled to, Any.[2] if you pleas to favour me with your Answer, direct for me at Mr Jacob Sampson Baltimore[3] I am your Hbl Servt Joseph Hague

RC (Adams Papers); internal address: "John Adams Esqr."

[1] For the mechanical operation of Hague's machine, see Descriptive List of Illustrations, No. 5, above. During the Revolutionary War, Hague supplied Pennsylvania merchants James Mease and Samuel Caldwell with textile goods. In 1783 Hague acquired several carding and spinning machines for resale, which were likely smuggled from Liverpool. Owing to difficulties with their assembly, the machines were sent back to England in 1787. Unwilling to cede or share control of the new technology, members of the Pennsylvania Society's manufacturing committee petitioned the state legislature to forbid the export of the machines and to discourage the emigration of trained workmen. Hague's brother, John, moved to Virginia and in 1790 established a cotton factory near Nashville, Tenn. Another Philadelphia partner in their business, John Butler, was a carpenter (David J. Jeremy, "British Textile Technology Transmission to the United States: The Philadelphia Region Experience, 1770–1820," *Business History Review*, 47:33, 40, 50 [Spring 1973]; Washington, *Papers, Revolutionary War Series*, 13:166; Samuel C. Williams, "The South's First Cot-

ton Factory," *Tennessee Historical Quarterly*, 5:213, 216–217 [Sept. 1946]; *Philadelphia Directory*, 1785).

Hague's appeal to JA likely stemmed from the publication of the 10 April Patent Act, which appeared in the Philadelphia *Federal Gazette*, 15 April. For the many inventors who sought JA's aid in obtaining patents and for his responses, see, for example, Thomas McKean's 20 Jan. letter, above, and JA's 19 May reply to Benjamin Lincoln, below.

[2] Staunton, Va., lawyer John Brown (1757–1837) served as the Virginia representative for Kentucky from 1789 to 1792 and opened a textile factory in Danville, Ky. (*Biog. Dir. Cong.*; *First Fed. Cong.*, 14:890).

[3] Jacob Sampson (1752–1822), a speculator from Sheffield, England, moved to Baltimore in 1775 and there sold slaves, land, and livestock (Lilla Briggs Sampson, *The Sampson Family*, Baltimore, 1914, p. 192; *Maryland Journal*, 11 Jan. 1780, 27 Aug. 1790).

From Thomas Crafts Jr.

My Dear Sir — Boston May 17. 1790

I recieved yours of april 4th and should have wrote sooner but thought it best to wait sometime that I might answer your Queries with more certainty. I thank you for Your Polite & unremitted attention to my Application in favour of Mr Martin B Sohier, Have waited with some degree of impatiance for the result of the Secretary of War's determination on that subject, Cannot doubt from what you write of his best disposition to serve him, after Your interposition & influence in his favour. but that I shall rest satisfye'd with his Decision—

Commerce & Business in general here is extreamly dull, perhaps it was never more so except at the time of the Port-Bill— Business is supposed not to be so brisk & florishing as it has been for several Years past and many suppose it is in Consequence of the large sums of Money locked up in the different custom houses and by that means kept out of Circulation or for ought we know sent to the Seat of Government— You ask if no Benign influence has as yet been felt in Consequence of the New Goverment— The not assuming the State Debts has had, a most disagreeable and banefull Effect here, and I am perswayded has made more persons disaffected to the New Goverment, than any other matter could possably have done. The long time Congress spent in disputing on the Quakers petition in favour of the Negro's & the warmth with which it was supported by the Eastern Members—has given great unesiness to many Persons— It being said here that was the cause of sowering the minds of the Southern members against an Assumtion of the State Debts—[1] The Price of Bills of Exchange have fallen here 10 pr Cent that is they were 5 pr Cent above parr & are now 5 pr Cent below parr. But it seems this was more by Accendent—(The great demand for Grain from Europe) then from any benign Influencee of the New Government.[2] And this has opperated rather against this Town, as large sums of Money, in addition to what is already Shut up has been sent to New York Philid[a] &c to purchase Bills— You inquire if the Ship Carpenters are Employ'd I answer. that they are wholly out Business as are most other Tradesmen, And I assure you the Situation of this Town, is truly Melancholy and Distressing. The sound of the Ax or the Hammer is hardly to be heard in any part of It— The Tradesmen, almost totaly discouraged. No work to be done, High Taxes & no prospect of Releiaf— You will see by Little attention paid to the Choice of Representives but 200 Voters. Then more then 20 Candidates— No list presented or prepared & when called upon to Vote. in general answerd they care'd not who were Chosen, they could not be worse off and, that it was not probable they should be better distress & poverty being thier portion & they appear to me to be quite discouraged—[3]

Cannot something be done to Encourage the Cod & whale Fisheries—

Must the Ship building be wholly Annihilated in the Eastern States—

Must the Assumtion of the State Debts be giving up for this Sessions—

Will not Congress take some measures that the Monies collected for Imposts may be brought into Circulation again as soon as posable

I am with great esteem & regard / Your most ob[t] Serv[t]

Thomas Crafts

RC (Adams Papers); internal address: "Excellency John Adams Esq[r]"; endorsed: "ans[d.] 25. 1790."

[1] For the "Quakers petition," see Benjamin Franklin's letter of 9 Feb., and note 1, above. On 4 June the Mass. General Court resolved that the U.S. government must assume the state's debts (Hall, *Politics without Parties*, p. 324).

[2] Crafts' source for these figures has not been identified. Because of poor harvests in 1789 and an influx of refugees fleeing political turmoil, France's grain famine spread to Switzerland. In early 1790, the American press reported on the "pinching scarcity of provisions" and projected that the crisis in France would escalate without the aid of U.S. imports (*Norwich-Packet*, 29 Jan.; Stockbridge, Mass., *Western Star*, 2 March; *Pennsylvania Packet*, 4 March; *Boston Gazette*, 15 March). See also John Bondfield's letter of 20 Nov. 1789 and note 4, above.

[3] Two hundred Boston voters turned out in the spring of 1790 to choose the Massachusetts governor and lieutenant governor and representatives for the General Court. After two rounds of voting, John Hancock and Samuel Adams were selected as governor and lieutenant governor, respectively, with Adams reinforcing his popularity by garnering 84 percent of the vote (A New Nation Votes; Hall, *Politics without Parties*, p. 325).

To Oliver Whipple

Dear sir New York May 18. 1790

With much pleasure I received your favour of the 26. of April: it brought fresh to my Memory the many hours We Spent together, in the Chamber where I first saw the Light of the sun.

I believe there are few Persons, who run through a public Career, especially one that interests the Passions of the People; without finding Persons to recollect Prophecies that great Things would one day be his Lot.— The political Path, in which I sat out [in] Life must lead either to destruction or to great success.— As I know there were not wanting Persons to predict that I should rise high, and among these were Men of Merit: so on the other, I believe there were many more who prosphecied that I should ruin myself Family and Country, and reach nothing but Infamy. I am not sorry as you may well imagine that the Prognostications of the latter sort are not fulfilled.

The Representation of your independent and respectable Circumstances gives me much Pleasure.— The sense of Congress seems to be so much against many missions abroad, that I apprehend you could find no Chance from that branch, in which so many have already been employed with Reputation, who are now out of office.— I really think you will find no office much better than a Lawyers office.— Mine I know while I held it, was the best office I ever enjoyed.

As the Executive department by the Constitution is wholly in the President, I make no Promisses to any one, and interfere as little, as possible in appointments.— I should however have much pleasure in concurring with the Friends You mention, in recommending you, as far as the public service may justify.[1]

With great Esteem and regard I have honour to / be, sir your most obedient servant John Adams

RC (private owner, 2007); internal address: "Oliver Whipple Esqr / Portsmouth. New Hampshire"; endorsed: "Vice Presidents Letter." LbC (Adams Papers); APM Reel 115. Text lost due to removal of the seal has been supplied from the LbC.

[1] Whipple renewed his request for patronage in a letter of 22 Nov., telling JA that "a Word from you in this Matter, will produce the desired Effect" (Adams Papers).

To William Ellery

Dear Sir New York May 19 1790.

I have received your favor of the 13th, as I did that of march in due season—[1] One wishes to be informed of all facts in which the public is interested: but the detail of Rhode Island manœuvres is distressing. The Senate yesterday passed a bill, which cutts off all communication with Rhode Island, if she chooses such a solitary selfish and unsocial system. The bill passed by a great majority, and the Senators appear very decided in this business. I would send you a copy of the bill, if I had one, but it is not necessary to send to town to get one, because the newspapers have already contained the substance of the bill, and the true bill as it passed will be with you in the gazetts before this letter.[2]

If the inland part of your people are so abandoned as to refuse still to ratify the Constitution, there will be no part left for the Seaports, but to do what I think they ought to have done long ago, meet and adopt the Constitution for themselves and petition congress to be received and protected. Your views, and wishes I have communicated to several gentlemen in confidence, but not to the President. He has been very ill and unable to attend to business.[3] It is a rule with me to meddle as little as possible in appointments; and I know not who are candidates for the office you speak of at New Port. Whenever my opinion is asked concerning any candidates within my acquaintance I always give it according to my best judgment— I presume that the applications of your Antis, are made to other men, to such as they have consulted with already too long.— Your convention meet next monday— Our bill cannot pass the house soon enough to reach you till many days after. I sincerely hope that your people will adopt the Constitution and send us an account of it before the bill passes the house.— I know not the character of the Govenors friend Mr Thompson: but possession you know is eleven points and if there is not any pointed objection against him, it would not I presume be difficult to gratify the Governor. John Adams

LbC in CA's hand (Adams Papers); internal address: "Hon Willm Ellery / New-Port"; APM Reel 115.

[1] Of [*ca.* 6] March, above. Ellery's letter of 13 May (Adams Papers) informed JA that Rhode Island legislators favored ratification of the Constitution with amendments but that Gov. Arthur Fenner's support of ratification hinged on whether his ally Ebenezer Thompson (1735–1805) kept his post as port collector of Providence. Ellery also solicited JA for the

collectorship of Newport. On 14 June George Washington nominated Ellery for the position, and his appointment was confirmed the same day. Ellery held the post until his death on 15 Feb. 1820. Thompson remained in his position from 1789 to 1790 and then served as naval officer from 1790 until his death in 1805 (U.S. Senate, *Exec. Jour.*, 1st Cong., 2d sess., p. 51; *Biog. Dir. Cong.*; Washington, *Papers, Presidential Series*, 5:414–415).

[2]The question of how the U.S. government should handle Rhode Island's outlier status took a turn on 28 April 1790, when Maryland senator Charles Carroll moved to form a committee to address the issue. Members Carroll, Oliver Ellsworth, Robert Morris, Ralph Izard, and Pierce Butler drafted the Rhode Island trade bill, which prevented "bringing goods, wares and merchandizes from the State of Rhode-Island and Providence Plantations, into the United States; and to authorize a demand of money from the said State." It was read in the Senate on 13 May and passed five days later in a vote of 13 to 8. William Maclay led the opposition, claiming it was meant to "impress the People of Rhode Island, with Terror," in "the same Way That a Robber does a dagger or a Highwayman a pistol." Newspaper accounts of the debates nurtured a new groundswell of Federalist sentiment. The Providence *United States Chronicle*, 20 May, reported that senators were weighing a bill to restrict the state's trade as of 1 July and demanding a $27,000 payment due 1 August. The bill was read in the House of Representatives on 19 and 20 May but referred to committee. Rhode Island's brinkmanship with the federal government ended with ratification of the Constitution on 29 May (*First Fed. Cong.*, 1:294–295, 309, 311, 312, 313–314; 9:225, 271).

[3] Struck by the influenza epidemic in New York, Washington battled a nearly fatal case of pneumonia from 10 to 20 May. He resumed his duties on 30 May but remained weak. AA was sensitive to the political implications of Washington's second grave illness in a few months, observing that "most assuredly I do not wish for the highest Post. I never before realizd what I might be calld to, and the apprehension of it only for a few days greatly distresst me" (Washington, *Papers, Presidential Series*, 5:393, 394, 395, 396, 398; *AFC*, 9:62).

To Benjamin Lincoln

Dear Sir New York May 19 1790

I have duly received but not duly answered your favor of April 3^d^.[1] It is a misfortune that a man can never be spoken to by a projectors without being misunderstood or misrepresented I told Mr. Forbisher that if he expected any thing from the general government, he must apply to it by petition. But I never told him, that I had the least suspicion that the general government would ever do anything for him.— How should they? He is in possession of no secret; if he was an inventor or discoverer he has long since made his art public; he therefore cannot obtain a patent.— One is harrassed through life with an hundred of these dreamers who will never take no! for an answer. if he will beleive that Congress will assist him why does he not petition? I have no such faith: if the state would not assist him, why should the Continent? We have been much allarmed, at the sickness of the President: but thank God, he is better and recovering fast. The house do not harmonize in the right system, so well as we could wish: but the prosperity of the Country, has been so greatly promoted by the government, that I hope we shall not throw it away.— The Massachusetts have appeared to me to waver as much as any State: but the elections this year I hope are more favorable—

Your[s] &c John Adams

LbC in CA's hand (Adams Papers); internal address: "Hon Benj[a] Lincoln."; APM Reel 115.

[1] Lincoln's letter of 3 April (Adams Papers) introduced William Frobisher (ca. 1724–1807). The Boston merchant, who had discovered a new method of making potash, failed to earn compensation from the Massachusetts legislature for his invention and sought JA's aid in securing it from the federal government. In his Diary, JA recalled meeting Frobisher on 28 June 1770 and hearing "a Narration of his Services to the Province," commenting, "Thus Projectors, ever restless." Frobisher was granted a federal patent on 17 Nov. 1796 (JA, *D&A*, 1:353; "The Records of Trinity Church, Boston, 1728–1830," Col. Soc. Mass., *Pubns.*, 56:821 [1982]; Henry L. Ellsworth, *A Digest of Patents, Issued by the United States, from 1790 to January 1, 1839*, Washington, D.C., 1840, p. 154).

To William Smith

Dear Sir, New York May 20 1790

Your agreable favour of the 24th of April, was brought to me in season and I thank you for it; though my thanks are not in good season.—Your sentiments concerning the assumption of the State debts, the encouragement of American navigation and the establishment of a national bank, are conformable to those of about one half The Continent and contrary to those of the other half. How shall we contrive to make the Clocks all strike together? Virginia begins to be convinced of the necessity of uniting with the States on this side of her, in measures to encourage our shipping, and give it an advantage over foreigners; but your cousin of Carolina, who is one of the most judicious men in the house, is you see quite an enemy to such measures. The Carolinas and Georgia, I suppose will be longer in their conversion, than Virginia has been.—[1] It may require a more United people and a stronger government to take those steady measures, necessary to support our navigation: but my sentiments on this point are no secret to Congress: I wrote them continually from England: and I still think for us to build man, and maintain twelve hundred ships for a foreign nation, out of the labour of our husbandmen is very ill contrivance for the interest of Agriculture, whatever our friend Smith may say.

Division of sentiments about every thing—some inclining to the French, some to the English; one party to the south and another to the north; one sett advocates for the interest of Agriculture; another for those of commerce a third for those of manufactures—every party pushing their own principles too far, and opposing others too much—

How few minds look through the mighty all, with a steady eye, and consider all its relations and dependences![2] How few aim at the good of the whole, without aiming too much at the prosperity of parts?— These questions have occurred ever since I was born, and will as long as I live, or you either. The turbulent maneuvres of a faction in the Massachusetts weaken and embarrass us, as much or more than Rhode Island. I despair of New England: they upon principle tie the hands and destroy the influence of every man who has any chance and any desire to serve them— So says and so feels, by cruel experience yours

J Adams—

LbC in CA's hand (Adams Papers); internal address: "Mr Wm Smith Boston"; APM Reel 115. Tr (Adams Papers).

[1] As the Anglo-American trade war dragged on, British merchants extended credit to southern planters in need of manufactured goods and agreed to carry their grain in exchange. On 17 May James Madison, leading a committee comprising Theodore Sedgwick of Massachusetts and Thomas Hartley of Pennsylvania, introduced a trade bill to increase tonnage duties on foreign ships. South Carolina representative William Loughton Smith opposed it, claiming in his speeches to the House on 17 and 18 May that the proposal was squarely aimed at Great Britain. W. L. Smith recommended that the executive branch should determine all questions of tonnage and warned Congress that it was "highly impolitic to enter into a commercial warfare with Great Britain." The bill was read again on 18 May and for a third time on 25 June, when the House voted to consider it further, but it was not passed. British newspapers reported avidly on the congressional debates, noting that the absence of an Anglo-American commercial treaty would injure British profits (George C. Rogers, *Evolution of a Federalist: William Loughton Smith of Charleston (1758–1812)*, Columbia, S.C., 1962, p. 173–175; *First Fed. Cong.*, 3:411, 413, 415, 477, 822; *New-York Daily Gazette*, 17, 18 May; London *English Chronicle*, 22 July; London *Diary*, 11 Aug.; London *Public Advertiser*, 7 Sept.).

[2] CA emphasized this sentence in the left margin of the LbC with a manicule.

To Thomas Crafts Jr.

Dear Sir

New York 25th [*May*] 1790

I have received with a mixture of pleasure and gloomy melancholy your favour of the 17th. What motives the eastern members can have to support the silly petition of Franklin and his Quakers, I never could conceive: but it was not that conduct which sowered the minds of the Southern members against an assumption of the State debts. The seat of government is more likely to have had such an effect on some minds.[1] What is the reason that bills should be ten or twelve per Ct below par here, and only five at Boston The demand from Europe for grain would not alone have produced so great and sudden a change in the price of bills. The sudden rise of stock which was certainly occasioned by the new government contributed a great share to this symptom of prosperity. If no measures would ever be carried in the State Legislature to encourage the fisheries I leave you to Judge whether it is probable that bounties can be obtained from the general government.

Ships before the revolution were built upon British capitals. There are no capitals in Boston I fear but such as consist in credits to the nation or the State or employed in speculations in the Stocks. The carrying trade is the only resource for shipbuilding. The English are in possession of this. They not only have ships ready; but they own the crops for the most part. To dispossess the English from this business requires a system of measures and a course of time and our people are so fickle and unsteady, that it is doubtfull whether they would bear with patience the trial of a fair experiment The Massachusetts a few years ago, made a navigation act, which if it had been preserved to this day would in my opinion have found full employment for her shipwrights: but M[r] Sullivan and Parson Thatcher, I heard in London became declaimers if not preachers against it and it was repealed.[2] If Congress should make a similar law, it will be opposed by powerful interests, who will continually grumble against it and there is neither vigour nor constancy enough in the government, I am afraid, to persevere. That Congress will take some measures to bring into circulation the monies locked up, I cannot doubt. This must be done— I am assured that considerable sums of money are ordered to America from Europe, so that I hope we shall not have so great a scarcity of money long. The State debts, I fear will not be assumed this session.

Without a national government and steady measures we shall never be prosperous, and there is too powerful a party in Massachusetts against both. I hope we shall see better times, but my hopes are not sanguine

Yours &c J A

LbC in CA's hand (Adams Papers); internal address: "Thomas Crafts Esq[r] Boston"; APM Reel 115.

[1] By late spring, congressional battle lines were drawn over two major issues: settling war debts and siting the capital. Within Congress, Massachusetts and South Carolina favored the federal assumption of state debts, while Virginia and North Carolina stood opposed to it. An antislavery petition, submitted by Benjamin Franklin, complicated both sets of debates. James Madison joined New England representatives in supporting calls to end slavery, but he led the opposition in the House of Representatives regarding assumption (Elkins and McKitrick, *Age of Federalism*, p. 147, 152, 160).

[2] The Mass. General Court's navigation act of 23 June 1785 prohibited imports sent via British ships, restricted foreign ships to entering only three regional ports, and laid duties on all other foreign ships that were double those paid by American ships. Massachusetts politician James Sullivan backed the measures, but he worried that internal division

and a love of luxury kept Americans under Great Britain's economic sway, writing: "Our Merchants have a supreme regard to her Commerce perhaps the large Sums they owe there keeps them in Awe." Peter Thacher (1752–1802), Harvard 1769, who was the General Court's chaplain, sided with Sullivan. On 29 Nov. 1790 Massachusetts lawmakers repealed the restrictions and heavy duties on foreign vessels, retaining the provisions against British ships (vol. 17:83, 535, 605; *Sibley's Harvard Graduates*, 17:237, 245, 246).

From Thomas Brand Hollis

Dear Sir 28 May. 1790 Chesterfeild Street

Having an opportunity of writing by Mr Rutledge[1] I embrace it with great pleasure to convey to you a few lines & some tracts & to convince you that you are often in my memory & could I find conveyances easy you would hear often from me being interested in the progress that Novi homines new men make in virtue & knowledge.

The state of the publick in general is astonishingly changed since we parted & I see with rapture the scenes which are opening on this world of ours from the English revolution the seeds of Freedom were sown you encouraged & promoted their progress to a Surprising degree of perfection the French Nation tho suffering from every quarter the utmost indignities that human nature could bear were not deterred from aiding & assisting the culture till at last the Sun of Liberty arose with healing in his wings & with undiminished splendor brought forth fruits worthy of Paradise to maintain envigorate & illumine mankind.

This last revolution being supernatural the hand of heaven is still with them to effect greater purposes This affair of Nootka Sound will have its consequences whither a war or not it will open that sea to America[2] Khamchatzar will be well known Japan will be practised & open to people of that Hemisphere Mexico will be independent Quebeck will gain a free constitution not granted by the English & United with America[3] the Chinese will alter their manners the Malese will navigate those seas as the inhabitants of sandwich Island do at present in American ships— Persia India Tibet & the great Lama will be accessible Asia will throw of her Tyrants Egypt will be formed by the French into a regular government & Africa cease to be the market for slaves but enjoy their native innocent & peace which will prevail all over the world in spight of the Despots. the time is approaching fast when Dr Jebbs wish will be accomplished.[4] a general hunt of kings— in this universal regeneration I fear England will be the last.

when we consider how rapidly the french revolution took place like an electrical stroke we may hope such great events are not very distance & to the improvement of government Franklyn's Idea may succeed that old age may be kept of & even life prolonged for a great period if not continued.[5] do not think me wild Some of these events have happened & the progress of science & knowledge promise the consequences.

Bruce's travels to Abyssinia are published at length have just begun it—to condemn it is the fashion for wch there may be some reasons but it opens almost a new part of the world & there are many valuable facts the stile is that of a proud man unpractised in the mechanism of writing— the designs of antique buildings of wch he had many have been purchased some time past with publick money & kept from that publick which ought to have been gratified with the publication of them for which they have paid & are willing to pay liberally![6]

Poor Lidiard the American was lost for want of money probably he was to have gone to the internal parts of Africa from Cairo— it seems there is a tract from the River Gambia or serra leone of 700 miles mostly by water to mourzouk capital of Fezzan & Gonjah is only 46 days from Assenti the gold coast—wch is much shorter than from Tripoli wch is 3000 miles & through desarts

a pompous book is printed but not sold!

two large black cities inland Cushnak & Bornou civilized & mahomitons—perfect religious liberty—they are larger than tripoli—Caravans go there[7]

The dissenters for want of proper spirit have again lost their cause but the subject is more genally understood & next application will come with greater force & strength—[8] Vailliants account of Africa is a valuable work He reinstates the Apron & the Cameliopardalis of Pliny[9] the tract on The Feudal tenure is by a friend of yrs a good & excellent performance[10]

my best comp^ts^ to Mrs Adams herself & family are in perfect health at the Hide which I wish her sincerely to enjoy with her family— compts to m^r^ & m^rs^ smith

and am Dear Sir with great esteem / Your affectionate friend

T. Brand Hollis

In the chronicle of Kings is there an instance of a Jewish King having 6 millions in bank & 12 hundred thousand a year coming to his people to pay his Doctors bill?. in a recent application the struggle was who Should give most as it is said not to be a question which concerns the civil list!.[11]

RC (Adams Papers); endorsed by CA: "Thomas / Brand Hollis / May 28— 90"; notation by CFA: "T. B. Hollis. / May 28. 1790."

[1] John Rutledge Jr. was returning to the United States following his grand tour of Europe, for which see vol. 19:215. He sailed from Falmouth, England, on the British packet *Chesterfield*, Capt. Schuyler, and reached New York City on 2 Aug. (*New-York Journal*, 3 Aug.).

[2] Competition for the lucrative fur trade and access to the Northwest Passage drew British, Spanish, and Russian merchants to the largely undeveloped trading post of Nootka Sound, located on the coast of present-day Vancouver Island, British Columbia, Canada. For the diplomatic crisis that challenged American neutrality throughout the summer and autumn of 1790, see John Brown Cutting's letter of 3 June, and note 1, below.

[3] Responding to loyalists' dissatisfaction with the terms of the 1774 Quebec Act, Parliament passed the Constitutional Act of 1791, splitting the province into Upper and Lower Canada. Each region operated under a separate government with a representative assembly and a governor (Donald Grant Creighton, *The Commercial Empire of the St. Lawrence 1760–1850*, Toronto, 1937, p. 114–115).

[4] Under John Jebb's ideal constitution, the people were empowered to bestow and to revoke the status of monarchs and nobility (Anthony Page, *John Jebb and the Enlightenment Origins of British Radicalism*, Westport, Conn., 2003, p. 203).

[5] Writing to Joseph Priestley on 8 Feb. 1780, Benjamin Franklin speculated that "all Diseases may by sure means be prevented or cured, not excepting even that of Old Age, and our Lives lengthened at pleasure even beyond the antediluvian Standard" (Franklin, *Papers*, 31:455–456).

[6] Scottish explorer James Bruce (1730–1794), of Kinnaird, published *Travels to Discover the Source of the Nile*, 5 vols., Edinburgh, 1790. During his travels in Algiers and Tunis, Bruce made three volumes of drawings of classical ruins that he presented to George III (*DNB*).

[7] Great Britain's African Association hired American explorer John Ledyard to travel south from Egypt. Ledyard arrived in Cairo in Aug. 1788 but died of a "bilious disorder" several months later. Hollis read an excerpt of secretary Henry Beaufoy's *Proceedings of the African Association*, London, 1790, which had appeared in the London *St. James's Chronicle*, 8 April 1790, and described the trading capitals of Cashnah (now Katsina, Nigeria) and the former empire of Bornu, Nigeria (vol. 18:96; A. Adu Boahen, "The African Association, 1788–1805," *Transactions of the Historical Society of Ghana*, 5:45, 56 [1961]).

[8] For the parliamentary debates over the repeal of the Test and Corporation Acts, see Hollis' letter of 29 March, and note 7, above.

[9] Pliny the Elder wrote about wild boars and giraffes in the eighth book of his *Natural History*, as did François Le Vaillant in his *Travels from the Cape of Good-Hope, into the Interior Parts of Africa*, 2 vols., London, 1790, 2:184, 457.

[10] Hollis meant the Abbé de Mably's *Observations sur l'histoire de France*, Geneva, 1765, a copy of which is in JA's library at MB. Widely reprinted in 1788, Mably's work chronicled the social history of rural feudalism and aristocratic tyranny (vol. 17:72; *Catalogue of JA's Library*).

[11] Under the Civil List Act of 1782, Parliament oversaw the expenditures of the monarchy. On 17 May 1790 George III requested a pension for his doctor, Francis Willis (1718–1807), of Lincoln, England. Ten days later, Parliament granted Willis an annual sum of £1,000 for 21 years (vol. 19:195; London *St. James's Chronicle*, 18, 29 May, 8 July; *DNB*).

From Bartholomew Burges

New York 29th. May '90

May it please your Excellency—

Sir, You did me the honor the winter before last to subscribe to a little Astronomical essay of mine and on my presenting the work I was honor'd by your invitation at Braintree, which gain'd me access to your Excellency: when on your understanding that I had been some many years in the East Indies, Your Excellency was pleas'd to intimate that you would present to your friends in Congress a memorial if I prepar'd one pointing out the eligibility of the Ameicans establishing factories in the East Indies, and of striking up Commercial treaties with the Indostan, and other Asiatic powers: a sufficient inducement for me to have digested into a Narrative the materials in my possession and the India matters I had then in speculation; and propos'd within my self to have effected this work, as soon as I should have received the profits of my little litarary undertaking, but disappointed therein by my having intrusted a man with my list of Subscribers and a second Edition of my Work who laying himself in with Edes the Printer at Boston and my Engraver; both equally dispos'd to wrong me, under the colour of Partnership, sequester'd the work out of my hands, and left me in a very ridiculous position at Boston, depriving me of all the advantages I expected to have reap'd from it; when in order to retrieve my self I set about composing and protracting a Sett of Charts of the Coast of America which are all now engraved, & publish'd in Boston;[1] a laborious peice of work that I compleated under very disadvantageous circumstances: when after having run my self in debt, in originating it, and bringing it forward by obtaining the patronage of the Honorable Mr. Bowdoin, Mr. Tommy Russel, Major Covin &c. &c; oblig'd to give it up and leave unpaid these demands, and forfeit my Engagements with the Public, or surrender it up to an artful fellow upon very disadvantageous terms I choos'd the latter, which man disappointing me in every shape, thro' out the series of the whole business, at the latter end I found my self, and family (remov'd by this time by me to Boston) in sudden extremity in a severe season of the year, and finally reduc'd to the alternative of being beholden to some four or five Honorable Gentlemen for assistance, or of seeing my wife, & three Children suffer; for however dispos'd to stoop to any thing for their support Gentlemen, and Merchants, on the one hand; to whom I was known, averse to employ a person in a low station, who had been in company and conversation with them, and with men of rank, and was; as they were pleas'd to say calculated for something better; added to my having been considerably incapacitated from getting a Livelyhood by daily labour, by reason of a shot—ie. or large iron ball, I received in India that enter'd my breast, and pass'd thro' my shoulder blade, in seising on an English ship in the Gulph of Gugzerat while in the service of Gillumnabby the Prince of Sinde;[2] and men who had been a long time in the line of Tuihin bendes the number of Newcomers acting in that sphere leaving no opening for my succeeding that way on the other hand and our furniture and things dispos'd of to buy bread; not resolution enough to snatch my self from my family immers'd in such distress, and go farther afield for their releif however expedient the step— in this provoking situation I remaind 'till about the middle of this month, when rather than leave my family so situated, by going to India at this time of life without securing to them some aid in my absence as some had advis'd me to do I form'd the resolution of gaining this Metropolis where was the seat of Government and where your Excellency residing something perhaps might be hop'd for, for the meliorating my condition, at least if any countenance could be given to any plan I might adopt for that purpose, that at the same time should have a tendency to national utility, and induc'd by these hopes, and urg'd by the above motives I came here and publish'd last Thursday the accompany'd Proposals: your Excellency's patronage to which, can I but obtain, by your honoring me with your name thereto, and the illustrious Presidents name to crown my endeavours, it will most undoubtedly answer my most sanguine expectations as it will be the means of not only bringing about a temporary assistance for me, but enable me to open a private Marine Academy for the improvement, and instruction of the Seafaring line in general, and a Marine Intelligence Office at the same time, where when Captains of Vessels of all denominations should be supply'd with Charts, and nautical directions and naval, and commercial information adapted to their Voyages from the most modern and authentic authorities to any part of the World, and enable me to prepare materials for an Edetion of large Terraqueous Globes, and the Superfices for Engraving; a business I am thoroughly acquainted with which would have a Tendency towards promoting useful Knowledge in this Empire, and of reestablishing my self again in life. Then please your Excellency being my Ultimatum should I not with the benevolent disposition you inherit succeed in this application I should conclude that some fatality must attend my proceedings that defeats all my attempts in these parts however honest my endeavours and despair of succeeding on the Continent of America! But reflect then please your Excellency on the situation of mind that dictated these sentiments and I should have hopes that this intrusion on your hours; to your self & the world of such importance, and of my particulars might plead you to pardon the liberty I have taken and to pay some little attention to my request begging leave to subscribe myself with the greatest respect, May it please Your Excellency Your Excellency's most Obedient & / devoted humble servant Bartholomew Burges

RC (Adams Papers); internal address: "The Honorable John Adames Esquire / L.L.D. Vice President of the United States &c."

[1] Bartholomew Burges (ca. 1740–1807) taught navigation, surveying, and astronomy in Ipswich, Mass. He wrote *A Short Account of the Solar System, and of Comets in General*, Boston, 1789, Evans, No. 21722. His most recent publication was *A Series of Indostan Letters*, N.Y., 1790, Evans, No. 22380, which he advertised in the *New-York Packet*, 27 May. Along with engraver John Norman (ca. 1750–1817) and auctioneer Matthew Clark (ca. 1747–1798), Burges produced *A Complete Chart of the Coast of America, from Cape Breton into the Gulf of Mexico*, Boston, 1790, Evans, No. 21738.

Several prominent authors, including David Ramsay and Jedidiah Morse, joined Burges in petitioning Congress for copyright protection. On 23 June 1789 Benjamin Huntington of Connecticut introduced a bill in the House of Representatives "to promote the progress of science and useful arts, by securing to authors and inventors the exclusive right to their respective writings and discoveries." Members of the House postponed debate on the bill until the next session, presenting a revised proposal "securing the copyright of books" on 28 Jan. 1790. One month later, Elias Boudinot made another key change, expanding the privilege to maps, charts, and other writings. Congress then passed the Copyright Act, which secured authors' rights for fourteen years, and George Washington signed it into law on 31 May (David Bosse, "Matthew Clark and the Beginnings of Chart Publishing in the United States," *Imago Mundi*, 63:22, 24, 26 [Jan. 2011]; *First Fed. Cong.*, 1:723, 728; 3:22, 56–57, 94, 306; New York *Gazette of the United States*, 5 June). See also Richard Cranch's 22 Jan. letter, and note 1, above.

[2] Fom 1757 to 1772, Ghulam Shah Kalhora ruled Hyderabad, located in present-day Pakistan's Sindh province (James Wynbrandt, *A Brief History of Pakistan*, N.Y., 2009, p. 100).

From Henry Marchant

Most respected Friend Newport May 29th. 1790—

'tis done,—'tis done— The Constitution this Day was adopted by Our State Convention, by a Majority of two— Never were Days of more anxiety, Labor and Assiduity, Hope and Fear, than the last six— It is a happy Circumstance that the Convention was adjourned to this Town, where we had the largest fœderal Interest, and little Influence of the Country Anties— The late Act passed by the Senate of Congress was an Instrument which we weilded with much Success and Execution:—Nothing could be more timely—[1] It would take a Quire of Paper to give You the entertaining particulars of this Week:— But I know not how soon an Opportunity may offer to New York—Therefore to Business

Congress may soon rise, and may find it necessary to make the Acts proper to the Introduction of this State into the Union, before Our Members may be able to reach Congress— Our Assembly will sit three Weeks from next Monday: The Senators may be chosen then; The Representative cannot be, till four Weeks after:—[2] I have therefore inclosed You the Revennue Act of this State; passed as nearly as possible to that of Congress—[3] Here you will find all the Ports marked out and well described, and every Thing necessary for forming Your Acts or Bills— Names for Officers I dare say have gone forward in Abundance long ago, and are in the Care and Charge of one Member or another.—[4] But if Satisfaction cannot yet be had on that Subject, or not untill Congress should rise,—the Act may provide for this State, that the President have the intire Power of Appointment; at any Rate untill Congress meet again—

I don't know but I am impertinent in this Business:—but my Wish is to advance the publick Weal, and to give every Aid in my Power, that the Wheels of Government, and Revennue, may be in Motion— What is well You may retain; You have been used to refine;—The Dross You may throw away.—

Upon this happy Occasion I congratulate You Sir,—And thro' You Sir, I desire to congratulate the President, Our fœderal Head and Father;—Congress and all well Wishers to the building up Our grand fœderal Cause and Government— With sincere Respects to Mrs. Adams, Compts. to the Family and all Friends, without Time to add; having come this Moment out of Convention, and amidst the din & Noise of Bells, Huzzas and Guns, I am most respectfully Your devoted / Friend & Servt. Hy: Marchant

P:S: Amidst my hurry I had forgot to acknowledge the Honor done me by yours of the 20th. of March, which would have been answerd before, but that I was tired of Conjectures, and wish'd for something substantial to communicate— Part of Yours will hereafter require further Attention—

RC (Adams Papers); internal address: "His Excellency John Adams Esqr."; endorsed: "Mr Marchant / May. 29. 1790."

[1] For the Rhode Island trade bill, see JA's letter of 19 May to William Ellery, and note 2, above.

[2] The Rhode Island legislature appointed Providence lawyer Theodore Foster (1752–1828), Brown 1770, and Col. Joseph Stanton Jr. (1739–1821), of Charlestown, as U.S. senators. Both men joined their colleagues in New York on 25 June. The election for U.S. representative was held on 31 Aug., with six candidates vying for the position. Benjamin Bourne (1755–1808), of Bristol, R.I., Harvard 1775, was chosen, and he took his seat on 17 Dec. (*Providence Gazette*, 19 June; *Biog. Dir. Cong.*; *First Fed. Cong.*, 1:371, 3:635; A New Nation Votes).

[3] Marchant's enclosure, not found, was a copy of the Impost Act of 1789, which levied and collected duties within Rhode Island. It was passed by the state legislature in Sept. 1789. It listed commodities, assigned duties and penalties, identified ports of entry, and itemized collectors' responsibilities (Evans, No. 22108).

[4] Under the Impost Act of 1789, Rhode Island was divided into the districts of Newport and Providence. A collector, naval officer, and surveyor staffed each major port, with six additional surveyors left to man a set of smaller ports. In May 1790, prior to ratifying the Con-

stitution, the General Assembly appointed twelve officials to those posts. On 14 June George Washington began making nominations for the Rhode Island ports, replacing nearly all of the officeholders. Foster, who retained his post as naval officer at Providence, wrote to Washington on 26 June, requesting that Ebenezer Thompson assume his local duties (Providence *United States Chronicle*, 27 May; *First Fed. Cong.*, 2:80, 83; Washington, *Papers, Presidential Series*, 5:557).

To Thomas Brand Hollis

My dear friend NewYork June 1 1790

Nothing mortifies me more than the difficulty I find to maintain that correspondence with you which when I left England I thought would be some consolation to me for the loss of your conversation.

We proceed by degrees to introduce a little order into this Country, and my public duties require so much of my time, that I have little left for private friendships however dear to me. By General Mansell I send you a small packet which will give you some idea of our proceedings.[1] The French seem to be very zealous to follow our example: I wish they may not too exactly copy our greatest errors and suffer in consequence of them greater misfortunes than ours. They will find themselves under a necessity of treading back some of their too hasty steps as we have done.—

I am situated on the majestic banks of the Hudson, in comparison of which your Thames is but a rivulet; and surrounded with all the beauties and sublimities of nature. Never did I live in so delightful a spot— I would give—what would I not give to see you here?— Your library and your cabinets of elegant and costly curiosities, would be an addition to such a situation which in this country would attract the attention of all. In Europe it is lost in the croud. Come over and purchase a paradise here, and be the delight and admiration of a new world; marry one of our fine girls and leave a family to do honor to human nature when you can do it no longer in person. Franklin is no more, and we have lately trembled for Washington— Thank God he is recovered from a dangerous sickness and is likely now to continue many years. His life is of vast importance to us.— Is there any probability of a fermentation in England, sufficient to carry off, any of her distempers? I wish her happy and prosperous, but I wish she would adopt the old maxim—"Live and Let live." Will there be a compleat revolution in Europe both in religion and government? Where will the present passions and principles lead and in what will they end? In more freedom and humanity I am clear: but when? or how?— My affectionate regards to Doctor Price and all our good friends—and beleive me yours dum spiro John Adams.

Rhode Island is become one of us on the 29 May.

LbC in CA's hand (Adams Papers); internal address: "Thomas Brand Hollis Esq[r] / Chesterfield Street Westminster."; APM Reel 115.

[1] British Army officer John Maunsell (1724–1795), a veteran of the Seven Years' War, held land grants to property in New York State and Vermont. He departed New York City on 3 June aboard the British packet *Queen Charlotte*, Capt. John Fargie, which reached Falmouth, England, on 3 July. JA's packet for Hollis included congressional journals (Jefferson, *Papers*, 18:263; *New-York Daily Gazette*, 2 June; London *Public Advertiser*, 5 July; from Hollis, 19 Oct., and note 4, below).

To Alexander Jardine

Sir New York June 1st 1790

I take the opportunity by General Mansell to acknowledge the receipt of your polite letter of the 29 of May 1789 and to present you my thanks for the valuable present of your entertaining travels.[1] Your compliments upon so hasty a production as my book are very flattering. It would give me pleasure to pursue the subject through all the known governments, and to correct or rather new make the whole work. But my life is destined to labor of a much less agreable kind.—I know not how it is but mankind have an aversion to the study of the science of government. Is it because the subject is dry? To me, no romance is more entertaining. Those who take the lead in revolutions are seldom well informed, and they commonly take more pains to inflame their own passions, and those of society than to discover truth: and very few of those who have just ideas, have the courage to pursue them. I know by experience that in revolutions the most fiery spirits and flighty genius's frequently obtain more influence than men of sense and judgment: and the weakest men may carry foolish measures in opposition to wise ones proposed by the ablest. France is in great danger from this quarter. The desire of change in Europe is not wonderful Abuses in religion and government are so numerous and oppresive to the people, that a reformation must take place or a general decline. The armies of monks, soldiers and courtiers were become so numerous and costly that the labor of the rest was not enough to maintain them. Either reformation or depopulation must come.

I am so well satisfied of my own principles, that I think them as eternal and unchangeable as the earth and its inhabitants. I know mankind must finally adopt a ballance between the executive and legislative powers, and another ballance between the poor and the rich in the legislature; and quarrel till they come to that conclusion— But how long they must quarrel before they agree in the inference I know not—

John Adams

LbC in CA's hand (Adams Papers); internal address: "Major A Jardine / Woolwich near London."; APM Reel 115.

[1] Jardine last wrote on 26 May 1789 to praise JA's *Defence of the Const.*, which had "advanced the subject more than any thing that has appeared since Montesquiu" (Adams Papers).

To Henry Marchant

Dear Sir

New York June 1. 1790

Your obliging Letter of the 29. Ult. was brought to me Yesterday at my house, and as there happened to be a few Freinds with me, we joined in Wishing Happiness and Prosperity to Rhode Island with great Cordiality. This morning the President did me the honour of a Visit and I had the Pleasure of congratulating him on this pleasing Event and presenting to him your affectionate Respects.

Congress I conjecture will wait the Arrival of your Senators, before they pass any Act.[1]

My hopes of the Blessings of Liberty from this Government, are much increased Since Yesterday. United We Stand but divided We fall. Join or die. these were our Maxims, twenty five or thirty Years ago, and they are neither less true nor less important now than they were then.

The renovation of that Union, which has acquired such renown in the World, by tryumphing, over Such formidable Ennemies, and by Spreading the Principles which are like to produce a compleat Revolution both in Religion and Government in most parts of Europe; cannot fail to res[tore] respectability to the American Name, and procure Us Consideration among nations.

I earnestly wish to see your Senators here and your Representative in the other house, and I cannot but hope that you will be one of the former.

With Sincere Esteem I am / dear sir your Friend and servant

John Adams

RC (MWelC:Special Colls.); internal address: "The Honourable / Henry Marchant"; endorsed: "V. P. J. Adams / June 1st. 1790—" Some loss of text due to wear at the edge.

[1] On the same day that JA wrote this letter, the House of Representatives appointed a committee to draft three pieces of legislation bringing the thirteenth state in line with the union. The first, the Rhode Island Act, was introduced on 2 June and signed by George Washington on 14 June, extending all previous federal laws. The second, the Rhode Island Judiciary Act of 23 June, established federal courts. Finally, the Rhode Island Enumeration Act of 5 July implemented the Census Act of 1 March (*First Fed. Cong.*, 1:727; 3:441–442, 822, 823).

From John Brown Cutting

Dear Sir London June 3d 1790

I inclosed You a few days ago a parcel of printed papers some of which I conceived might contain interesting intelligence especially if the dispute between Britain & Spain shoud terminate in hostilities, as in such an event the government of the United States woud at least be involved in discussions of considerable importance to our country with one or both of those nations.

Among the rest you have an authentic copy of the memorial or narrative of Mr Mears on the seisure of the british vessels in Nootka sound—as also a sketch of the debate in parliament occasion'd by the message of his britannic majesty on that affair.[1] You will not however obtain from the sketch an adequate conception of the high tone in which the minister spoke. It was thoroughly understood on all sides of the house—(I speak this from having been an auditor) that in unanimously promising his majesty national support against the insult of Spain the minister on his part was pledged to obtain not only pecuniary reparation for the confiscated property and for the insult offered to the british flag, but also a full dereliction from the Court of Spain of its claim to exclusive sovereignty over the coasts in the vicinity of Nootka Sound and on the northwest coasts of America and of exclusive navigation and commerce in those seas. A categorical answer to a demand of this sort is pretended by the Court of London to be expected from Madrid by the return of a messenger sent with it just four weeks ago. Meanwhile the warlike preparations in every port and corner of the Island are most vigourous and extensive. Ever since the summer of 1787 Spain has been putting her fleets in the most formidable condition.— Nor can one believe that the mere menace of Britain will make her under such circumstances yield the point in contest. In such a crisis it was natural for both nations to turn their eyes on France with considerable anxiety. The late discussion and determination in her national assembly of the great constitutional question whether the power of declaring war shou'd be lodged with the Legislature or be confided to the Executive was doubtless hasten'd by this anxiety. The settlement of this point in favour of the Legislative body is conceived by many here as decisive that the french nation will take no part in a war between Spain and Britain. But a more erroneous conclusion never was made. The military spirit of the nation is more alive than ever—and if a majority of its representatives shou'd after public discussion and debate decree to go to war, it wou'd be carried on with more vigour than ever. A partial sale of the ecclesiastical remains for a paper currency has opend a resource of finance that in case of state necessity might be vastly amplified.[2] And as to the supposed hazard that Spain might interfere to attempt a counter-revolution in France the idea is already scouted by the partizans of the reform. Two points only are wanting to produce a decree of the french national assembly for war. 1. A persuasion that the spanish have justice on their side in the present quarrel. and 2dly: That it is for the interest of the french that the mines of South America shoud not become british property. I expect to see both positions established by fact and argument shoud Britain manifestly overstep the limits of equity in her claims. In the interim the naval preparations in the ports of France will keep pace with those in the ports of Britain.

From the moment that a spanish war was publicly known to be impending—the people of the United States began to rise in the estimation of all ranks of men here. Instead of being considered as heretofore a sort of republican banditti enemies to kings and good order on land, and on the ocean one grade above the algerines only—in the course of a very few days we became popular in the City and bearable I am told even in the Cabinet![3] The unkind behaviour of Capt Hendricks an american navigator at Nootka sound—in not quarreling with the spanish Commodore was overlooked:[4] and the leading Editors of the ministerial newspapers have now orders to affirm that the offer of a treaty offensive and defensive between Britain and America is already dispatchd across the atlantic.[5] The principal inducements to an acceptance of such a treaty on the part of Congress—is a guarantee of a free navigation of the river Missisippi—a participation of some farther indulgencies as to the west india traffic—an adjustment of all disputed boundaries and a speedy surrender of the posts.

I wish the present juncture cou'd be improved for the adjustment of some criterion whereby our seamen might be discriminated from british seamen and consequently exempted from the outrages of the british press gangs. The great point to be guarded against on our part is—the first violence of having our mariners forced from on board our ships under a pretext that they are britons.— To do away all colour for committing it some palpable species of prima facie evidence is wanted—such as being immediately produced might stare every officer of a press gang in the face and leave him without excuse if he ventured to depart from the orders of the Admiralty Board by which he is ever directed to take no foreigners. A few days after I had memorializ'd the Lords of the Admiralty and almost exacted by dint of diligent and remonstrating assiduity the liberation of those six crews, or parts of crews which had been impress'd, Mr Governeur Morris to whom I had communicated my toils and their termination sent a note to the duke of Leeds and asking for an hours conversation with him—stated verry forcibly to him the pernicious effect that impressing our mariners must have on the commerce of Britain.[6] The Duke listen'd to him, thanked him, seemed to believe him and said orders shou'd be issued and measures taken to prevent the american seamen from being impress'd in future. But there are real difficulties in the business that general commands of this nature do not meet. As a zealous citizen I do wish some effectual remedy to such a national mischief and indignity coud be devised. No moment can be more favourable for attempting something of the sort than the present. The perfect protection of our mariners from being impressed or impeded is just now a desirable object to the commercial part of this nation. In former wars when the british seamen were press'd to mann the navy—the merchants coud generally procure Swedes Hollanders and other european seamen to supply their places—but at present all those foreign seamen are engaged by their sovereigns ~~in war~~ or by their fellow subjects—and the british merchant will be compeld to resort to the United States for american seamen in lieu of them.

As I send this letter one post later than that by which the mail is conveyed to Falmouth—it is necessary for me to close it immediately to obtain the chance of its reaching Mr Rutledge at Falmouth.

I intreat Mrs Adams to accept with yourself the best compliments and sincere good wishes of / Your respectful affectionate / and most obedt sert:

John Brown Cutting

RC (Adams Papers); endorsed by CA: "J B Cutting"; notation by CFA: "J. B. Cutting / June 3d 1790."

[1] For John Meares, see Descriptive List of Illustrations, No. 6, above. In 1789 Spanish officers, acting in the name of King Carlos IV of Spain, seized Meares' ships and his trading post at Canada's Nootka Sound for "good and lawful prize." Meares took it as a private loss of profit and, more significantly, as a public humiliation of the British flag. In April 1790 he brought his grievances to London, where he won powerful supporters who readied for war. George III addressed Parliament on 5 May, denouncing Spain's exclusive rights to

the Pacific Coast. William Pitt gave an "animated" speech of support the next day. M.P.'s unanimously approved outfitting forty ships of the line. Cutting enclosed Meares' 30 April account of the affair, titled *Authentic Copy of the Memorial to the Right Honourable William Wyndham Grenville . . . Containing Every Particular Respecting the Capture of the Vessels in Nootka Sound*, London, 1790.

When Meares traveled to London to press the House of Commons for military reprisal and personal compensation, the Nootka Sound conflict erupted into a full-blown international incident. Over the following months, the crisis laid bare the unequal strength of two major European pacts: the Family Compact, last renewed in 1761, which committed France to aid Spain; and the 1788 Triple Alliance of Britain, the Netherlands, and Prussia. While the Dutch Navy swept to Britain's side, Spain had a tougher time persuading France to uphold their agreement. In the first major foreign-policy decision of the new French National Assembly, lawmakers resolved to abstain from all wars of conquest. Following some diplomatic pressure, France relented slightly. It outfitted fourteen ships of the line in a show of solidarity with Spain and offered to mediate the dispute. Diplomatic efforts continued apace, with British and Spanish negotiators meeting at Madrid in mid-summer to craft an agreement (vol. 19:309; London *World*, 6, 7 May 1790; Black, *British Foreign Policy*, p. 233–246).

[2] The French National Assembly voted on 2 Nov. 1789 to seize ecclesiastical property as partial payment for the national debt, and on 19 Dec. it began auctioning off 400 million livres' worth of land. Turning its focus to foreign affairs, the assembly took the dramatic step, on 22 May 1790, of renouncing war for military conquest. This was a critical shift of policy, for if the Nootka Sound conflict triggered an Anglo-Spanish war, then France would be expected to uphold the Family Compact and aid Spain in safeguarding its colonial possessions in South America (Bosher, *French Rev.*, p. xviii, 145; Schama, *Citizens*, p. 487; Black, *British Foreign Policy*, p. 237).

[3] In Oct. 1789 George Washington dispatched Gouverneur Morris to London to resolve some of the issues lingering from JA's ministerial tenure, namely, the ongoing impressment of American seamen and the British Army's refusal to evacuate the frontier posts. The president instructed Morris, acting as an unofficial envoy, to renew negotiations for an Anglo-American commercial treaty and to raise the possibility of exchanging ministers. Morris met with the Marquis of Carmarthen and Pitt several times throughout the spring, but he made no headway on any front. At the same time, Morris convened with the French foreign ministry in London and he socialized with Pitt's rival Charles James Fox, factors that hindered prospects of diplomatic success. Reporting to Washington on 29 May 1790, Morris wrote: "It now stands on such Ground that they must write a Letter making the first Advance . . . and to that Effect I warned them against sending *a Message* by one of their Consuls" (Washington, *Papers, Presidential Series*, 4:179–181; 5:322–323, 430–438).

[4] Capt. John Kendrick (ca. 1740–1794) commanded the 1787–1789 expeditions of the *Columbia Rediviva* and *Lady Washington* to China. Kendrick was at Nootka Sound when Meares' ships were seized, and Meares claimed that Kendrick supported the action (vol. 19:xiii; *AFC*, 9:91; London *Public Advertiser*, 22 May 1790).

[5] As the Nootka Sound conflict heightened, the British press speculated that if the United States signed an offensive and defensive treaty with Britain, then Britain would intervene with Spain to guarantee American navigation of the Mississippi River (London *Whitehall Evening Post*, 1–3 June; London *Public Advertiser*, 3 June).

[6] For Cutting's efforts to counter the British Navy's impressment of American sailors, see his letter of 5 July, and note 5, below.

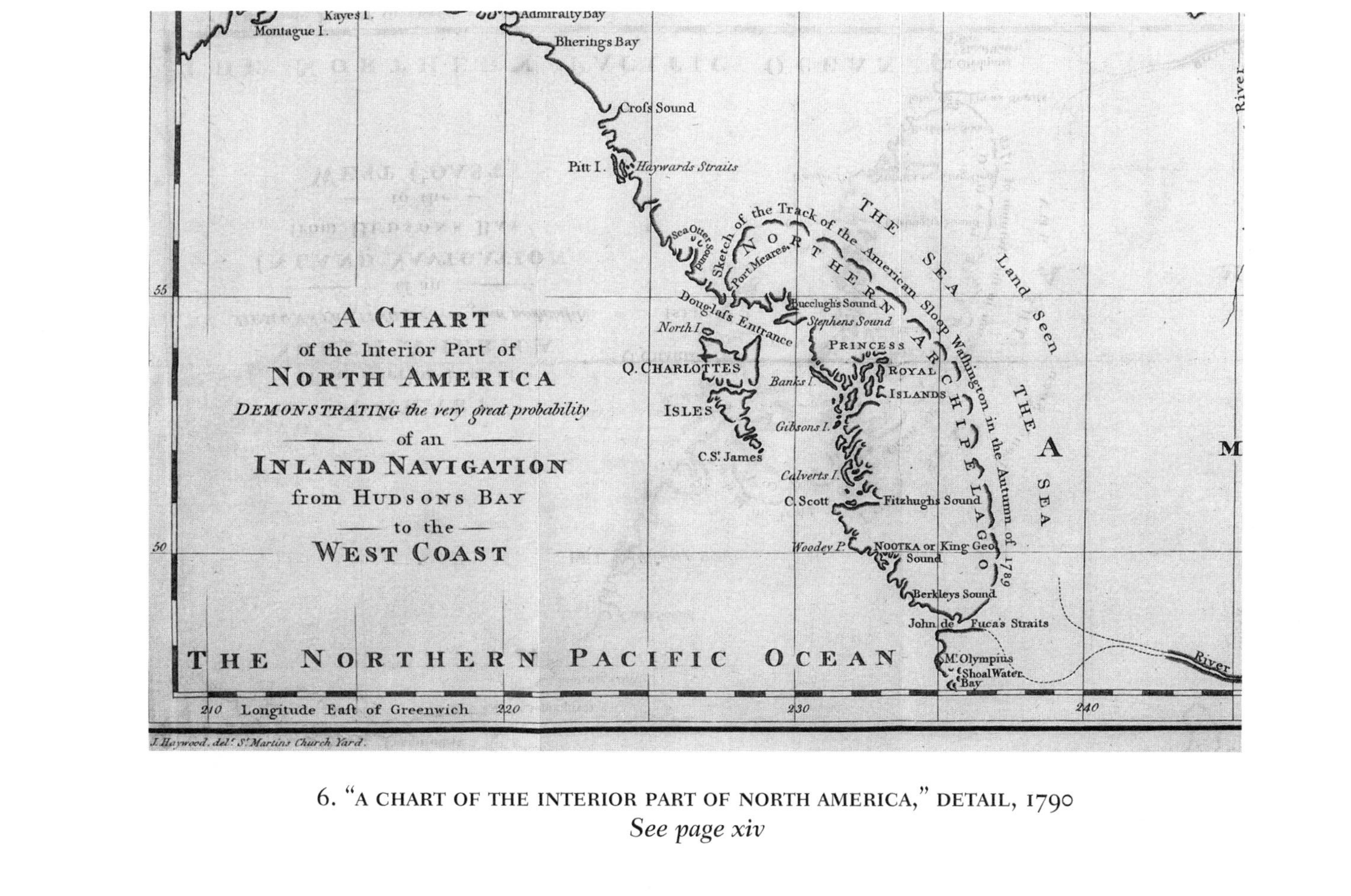

6. "A CHART OF THE INTERIOR PART OF NORTH AMERICA," DETAIL, 1790
See page xiv

From John Trumbull

Sir Hartford June 5th. 1790.—

Since I had the honor of receiving yours of April 25th., my time has been wholly taken up in attending on our Supreme Court of Errors, & the Session of our General Assembly, which with us is a kind of extrajudicial Court for the trial of private causes on Petition— I had also to conduct an application from the Mercantile Interest for the Repeal of our Excise-Laws—in which by influencing the leaders of the House of Representatives, & intimidating our opposers in the Council, by making our cause appear popular & calling the Excise antifederal, we procured a repeal with the greatest apparent unanimity, tho' I believe in my conscience, against the real wishes of a majority in both houses.[1]

Man is a strange being. His vice & depravity is every where seen—but his folly & dishonesty is no where so conspicuous, as in a popular assembly. Every man who pretends to form an opinion for himself & impose it on others, chuses his party, & takes his side, from motives of passion, interest or ambition. When this is completed, he employs what reasoning talents heaven has given him in the subsequent stage of the business, in forming arguments to justify his opinions. Nothing can be more ridiculous than to hear us then pretend to be governed only by reason, & spend hours of debate in acting the farce of rationality.

We are alarmed at the present situation of affairs in Congress. Of the Senate we hear little—but in the House of Representatives every thing seems conducted by Party, Intrigue & Cabal. We constantly hear of bargains between Members from different States for Votes on the most important questions— If State policy & local attachments are to continue their predominating influence—if they are to govern, or if not govern, to embarass, the affairs of the Union—we may bid adieu to the hopes of a Fœderal Government. One half of the People, as You truly observe do not wish to have any Government, & I believe we may add that the other half are not disposed to agree upon its form.

As to our debate on signs & ceremonies, I fully subscribe to their efficacy in government; but I firmly believe that from the present temper of the People, none of any significance or importance could at present be established or imposed without occasioning the most serious alarm. We might almost as safely introduce the Papal ceremonies in Religious worship. We neither fear God nor regard Man, but in a manner wholly democratical. But should the government continue, signs, ceremonies & external parade will naturally & gradually be introduced by the people themselves, who, as You justly observe, are equally fond of them, as the rest of mankind.

Our Clergy have shed their wigs & laid aside their red gates & board fences— They retain no mark of distinction but the Band on Sundays. At the same time they have lost nine tenths of their dignity & influence. I do not however ascribe this chiefly to the loss of the sign, but am opinion that from the cooperation of other causes, the wig & the dignity naturally fell together—for when the Dignity was gone, the wig was unable to support itself—

I hinted in my last letter, some dissatisfaction at the Secretary's reports. I will explain myself. He recommends the immediate Assumption of the State-debts, & yet discards all idea of direct Taxation.[2] When, in the name of Common Sense, are direct Taxes to be wanted, when can they with propriety be demanded, if not now? Does he mean to give them up forever, & lose the most important resource of the Empire? Is he ignorant that direct Taxation to a moderate amount is the strongest link in the chain of Government, & the only measure, which will make every man feel that there is a Power above him in this world? Does he fear the unpopularity of the measure? Is it more unpopular than the Assumption? Would not both be advocated and opposed from the same quarters? Ought not both to be proposed together? And has he not by discarding direct Taxation furnished the opposers of the Assumption with their strongest argument—that his proposed resources will fail him?

A direct Tax of one Cent on the Pound according to *our lists* once laid & submitted to by the People, as I have no doubt it would be, would establish the Fœderal Government.

I have a very high opinion of the Secretary—but must think that in this matter he has either gone too far or not far enough—and that if both measures could not be ventured at once, a small direct tax would be of more importance to the Government, than the immediate assumption of the State Debts without it.

The Secretary was warmly your Friend, & wished as much as any man in the States for your election to your present office—but, if the representation of Col. W. may be depended on as to the part he took in that affair, he was duped by the Antifederalists.[3] I hope he has no inclination to intrigue, & am sure both in that affair, & in his opposition to Clinton's re-election, he displayed no extraordinary talents for it. He absolutely scribbled against Clinton on topics calculated to make his enemy more popular. Let him keep to his Fort–Sterling abilities & Independent Honesty, joined with indefatigable industry.

I have to thank You for the Defence of the American Constitutions, & the two Pamphlets, which I received by Col. Wadsworth.[4] The Letters to Calkoen were not new to me—but I do not recollect to have seen before, the History of the American dispute—a performance, which ought to be preserved for Posterity, as it gives the most just & clear account of the transactions of those times, that has ever appeared in print.

Is not the *Defence of the American Constitutions* almost a Misnomer? Had we at that day, have we now in the new Constitution, a proper balance of the three Estates? It is true, we are defensible, as far as we have attempted it—but we have as yet effected little— We are unwilling to give effectual Power, & yet are capital artists at devising & multiplying checks—till we have made the machine too complicated to be set in motion—or I might rather say at present, that Franklyn's team at the tail have overpowered the progressive force, & that it has been sometime going retrograde with tolerable rapidity— You have taken great pains to instruct mankind in the fundamental principles of Government. You have demonstrated your positions by argument, authority & history. But the feelings of even civilized nations are I fear some centuries behind You. A spirit of liberty has indeed gone forth—a disposition to pull down Kings, nobilities & hierarchies—but where is the disposition to establish just governments on their ruins? The opposers of arbitrary power are apt to consider all power as arbitrary— To say no more of America, what is now doing in France? Great things I must own—& France may perhaps be as near the period when a regular, wellbalanced constitution may be formed, as England was in the days of our wise Namesake, *King John*. I hope nearer—for they are a far more enlightened people at this day, & have the benefit of the experience of others. Heaven grant they may profit by it— I wish every Member of their National Assembly were obliged under pain of expulsion, to read your Defence, & either adopt your Principles or confute them.

Fame has certainly been very liberal to Franklyn in his lifetime—but I doubt She will hereafter reclaim a great part of her donations. I could never view him as the extraordinary Genius, either in Politics or Literature which he has been called. Except his invention of Electric rods, I know no claim he has to merit as a Philosopher. He certainly never rose to high eminence as a literary character, & tho' always busy in politics & party, seems not to have been well versed in the Science of Legislation, or the Theory of Government.

Maddison's character is certainly not rising in the public estimation— He now acts on a conspicuous stage, & does not equal expectation. He becomes more & more a Southern Partizan, & loses his assumed candor & moderation. Indeed no man seems to have gained much reputation in the present session of Congress. Even Ames, who succeeded to King as the temporary Idol of Massachusetts, & whose praises were so much trumpeted forth in the last session, seems to be losing part of his Votaries.

Our Legislature seem determined to make no provision for the State Debt. We insist that we have paid beyond our proportion already, which I believe is true—but I suppose other States talk in the same strain. The State debts must be assumed by Congress, or they will never be paid—& before the period of their assumption, will probably in many of the States be so much depreciated as to afford Maddison & his adherents, new arguments for a discrimination.

Since I began writing we have the news of the accession of Rhode-Island to the Union. I hope it may prove a just subject of congratulation—but fear their members will join you, full fraught with State-politics, & a tolerable infusion of Antifederalism. The real friends to an efficient Government are so few, that we have reason to dread any accession to the number of its opposers.

I have the honor to be with the / greatest Respect, / Your Obliged & most Obed[t.] / Humble Serv[t.] John Trumbull

RC (Adams Papers); internal address: "The Vice President"; endorsed: "M[r] Trumbull / June 5. 1790 / ans[d] Jan 23. 1791."

[1] The Connecticut legislature met in Hartford on 13 May and adjourned two days later. It repealed a set of excise laws passed in May 1785 (Conn., *Acts and Laws*, 1785, p. 318; 1790, p. 391, Evans, Nos. 18965, 22421; *Connecticut Courant*, 17 May 1790).

[2] Trumbull referred to his letter of 30 March, above. In his 4 March and 22 April reports to Congress, Alexander Hamilton called for the improved collection of import duties as the preferred alternative to imposing a direct tax (Hamilton, *Papers*, 6:287–288; Chernow, *Alexander Hamilton*, p. 342).

[3] From 20 Feb. to 29 April, Hamilton printed sixteen letters under the pseudonym "H.G.," and sent open letters to the New York electorate, attacking George Clinton's conduct during the Revolutionary War and emphasizing his Antifederalist views. Clinton was reelected governor of New York, defeating Federalist Robert Yates (Hamilton, *Papers*, 5:262; Chernow, *Alexander Hamilton*, p. 274, 275). For Samuel Blachley Webb, see Trumbull's letter of 30 March, and note 7, above.

[4] Col. Jeremiah Wadsworth represented Connecticut in the House of Representatives from 1789 to 1795 (vol. 18:20; *Biog. Dir. Cong.*).

From Joseph Willard

Sir, Cambridge June 8. 1790.

I take the liberty of enclosing a petition to the National Legislature, from the Convention of the Congregational Ministers in this Commonwealth, by a Committee of the Body, upon a very important subject, viz. that of preventing incorrect editions of the Bible from being published among us.[1] The Committee have desired me to request your Excellency to take the charge of this petition, and to introduce it, at such time, as you may judge most expedient. They have full confidence in your Excellency, that you will do every thing in your power, that the American editions of that sacred Book, which contains the foundations of our holy religion, and for which, they are persuaded you have the sincerest regard, may come forth as correct as possible.

The Committee, by the direction of the Convention, are preparing letters to be sent to the Ministers of the various denominations of Christians, in the United States, requesting them to join in applications to the Congress, in this important business; and they hope, that the cause of true religion will be subserved by these exertions.

I am, Sir, / with sentiments of the highest respect / your Excellency's most humble / and obedient servant Joseph Willard

RC (Adams Papers); internal address: "His Excellency / John Adams Esquire."

[1] Willard's proposal for a federally sanctioned Bible echoed a 12 Sept. 1782 resolution of the Continental Congress regarding a similar request from Philadelphia printer Robert Aitken. JA laid Willard's petition before the Senate, where it was read on 14 June 1790. Various Baptist associations of New England submitted related petitions, which were read in the House of Representatives on 5 and 19 Jan. 1791. Congress took no further action on the matter (Washington, *Papers, Presidential Series*, 5:495; *JCC*, 23:574; *First Fed. Cong.*, 1:351; MHS, *Procs.*, 1st ser., 5:107).

To Thomas Brand Hollis

Dear Sir New York June 11th 1790

I have received your kind letter of March 29th and the packet of pamphlets, and I pray you to accept of my best thanks for both— I sent you lately by Genl Mansel, some of our rough matters.[1] The boxes of books you sent by Captain Bernard arrived safely, I know.—[2]

You seem to suppose our coast in danger from African pyrates; in this I presume you are deceived by the Artifices of the London insurance offices, for we are in no more danger than the Empire of China is.—

The great revolution in France is wonderful but not supernatural. The hand of Providence is in it, I doubt not; working however by natural and ordinary means, such as produced the revolution in the fifteenth century.— That all men have one common nature, is a principle which will now universally prevail: and equal rights and equal duties, will in a just sense I hope be inferred from it: but equal ranks and equal property never can be infered from it, any more than equal understanding agility vigour or beauty. Equal laws are all that ever can be derived from human equality. I am delighted with Doctor Price's sermon on patriotism; but there is a sentiment or two which I should explain a little. He guards his hearers and readers, very Judiciously against the extreme of adulation and contempt. The former is the extreme he says to which mankind in general have been most prone. "The generality of Rulers have treated men, as your English Jockies treat their horses—convinced them first that they were their masters and next that they were their friends, at least they have pretended to do so." Mankind have I agreed behaved too much like horses: been rude wild and mad untill they were mastered, and then been too tame gentle and dull.— I think our friend should have stated it thus. The great and perpetual distinction in civilized societies, has been between the rich who are few, and the poor who are many. When the many are masters, they are too unruly and then the few are too tame and afraid to speak out the truth. When the few are masters they are too severe, and then the many are too servile. This is the strict truth. The few have had most art and union, and therefore have generally prevailed in the end. The inference of wisdom from these premisses, is, that neither the poor, or the rich, should ever be suffered to be masters. They should have equal power to defend themselves: and that their power may be always equal, there should be an independent mediator between them, always ready, always able and always interested to assist the weakest. Equal laws can never be made or maintained without this.— You see I still hold fast my scales, and weigh every thing in them. The French must finally become my disciples, or rather the disciples of Zeno: or they will have no equal laws, no personal liberty, no property, no lives.—

I am very much employed in business, and this must be my apology for neglecting so much to write to you: but I will be as good a correspondent as I can— I hope you will not forget your old friend.—

In this Country the pendulum has vibrated too far to the popular side, driven by men without experience or Judgment, and horrid ravages have been made upon property, by arbitrary multitudes or majorities of multitudes. France has severe tryals to endure from the same cause— Both have found or will find, that to place property at the mercy of a majority who have no property is "Committere agnum lupo" My fundamental maxim is never trust the lamb to the custody of the wolf. If you are not perfectly of my mind at present, I hereby promise and assure you that you will live to see that I am precisely right— Thus arrogantly concludes your friend John Adams

LbC in CA's hand (Adams Papers); internal address: "Thomas Brand Hollis Esqr"; APM Reel 115.

[1] Of 1 June, above.
[2] For this shipment of books for Harvard, see Hollis' letter of 29 March, and note 3, above.

From William Smith

Dear Sr. Boston. 12th. June. 1790.

I have to acknowledge the Rect. of your esteem'd favor of the 20 Ulto. Our Genl. Assembly are now in Session.[1] their Conduct thus farr has been perfectly Fœderal, how long it may continue is uncertain. I am sorry that the assuming the State Debts & funding the Continental Debt are so long delay'd. so long as we are kept in suspence we are a prey to Speculators as most of our circulating Cash is employ'd in trading in paper.— 'till the Debt is fix'd but very little other Business can be carr'd on.— I do not find in the funding Bill any provision made for the New Emission Money, which runs on Interest & which Congress pledg'd their Faith to redeem & pay the Interest annually, provided the States neglected to make provision.[2] One Years Interest *only* has been paid. I have a considerable sum in this kind belonging to my father's Estate, which has lain for a number of Years.—[3] Our Court has given up the Light Houses in this State to Congress, it will be necessary for Congress, soon to make the Law regulating Pilots. &c at present the Pilots of this port are under no controul. shou'd this Law be bro't forward, the Marine Society of this port, wou'd be happy to render their services to put the Pilots on a proper footing.[4]

Mrs. Smith joins me in respects to Mrs. A— & yourself.—

Yrs. Most Respectfully Wm. Smith.

RC (Adams Papers); addressed: "The Vice-President / of the United States / New-York."; endorsed: "Mr W. Smith / 12. June 1790."

[1] The Mass. General Court met from 26 May to 25 June (Mass., *Acts and Laws*, 1790–1791, p. 91; Stockbridge, Mass., *Western Star*, 6 July).

[2] On 18 March 1780 Congress replaced Continental currency with a "new emission" that was guaranteed as national legal tender and earned 5 percent interest (Ferguson, *Power of the Purse*, p. 51).

[3] Isaac Smith Sr., who died three years earlier, had suffered several financial setbacks from the depreciation of public securities and the loss of two merchant ships (*AFC*, 8:196, 210).

[4] The Mass. General Court passed an act on 10 June 1790 transferring all ownership deeds and maintenance duties of several public lighthouses to the U.S. government. Federal oversight, however, remained murky. The Lighthouse Act of 7 Aug. 1789 stipulated that pilots would be supervised by the states until Congress made new legislation. Although Congress amended the Lighthouse Act on 19 July 1790, and George Washington signed it into law three days later, it contained no guidelines for pilot regulation (Mass., *Acts and Laws*, 1790–1791, p. 7–9; *U.S. Statutes at Large*, 1:53–54, 137; *First Fed. Cong.*, 1:422, 440).

From Jabez Bowen

Sir Providence June 14. 1790

I most sincearly Congratulate you on The accession of Rhode Island to the Union. by this event the Chain seems compleat. may our publick deliberations be conducted with that wisdom as shall insure Happiness to this great Nation.

I have just return'd from attending our Gen[l] Assembly, Convened on purpose to Elet Senators and prescribe the mode of Choosing the Representative. Your Humble Servant was a Candidate for a Senator, but was not able to obtain; the whole of the Paper Money and Antifederal Intrest being oposed to him. Theodore Foster Esq[r.] who is appointed is and has been Federal. but being Brother in Law to Gov[r] Fenner we fear will be totally against the Assumption. Joseph Stanton the other Senator is a full blooded Anti and a strong advocate for paper Money. hope they will both be for promoting the General good when deteached from their old Connections.[1]

I have wrote the President of the United State praying him to appoint my Son Oliver Bowen to the place of *Navel Officer* for the District of Providence he is about Twenty two Years of Age has had a Liberal Education and at present attends an Apothecarys Shop. the U. States owe me nearly Twenty Thousand Dollars which I lent them in the Years 1776 & 77, which puts it out of my power to provide for him at present. Theodore Foster Esq[r] was the Navel Officer. by his appointment as a Senator it will become vacant. if you will be so kind as just to second my application to the President shall esteem my self under many Obligations to you therefor.[2]

I Remain with sentiments of the / highest Esteeme your Excellencys / most Obedient Humb. Servant Jabez Bowen

P.S. The Bill which originated in the Senate for stopping intercourse with R^{d} Island & the demand for 27. thousand Dollars. were the procuring Causes of the Adoption of the Constitution.[3]

RC (Adams Papers); internal address: "~~Honble~~ Excellency John Adams"; endorsed: "Jabez Bowen / 14. June. 1790."

[1] Antifederalist Arthur Fenner (1745–1805) was the clerk of the Providence Court of Common Pleas. The Rhode Island legislature elected him governor on 5 May, and he served until his death (*AFC*, 14:299; *DAB*). For the election of Rhode Island's members of Congress, see Henry Marchant's letter of 29 May, and note 2, above.

[2] Bowen had written to George Washington a day earlier, soliciting a post for his son Oliver (1767–1804), Brown University 1788, but he was unsuccessful (Washington, *Papers, Presidential Series*, 5:516, 517).

[3] For the Rhode Island trade bill, see JA's 19 May letter to William Ellery, and note 2, above.

From John Brown Cutting

Dear Sir London 14 June 1790

By a vessel that sails for Boston tomorrow I inclose You the british king's speech on the adjournment prior to the late dissolution of parliament—for which dissolution the next day a royal proclamation issued. From the tenor of this speech a general european war is expected.[1] Meanwhile the most extensive naval armaments are preparing in the ports adjacent to all the great dockyards of this kingdom—and the most vigourous measures are pursuing to mann upwards of thirty sail of the line which are already put in commission with the usual proportion of frigates and sloops of war. Parliament will assemble on the tenth of august. Before that time it is said the answer of the Court of Spain to the demand of that of St James's will be had. But in the interval the monarch and minister of this nation have the whole game of war in their hands and will probably play it The affair of Nootka Sound afforded the minister a good pretext for arming but no well informed person can believe that an attack of the spanish nation or a determination to exact satisfaction for the seizure of those fur ships cou'd alone have given occasion to the efforts that are now making here. More especially when it is considered that the courts of Berlin Warsaw Constantinople Stockholm and the Hague are linked with that of St James's in a hostile confederacy against the sovereigns of Russia Germany Spain Portugal and Denmark. In fine it is expected and I think on rational grounds that a british squadron or a dutch or perhaps both will enter the Baltic within a very few weeks. shou'd another be detach'd into the mediterranean and a third towards the west india's before September it woud not surprize me.

It is my intention to put this note with some newspapers into the ship's bag immediately—and write You a seperate letter via Gravesend tomorrow.

With the greatest respect & esteem / Yours J B. Cutting.

RC (Adams Papers); internal address: "John Adams Esquire V. P. U. S."

[1] Cutting sent this letter via the *Marietta*, Capt. Fitzwilliam Sargent (Sergeant), which sailed from Gravesend, England, on 17 June and reached Boston on 23 August. Addressing Parliament on 10 June, George III alluded to the Nootka Sound negotiations with Spain, hoping for "Peace on just and honourable grounds" but advising that preparation for war was "indispensably necessary." The next day he signed a proclamation dissolving Parliament and calling for the first round of national elections since 1784 (London *Public Advertiser*, 11, 12, 19 June 1790; London *Diary*, 11, 12 June; Boston *Herald of Freedom*, 24 Aug.; Jefferson, *Papers*, 18:328).

From John Brown Cutting

Dear Sir, London 16 June 1790

I write this note just to inclose you a couple of newspapers.[1]

Such is the variable & distracted state of affairs at present here and all over Europe that it is impossible to form an opinion one day that events of the next will not overturn.

The cabinet of St Jame's having involved this nation in the fortunes of Prussia—it is next to impossible that a general war shou'd not ensue.[2] France has offered to mediate between Spain and Britain . . .[3] and since the credit of the paper money begins to be establish'd on the sale of the ecclesiastical territory which the national assembly have ordered she is again respectable here.—

Our country will be equally courted by both sides . . . and will I trust profit from the present crisis.—[4]

With the greatest esteem & respect / I have the honor to be / Your Most Obed[t] Ser[t:] John Brown Cutting

RC (Adams Papers); internal address: "John Adams Es[q] V. P. U. S."

[1] Enclosure not found.

[2] Cutting referred to the Triple Alliance with Prussia and the Netherlands, which committed Great Britain to aiding Prussian diplomatic efforts with both Austria and the Ottoman Empire. On 20 June Frederick William II, king of Prussia, ratified a Prusso-Turkish treaty. On 27 July Prussia and Austria negotiated the Convention of Reichenbach, resolving their conflicts with the Ottoman Empire and the Austrian Netherlands (vol. 19:309; Black, *British Foreign Policy*, p. 261, 262).

[3] Ellipses here and below in MS.

[4] The *Gazette d'Amsterdam*, 8 June, projected that an Anglo-Spanish war would significantly benefit the United States, because either European power would assist Americans in obtaining free navigation of the Mississippi River (William Ray Manning, *The Nootka Sound Controversy*, Washington, D.C., 1905, p. 421).

From François d'Ivernois

Monsieur Kensington ce 18 Juin 1790

Votre patience à lire le premier volume de l'histoire dont j'ai l'honneur de vous envoyer la suite m'autorisait suffisamment à cette liberte et je l'embrasse avec d'autant plus d'empressement qu'elle me procure l'o[cca]sion de me rappeler à l'un des hommes dont le souvenir m'est le plus précieux. J'y ai joint un double exemplaire complet afin que vous pussiez le remettre à quelque traducteur dans le cas ou vous auriez lieu de présumer, que présentant les objets les plus familiers aux Américains cet écrit vaudrait la peine d'etre traduit pour eux.[1]

Me voila depuis deux mois de retour d'un long voyage que vous m'avez vu commencer Monsieur, et dont la fin m'a présenté des tableaux bien plus satisfaisans que celui que nous offrit la Hollande en février 1788. Je retourne avec le fils de L^d. Eardley recommencer une nouvelle course pour la quelle dans les conjonctures actuelles de l'Europe nous aurions bien besoin de yeux aussi exercés que les votres, et je n'ai pas besoin de vous dire, je pense, avec quel plaisir je remplirais les ordres que vous voudriez me faire passer par l'adresse de *D^d Chauvet ^Esq. Kensington square Kensington*.[2]

Je viens d'adresser à un tres bon littérateur Mr Berenger deLausanne vos deux volumes sur la Constitution d'amérique en l'invitant à en entreprendre la traduction, et à la tenir prete pour la seconde Législature des français—[3] La non division de leur Corps Législatif qui était peut etre si nécessaire pour qu'il put édifier me parait presqu'inconciliable avec la marche nécessaire pour maintenir, et je ne serai vraiment rassuré sur la durée de la liberté française que lorsque le Corps Legislatif y sera partagé en deux factions.

J'ai l'honneur d'etre avec un profond respect / Monsieur / Votre tres humble / & tres obeissant serviteur F d'Ivernois

TRANSLATION

Sir Kensington, 18 June 1790

Your patience in reading the first volume of the history of which I have the honor to send you the sequel encouraged me enough to take that liberty, and I embrace it with even greater alacrity as it gives me the chance to reach out again to one of the men whose memory is most precious to me. I enclosed a complete duplicate copy so that you may hand it to a given translator in case you have cause to consider that, by presenting topics most familiar to Americans, this written work would be worth the trouble of translating it for them.[1]

It has now been two months since my return from a long voyage which you witnessed me begin, sir, and the conclusion of which presented me far more gratifying perspectives than those which Holland offered us in February 1788. I return with Lord Eardley's son to take up a new course for which, in the present conditions in Europe, we would well need eyes as experienced as yours, and I need not tell you, I believe, with how much satisfaction I would fulfill the orders you may wish to forward to me at the address of *David Chauvet Esquire Kensington square, Kensington*.[2]

I have just addressed your two volumes on the American constitution to a very good literary agent from Lausanne, Mr. Berenger, inviting him to undertake its translation, and to have it ready for the second French Legislative Assembly.[3] The non-division of their legislative body which was perhaps so necessary for its establishment seems to be nearly irreconcilable with the necessary means to maintain it, and I will be truly reassured of lasting French liberty only when the legislative body shall be shared between two parties.

I have the honor to be, with a profound respect, sir, your most humble, and most obedient servant F d'Ivernois

RC (Adams Papers); internal address: "To John Adams Esq." Some loss of text due to wear at the edge.

[1] A copy of d'Ivernois' *Tableau historique et politique des deux dernières révolutions de Genève*, 2 vols., London, 1789, is in JA's library at MB (*Catalogue of JA's Library*).

[2] D'Ivernois served as a tutor to Sampson and William, the sons of Sampson Eardley, 1st Baron Eardley (1745–1824). The London home of Swiss politician David Chauvet (1738–1803), a native of Geneva, became a haven for Dutch Patriot refugees (*DNB*; Lodge, *Peerage*, 1848; Laurens, *Papers*, 8:405).

[3] Jean Pierre Bérenger (1737–1807), a Swiss politician and author, did not publish a French translation of JA's *Defence of the Const.* (vol. 19:84; Franklin, *Papers*, 26:4).

From François Adriaan Van der Kemp

Sir! Kingston 19 Jun. 90.

Your Excellencÿ's favour of March 27. I received the 17 apr.—and was it not for a particularity attending this Letter, I would not so soon have troubled you with these. Your Superscrbed the cover with your name, joining to it, *Free*— this word together with your name was erased, and in their place put *none free*— Is this a consequence of the new regulations of the Post-office?[1]

With regard to France, mÿ ideas of this People are perhaps, less favourable than those of Others, and this maÿ afford a Sufficient reason, that I entertained Some doubts and Suspicions with regard of the consistency of their new-model'd government as wel, as in respect of the Blessings, which the people at large Should enjoÿ bÿ this change of measures— Love of mankind and Liberty make me wish, that Liberty maÿ prevail in everÿ part, althoug I fear that she is more and more declining in Europe— The Franch people are the last, to enjoÿ it; verÿ few of their general assemblÿ would be willing to coöperate to this view, and the Bulk of the nation would, after the first delinien is passed, join the first Power, to restore their Royal Master in his ancient despotic the Prærogatives. Your own observation, that the Defence &c must displease Violent Monarchians Aristocrates, and Demagogues, wil afford a reason, that it is not yet translated into French—and gives no great proof of the Sincerity of Some leading men together with their inferiors, to knew Such a work and be Silent— But how Sir! can this Silence Surprise Us who See american Scriblers abuse a performance, who Should eternise their obscure names, if theÿ dared to make them public—

I recommended the defence to the Baron D'averhoult, en champagne, and be impatient for his answer, which I intend to communicate to your Excellencÿ, as Soon as I receive it.[2]

I received, by order of the President, a Polite refusal upon mÿ petition for his intercession, as far he thought it convenient;[3]

It wil be pleasing to me to receive an occasion to Shew Your Excellency which what perfect esteem and considerations / I am / Sir! / Your most obedient and / Obliged Servant Fr Advdkemp.

P.s. know your Sir, Who was at the bottom of that daring Intrigue, mentioned in your last?[4] can his name be Spelled with a double T?

RC (Adams Papers).

[1] Prior to the Postal Act of 1792, it was unclear if the vice president had franking privileges, or how the entire postal system would operate. Seeking "some immediate provision by law" to govern the new entity, postmaster Ebenezer Hazard petitioned the House of Representatives on 17 July 1789. A committee comprising Elias Boudinot, Benjamin Goodhue, and Richard Bland Lee recommended on 9 Sept. that Congress regulate the U.S. Post Office. The Senate rejected the House's subsequent resolution but passed a similar bill, which George Washington signed into law on 22 September. While the president, members of Congress, and other government officials were exempt from paying postage, the Post Office "would not permit Franks even to the V. P.," as AA discovered (*AFC*, 9:2, 95; *First Fed. Cong.*, 1:170–171, 719; 3:113–114, 198; *U.S. Statutes at Large*, 1:70, 232, 237).

[2] By 1788 Dutch Patriot Jan Anthony (Jean Antoine) D'Averhoult (1756–1792), of Utrecht, had fled to France, where he briefly presided over the National Assembly from Jan. to Aug. 1792 (Bart Boon, "Jan Anthony d'Averhoult door Louis-Léopold Boilly: de Geschiedenis achter een ongewoon portret," *Oud Holland*, 111:253 [1997]; Hoefer, *Nouv. biog. générale*).

[3] See Van der Kemp's letter of 17 March 1790, and note 1, above.

[4] JA last wrote to Van der Kemp on 27 March, but for Alexander Hamilton's electoral intrigues, see JA's letter to Benjamin Rush of 9 June 1789, and note 2, above.

From Alexander Hamilton

June 23th [1790]

Mr. Hamilton will have the honor of Dineing with the Vice President on the 30th. of June agreeably to his Obliging invitation[1]

RC (MHi:Adams-Hull Coll.); addressed: "The Vice President of the United States"; endorsed by CA: "Mr Hamilton."; notation by CA: "Van Berckel Sen / Van Berckel Jun / Gen Knox / Viar / Jefferson / Hamilton / Otto / Andriani / Cazenove / Izard / Butler / Smith / Morris / Kaine / Barclay / Jay / Coxe."

[1] For JA's social responsibilities as vice president, see Roger Sherman's note of 16 Aug. [1789], and note 1, above. A year later, JA's guest list had expanded significantly to include members of Congress, his colleagues in the president's cabinet, and a rotating set of foreign diplomats.

From John Brown Cutting

Dear Sir London 5th July 1790

There are so many rumours concerning the present state of the dispute between Spain and Britain and so many individuals interested to misrepresent it that it is with much diffidence that I venture to offer you any opinion on that subject.

The british parliament the members of which are now chiefly elected will not be assembled before the middle of august.[1] Till then very little that can be depended on relative to the spanish rupture will be known—unless some unforseen event shou'd precipitate hostilities.

Mr Fitzherbert the british ambassadour is now at Madrid—negociating.[2] I believe it may be relied on that he is instructed to demand 1s. Satisfaction for the seisure of the british ships in Nootka Sound—and for the destruction of the factory establish'd on the coast. 2. An acknowledgment of a right in great Britain to navigate the South Seas and carry on fisheries and commerce throughout those seas and coasts. 3dly Payment of a million sterling the computed cost of the present armaments here. The second of these points is that which Spain is most loth to give up—and from which the minister of this country is determin'd not to recede.

Both nations however are willing to negotiate—Britain because she is not ready to begin maritime hostilities with vigour till her west india merchantmen come in with seamen to mann the fleet—which at present is very thinly mann'd: Spain because tho' ready herself—

her new ally Portugal is not—and because she is desirous to ascertain what reliance may be had on her old ally France for aid in the war.

Meanwhile both parties to this dispute must be desirous of the friendship of the United States. I hope our country without embroiling herself will obtain considerable points of both.[3] The court of Lisbon have already appointed M. Friere their late resident at this court—to be minister, resident with Congress.[4] And I understand from good authority that the navigation of the Missisippi is already tacitly ceded to the United States—by orders issued to the Vice Roy of Mexico. Be this so or not the present period seems a most auspicious one to gain whatever points the United States are most desirous of gaining either of Spain or Britain.

Shou'd the latter be disposed to treat—I hope the moment will not be neglected to agree upon some criterion whereby the american seamen may be properly discriminated from the british and consequently protected from the insults of their press gangs and the management that is now practiced to get them on board their ships of war. For two months past I have diligently discharged the duty which I think incumbent upon a republican citizen—in contributing to rescue our seamen from an abhorred servitude in the british fleet Altho' I have succeeded in most instances—in some I have wholly failed. Whatever of industry or ability I possess has been on this occasion exerted and for the present this exerition is likely to continue because it is likely to be needed.

But as I have repeatedly written both to yourself and to Mr Jefferson on this subject—I shall not trouble You with a fresh repetition of what I considered it my duty at the time zealously to represent.[5]

I send you a parcel of newspapers— The Editor is violently ministerial; but is reputed to possess better sources of foreign intelligence than most of his co-temporaries.[6]

Mrs Adams and the rest of your family will please to accept the best compliments of / Your respectful affectionate / and most obedt sert

John B. Cutting

RC (Adams Papers).

[1] Originally slated to reconvene on 10 Aug., Parliament was twice prorogued in order to accommodate George III's call for a general election, a move largely engineered by William Pitt. Great Britain's surge in prosperity and talk of a war with Spain shaped the poll results, which enlarged the ranks of Pitt's supporters in the House of Commons and burnished his popularity. In his 26 Nov. opening speech, the king proclaimed an "amicable termination" of the Nootka Sound crisis, for which see note 2, below (from Cutting, 14 June, and note 1, above; Hague, *Pitt*, p. 238; *London Chronicle*, 3 Aug., 27 Nov.; London *Diary*, 13 Oct.).

[2] For the origins of the Nootka Sound conflict, see Cutting's letter of 3 June, and note 1, above. The first real breakthrough in nego-

tiations came on 24 July, when British diplomat Alleyne Fitzherbert exchanged a key set of declarations with the Spanish foreign minister, José de Moñino y Redondo, Conde de Floridablanca. As talks continued for the next few months, the British kept their fleet at the ready, rebuffing Spanish proposals for mutual disarmament. The diplomatic process was extended repeatedly, by the late promise, on 28 Aug., of French ships to aid Spain and by the debate over the terms of the preliminary armistice. Ultimately, in November, Spain agreed to pay reparations as stipulated by Britain, but the larger question of upholding sovereignty without settlement remained (Black, *British Foreign Policy*, 246–256).

[3] JA and others in the federal government grew concerned that an Anglo-Spanish war on the Pacific coast would incur foreign requests to march troops across the neutral nation, for which see George Washington's letter of 27 Aug., and note 1, below.

[4] Like JA and others, Cutting mistakenly anticipated the imminent finalization of the proposed Portuguese-American Treaty of Amity and Commerce, for which see vol. 18:256–271. Ciprião Ribeiro, Chevalier de Freire, who served as Portugal's minister to the United States until 1799, presented his credentials to Congress in Oct. 1794. Cutting's information regarding other developments, however, was less accurate. Spain did not concede free navigation of the Mississippi River to the United States until 1795, as part of Pinckney's Treaty (vol. 17:19; *AFC*, 6:474; Washington, *Papers, Presidential Series*, 16:101).

[5] Emphasizing his efforts to counter British impressment of American seamen, Cutting wrote to JA on 31 May 1790 (Adams Papers) and 3 June, above. He provided similar reports to Thomas Jefferson, who forwarded a selection of Cutting's letters to Washington. To Cutting, the secretary of state expressed thanks for "the fatiguing exertions which your humanity and patriotism have led you to make for the relief of so many of our countrymen." Cutting's work failed to secure him the U.S. consulship at London, but Jefferson enclosed £50 as compensation (Jefferson, *Papers*, 16:415; 18:330).

[6] Cutting sent several issues of the London *Diary*, edited by journalist William Woodfall (1745–1803), who was known for his highly detailed parliamentary coverage (*DNB*).

From Alexander Hamilton

Sir — Monday July 5 [*1790*]

I have the honor to inform the Vice President of the United States and to request him to ~~inform~~ cause an intimation to be given to the Honoble The Members of the Senate that at one oClock to day, an oration will be delivered at St Pauls Church in commemoration of the declaration of Independence by a Member of the Society of the Cincannati and that seats are provided for his and their accommodation. Peculiar circumstances prevented an earlier communication. The Requisite number of tickets ~~accompany this~~ have been sent to the Secretary of the Senate.[1]

I have the honor to be with the / most perfect respect Sir / Your Obed Hum st

A Hamilton
Vice President of the NY Society of the Cin:

RC (DSI:Adams-Clement Coll.); addressed: "The Vice President of the United States"; internal address: "Vice President of the United States"; endorsed: "Col. Hamilton / 5. July 1790."

[1] The Fourth of July fell on a Sunday in 1790, shifting national celebrations to the next day. In New York City and across the country, Americans marked the anniversary with military parades, cannon salutes, and public readings of the Declaration of Independence.

JA evidently made use of the tickets, and Hamilton's itinerary was accurate. Adjourning for one afternoon, a large contingent of senators and representatives joined JA and George Washington at the president's house for wine, punch, and cake. They proceeded to St. Paul's Chapel on Wall Street, where New York lawyer Henry Brockholst Livingston gave a "well adapted" oration that was "received with great applause." In Boston, the church bells rang at daybreak, and government officials gathered at the Old South Meeting House for festivities. Philadelphia residents set off fireworks that evening at the statehouse (Maclay, *Journal*, p. 315–316; Washington, *Diaries*, 6:85–86; *New-York Journal*, 9 July; Boston *Columbian Centinel*, 7 July; *Pennsylvania Mercury*, 8 July).

From David Humphreys

Sir New York July 8th. 1790.

On Saturday next, the President proposes to go, with Mrs Washington and his family, to view the remains of the old fortifications near Kingsbridge. He has understood from Mrs Washington that Mrs Adams was desirous of gratifying her curiosity on the same subject.[1] If you should find it convenient to make the ride, with Mrs Adams and your family, he will be happy in the pleasure of all your Company at dinner at the White House (i.e. the House which was Colo. Morris's) where he has already ordered provision to be made for a small party. The President intends setting off from his House, at a little after nine in the morning.

I shall be much obliged by being honored with information whether it will be convenient for you to be of the party.

With sentiments of perfect respect / I have the honor to be / Sir / Your most obedt & / most humble servant D. Humphreys

RC (Adams Papers); internal address: "The Vice President / &c &c &c."

[1] On 10 July George Washington set off with a large party that included his cabinet and staff and their wives, as well as JA, AA, Martha Washington, and several family members. They toured Fort Washington, located at the northern tip of Manhattan, where the American general had suffered one of his greatest tactical defeats during the Revolutionary War. The group dined at Washington's former headquarters, now the Morris-Jumel Mansion, which was previously owned by British Army colonel Roger Morris (1727–1794), who fled to Yorkshire, England. The New York State legislature seized the estate in 1777 and sold it to John Berrian and Isaac Ledyard in 1784 (vol. 5:ix–x; Washington, *Diaries*, 6:92–93; *ANB*).

From George Joy

Monday 12th: July 1790

Mr: Joy presents respectful Compliments to the Vice-President and takes the liberty to hand him a sample of American made sugar which he had put up in Philadelphia for that purpose— Mr: J. is well acquainted with the Gentn: concern'd in promoting this valuable

Manufacture and can with Confidence assure Mr: Adams that the sample now sent is the genuine product of the American Maple—[1]

Judging as well from the Number of Boilers that have been order'd as from other Circumstances Mr: J. is also persuaded that a great increase of the Article may be reasonably expected.—

RC (Adams Papers); endorsed by CA: "Mr Joy July 12— 90."

[1] Merchant George Joy (ca. 1776–1834) was the scion of a loyalist family that left Boston in 1776 and eventually resettled in London. His supplier was Quaker merchant Henry Drinker, who established a 3,000-acre farm and maple sugar business in eastern Pennsylvania, providing an alternative to the West Indian cane sugar that relied on enslaved labor. By 1795, many of Drinker's investors had withdrawn from the costly project, and his venture failed (Bradford Perkins, "George Joy, American Propagandist at London, 1805–1815," *NEQ*, 34:191 [June 1961]; *Extracts from the Journal of Elizabeth Drinker, From 1759 to 1807*, ed. Henry D. Biddle, Phila., 1889, p. 220; David W. Maxey, "The Union Farm: Henry Drinker's Experiment in Deriving Profit from Virtue," *PMHB*, 107:612, 613, 617, 628 [Oct. 1983]).

From John Brown Cutting

Dear Sir London 17th July 1790

I embrace the opportunity afforded me by a vessel that sails to day for Philadelphia to send you some newspapers and to tell You that the condition of the american seamen here claims the immediate attention of the Government of the United States.[1]

In the absence of any person invested with consular or ministerial authority from Congress—I cou'd not endure to see my fellow citizens first subjected to the outrages of british press gangs—and then drag'd on board british ships of war to be scourged at the mere will and base discretion of every mean or malignant petty officer of the navy into the performance of ~~duties~~ services which our native seamen dread and detest. In this crisis I came forward and did and have done and am continually doing all that a zealous persevering individual cou'd or can do in his private capacity.

It is now necessary to state that every seaman of the United States is impress'd for and retain'd in the service of his britannic majesty as a british subject—unless the Captain who ship'd him in America will positively swear that he was actually born in the United States and is a subject of them. No Commander of a british bottom in the American Trade can take such an oath: consequently every american seaman who happen'd to arrive here since the 4th of last May in a british bottom is now on board a british ship of war. Several applications have been made to me by seamen in this predicament—and some of these accompanied with strong evidence that the applicants were really natives of the United States. In the next place there are several natives of G— Britain and Ireland who command american bottoms—but are unable—possibly unwilling to identify their american seamen by such an oath. And lastly when an american commander of an american bottom has sworn point blank that such and such seamen are natives & subjects of America—and in consequence thereof I have press'd the Lords of the Admiralty for their discharge and for a written exemption against another impress and have obtain'd both—both have been violated—by a new press-gang. On Wednesday evening last for instance such discharges and protections were totally disregarded: almost every american seaman in the thames—as well as mates of vessels and apprentices—were swept off in the night—some of these have been hardly treated by inferior officers of the british navy.[2]

It must be owned there are intrinsic difficulties in some cases to furnish even reasonable proof that a particular seaman is a subject of the United States: but in some of the cases to which I allude the most clear and absolute proof had been given and in the manner prescribed by the Lords of the Admiralty themselves.

Perhaps no *immediate remedy* that wou'd be effectual can be invented by Congress. A *palliative* wou'd be—the appointment of a consul here who might substitute prudence and management sustain'd by a suitable *authority* from the American government—in lieu of *clear rules* of *proceeding* and *loftier powers* than cou'd be now exercised here with utility to our country.[3]

Clad with that mild and modest capacity—I am vain enough to believe that even I shoud be enabled just now to render the United States essential service—which the experience and local knowledge of the past six weeks have afforded me peculiar facilities for performing in future. But at any rate I feel it my indispensable duty to continue exerting every nerve in endeavours to procure the release of as many of these impressed american seamen as possible. Before the late rigourous impress I had paved the way for liberating many of them—who have returned home rejoicing. Nor do I now despond of procuring the discharge of some—to the birth and citizenship of whom their commanders are this day again to swear. Patience, vigilance prudence and unwearied perseverance—are our only weapons.

I consider a war between Britain & Spain as inevitable—between Prussia and Austria as in the highest degree probable. *Manifestos* are expected to be published this evening.

I write this in the greatest haste— / very respectfully & affectionately / Yrs.

J. B. Cutting

RC and enclosures (Adams Papers).

[1] Cutting enclosed a copy of a 30 June letter from Williamsburg, Va., sailor Hugh Purdie, who was appealing for aid. For Purdie's impressment by the British Navy, documentation of the severe floggings and abuse he suffered aboard the *Crescent*, and the secretary of state's intervention in his liberation, see Jefferson, *Papers*, 18:310–342. This packet reached JA via the *Marquis de la Fayette*, Capt. Cain, which sailed from Gravesend, England, on 19 July and arrived in Philadelphia on 28 Sept. (London *Public Advertiser*, 21 July; *London Chronicle*, 22 July; Philadelphia *Federal Gazette*, 28 Sept.).

[2] Cutting's account of the British Navy's ongoing "hot press" was accurate. On the evening of 14 July, over 1,000 sailors were violently impressed near the Thames River and "outward-bound ships stripped of every hand" (London *Whitehall Evening Post*, 15–17 July).

[3] The U.S. consulship in London drew a crowd of contenders, including Cutting, New York merchant Stephen Sayre, and JA's top choice, Thomas Barclay. Thomas Jefferson, however, recommended Joshua Johnson. George Washington nominated Johnson on 2 Aug., and the Senate confirmed his appointment the next day. Johnson served until 1797 (vol. 17:487; *AFC*, 11:275; Washington, *Papers, Presidential Series*, 1:184, 231; 6:503, 676; Jefferson, *Papers*, 17:254, 18:315; *First Fed. Cong.*, 2:84, 85).

To Eliphalet Fitch

Dear Sir

New York July 18. 1790

I have received the polite and obliging Letter, you did me the honour to write me, on the Seventh of May.—[1] Although an intimate and frequent Correspondence with you, considering the relation between Us, and the agreable Acquaintance, I had with you in France and England would have been always agreable to me; Yet considering the different Countries and Governments in which We live, and the Avocations of Business, which demand the Attention of both of Us, I never expected more Intercourse than there has been.—

Your Countrymen, I dare say, would be very happy to see you in North America; and none of them more than myself: Yet considering the importance of your Affairs, where You are it is a favour little to be expected. Next to the Pleasure of seeing you here, I should esteem that of frequently hearing of your health and that of your family. You were not so kind in your Letter as to let me know the Situation of your son, whom I saw in London, and in whose good fortune I interest myself very much.—[2] The last of my three sons is to commence at Cambridge this Week, and like his two elder Brothers is destined to the Bar.— My only Daughter married to Col. smith of New York, has two fine Boys, and a third perhaps not far from Seeing the light of our sun.[3]

Far advanced in my fifty fifth Year, and having run through a great Variety of scænes in Life, I can very heartily join with You Mr Burke the King of Prussia and King solomon, in pronouncing all Vanité des Vanités.—

Yet I have lived to see my Country free and prosperous, rapidly Advancing to Wealth and Grandeur, after having seen her in great danger and deep Distress: I have lived to see, Europe become the Pupil of Harvard Colledge and the Town of Boston; and if I were Sure she would profit of her Lesson as much as this Country has done, I should think I had lived and seen enough.

M[rs] Adams joins with me and all mine in most respectful Compliments to yourself, M[rs] Fitch and your son: and in grateful Acknowledgments for the very handsome present in Sugar, Wine and Spirits which you had the Generosity to Send Us, and which We have received in good order.

Your Packet to the President I had the honour to present to him, with my own hand.

With great and sincere Esteem, I have / the honour to be, dear sir, your most / obedient and obliged servant John Adams

RC (InHi:Arthur G. Mitten Coll.); internal address: "Eliphalet Fitch Esqr / Receiver General of the / Island of Jamaica." LbC (Adams Papers); APM Reel 115.

[1] For this letter and the packet that JA presented to the president, see Fitch's letter of 10 May, and note 1, above.

[2] JA frequently socialized with Fitch's family, including wife Mary (ca. 1748–1808) and son Jeremiah (1778–1840), throughout his diplomatic tenure in Europe. Fitch replied on 11 March 1791 (Adams Papers) with the news that his son was an apprentice with the Jamaican law firm of Farmer & Moore (vol. 14:430; *AFC*, 10:33; MHS, *Procs.*, 50:196 [1916–1917]).

[3] AA2 gave birth to her third son, Thomas Hollis Smith, on 7 Aug. 1790 (*AFC*, 9:84, 92).

From Pierre Delivet

Dear Sir— Baltimore Goal Jully 21th. 1790

The first cause that the federall Court of anapolis had on there dockett, To Judge, Since Its Erection, Was on a Process of accompt Between two french Merchents, Belonging to france & actual Subjects of his Most Christian Majesty,[1] Which as I aprehend, That Court has No Right to take Cognisance of It Beeing Not only Diamatrically oposite to the Laws of france, But Contrary to the Stipulated articles Between H.M.C. King & the United States, Notwithstanding which, thay have Risolved from the french Consulatory Court of Baltimore To a Judgment Which is appeal to france; off the three Judges of the Consulatory Court that have Given Judgment, two of them Are Parties in the Cause, and in order to have the Execution of there Sentencess to proceed agreable to there Minds, thay have had Recourse to the federal Court of Anapolis, Which is Well Known, to Be Contrary to the Laws of Both Nations, I therefore Conclude that the federal Court have Not Been So Circumspect in there audience as the Nature of the Case Required, & on the 7th. & 8 of may Last, in Said Court there Was So little Atention Paid to the Convention of Both Courts that I who am a Partey Conserned, was Sentensed. By the federal Court to Imprisonment, in Violation of a XII article Between the Court of france & the United States, But whether this Sentence, Proceeded from, Inatention, Ignorence, Partiality, or any other Cause, I am Not in a Sittuation to Determine But as it has been Puntually Executed, have only to inform Yours Honour, of the Cause & Effect, & Desire that You Will Extend Yours humanity & Power with the federal Court So far towards My Releasment, from this obscure and Humeliateing Goal, from whence I have the honour of adressing You, That thereby I may have an opertunity of Makeeng a Proper aplycation, for Damages Sustaind from Insult & Injustice.

Your Kind Interposition in this My time of Eligal & abusive treatment will Ever be Most Graatfully acknowledged; By Your Sinceer and Humble Servent

Delivet 2d. Lietnd:
of His M C Majesty Navy

RC (Adams Papers).

[1] A consular court in Baltimore heard the dispute between French Navy lieutenant Pierre Delivet (b. ca. 1735) and a group of French merchants based in Le Havre, Rouen, and Paris. Once the judges invoked Maryland law, however, the case shifted to the federal district court in Annapolis. Delivet's complaint was rooted in Art. 12 of the consular convention of 9 Sept. 1789, which stipulated that a French consul must adjudicate any such matter. Instead, Delivet was remanded to the Baltimore city jail in March 1790 and moved to the Annapolis prison on 6 May. He appealed to Thomas Jefferson for aid at least three times throughout the summer, additionally citing Arts. 4, 5, and 6, which outlined contractual relationships between consuls and crews. The secretary of state took action on 23 Aug., asking Maryland attorney general Richard Potts to investigate the case. Eventually freed, Delivet identified himself to James Madison in a letter of 26 May 1813 as "a frenchemen Born over 78 Year of age officer of the Royal Navy un tell the french Revolution that I Came to America and Naturalise" (Jefferson, *Papers*, 14:173–174, 176–177; 17:399–400; 23:273; Madison, *Papers, Presidential Series*, 6:347–351).

From Richard Varick

Sir

New York July 21st. 1790.

The Corporation of this City have applied to the President of the United States to permit Colo. John Trumbull take his Portrait to be placed in the City Hall, to which the President has consented & M^r. Trumbull has suggested to me that as the Portrait will be large the Room in the Hall in which those of the King and Queen of France are placed will be most eligible to perform the Painting in & that he will take Care that no Possible Injury or Inconvenience shall be occasioned by this Indulgence to him.

The whole of the Hall being devoted to the Use of Congress, I take the Liberty of thus Addressing You Sir, as well as the Speaker of the House of Representatives on the Subject & of soliciting your Permission, under a Persuasion that your respective Assent will be sufficient, without troubling the Senate or House of Representatives.[1]

I pray Your Answer on this Subject, & have the Honor to be with great Respect / Sir / Your Obed^t. & very / Hble Servt.

Rich^d: Varick

RC (Adams Papers); internal address: "Honble. John Adams Esqr. / Vice President / of the United States."

[1] New York mayor Richard Varick (1753–1831), former secretary to George Washington, guided the decoration of Federal Hall. JA and his congressional peers sat near copies of two full-length portraits, Antoine François Callet's "Louis XVI in Coronation Robes" and Élisabeth Louise Vigée Le Brun's "Marie Antoinette in Ceremonial Dress." The city council recruited Col. John Trumbull to produce additional artwork. For Trumbull's portrait of Washington, see Descriptive List of Illustrations, No. 7, above (*ANB*; Washington, *Papers, Presidential Series*, 6:103; T. Lawrence Larkin, "A 'Gift' Strategically Solicited and Magnanimously Conferred: The American Congress, the French Monarchy, and the State Portraits of Louis XVI and Marie-Antoinette," *Winterthur Portfolio*, 44:31, 49, 53–54 [Spring 2010]).

To Richard Varick

Sir New York— July 22. 1790

I received Yesterday the Letter you did me the honour to write me, Soliciting Permission for Mr Trumbul, to paint the Portrait of the President in that room of the City Hall, in which the Portraits of the King and Queen of France are placed.

This morning I took the Liberty to read your Letter, Sir, in Senate, and have the orders of the members to inform you, that they consent with Pleasure to Mr Trumbuls request. I am happy, sir in the opportunity, of obliging Mr Trumbul as well as Yourself and have the honour to be, with great Esteem / your most obedeint and most humble / servant John Adams

RC (private owner, 1979); internal address: "The Honble Richard Varick Esqr / Mayor of the City of New York."

7. GEORGE WASHINGTON, BY JOHN TRUMBULL, 1790
See page xiv

From C. W. F. Dumas

Monsieur, Lahaie 23 Juillet 1790

Quoique je puisse & doive être certain que V^e. Exc^e. a régulierement connoissance de mes Dépeches à l'hon^ble. Départment des Aff. Etr., j'ai néanmoins cru devoir prendre la liberté de m'adresser directement à Elle, pour Solliciter, Monsieur, votre Attention Spéciale à un Article dans celle du 14 au 23 de ce mois, & aux annexes, où il est question de l'honneur qui nous est fait par l'Académie Américaine des Arts & des Sciences à Cambridge en Massachusetts, à Mr. le Profess^r. Luzac & à moi; & par conséquent au desir, bien naturel, que nous avons de Savoir à qui nous somes redevables d'avoir été proposés pour cette faveur, afin de pouvoir Lui en témoigner notre juste gratitude.[1]

Voilà, Dieu merci, la vraie liberté civile, la vraie Majesté, celle du Peuple, hautement reconnue & établie par deux puissantes nations, capables de donner le ton, l'une au nouveau monde, l'autre à l'ancien, plus que jamais dignes amies l'une de l'autre, faisant ensemble une masse de près de 30 millions d'humains:— un Roi citoyen plus solidement puissant que tous ses Confreres: tous les autres trônes, Gothiques, fondés sur d'antiques opinions & préjugés, ébranlés par l'abolition de la Noblesse héréditaire & de l'hiérarchie en France, leur politique déroutée par le Décret de renonciation à tout Esprit de conquête; frémissants, tremblants, ne sachants quel parti prendre pour contenir les millions assujettis à leurs Dictatures.— *Novus rerum nascitur ordo*.— Et moi, septuagénaire, je verrai encore une partie de tout cela, petit Diogene, seul & rencoigné dans le vaste tonneau de l'hôtel Américain, ne desirant rien des Alexandres, sinon de ne pas m'intercepter le Soleil par leur ombre.

Veuillez, Monsieur, pendant le reste de cette vie, m'honorer de vos bonnes graces, agréer l'homage de mes respects pour Mad^e. Adams, le tribut de mes voeux pour votre constante prospérité & pour celle de vos chers Enfans, & être persuadé du sincere respect avec lequel je suis pour toujours Monsieur, De Votre Excellence, les très-humble & très-obéissant serviteur, Cwf Dumas

TRANSLATION

Sir The Hague, 23 July 1790

Though I may and should be certain that your excellency is regularly informed of my dispatches to the honorable Department of Foreign Affairs, I nevertheless found it necessary to take the liberty to address myself directly to you to solicit, sir, your particular attention to an article in that of the 14th to 23rd of this month, and to the enclosures which touch upon the honor done to Professor Luzac and to me, by the American Academy of Arts and Sciences in Cambridge, Massachussetts; and consequently, to the very natural desire that we have to know to whom we are obliged to have been recommended for this favor, in order that we may express our proper gratitude.[1]

Here, thanks be to God, is real civil liberty, true majesty, the people's, highly commended and established by two powerful nations, capable of setting the bar, one for the new world, the other for the old, more than ever worthy friends one of the other, together making up a population of almost 30 million humans. A citizen king more firmly powerful than all of his peers: all of the other thrones, Gothic ones, founded upon ancient opinions and prejudices, undermined by the abolition of hereditary nobility and hierarchy in France, their politics deterred by the decree renouncing all spirit of conquest; quaking, trembling, not knowing what decision to make in order to contain the millions subjected to their dictatorships. *A new order of things is born.* And I, a septuagenarian, shall yet see a little part of all this: little Diogenes, alone and crouched within the vast barrel of the Hôtel des États-Unis, undesirous of anything from the Alexanders of the world, so long as they do not block my sun with their shadow.

Would you be pleased, sir, for the remainder of this life, to honor me with your good graces, to accept the extension of my respects for Mrs. Adams, the tribute of my wishes for your steady prosperity and for that of your children, and to be persuaded of the sincere respect with which I am now and always, sir, your excellency's most humble and most obedient servant

Cwf Dumas

RC (Adams Papers); internal address: "A Son Excellence Mr. J[n.] Adams, Président du Senat en Congres des Et. un."; notation: "Pr."

[1] On 26 May 1789 Dumas and Jean Luzac were elected foreign members of the American Academy of Arts and Sciences. Blending personal and political news, Dumas wrote nine letters to John Jay from 19 June to 2 Dec., and from 15 Nov. to 14 July 1790, he sent six more reports on foreign affairs to Thomas Jefferson (from Dumas, 13 June 1789, above; Portland, Maine, *Cumberland Gazette*, 19 June; *Dipl. Corr.*, 1783–1789, 3:605–653; Jefferson, *Papers*, 16:193–194, 265–266, 415–416, 442–443; 17:208–210; Nationaal Archief:Dumas Papers, Microfilm, Reel 3, f. 1043–1045).

From George Walton

Sir,

Augusta, 23 July, 1790.

By some intelligencies lately from Europe, it is said that Great-Britain is zealously endeavoring to repossess the Floridas; and I have no doubt of the fact, because her interest is greatly concerned in the event, and in general she has seen it better than any other Nation.[1] Her frozen possessions to the North are not calculated for Caribean supplies. West-florida is very much so; and the possession of the Navigation of the Mississippi would secure an exclusive right to the advantages of the immense agricultures of the west; and which would encrease by that event. The posts that Nation keeps contrary to her engagements with America, is the link which is intended to connect her power from the North to the South; and the Bourbon scheme, which aimed at deriving abundance from a wilderness, is now reviving with the felling axe and hoe. If care is not taken that enterprising and Commercial Nation will generate another Revolution in America. Independence west of the Mountains would draw one half of the Eastern Inhabitants. The result taken from the Union, and put in the scale of Great-Britain, would greatly compensate her late losses. I take it for certain that an arrangement so fatal will be defeated, by alarming the Spanish Nation with the formidability of such a neighbor. To me it appears one of the most important objects that Nation has latterly contemplated; And success will be equally productive of Wealth, power and revenge. As I shall be very much obliged to you for your opinion upon this subject, and of the detention of the Posts, I have taken the liberty of addressing this scrawl, being with the highest respect & Esteem, / Sir, / Your Most Ob[t.] Serv[t.]

Geo Walton.

P.S.

M[r.] John Gibbons, in point of character and ability, is qualified to be the Accountant in this state for the United States.[2]

RC (Adams Papers).

[1] At the Nootka Sound conflict's peak, U.S. newspapers reported that Vincente Manuel de Zéspedes y Velasco, Spanish royal governor of Florida, was improving the military fortifications of St. Augustine with the expectation that "England will make a bold push to regain those valuable provinces." Although press reports exaggerated several scenarios of possible European aggression, there was a kernel of truth to some of the accounts. William Pitt, for example, met secretly with Venezuelan revolutionary Francisco de Miranda to discuss the possibility of Britain's gaining control over Spain's colonial possessions, including Cuba, Florida, and portions of the Mississippi Valley (vol. 17:301; *Pennsylvania Mercury*, 6 July; *New-York Packet*, 8 July; *Connecticut Courant*, 12 July; *ANB*; William Ray Manning, *The Nootka Sound Controversy*, Washington, D.C., 1905, p. 412–414).

[2] Savannah auctioneer John Gibbons (1758–1814), who was an auditor of Georgia's public accounts in 1782, did not earn a federal post ("Historical News and Notices," *Journal of Southern History*, 24:137 [Feb. 1958]; Charles C. Jones Jr., *The History of Georgia*, 2 vols., N.Y., 1883, 2:521; Thomas Gamble Jr., *A History of the City Government of Savannah, Ga., from 1790 to 1901*, Savannah, Ga., 1900, p. 494).

To Henry Marchant

Dear Sir New York 25 of July –90

I have rec^d your favour of the 19th– I presume your answer to Mr Jefferson will be sufficient: but If you write to the President, it will do no harm– Your letter to the President came to me after your appointment, so that I have never delivered nor mentioned it to any one; and shall keep it and all that came with it till your farther orders.– It is best it should not now be conveyed to the President, as it is become unnecessary.[1]

I thank you my dear Sir for your friendly politeness. I shall certainly never pass New Port without seeing you and your family, I hope in prosperity. I should have written you before but for a cause which makes it difficult to write now, an inflamation in my eyes.[2] He will not be less friendly to you, if you should ever hear of poor old blind

John Adams.

LbC in CA's hand (Adams Papers); internal address: "Hon Hen Marchant / New Port."; APM Reel 115.

[1] Soliciting the post of Rhode Island district judge, Marchant wrote to JA on 7 June (Adams Papers) and enclosed a letter of the same date for JA to forward to the president. Two weeks later, Marchant sent JA several letters of recommendation supporting his application (Washington, *Papers, Presidential Series*, 5:488–490; from Marchant, 16 July 1789, and note 1, above).

[2] Owing to ill health, JA's letter writing lapsed noticeably after 11 June 1790, resuming on 15 July.

From Elbridge Gerry

My dear sir New York 26 July 1790

As you were so obliging on saturday last as to inform me of your design to recommend my brother Samuel Russel Gerry to the office of collector for the port of Marblehead, I think it necessary to inform you that of all the candidates, he is the only one who has received any appointment under the State & he has received three offices commissary, naval officer, & collector of excise.[1] in the two former he gave great satisfaction to the inhabitants of the town as well as to the State, & his reputation was so fair with the General court, as that a member of the Committee for liquidating accounts informed me, whenever Mr Gerry's accounts were presented, they were so fair & so well vouched as to require but a few moments examination. his popularity in the town is manifest by the voluntary petition of the merchants & traders to elect him, directed to the President of the U.S. thus much I am in justice bound to say for him, he is a man of strict honor & integrity & assiduous in his undertakings. he has been very unfortunate by the war & has a large family to maintain, but I will not trouble you further being my dear sir yours with every sentiment / of esteem & respect E Gerry

RC (Adams Papers); internal address: "The Vice-President of the U States."

[1] Marblehead, Mass., merchant Samuel Russel Gerry (1750–1807) was one of Elbridge Gerry's younger brothers. The elder Gerry enclosed a petition, not found, supporting his brother's bid for the collectorship and signed by 57 local merchants. George Washington nominated Samuel for the office on 2 Aug., and the Senate confirmed his appointment the next day. Samuel's poor record keeping plunged him into debt, and he lost his post in 1801 (Washington, *Papers, Presidential Series*, 6:124–125).

From Jeremiah Allen

Sir Boston July 29. 1790

When I had the Honor of being with you, a Conversation turn'd upon the Consul for Russia, I observed it would not do, unless some pay or Emolument, was with it, as Consuls at St. Petersburg by Custom Were obliged, to Ride with four Horses, Merchants by Law forbid to Ride with more then two

since my Return some of my Friends have advised me, to apply for the appointment, I think if it was consistent, and I could be appointed for Russia, Sweden & Denmark perhaps something might be allowed untill the Consulage was sufficient— It was Judge Dana's Opinion, that one Consul for those Powers would be Competant to every purpose

Your Excellency knows that all Ships going into the Baltic must enter at Elsinuer

If a General War takes place, it may be Well for the Continent to have a Person, in the Northern part of Europe to be on the Watch, to take any advantage that chance may throw in the Way for the benefit of the Commerce of this Country— I recollect when I had the Honor of a Conversation with Your Excellency at Mr Jays, you observed that every Man, who Wishd an office, ought to apply, and that applications Were pleasing, therefore I address myself to you, the Reasons why I apply are, when I went to Russia, I was the First American. whos Name was enter'd at the Custom House, and put into the Gazette—in Consequince the Dutchess of Kingston sent for me, and by my means sent Her Ship to Boston, which opend the Trade— When I arrived, I advertized in the papers that I would give every information Relative to the Trade &c Mr Cabot had a Ship going there, I wrote a letter to Prince de Narisken, Master of the Empresss Horse—setting forth, that Our Captains Were unacquainted with the Trade, and in case of any mistake, Requested him to befriend them—[1]

That Letter he got the English Minister Mr Fizt Herbert to translate into French, and a Merchant who understood Russ. to translate it into that Language, and shew them to The Empress, She told him, to Inform me, that every indulgence, that was reasonable should be granted— after I went again to Russia, and carried a present for The Empress of diffirent Birds & Squrrells

She Received them Graciously, and sent word if I had any favor to ask of the Government it should be granted, I reply'd to the Nobleman that personally, I had nothing to ask, perhaps my Country might, at a future period— from these Circumstances, presuming upon your Friendship and Judgment, I request the favor, that you will be so good, as to mention my Request to The President, shew him this, or an Extract if proper, for which I shall ever Esteem myself under the greatest Obligation to you— I have neither Wrote or Spoke to any person upon the Subject before—it will be adding to the favor if Your Excellency will condecend to Write a line what I may expect, or if necessary for me to go to New York— Mrs Browne joins in Respects to you and Mrs Adams

I take the liberty to enclose a list of the Exports from Russia for the Year 1786

I have the Honor / to be with Respect / and Esteem Your / Excellency most Humbe. / and obedient servt Jeremiah Allen

RC and enclosure (Adams Papers); internal address: "The Vice President"; endorsed by CA: "Jeremiah Allen / July 29— 90."

[1] Allen, a Boston merchant who first met JA aboard *La Sensible* in Nov.–Dec. 1779, made his initial trip to St. Petersburg in 1783 and returned via the Duchess of Kingston's ship, the *Kingston*, on 13 December. Abroad, Allen contacted Lev Alexander Naryskin (1733–1799), grand equerry to Catherine II, and made his presence known in the St. Petersburg *Vedeomosti*. He advertised widely in Massachusetts newspapers, offering "every possible Information" about the logistics of Russian trade. Beverly, Mass., merchants John and Andrew Cabot sent the *Sebastian*, Capt. James Worsley, which left Salem on 17 May 1784 and returned on 21 November. Another Cabot ship, the *Commerce*, Capt. Tuck, soon completed the same route. With this letter, Allen enclosed a detailed 1786 report showing that ten American vessels were outbound from St. Petersburg to New England ports, laden with iron and hemp. He was unsuccessful in obtaining a government post, and the role of U.S. consul to Russia was not filled until 1803 (vols. 9:87; 15:182, 307; 17:151; Alfred W. Crosby Jr., *America, Russia, Hemp, and Napoleon: American Trade with Russia and the Baltic, 1783–1812*, Columbus, Ohio, 1965, p. 40–42; *Boston Gazette*, 22 Dec. 1783, 19 Jan. 1784; Boston *Continental Journal*, 1 April; *Salem Gazette*, 18 May, 5 Oct.; Newburyport *Essex Journal*, 24 Nov.; Catherine II, *Selected Letters*, transl. Andrew Kahn and Kelsey Rubin-Detlev, Oxford, 2018, p. 421; LCA, *D&A*, 1:292).

From William Cushing

Dear Sir, Middletown Saturday Eveng 7th. Augst. 1790

I intended myself the pleasure of calling to pay my respects to you before leaving the city, & for that purpose had engaged a hack to carry me out Thursday Morning, but the hack failed & disappointed me & the packet I had bespoke a passage in, being soon ready to sail, I stepped aboard & reached the harbour of Newhaven that Evening; which saved much jolting over horseneck rocks.— So I hope you will excuse my neglect.—

Our Session was short, having not much to do, besides determining what rout we were to take respectively the next Circuit Court; & it being the general opinion that a rotation was not necessary in the Contemplation of law; the Chief Justice & I are to begin in october at Albany & circulate Eastward, Ending with Providence the beginning of December.[1] Before our Circuit begins I hope to hope to have the pleasure of Seeing you Eastward if you make a visit that way. I present my respects to Mrs. Adams & am Sir your affectionate humble servant Wm Cushing—

RC (Adams Papers).

[1] The fall session of the eastern circuit opened in Albany, N.Y., on 4 October. Judges heard cases in Hartford, Conn.; Boston; and Exeter, N.H., before adjourning in Providence, R.I., on 7 Dec. (*Doc. Hist. Supreme Court*, 2:536, 541, 542).

From John Brown Cutting

Dear Sir, London Aug. 11. 1790

If ever there was a time when the volunteer exertions of a citizen of America became a duty incumbent upon him in a foreign realm—that period has existed here.

For many weeks past I have not been absent a single day from the Admiralty—sundays only excepted. It is not for me to say how efficacious in resisting individual oppression or national mischief this unintermitting attention has proved.

I have not yet leisure to transmit either to Yourself or to Mr Jefferson a full detail of facts. By the inclosed papers however You will obtain some information.[1]

The *press* notwithstanding pacific appearances in the newspapers yet continues, throughout the british ports: but whether the british fleet is rendering thus formidable for warlike enterprize or only politic intimidation, the best informed people here can only conjecture.

The preliminary articles of a pacification between the courts of Berlin and Vienna are signed— By these it is said the house of austria must relinquish every fruit of their war with Turkey except the dismantlement or demolition of a few turkish fortresses.[2] The reduction of the revolted Netherlands—is a measure that Leopold is resolved on.[3] Nobody will pity a race of revolutioners so debased by bigotry as to pass contentedly from the imperial yoke to that of priestly and aristocratic fabrication.

The empress of Russia has signified her consent to the Emperor that is to be—of Germany—to make a seperate peace for himself—if his affairs require it. Firm and haughty she defies her foes and relies on her own resources for carrying on a war with Sweden & the Porte.[4]

Very respectfully Your affectionate and most obed ser[t]

John Brown Cutting

RC (Adams Papers).

[1] The enclosures have not been found, but for Cutting's efforts on behalf of American sailors, see his 17 July letter to JA, and note 2, above. He documented the struggle in his *Facts and Observations, Justifying the Claims of John Browne Cutting*, Phila., 1795, Evans, No. 28522. Cutting claimed that he assisted more than 700 American seamen, spending nearly $7,000 of his own funds, and he asked Congress for reimbursement. He received a partial payment of $2,000 in 1792 (Jefferson, *Papers*, 23:105, 106).

[2] Leopold II, emperor of Austria, agreed to a truce with the Ottoman Empire on 19 Sept. 1790 and signed the Treaty of Sistova on 4 Aug. 1791. Austria relinquished portions of Bosnia, Serbia, Moldavia, and Wallachia (Black, *British Foreign Policy*, p. 262, 263; Mehrdad Kia, *The Ottoman Empire: A Historical Encyclopedia*, 2 vols., Santa Barbara, Calif., 2017, 1:49).

[3] For the revolt in the Austrian Netherlands, see John Bondfield's letter of 20 Nov. 1789, and note 2, above.

[4] The Russo-Swedish War ended on 14 Aug. 1790 with the Treaty of Varala. The Russo-Turkish War continued until 1792, culminating in the Treaty of Jassy (vol. 19:42; from John Paul Jones, 20 Dec. 1789, and note 3, above).

To Richard Varick

Sir, New-York, August 12, 1790

It is with great pleasure, that, in obedience to an order of the Senate of the United States, I have the honor to enclose their Resolution of this date, which was unanimously agreed to; and in behalf of the Senate, I request that you will be pleased to communicate the same to the Corporation of this city, and at the same time signify to them, that it is the wish of the Senate, that the Corporation will permit such articles of furniture, &c. now in the City-Hall, as have been provided by Congress, to remain for the use of that building.[1]

I am, Sir, your most obedient / Humble servant,

John Adams
Vice President of the United States,
and President of the Senate

MS not found. Printed from *First Fed. Cong.*, 1:490–491.

[1] JA enclosed a copy of the 12 Aug. Senate resolution thanking the New York City legislature "for the elegant and convenient accommodations provided for Congress." Once Congress relocated to Philadelphia, the Federal Hall building served as City Hall until 1812, when it was sold and demolished (*First Fed. Cong.*, 1:490; Eric Homberger, *New York City: A Cultural and Literary Companion*, N.Y., 2003, p. 55).

From Sylvanus Bourne

Dr Sir— Boston Augt 15th 1790

Observing by the Papers that you are one of the Commrs: appointed for purchasing part of the public Debt at Markett in which you will ~~doubtless~~ probably wish to employ an agent—if this should be the Case—Mr Woodward occurred to my mind as a person well calculated for such an employ—both for integrity & a thourough acquaintance in this kind of buisness—having been for a long enrolled in the list of speculators in Boston & with reputation— should it be convenient to employ him as an agent while you will serve the publick—you will also confer an essential favour on a meritorious Individual—[1]

I am at a loss to determine why the Consular Bill has been short of sight—it will prevent my Departure for some time[2]

I have the honour to be with great / Respect Yr Ob Servt

Silva. Bourne

RC (Adams Papers); endorsed by CA: "Silv. Bourn / Augst. 13— 1790."; notation by CFA: "S. Bourne. / Augt 13th 1790."

[1] Approving a key component of Alexander Hamilton's economic plan, Congress on 9 Aug. passed an act "making provision for the reduction of the public debt," which George Washington signed into law three days later. JA was one of five commissioners empowered to purchase public debt on behalf of the federal government. However, JA did not need an agent, since state loan officers were deputized to handle the sale of securities. Bourne recommended Braintree surveyor of highways Joseph Woodward, who wrote to JA on 15 and 30 May 1789 (both Adams Papers), soliciting the Boston collectorship (*U.S. Statutes at Large*, 1:186; *First Fed. Cong.*, 3:567–568; *AFC*, 8:360, 9:108, 109).

[2] On 15 July 1790 Elbridge Gerry introduced a bill in the House of Representatives to establish salaries for U.S. consuls, and it was passed six days later. The bill was read in the Senate on 21 and 26 July but postponed until the next session (*First Fed. Cong.*, 3:514, 522, 824).

To Chrétien Guillaume de Lamoignon de Malesherbes

New York, August 19th, 1790.

Mr. Ducher, a French gentleman, whom you did me the Honor to introduce to me formerly by letter, and who is well esteemed in this country, will have the honour to deliver you this.[1]

The news of the death of my worthy friend Count Sarsefield has afflicted me the more as I have never been able to learn the circumstances of it or of his last sickness, or in what situation he has left his affairs, and especially his Manuscripts. He once told me it was his intention to request the Earl of Harcourt, his friend in England, to publish some of his writings after his death.[2]

I should esteem it a favour if you would inform Mr. Ducher of any particulars, or indicate to him any person who can give him information which he will be so good as to convey to me. Knowing as we do by experience the distresses and dangers of a revolution, we are very anxious for our friends in France, to whom we wish all success and happiness.

With great and sincere consideration, I have to be, &c.

MS not found. Printed from Alfred Morrison, comp., *The Collection of Autograph Letters and Historical Documents*, 2 vols., 2d ser., London, 1893–1896, 1:10.

[1] The famed jurist Malesherbes, now acting as the French minister of state, wrote to JA on 29 Aug. 1782 (Adams Papers) to introduce lawyer Gaspard Joseph Amand Ducher (1744–1804), of Châteldon. Ducher served as the French vice consul at Portsmouth, N.H., from 1786 to 1787, and at Wilmington, N.C., from 1787 to 1789. A copy of Ducher's *Coutumes Generale et Locales de Bourbonnois,* Paris, 1781, is in JA's library at MB (vol. 9:229; Societe d'Emulation & des Beaux Arts du Bourbonnais, *Bulletin Revue*, Moulins, France, 1899, p. 219, 220; Frederick L. Nussbaum, *Commercial Policy in the French Revolution: A Study of the Career of G. J. A. Ducher*, Washington, D.C., 1923, p. 14, 17, 34–35).

[2] Guy Claude, Comte de Sarsfield, died in Paris on 26 May 1789. George Simon, 2d Earl of Harcourt (1736–1809), did not proceed with plans to publish Sarsfield's papers (vol. 17:411; London *Diary*, 5 June; London *Oracle*, 2 June).

From John Codman Jr.

Dear sir

Boston 27 August 1790

Enclosed is an Account of the Cost of your two Casks of Wine & the charges which I have paid upon it— agreeably to your desire I shall acquaint Doctor Tufts of the amount that he may discharge it when convenient[1]

I understand our friend Mr Harrison does not accept the appointment of Consul at Cadiz— My Brother Richard whom I believe is honored with being personally known to you I am flattered to suppose would not discredit such an office, he has had as good an education as this country affords & since that time has spent several years in my compting house but lately being out of health he has taken a tour into France Spain & Italy which has given him an acquaintance with some of these languages & finding the climate beneficial to him is a good deal attached to a residence in that part of the world[2]

As your influence must greatly prevail with the President & the Sec^y^ of foreign affairs. I have taken the liberty in this instance to solicit your interest in his favour— The Consulship at Cadiz would be more acceptable than any other because I should have it in my power to serve my brother in the course of business better there than elsewhere and had it not been that I conceived Mr Harrison entitled to a preference, this application would have been made at an earlier period when the appointments from Massachusets were not so disproportionate as at present, which I have understood would probably prevent further appointments from this quarter, but when it is considered that the Education of the Young Gentlemen of this state especially of the Commercial kind is more attended to than in some of the States in the union, where Merchants are made up principally of foreigners it will not seem extraordinary that more candidates should offer from hence, than from them.

Was it necessary to furnish letters of recommendation from more disinterested persons I would thank you to mention it & I will forward them, I cannot however forbear to solicit your forgiveness for this intrusion on your goodness & to assure you that if you should feel satisfied to interest yourself in behalf of my brother you will confer a lasting obligation on him as well as on Your obed^t^ & respectful Hum^l^ Servt. John Codman jun

RC (Adams Papers); internal address: "His Excellency John Adam Esqre."; endorsed: "John Codman Junr. / 27. Aug. Ans^d.^ 10 Oct^r.^ / 1790."

[1] Boston merchant John Codman Jr. (1755–1803) shipped two casks of wine from Spain. Replying on 15 July 1791 (Adams Papers), JA arranged for Cotton Tufts to send the shipment to his new residence in Philadelphia and to pay the bill (*AFC*, 7:111).

[2] For the appointment of a U.S. consul at Cádiz, see Sylvanus Bourne's letter of 8 Sept. 1789, and note 1, above.

From George Washington

Sir, New York, August 27th: 1790.

Being very desireous of obtaining such aids and information as will enable me to form a just opinion upon the subject of the enclosed paper, in case the events therein mentioned should take place; I have taken the liberty to submit it to you for your consideration, requesting that you will favor me with an opinion thereon.[1]

With very great esteem & regard / I am / Sir, / Your most Obedt: Hbe. Servt. Go: Washington

ENCLOSURE

(Secret)

United States August 27th: 1790

Provided the dispute between Great Britain and Spain should come to the decision of Arms, from a variety of circumstances (individually unimportant and inconclusive, but very much the reverse when compared and combined) there is no doubt in my mind, that New Orleans and the Spanish Posts above it on the Mississippi will be among the first attempts of the former, and that the reduction of them will be undertaken by a combined operation from Detroit.[2]

The *Consequences* of having so formidable and enterprising a people as the British on both our flanks and rear, with their navy in front, as they respect our Western settlements which may be seduced thereby, as they regard the Security of the Union and its commerce with the West Indies, are too obvious to need enumeration.

What then should be the answer of the Executive of the United States to Lord Dorchester, in case he should apply for permission to march Troops through the Territory of the said States from Detroit to the Mississippi?[3]

What notice ought to be taken of the measure, if it should be undertaken without leave, which is the most probable proceeding of the two?

Mr. Adams will oblige the President of the United States by giving his opinion in writing on the above statement.

Go: Washington

RC and enclosure (Adams Papers); internal address: "Mr. Adams—" and "Mr. Adams."; docketed by JA: "No. 1." and "No. 2."

[1] With minor alterations in wording, Washington sent the same query to his entire cabinet. Most of them replied immediately, anxious to resolve the first test of American neutrality. JA, John Jay, and Henry Knox all cited law of nations theory—especially the works of jurists Emmerich de Vattel, Hugo Grotius, and Samuel von Pufendorf—and strongly advised sitting out the Nootka Sound conflict until either Great Britain or Spain formally approached with a request to move troops through American territory. Thomas Jefferson outlined a more aggressive path of preemptive denial, to be underlined by force if necessary. Alexander Hamilton, replying a month later, upheld the majority view. Just as JA observed in his reply of 29 Aug., below, Hamilton emphasized that the United States lacked the military, the money, and the popular support needed to go to war. He wrote: "There are causes which render war in this country more expensive, and consequently more difficult to be carried on than in any other. There is a general disinclination to it in all classes" (Washington, *Papers, Presidential Series*, 6:353–361, 439–460). See also Descriptive List of Illustrations, No. 6, above.

[2] Spain held regional posts in St. Louis and Natchez, Mississippi (Abernethy, *The South in the New Nation*, p. 208).

[3] False rumors that Benedict Arnold was reviewing the Detroit, Mich., militia fueled concern that the British planned to invade Spanish Louisiana. Arnold, however, was mired in a series of lawsuits in St. John, New Brunswick, Canada, during 1790 (vol. 19:48; Washington, *Papers, Presidential Series*, 6:344–345).

To George Washington

Sir New York August 29 1790

That New Orleans, and the Spanish Posts on the Missisippi, will be among the first attempts of the English, in case of a war with Spain, appears very probable: and that a combined operation from Detroit, would be convenient to that end cannot be doubted.

The Consequences, on the western Settlements, on the commerce with the West Indies, and on the general Security and tranquility of the American confederation, of having them in our rear, and on both our flanks, with their navy in front, are very obvious.

The interest of the United States duely weighed, and their Duty conscientiously considered, point out to them, in the case of Such a War, a neutrality, as long as it may be practicable. The People of these States would not willingly Support a War, and the present Government has not Strength to command, nor enough of the general[1] Confidence of the nation to draw the men or money necessary, untill the Grounds, causes and Necessity of it Should become generally[2] known, and universally approved. A pacific Character, in opposition to a warlike temper, a Spirit of Conquest, or a disposition to military Enterprize, is of great importance to us to preserve in Europe: and therefore We Should not engage even in defensive War, untill the Necessity of it, Should become apparent, or at least until We have it in our Power to make it manifest, in Europe as well as at home.

In order to preserve an honest Neutrality, or even the Reputation of a disposition to it, the United States must avoid as much as possible, every real Wrong, and even every Appearance of Injury to either Party. To grant to Lord Dorchester in case he Should request it, permission to march troops through the territory of the United States, from Detroit to the Missisippi, would not only have an appearance offensive to the Spaniards, of partiality to the English, but would be a real Injury to Spain. The Answer therefore to his Lordship Should be a refusal, in terms clear and decided, but guarded and dignified, in a manner, which no Power has more at command than the President of the United States.

If a measure So daring offensive and hostile, as the march of Troops through our Territory to Attack a Friend, Should be hazarded by the English, without leave, or especially after a refusal, it is not So easy to answer the Question, what notice ought to be taken of it.

The Situation of our Country is not like that of most[3] of the nations in Europe. They have generally large numbers of Inhabitants in narrow territories: We have Small numbers Scattered over vast regions. The Country through which the Brittons[4] must pass from Detroit to the Missisippi, is, I Suppose, so thinly inhabited, and at Such a distance from all the populous Settlements, that it would be impossible for the President of the United States to collect Militia or march troops Sufficient to resist the Enterprize. After the Step shall have been taken there are but two Ways for Us to proceed one is War and the other negotiation. Spain would probably remonstrate to the President of the United States but whether she should or not, the President of the United States should remonstrate to the King of Great Britain. It would not be expected I Suppose by our Friends or Ennemies that the United States should declare War at once. Nations are not obliged to declare War for every Injury or even Hostility. A tacit Acquiescence under Such an Outrage, would be misinterpreted on all hands; by Spain as inimical to her and by Brittain,[5] as the effect of Weakness, Disunion and Pusillanimity. Negotiation then is the only other Alternative.

Negotiation in the present State of Things is attended with peculiar difficulties. As the King of Great Britain, twice proposed to the United States, an Exchange of Ministers, once through Mr Hartley and once through the Duke of Dorsett, and when the United states agreed to the Proposition, flew from it: to Send a Minister again to st James's till that Court explicitly promises to send one to America is an humiliation to which the United States ought never to Submit.[6]

A Remonstrance from Sovereign to sovereign cannot be Sent, but by an Ambassador of some order or other: from Minister of State to Minister of State, it must be transmitted in many other Ways: A Remonstrance in the form of a Letter from the American Minister of State to the Duke of Leeds, or whoever may be Secretary of State for foreign affairs, might be transmitted, through an Envoy, Minister Plenipotentiary, or Ambassador of the President of the United States, at Paris, Madrid or the Hague and through the British Ambassador at either of these Courts. The Utmost length, that can be now gone, with Dignity would be to send a Minister to the Court of London, with Instructions[7] to present his Credentials, demand an Audience, make his Remonstrance, but to make no Establishment and demand his audience of leave and quit the Kingdom in one, two or three Months if a Minister of equal degree were not appointed and actually sent to the President of the United States, from the King of Great Britain.

It is a Misfortune that in these critical moments and Circumstances, the United States have not a Minister of large Veiws, mature Age Information and Judgment, and Strict Integrity at the Courts of France Spain London and the Hague.[8] Early and authentick Intelligence from those Courts may be of more importance than the Expence: but as the Representatives of the People, as well as of the Legislatures, are of a different opinion they have made a very Scanty Provision for but a part of Such a system. As it is, God knows where the Men are to be found who are qualified for Such Missions and would undertake them. By an Experience of ten Years which made me too unhappy[9] at the time to be ever forgotten, I know, that every Artifice which can deceive, every temptation which can operate on hope or fear, Ambition or Avarice, Pride or Vanity, the Love of Society Pleasure or Amusement will be employed to divert and warp them from the true line of their Duty and the impartial honour and interest of their Country.

To the Superiour Lights and Information derived from office; the more Serene[10] temper and profound Judgment of the President of the United States, these crude and hasty thoughts[11] concerning the Points proposed, are humbly Submitted, with every sentiment of respect and / Sincere attachment, by his most obedient / and most humble servant John Adams[12]

RC (DLC:Washington Papers); internal address: "The President of / the United States."; endorsed: "From / The Vice-President / 29th. Augt. 1790." Dft (Adams Papers). FC (Adams Papers).

[1] In the Dft, JA wrote "unanimous."

[2] In the Dft, JA wrote "publick and notorious."

[3] In the Dft, JA wrote "any."

[4] In the Dft, JA wrote "English."

[5] In the Dft, JA wrote "England."

[6] For David Hartley's and the Duke of Dorset's proposals for the exchange of ministers, see vol. 17:19–20.

[7] In the Dft, JA added here, "not to present his Credentials nor ask an Audience untill a Minister of equal Degree should be appointed at st James's to come to the United States, and with further Instructions to quit the Kingdom, without communicating his Credentials, to the King if a Counter Minister were not appointed within one Month."

[8] Of the cabinet members who replied to Washington with advice on the Nootka Sound conflict, only JA and John Jay used the opportunity to advocate for sustaining and deepening the American diplomatic presence in Europe. On 22 Dec. 1791 Washington nominated Gouverneur Morris to serve as U.S. minister to France and William Short as minister to the Netherlands. Senators debated the merits and expenses of maintaining resident diplomats before confirming both appointments in mid-Jan. 1792. Morris served until 1794; Short was reassigned to Spain, where he was the U.S. minister from 1794 to 1796 (U.S. Senate, *Exec. Jour.*, 2d Cong., 1st sess., p. 92, 93, 96, 98; 3d Cong., 1st sess., p. 157; 4th Cong., 1st. sess., p. 269).

[9] In the Dft, JA wrote "miserable."

[10] In the Dft, JA wrote "calm" but then canceled it and interlined "Serene."

[11] In the Dft, JA added "which contain the best opines he can form."

[12] Following the advice of JA and others, the president's decision to wait out the negotiations at Madrid proved fruitful, and French nullity proved fortunate. By late October the British and Spanish negotiators had hammered out the first of three Nootka Sound conventions, formed between 1790 and 1794, that opened the territory to both nations for trade. Widely hailed as a British diplomatic win, the Nootka Sound conflict demonstrated the Triple Alliance's military power and, more critically, eroded the longstanding belief that land claims must be supported by settlement (Black, *British Foreign Policy*, p. 233–256).

To Samuel Adams

Dear Sir New York September 12th 1790

Upon my return from Philadelphia to which beloved City I have been, for the purpose of getting an house to put my head in next Winter[1] I had the pleasure of receiving your favour of the Second of this month. The Sight of our old Liberty Hall, and of Several of our old Friends, had brought your venerable Idea to my mind, and continued it there, a great part of the last Week, so that a Letter from you on my Arrival Seem'd but in continuation. I am much obliged to the "confidential friend["] for writing the short Letter you dictated, and shall beg a continuance of Similar good offices.[2]

Captain Nathaniel Byfield Lyde, whom I know very well, has my hearty good Wishes. I Shall give your Letter and his to the Secretary of the Treasury, the Duty of whose Department it is to receive and examine all applications of the kind. applications will probably be made, in behalf of the Officers who Served the last War in the Navy, and they will be likely to have the preference to all others: but Captn Lydes Application Shall nevertheless be presented and have a fair Chance.

My Family as well as myself are I thank God in good health, and as good Spirits as the prospect of a troublesome removal will admit. M[rs] Adams desires her particular regards to your Lady and yourself.

What? my old Friend is this World about to become.? Is the Millenium commencing? Are the Kingdoms of it, about to be governed by Reason? your Boston Town Meetings, and our Harvard Colledge have Sett the Universe in motion. Every Thing will be pulled down. So much Seems certain. But what will be built up? Are there any Principles of political Architecture? What are they? Were Voltaire and Rousseau Masters of them? Are their Disciples acquainted with them? Lock taught them Principles of Liberty: but I doubt whether they have not yet to learn the Principles of Government. Will the Struggle in Europe, be any Thing more than a change of Impostors and impositions?

With great Esteem and Sincere affection / I am my dear sir your Friend / and Servant
John Adams.

RC (NN:George Bancroft Coll.); addressed: "His Honour / Samuel Adams Esq[r] / Lt Governor of the / Massachusetts / Boston"; internal address: "His Honour / Samuel Adams Esqr / Lt Governor of the / Massachusetts."; endorsed: "Letter from John Adams / to Saml. Adams / dated New York Sep[r] / 12 1790"; notation: "Free / John Adams." LbC (Adams Papers); APM Reel 115.

[1] JA visited Philadelphia in early September. He leased Bush Hill, a mansion located two miles outside the city, which became the Adamses' home until spring 1791 (*AFC*, 9:xii–xiii, 103). For Congress' relocation, see Descriptive List of Illustrations, No. 8, above.

[2] Adams wrote on 2 Sept. 1790, recommending Capt. Nathaniel Byfield Lyde to command the Massachusetts revenue cutter. Lyde, who frequently carried letters and goods for JA and AA, also made a direct appeal to the vice president in an undated letter enclosed by Adams (both Adams Papers). JA forwarded Adams' letter and Lyde's application to Alexander Hamilton on 27 or 28 September. Lyde did not receive a federal post, and by 4 Dec. John Foster Williams had been named to fill the command (vol. 12:238; *AFC*, 7:index; Hamilton, *Papers*, 7:97, 192).

From the Abbés Chalut and Arnoux

Paris 13. 7bre 1790

Les abbés Chalut et Arnoux ont l'honneur de faire leurs sinceres Compliments à Monsieur Adams et de l'assurer de leur estime et de leur amitié; ils lui envoyent un exemplaire de deux ouvrages posthumes de M. l'abbé de Mably. ces deux ouvrages sont en deux volumes. il en paroitra encore Cinq on aura soin de les lui faire parvenir à mesure qu'ils paroitront[1]

Les abbés Chalut et Arnoux presentent leurs hommages respectueux à M[de.] Adams et à M[de.] votre fille, ils font leurs amitiés à M.M. vos fils.

8. "ROBERT MORRIS MOVING THE CAPITOL," CA. 1790

See page xv

TRANSLATION

Paris, 13 September 1790

The Abbés Chalut and Arnoux have the honor of extending their sincere compliments to Mr. Adams and of assuring him of their esteem and friendship; they send him a copy of two posthumous works of the Abbé de Mably. The two works are in two volumes. Another five will be published and will be sent as they become available.[1]

The Abbés Chalut and Arnoux present their dutiful respects to Mrs. Adams and to Madam your daughter. They send their friendly regards to Messrs. your sons.

RC (Adams Papers).

[1] With their final extant letter to JA, Chalut and Arnoux enclosed the first two volumes of the Abbé de Mably's *Oeuvres Posthumes*, Paris, 1790, which are in JA's library at MB (*Catalogue of JA's Library*).

From Cotton Tufts

Dear S^r. Weymouth Septemb^r. 18. 1790

Accounts have been exhibited to me by several Dep^y. Sheriffs for Service of Writs committed to them by You while in the Practice of Law. I have found myself embarrassed with Respect to the Payment of them not being fully acquainted with your Mode of transacting Business with them. I have found it necessary to examine Your Writ Execution & Account Books; in some Cases where the Minutes in them rendered it probable that You charged & rec^d. the Service and that neither You nor the Plaintiff had accounted for the Service I have paid it—but least I should make Blunders I wish You to give me some Directions relative to the Payment of such Accounts

I find in Your Acc^tt. Book a Ballance of £20. or more standing against Thos. Boylstone Esq. If it is due, Would it not be best to render in the Acc^tt. to M^r. Gill— There is also a Ballance of £15.5.2 against Simon Joy of this Town (lately dec^d) I have presented the Acc^tt. to his Adm^rs. who informd me that he has a Receipt of £12 or 14£ but could not then ascertain the Sum being from Home. I have examind the Writ Book and find the following Entries

Viz. "Jany. C^t. 1771. John Adams V^s. Simon Nehemiah, David & William Joy. Writ & Serv^d. 8/6 rec^d. 8/6 Agr^d."[1]

"Jany C^t. 1774. John Adams V^s. Simon Joy & At^s. Bond. 9/4 serv^d. rec^d. 16/ Cost and £12.10.1 in Part of the Bond for which I gave a loose Recipt. Jany 4. 1774"— The abovement^d. is formed from An Account begun in 1770 & continued to 1773– no Credit is given therein And as an Action was brought against Simon Joy & Sons on Bond in 1771 Jany C$^{t.}$ and the Account was then open I suppose the Receipt mentioned by the Adm$^{rs.}$ must undoubtedly be the Receipt You gave Jany 4. 1774 on Acc$^{tt.}$ of the Bond and that the Account is still due– whether I am right in my Idea of the Business You can best determine– But as the Sum in Question is worth attending to Youll be pleased to give me such Information as You may think necessary for the proper Settlement of the Acc$^{t.}$

I enclosed in my last Letter to M$^{rs.}$ Adams a List of Your public Seccurities–[2]

Be so good as to write to me upon the Matters abovementioned by the first Opp$^{y.}$ I wish You an agreable Scituation at Philadelphia, but at the same Time cannot but sympathise with You in the misfortune of removing from so delightful a Spot as that You have lately occupied. I sometimes think that had You been less conversant with Removes, You would enjoyed a less Share of Health, However those which You have undergone, must have been attended with great Fatigue Trouble & Expence– Be pleased to present my affectionate Regards to M$^{rs.}$ Adams & Family

I am with sincere Respect / Yours Cotton Tufts

Octob. 21.

This day rec^{d} Y$^{rs.}$ of the 10^{t} Ins$^{t.}$ & shall comply with Your Request–

RC (Adams Papers); internal address: "Hon John Adams Esq."

[1] Tufts was resolving several outstanding debts with regard to JA's law practice, including money owed to JA by Boston merchant Thomas Boylston, whose brother-in-law was Moses Gill, and by Weymouth farmer Simon Joy (1697–1789) and his sons William (1721–1811), Nehemiah (1726–1802), and David (1738–1820) (*AFC*, 1:213; James Richard Joy, *Thomas Joy and his Descendants*, N.Y., 1900, p. 71).

[2] Not found. For JA's related instructions, see his 10 Oct. reply to Tufts, below.

From Samuel Adams

Dear sir Boston Oct$^{r.}$ 4$^{th:}$ 1790

With pleasure I received your Letter of Sept$^{r.}$ 12th; and as our good friend, to whom I dictated my last is yet in Town; I have requested of him a second favour–

You ask what the World is about to become? and, Is the Millenium commencing? I have not studied the Prophesies, and cannot even conjecture. The Golden Age so finely pictured by Poets, I beleive has never yet existed; but in their own imaginations. In the earliest periods, when for the honor of human nature, one should have thought, that man had not learnt to be cruel; what Scenes of horror have been exhibited in families of some of the best instructors in Piety, and morals! Even the heart of our first father was grievously wounded at the sight of the murder of one of his Sons, perpetrated by the hand of the other.— Has Mankind since seen the happy Age? No, my friend. The same Tragedy's have been acted in the Theatre of the World; the same Arts of tormenting have been studied, and practiced to this day; and true religion, and reason united have never succeeded to establish the permanent foundations of political freedom, and happiness in the most enlightened Countries on the Earth.— After a compliment to Boston Town meetings, and our Harvard College as having "set the universe in Motion"; you tell me Every Thing will be pulled down; I think with you, "so much seems certain," but what say you, will be built up?

Hay, wood, and stuble may probably be the materials, 'till Men shall be yet more enlightned, and more friendly to each other— "Are there any Principles of Political Architecture"? Undoubtedly. "What are they?"— Philosophers ancient, and modern have laid down different plans, and *all* have thought themselves, Masters of the true Principles. Their disciples have followed them, probably with a blind prejudice, which is always an Enemy to truth, and have thereby added fresh fuel to the fire of Contention, and increased the political disorder— Kings have been deposed by aspiring Nobles, whose pride could not brook restraint— These have waged everlasting War, against the common rights of Men.— The Love of Liberty is interwoven in the Soul of Man, and can never be totally extinguished; and there are certain periods when human patience can no longer endure indignity, and oppression. The spark of liberty then kindles into a flame; when the injured people attentive to the feelings of their just rights magnanimously contend for their compleat restoration But such contests have too often ended in nothing more than "a change of Impostures, and impositions." The Patriots of Rome put an End to the Life of Cæsar; and Rome submitted to a Race of Tyrants in his stead. Were the People of England free, after they had obliged King John to concede to them their ancient rights, and Libertys, and promise to govern them according to the Old Law of the Land? Were they free, after they had wantonly deposed their Henrys, Edwards, and Richards to gratify *family pride*? Or, after they had brought their first Charles to the block, and banished his family? They were not— The Nation was then governed by King, Lords, and Commons, and its Libertys were lost by a strife among three Powers, soberly intended to check each other, and keep the scales even. But while we daily see the violence of the human passions controuling the Laws of Reason and religion, and stifling the very feelings of humanity; can we wonder, that in such tumults little, or no regard is had to Political Checks, and Ballances? And such tumults have always happened within as well as without doors. The best formed constitutions that have yet been contrived by the wit of Man have, and will come to an End—because "the Kingdoms of the Earth have not been governed by Reason." The Pride of Kings, of Nobles, and leaders of the People who have all governed in their turns, have dissadjusted the delicate frame, and thrown all into confusion— What then is to be done?— Let Divines, and Philosophers, Statesmen and Patriots unite their endeavours to renovate the Age by impressing the Minds of Men with the importance of educating their *little Boys*, and *Girls*—of inculcating in the Minds of Youth the fear, and Love of the Deity, and universal Phylanthropy; and in subordination to these great principles the Love of their Country—of instructing them in the Art of *self* government, without which they never can act a wise part in the Government of Societys great, or small—in short of leading them in the Study, and Practice of the exalted Virtues of the Christian system; which will happily tend to subdue the turbulent passions of Men, and introduce that Golden Age beautifully described in figurative language; when the Wolf shall dwell with the Lamb, and the Leopard lie down with the Kid—the Cow, and the bear shall feed; their Young ones shall lie down together, and the Lyon shall eat straw like the Ox—none shall then hurt, or destroy—for the Earth shall be full of the Knowledge of the Lord— When this *Millenium* shall commence, if there shall be any need of Civil Government, indulge me in the fancy that it will be in the Republican form, or something *better*—

I thank you for your Countenance to our friend Lyde— Mrs. Adams tells me to remember her to yourself, Lady, and Connections; And be assured that I am sincerely / Your friend— Saml Adams

RC in Joseph Willard's hand (Adams Papers); internal address: "The Vice President of the United States"; endorsed: "Lt Governor Adams / Octr. 4. ansd. 18th. 1790."

To John Codman Jr.

Dear Sir, New York October 10 1790.

I duely received your obligin letter of the 27th of August; but a journey to Philadelphia, and the confusion of preparations to remove to that City, have prevented an earlier answer to it. I concur very freely and very fully with you, in your sentiments respecting the appointments of Consuls abroad; but I find the President and Secretary of State, are impressed with an apprehension of censure, for appointing too many from one State.[1] Before your letter arrived to me, the President and Mr Jefferson were both gone to Virginia— When I meet them at Philadelphia, I will deliver the letter to the latter, and heartily wish your Brother success.[2] I think it is adviseable for you to send on to me the best letters of recommendation of your Brother, that you can readily obtain; and they shall be communicated too.

The Wine you received for me from Spain, I should be obliged to you, to Ship by the first good opportunity addressed to me at Philadelphia; I shall remove in ten days, and be there ready to receive it, before it will arrive.

I am Sir with much esteem your obliged humble Servant,

John Adams.

LbC in CA's hand (Adams Papers); internal address: "John Codman / Junr $Esq^{r:}$ / Boston"; APM Reel 115.

[1] Of the eighteen consuls nominated by the president on 4 June and 2 Aug., four men were from Massachusetts, three apiece were from Virginia and New York, and two were from Maryland. The remaining six were not Americans, which proved the greater controversy. Senators hotly debated the issue, finally resolving to support the candidates by midsummer. Tension lingered over the perceived regional favoritism of the appointments. Reviewing the whole process on 26 Nov., Thomas Jefferson observed that "so many Massachusetts men have already obtained Consular appointments as to endanger considerable discontent in the other states" (Washington, *Papers, Presidential Series*, 5:473–476, 6:183; Jefferson, *Papers*, 18:80).

[2] George Washington departed New York on 30 Aug. and visited Philadelphia for several days, reaching Mount Vernon on 11 September. Jefferson left for Monticello by 2 Sept., arriving home on 20 Sept. (Washington, *Papers, Presidential Series*, 6:380, 392, 393, 410; Jefferson, *Papers*, 17:473, 511; Philadelphia *Federal Gazette*, 4 Sept.).

To Cotton Tufts

Dear Sir, NewYork October 10th 1790.

I write at this time only to authorise and request you, to subscribe for me, to the new loan, all the final settlements, Loan Office Certificates, Indents, or other paper securities whether of the United

States, or particular States, which you have in your hands belonging to me.[1] I know not that any more particular power is necessary; if it is, upon notice, I will send it immediately. We remove to Bush-Hill, about two miles out of the City of Philadelphia, in about ten days; Can't you spare the time make us a visit?[2] You would make us very happy. Compliments to Mrs Tufts; should be very glad to see her with you. With usual affection, yours John Adams.

LbC in CA's hand (Adams Papers); internal address: "The Honble / Cotton Tufts / Esqr."; APM Reel 115.

1 Under the Funding Act of 4 Aug., three types of federal securities were eligible for sale. JA invested $2,036.32 at 6 percent per annum and $1,784.57 at 3 percent per annum, both beginning 1 Jan. 1791, and $1,018.16 at 6 percent per annum beginning 1 Jan. 1801. AA made similar investments totaling $3,164. Significantly, in tandem with the Adamses' investment activities, JA also served as a commissioner of the Sinking Fund, for which see the board's summary report to Congress of 21 Dec. 1790, and note 1, below (JA to Tufts, 23 Dec., MBBS:Colburn Autograph Coll.; *AFC*, 9:xiv, 95, 197).

2 The Adamses departed the city on 7 Nov. on the New York packet, Capt. Corwin, and reached Philadelphia five days later (*AFC*, 9:142, 150, 507; *New-York Daily Gazette*, 8 Nov.; *Pennsylvania Mercury*, 13 Nov.).

To Thomas Welsh

Dear Sir New York Octr. 10 1790

It would give me great Pleasure to comply with your request, and to be of Service to you, in any Way in my Power: but I am not at Liberty to communicate the most distant hint to any one, relative to the Subject.[1]

One Anecdote which flatters my Pride, if it does not comfort my Conscience, among the many mortifications of my Social Feelings, which I am obliged to submit to, I will relate to you.

My Friend Count Sarsefield, one of the most learned and Sensible french Noblemen I ever knew, asked me in London to import some Mirror Plates, alias Looking Glasses from France, which he wanted to give in Presents to his friends, under my Priviledge as an Ambassador. I answered him that Although I should be very happy to oblige him, I had never done Such a Thing in any Country, and could not think of doing it.— I expected Such an Answer, Said the Count "Il ne vaut pas, un Sou, d'etre votre Ami." "It is not worth a Shilling to be your Friend."— I am afraid that my Friends will all find, as long as I live, that my friendship is not worth a groat.

Whether worth a penny or not, I am however / your friend

John Adams

RC (MHi:Adams-Welsh Coll.); addressed: "Dr Thomas Welsh / Boston"; internal address: "Dr Welch."; endorsed: "Vice President / Octob^r: 9 1790"; notation by JA: "Free / John Adams." LbC (Adams Papers); APM Reel 115.

[1] For Welsh's repeated requests to JA for inside information on the newly established Sinking Fund, see *AFC*, 9:114–116.

From Nicolaas & Jacob van Staphorst and Nicolaas Hubbard

Amsterdam 11. October 1790.

We beg leave to introduce to your Excellency's acquaintance, the Bearer M^r. Joseph Ceracchi Native of Rome & an eminent Sculptor, requesting your Excellency to render him every Service and civility in your Power, under our assurance of his being well worthy of them, and that your Excellency will thereby particularly oblige those who on similar & all other occasions are with great regard & respect.[1] / Your Excellency's. / Most obid^t. & humble Servants

N & J. Van Staphorst & Hubbard

RC (Adams Papers); internal address: "His Excell^y. John Adams Esqr. Vice President of the / United States.—"

[1] Italian sculptor Giuseppe Ceracchi (1751–1801) arrived in Philadelphia by March 1791. He created terra-cotta or marble busts and medallions of George Washington, Thomas Jefferson, James Madison, and Alexander Hamilton, among others. AA likely donated Ceracchi's medallion of JA to the American Academy of Arts and Sciences in 1794, but both the medallion and the bust have since been lost (*AFC*, 10:284; Oliver, *Portraits of JA and AA*, p. 211–213; Oxford Art Online).

From William Temple Franklin

Sir, Philadelphia, 13, Oct. 1790.

Permit me to inform your Excellency, that in consequence of pressing Letters from my Friends in England and France, urging me to go over immediately with my Grandfathers Papers, in order to derive that Advantage in the Publication of them, which, they say, delay would diminish;—& having likewise some other private Business to transact; I have concluded to go in the Pigou, which will sail for London the latter end of this Month.—[1] It will give me great Pleasure, Sir, to be honor'd with yours & your Ladys Commands for that City, or Paris; whither I propose going sometime in January: And if during my stay in Europe I can in any way be useful to your Excellency, I beg you will command me freely, & be assur'd that I shall at all times be happy to prove to you my Gratitude for past Favors, and how sincerely I am, / Sir, / Your Excellency's / most obedient and / faithful humble Ser$^{t:}$ W. T. Franklin

My best Compliments to your Son.—

RC (Adams Papers); internal address: "His Ex^{y} / John Adams Esqr."

[1] Franklin inherited more than 15,000 documents belonging to his grandfather Benjamin, and he carried 3,000 of them to England. He sailed via the *Pigou*, Capt. Collet, from Philadelphia on 5 Nov., before the Adamses departed New York. In 1818 he published a London edition of his *Memoirs of the Life and Writings of Benjamin Franklin* (Jefferson, *Papers*, 18:87, 88; Philadelphia *Federal Gazette*, 4 Nov. 1790; Philadelphia *General Advertiser*, 5 Nov.).

To William Temple Franklin

Sir New York, October 16 1790.

Last night I had the pleasure to receive your obliging letter of the 13 of this month, and thank you for your information of your intention to embarke for Europe. The advice of your friends in France and England, to be as early as possible in the publication of your Grandfathers papers, is probably judicious; as a certain ardor of curiosity wears off in such cases commonly, in time. Your friend my dear M$^{rs.}$ Adams is ill in bed, of a fever; and which renders the misfortune more severe, we were all packed up for a removal to Philadelphia.[1] I am however still in hopes that we shall, be at Bush-hill before you embark; in which case I shall request the favor of you to take a small Packett or two. But, if contrary to my hopes, and expectations, we should not see you before you Sail, present my affectionate regards to all our good friends in France and England, especially the marquis and his Lady, Mr Grand and family, and the Abbys De Chalut and Arnoux; In England to Mr Hartly Dr Price Mr Brand Hollis and the Vaughan Family. I shall be glad to hear of your wellfare, and to read your observations upon the progress of Liberty in Europe. I am Sir with much esteem and regard your most obedient Serv$^{t.}$

John Adams

LbC in CA's hand (Adams Papers); internal address: "William T / Franklin Esqr"; APM Reel 115.

[1] AA had been suffering from intermittent shaking fits and "voilent fever," likely malaria, since 10 Oct., and she began to recover in early November (*AFC*, 9:140, 141, 142).

To Samuel Adams

Dear Sir New York Oct. 18. 1790

I am thankful to our common friend as well as to you for your favour of the 4th. which I received last night.— My fears are in Unison with yours, that Hay, Wood and Stubble will be the materials of the new political Buildings in Europe, till Men shall be more enlightened and friendly to each other.

You agree, that there are undoubtedly Principles of Political Architecture: but instead of particularizing any of them, You Seem to place all your hopes in the universal or at least more general prevalence of Knowledge and Benevolence. I think with you that Knowledge and Benevolence ought to be promoted as much as possible: but despairing of ever Seeing them Sufficiently general for the Security of Society, I am for Seeking Institutions which may Supply in some degree the defect.— If there were no Ignorance Error or Vice, there would be neither Principles nor Systems of civil or political Government.

I am not often Satisfied with the opinions of Hume but in this he Seems well founded that all Projects of Government founded in the Supposition or Expectation of extraordinary degrees of Virtue are evidently chimerical.[1] Nor do I believe it possible, humanly Speaking that Men should ever be greatly improved in Knowledge or Benevolence without assistance from the Principles and system of Government. I am very willing to agree with you in fancying, that in the greatest Improvements of Society, Government will be in the Republican form. It is a fixed Principle with me that all Good Government, is and must be Republican. But at the Same time, your Candour will agree with me, that there is not in Lexicography, a more fraudulent Word. Whenever I Use the Word Republick, with approbation I mean a Government, in which the People have, collectively or by Representation, an essential Share in the Sovereignty. The Republican Forms of Poland and Venice, are much worse, and those of Holland and Bearn very little better, than the Monarchical form in France before the late Revolution. By the Republican form, I know you do not mean, the Plan of Milton, Nedham or Turgot: for after a fair Tryal of its miseries, the Simple monarchical form will ever, be, as it has ever been, preferred to it, by Mankind. Are We not, my Friend, in danger of rendering the Word Republican, unpopular in this Country, by an indiscreet, indeterminate and equivocal Use of it.? The People of England have been obliged to wean themselves from the

Use of it by making it unpopular and unfashionable, because they found it was artfully Used by Some and Simply understood by others, to mean the Government of their Interregnum Parliament. They found they could not wean themselves from that destructive form of Government, So entirely, as that a mischievous Party would not Still remain in favour of it, by any other means, than by making the Words Republick and Republican unpopular. They have Succeeded to Such a degree, that with a vast Majority of that nation, a Republican is as unamiable as a Witch a Blasphemer, a Rebel or a Tyrant. If, in this Country, the Word Republick should be generally understood, as it is by some, to mean a form of Government inconsistent with a mixture of three Powers forming a mutual ballance We may depend upon it, that Such mischievous Effects will be produced by the Use of it, as will compell the People of America to renounce, detest and execrate it, as the English do. With these Explanations, Restrictions and Limitations I agree with you in your Love of Republican Governments, but in no other Sense.

With You, I have also the honour most perfectly to harmonize, in your Sentiments of the Humanity and Wisdom of promoting Education in Knowledge Virtue and Benevolence. But I think that these will confirm mankind in the opinion of the necessity of preserving and Strengthening the Dykes against the Ocean, its Tides and Storms. Human Appetites, Passions, Prejudices and self Love, will never be conquered by Benevolence and Knowledge, alone introduced by human means. The millenium itself neither Supposes nor implies it. All civil Government is then to cease and the Messiah is to reign. That happy and holy State is therefore wholly out of this question. You and I agree in the Utility of universal Education: But will nations agree in it, as fully and extensively as We do? and be at the Expence of it? We know with as much certainty as attends any human Knowledge that they will not. We cannot therefore Advize the People to depend for their Safety, Liberty and Security, upon hopes and Blessings, which We know will not fall to their Lot. If We do our duty then to the People We shall not deceive them, but advise them to depend upon what is in their Power and will relieve them.

Philosophers ancient and modern do not appear to me to have Studied Nature, the whole of Nature, and nothing but nature. Lycurgus's Principle was War and Family Pride: Solons was what the People would bear. &c. The best Writings of Antiquity upon Government those I mean of Aristotle, Zeno and Cicero are lost. We have human Nature, Society, and universal History to observe and Study, and from these We may draw, all the real Principles which ought to be regarded. Disciples will follow their Masters, and interested Partisans their Chieftains, let Us like it, or not. We cannot help it. But if the true Principles can be discovered and fairly fully and impartially laid before the People, the more light increases the more the Reason of them will be Seen, and the more disciples they will have. Prejudice, Passion and private Interest, which will always mingle in human Enquiries, one would think might be enlisted on the Side of Truth, at least in the greatest number, for certainly the Majority are interested in the Truth if they could See to the End of all its Consequences. "Kings have been deposed by aspiring Nobles"[2] True, and never by any other. "These" the Nobles I Suppose "have waged everlasting War against the common Rights of Man." True, when they have been possessed of the Summa imperii, in one body, without a Check. So have the Plebeians—so have the People, so have Kings—So has human Nature in every shape and Combination, and So it ever will. But on the other hand the Nobles have been essential Parties in the preservation of Liberty, whenever and wherever it has existed. In Europe they alone have preserved it, against Kings and People, wherever it has been preserved: or at least with very little assistance from the People. one hideous Despotism, as horrid as that of Turkey would have been the Lot of every nation of Europe, if the Nobles had not made Stands. By Nobles I mean not peculiarly, an hereditary Nobility, or any particular modification, but the natural and actual Aristocracy among Man kind. The Existence of this You will not deny. You and I have Seen four noble Families rise up in Boston the Crafts's Gores, Daws's and Austins. These are as really a Nobility in our Town, as the Howards, Sommersets, Berties &c in England.[3] Blind undistinguishing Reproaches, against the Aristocratical part of Man kind, a Division which Nature has made and We cannot abolish, are neither pious nor benevolent. They are as pernicious as they are false. They serve only to foment Prejudice Jealousy, Envy Animosity and malevolence. They Serve no Ends but those of Sophistry, Fraud and the Spirit of Party. It would not be true, but it would not be more egregiously false, to say, that the People have waged everlasting War against the Rights of Men.

"The Love of Liberty, you Say is interwoven in the Soul of Man." So it is, according to La Fontaine, in that of a Wolf. and I doubt whether it be much more rational generous or Social, in one than in the other untill in Man, it is enlightened by Experience, Reflection, Education and civil and political Institutions, which are at first produced and constantly Supported and improved by a few, that is by the Nobility. The Wolf in the Fable, who preferred running in the forest, lean and hungry, to the Sleek plump and round Sides of the Dog, because he found the latter was sometimes restrained, had more Love of Liberty than most Men. The Numbers Men in all ages have preferred Ease, Slumber and good chear, to Liberty when they have been in Competition. We must not then depend alone upon the Love of Liberty in the soul of Man, for its Preservation. Some political Institutions must be prepared to assist this Love, against its Ennemies. Without these, the Struggle will ever end, only in a Change of Impostors.[4] When the People who have no Property, feel the Power in their own hands to determine all questions by a Majority, they ever attack those who have Proper[ty] till the injured Men of Property, loose all Patience and recur to finesse, Trick and Stratagem, to outwit those, who have too much Strength because they have two many hands, to be resisted any other Way. Let Us be impartial then and Speak the whole Truth. Till We do We shall never discover all the true Principles that are necessary. The multitude therefore as well as the Nobles must have a Check. This is one Principle.

"Were the People of England free, after they had obliged King John to conce[de] to them, their ancient Rights." The People never did this.— There was no People who pretended to any Thing. It was the Nobles alone. The People pretended to nothing but to be Villains Vassals, and Retainers to the King or the Nobles. The Nobles, I agree, were not free, because all was determined by a majority of their Votes, or by Arms, not by Law. Their feuds deposed their "Henrys, Edwards, and Richards," to gratify Lordly Ambition, Patrician Rivalry and "Family Pride." But if they had not been deposed those Kings would have become Despots, because the People would not and could not join the Nobles in any regular and constitutional opposition to them. They would have become Despots, I repeat it, and that by means of the Villains Vassalls and Retainers aforesaid. It is not Family Pride, my Friend, but Family Popularity that does the great Mischief, as well as the great good. Pride in the heart of Man, is an evil fruit and concommitant of every Advantage; of Riches, of Knowledge; of Genius, of Talents, of Beauty of Strength, of Virtue, and even of Piety. It is Sometimes ridiculous, and often pernicious: but it is even sometimes and in Some degree Useful. But the Pride of Families would be always and only ridiculous, if it had not Family Popularity to work with. The Attachment and Devotion of the People to some Families, inspires them with Pride. As long as Gratitude or Interest, ambition or avarice, Love, hope or fear Shall be human motives of Action, So long will numbers attach themselves to particular Families. When the People will, in Spight of all that can be Said or done, cry a Man or a Family up to the Skies, exaggerate all his Talents & Virtues not hear a Word of his Weakness or faults, follow implicitly his advice detest evey Man he hates, adore evey Man he loves, and knock down all who will not swim down the Stream with them, where is your Remedy? When a Man or Family are thus popular, how can you prevent them from being proud. You and I know of Instances in which Popularity has been a Wind, a Tide, a Whirlwind— The History of all Ages and Nations is full of Such Examples. Popularity that has great Fortune to dazzle; Splendid Largesses to excite warm Gratitude, Sublime beautiful and uncommon Genius or Talents to produce deep Admiration; or any Thing to support high hopes and Strong Fears, will be proud, and its Power will be employed to mortify Ennemies, gratify friends, procure Votes, Emoluments, and Power. Such Family Popularity ever did and will govern, in every nation in every Climate, hot and cold wet and dry—among civilizd and Savage People: Christians and Mahometans Jews and Heathens. Declamation against Family Pride is a pretty Juvenile Exercise: but unworthy of Statesmen. They know the Evil and danger is too Serious to be Sported with. The only Way, God knows, is to put these Families into an Hole by themselves, and Sett two Watches upon them; a Superiour to them all, on one side, and the People on the other.

There are a few Popular Men in the Massachusetts, my Friend who have I fear less honour, Sincerity and Virtue than they ought to have. That if they are not guarded against may do another Mischief. They may excite a Party Spirit, and a mobbish Spirit instead of the Spirit of Liberty, and produce another Wat Tylers Rebellion. They can do no more. But I really think their Party Language ought not to be countenanced; nor their Shiboleths pronounced. The miserable Stuff that they utter about the Well-born is as despicable as themselves. The ευγενειϭ[5] of the Greeks, the bien neés of the French, the Gewellgebornen of the Germans & Duch, the beloved Families of the Creeks, are but a few Samples of national Expressions of the Same Thing, for which every nation on Earth has a Similar Expression.—[6] one would think that our Scribblers were all the sons of Redemptioners or transported Convicts They think with Tarquin In novo populo, ubi omnis repentina atque ex virtute nobilitas Sit, futurum locum forti ac Strenuo viro—[7]

Let Us be impartial. There is not more of Family Pride on one Side, than of Vulgar Malignity and popular Envy on the other. Popularity in one Family raises envy ~~in another and~~ in others. But the Popularity of the least deserving will tryumph over Envy and Malignity, while that which is acquired by real Merit will very often be over born and oppressed by it.

Let Us do Justice to the People and to the Nobles for Nobles there are as I have before proved in Boston as well as Madrid. But to do Justice to both, you must establish an Arbitrator between them. This is another Principle.

It is time that you and I should have some Sweet Communion together. I dont believe, that We who have preserved for more than thirty Years an uninterupted Friendship, and have So long thought and acted harmoniously together in the worst of times, are now so far asunder in sentiment as some People pretend. in full confidence of which I have used this freedom, being / ever your warm friend

John Adams

RC (NN:George Bancroft Coll.); addressed: "Honorable Samuel Adams / Lieutenant Governor of Massachusetts / Boston"; internal address: "His Honour / Samuel Adams Esqr / Lieutenant Governor of Massachusetts"; endorsed: "Letter from John / Adams dated New / York Oct. 18. 1790"; notation: "Free / John Adams." LbC (Adams Papers); APM Reel 115. Text lost due a tight binding has been supplied from the LbC.

[1] David Hume, "Idea of a Perfect Commonwealth," *Essays and Treatises on Several Subjects*, 2d edn., 4 vols., Edinburgh, 1777, 4:252.

[2] JA quoted Adams' letter of 4 Oct., above.

[3] Prominent members of these Boston families included lawyers Christopher Gore and Thomas Dawes Jr. as well as merchants Benjamin Austin Jr. and Col. Thomas Crafts Jr. The Howards, Somersets, and Berties were families who held major posts in the English government over multiple generations (vol. 19:index; *AFC*, 2:225, 9:index; *DNB*).

[4] In the LbC, CA wrote "impositions, and."

[5] Well-born.

[6] From this point, the LbC is in an unknown hand.

[7] "Among a new people, where all rank was of sudden growth and founded on worth, there would be room for a brave and energetic man" (Livy, *History of Rome*, Book I, ch. 34, lines 6–8).

From Thomas Brand Hollis

my Dear Sir — Harvard octo. 19th. 1790

amidst the numerous & important concerns in which you are engaged, & for which I rejoice that you should sometimes think of me gives me a heartfelt satisfaction & I trust to have some claim to the continuance of your friendship & correspondence, if being conscious, my regard for you was always sincere & interested from principle, in the cause of your country.

I begun this letter on a pleasing spot in Dorsetshire called *Adams* a portion of a large farm nominated Harvard there you stand not alone; but in the midst of a commonwealth surrounded by your american friends & Hero's; Cotton Mather Vane Hutcheson Mayhew Hancock & others indeed the whole state is peopled with American Patriots & martyrs. think then what pleasing reflections must there occur from the glorious effects of the principles of these noble writers & actors, Ludlow, Sidney, Marvell, Harrington, Milton Neville Locke all surrounding Harvard have operated, to emancipate your Hemisphere & the same divine light has dispersed no small clouds & illumined our Horizon which will direct to more extended future views.[1]

France will succeed to her utmost wishes the Assignats do pass currently & the Lands sell at 22 years purchase & it is imagined the Lands of the chruch will sell higher as the purchase is more convenient. the government will be formed & fixed by January & a new election of members which will strenghen the present System.[2]

I never despaired of the French revolution there is one will all acting to one point the general happiness, & the oppression which was enormous drove to this & discover'd to the body of the Nation that the welfare of 30 millions of people was an object of greater consequence to them who made that number than the parade & pomp of one family or of one man to whose fantastick power they were Subject. what a divine afflatus to break out all at once!

to such a phantom of a King as now is, perhaps I should have no objection but the name, the Hebrew Superstition still remaining; its probable he may be of use for Suspence & deliberation.

two councils would not have been born in France the Nobility would have torn the other house in peices & no regeneration could have succeeded the peerage remaining.

what fermentation can you expect here? we are not sick enough for any bleeding nor yet ripe for any cure! you have touched on a capital principle, live & let live have we not extended the monopoly even to Liberty but is not this the spirit of trade?— take warning, has not cicero said something like this 2000 years agoe?

that more humanity more knowledge & freedom will be the consequence of these fermentations I have no doubt & will all tend to Essential good.

The pope precipitates his fall by folly ignorance & avarice— status Ecclesia a large & severe work published a great sale of books of an Italian Dr: Paitoni of venice cheifly Physick & natural knowledge a small tract from Paris sur la vente &c not capital which may be satisfactory to you. will come next time—[3]

I can say with great truth no american wishes prosperity to that country more than I do & therefore rejoice to hear that you are getting into order & that Rhode Island is united with you.

I cannot say the french have been hasty they have done much it is true & much remains to do.

I am glad to hear of your pleasing situation as no one has a greater claim to be happy for the services he has done & is doing. your Journals entertained me & add to my american library. m[r] Knox conveyed to me Winthrop & the confederalist[4] this I have read some time since & is valuable the other is curious as a History of a persecuted Colony.

I do not want inclination to see your country but the objection my amiable friend makes to repeat her visit here, operates strongly with me with the additional circumstance of eternal Blue & gold.

one unlucky circumstance regarding marbles in your country & I fear will prevent the use of them is that the flies will entirely cover them with a Patina not of the most pleasing or antique colour.

if no americans were ever prisoners at algiers or Morrocco you need have no fears of the plague but we have heard lately & most truely of some dying there[5] & the transportation is most easy by goods—however Howards book is most excellent of its kind & therefore sent it wishing you to have every capital Book as it is said you are the first Library. am told you have Piranesi works?[6] we only differ about the wolfe & what is the best guard against him under whatever name he may go we had a singular meeting on the 4th. November D[r] Price in the chair as a triumph over Burke— Horne Tooke one of the stewards supporting him on one side!

many excellent toasts from D. P. may the Parliament of England be the National assembly.[7]

I cannot but send you Burke's reflection on the French revolution tho unwilling to disperse them illiberal & indecent full of misrepresentations & Sophistry inveterate prejudices disappointed ambition tending almost to raving, talents misapplied eloquence & Brilliancy of stile perverted to wrong purposes, thus all the amiable excellencies & knowledge & science are become mischeivous & detrimental to the best interests of mankind! yet notwithstanding this work is become the engine of party to scandalize the most independent & best of men.[8]

The Bernois have made a Cordonn of 3000 men with increase of pay to keep out the french refugees! vain cord! Burke will remind you of filmer in the 18 century![9] some french speeches will entertain you. wch I wish this letter may do for it has tired me— is there a good Library at N. York on a liberal plan? on the 4th. we had the news of the spanish affairs to settled on 27.[10] by Gazeete a matter of triumph to our young man & the only Equivalent for his enormous expences I rejoice that France will not now be disturbed in her new constituion not that it is the general wish here of politicians.

the Czarina has made peace without the P. Tyrant interfering[11]

RC (Adams Papers).

[1] Hollis interspersed with Americans Cotton Mather, Thomas Hutchinson, and John Hancock a set of famed British politicians, rebels, and writers, including Sir Henry Vane, Jonathan Mayhew, Edmund Ludlow, Algernon Sidney, John Milton, James Harrington, Andrew Marvell, and Henry Neville (vols. 1:198, 4:48; JA, *D&A*, 1:6; *DNB*).

[2] Emboldened by the profits made from its 2 Nov. 1789 seizure of church property, the National Assembly by April 1790 began acquiring aristocrats' private estates. These lands were sold in exchange for assignats, which became the legal tender on 17 April. On 19 June the assembly abolished the titles and privileges of all hereditary nobility (Bosher, *French Rev.*, p. xviii, 145).

[3] In early November, British newspapers announced the sale of the vast library of Venetian author Giovanni Battista Paitoni (1703–1788). Hollis sent to JA Laurent Le Couteulx, *Observations sur la Vente des Domaines Nationaux et son Influence sur le Credit Public*, Paris, 1790 (London *Gazetteer*, 4 Nov.; London *World*, 6 Nov.).

[4] JA sent congressional journals with his letter of 1 June, above. For John Winthrop's journal, see Jeremy Belknap's 18 July 1789 letter, and note 2, above.

[5] According to Joshua Johnson's 25 Feb. 1791 report to Thomas Jefferson, six American sailors died of the bubonic plague between Jan. 1787 and Aug. 1788 (Jefferson, *Papers*, 19:332).

[6] John Howard, *State of the Prisons in England and Wales: With Preliminary Observations, and An Account of Some Foreign Prisons*, London, 1777, and Giovanni Battista Piranesi, *Carceri d'Invenzione*, Rome, 1750.

[7] Hollis evidently completed this letter a few weeks later, for he reported on the nearly 300 members of the Revolution Society who met in the London Tavern on 4 Nov. 1790 to mark the anniversary of King William III's 1688 arrival in England. Chairman Richard Price offered toasts to the French National Assembly and to the British Parliament, while British radical John Horne Tooke (1736–1812) criticized M.P. Edmund Burke's views as "The Lamentations of the Priesthood, for the loss of their Cake" (London *General Evening Post*, 11 Nov. 1790; London *World*, 5 Nov.; *DNB*).

[8] Edmund Burke, *Reflections on the Revolution in France*, London, 1790.

[9] Sir Robert Filmer (ca. 1588–1653), of Kent, England, was a political theorist who upheld the divine right of kings (*DNB*).

[10] The London *Whitehall Evening Post*, 2 Nov., reported the anticipated signing of the second Nootka Sound convention on 27 November.

[11] Owing to Prussian mediation, the Russo-Swedish War ended on 14 Aug., for which see John Paul Jones' letter of 20 Dec. 1789, and note 3, above.

To Thomas Brand Hollis

Dear Sir, New York, November 3, 1790.

By Mr. Broom, a worthy citizen of our states, I take the pleasure to inform you, that I have received your kind letter, and have sent the two packets to Dr. Willard and to Harvard college.[1] As these packets have been delayed by their address to me, I beg the favor of you in future to address any favors of the kind, intended for the college, to the care of my son, "John Quincy Adams, counsellor at law, Court-street, Boston," who will think it an honor and a pleasure to obey your orders. Your favors to me, you will please to address to me at Philadelphia, to which city I am to remove with my family to-morrow.

Philadelphia is to be my residence for the future, and the seat of government. My address will be, John Adams, vice-president of the United-States, Bush-hill, Philadelphia.

This country, sir, is as happy as it deserves to be. A perfect calm and contentment reigns in every part. The new national government enjoys as much of the confidence of the people as it ought to enjoy, and has undoubtedly greatly promoted their freedom, prosperity and happiness. Nothing can be more acceptable, than the little pamphlet you have sent me, and I pray you to accept my best thanks.

We are very anxious for the cause of liberty in France, but are apprehensive that their constitution cannot preserve their union.[2] Yet we presume not to judge for them when will be the proper time, and what the method of introducing the only adequate remedy against competitions. You know what I mean. My family, your friends, are all well. Pray write as often as you can to him who is, for life, / with great esteem / your friend and humble servant, John Adams.

MS not found. Printed from Disney, *Memoirs*, p. 38; internal address: "Thomas Brand-Hollis, esq."

[1] See Hollis' 29 March query, and note 3, above. New Haven merchant Samuel Broome (ca. 1734–1810) delivered two packages of books intended for Harvard (vol. 16:522; New York *Columbian*, 9 July 1810; *Connecticut Herald*, 17 July).

[2] On 3 Sept. 1791 the National Assembly adopted the Constitution of 1791. It was the country's first written document of its kind, and Louis XVI signed his assent eleven days later. The Declaration of the Rights of Man and the Citizen, of 26 Aug. 1789, prefaced the constitution, which stipulated the establishment of a unicameral legislature and espoused a figurehead monarchy. The framers of this constitution made a hard distinction between "active" and "passive" citizens; voting rights were restricted to men 25 years of age or older who paid taxes equivalent to three days' labor. The French constitution's text first appeared in the New York *Daily Advertiser*, 6 Oct. 1791, and it was widely reprinted in the American press (Bosher, *French Rev.*, p. 133; William Doyle, *The Oxford History of the French Revolution*, Oxford, 1989, p. 118, 120, 123, 124; Philadelphia *General Advertiser*, 10 Oct.; Boston *Argus*, 28 Oct.).

From Samuel Adams

My dear Sir Boston Novem[r:] 25[th:] 1790

I lately received your Letter of the 18[th:] of October.— The Sentiment, and observations contained in it demand my attention.

A Republic, you tell me, is a Government in which "the People have an essential *share* in the Sovereignty"; Is not the *whole* sovereignty, my friend, essentially in the People? Is not Government designed for the Welfare, and happiness of all the People? and is it not the uncontroulable essential right of the People to amend, and alter, or annul their Constitution, and frame a new one, whenever they shall think it will better promote their own welfare, and happiness to do it? That the Sovereignty resides in the People is a political doctrine which I have never heard an American Politician seriously deny. The Constitutions of the American States reserve to the People, the exercise of the rights of Sovereignty; by the annual, or biennial elections of their Governours, Senators, & Representatives: and by empowering their own Representatives to impeach the greatest officers of the State, before the Senators who are also chosen by themselves.[1]

We the People is the stile of the fœderal Constitution— They adopted it; and conformably to it, they delegate the exercise of the Powers of Government to particular persons, who after short intervals resign their Powers to the People: and they will re-elect them, or appoint others, as they think fit.

The American Legislatures are nicely balanced: They consist of two branches, each having a check upon the determinations of the other: they sit in different chambers, and probably often reason differently in their respective Chambers on the same questions—if they disagree in their decisions, by a conference their reasons, and Arguments are mutually communicated to each other: Candid explanations tend to bring them to agreement; and then according to the Massachusetts constitution, the matter is laid before the first Majistrate for his revision— He states objections, if he has any, with his Reasons, and returns them to the Legislators, who by larger Majorities ultimately decide. Here is a mixture of three Powers founded in the Nature of Man; calculated to call forth the rational Faculties, in the great points of Legislation, into exertion; to cultivate mutual Friendship, and good humour, and finally to enable them to decide, not by the impulse of passion, or party prejudice, but by the calm

Voice of Reason, which is the Voice of God:— In this mixture you may see your "natural, and actual Aristocracy among mankind," operating among the several Powers in Legislation, and producing the most happy Effects— But the Son of an excellent Man may never inherit the great qualities of his father; this is common observation and there are many instances of its truth: Should we not therefore conclude that hereditary Nobility is a solecism in Government? Their Lordships Sons, or Grand sons may be destitute of the faintest feelings of honor, or honesty; and yet retain an essential share in the Government by right of inheritance from Ancestors, who may have been the Minions of Ministers—the favourites of Mistresses, or Men of real, and distinguished Merit. The same may be said of hereditary Kings; Their Successors may also become so degenerated, and corrupt as to have neither inclination, nor capacity to know the extent, and Limits of their own Powers, nor consequently those of others— Such kind of Political Beings, Nobles, or Kings, possessing hereditary right to essential shares in an equipoized Government are very unfit persons to hold the scales; Having no just conception of the Principles of the Government, nor of the parts which they, and their copartners bear in the administration; they run a wild career, destroy the checks, and ballances, by interfering in each others departments, till the Nation is involved in confusion, and reduced to the danger, at least, of Bloodshed to remove a Tyranny, which may ensue— Much safer is it, and much more does it tend to promote the Welfare and happiness, of Society to fill up the offices of Government after the mode prescribed in the American Constitution, by frequent Elections of the People. They may indeed be deceived in their choice; they sometimes are; but the Evil is not incurable; the Remedy is always near; they will feel their mistakes, and correct them.—

I am very willing to agree with you in thinking, that improvement in Knowledge, and Benevolence received much assistance from the principles, and Systems of good Government: But is it not as true that without knowledge, and benevolence Men would neither have been capable or disposed to search for the principles, or form the System— Should we not, my friend, bear a gratefull remembrance of our pious and benevolent Ancestors, who early laid plans of Education; by which means Wisdom, Knowledge, and Virtue have been generally diffused among the body of the people, and they have been enabled to form and establish a civil constitution calculated for the preservation of their rights, and liberties— This Constitution was evidently founded in the expectation of the further progress, and "extraordinary degrees" of Virtue. It injoyns the encouragement of all Seminaries of Literature, which are the nurseries of Virtue depending upon these for the support of Government, rather than Titles, Splendor, or Force— Mr. Hume may call this a "Chimerical Project";— I am far from thinking the People can be deceived by urging upon them a dependance on the more general prevalence of Knowledge, and Virtue: It is one of the most essential means of further, and still further improvements in Society, and of correcting, and amending moral sentiments, and habits, and political institutions; 'till "by human means" directed by divine influence; Men shall be prepared for that "happy, and holy State" when the Messiah is to reign—

"It is a fixed Principle that all good Government is, and must be Republican."— You have my hearty concurrence; and I believe we are well enough acquainted with each others Ideas to understand what we respectively mean when we "use the Word with approbation"— The Body of the People in this Country are not so ignorant as those of England were in the Time of the Interregnum Parliament.— They are better educated: they will not easily be prevailed upon to believe that a Republican is "as unamiable as a Witch, a Blasphemer, a Rebel, or a Tyrant." They are charmed with their own forms of Government, in which is admitted a mixture of Powers to check the human passions, and controul them from rushing into exorbitances— So well assured are they, that their liberties are best secured, by their own frequent, and free Election of fit persons to be the essential sharers in the administration of their Government; and that this form of Government is truly *Republic*, that the body of the People will not be perswaded, nor compelled to "renounce, detest, and execrate the very Word Republican as the English do."— Their Education has confirmed them ["]in the opinion of the necessity of preserving, and strengthening the Dykes against the Ocean, its Tydes, and Storms," and I think they have made more safe, and more durable Dykes, than the English have done—

We agree in the Utility of univeral Education, but "will nations agree in it as fully, and extensively, as we do?["] Why should they not? It would not be fair to conclude, that because they have not yet been disposed to agree in it, they never will. It is allowed, that the present age is more enlightened, than former ones. Freedom of enquiry is certainly more encouraged: The feelings of humanity have softned the heart: The true principles of civil, and religious Liberty are better understood: Tyranny, in all its shapes, is more detested, and bigotry, if not still blind, must be mortified to see that she is despised. Such an age may afford at least a flattering Expectation that Nations, as well as individuals, will view the utility of universal Education in so strong a light as to induce sufficient national Patronage, and Support.— Future Ages will probably be more enlightned than this.

The Love of Liberty is interwoven in the Soul of Man— "So it is in that of a Wolf"; However irrational, ungenerous, and unsocial the love of liberty may be in a rude Savage, he is capable of being enlightned by Experience, Reflection, Education, and civil, and Political Institutions. *But the* Nature of the Wolf is, and ever will be confined to running in the forest to satisfy his hunger, and his brutal appetites; the Dog is inclined in a more easy way to seek his living, and fattens his sides with what comes from his masters kitchen.— The Comparison of La Fontaine is in my opinion ungenerous, unnatural, and unjust.—

Among the Numbers of Men, my friend, are to be found not only those who have "preferred ease, slumber, and good chear to liberty"; but others, who have eagerly sought after Thrones, and Sceptres, hereditary shares in Sovereignty Riches, and Splendor, Titles, Stars, Garters, Crosses, Eagles, and many other childish play things, at the expence of real Nobility, without one thought, or care for the liberty, and happiness of the rest of Mankind.— "The People, who have no property feel the Power of governing by a majority; and ever attack those who have property."— "The injured Men of Property recur to finess, trick, and Stratagem," to outwit them: True; These may preceed from a Lust of domination in *some* of both parties.— Be this as it may; It has been known, that such deceitfull tricks have been practiced by some of the rich upon their unsuspecting fellow Citizens; to turn the determination of Questions, so as to answer their own selfish purposes, to plunder or filch the rights of Men are crimes equally immoral, and nefarious; tho committed in a different manner: Neither of them is confined to the Rich, or the Poor; they are too common among both. The Lords as well as commons of Great Brittain by continued large majorities endeavoured by Finess, Tricks, and Stratagems, as well as Threats to prevail on the American Colonies to surrender their Liberty and Property to their disposal.— These failing, they attempted to *plunder* our rights by force of Arms— We feared their Arts more than their Arms. Did the Members of that hereditary House of Lords, who constituted those repeated majorities, then possess the spirit of Nobility? Not so, I think: That Spirit resided in the *illustrious* Minorities in both Houses.— But "by Nobles" who have prevented "one hideous Despotism as horrid as that of Turkey from falling to the lot of every Nation of Europe["]; you mean "not peculiarly, an hereditary Nobility, or any particular Modification,["] but "the natural, and actual Aristocracy among Mankind"; The existence of which, I am not disposed to deny.— Where is this Aristocracy to be found? Among Men of all Ranks, and Conditions. The Cottages may beget a wise Son; the Noble, a Fool: The one is capable of great Improvement—the other not. Education is within the Power of Men, and Societys of Men—Wise. and judicious Modes of Education, patronized, and supported by communities, will draw together the Sons of the rich, and the poor, among whom it makes no distinction; it will cultivate the natural Genius, elevate the Soul, excite laudable Emulation to excel in Knowledge, Piety, and Benevolence, and finally it will reward its Patrons, and Benefactors by shedding its benign Influence on the Public Mind.— Education inures Men to thinking, and reflection, to reasoning and demonstration. It discovers to them the moral and religious duties they owe to God, their Country and to all Mankind.— Even Savages might, by the means of Education, be instructed to frame the best civil, and political Institutions with as much skill and ingenuity, as they now shape their Arrows. Education leads youth to "the Study of human nature, society, and universal History" from whence they may "draw all the Principles" of Political Architecture, which ought to be regarded— All Men are "interested in the truth." Education by shewing them "the End of all its consequences" would induce, at least, the greatest numbers to inlist on its side. The Man of good understanding who has been well educated, and improves those advantages as far as his circumstances will allow, in promoting the happiness of Mankind, in my opinion, and I am inclined to think in yours is indeed "well born."— It may be "puerile, and unworthy of Statesmen" to declame against *Family Pride*; but there is and always has been such a ridiculous kind of Vanity among Men. "Statesmen know the evil, and danger is too serious to be sported with." I am content they should be put into one hole; as you propose, but I have some fears that your Watchmen on each side will not well agree. When a Man can recollect the *Virtues* of his Ancestors; he certainly has abundantly more solid satisfaction, than another who boasts that he sprang from those, who were *rich*, or *noble*; but never discovers the least degree of Virtue, or true worth of any kind, "Family Popularity," if I mistake not, has its source in family pride; It is by all means sought after, that hommage may be paid to the name of the Title, or Estate, to supply the want, in the possessor, of any great, or good quality whatsoever— There are *individuals* among Men, who study the art of making themselves popular, for the purpose of getting into Places of Honour, and Emoluments, and by these means of gratifying hereafter the noble Passion—Family Pride— Others are so inchanted with the Musick of the sound, that they conceive it to be supreme felicity. This is indeed Vanity of Vanities, and if such deluded Men ever come to their Senses, they will find it to be vexation of Spirit. When they reflect on their own folly, and injustice in having received the breath of Applause with avidity, and great delight, for Merrit which they are conscious they never had; and that many who have been the loudest in sounding their praises, had nothing in view, but their own private, and selfish interests, it will excite in them the feelings of shame, remorse, and self contempt—

The truly virtuous Man, and real Patriot is satisfied with the approbation of the wise, and discerning; he rejoices in the contemplation of the Purity of his own Intentions, and waits in humble hope for the Plaudit of his final Judge—

I shall hardly venture again to trespass on the Benevolence of our Confidential Friend— You will not be sorry; it will afford you Reliefe, for in common Civility you *must* be at the Trouble of reading ones Epistles. I hope there will be a Time when we shall have "sweet Communion" together. In the mean Time let me not lose the Benefit of your valuable Letters. Adieu. Believe me / Your sincere Friend

Sam[l] Adams

RC in Joseph Willard's hand (Adams Papers); internal address: "Vice President of / the United States."

[1] Nine state constitutions had articles providing for impeachment of the executive; Maryland's and North Carolina's did not. Connecticut and Rhode Island continued to operate under colonial charters, which contained no mention of executive (royal) authority (Gordon S. Wood, *The Creation of the American Republic*, Chapel Hill, N.C, 1969, p. 133, 141, 142).

From Thomas Jefferson

Dear Sir Philadelphia Nov. 26. 1790.

From a letter received from the President mr̃ Lear is satisfied he cannot be here to-day and doubts even the possibility of his arrival tomorrow.[1] of course our expedition of to-day would be certainly fruitless, and is therefore laid aside agreeably to a message I have received from Gen[l.] Knox & the attorney Gen[l.]

Your's affectionately & respectfully Th: Jefferson

RC (Adams Papers); addressed: "The Vice-president of the United / States / at / Bush-hill"; endorsed: "Mr Jefferson / Novr 26. 1790."

[1] Tobias Lear (1762–1816), of Portsmouth, N.H., Harvard 1783, was George Washington's private secretary from 1786 to 1793. Explaining to Lear that he had been repeatedly delayed by the "most infamous roads that ever were seen," the president reached Philadelphia at eleven o'clock on the morning of 27 Nov. 1790. Jefferson and other members of Washington's cabinet postponed their plans to escort him from Gray's Ferry into the city (*AFC*, 8:380; Washington, *Papers, Presidential Series*, 6:689, 690; same, *Confederation Series*, 3:600; Jefferson, *Papers*, 18:78; New York *Daily Advertiser*, 1 Dec.; Boston *Independent Chronicle*, 9 Dec.).

From Wilhem & Jan Willink

Sir Amsterdam 2 Decemr. 1790.

Deprived of your agreable favors since we had the honor of Paying you our respects under date of 1 febry, the present will principally Serve to advise the drawing of the Lottery of the american 4 Per Cts: in which we are sorry to find that the Numbers of your obligations do not class among the fortunate ones; by this opportunity we beg leave to remind you of the prize of *f* 1000.—which fell to your lot the former drawing, we pray you to send us a receipt for the amount together with the Coupons that are due, ordering us at the same time in what manner to dispose of the amount.—[1]

It gives us a very singular Satisfaction to observe the influence made on the Public Credit of America by the Wisdom with which the Legislative acts of Congress are fraught, we sincerely hope the same sage Councils may continue to direct their proceedings & that their encreasing Credit may arrive e're long at the highest pitch.—

Our Ladies join us in respectfull Compliments to you & Lady praying you to be assured of the Esteem with which we have the honor to remain / Sir / Your most obedt Hmble Servants

Wilhem & Jan Willink

RC (Adams Papers); internal address: "To / The Honble John Adams Esqr: / Vice President of the United States / Philadelphia."

[1] For JA's prize in the Oct. 1788 private lottery held by the Dutch loan consortium, see vol. 19:435.

From William Stephens Smith

Dear Sir— New York December 3d. 1790.

Permit me to introduce to your acquaintance Mr. Blodget, tho' I believe you may recollect seeing him in London—he will present himself to the President being charged with the prosecution of a plan relative to the building of the fœdral City,[1] he is a young man of great property and supported in his project by most undoubted security, he will if you give him an opportunity communicate his intentions out of civility and respect for your Character and station but has not the most distant wish, that you should in any manner interest yourself in the business, but as it will doubtless become a matter of conversation, your knowing from himself the principles of his project will be sufficient master of the subject to say when it is mentioned what you think of it, founding your observations on the engenuity of the project the Genius of a Boston Lad, & the effect it will have on the public purse— You will oblige me by telling him I have written to you on the subject as I promised him I would, & as a young rising Genius, I think him at least entitled to smiles and protection, remember me to Mrs: Adams Mr. Thomas & kiss my dear boy for me.[2]

I am Dr. Sir—yours sincerely W: S: Smith

RC (Adams Papers); internal address: "The Vice President—"

[1] Goffstown, N.H., native Samuel Blodget Jr. (1757–1814) was a real estate speculator and amateur architect. News of the president's October tour of the Georgetown, D.C., area, which was designated for the capital, sparked the interest of investors like Blodget. Once the president finalized the federal seat's location on the Potomac River in a 24 Jan. 1791 message to Congress, construction proposals poured in. Only then did Blodget act, purchasing five lots of land for $10,000 at the first auction, on 17–19 October. He also put forth an ambitious proposal to create a main thoroughfare in the new capital, but it was rejected (Jefferson, *Papers*, 23:225; 34:xli; Bryan, *Hist. of the National Capital*, 1:108–109, 119, 187–190; Washington, *Papers, Presidential Series*, 9:196, 230–231, 391; 10:649).

[2] Shortly after writing this letter, WSS made a "sudden and unexpected" trip to England to settle family debts and to pursue a speculative business venture. In London he met unofficially with William Wyndham Grenville, 1st Baron Grenville, the British home secretary, on 9 April, and discussed the possibility of sending a minister to the United States. Failing to achieve success on any front, WSS returned to New York City on 5 June and relayed his private conversation to George Washington, who thanked WSS for his efforts (*AFC*, 9:156, 157, 222).

To Thomas Mifflin

7th. December. 1790—

The Vice President of the United States presents his compliments to Governour Miflin, & informs him, that the President of the United States has signified his pleasure to meet Congress in the Senate Chamber, to morrow at 12. O'Clock, and that a Seat is ordered for Governour Miflin if it should be agreeable to him to be present—[1]

RC (PHi:Autograph Coll.); addressed: "His Excellency / The Governour / of the State of / Pennsylvania"; endorsed: "1790 / December / 7th: / From the / Honorable / John Adams Esqr. / Vice President of the United / States—"

[1] The third session of the first Congress convened in Philadelphia on 6 December. George Washington addressed both houses two days later. The president opened his speech by praising the nation's prosperity, Kentucky's imminent statehood, and the 7 May ratification of the fifth Dutch-American loan. Washington emphasized a need to meet "certain banditti" on the Ohio frontier with military force. Pointing to the "disturbed situation of Europe, and particularly the critical posture of the great maritime powers," Washington underlined his support for the American carrying trade and the pressing need for a consular convention. Members of the House and the Senate made their replies on 13 December. Writing to JQA, JA confided that he found "the opening of this Sessions has been auspicious and agreable" (Washington, *Papers, Presidential Series*, 7:45–49, 65–68; JA to JQA, 8 Dec., Adams Papers).

To the Commissioners of the City and County of Philadelphia

Gentlemen: Thursday, December 9, 1790.

The Senate have considered the letter that you were pleased to address to the Senate and the House of Representatives, on the 6th instant, and they entertain a proper sense of the respect shown to the general government of the United States, by providing so commodious a building as the commissioners of the city and county of Philadelphia have appropriated for the accommodation of the Representatives of the Union, during their residence in this city.[1]

I have the honor to be, / Your most humble servant,

John Adams,
Vice President of the United States,
and President of the Senate.

MS not found. Printed from U.S. Senate, *Jour.*, 1:218–219.

[1] One of the first orders of business of the new session of Congress was to consider the 6 Dec. letter inviting members to meet in the former Philadelphia County Courthouse, located at the corner of Sixth and Chestnut Streets. Newly renovated to accommodate 300 people, the building included a first-floor gallery, where the House of Representatives met, and space for the Senate to meet on the second floor. The building was renamed Congress Hall (Edward M. Riley, "The Independence Hall Group," Amer. Philos. Soc., *Trans.*, 43:26, 27, 28 [1953]).

From William Cranch

Sir, Braintree Dec[r.] 11. 1790.

Having neglected writing to you for so long a time, for which I can form no possible Apology, except a general aversion to writing, I feel a degree of diffidence, in again addressing you—and being destitute of political information, I am ignorant how I shall render a letter acceptable.[1] I have yet to acknowledge the receipt of two favours from you, of the 14th, & 31st of last *March*, the latter of which inclosed the Character of an honest Lawyer. I obeyed your commands respect the printing of it, as far as I could. I regret that the vices of indolence, drunkeness, captiousness & ignorance should render it inapplicable to so great a number of the profession in this County. There are however enough left yet, I hope, to keep up the remembrance of that Character, and to invalidate that popular opinion, that every lawyer must be a dishonest Man.

I am sorry to hear that the County of Barnstable, have probably made choice of one of the Profession, for their Representative in Congress, whose intemperance has already ruined his own Character, and will, I fear bring disgrace upon the Commonwealth. It is said that the influence of General Freeman, decided the choice. His utmost Exertions were used, in order to remove Mr Bourne, that the General's Son, who has just entered the Profession, may step into Mr Bourne's business.[2] A selfishness of Principle which, it appears to me, the good People of the District ought to resent.

All this, Sir, you may possibly have heard before—I am so little engaged in the political way at present, that I am almost the last person in the County to whom the News comes. My Sphere of Politics, like the Magician's Circle, includes only myself; and my principle object in view at present is to obtain a support. It is extremely disagreable to me to be obliged to be dependant, even upon the goodness of a Parent, after having arrived at the Age of Manhood— I am still, however, necessitated to submit to that Condition. I do not complain that business comes no faster. I know not what right I have to expect more. For some time at least, it must be accident only that can bring me Clients—

I find myself, Sir, very ignorant of the Civil law. Where shall I begin my Course of Study in that branch? I have presumed, Sir, to trouble you with this request, relying upon that readyness to afford Instruction which I have so often experienced, and for which I hope I shall always feel Grateful.

Our friends here are all well— We feel extremely [an]xious concerning my Aunt's health— We have not yet heard of her Arrival at Philadelphia— We regret that your distance from us is increased & are waiting with impatience for the Spring in Expectation of a visit from you & my Aunt, when none of your friends or Relations will receive you with more sincere Respect, duty or Affection than your obliged Nephew William Cranch.

RC (Adams Papers); addressed: "The Vice President / Of the United States / Philadelphia"; internal address: "The Vice President—" Some loss of text where the seal was removed.

[1] Cranch last wrote to JA on 24 Jan., above.

[2] Barnstable, Mass., lawyer Shearjashub Bourne (1746–1806), Harvard 1764, defeated fourteen other candidates, including the incumbent, George Partridge, to become the new congressional representative for Plymouth County. Cranch referred to the political impact of Brig. Gen. Nathaniel Freeman (ca. 1741–1827), of Sandwich, Mass., and his son, lawyer Nathaniel Jr. (1766–1800), Harvard 1787, a classmate of JQA's (*AFC*, 8:139, 9:159; *Biog. Dir. Cong.;* A New Nation Votes; Heitman, *Register Continental Army;* Boston *Columbian Centinel*, 26 Sept. 1827).

From William MacCreery

Dear Sir — Baltimore 11 December 1790

Altho' it be the fate of persons high in power to be exposed to the importunity of the many, and they are obliged not only to suffer, but submit to it, I assure you I feel much repugnance in troubling you with this letter.[1]

The arrival of a Vessell here in the last summer with a number of German-passengers after a very tedious voyage, having communicated a contagious distemper to some of the inhabitants, hath at last convinced us of the necessity of a Pest-house near this Town, and consequently of the appointment of a health-officer; and having of late been rather over stock'd with Gentlemen of the Faculty, not less than seven have started for this small plate![2] It is for this reason that I have interested myself in behalf of my Freind & Neighbour Doctor John Coulter—not merely because he is my Freind and neighbour, but because he is well qualified for the place, and has, in my oppinion, a better claim to it than any other person whatever. He has resided in this Town upwards of Twenty Years; has been a steady, uniform patriot, served in our Navy, and several Years on the Bench with much reputation. He has rendered most essential service to his Country in the late conflicts with the enemies of the present Constitution; having served in our assembly that Year to the no small prejudice of his Family. All this is well known to M^r. Carroll of the Senate, & to M^r. Smith of the lower House, to whom I beg leave to refer you. Doctor Coulter wou'd not have needed my recommendation on this occasion, had not his competitors got a great start of him in their applications for Petitions & certificates; as they reside in Town, & he at the Point—the latter however is the most eligible situation for the office he solicits. If the appointment rested with the inhabitants of this Town at large, there is no doubt but D^r. Coulter wou'd carry it by a very large Majority; Doctor Gilder (one of the applicants) having served all, or most of the war as surgeon in the Army, has certainly strong claims on the *public*, but Doctor Coulters situation, long residence and services amongst us, gives him I think, a superior claim to the place in question, to all the other candidates.

Let me therefore beg of you, Sir, in virtue of that goodness you were wont to shew me on former occasions, that any services you can render Doctor Coulter in this bussiness, with propriety, may be done, and placed to my debit—for his good conduct therein, if appointed, I venture to hold myself responsable—

With the greatest respect, & most sincere attachment I have the honor to be / Dear Sir / Your Obliged H^le^ Servt.

Will MacCreery

RC (Adams Papers); internal address: "Honorable J. Adams V. P. U. S. Philadelphia"; endorsed: "Mr MacCreery / 11. Decr. ans^d^ 27. / 1790."

[1] Ulster, Ireland, native MacCreery (1750–1814) was a Baltimore merchant who transmitted goods for the Adamses during the Revolutionary War. He represented Maryland in the House of Representatives from 1803 to 1809 (vol. 5:299; *Biog. Dir. Cong.*).

[2] This may have been the Baltimore-bound brigantine *Venus*, Capt. Pajeken, which sailed from Bremen on 6 Oct. 1789 and did not return there until 20 July 1790. To address a growing need on the docks, MacCreery recommended the appointment of John Coulter (ca. 1751–1823), of County Down, Ireland, who had been a Continental Navy surgeon. Five more local physicians applied: George Buchanan, Reuben Gilder, James Wynkoop, John Ross, and Capt. Benjamin Dashiell.

Taking up the issue on 16 Dec., the House of Representatives read a petition from Baltimore citizens requesting a health officer to protect the city from foreign diseases, and it was referred to committee. On 21 Dec. the committee advised the establishment of health officers in U.S. ports and began to draft legislation, but the project languished until 6 June 1794, when the House consented to a Maryland state law of 28 Dec. 1793 appointing Baltimore doctors John Ross, Thomas Drysdale, and John Worthington as health officers (*Maryland Journal*, 6 Oct. 1789, 20 July 1790; Jefferson, *Papers*, 18:472; Washington, *Papers, Presidential Series*, 7:107, 108, 116, 174, 255; 13:518; Baltimore *American & Commercial Daily Advertiser*, 29 May 1823; John R. Quinan, *Medical Annals of Baltimore from 1608 to 1880*, Baltimore, 1884, p. 18, 19).

Address from the Senate to George Washington

Monday December 13th 1791 [*1790*]

At twelve o'clock the Senate attended upon the President of the United States at his own House, when the President of the Senate delivered the following Address.[1]

To the President of the United States of America.

We receive, Sir, with particular satisfaction the communications contained in your Speech, which confirm to us the progressive State of the public Credit, and afford at the same time, a new proof of the solidity of the foundation on which it rests; and we chearfully join in the acknowledgement, which is due to the probity and patriotism of the mercantile and Marine part of our fellow Citizens, whose enlightened attachment to the principles of good government is not less conspicuous in this, than it has been in other important respects.

In confidence that every constitutional preliminary has been observed, we assure you of our disposition to concur in giving the requisite Sanction to the admission of Kentucky as a distinct member of the Union, in doing which, we shall anticipate the happy effects to be expected from the sentiments of attachment towards the Union and its present government, which have been expressed by the Patriotic inhabitants of that District.[2]

While we regret that the continuance and increase of the hostilities and depredations which have distressed our north western Frontier, should have rendered Affensive measures necessary, we feel an entire confidence in the sufficiency of the motives which have produced them, and in the wisdom of the dispositions which have been concerted in pursuance of the powers vested in you; and whatever may have been the event, we shall chearfully concur in the provisions which the expedition that has been undertaken may require on the part of the Legislature, and in any other which the future peace and safety of our frontier Settlements may call for.

The critical posture of the European Powers will engage a due portion of our Attention, and we shall be ready to adopt any measures, which a prudent circumspection may suggest, for the preservation of the blessings of Peace: The navigation and fisheries of the United States, are objects too interesting not to inspire a disposition to promote them, by all the means, which shall appear to us, consistent with their natural progress, and permanent prosperity.

Impressed with the importance of a free intercourse with the Mediterranean, we shall not think any Deliberations misemployed which may conduce to the adoption of proper measures for removing the impediments that obstructed it.

The improvement of the judiciary system, and the other important objects, to which you have pointed our attention will not fail to engage the consideration they respectively merit.

In the course of our deliberations, upon every subject, we shall rely upon that co-operation which an undeminished zeal, and incessant anxiety for the public welfare on your part, so thoroughly ensure; and as it is our anxious desire, so it shall be our constant endeavour, to render the established Government more and more instrumental in promoting the good of our fellow citizens, and more and more the object of their attachment and confidence.

United States of America.

In Senate December the 13th 1790

John Adams.
Vice President of the United States
and President of the Senate.—

FC (DLC:Washington Papers).

[1] Senators Oliver Ellsworth, Rufus King, and Ralph Izard prepared the formal response to George Washington's 8 Dec. address to Congress, for which see JA's letter to Thomas Mifflin of 7 Dec., and note 1, above. At noon on 13 Dec., JA accompanied the senators to the President's House, located at Sixth and Market Streets, where he read the address (*First Fed. Cong.*, 1:501, 505, 506, 507).

[2] Residents of Kentucky, then part of Virginia, petitioned Congress on 29 Feb. 1788 seeking statehood. On 3 July their request was deferred pending the implementation of the U.S. Constitution. Virginia lawmakers, mindful of a faction within Kentucky interested in Spanish sovereignty in exchange for access to the Mississippi River, passed an act of separation on 18 Dec. 1789, scheduling a special convention on 26 July 1790 and mandating that the new state join the union. The convention met and accepted the terms. Congress passed an act approving the petition for statehood on 4 Feb. 1791, and Kentucky was admitted on 1 June 1792 (Abernethy, *The South in the New Nation*, p. 51, 69; Lowell H. Harrison and James C. Klotter, *A New History of Kentucky*, Lexington, Ky., 1997, p. 61).

From James Greenleaf

Duplicate

Sir — Amsterdam Decr. 14. 1790

The partiality of some of my American friends, has induced them to consider me, as not altogether uneligible, as Resident, from the United States, to the Court at the Hague; & they have in consequence named me, to his Excellency the President, as Candidate for that Appointment—the kind interest, I am informed, your Excellency has been pleased to express in my behalf, claims my gratitude, & leads me to hope, I may need no apology for the present intrusion—[1]

So far as talents for public affairs—a mature age & experience, find their due weight, I cannot be considered as so eligible to the appointment in question, as many, who, perhaps, may alike stand candidates—but if, what may be found wanting on this side, can in any measure be compensated for, by the few accidental *local* advantages I possess—I might, perhaps, with the aid of your Excellencys kindness, flatter myself, with some hopes of obtaining, the suffrage of his Excellency the President in my favour—

My numerous friends & family connections, in the several departments of the Government of this Country—my long acquaintance with the manners of its inhabitants; and my Knowledge of the languages most used here; constitute the principle advantages above alluded to—

It may perhaps also, not be improper I should mention to your Excellency, the circumstance of my having been once honoured by an application from the Grand Pensionary of Holland, for the procurement of a large quantity of Grain, at a time when a dearth was apprehended—which, together with that, of my having had repeated occasion to decline the acceptance of Offices under this Government, prove, that I enjoy here no small share in the public confidence—[2]

But I can urge no circumstance, on which to ground, any particular claim, to the confidence of my Countrymen—unless it be, the unasked for, & almost unknown influence, I have, in more than one instance, used with the Admiralty here, for the releasement of American Vessels, arrested on suspicion, or proof of frauds—together with the circumstance, of my having obtained authorization for the subscription of about half a Million dollars, to the new Loan of Congress, with the view of lessining the influence of a powerfull party of Annuitants, whose declared intentions are, to protest against the Act of Congress, lessening the rate of Interest, on the national debt—

Unwilling to intrude further on your Excellencys time, I would only add, that should it please his Excellency the President, to nominate me Resident; it would be my wish, that the salary allowed, may be as small as propriety will admit of, & to be increased, only, as my services may deserve—

I have the honour to be, / with the utmost esteem & veneration / Your Excellencys respectfull / and most obedient Servant

James Greenleaf.

RC (Adams Papers); internal address: "His Excellency John Adams Esquire / Vice President of the United States / President of the Senate &c. &. &c / Philadelphia—"; endorsed by CA: "James Greenleaf / Decem 14 1790."

[1] Boston merchant James Greenleaf (1765–1843), who represented the New York firm of Watson & Greenleaf in Amsterdam, married the Baroness Antonia Cornelia Elbertine Scholten van Aschat in 1788. Boston lawyer Thomas Dawes Jr. sent a letter of support to JA on 27 April 1789 (Adams Papers) and to George Washington on 25 May, highlighting Greenleaf's long residence in Amsterdam as well as his fluency in Dutch and French. The president nominated him to serve as the U.S. consul to the Netherlands on 1 March 1793, and the Senate confirmed his appointment the next day. Greenleaf held the post until 1795 (*AFC*, 10:156, 408; Washington, *Papers, Presidential Series*, 2:387; U.S. Senate, *Exec. Jour.*, 2d Cong., 2d sess., p. 136).

[2] Laurens Pieter van de Spiegel (1737–1800), of Middelburg, Netherlands, served as the grand pensionary from 1787 to 1795 (Biografisch Portaal van Nederland).

To Elkanah Watson Jr.

Sir Philadelphia Decr 16. 1790

I have this moment received your favour of Nov. 30, and the Volume inclosed with it: an acceptable Present for which I thank you.[1]

I have not yet had the time to read it, and cannot therefore form any Opinion of its merits. By a kind of [*Sortes virgiane*] I Stumbled on the Anecdote of the Child drowning in [the Canal] at the Hague, which brought strongly to my Recollection the feelings We both experienced in that disstressing moment, which were abundantly compensated by the Joy at the unexpected deliverance of the little Urchin.

If upon reading the Book, any remarks should occur to me worthy your Attention I may at some leisure moment, communic[ate them to you.]

I am obliged to you for informing me where you are situated: and I hope your Prospects are there agreable, and will answer to your Expectations.

My Rambles abroad appear to me like a Dream: and if your Book had not recalled the Scene of the drowning Babe I might never have thought of it more. My Imagination is always refreshed with the Recollection of my Walks and rides about the Hague which are charming: and with those in the Bois de Boulogne, more than with the more Splendid Scenes at Courts or in Cities.

I am sir with Sincere regard / Your most obedient sert

John Adams.

P.S. I remember now that you once told me at the Hague "That the American Tories and refugees [in England] dreaded me more than any other or than all other men in the World." These Expressions, although they are very Strong are of ambiguous Signification.— there were some forged Letters printed in my Name in the London Newspapers breathing Vengeance against that description of People which was never in my feelings nor consistent with my Principles. from these Counterfeits they might be led to expect from me vindictive measures against them, which I never dream'd of.[2]

The Refugees moreover, might entertain hopes, however weak and visionary, of again Seeing the Domination of Britain reinstated in America, and might think me their most determined opponent.— in Such a Guess as this they would not have been much out. however as you Said you knew their Sentiments from Conversations with them, I wish you would explain the matter to. J A.

RC (N:Elkanah Watson Papers); internal address: "Mr Elkanah Watson Junr / [. . .] Albany." Text lost due to a torn manuscript has been supplied from a FC (N:Elkanah Watson Papers).

[1] Watson wrote to JA on 30 Nov. (Adams Papers), alerting him that he had resettled in Albany, N.Y., and enclosing a copy of his *Tour in Holland, in MDCCLXXXIV. By an American*, Worcester, Mass., 1790, Evans, No. 23039. There, Watson related JA's 1784 attempt to rescue a child drowning in a Delft canal, for which see vol. 16:275.

[2] The London *Lloyd's Evening Post,* 11 July 1781, printed an extract of a 15 Dec. 1780 letter allegedly written by JA to Massachusetts lieutenant governor Thomas Cushing and discovered aboard a seized brigantine, the *Cabot.* In it, JA reportedly recommended "to fine, imprison, and hang" all loyalists, adding: "I would have hanged my own brother, if he had took a part with our enemy in this contest." Several Massachusetts newspapers reprinted the forged letter on 8 Nov. 1781, but the Boston *Independent Ledger*, 12 Nov., labeled it "spurious," noting that Cushing had not written to JA as the text claimed; that JA could not have known of Cushing's political appointment as of the letter's dateline; and, most significantly, that JA had publicly denounced the document as fake. Loyalist propaganda bedeviled JA during his diplomatic tenure in London, but the 1780 forgery remained a particular burr in his thought for many years. Writing to John Marshall on 10 Feb. 1801 (Adams Papers), JA reiterated that the views held therein were "inconsistent with the whole tenor of my life & all the feelings of my nature" (vol. 9:318; Boston *Independent Chronicle*, 8 Nov. 1781; *Salem Gazette*, 8 Nov.).

From Johannes Altheer

A Son Exellence ce 16e Dec: 1790.

Du Temps de votre Ambassade nous eumes l'honeur de vous voir en cette Ville et meme à notre magazin de Livres ou vous avez achettés entre autres le Tableau de l'hist. des Provinces Unies par Cerisier imprimé chez nous & dont nous vous addressames les 3 derniers volumes à la Haye en 1783: pour. *f*5:8—dholl.[1]

Comme mon Oncle le Sr. Wild par l'augmentation de ses années et le Changement de systeme est resolû de se retirer il m'a cedé tout son commerce me chargeant de la liquidation. je prends la liberté de vous addresser celle ci, en vous sollicitant de faire connoitre notre magazin à quelque Libraire de Philadelphie sur lequel nous pouvons faire fond: ce seroit trop de vous solliciter à nous envoyer quelque bonne addresse de Libraire chez Vous, ne fut ce que par un de vos secretaires: Nous sommes en etat de fournir presque tous les livres d'Etudes, grecs ou latins comme vous verrez par le Catalogue, que nous avons remis à Mr. Dumas pour votre Exellence.

C'est àvec une Consideration non alterable que j'ai l'honeur d'etre sincerement de / Votre Exellence / tresh & tres obt servr.

J: Altheer

TRANSLATION

To his excellency 16 December 1790

During the period of your mission, we had the honor of seeing you in this city and also at our bookstore where you bought, among others, *Tableau de l'histoire des Provinces Unies* by Cerisier, published in house, of which we delivered the three last volumes to The Hague in 1783 for 5:8 Dutch florins.[1]

As my uncle, Mr. Wild, is getting on in years and due also to the change in government, he has decided to retire and to leave me his entire business, charging me with its liquidation. I take the liberty to address to you this letter, and I beg you to make our store known to some bookseller in Philadelphia with whom we can establish our trust. It may be too much to solicit from you some good address of a bookseller of yours to send to us, even if it is via one of your secretaries. We are able to provide almost all books of study, Greek or Latin, as you will see in the catalogue which we have delivered to Mr. Dumas for your excellency.

It is with unwavering consideration that I have the honor sincerely to be your excellency's most humble and most obedient servant J: Altheer

RC (Adams Papers); notation: "Notre addresse est B. Wild & J: Altheer / Libraires à Utrecht."

[1] Utrecht booksellers Bartholomé Wild (d. ca. 1809) and Johannes Altheer (1758–1840) published Antoine Marie Cerisier's *Tableau de l'histoire générale des Provinces-Unies*, 10 vols., Utrecht, 1777–1784, two sets of which are in JA's library at MB (vol. 10:276; *Catalogue of JA's Library*).

To John Jay

Dear Sir Philadelphia Decr 20. 1790

Permit me in this Severe Season, to Salute your fireside, and congratulate you on your return from the Northern Circuit.[1]

As the time approaches when We are to expect the Pleasure of Seeing you at the Supream Court in Philadelphia, you will give me leave to solicit the Honour and the Pleasure of your Company and that of M[rs] Jay, and whoever else of the Family who may accompany you, at Bush Hill, during the time you may have occasion to Stay at Philadelphia.

This Satisfaction I have here requested as a favour, in hopes that there will be no Hesitation or Delicacy, to prevent you from readily granting it: but if I should be mistaken in this hope I shall certainly demand it as a right: because the Rights of Hospitality are not only Sacred but reciprocal.

As you are a Roman, the Jus Hospitii will not be disputed by You: and as I wish that I was one, I shall respect it and claim it.— We have an handsome and convenient Room and Chamber, and a decent Bed at your Service; and instead of the smallest Inconvenience to Us, you will confer a real Obligation, on Mrs Adams who joins with me in the request, to Yourself and Mrs Jay, and on your assured Friend and / humble servant John Adams

RC (NNC:John Jay Papers); addressed: "The Chief Justice of the / United States, at his / House in / New York"; internal address: "Chief Justice Jay."; endorsed: "Vice Presid$^{t.}$ Adams / 20 Decr 1790 / rec$^{d.}$ 3 Jan / an$^{d.}$ 4 Jany 1791—"; notation: "Free / John Adams."

[1] Fulfilling the constitutional duties outlined for the U.S. Supreme Court under the Judiciary Act of 1789, Jay acted as circuit justice for the Eastern Circuit from 28 Sept. to 15 Dec. 1790. He began his federal duties as chief justice of the Supreme Court in Philadelphia on 7 Feb. 1791, staying with the Adamses from 30 Jan. to 14 February. His wife, Sarah Livingston, and their family remained in New York (from Jay, 4 Jan., below; *AFC*, 9:186; Jay, *Selected Papers*, 5:277, 284, 308).

The Board of the Sinking Fund to Congress

Philadelphia Decem$^{r:}$ 21$^{st.}$ 1790

The Vice President of the United States and President of the Senate, The Chief Justice, The Secretary of State, The Secretary of the Treasury, and the Attorney General—

Respectfully report to the Congress of the United States of America:

That, pursuant to the Act intitled an Act making provision for the Reduction of the Public Debt, They on the 26$^{th:}$ day of August last convened at the City of NewYork and entered upon the execution of the trust thereby reposed in them.[1]

That in conformity to a resolution agreed upon by them, on the 27th, and approved by the President of the United States, on the 28$^{th.}$ of the said Month, they have caused purchases of the said Debt to be made, through the Agency of Samuel Meredith Treasurer of the United States; which on the 6$^{th.}$ day of December instant amounted to Two hundred and seventy eight thousand, Six hundred and eighty seven dollars & thirty Cents, and for which there have been paid One hundred and fifty thousand, Two hundred & thirty nine dollars & twenty four Cents, in Specie; as will more particularly appear by a return of the said Samuel Meredith, confirmed by an authenticated Copy of his Account settled at the Treasury of the United States, which are herewith submitted, and prayed to be received as part of this report and in which are specified the places where, the times when, the prices at which, and the persons of whom the said purchases have been made.[2]

Signed by order of the Board John Adams.

RC in CA's hand (DNA:RG 46, Records of the U.S. Senate); notation in JA's hand: "Report of the / Commissioners / for the / reduction of the / national debt / Read. / Decr 21 / 1790" and: "3$^{d:}$ Sess: 1$^{st.}$ Con:" and: "N$^{o.}$ 19." and: "N$^{o.}$ 3. Series / Dec$^{r.}$ ~~19~~ 20."

[1] Following the Funding Act of 4 Aug., Congress moved quickly to draft and pass the remaining economic legislation needed to secure Alexander Hamilton's grand plan for U.S. financial stability. Both houses of Congress resolved on 9 Aug. to establish a sinking fund from the surplus in the U.S. Treasury. Three days later, George Washington signed the Sinking Fund Act, which named JA, Hamilton, John Jay, Thomas Jefferson, and Edmund Jennings Randolph as commissioners. See also Sylvanus Bourne's letter of 15 Aug., and note 1, above.

Under the Sinking Fund Act, the commissioners determined the logistics of buying and selling public debt. At their first meeting, on 27 Aug., they approved Hamilton's proposal for purchases to begin in New York on 1 Sept. and in Philadelphia on 1 November. U.S. treasurer Samuel Meredith was tasked with making purchases, keeping records, and providing quarterly reports; further, the monthly sum borrowed by the treasury was not to exceed \$50,000. JA immediately sent Washington a brief report laying out the sinking fund's protocols, which the president approved on 28 August. When the commissioners reconvened on 18 Dec., they decided to submit an account of the sinking fund's initial activities to Congress, with JA slated to sign an accompanying report on the board's behalf. For the report, which Hamilton sent to JA and the Senate on the day it was due, see his letter of 21 Dec., below (*First Fed. Cong.*, 1:484, 486, 490; 3:558, 560, 561; *Amer. State Papers, Finance*, 1:81–82, 235; Washington, *Papers, Presidential Series*, 6:347–348).

[2] From this point, the report is in JA's hand.

From Alexander Hamilton

Dec$^{r.}$ 21. 1790

The Secretary of the Treasury presents his respects to the Vice President and sends him the report of the Trustees of the Sinking Fund with the Documents referred to in it, in Triplicates according to the direction of the Board—[1] He begs leave to remind The Vice President that this is the last day; of course it is necessary it should be presented to day. He is sorry that it could not have been prepared sooner. But that for the President is under cover directed to him & that for the House of Representatives is under cover directed to the Speaker so that nothing remains but to sign & transmit

RC (Adams Papers).

[1] According to the board's 21 Dec. report to Congress, initial sales of the public debt generated \$278,687.30, although the treasurer had thus far collected only \$150,239.24 in specie (*Amer. State Papers, Finance*, 1:81–82).

To Mercy Otis Warren

Madam Philadelphia Dec[r] 26— 1790

Yesterday I had the pleasure of receiving your favour of September the 24th with an elegant copy of your poems dramatic and miscellaneous; for both which I pray you to accept my best thanks[1] It is but a few days since we received three other copies addressed to me but without a letter or any other indication from whom or whence they came. As we were subscribers for the publication these might come from some Book seller who in due time will produce his account which we shall be ready with pleasure to discharge. If they came from you Madam, we are so much the more obliged and thankful to you: and shall hereafter receive from a Bookseller those for which we subscribed: all will not be too many and we shall know very well how to dispose of them with pleasure and advantage. The poems are not all of them new to me by whom some of them have been read and esteemed some years ago. However foolishly some European writers may have sported with American reputation for genius literature and science: I know not where they will find a female poet of their own to prefer to the ingenious author of these compositions. I am ignorant Madam of any foundation you may have for the distinction you make between The Vice President and M[r] Adams or for an insinuation that either may have forgotten M[rs] Warren is certainly indebted to the Vice President and M[r] Adams in partnership for the last letter. Be pleased Madam to present my respectful regards to General Warren and all friends

With great esteem I have the honor to be / Madam your most obedient and most humble / servant John Adams.

LbC in CA's hand (Adams Papers); internal address: "M[rs] Mercy Warren / Plymouth—"; APM Reel 115.

[1] With her brief note of 24 Sept. (Adams Papers), Warren sent a copy of her *Poems, Dramatic and Miscellaneous*, Boston, 1790.

From Elkanah Watson Jr.

Sir Albany. 26[th.] Dece[r.] 1790

I have unexpectedly been hon'd with a letter from your Excellency.[1] The present edition of the Little performance I sent you, consists of only 350, most of which have run off beyond my expectations; some of my eastern friends have advised me to secure a copy right, & prepare for a 2d. edition upon a more enlarg'd scale: should this be tho't expedient or not any remarks you may please to furnish me, will confer a particular favour. Should I attempt a second edition I have thoughts of interspersing the work with extracts either from my Journals in America, France, the Netherlands or in England, haveing always kept a regular diary from day to day in all my perigrinations since the year 77. My tour in Holland was so limitted, & my stay there so short, that I must necessarily have been led into many inaccuracies.

In some of my general reflections particular in respect to America, I have adopted several Ideas I catch'd from you when at the Hague.

Your friendly solicitation for my wellfare claims my fervent gratitude. Altho' my former commercial exertions in Europe terminated most fatally to my purse, & peace of mind; yet I cannot reproach myself for any misconduct or inattention; and I have the pleasing consolation of haveing Left England with honour & advantage; because I obtained my compleat discharge, in addition to an allowance of about £700—from my assignees. this Sir, with small speculations, & strict economy has enabled me to subsist my Little family with decency, without invadeing this small Stock. As I had from the begining taken a decisive part in exerting my little mite to promote the progress of the new constitution, I had form'd some hopes of obtaining under the new government a small appointment adequate to my experience on the active stage of business.

From a personal acquaintence with several members of both houses, who appeared anxious to promote my views; I was Led to cherish such hopes—but Alas! I soon found myself lost in a host of greedy applicants. You see Sir—I write with freedom and without reserve—the familiar stile of your letter, seems to warrent it, by your removeing the barrier, which places your elevated Station, from my obscurity at such an immense distance.

Respecting the Tory business, the whole matter had escaped my mind; but I recolect now to what I had perticular referencce. In the year 82 as well as 84 I spent about a month in each year in Birmingham; where resided Judge Oliver, Elisha Hutchenson, Doctr. Oliver, & many other refugees— you may recollect Sir our family connection by intermarriages—so in fact, I was upon the most familiar footing—divested of political prejudices: Your name being frequently on the carpet—the Judge in perticular seem'd fill'd with rancour & mortification— Indeed he appear'd to lay all his reverse of fortune at your door, as the original & principal cause of the revolution, as well as the persecution of the tories.[2]

I am (with respects to M[rs.] Adams family) Very respectfully / Your devoted & Oblig'd H[l.] S[t.] Elk[a.] Watson J[r.]

RC (Adams Papers); addressed: "His Excellency John Adams Esq[r.] / Vice President / of the / United States / In Congress"; internal address: "His Excell[y.] John Adams Esq[r.]"; docketed by JA: "Elkanah Watson / Albany Dec[r] / 1790."

[1] Of 16 Dec., above.

[2] Loyalist Peter Oliver, with his son Peter Jr., fled to England during the Revolutionary War. Peter Sr.'s daughter, Elizabeth (1735–1767), married Watson's half-brother, George (1718–1800). Boston merchant Elisha Hutchinson (1745–1824), Harvard 1762, was a son of Massachusetts' last royal governor, Thomas Hutchinson (*Sibley's Harvard Graduates*, 8:760, 761; 15:85, 86, 264; Augustus Thorndike Perkins, *A Sketch of the Life and a List of Some of the Works of John Singleton Copley*, Boston, 1873, p. 126, 127).

To William Cranch

My dear Sir Philadelphia Dec[r] 30 1790

I have had the pleasure of receiving your letter[1] and should be happy to furnish you with any hints concerning the study of the Civil Law, which may occur to me after having laid aside all such studies for many years. Under the general phrase Civil law is often understood what is commonly considered the learning necessary to obtain a degree of Doctor of Laws LLD the common abreviation signifies Legis Legum Doctor or Utriusque Juris Doctor. One branch of the division is the Law of Nature and Nations and the other the Roman Law.

Of the first of these, Grotius, Puffendorf, Burlamaque, Vattel Heineccius, Bynkershoeck, Noodt, are the writers most in use and I suppose as good as any— Of the last, if your intention is to confine your inquiries to the English language, Woods institute of the Civil Law, Domat, D[r] Taylor and Wiseman's Law of Laws may answer your purpose. But if, as I presume it will, your ambition and curiosity should prompt you to become a master of this divine science as it used to be called, you will in the first place find it necessary to increase your familiarity with the Latin language and the Roman learning in general. The institutes of Justinian, the Code the Novells and the digest are all in latin. Commentators on all these writings are innumerable. But Hoppius, Vinnius, Gail and Cujaicius with Oughtons Ordo Judiciorum are esteemed the best.[2] There are many little Compendium's or abridgments in latin of the institutes, which you may read to advantage— They will frequently fall in your way at sales and may be purchased cheap. But if you read carefully the institutes and acquire a familiarity with the titles and indexes of the Corpus Juris, So that you may be able readily to Search a point as you may have occasion, you will find it very useful and agreeable.— Those who pretend to be very learned in this way Study the Greek translation of Theophilus, of the institutes of Justinian which is indeed rather a commentary I wish you much pleasure and profit at the bar and am with much affection your friend as well as Uncle John Adams.

LbC in CA's hand (Adams Papers); internal address: "Mr William Cranch. Braintree."; APM Reel 115.

[1] Of 11 Dec., above.

[2] JA's recommendations fell into three categories, and nearly all were drawn from various editions held in his library at MB. JA's recommended reading on the law of nations included: Hugo Grotius, *The Rights of War and Peace*, London, 1738; Samuel von Pufendorf, *Law of Nature and Nations*, London, 1729; Jean Jacques Burlamaqui, *The Principles of Natural and Politic Law*, 2 vols., London, 1763; Emmerich de Vattel, *The Law of Nations, or Principles of the Law of Nature, Applied to the Conduct and Affairs of Nations and Sovereigns,* London, 1793; Johann Gottlieb Heineccius, *A Methodical System of Universal Law*, 2 vols., London, 1741; Cornelius van Bynkershoek, *Opera Omnia*, Leyden, 1767; and Gerard Noodt, *Opera Omnia*, Leyden, 1760. For the second category, of civil law, JA advised reading these works: Thomas Wood, *A New Institute of the Imperial or Civil Law*, London, 1704; Jean Domat, *Civil Law in Its Natural Order*, transl. W. Strahan, 2 vols., London, 1722; John Taylor, *The Elements of Civil Law*, Cambridge, 1755; and Sir Robert Wiseman, *The Law of Laws*, London, 1656. JA's final category, of suggested reading in Roman law, included: Justinian, *Codex, Digesta, Institutiones*, and *Novellae*; Joachim Hoppe, *Commentatio succincta ad Institutiones Justinianeas*, Danzig, 1693; Arnoldus Vinnius, *Commentarius . . . institutionum imperialium*, Leyden, 1642; Andreas von Gail, *Practicarum observationum, tam ad processum judiciarium, praesertim imperialis camerae*, Cologne, 1578; Jacques Cujas, *Opera omnia, in decem tomos distributa*, 10 vols., Paris, 1658; and the Greek translation of Theophilus' *Institutes of Justinian*, The Hague, 1751 (*Catalogue of JA's Library*).

From the Boston Marine Society

Sir Boston 3rd. Jany. 1791.

In behalf of the Marine Society of this Town, we have the Honor of addressing you on a subject that has long engaged the attention of that Corporation.— The encouragement & preservation of our Seamen must interest every man who considers how valuable the labours of that class of Men are to a commercial Country, nor will the Interest be lessen'd from the veiw of them, in time of War, as the maritime Barrier of the United States.— From your exalted Rank in the National Government, uniform & ardent attachment to, & extensive knowledge of the best & greatest Interests of our Country, the Society have directed us their Committee to transmit the papers which accompany this Letter for your Consideration.—[1] And, if the proposals included in them should meet your Approbation, to request your assistance in Congress on the business. There is an additional Argument, omitted in the petition, which might be urged for the Erection of an Hospital, That sick Sailors are compelled to take up their Lodgings in Houses very illy provided for their accommodation, not to add the variety of gross Impositions they are subjected to. Numbers of them annually perish, whose lives might be preserved were they admitted into a Hospital, where they would find the best medical aid, good nursing & comfortable Lodging & diet on easy Terms.

Should you approve this application, We must beg you to be at the Trouble of conversing with the Gentlemen who represent this State in both Houses of Congress, to whom we have addressed a Letter.

From the partial & flattering Consideration of numbering You among their Members, the Society have been induced to sollicit your Advice & Services in this Business.

We are with sentiments of the most affectionate respect & sincere personal attachment / Dear Sir / Your faithful humble Servants.

Wm Tudor
Alexr Hodgdon
Aaron Dexter
Wm. Deblois—
Sheml. Russell—
Mungo Mackay
W Scollay

The Society are desirous of knowing whether any measures were adopted in consequence of the application of the Merchants to the President of the United States on the Subject of the Pilotage and Regulations of the Harbour of Boston— As you were so obliging as to take charge of those Papers we would thank you for any Information respecting them. The Merchants are equally anxious with the Society on this Subject.—[2]

RC (Adams Papers); internal address: "His Excellency the Vice President / of the United States."; docketed by JA: "Marine Society."

[1] JA, who was a member of the Boston Marine Society, sent this petition to the House of Representatives, which received it on 27 January. Two weeks later, it was referred to Alexander Hamilton. On 17 April 1792 Hamilton presented his report on marine hospitals, advising Congress to establish at least one in the United States, to be funded by a ten-cent deduction from sailors' monthly wages, as it would benefit trade and protect "a very needy class of the Community." Disabled seamen and sailors' widows and children were eligible to draw from the same fund, which would be guided by a board of 25 directors. Congress

took action on 14 July 1798 when it passed an act with Hamilton's terms largely intact. As president, JA signed it into law two days later (Hamilton, *Papers*, 11:295, 297).

[2] For the lack of piloting regulations, see William Smith's letter of 12 June 1790, and note 4, above.

From John Jay

Dear Sir

New York 4 Jany 1791—

a weeks absence on a visit to my friends at Rye, from whence I returned last Evening, prevented my having 'till then, the Pleasure of recieving your very obliging Letter of the 20 Dec^r.^—

For the Invitation with which you honor me, be pleased to accept my cordial acknowledgements— It is conveyed in Terms which enhance the compliment, & I accept it with that Satisfaction which Politeness united with Sincerity seldom fail to excite.—

The Season of the Year and the objection of being both so long absent from our family, will not permit Mrs. Jay (who as well as two of the Children are but lately recovered from the malignant sore Throat) to favor me with her Company to Philadelphia— I regret this the more as such an Excursion would otherwise conduce to her Health, and as my present official Duties separate us so often and so long. She joins with me in requesting the favor of you to present our best wishes & the Compliments of the Season to Mrs. Adams— Accept the same from / Dear Sir / Your friend & Servt

John Jay—

RC (Adams Papers); internal address: "His Excellency / John Adams Esqr."

From John Redman

Sir,

Philadelphia, Jan. 5, 1791.—

It is with great pleasure I obey the Orders of the Corporation of the 2^d:^ Presbyterian Church, in Arch-Street, by communicating their Resolution of the 29th. Ultimo, appropriating the large pew fronting the pulpit, & the two pews adjoining it, for the use of the Vice-President of the United States, & such members of both Houses of Congress, as choose, during their Sessions, to worship in that Church.—[1]

I have the honor to be, / With the greatest respect & esteem, / Your most obedient & very humble servant,

John Redman, President.

ENCLOSURE

At a Meeting of the Corporation of the 2d. Presbyterian Church on Wednesday 29th. December 1790—

On Motion

"Resolved that the following Pews Vizt. No. 24, 25, & 150 be appropriated for the purpose of Accommodating the Vice President of the United States & such Members of Congress as during the Sessions thereof, may choose to Worship in the said Church, & that the President of the Board give Notice Accordingly."

Extract from the Minutes Robert Smith, Secty

RC and enclosure (Adams Papers); internal address: "John Adams, Vice President of the United States, & / President of the Senate.—"

[1] Dr. John Redman (1722–1808) was an elder of Philadelphia's Second Presbyterian Church and later served as president of the city's College of Physicians (vol. 3:245; Whitfield J. Bell Jr., "John Redman, Medical Preceptor, 1722–1808," *PMHB*, 81:157, 164 [April 1957]).

To John Redman

Sir Philadelphia Jan. 5. 1791

I received this morning the Letter you did me the honour to write me, communicating the resolution of the Second Presbyterian Church in Arch Street, of the 29th Ultimo, appropriating the large Pew fronting the Pulpit, and the two Pews adjoining it, for the Use of the Vice President of the United States and Such members of both Houses of Congress as choose during their Sessions to worship in that Church: and immediately communicated it and the Resolution inclosed in it, by reading both in the Senate of the United-States.

Permit me Sir to express to you and to the Corporation, my Thanks for this obliging Mark of their respectful Attention to your and their most obedient and most humble servant John Adams.

RC (PPPrHi:Rare Documents Coll.); addressed: "Mr John Redman / President of the Corporation / of the Second Presbyterian / Church in Arch Street / Philadelphia"; internal address: "Mr John Redman President / of the Corporation of the Second / Presbyterian Church in Arch street"; endorsed: "Letter from / The Honble. Jno. [Adam]s— / 5th. January [1791]." Some loss of text where the seal was removed.

From William Smith

Dear S[r.] Boston. 16 Jan[y.] 1791.

By one of the last Posts, by direction of the Boston Marine Society, I forwarded you a number of Papers respecting a Marine Hospital. I now forward you by the Bearer M[r] Adams a Plan & Elevation of the Hospital that wou'd be erected by the Society cou'd they obtain permission you will please to make what use of it you may think proper.[1] this Building on the place that is propos'd wou'd add greatly to the Beauty of the Harbour & relieve a great number of distress'd objects—In a time of Warr wou'd give spirits to Seamen in the public service to know that if any misfortune happen'd to them, they had an Assylum for the remainder of their Days. The Society have a handsome Capitol at Interest, which they wou'd Invest in such a Building, to receive the Interest of their Money untill the Revenue of the Hospital was sufficient to return it.—

M[rs.] Smith joins me in Affec[te.] Regards to you S[r.] & M[rs.] Adams and we are happy to hear that she has again recover'd her Health—

I am with Respect / Y[r] Most H Ser[t] W[m.] Smith

RC (Adams Papers); internal address: "His Ex[y.] John Adams Esq[r.]"

[1] The enclosure has not been found, but for JA's role in the creation of these hospitals, see the Boston Marine Society's letter of 3 Jan., and note 1, above.

From Thomas Jefferson

Sir Philadelphia. Jan. 17. 1791.

I have the honour to enclose you a Postscript to the Report on Measures, Weights & coins now before your house. this has been rendered necessary by a small arithmetical error detected in the estimate of the cubic foot proposed in that report. the head of Superficial measures is also therein somewhat more developed.[1]

Nothing is known, since the last session of Congress of any further proceedings in Europe on this subject.

I have the honour to be with sentiments of the most profound respect sir / Your most obedient / & most humble serv[t]

Th: Jefferson

RC (DLC:Jefferson Papers); internal address: "The honourable the President of the Senate."

[1] Adhering to a 15 Jan. 1790 resolution of the House of Representatives, Jefferson set to work in April drafting a uniform system of weights and measures meant to regulate trade and currency. He worked on the project with singular focus for several months, battling intense headaches caused by spending long hours on complex calculation. Along the way he consulted Alexander Hamilton, James Madison, Philadelphia watchmaker Robert Leslie, and astronomer David Rittenhouse. Jefferson sent the final report to the House on 4 July, and it was printed in several New York newspapers during the first week of August. Sensing popular interest in Jefferson's great effort, George Washington urged Congress to take action on 7 Dec. and again on 25 Oct. 1791, but it was not until 1792 that senators began to debate the report (Jefferson, *Papers*, 16:604–607, 614–616).

From Mercy Otis Warren

Sir. Plimouth Jan 17th 1791

An unsealed letter from you came to my hand this day.[1] for the letter I thank you. as it contained expressions of regard & esteem which I have been used to receive from your pen. for the manner I own myself at a loss—

Dos not an unsealed letter from you sir appear like a diminution of that Confidential intercourse that long subsisted? and Conveyed warm from the heart the strong expressions of friendship in many a close sealed packet.

Was you sir apprehensive that your own reputation might suffer by an attention to any one of a family you *had been used to hear spoken off with respect and affection by all*? only, the public first inspected the Correspondence. Yet perhaps you might mean to do me honour by leting the world see your polite encomium on a late publication.

Indeed I feel myself flattered by the Compliment. & yet more by its being in the stile of my old friend.—

I acknowledge I stand indebted to the vice president for one letter before his of the 26 Decmber.—[2]

But You must permit me to say some expressions in that letter appeared so irreconcilable with former sentiment that I was impeled much against my inclination to consider it as forbiding any further interruption.—

Delicate friendship Confines as its own disinterested attachment is easily wounded.— I might perhaps feel too sensibly some former impressions that may hereafter be explained.— but I can never tax myself with a voluntary neglect of punctuallity: or the want of attention in any other instance towards friends I thought unimpressable by the *Ebullitions* [. . .] party or political malice.—

A Copy of the work you informed me you had just received I forwarded immediatly in publication. I knew not what should thus long have retarded its passage.

Nor can I inform you sir from whom you received three other Volumes. but Could I have supposed as you obligingly intimate that you Could have disposd of so many with *pleasure* & *advantage*. they should have been much at your Service from the hand of the author.—

M[r] Warren returns both friendly and respectful regards.— You will present me also to M[rs] Adams.

I am Respected Sir with Sincere Esteem / Your most Obedit / Humble Servant

M Warr[en]

RC (Adams Papers); addressed: "Hon[ble] / M[r] Adams / Vice president of the / United States"; endorsed: "M[rs] Warren"; notation by CFA: "Jan[y] 14th 1791." Some loss of text where the seal was removed. Filmed at 14 Jan. 1791.

[1] Of 26 Dec. 1790, above.

[2] JA had previously written to Warren on 29 May 1789 (vol. 19:483–484).

From Thomas Jefferson

Sir

Philadelphia Jan. 20. 1791.

I have the honor to inclose you a letter from one of our captive citizens of Algiers, if I may judge from the superscription and from the letters from the same quarter which I have received myself. as these relate to a matter before your house, and contain some information we have not before had, I take the liberty of inclosing you copies of them.[1]

I have the honour to be with sentiments of the most profound respect & attachment sir / Your most obedient / & most humble serv[t.]

Th: Jefferson

RC (DLC:Jefferson Papers); internal address: "The President of the Senate."

[1] For the plight of the American sailors seized and held in Algiers since 1785, see the indexes to vols. 17, 18, and 19. Jefferson tackled the question of their ongoing imprisonment early in his tenure as secretary of state, passing along advice to George Washington on 12 July 1790 that a show of force was needed to deter captures by Barbary corsairs. He renewed his proposal on 28 Dec., submitting a report to the president. Jefferson focused on the state of American trade in the Mediterranean, and the second offered an analysis of the Algerian captives' ordeal. Jefferson outlined in detail the failed missions to liberate them, undertaken by John Lamb and members of the Mathurin order. He also raised questions about the constitutional powers in play, especially how the president and Congress might cooperate in order to set ransoms, pay tributes, and declare war. Finally, Jefferson cautioned that Americans needed to raise a fleet of their own: "Should the United States propose to vindicate their Commerce by Arms, they would, perhaps, think it prudent to possess a Force equal to the Whole of that which may be opposed to them. What that equal Force would be, will belong to another Department to say."

Jefferson then sent this letter to JA, who laid it before the Senate with multiple enclosures on 21 Jan. 1791. He included copies of three letters written by one of the captives, Capt. Richard O'Bryen, from May to July 1790, that documented Lamb's mismanagement of the negotiations with Mohammad ibn Uthman, dey of Algiers. O'Bryen supplied intelligence on the size and scope of the Algerian fleet, recommending that the U.S. government "embrace every opportunity of trying for a Peace" in order to safeguard trade and to stabilize skyrocketing insurance rates. The Senate resolved on 1 Feb. 1791 that the president should "take such measures as he may think necessary for the redemption of the citizens of the U.S. now in captivity at Algiers," although they capped the total expenses at $40,000. The president agreed on 22 Feb., promising to move forward "so soon as the monies necessary shall be appropriated by the legislature," but no further steps were taken toward the Algerian captives' emancipation until March 1792 (Jefferson, *Papers*, 18:403, 414, 428–429, 431–433, 437, 439, 443, 444–445).

From William Smith

Dear Sr. Boston. 21st. Jany. 1791

I take the freedom to introduce to your notice Major Kent. a Grandson of the late Cap Kent of Charlestown. he goes to Philadelphia, to procure from Congress the same compensation for his services as the other Officers of the late Army receiv'd.—[1] He enter'd the Army as a private in Col. Henry Jackson's Regt. by his good conduct was soon promoted as an Officer and continued in the service 'till the Fall of the Year 1782. when his Health was so impair'd from continued attention to his Duty, that by advice of his Physician & consent of the Commander in Chief he resign'd his Commission. unfortunately abt. two Months before the Resolve of Congress was passd. allowing five Years pay.— as he faithfully perform'd his duty & retir'd with honor to recover his Health impair'd in the service of his Country. his Friends have recommended his applying, as his case is singular no other Officer being in the same situation. some Officers recd. this Allowance who had been in the service but a few Months—

I observe by the Papers that the Report of the Secy. for an additional Duty on Rum & the Excise wou'd probably be adopted.[2] the present Duty is now exceeding high & principally falls on the Importer I think it wou'd be just to pospone the commencement of the New Duty on Imported Rum to the 1st. July to give those who have sent their Vessells on Rum Vo. an oppertunity to return. as it was expected when their Vessells sail'd to pay only the present Duty & had calculated their Vo. on that duty. this delay can be of no detriment to the publick, as the Interest does not commence for a Year for which these dutys are said [. . . .] of payment of the Duty on Rum shou[. . . .] extended to 6 or 9 Ms.—

Mrs. S. joins me in our best regards to you & Mrs. Adams—

I am with great Respect / Yr Most H Sert Wm. Smith

RC (Adams Papers); addressed: "The Vice-President / of the / United States."; internal address: "His Exy. John Adams Esqr."; endorsed: "Mr Smith"; notation: "Major Kent." Some loss of text where the seal was removed.

[1] Former Continental Army major Ebenezer Kent Jr. (1759–1812) was the grandson of Capt. Ebenezer (1700?–1776) and therefore a distant relation of AA's by marriage. Major Kent, who served in Col. Henry Jackson's artillery regiment from Feb. 1777 to Jan. 1781, appealed to Congress for a pension because he had "injured his constitution by great exertions" at the Battle of Monmouth on 28 June 1778. Kent's claim and those of many more veterans were laid before Congress on 15 Oct. 1792. Progress on their requests was hindered by a lack of muster rolls and a dearth of clear record-keeping during the Revolutionary War (Heitman, *Register Continental Army*; *AFC*, 1:220, 10:360; *Amer. State Papers, Claims*, p. 57, 63, 111).

[2] Congress was still working to enact legislation based on the terms and duties proposed in Alexander Hamilton's 14 Jan. 1790 report on the public credit, for which see Stephen Higginson's letter of 1 March, and note 2, above. Six days after Smith wrote this letter, the House of Representatives passed, by a vote of 35 to 21, the Whiskey Act, a controversial piece of legislation that laid an excise on domestic and imported liquors. Farmers in western Pennsylvania, who reaped extra revenue by distilling surplus grain into liquor, were incensed that the heavy federal tax fell on small producers. Their outrage gave rise to the Whiskey Rebellion in 1794 (U.S. House, *Jour.*, 1st Cong., 3d sess., p. 364–365; *AFC*, 9:320, 10:index).

From James Lovell

Sir — Boston Jany. 22d. 1791

From the Borders of the Grave, revived, and even established in Health, I once more present my Respects with my accustomed Fervency to You and Yours.

But, with my Respects I must also send my Complaints and Supplications.

In a Transaction where you was only, according to your own chosen Expression, Teste di Legno, I was fretted disgraced & beslaved; and have taken some Measures for Emancipation. You will know *why* I was not Collector of this Port; but I have never told you how perfectly *you* reconciled me *at first* to my present Office, or how I ceased *afterwards* even to wish for any Change during the Remainder of my Days. But, Sir, what tended heretofore to give me Tranquillity serves at present to heighten my Chagrin. Possessing the good Will of the President and yourself I am martyred by one or more Committee-Men who have carried private Friendship and Relationships into their public official Doings. I know but two of the Committee one of whom can give no better Rationale of the inimical Transaction than because the other "perhaps was more a Friend to the Collector than to the Naval officer," while in fact he was himself brother in Law to a Surveyor, and the Naval Officer is sacrificed to both.

This will appear œnigmatical till you have read my Letter to m^{r} Gerry.[1] I intreat you to do that; and to quiet me by a Condemnation of my Discontent, or by promoting Redress—according to the Verdict of that sound Judgement to which I now submit myself.

Be so good as to allow me to present my respectful Love to your Lady, and to think me continuing devotedly / Sir / Your obedient / Friend & Humble / Servant James Lovell

RC (Adams Papers); addressed: "The Vice President / of the United States / His Excellency / John Adams Esqr / Philadelphia"; endorsed: "Mr Lovel"; notation by Lovell: "fav^{d} by / Maj^{r} Gen$^{l.}$ Lincoln"; and by CFA: "Jany 22^{d} 1791."

[1] Lovell also wrote to Elbridge Gerry on 22 Jan., complaining that personal connections between members of Congress and those applying for jobs in the revenue service meant that Gerry and his colleagues were biased enforcers of the Collection Act. He wrote: "As there are 67 Collectors 54 Surveyors and but 13 Naval Officers it is evident how the Proportion of *Relations Friends* and *Patrons* will *naturally* stand in the Great Assembly." Lovell trained his criticism on appointments made for the ports of Baltimore, Philadelphia, Newburyport, and Salem, Mass., where, he observed, "Rivalry & Heart-burnings" for federal posts dominated local politics. Equally troubling, in Lovell's view, was the hazy status of officers' duties, their annual salaries, and their treatment of emoluments (*First Fed. Cong.*, 21:494–497).

To John Trumbull

Dear Sir Philadelphia Jan. 23. 1791

I have been So much of an Antiœconomist as to leave your Letter of June the fifth unanswered to this day.

The Defence of the American Constitutions, is not I apprehend a "Misnomer." Had the Patriots of Amsterdam repulsed the Duke of Brunswick from the Haerlem Gate, an History of the Action, might have properly been called an Account of the Defence of Amsterdam: although the City, on the Side of the Leyden Gate and Utrecht Gate, had been so ill fortified as to have been indefensible, had the Prussian Attack been made on either of those Quarters.[1]

My three Volumes are a Defence of the American Constitutions, on that Side on which they are attacked. Mr Turgot attacked them for aiming at three orders and a Ballance. I defended them in this Point only. Had he attacked them for not making their orders distinct and independent enough: or for not making their Ballances compleat, I should have been the last Man in the World to have undertaken their Defences. If another Edition should ever be published I would insert in the Title Page "A Defence &c against the Attack of Mr Turgot.["] This I apprehend would cure all Defects, in Point of Title.

But as you observe the Feelings of Mankind are so much against any rational Theory, that I find my labour has all been in vain: and it is not worth while to take any more Pains upon the subject.

The Rivalry between the State Governments and the national Government, is growing daily more active and ardent. Thirteen Strong Men embracing thirteen Pillars at once, and bowing themselves in concert, will easily pull down a frail Edifice. If the Superiority of the national Government is not more clearly acknowledged, We shall soon be in a confusion, which We shall not get out of, for twenty Years.

There was never more occasion for firmness, in all who wish in Sincerity for Peace, Liberty or Safety.

The Secretary of the Treasury is all that you think him. There is no office in the Government better filled. it is unhappy that New York has taken away one of his Supports. Your Sentiments of other Characters, and of Measures in general appear to me to be so just, that I cannot but wish that You had more to do in public affairs. But they say that you "love Wit better than your friend": and although I dont believe this, I expect from you, by Way of revenge for this Piece of information, a sheet or two of their Sarcasms upon me. I know that altho the ridiculous can never escape your observation, in a friend or an Ennemy; yet you love the former and have no ill Will against the latter.

The Independence of your fame and fortune, and your happiness in private Life are more to be envied than any public office or Station. For myself I find the office I hold, tho laborious, so wholly insignificant, and from the blind Policy of that part of the World from whence I came, So Stupidly pinched and betrayed that I wish myself again at the Bar, old as I am. My own Situation is almost the only one, in the World in which Firmness and Patience are Useless. I have derived so much pleasure from your Correspondence, that notwithstanding the long interruption of it, I hope you will not deny it in future / to your friend & humble ser^t^ [. . . .]

RC (NjP:Andre De Coppet Coll.); internal address: "Counciller Trumbull."; endorsed: "Honble. John Adams / Jany 23^d.^ 1791." LbC (Adams Papers); APM Reel 115. Some loss of text due to a cut manuscript.

[1] Karl Wilhelm Ferdinand, Duke of Brunswick, was instrumental in restoring the stadholder during the Prussian invasion of the Netherlands in 1787 (Schama, *Patriots and Liberators*, p. 129).

To Samuel Tucker

Sir Philadelphia Jan. 27. 1791

I have received your Several Letters and Should have been glad of the opportunity to have Served you as far as might have been in my Power: but before the receipt of your first Letter the Place you Solicited had been filled by the President of the United States.[1]

I have represented your Character in the most favourable light to the Secretary at War, and if you think of any other Way, or any particular affair in which I can befriend you please to let me know it. The Ships Journal of our Voyage, I wish you would Send to my son John Quincy Adams in Boston, who will preserve it for, sir / your humble serv[t] John Adams

RC (MH-H:Tucker Papers); internal address: "Captain Tucker."

[1] Capt. Samuel Tucker (1747–1833), who commanded the *Boston*, a 24-gun Continental frigate, wrote to JA on 1 Oct. 1790, 10 Nov., and 30 Dec. (all Adams Papers), seeking a federal appointment to the Massachusetts revenue cutter. Tucker was not successful despite his long personal acquaintance with the vice president and his family, which stretched back to the Revolutionary War. JA and JQA secretly embarked for France in Feb. 1778 via the *Boston*. Tucker kept a 62-page log of the voyage, titled "An Abstract of a Journal," which he sent to JQA at an unknown date (M/Non-Adams/13, APM Reel 342; *AFC*, 1:xv–xvi; 2:389).

From Thomas Jefferson

Sir Philadelphia February 2[d.] 1791.

As the information contained in the enclosed extracts from a letter of M[r.] Short's lately arrived, has some relation to a subject now before the Senate, I have thought it my duty to communicate them,[1] and have the honor to be with sentiments of the most profound respect and attachment. / Sir / Your most obedient and / most humble Servant:

FC and enclosure (DLC:Jefferson Papers); internal address: "The President of the Senate."

[1] Jefferson enclosed extracts of a 21 Oct. 1790 letter from William Short outlining the state of Franco-American trade. According to Short, the French National Assembly balked at paying the same foreign tonnage duties to the United States that had been levied on Great Britain since 20 July. French legislators were also reconsidering the favorable treatment previously granted to American imports of tobacco and whale oil. On 18 Jan. 1791 Jefferson edited and used Short's intelligence to communicate this news in a formal report to the president, along with his recommendation to heed the French appeals. George Washington transmitted Jefferson's report to the Senate on 19 January. It was referred to com-

mittee on 27 Jan. and was still under consideration when Jefferson sent this information, a key source of his report, separately to JA. The resulting debate exposed supporters of British and French interests alike in Congress. But any meaningful step toward formulating an American policy in response was preempted in June, when the National Assembly terminated all past favors awarded to American-built ships, tobacco, and whale oil (Jefferson, *Papers*, 18:544, 546, 555, 565, 570; 19:238–239; U.S. Senate, *Exec. Jour.*, 1st Cong., 3d sess., p. 66, 72).

From John Trumbull

Dear Sir Hartford Feby. 5th. 1791—

You cannot doubt how much I esteem myself honored by your Correspondence— But in a Correspondence with Great Folks, it is my rule to consider myself only an Echo—and like that, I will answer punctually—

The Title of your Volumes is not a Misnomer, in the light you place it— Our Constitutions were indeed attacked by Mr. Turgot on the only side capable of *A Defence*. But I think Sir, You have too humble an opinion of the success of that work— It has been abused by those, who did not understand it in addresses to those, who never read it— But your Principles are daily gaining ground among that part of the Community, who are, or wish to be, well informed— You cannot expect them to be very popular among the Shayites of Massachusetts, or the Gougers of Carolina. But the clamour raised against them was a proof of the necessity of such a work.

Your present Office is far from being insignificant to the Public or Yourself. It must give You every advantage of influence—& we are at least indebted to your Casting Voice, for some of the most important decisions in the National Legislature.

The Rivalry between the National Government & the State Legislatures was an event naturally to be expected. But I cannot consider it as immediately dangerous. The National Government must on any question yield to the State Legislatures, if united— But such an union on any question is improbable. It is morally impossible that Congress should pass any Law, which every State would feel interested to oppose—& it is highly improbable that any Law would be enacted disagreeable to a Majority of the States— Should such a case happen the law would be repealed without the ruin of the National Government.

A change of our Government is, in my opinion, more likely to take place at some future period from a division of the American Empire, than from a Coalition of the State-Legislatures. You can scarcely conceive with what contempt the Resolves of N. Carolina & Pennsylvania are viewed here.[1]

I observe You have given no opinion on the remarks I made on the Subject of direct Taxation. My general Idea is that a Revenue ought to be drawn from two sources only—a Land-tax & Duties on Commerce &c—and that these Taxes, if properly adjusted, will most equally embrace every object of taxation. I am sensible that the constitution precludes a general Land-tax—a direct Tax is therefore the only equivalent. I am sensible of the very great, but I cannot believe insuperable, difficulties in devising an effectual mode of imposing & collecting a direct tax in all the States in the Union. Perhaps it could not be done immediately. Yet I must think it unequal to collect our whole revenue from our infant Commerce, impolitic to depend only on that Resource, & still more so, to hold out the Idea that direct Taxes will never be required, unless in some unforeseen & extraordinary emergency. Unless we are more successful in protecting & consequently in disposing of our Western Territory, we shall be necessitated to have recourse to direct Taxation much sooner than seems to be expected. The Patriotism of our Merchants, however justly complimented at present, cannot always be depended on as the sole preservative against smuggling—and we may soon be obliged to expend one half of our commercial revenue to secure the other.

The Secretary of the Treasury rises in my estimation on every Report he makes—though I do not pretend to be an accurate Judge on some of the subjects, for instance on the National Bank— I am sorry that he is deprived of any of his supports—but I believe he has yet a very able one in my Friend *Wolcott*.[2] I cannot doubt You are before this time acquainted with his merit—his honesty, independence of sentiment, indefatigable attention to business, regard for the public interest, & contempt of all praise or popularity, that might be gained by servility or adulation, or the desertion of a single principle of Rectitude.

You tell me, they say "I love Wit, better than my Friend"— I believe there is no Person, whom the world allow to possess both wit & humour (and the last I consider as more particularly my talent) who more cautiously avoids any display of it, than myself. In my Profession I am sure there is not an Attorney at the Bar, possessed of any genius in that line, who does not oftner endeavour to show it. Indeed I have for many years been endeavouring to avoid all ostentation of Wit, Brilliance, or Poetical Genius, at the bar, & to learn to talk plain common sense to Connecticut Juries. And I have the vanity to think, that in this I have succeeded. In the course of the present week, I have argued nine causes to the Jury, before our County Court now sitting, and have gained every cause. You will judge whether this effect could be produced by wit.

As a satirical Writer, I do not recollect that I ever published any composition, written on grounds of mere personal enmity. I have often engaged deeply in political Satire, but never where I did not think the subject essentially important to the national welfare. Having no popular views, I have written with a boldness of censure on characters, as well as measures, on which very few others would have ventured. I do not wonder that the heads of our former political factions, still feel the smart of their old wounds. The leading characters on the side I engaged never found me a Tool to be depended on. I supported them, when I thought them right & censured them when they deserted their principles. If I was not always right, I was always independent—so that I naturally acquired the hatred of one party, & had nothing to expect from the cold esteem of the other.

But I have disbanded my satirical Muses, since the adoption of the Constitution, & wish to have no second necessity of embodying them— Yet I have been as active, & I believe as useful in public affairs in this way, as I could have been in any public office, for which I could imagine myself qualified.

I am sorry to disappoint You of the sheet or two of sarcasms You expected. But I had so far exhausted the subject at first, & have heard so little upon it lately, that I must defer it, till I can obtain some further information. Indeed the conversation on that subject has subsided, & I believe You might depend on the firm support of the Northern States, on any future occasion.

How is the affair of the permanent residence of Congress relished at present? Will it not continue to occasion some uneasiness? That ugly name, *Connegocheague*, does not seem well adapted to our New-England wind pipes.[3] We have some thoughts of applying to *Webster* to soften it by his new mode of spelling, & perhaps it might make an elegant figure in Franklyn's new-invented types. In the mean time we expect to hear, that General Harmar, the great Defender of the West, is called out to guard the future Wigwam of Empire, and assist in running the four Lines of Experiment.[4]

An attachment to Fœderal Principles seems evidently to increase in Congress. The divisions in the house of Representatives are by no means so nearly equal on popular questions, as they were in former questions. Maddison in his constant opposition to every plan of the

Secretary of the Treasury, seems dwindled from the Great Politician we once supposed him, to the insignificant leader of an impotent Minority— No man ever more mistook his real Interest, or the line of Policy he ought to have pursued. He has lost all his popularity in this quarter. I cannot but think that our Government, on the whole, acquires strength & energy, & that the people in general are so happy under its administration, that little danger is at present to be feared from the efforts of political factions.

I am Sir with the greatest Respect / Your most Obed[t.] Serv[t]

John Trumbull

RC (Adams Papers); internal address: "The Vice President"; endorsed: "M[r] Trumbul."

[1] For the progress of the Bill of Rights, see James Sullivan's letter of 2 July 1789, and note 2, above.

[2] Oliver Wolcott Jr. (1760–1833), Yale 1778, was the first comptroller of the U.S. Treasury (*AFC*, 9:418).

[3] According to the Residence Act of 16 July 1790, the federal capital could be built anywhere on the Potomac River between its eastern branch (now Anacostia River) and the Conococheague Creek, located near Williamsport, Md. (Madison, *Papers, Congressional Series*, 13:261–262). See also First Congress, Second Session, 4 Jan. – 12 Aug. 1790, Editorial Note, above.

[4] Brig. Gen. Josiah Harmar (1753–1813), originally of Philadelphia, had carried a copy of the ratified Anglo-American peace treaty to Europe in 1784. On 24 April 1787 the Continental Congress sent Harmar to Vincennes, Ky., to "take immediate and efficient measures for dispossessing a body of men who have in a lawless and unauthorized manner taken possession of post St Vincent in defiance of the proclamations and authority of the United States." At first, Harmar trained his efforts on curbing the violence of hunters and squatters who sought to edge out roving speculators in staking out land claims. But by the summer of 1790, Harmar had shifted his focus, instead preparing to launch a wide-ranging campaign against the Miami, the Shawnee, and the Delaware near present-day Fort Wayne, Ind. In September Harmar's forces clashed with the Shawnee near the Miami villages on the Maumee River, and the U.S. troops were defeated (vol. 15:449–450; Washington, *Papers, Presidential Series*, 2:293–294, 6:583–584; Washington, *Diaries*, 6:91–92; William H. Bergmann, *The American National State and the Early West*, Cambridge, Eng., 2012, p. 29–31, 44–45).

From Peter Thacher

Hon[d.] & d[r] sir　　　　Boston Feb. 8 1791

I must make an apology for asking you to accept of the sermon inlosed herewith.[1] You knew and loved the man whose death occasioned it, and this circumstance may render it pleasing to you to receive it. Besides, you loved the father of the author and have always been kind and friendly to him in person, and by these means the candor which it needs will be secured in your perusal of it.

Excuse me, sr, for saying that I feel the most lively gratitude for the services which you have done your country, and that you have my constant wishes and prayers for your health and happiness. M[rs] Adams, with your good family, share in my best regards, and I am, / sr, with the utmost / respect, / Yr sincere friend & Ser[t]

Peter Thacher

RC (Adams Papers); internal address: "Hon. J Adams Esq[r] / Vice president of the / united states."

[1] Thacher was the son of Oxenbridge Jr. (1719–1765), a prominent Boston lawyer long esteemed by JA (vol. 1:98). The younger Thacher likely enclosed a copy of his *Sermon, Preached to the Society in Brattle Street, Boston, November 14, 1790: And Occasioned by the Death of the Hon. James Bowdoin, Esq. L.L.D. Lately Governor of the Commonwealth of Massachusetts*, Boston, 1791, Evans, No. 23825.

From Samuel Tucker

sir

Marblehead Feb[ry.] 11— 1791.

I Yesterday receivd Your very Polite Letter[1] by which I think myself highly Honour'd on this reception, from so great a Character, and shall strictly attend to the Purport thereof. as it is Probable their will be more Cutters than one stationd on our Coast the sea part being so Extensive, I should be glad of such a command should this not be, Please to offer me a Candidate, to the President, to any Post or office You may think me qualified for and be assur'd that no Gentleman, while I have Existence shall have the least reason to reflect on themselves, from any Recommendation they may be pleas'd to give me, though I sometimes think seriously on my being by our Governor and Gen[l.] Lincoln omitted, in their Letters they wrote for Candidates, and my not knowing anything of the cutters being Built, or I should have made an early application for the Cutter in this State, as my claim was so just 'tho never desirous, of holding any Post in Public service was it not meritted.

I shall take Particular care to give M[r.] John Q Adams the Journal you mention myself in the course of the next Week; and must say Your very favourable expressions shall be ever gratefully acknowledg'd by, / Sir your most Obedient and very / Humble servant

Samuel Tucker.

RC (Adams Papers); internal address: "The Hon[ble] John Adams"; endorsed: "Capt. Tucker."

[1] Of 27 Jan., above.

From Thomas Brand Hollis

Feb 12. 1791.

Mr Brand Hollis having met with this second volume of the History of Bologna by Ghiradacci requests Mr Adams to accept of it from gratitude to him for having produced to the publick the act of the 3 of June 1257 by which all the Slaves & villains were manumitted.[1] The book containing it is intitled The Paradise of pleasure.

1605. Ghirardacci lib VI. p. 194 con Licenza de Superiori.

There has been 3. Edit of this 2 vol book. 1657. Edit. 3d.

RC (Adams Papers).

[1] Cherubino Ghirardacci, *Della Historia di Bologna*, 2 vols., Bologna, Italy, 1605, two copies of which are in JA's library at MB with significant annotations. Approximately 5,855 serfs of Bologna were freed on 3 June 1257; the *Liber Paradisus* lists the names of the emancipated and their former masters (*Catalogue of JA's Library;* Christopher Kleinhenz, ed., *Medieval Italy: An Encyclopedia*, 2 vols., N.Y., 2004, entry on Bologna).

To Mercy Otis Warren

Madam. Philadelphia February 14th 1791—

By the last post I received your letter of January 17th, and was as much surprised at the information that my last letter to you arrived unsealed, as you could be at the receipt of it.[1] It was most certainly no intention of mine that it should have gone unsealed; nor can I account for the fact.[2] My conjecture is that the person, one of my sons who copied into my letterbook, either inadvertently sent it, or suffered a servant to take it off the table to the post office without putting a wafer into it according to his usual practice. Neither "The ebullitions of party, nor political malice" have made any impressions on me. The expressions you allude to, were the result of very sober reflection upon facts proved to me, by the testimony of many witnesses of unquestionable veracity among whom were not a few of the best friends General Warren ever had in his life.—

A civil war Madam, is in my opinion a very serious thing. This Country has once at least been within a hairs breadth of a very bloody one: nor is it likely to be soon so secure against the probability of another, as I wish it. There is more than one among those persons whom twenty years ago, I counted among my friends who are not so explicit and decided as I presume to think they ought to be, in favor of those principles and measures, which appear to me indispensable to preserve the liberty, peace and safety of this people. As long as this indecission remains, it is impossible there should be the same confidence between them and me, which there was once.— The affection for them which I once had will never be forgotten, nor can it ever be destroyed, but confidence can never be the same, without the same foundation for it

With[3] much esteem I am Madam / your most obedient servant

John Adams.[4]

LbC in CA's hand (Adams Papers); internal address: "Mrs Warren."; notation by CA: "Not sent."; APM Reel 115. Dft (Adams Papers).

[1] In the Dft, CA also wrote, "in that unguarded condition."

[2] In the Dft, CA also wrote: "The only conjectures that I can form are that the person who copied it into my letter book either inadvertently sent it or suffered a servant to take it off the table to the post office, without putting a wafer into it, according to his usual practise. The other copies of the poems, which I mentioned, appear to have been sent by a bookseller, who has since sent in his account as for the copies we subscribed for. A poem under the title of the 'Virtues of nature' attributed to Mrs Morton is now circulating here and meets with much applause. The fine arts appear to be growing in this Country at least as fast as science, agriculture, commerce and manufactures— Yet I think there are scarcely so many readers as before the Revolution—"

[3] In the Dft, CA wrote, "With usual regards to Genl Warren."

[4] JA and Warren did not exchange letters again until Aug. 1803 (*Warren-Adams Letters*, 2:344–345).

To William Tudor

Dear Sir Philadelphia Feb. 15. 1791

My good Genius this morning has thrown in my Way, by perfect Accident, your oration of the 4. July last, and although I read it with much pleasure, in its Season it now appeared to me, new and beautiful as ever.[1]

I am afraid I never thanked you for the handsome Compliment paid to me in a Note. Indeed I now and then get a Compliment, and do not always give thanks for it. I am informed, within a few days, of an Eulogium passed upon me at Birmingham by our old C. Justice Oliver: and I question whether I Shall Send him Thanks for it at all,. To a Gentleman in Company with him, he complained bitterly of John Adams, as "the Author of all his misfortunes and the Sole Contriver of the Revolution." What a divine Compliment! Did you ever hear or read Such a Panegyrick? Your Compliment, goodly as it is, is flat and insipid in Comparason.

The Secret is that I was the "Original Inventor" of the Impeachment against him and that Impeachment excited the Grand and Petit

Jurors in all the Counties of the Province to refuse to Act under him or his Court, and those Refusals really did produce the Revolution.

I must plead guilty to the Charge. I really was the very Midwife, who brought that Same impeachment into the World. I never before Suspected however, that Oliver was So well informed of our Secret History. at Table at Sam. Winthrops with a large Circle of Whigs, Dr John Winthrop, turned to me, and asked Mr Adams what can be done to avoid this fatal Stroke, the Royal Salaries to the Judges? "Impeach of High Treason, before the Governor and Council, the Chief Justice," was the answer, and this was the first time the Word Impeachment as I believe was pronounced. Major Hawley Soon heard of it, and came to me to know the grounds of my Strange Opinion. I Shewed him Book Chapter and Verse.[2]

I owed Oliver however no ill Will. His Compliment is not merited.— for altho I was really the first Cause of the Impeachment, it is my full Belief that the Revolution would have happened, if I had not existed. British Pretentions, could never have been carried into Execution, over such a Country and Such a People, even although there had never existed a Washington or an Hancock a Franklin Adams or Warren.

Dont, I pray you quite forget, your old / Friend J. Adams

RC (MHi:Tudor-Adams Correspondence); internal address: "William Tudor Esqr"; endorsed: "Vice President. / 15 Feb. 1791." LbC (Adams Papers); APM Reel 115.

[1] William Tudor, *A Gratulatory Address, Delivered July 5th, 1790, before the Society of the Cincinnati, of the Commonwealth of Massachusetts*, Boston, 1790, Evans, No. 22947.

[2] For JA's role in the Mass. General Court's 1774 impeachment of Peter Oliver, chief justice of the province, see vol. 2:vii, 7–17.

From Stephen Hall

My dear & honour'd friend; Portland 19. Feby. 1791.

I have not forgot the Chagrin I suffered in not obtaining the Collectorship of Impost at this Port.[1] Mr. Thacher, I suppose, remains my determined enemy; & would gladly see me excluded from any share in collecting the Excise. I wish however to be employed in it. My natural activity I think is no objection to it. I have nothing to say of other qualifications. Those who know me are the best judges. Permit me to renew my request of your friendship in the Case.—

Sincerely wishing You the choice of heaven's blessings, give me leave to / subscribe your devoted friend, / & very humble Servant;

Stephen Hall.

RC (Adams Papers); addressed: "[. . . .] / Vice President of the United States / Philadelphia."; internal address: "His Excellency John Adams. Esqr."; endorsed by CA: "S Hall / 19 Feb 1791." Some loss of text due to a torn manuscript.

[1] See Hall's letter of 15 Aug. 1789, and note 1, above.

From Henry Marchant

Dear Sir, Newport Feby. 19th. 1791—

The Congress of the United States are once more seated at Philadelphia. I wish the People there may be more conscious of the Honor and Advantage of the Residence of that Body with them than heretofore—And that They will discover less of a mobish Disposition— I am sorry to see Petitions and Remonstrances beat up about the Streets against Acts merely in Contemplation— I wish also Virginia so anxious for the Honor of abtaining the final Residence of Congress within the Dominion, would not take the Lead in lessening the Authority and necessary Powers of Congress, and thereby lessening the due Influence of Government.—

I hope the speculating Genius of Georgia upon Indian Lands and Furs will subside I did hope the paper Mony Madness of North Carolina would have ceased with that of this State:— Or however averse to the Assumption, as puting an End to the artful Views of some miserable wicked Pollliticians,—They would not have contended, or shewn Their Temper after, and upon the most mature Deliberation, the Wisdom of the Nation had determined the Subject— Maryland too almost resolved to lead down the Virginia Dance. Amongst many Disappointments, there will be some Capers cut.— This State I do pronounce has come down to as contented and steady Fœderalisim as any one State in the Union— Some of the Leaders of Our late unhappy Measures have since, and particularly after an Attendance upon the Circuit Court declared, if possible, They would unsay all They had said & done:—And that They were happily undeceived.—

People in Office cannot take too much Pains to concilliate Minds; and cautiously carry Themselves in Their respective Offices. Let me say, that as in England the Clerks &c carry a hautiness and Consequence about them, above the Heads of their Departments, so, such Persons may, perhaps in some Instances do, feel too important— Their Conduct is heard of further than They conceive— The Heads of Departments I hope will be careful to check such a Temper and Carriage in those under them— Americans cannot bear such little Tyrannies— Let them study by all means to oblige— Those Things are more leading in their Consequences than may be imagined— When a Person goes to a publick Man, or a publick Office;—He carries a Report Home and to His Neighbours highly influential upon Their Minds, as it may be favourable or otherwise— The Report whatever it be inlarges Circle beyond Circle;— As when a Stone is thrown into a smooth Water—

It appears the Intent of Congress is to rise the first of March— To me it seems almost impossible, when I consider the amazing Business before Your honorable Body.— But I find the Heads of Departments greatly relieve the Legislature— The Secretary of the Treasury by his Ingenuity and astonishing Industry amases all— I beg They will not destroy his Health.— It was little conceived that such a Character existed amongst Us:—But a kind Providence does every Thing for America—

We are suffered however to be chastised in Our Frontiers— We hope the most decisive Measures and upon a large Scale will be adopted, to put a final End by the Blessing of Heaven to any future Ravages of the Indians— Such Measures in the End may prove not only most for Our Peace, but the cheapest— You will excuse me my dear and honored Sir;—but I love to write You now and then, however unimportant, because You are always so kind as to let me hear of You in Return—And to hear that You and Yours are well, gives sincere Pleasure to Sir, Your / most affectionate Friend / and very humble Serv[t.]

Henry Marchant

RC (Adams Papers); internal address: "His Excellency / John Adams Esq[r.] / Vice President &c."; endorsed: "M[r] Marchant. 19. Feb. / ans[d.] 2. March. 1791."

From Hannah Adams

Sir, Medfeild. Massachusets. Feb— 21. 1791.

Desirous to gain the patronage of so distinguished a character, with the utmost diffidence I request your acceptance of the inclosed dedication to my View of Religions. Your permission to adorn my book by prefixing your name will do me the greatest honour,[1]

I am with the highest respect, / Sir, / Your most obedient humble servant,

Hannah Adams.

RC (Adams Papers).

[1] For Adams and her dedication of *View of Religions, in Two Parts*, see Descriptive List of Illustrations, No. 9, above.

9. HANNAH ADAMS, BY CHESTER HARDING, CA. 1827
See page xv

From Perez Morton

Sir — Boston Feby 23^{d} 1791

At the request of Miss Hannah Adams, I enclose & forward to you her Request to honor a publication, she intends making to the World, with Your Patronage by fixing your Name to it in a dedicatory Address—this is forwarded for your perusal.— The Merits of the Work I am totally a Stranger to having never perused—but being informed it is a *correction*, *enlargement*, & *amendment* of a former Work of hers on the same Subject, I have very little doubt, but that she will do herself great Credit by the Performance, & that while your name may add Lustre to the Authors, it will receive no diminution of its own by this Indulgence— She wishes, should you accept the Dedication— You would be pleased to furnish her with the various literary Titles you sustain, & your Sentiments on the Propriety of adding any other title to your political Character than that of ~~"Presid~~ "*Vice-President of the United States*"

Your obliging Attention to Miss / Adams's request will confer / an honor on Your most / Obed$^{t.}$ & very hu^{l} Servt — Perez Morton[1]

RC (Adams Papers).

1 Although JA was not acquainted with his distant cousin Hannah Adams, Morton likely knew her from the New England literary circle that included his wife, the author Sarah Wentworth Apthorp Morton (JA to Perez Morton, 10 March, LbC, APM Reel 115; *AFC*, 1:141).

To Benjamin Waterhouse

Dear Sir — Philadelphia Feb. 24. 1791

It was not, till yesterday that I received your kind Letter, with your Discourse on Animation; for both of which obliging favours I pray you to accept of my best Thanks.[1]

My incessant Drudgery for three and thirty Years in the dull fields and forests of Law and Politicks, has rendered it impossible for me to Spare much of my time, in disquisitions of natural Knowledge. Whenever any Thing of the kind however has accidentally fallen in my Way, it has revived the fond Attachment of my Youth, and given me more pleasure than I can account for.

There is no Physical Subject has occurred oftener to my Thoughts, or excited more of my Curiosity, than that which you chose for your Discourse, *Animal Life*. It has long appeared to me astonishing, that it should be impossible to discover, what it is, which the Air conveys into our Lungs and leaves behind it, in the Body when We breathe. This, whatever it is, Seems to be, the Cause of Life, or at least of the continuance and Support of it, in the larger Animals. whether the Air, in any Similar manner, Supports the Animalcules which We discover by Microscopes, in almost every kind of substance I know not.

Dr Franklin has sometimes described to me in Conversation, experiments which he made in various parts of his Life relative to this subject, which I hope will be found among his Papers. I should be afraid, upon mere memory of transient Conversation to repeat some facts which he related to me, of the revival of animalcules to perfect Life and Activity after ten Years of Torpor, in a Phyal which he left in Philadelphia when he went to England and which had not been handled till his return.

Pray where is the Evidence of the Existence of a Subtle Electric fluid which pervades the Universe? and if that fact were proved, where is your Authority for Saying that Such an Electrick fluid is the Cause of Life? Why may it not as well be Magnetism? or Steam, or Nitre? or fixed Air? These are all tremendous Forces in nature. But where and what is the Principle or Cause of Activity in all of them?

The Cause of Motion in all these Phænomena, as well as in the Emanations of Light, or the Revolutions of the Heavens or Gravitation on Earth, is Still to seek.

Your Discourse, my dear sir has given me great Pleasure, and, (if my Opinion is worth your having tho indeed I must acknowledge it is of very little value in Such Things) does honour to you, and to the Societies to which You belong.

With great Esteem, I am, dear sir / your most obedient & most / humble servant John Adams

RC (MHi:Adams-Waterhouse Coll.); addressed by JQA: "Doctor Benjamin Waterhouse. / Cambridge— / Massachusetts."; internal address: "Dr Benjamin Waterhouse / Cambridge"; notation: "Free / John Adams." LbC (Adams Papers); APM Reel 115.

[1] Waterhouse's letter has not been found. He sent a copy of his address *On the Principle of Vitality. A Discourse Delivered in the First Church in Boston, Tuesday, June 8th, 1790. Before the Humane Society of the Commonwealth of Massachusetts*, Boston, 1791, Evans, No. 23038.

To Peter Thacher

Dear sir, Philadelphia Feb$^{ry:}$ 25$^{th:}$ 1791.

I received by the last Post, and have read with great pleasure your obliging letter;[1] and the Sermon which accompanied it on the death of His Excellency Governor Bowdoin, for whose person I had an affection, and for whose character I had in common with all men, a sincere esteem; I say in common, because I really know of no Party or individual, that had not such an Esteem for him. The Sermon, which as it avoids on the one hand all fullsome flattery, and extravagant Panegyrick, and on the other is not deficient in the just praise which it becomes a Man, a Christian, and a Divine to give, is full of excellent moral and religious sentiments, expressed in elegant language. The recollection of your Father excited much tenderness of sentiment. He was a friend in my youth, who of all my friends at the Bar, entertained sentiments the most like my own.

As we advance in life Friends with whom we have cooperated, and Enemies with whom we have contended fall around us. For my own part mine have fallen in such numbers, both in Europe, and America, within a few years, that I begin to feel almost alone in the World; At my age, new Friends are not easy to procure, and indeed new Enemies if we have any such, appear of much less consequence. An Old man really seems to me sometimes, to have more regard even for his old ennemies, than his new friends. My generation is going fast off the stage, and another rushing on, and with its opinions, Moral, Metaphisical, Political and Civil, which I comprehend not. There are in Europe appearances, which indicate such changes, that it is not extravagant to say, that there may be countries in another Century intollerant not only of Chistianity but of Theism; Martyrdom at the Stake for professing the Belief of a God, and a future State, seems beyond credibility but it would be but a natural consequence of opinions and systems now propagating with the Zeal of Proseliteism. For your benevolent Prayers accept of my sincere thanks.

I am with great esteem Dear sir your Obedient ser$^{t.}$

John Adams.

LbC in CA's hand (Adams Papers); internal address: "The Revd Peter Thacher"; APM Reel 115.

[1] Of 8 Feb., above.

From William Temple Franklin

Sir, London, 25th: Feb. 1791.

In the Letter you did me the honor of writing to me[1] previous to my Departure from Philadelphia, you intimated a Wish to be informed of the Progress of French Liberty.— I have not yet been able to go over to the Continent—but shall in a few Weeks, when I will endeavor to comply with your Desire, relative to the Revolution that is effecting in France.—

In the meantime, I have taken the Liberty of sending you (by the Pigou) some important Works, that that Event has given rise to lately; and which indeed interest the Liberties of Mankind in general.—[2]

From every thing that I have hitherto been able to learn of the Proceedings in France,—I have no Doubt of the Revolution terminating favorably to Liberty—& Good-Government.— And notwithstanding the present apparent Prosperity & Tranquility of this Country, I think the Seeds of a Revolution are sown here, and the Harvest not far off:—for however the theoretical Part of the Constitution may be justly admired, the *practical* Part is replete with Corruption; which must ere long, produce a violent Fermentation.— Happy!—thrice happy, America!!

With sentiments of Respect & Esteem, / I am, Sir, Your most obedient / & very humble Sert.— W. T. Franklin.—

RC (Adams Papers); internal address: "The honble / J. Adams Esqr. / &c.— &c—"; endorsed by CA: "W T. Franklam / Feb 25th: 1791."

[1] Of 16 Oct. 1790, above.

[2] The *Pigou*, Capt. Collet, reached Philadelphia on 23 April 1791 (Philadelphia *Federal Gazette*, 23 April).

From William Tudor

Dear Sir Boston 27 Feb. 1791

I was greatly obliged by your Letter of the 15th Instant, although it gave me some Mortification arising from the Reflection that I might set it down to my own Inattention that I have been so long without such a Mark of your Friendship.

It is impossible not to smile at hearing Mr. Oliver complain of his Misfortunes. No Man who deserved so little, has been more fortunate. Unless to be removed from a State of humiliating pecuniary

Perplexity, & relieved from a Station which he had neither Learning or Talents to dignify or render easy, & to be placed in affluence & Repose, is to be considered by a Man on the wrong Side of Seventy as an Evil.

I have full Faith in the Feelings, Sense & Resentments of my Countrymen; but I am also persuaded that the Revolution was hastened by a few choice Spirits, much fewer than present Envy & Rivalship admit, & Whom posthumous History will select & perhaps do Justice to. The anti-revolution domestic Enemies of America to a Man supposed that You was the most energic Plotter, & intrepid Projector of all the Authors of the Revolution. And they too may have their Historian. Thus my dear Sir, I don't see how it is possible for this Truth to escape the knowlege of Posterity.

Congress having dispatched so much Business this Session, or being thought to have done it, are rising into Popularity. There is no People on Earth who would more cheerfully submit to Taxation, which is not direct, than the Subjects of this State. The Excise Bill which the southern Patriots affect to deprecate & dread so much, is generally here approved of. Indeed Humanity, Policy, Revenue, Morals call for a Tax on ardent Spirits. And it is supposed that if the Collection is inforced as vigourously & steadily as the Impost, that it will exceed in Product the Calculation of the Secretary Hamilton.

I was rejoiced to learn from Mr Cranch your Intention to spend your Summer at Braintree.[1] As a Farmer You must do good there. The North Precinct have petitioned the Legislature for a Seperation, & would have succeeded, could they have got more of the Inhabitants of Squantum to have united with them in the Petition.[2]

Our Sup. Jud. Ct. is now sitting, but the civil Business is greatly impeded by the Number of Criminal Trials, which grand & petty Villainy furnish. We much Want a New System of criminal judicial Process especially in Suffolk.

Yours, most faithfully, Wm Tudor

RC (Adams Papers); internal address: "Mr. Adams"; endorsed: "Mr Tudor Feb. 27. / ansd. March 15. 1791."

[1] The Adamses left for Braintree on 2 May, returning to Philadelphia in late October (*AFC*, 9:508, 509).

[2] A month earlier, citizens of Braintree had begun the lengthy process of incorporation as a new town. Approximately 150 men, a combined force of residents hailing from Braintree's north and middle precincts as well as Dorchester and Milton, petitioned the Mass. General Court for the change. State senators began debating the request on 28 Jan. and invited representatives from Braintree to comment at a special hearing on 16 Feb. (*AFC*, 9:236).

To Ebenezer Hazard

Senate Chamber Feb. 28. 1791

Mr Adams presents his Compliments to Mr Hazard, and returns, with Pleasure, the Proposal for printing his valuable Collection of State Papers, with a Subscription.[1]

RC (NHi:Gilder Lehrman Coll., on deposit); endorsed: "Vice Presidt. Adams."

[1] New York City bookseller Ebenezer Hazard (1744–1817) widely advertised his plans to compile and print his *Historical Collections; Consisting of State Papers . . . Intended as Materials for an History of the United States*, 2 vols., Phila., 1792–1794. He wrote to JA on 26 Feb. (Adams Papers) soliciting his patronage in publishing the work that JA had identified thus in 1774: "Hazard is certainly very capable of the Business he has undertaken—he is a Genius." A full set of Hazard's edition, once in JA's library at MB, has been lost (vol. 4:492; JA, *D&A*, 2:109; *Catalogue of JA's Library*).

Appendix

Appendix

LIST OF OMITTED DOCUMENTS

This list includes 128 documents omitted from volume 20 of the *Papers of John Adams* and 1 document that has come to the editors' attention since the publication of the volume in which it would have appeared. Entries contain the date of the document, the correspondent, the form in which it exists (Dft, FC, LbC, LbC-Tr, MS, RC), its location, and its place of publication, if any. Where there are multiple instances of publication, the most recent has been indicated to facilitate accessibility. All copies existing in the Adams Papers have been indicated.

1764

[*April*]	To Nathaniel Perkins, RC (private owner, 2019).

1789

4 June	To Robert Duncan, LbC (Adams Papers), APM Reel 115.
4 June	From Thomas Melvill, RC (Adams Papers).
5 June	From Joseph Willard, RC (Adams Papers).
9 June	From Stephen Hall, RC (Adams Papers).
11 June	To Thomas Melvill, LbC (Adams Papers), APM Reel 115.
12 June	From Uzal Ogden, RC (Adams Papers).
20 June	To Robert Henry, LbC (Adams Papers), APM Reel 115.
20 June	To Cotton Tufts, LbC (Adams Papers), APM Reel 115.
20 June	From William Davis, RC (Adams Papers).
25 June	From George Mason Jr., RC (Adams Papers).

26 June	To Stephen Hall, LbC (Adams Papers), APM Reel 115.
28 June	To William Davis, LbC (Adams Papers), APM Reel 115.
28 June	From James Sullivan, RC (Adams Papers).
28 June	From Elkanah Watson Jr., RC (Adams Papers).
30 June	From Nathaniel Falconer, RC (Adams Papers).
1 July	From John Jenks, RC (Adams Papers).
1 July	From the Society of the Cincinnati, RC (Adams Papers); Dupl (Adams Papers).
2 July	From William MacPherson, RC (Adams Papers).
2 July	From Benjamin Rush, RC (Adams Papers); PRINTED: Rush, *Letters*, 1:517–518.
3 July	From Thomas Mifflin, RC (Adams Papers).
4 July	To Nathaniel Falconer, LbC (Adams Papers), APM Reel 115.
5 July	From William Thompson, RC (Adams Papers).
6 July	From Frederick Phile, RC (Adams Papers).
7 July	From Thaddeus Burr, RC (Adams Papers).
7 July	From Stephen Hall, RC (Adams Papers).
13 July	From Peter Cunningham, RC (Adams Papers).
15 July	To Thaddeus Burr, LbC (Adams Papers), APM Reel 115.
16 July	To George Washington, LbC (Adams Papers), APM Reel 115; PRINTED: Washington, *Papers, Presidential Series*, 3:212–213.
16 July	From Benjamin Lincoln, RC (Adams Papers).
21 July	To Daniel McCormick, LbC (Adams Papers), APM Reel 114.
28 July	From Robert Morris, RC (MHi:Adams-Hull Coll.).
29 July	From Samuel Smedley, RC (Adams Papers).
30 July	From James Bowdoin, RC (Adams Papers).
30 July	From William Thompson, RC (Adams Papers).
3 Aug.	From Jeremiah Wadsworth, RC (MHi:Adams-Hull Coll.).
15 Aug.	From Benjamin Huntington, RC (MHi:Adams-Hull Coll.).
15 Aug.	From James Schureman, RC (MHi:Adams-Hull Coll.).
18 Aug.	From James Sullivan, RC (Adams Papers).
20 Aug.	From James Sullivan, RC (Adams Papers).

21 Aug.	From John Hathorn, RC (MHi:Adams-Hull Coll.).
21 Aug.	From James Jackson, RC (MHi:Adams-Hull Coll.).
21 Aug.	From Roger Sherman, RC (MHi:Adams-Hull Coll.).
30 Aug.	From George Walton, Dupl (Adams Papers).
1 Sept.	From Richard Bassett, RC (MHi:Adams-Hull Coll.).
1 Sept.	From William Paterson, RC (MHi:Adams-Hull Coll.).
1 Sept.	From Paine Wingate, RC (MHi:Adams-Hull Coll.).
5 Sept.	From Henry Wynkoop, RC (MHi:Adams-Hull Coll.).
14 Sept.	To John Warren, LbC (Adams Papers), APM Reel 115.
20 Sept.	From James Sullivan, RC (Adams Papers).
21 Sept.	From William Hunt, RC (Adams Papers).
22 Sept.	To Cotton Tufts, RC (private owner, 2012); LbC (Adams Papers), APM Reel 115.
23 Sept.	From Henry Knox and Lucy Flucker Knox, RC (MHi:Adams-Hull Coll.).
27 Sept.	From John Sullivan, RC (Adams Papers).
29 Sept.	From Hezekiah Welch, RC (Adams Papers).
30 Sept.	From Marston Watson, RC (Adams Papers).
1 Oct.	From Franco Petrus van Berckel, RC (MHi:Adams-Hull Coll.).
5 Oct.	From Nicolaas & Jacob van Staphorst and Nicolaas Hubbard, RC (Adams Papers).
16 Oct.	From William Cushing, RC (Adams Papers).
17 Oct.	To William Cushing, RC (MHi:William Cushing Family Papers).
2 Nov.	From Zechariah Paddock, RC (Adams Papers).
15 Nov.	From C. W. F. Dumas, RC (Adams Papers).
14 Dec.	From John Kean, RC (Adams Papers).
[*ca.* 1789]	John Adams' Memorandum of Guests, MS (Adams Papers).
[*1789–1791*]	From Aedanus Burke, RC (MHi:Adams-Hull Coll.).
[*1789–1791*]	From George Clymer, RC (MHi:Adams-Hull Coll.).
[*1789–1793*]	From Peter Silvester, RC (MHi:Adams-Hull Coll.).
[*1789–1793*]	From Thomas Tudor Tucker, RC (MHi:Adams-Hull Coll.).

1790

1 Jan.	From Gasparo Soderini, RC (Adams Papers).
9 Jan.	From François Adriaan Van der Kemp, RC (Adams Papers).
11 Jan.	Address from the Senate to George Washington, RC (DLC:Washington Papers).
20 Jan.	From George Duffield, RC (Adams Papers).
26 Jan.	From Benjamin Rush, RC (Adams Papers).
31 Jan.	From Thomas Crafts Jr., RC (Adams Papers).
13 Feb.	From Jeremy Belknap, RC (Adams Papers).
16 Feb.	From John Brown & John Brown Francis, RC (Adams Papers).
16 Feb.	From John Montgomery, RC (Adams Papers).
16 Feb.	From James Pemberton, RC (Adams Papers).
18 Feb.	From Samuel Allyne Otis, RC (Adams Papers).
28 Feb.	To Benjamin Rush, Dft (Adams Papers).
17 March	From John Hurd, RC (Adams Papers).
29 March	From Sylvanus Bourne, RC (Adams Papers).
31 March	To William Cranch, RC (MHi:Adams-Cranch Family Papers).
31 March	From Richard Price, RC (Adams Papers).
2 April	To John Trumbull, RC (NIC:Moses Coit Tyler Coll.); LbC (Adams Papers), APM Reel 115.
3 April	From Alexander Johnson, RC (Adams Papers).
3 April	From Benjamin Lincoln, RC (Adams Papers).
5 April	To John Hurd, LbC (Adams Papers), APM Reel 115.
16 April	To John Quincy Adams, RC (Adams Papers); Tr (Adams Papers).
26 April	From Benjamin Lincoln, RC (MHi:Endicott Autograph Coll.).
[*April*]	To Thomas Welsh, LbC (Adams Papers), APM Reel 115.
4 May	From Benjamin Rush, RC (Adams Papers).
7 May	From Eliphalet Fitch, RC (Adams Papers).
13 May	From William Ellery, RC (Adams Papers); PRINTED: *Doc. Hist. Ratif. Const.*, 26:866–868.
20 May	From James Lovell, RC (Adams Papers).
20 May	From Charles Christoph Reiche, RC and enclosure (Adams Papers); PRINTED: *First Fed. Cong.*, 19:1550–1551.

27 May	From Benjamin Lincoln, RC (Adams Papers).
31 May	From John Brown Cutting, RC (Adams Papers).
1 June	From William Ellery, RC (Adams Papers); PRINTED: *Doc. Hist. Ratif. Const.*, 26:1018–1019.
7 June	From William Ellery, RC (Adams Papers).
7 June	From Henry Marchant, RC (Adams Papers); PRINTED (in part): *Doc. Hist. Ratif. Const.*, 26:1039–1040.
11 June	From John Brown, RC (Adams Papers); PRINTED: *Doc. Hist. Ratif. Const.*, 26:1043–1044.
12 June	From Henry Marchant, RC (Adams Papers).
19 June	From Bartholomew Burges, RC (Adams Papers).
19 June	From Henry Marchant, RC (Adams Papers).
22 June	From Count Paolo Andreani, RC (MHi:Adams-Hull Coll.).
26 June	From Henry Marchant, RC (Adams Papers).
28 June	From John Montgomery, RC (Adams Papers).
5 July	From Henry Marchant, RC (Adams Papers).
15 July	To John Codman Jr., LbC (Adams Papers), APM Reel 114.
19 July	From Henry Marchant, RC (Adams Papers).
28 Aug.	From George Washington, FC (DLC:Washington Papers); PRINTED: Washington, *Papers, Presidential Series*, 6:347–348.
2 Sept.	From Samuel Adams, RC (Adams Papers); PRINTED: Adams, *Writings*, 4:339–340.
2 Sept.	From Thomas Fitzsimons, RC (MHi:Adams-Hull Coll.).
12 Sept.	To Nathaniel Byfield Lyde, LbC (Adams Papers), APM Reel 115.
24 Sept.	From Mercy Otis Warren, RC (Adams Papers); PRINTED: *Warren-Adams Letters*, 73:323.
1 Oct.	From Samuel Tucker, RC (Adams Papers).
10 Nov.	From Samuel Tucker, RC (Adams Papers).
22 Nov.	From Oliver Whipple, RC (Adams Papers).
23 Nov.	From Thomas Brand Hollis, RC (Adams Papers).
30 Nov.	From Elkanah Watson Jr., RC (Adams Papers).
4 Dec.	From Alexander Hamilton, RC (Adams Papers); PRINTED: Hamilton, *Papers*, 7:192.
27 Dec.	To Edward Tilghman, RC (MdHi:Tilghman Family Papers).

30 Dec.	From Benjamin Putnam, RC (Adams Papers).
30 Dec.	From Samuel Tucker, RC (Adams Papers).

1791

22 Jan.	From John Codman Jr., RC (Adams Papers).
24 Jan.	From George Richey Everson, RC (Adams Papers).
1 Feb.	From Rufus King, RC (MHi:Adams-Hull Coll.).
26 Feb.	From Ebenezer Hazard, RC (Adams Papers).

Index

NOTE ON THE INDEX

The index for volume 20 of the *Papers of John Adams* is designed to supplement the annotation, when possible, by furnishing the correct spellings of names; supplying forenames when they are lacking in the text; and indicating dates, occupations, and places of residence when they will aid in identification. Markedly variant spellings of proper names have been cross-referenced to what are believed to be their most nearly standard forms, and the variant forms found in the manuscripts are parenthetically recorded following the standard spellings. Subentries appear in alphabetical order by the primary word of the subentry. Abbreviations are alphabetized as if they were spelled out, thus "JA" is alphabetized under "Adams." Also, main entries for members of the British nobility are, with a few exceptions, at their titles rather than their given names.

Letters to and from John Adams are listed under the names of his correspondents at the end of each such entry; these correspondents are listed alphabetically by writer or recipient in two paragraphs under the John Adams entry. Branches, departments, and positions within the U.S. federal government are indexed individually under the name of the entity, with subdivisions as appropriate. For example, the Supreme Court is found as a subentry under "Judiciary, U.S." while "Presidency, U.S." stands as a main entry.

Only the English translations of foreign-language letters have been indexed. Book and pamphlet titles mentioned or cited by Adams and his contemporaries appear in shortened form under their authors' names, when known; full citations are found in the notes.

The index was compiled in the Adams Papers office.

Index

Index

¶The *Papers of John Adams* was composed in the Adams Papers office using Microsoft Office Professional with style sheets and programs created by Technologies 'N Typography of Merrimac, Massachusetts. The text is set in eleven on twelve and one half point using the Linotype-Hell Postscript revival of *Fairfield Medium*, a design by Rudolph Ruzicka that includes swash characters especially designed for *The Adams Papers*. Greek characters are set using Zeph Text, courtesy of the Loeb Classical Library. The printing and binding are by Sheridan Books of Ann Arbor, Michigan. The paper, made by Finch, Pruyn & Company and distributed by Lindenmeyr Munroe, is a grade named *Finch Fine Vanilla*. The books were originally designed by P. J. Conkwright and Burton L. Stratton.